McDonnell F-4
PHANTOM
Spirit in the Skies

McDonnell F-4
PHANTOM
Spirit in the Skies

Edited by Jon Lake

Aerospace Publishing London
Airtime Publishing USA

Published by
Aerospace Publishing Ltd
179 Dalling Road
London W6 0ES
England

Published under licence in USA
and Canada by
Airtime Publishing Inc.
10 Bay Street
Westport, CT 06880
USA

Distributed in the UK,
Commonwealth and Europe by
Airlife Publishing Ltd
101 Longden Road
Shrewsbury SY3 9EB
England
Telephone: 0743 235651
Fax: 0743 232944

Distributed to retail bookstores in
the USA and Canada by
Abbeville Press Inc.
488 Madison Avenue
New York, NY 10022
USA

US and Canadian readers wishing
to order by mail, please contact
Airtime Publishing Inc. at (203)
226-3580. The publishers also
welcome inquiries from model and
hobby stores.

Aerospace **ISBN: 1 874023 28 X**
Airtime **ISBN: 1-880588-04-8**

Publisher: Stan Morse
Editor: Jon Lake
Production Editors:
  Sheryl Fellows
  Karen Leverington
Picture Researcher and
Editorial Assistant: Tim Senior
Design: Barry Savage
  Robert Hewson
  Dennis Day
  Steve Page
Authors: Robert F. Dorr
  Jon Lake
  René J. Francillon
  Bill Gunston
  Bob Archer
  Pat Martin
  John Roberts
Artists: Keith Fretwell
  Grant Race
Typesetting: SX Composing Ltd
Origination and printing by
  Imago Publishing Ltd
Printed in Singapore

The publishers gratefully
acknowledge the assistance given
by Mr Lon Nordeen and Mr Lee
Whitney of McDonnell Douglas;
Mr Michael Hill of RAF Strike
Command; and Rear Admiral
Julian Lake, USN, Retired.

We would also like to acknowledge
the permission granted by Sphere
Books Limited to use pages 132-138
of their book *G-SUIT – Combat
Reports from Israel's Air War*.

**World Air Power Journal is
published quarterly and
provides an in-depth analysis
of contemporary military
aircraft and their worldwide
operators. Superbly produced
and filled with extensive color
photography, World Air Power
Journal is available by
subscription from:**

**UK, Europe and
Commonwealth:
Aerospace Publishing Ltd
179 Dalling Road
London W6 0ES
England**

**USA and Canada:
Airtime Publishing Inc.
Subscription Dept
10 Bay Street
Westport, CT 06880
USA**

CONTENTS

CHAPTER 1

FORGING THE
PHANTOM

Over St Louis on 27 May 1958, McDonnell test pilot Robert C. Little temporarily lowers the leading-edge flaps and landing gear of the first F4H-1 Phantom (BuNo. 142259) on its first flight. This portrait was shot from one of two F-101 Voodoo chase planes. Note the early air intake shape, Dayglo trim and absence of a second seat in the premier Phantom.

Developed from an unsuccessful contender for the requirement fulfilled by Vought's F8U Crusader, the Phantom was procured as an all-weather fleet defense interceptor. Unusually, everything worked, even the new high-tech radar, and service introduction was commendably rapid. The F4H soon demonstrated outstanding reliability and robustness, coupled with impeccable handling characteristics. The aircraft's potential as a multirole warplane was quickly recognized, both by the Navy and by new customers, including the USAF, who swallowed their pride and ordered a Navy airplane.

When McDonnell test pilot Robert C. Little taxied out from the flight test ramp at Lambert-St Louis Municipal Airport, on the morning of 27 May 1958, few present could have predicted how successful his aircraft, the brand new YF4H-1 prototype, would become. Among his audience were some of the McDonnell employees who had already put more than 6.8 million man-hours into the project, which had involved 1,500 aerospace firms spread through 28 states. While they were justifiably proud of their creation, even the most optimistic realized that the new aircraft was the prototype of a naval, carrierborne interceptor, and that as such was unlikely to enjoy a huge production run. With US Navy interest pointing more towards exotic strike aircraft, some well-informed observers even suspected that the aircraft would never progress beyond a handful of prototypes and test aircraft.

As Little advanced the twin throttles, the thunderous note of the J79 engines rose to a crackling roar. Engaging afterburner and releasing the brakes, the roar became an ear-splitting, sternum-rattling scream, and the streamlined gray and white machine, with its characteristic upturned wingtips and downturned tail, accelerated rapidly down the runway.

The new aircraft was designated F4H-1 and its project manager, Don Malvern, wanted to name it Satan. But the grand old man of the company, McDonnell himself, had made it clear that the new aircraft was to be named the F4H-1 Mithras, after the Persian god of light. No popular

Inset above: Bob Little poses beside the premier F4H-1 Phantom in November 1958. The aircraft now has a red tail, 18 months after its first flight. Most early test flying was carried out by McDonnell's Gerald (Zeke) Huelsbeck, who eventually lost his life in this prototype.

Left: The second F4H-1 Phantom (BuNo. 142260) flies over St Louis in January 1961. This ship was briefly known as 'Skyburner' when flown to an altitude record of 98,560 ft (30041 m) by Commander Lawrence E. Flint Jr on 6 December 1959. Later employed at Lakehurst, New Jersey, to test a carrier emergency landing restraint, ship two ended its career as a maintenance trainer in Memphis, but is now being restored to nonflying status by the New England Air Museum.

name had been given to the jet as yet, and in spite of the enormous investment, no one could be certain that more than the first two prototypes would be built.

Bob Little hauled back on the stick, eyed his gauges, watched the St Louis aerodrome slip away beneath the haze, and reached to pull up the landing gear. A chase plane tucked in neatly behind him. Four years earlier, Little had taken the prototype F-101 Voodoo to supersonic speed on its maiden flight, and he expected little difficulty doing the

same today. But as the gray/white F4H-1 climbed near the Mississippi River, Little began to experience hydraulic problems and did not like the feeling he got when the undercarriage raised. He pulled the gear handle again. His chase pilot confirmed that the nose-wheel door appeared to be stuck in the 'open' position, and Little realized that the only way he could achieve symmetry in flight was to lower the gear completely. A few seconds into its first flight and the Navy's new fighter was malfunctioning.

Forging the Phantom

Far right: A McDonnell F3H-2 Demon (BuNo. 143420) of VF-41 'Black Aces' on the starboard elevator of USS Independence (CVA-62) in May 1959. The Demon, the only single-engined fighter from McDonnell, strongly influenced the twin-engined F-4.

Right: The first Phantom: McDonnell's diminutive FH (originally FD) first flew in January 1945. Two XFD-1 prototypes were followed by 60 FH-1 production aircraft.

Below: When McDonnell started F-4 design work with the F3H-G mock-up, seen at St Louis on 18 May 1954, the company hedged its bets by designing the right side for a J79 engine and the left for a J65.

The aircraft was intended for a two-man crew but was being flown solo. It had a stubby, pointed nose, curiously bent wings and a stooped tailplane, and in years ahead men were going to call it 'Double Ugly'; yet it was to become a creation of beauty to many. It was flying now because the Navy wanted a new ground attack aircraft, yet it was being developed as an interceptor to defend the Navy's aircraft carrier battle groups.

Fighters, of course, had one-man cockpits, single engines and guns. But this fleet defense interceptor was configured with two seats, two engines and an armament consisting only of missiles. The new aircraft was not as maneuverable as the FJ-4 Fury that was currently being retired from Navy service, nor was it as fast as the F8U-3

Crusader III being developed by the competing Vought company. It was not even as fast as McDonnell's own F-101 Voodoo.

What future could this aircraft have? The US and USSR were rattling nuclear sabres at each other, but the world was essentially at peace (although the Americans saw hints that in the coming 1960s they might have to go to war in the Belgian Congo). In the Pentagon, the Navy did not have as much priority as the long-range strategic bombers of the Air Force. Within the Navy, an interceptor was not as appealing as a new attack aircraft, and there was no guarantee that more than a handful of test ships would be built.

Such were the prospects for a new, unproven airplane that was destined to become one of the true immortals – one of the handful in history to rise to true glory, worthy of mention in the same breath as Spitfire, Mustang and Sabre. And now the nose-wheel door was stuck! It was a frustrating start for the new fighter, which would not be named Satan or Mithras, but (because McDonnell changed his mind) would be called Phantom II.

New fighter

We know today that the F-4 Phantom II became the standard against which every other fighter of its generation would be measured. We also know that the Phantom took

men into battle in Vietnam, in the Israeli-Arab conflicts and, belatedly, in the Persian Gulf. Five thousand two hundred and one Phantoms, representing the largest production run of a Western fighter since the F-86 Sabre, served in 13 air forces and carried out a wide range of military missions. We know that MiGs fell before the Phantom, that aces flew it to fame and that the Phantom racked up at least 320 aerial victories worldwide. And we know, as a company advertisement proclaimed, that for a generation, "Phantoms rose from land and sea to take command of the air." Absolute command. But there were bumps along the road in the Phantom's upbringing, starting with that first flight.

Fighter pilots like Bob Little are an active, vigorous, spirited lot, but when they compose written words they inevitably write in the passive tense. "I started engines," is likely to be weakened into the passive, "The engines were started," when a fighter jock puts pen to paper. Bob Little's report on the first flight of the Phantom, written in fighter-jock passive prose, is a seminal historical document.

"The initial flight of the F4H-1 was successfully performed this morning. A brief evaluation of handling qualities in the basic and landing configuration showed excellent flight characteristics for all conditions tested.

"Takeoff was accomplished at an indicated airspeed (IAS) of 160 kt (184 mph; 296 km/h) with A/B power at gross weight of approximately 36,000 lb (16300 kg). The

Left: The first F4H-1 Phantom, with its unique air intakes showing clearly and dummy AAM-N-6 Sparrow missiles beneath the fuselage, plows through the sky on an early test flight. The first ship actually was not 'wired' for missiles, had no radar and was essentially a proof-of-concept air vehicle.

airplane lifted off briskly after about 2,000 ft (600 m). Takeoff characteristics were good. A nose-up trim change was noted at liftoff. Engine power was reduced to approximately military power very shortly after takeoff, and the remaining climb-out was made at this power setting. The right-hand engine developed an RPM (revolutions per minute) oscillation of plus or minus three percent with accompanying TOT (turbine outlet temperature) fluctuation of plus or minus 50-75°C (122-167°F) when power was reduced from A/B to military. This RPM fluctuation continued for two to three minutes even with throttle modulation below military power down to approximately 88 percent. After this brief period of unstable engine operation, the engine settled down at approximately 92 percent and operated normally thereafter. As the climb-out was continued, the pilot noted a hydraulic warning light on power control system No. 2 and the pressure dropped to zero. The chase pilot reported evidence of hydraulic fluid under the right wing at the same time. The flight was continued on power control system No. 1 pressure. The leading- and trailing-edge flaps were retracted normally with no perceptible trim change. The climb was discontinued at an altitude of 10,000 ft (3050 m) and speed was increased to 370 kt (426 mph; 684 km/h) IAS. At this time the chase pilot reported that the nose-gear door was not fully closed. However, no gear cycle was attempted at this time.

"The airplane handling qualities were briefly evaluated to 370 kt (425 mph; 684 km/h) IAS with satisfactory results on the lateral and longitudinal control system. Dihedral effect was mild and lateral-directional damping as a result of rudder input was good. Speed brakes were extended at 350 kt (403 mph; 647 km/h) IAS with no noticeable trim change. Airspeed was reduced to approximately 240 kt (276 mph; 444 km/h) IAS, where the landing gear was extended satisfactorily with no trim change. Airspeed was reduced further to 200 kt (230 mph; 370 km/h) IAS and the leading- and trailing-edge flaps were extended; trim change was not perceptible to the pilot. The flight was then discontinued since continued operation on one power control hydraulic system was considered inadvisable.

"Landing approach was made at 160 kt (184 mph; 296 km/h) IAS at approximately 81 percent RPM on the engines, with touchdown occurring at approximately 155 kt (178 mph; 287 km/h) IAS. Parabrake was deployed satisfactorily and the landing roll was easily controlled with moderate wheel braking.

Left: After the F3H-G replica, McDonnell built this mock-up of the F4H-1-to-be, seen in December 1955. The shape of the F4H-1 was now established, although the aircraft which followed had a different vertical tail and a 'bent' wing.

Below: While the F4H-1 (foreground) was taking shape, McDonnell built F-101 Voodoos. The 20th Voodoo, an F-101A, is pictured on the right. Behind the Phantom is an RF-101C recce ship.

F4H-1 Phantom speed/altitude records

Project Top Flight (altitude record)
6 December 1959
Edwards AFB, California
Commander Lawrence E. Flint, Jr
F4H-1 Phantom (142260)
98,560 ft (30041 m)

Speed record (500-km/ approx. 311-mile closed-circuit course)
5 September 1960
Edwards AFB, California
Lieutenant Colonel Thomas H. Miller (USMC)
F4H-1 Phantom (145311)
1,216.78 mph (1958.16 km/h)

Speed record (100-km/ approx. 62-mile closed-circuit course)
25 September 1960
Edwards AFB, California
Commander John F. (Jeff) Davis
F4H-1 Phantom
1,390.21 mph (2237.26 km/h)

Speed record (3-km/ approx. 1.9-mile closed-circuit course)
28 August 1961
Edwards AFB, California
Lieutenant Huntington Hardisty and Lieutenant Earl De Esch
F4H-1 Phantom (145307) 'Sageburner'
902.769 mph (1452.826 km/h)

Speed record (absolute)
22 December 1961
Edwards AFB, California
Lieutenant Colonel Robert B. Robinson (USMC)
F4H-1 Phantom (142260)
1,606.342 mph (2585.086 km/h)

Altitude record (sustained flight)
5 December 1961
Patuxent River, Maryland
Commander George W. Ellis
F4H-1 Phantom
66,443.8 ft (20252.1 m)

Project High Jump ('Time-to-climb' records)

Height (m)	Date	Pilot	Time (sec)	Previous
at NAS Brunswick, Maine:				
3000 (9,843 ft)	21 February 1962	Lieutenant Commander J. Young	34.523	35.624
6000 (19,685 ft)	21 February 1962	Commander D. Longton	48.787	51.429
9000 (29,528 ft)	1 March 1962	Lieutenant Colonel McGraw	61.629	64.760
12000 (39,370 ft)	1 March 1962	Lieutenant Colonel McGraw	77.156	95.740
15000 (49,213 ft)	1 March 1962	Lieutenant Commander D. Nordberg	114.548	131.100
20000 (65,617 ft)	31 March 1962	Lieutenant Commander T. Brown	178.500	222.990
at NAS Point Mugu, California:				
25000 (82,021 ft)	3 April 1962	Lieutenant Commander J. Young	230.440	266.030
30000 (98,425 ft)	12 April 1962	Lieutenant Commander D. Nordberg	371.430	904.920

Above: One of the final photographs of ship one (BuNo. 142259) shows preparations for Project Top Flight by test pilot Gerald (Zeke) Huelsbeck in September 1959. Just two weeks later, on 21 October 1959, Huelsbeck lost his life in this prototype. Ship two (BuNo. 142260), flying in much the manner of a crude ballistic missile, blasted skyward in a spectacular climb on 6 December 1959 to achieve Commander Lawrence E. Flint's altitude mark cited above.

Right: Lieutenant Colonel Thomas H. Miller eventually rose to three-star rank, was for a time the senior aviator in Naval and Marine aviation, and played a key role in bringing the Harrier to the United States. His closed-circuit speed record on 5 September 1960 was not made in the F4H-1 Phantom shown here. His record-setting ship was Phantom No. 12 (BuNo. 145311), which had smaller inlet warning stripes, no radome and a special nose pitot tube.

Above: The first 'Sageburner', alias Phantom No. 17 (BuNo. 145316), would have set a spectacular speed record if Commander J. L. Felsman (inset) had not thrown the F4H-1 into violent PIO (pilot-induced oscillation) resulting in the tragic loss of both plane and pilot.

Below: Lieutenant Huntington Hardisty and Lieutenant Earl De Esch (bottom) flew the second 'Sageburner', Phantom No. 8 (145307), to a 3-km closed-circuit speed record. Hardisty later commanded US Pacific forces, while 145307 went to Washington's National Air and Space Museum.

Above: The very busy No. 2 Phantom (BuNo. 142260) briefly carried the name 'Skyburner' while Marine Lieutenant Colonel Robert B. Robinson (top) established yet another F4H-1 speed record. The US Marine Corps wanted the Phantom from the start and had several pilots assigned to developmental work.

Below: Project High Jump was a massive attempt at a series of time-to-climb records. They were the only speed/altitude records to be achieved by production F4H-1 Phantoms. Among the participants was John Young, who later became an Apollo astronaut. This F4H-1 (BuNo. 148423) is one of the 'jumpers'.

An F4H-1F Phantom (originally F4H-1, and later F-4A), the third ship in the series (BuNo. 143388), takes on fuel from an A3D Skywarrior in March 1961, long after flight refueling trials were completed using other Phantoms and Skywarriors. The Phantom was also tested with a 'buddy' refueling store, but this was never used operationally.

F4H-1 Phantom No. 11 (BuNo. 145310), with a flush canopy but a splitter vane added to early-style air inlets, was assigned to weapons trials. Seen here in April 1961 with 22 of the US Navy's new 500-lb Mk 83 series, ship 11 dropped live ordnance at Fort Bragg, North Carolina, observed by President John F. Kennedy. The Phantom, a fleet defense interceptor, had air-to-ground duties added before becoming operational.

"Post-flight inspection revealed loss of hydraulic pressure due to a hydraulic line failure at the No. 2 power control system reservoir pressurization line. Inspection of the right-hand engine revealed no obvious cause of the RPM surge condition that occurred on takeoff. However, further inspection of the engine revealed foreign object damage to the compressor blades. The engine has been rejected and is being replaced prior to the second flight which is expected on 28 May."

No, it was not the best beginning for the US Navy's newest warplane.

McDonnell background

The original Phantom had been the McDonnell XFD-1 (later FH-1), a straight-wing twin-jet which was the first American jet to take off from and land on a carrier, flying from USS *Franklin D. Roosevelt* (CVA-42) on 21 July 1946, with Lieutenant Commander James J. Davidson as pilot.

The success of the FH-1 Phantom, McDonnell's first production aircraft, came in lean postwar years when other aircraft manufacturers were struggling to keep themselves in business. Mr Mac, as James S. McDonnell was always called, took on the challenge of convincing the US Navy and, later, the US Air Force, to buy new aircraft types from him before the production of older types was completed. The order for 100 Phantoms was followed by a contract for the XF2D-1 (later F2H-1) Banshee. McDonnell also developed the XP-85 Goblin parasite fighter and XF-88 Voodoo for the Air Force, but the Banshee became his second production type and was blooded in the Korean War (1950-53). Improved versions of the Banshee served as nuclear bomber (F2H-2B), night-fighter (F2H-2N), reconnaissance aircraft (F2H-2P) and all-weather fighter (F2H-3 and F2H-4). Thirty-nine examples of the F2H-3

Phantom at sea

The F4H-1 Phantom was to be the spearhead of a vigorous new Navy with modern carriers (some of them nuclear-powered), equipped with angled decks, steam catapults and mirror landing systems. 'Essex'- and 'Midway'-class carriers were imposing enough, but the US Navy's 'mix' of flat tops was dominated by its new 'Forrestal' class. McDonnell's big, bent-wing fleet interceptor had to take the impact of tailhook-retarded carrier landings and the acceleration of being launched from deck. The F4H-1 had to handle itself in a low-speed, high-risk flight regime near the 'boat'. Earlier, the US Navy had invested in 103 FJ-2 Furys, but carrier trials found them nearly useless for shipboard duty. Carrier suitability was designed into the Phantom, but nothing was proven until the F4H-1 Phantom went aboard USS *Independence* (CVA-62) and USS *Intrepid* (CVA-11) in 1960.

Above: Lieutenant Commander Paul Spencer taxis F4H-1 Phantom No. 6 (BuNo. 143391) during the carrier qualification trials aboard USS Independence (CVA-62), which proved that the McDonnell fighter could handle shipboard duties.

Below: A Piasecki HUP-2 hovers vigilantly in the plane-guard slot while F4H-1 Phantom No. 6 gets ready on 'Indy's' starboard elevator in April 1960. This Phantom landed and took off from the carrier with few problems.

Above: This F4H-1 Phantom has its tailhook deployed and is about to 'take the wire' for a successful carrier landing. The angled deck, introduced by the US Navy in the mid-1950s but a British invention, made the pilot's task far easier during landing and removed the risk that a poor landing would be followed by a collision with other aircraft on deck. The Phantom was bigger, heavier and more complex than most carrier aircraft of its era, and at first intimidated some of the maintenance personnel on the carrier.

Above: The F4H-1 Phantom's wings have been unfolded. Deckhands remove a tie down and prepare to help Lieutenant Commander Paul Spencer taxi off the elevator to Independence's deck. The name 'Phantom II', emblazoned on the fuselage, was for the benefit of the carrier's crew who had not seen an F4H-1 before.

Right: Phantom No. 6 is slammed into the void by Independence's steam catapult during 1960 carrier trials. The steam catapult was a British innovation, which was adopted by the US Navy in the mid-1950s and was standard throughout the fleet by the time the Phantom came along.

Forging the Phantom

Above: F4H-1 Phantom No. 11 (BuNo. 145310) poses with 22 500-lb Mk 83 bombs in February 1960. This load allowed for no external fuel and limited the Phantom's combat radius. As air-to-ground work was added to the Phantom's duties, a 'mix' of fuel plus bombs resulted in the F-4 being capable of delivering eight to 10 bombs on a target at a reasonable distance from the carrier.

Right: Though the original FH-1 Phantom is not included, this rare portrait depicts three of the four fighters built by McDonnell for the US Navy. Leading the pack is an F2H-3 Banshee (BuNo. 126486) which, by January 1959, belonged to the US Navy Reserve. In trail are an F3H-2N Demon (BuNo. 143476), still at the McDonnell plant, and an F4H-1 Phantom (BuNo. 143390), the rarely-depicted fifth aircraft in the F-4 series.

Right: Much of the early development work on the Phantom was carried out at NATC at Patuxent River in southern Maryland, where long runways and a zone of relatively little air traffic enabled crews to wring out the new fighter. Both 'NAVY' and 'MARINES' were painted on this early Phantom so that both services could be represented when the airplane was placed on a flatbed truck and towed down Pennsylvania Avenue at the inauguration of President Kennedy on 20 January 1961.

Banshee went to the Royal Canadian Navy, which operated them from the deck of HMCS *Bonaventure*.

McDonnell followed with the F3H Demon fighter, designed by a team headed by Richard Deegan. The Demon had an advanced airframe with sharply swept wing and tail surfaces, but the choice of the Westinghouse XJ40 turbojet engine proved disastrous. The XF3H-1 Demon prototype was flown on 7 January 1951 by Bob Edholm, but the production F3H-1N night-fighter version did not fly until 24 December 1953, and even then it was not much of a Christmas Eve gift. The F3H-1N suffered a series of crashes due to its low thrust and the unreliability of its engine. Production was halted after 58 had been built, and many were barged down the Mississippi to be used as ground instructional trainers at the Naval Air Technical Center in Memphis, Tennessee.

An Allison J71-powered F3H-2 Demon had a more successful career with the fleet, together with the F3H-2M version, which was noteworthy as the first US combat aircraft to carry the Sparrow radar-guided missile. Five hundred and twenty-one Demons were manufactured between 1949 and 1959. Meanwhile, the F-101 Voodoo was created by a design team headed by E. M. 'Bud' Flesh. The big, heavy Voodoo, first flown at Edwards Air Force Base, California, on 29 September 1954 with Bob Little at the controls, was eventually produced in F-101A and F-101C strike versions, F-101B interceptor and RF-101A and RF-101C reconnaissance aircraft. The RF-101C was the first US combat aircraft in Vietnam, and it routinely flew missions at speeds higher than any reached before or since by an aircraft in battle.

Phantom genesis

With this string of successes, it had to be frustrating for Mr Mac that arch-rival Vought had won the major Navy production order of the 1950s with its F8U Crusader. McDonnell's response was to task a design team under Herman Barkey to design an airplane that the Navy would want. In 1953-54 McDonnell and Davis S. Lewis traveled to Washington to question not only naval aviators but also their wives about the type of aircraft they needed. The same Navy fighter jock who demanded a hot-rod, single-engined jet in front of his buddies would confide in his wife his strong preference for twin-engined safety.

The Barkey team's new design began in mid-1953 as a single-place, long-range attack craft financed by the company and completed in mock-up form under the company designation F3H-G. A refined version existed on paper as the F3H-H. "It's never been acknowledged," says a company employee, "but the Phantom owes a real debt to the design work that went into the F3H Demon."

A marriage between a shortened Demon and a swept-wing Banshee, the F3H-G/H had straight tailplanes and in-

14

corporated a 'Coke Bottle' fuselage to enhance supersonic flight. It also took into account the 'weapon system' concept then in vogue in the Pentagon. Originally intended as a single-place, long-range attack aircraft, it was to be equipped with APQ-50 radar, armed with four 20-mm cannon and given external store stations for various ground attack weapons. The proposed powerplants were two 7,800-lb (34.7-kN) thrust Wright J65-W-2 (or W-4) turbojet engines, license-built versions of the Rolls-Royce Sapphire. The Navy was having several unrelated problems with this engine in its FJ-3 and FJ-3M Fury series of fighters, but it expected that the problems would be solved in time for a new fighter. Both Barkey's design team and the Navy were also looking at the General Electric J79, a far more powerful engine which had been developed for the Air Force's Convair B-58 Hustler bomber.

McDonnell submitted a formal development proposal for the F3H-G/H to the Navy in August 1954. This resulted in a letter of intent (in October 1954) for two prototype and one static test aircraft. At this time, the new aircraft was designated AH-1 to reflect its intended ground attack mission.

Commander Francis X. Timmes was the Navy's project officer for the McDonnell AH-1, and he found himself struggling to find a place in the fleet for the new design at a time when the Navy's attack people were married to the Douglas A4D Skyhawk and the Navy Fighter Desk was preoccupied with the Vought F8U Crusader. Barkey and Timmes worked closely together as the new design went through fits and starts. But on 26 May 1955, the designers settled upon a two-man crew for the new aircraft and its designation was changed again, from AH-1 to F4H-1. The Phantom-to-be never had an X prefix for 'experimental', so there was no XF4H-1 designation.

On 25 July 1955, the Navy and the manufacturer agreed to a detailed list of specifications for the new aircraft. The McDonnell design was now slated to have twin J79 engines (the J65 having been abandoned), AAM-N-6 Sparrow III radar-missile armament, improved air-intercept radar, a maximum speed of at least Mach 2 and a

two-man crew. The Navy committed itself to the purchase of two prototypes (BuNos 142259 and 142260), although not, as had been previously discussed, to a static test article. At the same time, the Navy authorized Vought to build two prototypes of the single-seat, single-engined, missile-carrying F8U-3 Crusader III to compete with the McDonnell design.

The flight surfaces of the new aircraft did not evolve, contrary to legend, from someone trampling on the blueprints. The original AH-1 had a low-set tailplane, but in the F4H-1 there was no place to put it. After much wind-tunnel work and consideration of more than 20 different arrangements, it was decided to apply 23° of anhedral. This gave the necessary degree of stability but still left the tailplane free of the jet efflux. This configuration contributed in the developmental phase to stall-recovery problems.

The wing underwent many changes. The center section of the wing had been envisioned as an immensely strong unit spanning 27 ft (8.23 m) from wingfold to wingfold, with a permanent manufacturing splice at the centerline. Barkey's engineers reached a point where, to avoid having to redesign the entire wing, they gave the outboard panels 12° of dihedral, resulting in an 'average' wing dihedral of 5°. In this remarkably casual manner, the wing shape of the future Phantom was determined.

Even after the final design of the F4H-1 had been decided, minor adjustments kept changing plans for the completion of the first airframe and for the first flight. Initially, the first F4H-1 was scheduled to fly in February 1958 and then, because of a company program for overtime work, in December 1957. Later, when the Navy decided it wanted to make the first flight at Edwards AFB, California, a March 1958 maiden flight was projected. These plans were changed once more when Commander Timmes' office directed McDonnell to fly the first aircraft at St Louis in April 1958. The first flight was eventually accomplished on 27 May 1958, with Bob Little doing the honors.

Chase pilot William S. Ross took the few photos of the first flight of the F4H-1, which show 142259 with its landing gear down for part of the time and up for the remainder (but with the nose-gear door always open). The first flight

The Phantom RAG

Captain Gerald G. O'Rourke, USN (Retired)

Jerry O'Rourke was a veteran of night-fighter operations in the Pacific and Korea when he took command of the first F4H-1 Phantom replacement air group, VF-101 Det. Alpha, in 1961. He later commanded the second F-4B Phantom squadron in the fleet, VF-102 'Diamondbacks', aboard USS *Enterprise* (CVAN-65), and experienced a tragic mishap in what may have been the first 'cold cat' launch of a Phantom from a carrier.

Above: Hitting the boat: an F-4B Phantom (BuNo. 148385), which had been designated F4H-1 until 1962, wears the plain markings of VF-101 'Grim Reapers', Det. Alpha, the East Coast training squadron. O'Rourke and others faced the challenges of 'bringing up' the RAGs which had not trained two-man fighter crews before.

Left: A trio of F-4B Phantoms belonging to VF-101 Det. Alpha in a 'tight' formation in March 1963. The protrusion beneath the F-4B's radome was for an IR sensor, although not all Phantoms with this nose shape had the device installed.

was far from a total success and things had to be improved. Prior to Little's second flight in 142259, the right engine was replaced and the inlet ramps were repositioned at 4°. Every item connected with the landing gear was checked thoroughly.

None of this did any good. On the second flight (29 May 1958), the nose landing-gear door still remained partly open. But things began to improve on the third and fourth flights (31 May 1958 and 2 June 1958) when the Phantom flew at Mach 1.30 to 1.68.

The Phantom and the competing Vought F8U-3 Crusader III were put through Navy Phase I Flight Evaluations at Edwards AFB. The Vought aircraft, which should have been designated F9U-1 and was the second, not the third, major version of the Crusader, was more powerful and faster and had enormous potential as an air-to-air fighter, but the F4H-1 Phantom won the competition with little difficulty.

With Navy cooperation, McDonnell now set forth to publicize its new Phantom fighter with a dramatic series of

speed and altitude record attempts. The first of these was Project Top Flight, which was to be mounted from Edwards AFB with the goal of flying higher than any other aircraft. The F4H-1 prototype was lost in a crash in October 1959 preparing for Top Flight, killing test pilot Gerald (Zeke) Huelsbeck.

Still, the Top Flight effort went ahead. The US Navy set a new world altitude record for aircraft on 6 December 1959, when Commander Lawrence E. Flint Jr flew the second F4H-1 (BuNo. 142260) to 98,560 ft (30,041 m). This bettered, by 3,902 ft (1189 m), the existing official record of 94,658 ft (28852 m) set in July 1959 by Major V. S. Ilyushin of the Soviet Union in a Su-T-43-1.

Commander Flint explained while the flight was under way that he took the F4H-1 up to 47,000 ft (14500 m), boosting its speed to nearly Mach 2.5, set the aircraft in a 45° angle of attack and climbed to 90,000 ft (27500 m), where he closed down the engines. The F4H-1 then coasted or zoomed to 98,560 ft (30,041 m). The aircraft's speed fell to an incredible 45 mph (72 km/h) as it went over the top

"In October 1959, I went to Key West to VF-101, the 'Grim Reapers'. This was the RAG which trained Navy pilots, and I was en route to being checked out in the Douglas F4D-1 Skyray. Captain Mickey Weisner, the squadron commander, saw me hanging around and said, 'What are you doing about that F-4 thing?' I thought he was referring to the Skyray. Then he said, 'You're supposed to be doing something about that Phantom stuff.' Those words were the only orders I ever received.

"The Navy was training future backseaters for the F4H-1 Phantom at James Connally AFB, Texas. On 13 December 1959, I flew to Connally to find out what was going on with the training of Phantom radar operators. When I landed, I was surrounded by guys. *They* all wanted to ask *me* what was going on. I realized we were deficient in training and preparing backseaters for the new Phantom.

"We moved the portion of VF-101 which trained Phantom crews from Key West to Oceana. This was VF-101 Det. Alpha, and I became the OIC. I felt strongly that we needed better training for the radar operators. We scrounged up a bunch of Douglas F3D-2T2 Skyknights, had them fitted with Demon radar, and used them for radar air engagements against F9F-8Ts. This was the only way future Phantom radar operators could get realistic training.

"My first Phantom flight was on 23 January 1961 in an early F4H-1F (BuNo. 148256) with Ken Stecker, a pilot who'd been flying the type at Patuxent. It was the most satisfying feeling I'd ever had in my life because it confirmed everything we'd heard about the aircraft. Compared with the F4D or F3H Demon, it was like going from a tricycle to a racing car.

"The Phantom had brute power. With two engines, when you threw burner in it would rattle your brain. A big surprise was its feeling of solidity. The F3D Skyknight had been rugged but slow. The F4H-1F Phantom had that same rock-solid rigidity but it was *fast*. And we knew the radar was good. The F4D-1 Skyray had had a good radar, but it was difficult to use and the weapon system on that airplane stank. I looked at this Phantom and said, 'It's the best aircraft in the world *and* it's a Navy aircraft with a tailhook!'

"At this time, the only armament was Sparrows. The Sidewinder did not come until later. The 'Gun Club Crowd' was pushing for a gun. I didn't want a gun because I didn't like the idea of guns going off right under the radar while you were trying to use the scope.

"In VF-101 Det. Alpha we trained the first three fleet squadrons to use the production F4H-1 Phantom (redesignated F-4B on 1 October 1961). These were VF-74 'Be-devilers' under Commander Julian Lake, VF-102 'Diamondbacks' under Commander Joseph Konzen, and VF-41 'Black Aces' under Commander Whit Freeman. Lake's VF-74 completed carrier qualifications on USS *Saratoga* in October 1961, the first in the fleet. A year later, I got orders to command VF-102 'Diamondbacks' aboard USS *Enterprise*.

"The one sad note in my experience with this great aircraft was a cold cat shot from USS *Enterprise* on 9 March 1963, which resulted in the loss of an aircraft and the death of a fine backseater, Dave Philo.

"We had an F-4B with three fuel tanks and it was to be a day launch, a cat shot with full burners. When we were ready to launch, I put it into full burner, and saluted. But there was no *whoomfh!* sending us off at 160 kt. Instead, I heard a *pop!* and we were doing about 30 kt. It was a cold cat shot. The catapult hadn't functioned.

"We did not have zero-zero ejection seats in those days. If we ejected while on deck, we wouldn't make it. 'Put on the brakes!' Dave shouted. This was wishful thinking. I had actually done this in an F3D Skyknight once, but in the Phantom it was impossible.

"I stood on the brakes. My left hand was frantically trying to get the engines out of burner. On the cat, the nose wheel was extended, so I had no nose-wheel steering and couldn't turn the aircraft. 'I'm getting out, I'm getting out!' Dave cried. I thought he was going to eject.

"Actually, he blew the canopy and tried to climb out, but he hadn't unclipped one of his connections to the airplane. I decided that I'd wait for the nose wheel to go over the bow of the carrier, then eject, and hope to get pushed forward.

"When the aircraft got to the end of its track I punched out. I felt myself going up into the air and then I hit the water head-first with my helmet. As an experienced swimmer, I got rid of the chute. I was confident I could swim to Sardinia if necessary and if only that fucking ship didn't hit me first.

"Though I hadn't realized it, for some reason the aircraft had turned to starboard 10° or so. This meant I was on the starboard side of the ship and was not going to get run over. I didn't see Dave. He had tried to jump over the side of the aircraft but was still attached and had gone in with it.

"As skipper of the squadron, I knew that we needed more practice for cold cat shots. In retrospect, we should have established procedures for this situation. It was one of many things we learned in the very early days in the Phantom."

and headed back to earth. Wearing exactly the same pressure suit as Project Mercury astronauts, Flint restarted his engines again at 70,000 ft (21500 m) and made a normal landing at Edwards AFB.

It was just the beginning of a spectacular series of records for the new McDonnell fighter. On 5 September 1960, Marine Lieutenant Colonel Thomas H. Miller claimed a new 500-km (approx. 311-mile) world-class speed record of 1,216.78 mph (1958.16 km/h) for a flight made in an F4H-1 (BuNo. 145311) at Edwards AFB. This improved on the existing record of 816.3 mph (1313.7 km/h) by nearly 50 percent. On 25 September 1960, Commander John F. (Jeff) Davis, flying an F4H-1, averaged 1,390.21 mph (2237.26 km/h) over a 100-km (approx. 62-mile) closed-circuit course, 45,000 ft (13700 m) above the Mojave Desert.

Tragic record attempt

The only record attempt to 'go wrong' was the low-level speed record on 18 May 1961, which ended in tragedy when Commander J. L. Felsman died in the crash of an F4H-1 Phantom (145316), the first of two ships to be nicknamed 'Sageburner'. Pitch dampener failure led to pilot-induced oscillation, causing the Phantom to break apart and explode in a fiery, spectacular crash.

On 24 May 1961, the US Navy launched Project LANA, a transcontinental Bendix Trophy Race speed dash by F4H-1 Phantoms refueled by A3D Skywarriors. Three of the four Phantoms participating in the flight established speed records for the trans-American journey from Ontario, California, to Floyd Bennett Field, New York.

Left: Jerry O'Rourke had flown the F3D Skyknight in night fighter missions against MiGs in Korea. Later, he went around the US locating Skyknights to employ as the F3D-2T2 in mock air combat to train radar intercept officers for the F-4 Phantom.

Below: These two F4H-1F Phantoms look almost identical, but the ship on the left belongs to the West Coast training squadron VF-121 while the lead Phantom has been painted with the tailcode of VF 101 Det. Alpha from the East Coast.

F4H-1F Phantom No. 38 (BuNo. 148266), coded as AD-182 with the 'Grim Reapers' of VF-101, was painted with yellow bands to become LANA 4 for its transcontinental speed run. As on other Project LANA aircraft, each of which acquired colorful trim, the bands extended across a portion of the wing. Despite noble efforts, the East Coast aviators of VF-101 were bested by the West Coast's VF-121, which entered only one of the five aircraft in the contest but made the fastest flight.

The top speed, set in aircraft 148270, was an average of 869.73 mph (1,399.66 km/h).

The Navy's second attempt at a 'Sageburner' low-level speed record proved more successful than the first. On 28 August 1961, Lieutenant Huntington Hardisty and Lieutenant Earl De Esch flew an F4H-1 (145307) to an average speed of 902.769 mph (1452.826 km/h) over the White Sands Missile Range, New Mexico, claiming a record for a 3-km (approx. 1.9-mile) course. Their success was followed on 22 December 1961 by a 'Skyburner' effort in which Lieutenant Colonel Robert B. Robinson (USMC) flew an F4H-1 (142260) to 1,606.342 mph (2585.086 km/h) for an absolute record. On Robinson's second run over the measured course, the Phantom was clocked at 1,700 mph (2736 km/h).

The incredible roster of speed and altitude records was capped off with a flight on 5 December 1961 at Patuxent River, Maryland, when Commander George W. Ellis claimed a new altitude record for sustained flight of 66,443.8 ft (20252.1 m), and by a series of 'time-to-climb' records set under Project High Jump in February, March and April 1962. Although the 'time-to-climb' effort may have been somewhat misleading in that the Phantom was not configured for an operational mission, with full fuel and armament, this was probably the only one of the various records which spoke with some eloquence about how the Phantom could fulfill a military role. It was not to be scoffed at when, on 3 April 1962, future Gemini astronaut Lieutenant Commander John Young took an F4H-1 Phantom (148423) to 25000 m (82,000 ft) in a scant 230.440 seconds.

The remarkable performance of the Phantom had been proven beyond doubt, and demonstrated to press, public and Congress. To quote McDonnell test pilot George S. Mills, "We had proven that we had a winner from the start."

Almost totally overlooked amid all this was the fact that the F4H-1 Phantom was not going to fly its *mission* at these incredible speeds and altitudes, and that the aircraft had been developed because it had a job to do. Production was forging ahead rapidly. Almost unnoticed amid the hoopla of speed and altitude efforts, on 25 March 1961, test pilot Thomas Harris flew the first production F4H-1 Phantom (148363). This was the 48th Phantom to be built and had J79-GE-8A or -8B engines with a revised inlet ramp. To distinguish the production machine from the less powerful Phantoms already flying (half with J79-GE-2A and half

Project LANA

To cap off the Phantom's successful speed and altitude efforts, the US Navy ran Project LANA, a transcontinental speed dash by five F4H-1Fs. The roman L signifying 50, LANA stood for '50th Anniversary of Naval Aviation' and was to demonstrate the Phantom's speed and reach. Pilots included key figures in the Phantom development story. Project LANA refueling problems handed the Bendix Trophy Race contest (24 May 1961) to VF-121's LANA 3 (BuNo. 148270), which flew from Ontario, California, to Floyd Bennett Field, New York, at an average of 869.73 mph (1399.66 km/h).

Above: In triumph, Lieutenant Commander Dick Gordon and B. R. Young grasp the Bendix prize in front of LANA 3, alias F4H-1F (BuNo. 148270), after completing the successful trip from Ontario to Floyd Bennett Field ahead of the three other LANA participants and the spare.

Below: LANA 3, flown by Gordon and Young, was resplendent in red trim. VF-121 'Pacemakers' succeeded in having their squadron designation painted in larger letters than the other squadron which provided aircraft for LANA, VF-101 'Grim Reapers'. Crews came from several squadrons.

Above: An F4H-1F Phantom (BuNo. 148261) of VF-101 practices for LANA by drinking from an A3D-2 Skywarrior (BuNo. 142650) of VAH-9. During LANA, tankers were too high (at 35,000 ft) and too early, and their pipes partly froze. Only LANA 3, Dick Gordon's Phantom, was able to feed from a fresh, untroubled A3D-2.

Left: Like all but the winning LANA Phantom, LANA 2 (BuNo. 148268, coded AD-184) had difficulties receiving fuel from the five participating A3D-2 tankers, and flew the cross-country dash slower than expected.

Right: LANA crews form a Phantom 'Who's Who'. Left to right: Cdr Paul Spencer VF-74 (pilot, LANA 4), Lt Cdr Tom Johnston VF-101 (RIO, LANA 2), Lt Ed Cowart VF-74 (RIO, LANA 1), Cdr Scott Lamoreux VF-101 (pilot, LANA 2), Cdr Julian Lake VF-74 (pilot, LANA 1), Lt jg B. R. Young VF-124 (RIO, LANA 3), CWO J. H. Glace VF-124 (RIO, LANA 5), Lt Cdr Dick Gordon VF-124 (pilot, LANA 3), Lt Cdr 'Stroke' Wagner VF-74 (RIO, LANA 4), Lt Cdr Ken Stecker VF-124 (pilot, LANA 5).

First with the fleet

VF-74 'Be-devilers', commanded by Commander Julian S. Lake, drew the historic task of becoming the first fleet squadron to operate the F4H-1 Phantom. The VF-74 skipper was tasked to run a flyoff against the Convair F-106. Included were head-on intercepts, "pretty exciting because the closing velocities were tremendous: Mach 4 in some cases." In the 1960s, many still thought of a jet fighter in terms of how fast it was, rather than how it performed its overall mission, and Lake rose to the challenge. "We loved to bug opponents at the officers' club by asking them if they'd been through the Mach lately. When they answered, 'Yeah,' we asked 'Which one?' rubbing it in that the Phantom [was the only jet which could] hit Mach 2." VF-74 took the new fighter aboard the Navy's new showpiece carrier, the USS *Forrestal* (CVA-59). "Being skipper of VF-74 was easy because they had given me so much real talent. The Navy had handpicked just about everybody in the squadron and it was a real pleasure to be in charge of it."

Below: A busy deckhand (the green vest signifies arresting gear crew) rushes to disengage the tailhook as an F4H-1 Phantom (BuNo. 148381, coded AJ-104 of VF-74) halts on the carrier. Said Lake: "The testers wanted to test the F4H until the wings fell off. I had to do conniving, scheming and politicking to get the Phantom freed up for fleet duty."

Right: The US Navy's first operational F4H-1 Phantoms in November 1961. Wags argued that VF-74 'Be-devilers' had a misplaced hyphen in their name and that the squadron's fliers, were really the 'Bed-evilers'. In fact there was little free time as Commander Lake pushed hard to get the Phantom operational.

with J79-GE-8 engines), the 47 preproduction airplanes were redesignated F4H-1F, while the 48th and subsequent production machines retained the F4H-1 nomenclature. This was misleading, since the first 47 Phantoms had little in common. Beginning with the 19th ship, all aircraft had the raised canopy and AN/APQ-72 32-in (81-cm) radar dish antenna and were identical to the production airplanes. A further change was to take place on 1 October 1962, when the F4H-1F and F4H-1 were redesignated F-4A and F-4B, respectively.

None of the speed or altitude records was going to be worth a hoot if the F4H-1 Phantom could not do its job, which was to engage aircraft attacking the Navy's carriers at a distance and protect the carrier battle groups from attack. Shipboard suitability trials were conducted using the sixth F4H-1 (143391) aboard USS *Independence* (CVA-62) off the Atlantic coast on 15-20 February 1960. A second set of carrier trials was made aboard the much smaller USS *Intrepid* (CV-11). Like early tests of the Phantom's radar (so vital to its intercept mission) and the AAM-N-6 Sparrow III radar missile (redesignated AIM-7C on 1 October 1962), the carrier trials proceeded without serious difficulty.

As early as 1960, the US Navy began to form the first RAG (Replacement Air Group), the squadron which would train future pilots and backseat RIOs (radar intercept officers). The first such squadron was VF-101 'Grim Reapers', then located at Key West, Florida, and which later moved to NAS Oceana, Virginia. The Navy had not

operated a two-seat fighter since the Douglas F3D-2 Skyknight in the Korean War (1950-53). One of VF-101's key members, Lieutenant Commander Gerald G. O'Rourke, spent part of his time as a Phantom pioneer scrounging up Skyknight relics at the 'boneyard' at Litchfield Park, Arizona, and having them field-converted to the training role with the designation F3D-2T-2 (changed to TF-10B on 1 October 1962).

As a US Navy aircraft, the Phantom was destined to operate from the decks of aircraft carriers, and carrier trials were an early hurdle that had to be overcome successfully. The sixth F4H-1 conducted initial carrier suitability trials aboard USS *Independence* during February 1960, even operating with dummy bombs on the centerline – a remarkable tribute to pilot Lieutenant Commander Paul Spencer's faith in the sturdiness and suitability of his mount. Spencer was aided by Larry Flint (the Top Flight pilot), and between them they made 18 catapult launches. A second set of trials was conducted aboard the much smaller USS *Intrepid* during April, and the aircraft proved entirely satisfactory, although some minor arrester hook adjustments were necessary. (The first front-line squadron's carrier qualifications were completed by VF-74 in October 1961, and the squadron later joined USS *Saratoga*.)

The other early Phantom RAG was VF-121 at NAS Miramar, California, and the first operational fleet squadron was VF-74 'Be-devilers' under Commander Julian S.

Above: VF-114 'Aardvarks' was one of the first Pacific Fleet squadrons to fly the Phantom operationally, and soon found itself and the F-4B pitted against the Soviets in the Cold War. A Tupolev Tu-16 'Badger-E/F' aiming its cameras at USS Kitty Hawk is stalked by an 'Aardvark' F-4B (BuNo. 149435, coded NH-402).

Left: An F-4B Phantom lands on USS Bon Homme Richard (CVA-31) in September 1963. Once production got under way the Phantom joined new air wings on many carriers.

Below: Still called F4H-1 but soon to be F-4B, an operational Phantom of VF-102 'Diamondbacks' (BuNo. 148413, coded AF-101) is bridled to the catapult.

In June 1964, there was no direct link between the McDonnell aircraft on the left and the Douglas 'Scooter' on the right, but all this changed with the mid-decade merger that created McDonnell Douglas. An F-4B Phantom (BuNo. 150431) of VF-142 'Ghostriders' refuels from an A-4C Skyhawk of VA-146 'Blue Diamonds'.

Below right: An F-4B Phantom belonging to VF-151 'Vigilantes' visits Andrews AFB, Maryland, and displays the rare markings of carrier air wing 16 (CVW-16). This F-4B (BuNo. 151003) later became an F-4N.

Below: During a ceremony at NAS Miramar to retire the US Navy's last F-3 Demon, an F-4B Phantom poses in the colors of VF-161 'Chargers' on USS Oriskany. The F-4 could operate from World War II carriers, but the US Navy limited it to 'Midway'- and 'Forrestal'-class ships.

Lake. Lake and O'Rourke worked vigorously at separate locations to improve the Phantom's performance and to persuade the Navy (heresy that it was) that its new fleet defense interceptor might even have an air-to-ground role.

VF-74, in particular, went for it in a big way, determined to prove its new mount. Its commander, Lake, had flown one of the four 'Project LANA' Phantoms used to shatter the intercontinental speed record, and he was equally concerned with proving that the new aircraft was more than a bomber-destroying BVR (beyond visual range) interceptor, and that it could dogfight with the best. He aggressively encouraged his VF-74 crews to take on USAF fighters and mix it.

Early Phantom pilots found that with some common sense they could outfight the USAF's new Convair F-106A Delta Dart in most regimes. This ability was later to be of crucial importance, as will be seen. There was absolutely no doubt that a Phantom could take off from a carrier with a load of four Sparrows and two wing tanks (the capability to employ six Sparrows, using inboard pylons in addition to the four under-fuselage wells, was rarely used), fly out to a combat radius of around 700 miles (1100 km) and pick off attacking bombers under BVR conditions.

The AN/APQ-72 radar had almost no teething problems. The Sparrow missile also became operational quite easily, although problems were discovered in later years when it was used in a role it was never intended for, namely fighter-versus-fighter actions. In 1962, the Navy was readily fielding operational Phantoms.

It was no accident that two key components of the F-4B – the Westinghouse APQ-72 radar and the AAM-N-6 (AIM-7C) Sparrow III radar-guided missile – found their way into the operational Phantom with almost no difficulty at all. There was good reason. The APQ-72, intended for use with Sparrow and developed at Patuxent River with input from the manufacturer, was an 'update' of the APQ-50, which had toted up eight years of proven fleet performance in the Douglas F4D-1 (F-6A) Skyray and was also flown in a few of the early F4H-1Fs. By the same token, the AAM-N-6 (AIM-7C) Sparrow III missile (very different from the trouble-prone Sparrow I and II models) also had years of proven fleet success with the F3H-2

As with any new aircraft, part of the success of the early Phantom program was attributable to people, among them Commander Gerald (Jerry) O'Rourke, who headed up the radar branch of NATC Patuxent River, flew early Sparrow trials, served in the first RAG, and then went on to command one of the first operational squadrons with the F-4B Phantom, the 'Diamondbacks' of VF-102 aboard the nuclear-powered USS *Enterprise* (CVAN-65).

Woolridge remembers, "In 1960-62, we practiced *all the time* on air-to-air intercept. We practiced head-on snap-ups for a situation where you had a differential of altitude between you and the bomber. We practiced from 200 ft (60 m) off the water up to the highest altitude we could reach." More than a few people were well aware that the Phantom might have other uses beyond its air defense application, and the US Air Force was beginning to express interest in a version to be designated F-110A. The Marine Corps, which existed primarily to support its troops on the ground, had been deeply involved in the Phantom program from the start and wanted some of the new airplanes for itself.

Marine officers were involved with the Phantom from

Demon. About the only issue to be debated was whether the Navy had chosen the right radar. E. T. Woolridge, who flew some of the early fleet defense interceptor trials in the Phantom, felt that a 'jazzed-up' version of the Demon's APQ-51 radar would have been even better than the improved version of the Skyray's APQ-50. "Nobody has ever agreed with me much on this," Woolridge admits, and the radar actually chosen for the Phantom was to become legendary as the farthest-reaching and most accurate of its era.

Above: An early F-4B Phantom of VF-143 'Pukin' Dogs' plugs into the buddy refueling store carried by an A-4C Skyhawk of VA-146 'Blue Diamonds' in February 1963. The Navy explored using Phantoms to refuel Phantoms, but deemed the idea uneconomical.

Below: On USS Constellation (CVA-64), an F-4B Phantom of VF-143, piloted by Commander Merrell (skipper) with the USAF's Major General Stillman in the backseat, is made ready for launch. The deck crewmen perform a rigorously choreographed routine to prepare for launch.

With the Marines

The United States Marine Corps, always a small and elite fighting force, had a strong need for the F-4 Phantom and was able to 'sign on' for the McDonnell fighter from the start – a dramatic change from a past history of 'making do' with obsolescent equipment. The Marines looked hard at the Phantom's range and ordnance-carrying capacity, expecting the Phantom to be ideal in supporting ground troops. VMF(AW)-314 'Black Knights' and VMF(AW)-531 'Gray Ghosts' both claimed to be the first Marine F-4 squadron, while the Corps quickly changed the style used to designate them – to VMFA-314 and VMFA-531. 'Fighter attack' was just the term for what the Marines had in mind. Even as the Phantom joined the Marines, the US commitment to South Vietnam was deepening and the close air support mission was taking on new importance.

Above: An F-4B Phantom of VMFA-115 'Silver Eagles' hauls a major load of bombs. Many Marine air-to-ground missions, especially close air support, spanned short to medium distances, allowing the tradeoff: more bombs, less fuel.

Below: Seen during October 1964, two F-4B Phantoms of VMFA-513 'Flying Nightmares', a one-time World War II night-fighter squadron. The black radome (right) gave way to a light-colored radome on most production ships.

Above: A VMFA-531 'Gray Ghosts'
F-4B Phantom (BuNo. 149455,
coded EC-14) makes a short-field
takeoff in 1964 tests at Camp
Lejeune, North Carolina, to
determine the Phantom's
compatibility with rough field
conditions. The Marines may have
been prescient, foreseeing
meager facilities in South
Vietnam.

Left: At times the scene on a
carrier deck could resemble a
macabre parody of the industrial
age. This early view of a Marine
Corps F-4B Phantom aboard the
USS Midway shows a green-
jacketed launch crew working on
the catapult shuttle, while the
F-4B waits with nose high and
leading- and trailing-edge wing
flaps down.

Above: One of the earliest views
of a fully operational US Marine
Corps Phantom is this portrait of a
VMF(AW)-314 Phantom. The short-
lived designation was soon
changed to VMFA-314 and the
'Black Knights' had a long and
successful career with the big
McDonnell fighter.

Right: A rare view of F-4B
Phantoms of VMF(AW)-513 'Flying
Nightmares' on a carrier deck.
This squadron never actually
made a full-length cruise on the
'boat'. The Phantom in the
background (BuNo. 148415) served
for more than 20 years, but by 1984
was being used for parts in the
QF-4B drone program.

Above: In St Louis snow in 1962, a US Navy F4H-1 Phantom (BuNo. 149405) poses as a Tactical Air Command (TAC) F-110A; the Air Force did not have Phantoms at the time. Two ships (149405 and 149406) were borrowed, feigning 'delivery' to TAC. Later, Navy F-4Bs were used in developmental work and for training.

Right: On 24 January 1962, World War II air aces Colonels Gordon Graham and George Laven drew the task of delivering the first F-110A Phantoms from St Louis to TAC's headquarters at Langley AFB, Virginia. The problem was that the USAF did not actually have any F-110A Phantoms (soon to be redesignated F-4C), so the two aircraft – to which Graham is here being handed a symbolic ignition key – were borrowed Navy F4H-1s. The takeoff of one of the ships is recorded in the lower picture.

Above: Wearing TAC badges, two USAF F-110A Phantoms (actually Navy F4H-1s) ply the skies. When the USAF finally started receiving its own Phantoms, they were delivered in the Navy's gull-gray/white paint scheme until camouflage was eventually adopted.

Far left: The Phantom looked rather handsome, with oversized TAC insignia, dated green anti-glare shield, early Navy-style air intake warning arrow and pre-1964 'buzz' number (FJ-406). F4H-1 Phantoms 149405 and 149406 toured the United States, showing USAF airmen what their future fighter would look like.

Above left: A borrowed F-4B Phantom takes off. This is an excellent portrayal of the USAF's early color scheme for its Phantoms – gull-gray/white paint, oversized national insignia, 'buzz' number and US AIR FORCE on the fuselage.

the beginning, both behind the scenes in the Pentagon and in the cockpit, where Lieutenant Colonel Robert J. Barbour flew F4H-1 No. 3 for the first time on 6 October 1959, beginning a long association with the Corps and the F-4. With a long history of receiving new types only after they had been in Navy service for a long time, the Marines were unhappy. They could see the Phantom's potential, and they wanted the airplane now! With a cadre of experienced Skyknight RIOs, the Marines were able to gear up for the new machine very quickly, and VMF(AW)-314 'Black Knights' and VMF(AW)-531 'Gray Ghosts' re-equipped during mid-1962 after their crews trained with the RAGs. The Marines were in little doubt that the Phantom was a fighter-bomber and not just an all-weather interceptor, and in August 1963 their squadrons were redesignated with a VMFA- prefix (signifying Heavier-than-air Marine Fighter Attack). It was with the Marines that the first RAF officers, Flight Lieutenant James Sawyer and Squadron Leader Ian Hamilton, became front-line Phantom aircrew.

If any doubt as to the capability of the Phantom could possibly remain, it was resolved during the October 1962 Cuban missile crisis when O'Rourke was skipper of

VF-102 on USS *Enterprise*. Every time a Cuban MiG got anywhere near crossing an imaginary line about 100 miles (160 km) away from USS *Enterprise*, "We were on top of him before he could sneeze," O'Rourke recalls. Much more important, as Americans girded for an expected invasion of Cuba, O'Rourke became more insistent that the Phantom had an air-to-ground role. As one squadron mate recalls:

"Jerry was being innovative and aggressive. He tried to figure out how to hang things on a Phantom to shoot at people. He sought approval for 5-in rockets to go on our pylons so we could go shoot at the Cubans. We also experimented with tail warning radar for the first time." But nobody was listening quite yet. O'Rourke at one point received a message rebuking him for his leadership and reminding him that the Phantom was an *interceptor*. It was not to remain so for long.

The Marines were just too late to see action in the Cuban crisis, but the 'Gray Ghosts' did make it to Key West, where they flew scrambles against Mexican airliners, lost lightplanes and even the odd Cuban MiG-17. After Cuban MiGs strafed a fishing boat 50 miles (80 km) southwest of

Forging the Phantom

Key West, Marine Phantoms were scrambled to investigate. Their crews soon discovered that the MiG-17 enjoyed a very short turn radius. As one of the MiGs closed onto the tail of his aircraft, one laconic RIO was heard to remark, "You'd better do some of that pilot shit, 'cause we're losing!"

For the US Air Force to assimilate a Navy fighter aircraft was remarkable, since for years the Navy had been seen as a repository of second-rate aircraft, compromised by the demands of carrier operation, and usually half a generation

behind their Air Force equivalents. Thus, while Air Force fighter pilots were tooling around in hot-rod, swept-wing F-86 Sabres, Navy fighter jocks were still in plank-winged Grumman Panthers, and when the Air Force was receiving F-100s (and even F-104s), the best the Navy had to offer were Tigers, Skyrays and the truly awful Demon.

Now the boot was on the other foot, and an official fly-off between the Air Force's best fighter, the F-106, and the Navy's new Phantom underlined the Phantom's superiority in virtually every parameter, in all regimes. And the Navy fighter could carry a truckload of 500-lb (227-kg) bombs without seriously compromising its performance or air-to-air capability. It was clearly a time to swallow some pride.

The US Air Force was so keen to get its hands on the new fighter that after the evaluation of two F-110A prototypes (actually borrowed, repainted Navy F-4Bs) it borrowed 29 more Navy F-4Bs to get the program moving, pending delivery of its own F-4Cs. Even this was little more than a minimum-change F-4B, with the same infrared seeker fairing below the radome (though the equipment was never required or delivered), for speed of procurement. Two wings (the 12th and 15th TFWs) were quickly re-equipped at MacDill AFB, Florida.

All three services soon deployed their new aircraft to Vietnam, where their versatility, ruggedness and sheer capability were to be fully revealed.

Front-line USAF fighter

Following President Kennedy's 20 January 1961 pledge to "pay any price, bear any burden" to combat Communism, the US Air Force launched an ambitious plan to modernize in the new decade, relying on two fighters – the F-110A Phantom and F-111A, or TFX. TFX turned out not to be a fighter and had to wait another decade for modest success in the strike role. The Phantom was left without serious competition as the backbone of the USAF's fighter force of the 1960s, a decade which began with Americans certain they would soon be fighting in the Belgian Congo or invading Cuba. Indeed, the Cuban missile crisis of October 1962 prompted the rapid formation of Phantom fighter wings. By 1963, when two F-4C wings had formed and the Phantom was in full production, Kennedy's advisers were still focusing on Cuba but had found time to announce a withdrawal of some of the few thousand Americans in a less-known trouble spot, South Vietnam.

Above: Phantoms were everywhere at MacDill AFB, Florida, when the USAF 'worked up' two Phantom wings at the same time: the 12th and 15th TFWs. The Phantom replaced aging F-84F Thunderstreaks.

Below: An F-4C Phantom (63-7478) after delivery to the US Air Force in 1963.

Below: The F-4C Phantom entered service soon after the KC-135 Stratotanker, which gave the USAF global 'legs'. In an early compatibility test, the first operational F-4C (63-7407) mates with a KC-135.

Below right: The USAF retained the US Navy's arresting system for short-field landings and evaluated it in rigorous trials with this early F-4C Phantom (63-7440). All USAF Phantoms thereafter continued to have a tailhook.

CHAPTER 2

BAPTISM OF FIRE

Above: An F-4J Phantom (BuNo. 155573) of VF-96 'Fighting Falcons' drops 500-lb Mk 82 bombs on a Vietnamese target, flying from USS Constellation (CVA-64). VF-96 made eight combat cruises and produced the war's only Navy aces.

Right: Colonel Robin Olds nearly attained ace status in three fighters, the P-38, P-51 and F-4. Olds' four MiG kills in 'Nam mattered less than his leadership of the 8th TFW 'Wolfpack'.

The Phantom was still a very new warplane when the US involvement in Vietnam slipped from being a small-scale semiclandestine COIN operation to an overt US military presence. The Phantom was soon involved, and the war quickly proved a tough testing ground for the aircraft and its crews. Best remembered are the MiG killers, but this should not obscure its primary role in Vietnam as a fighter-bomber.

Americans went to war in Vietnam confident in their purpose, training and technology. Innocents, they took for granted not just their inevitable victory but the righteousness of their cause. The first US advisers appeared in that hapless Asian backwater in 1959. In 1960, the US Navy delivered AD-6 Skyraiders and support personnel to the fledgling South Vietnamese air arm, and in 1962, the US Air Force deployed T-28 and B-26 prop-driven warplanes.

Violating an edict of warfare which holds that if you fight, you must fight to win, Americans went to war in increments. Between 1960 and 1965, in gradual steps started by Presidents Eisenhower and Kennedy and continued by Lyndon Johnson, the American presence grew. In 1965, a mammoth buildup of force began (as did bombing of North Vietnam), but not until 1969 did American troop strength peak at 565,000.

South Vietnam was less a country than a slab of real estate, where a government sat in Saigon but the hinterlands were dominated by insurgents, all of them South Vietnamese and some of whom were Communists. The upstarts belonged to the National Liberation Front (NLF), but Saigon called them Viet Cong (VC). Little influenced by Communist North Vietnam, they fought merely for change in the South. But as the United States presence escalated, Hanoi began supplying arms to NLF guerrillas.

1 November 1968 to 8 May 1972: Bombing halt – no air operations 'up North', with some limited or temporary exceptions.

26–30 December 1971: Operation Proud Deep Alpha – a five-day limited air effort against some North Vietnamese targets despite the bombing halt.

6 April 1972 to 7 May 1972: Operation Freedom Train – renewed but limited air operations against North Vietnam.

8 May 1972 to 23 October 1972: Operation Linebacker – the second major campaign of air operations against North Vietnam.

18–29 December 1972: Operation Linebacker II (also called the Eleven Day War) – the final air effort against North Vietnam spearheaded by massive B-52 bombing 'up North'.

Throughout the Vietnam War, starting in 1960, the US also fought in Laos. Early on, much of this was related to internal disputes, but by 1965 Operations Steel Tiger and Barrel Roll were directed against the North Vietnamese Army (NVA) in Laos. Beginning in the late 1960s, US airmen also fought in Cambodia. This continued beyond the end of the Vietnam War (27 January 1973) until 15 August 1973.

Above: On an early Vietnam sortie, this F-4C Phantom (63-7656) closes on the tanker with its dorsal fuel receptacle open. Note the unusual strike camera below the paired bombs on the inboard pylon. This Phantom wears the early Navy-style paint, a TAC tail badge and large 'buzz' number.

Below: A Phantom of VF-154 'Black Knights' is made ready for launch from its carrier off the coast of Vietnam. The typical carrier air wing had two fighter squadrons, two light attack squadrons (A-4 or A-7) and a medium attack squadron (A-1 or A-6).

When the American buildup began in earnest in 1965, Hanoi also built up its defenses, acquiring Soviet SA-2 'Guideline' surface-to-air missiles and MiG-15, MiG-17 and, shortly after, MiG-21 fighters. Oddly, American officials used the Chinese threat as a pretext for their build-up, though the Chinese, never kindly disposed toward their southern neighbors, consistently interfered with and impeded Soviet arms deliveries. Americans never understood that by intervening they forced North Vietnam into the war and enabled the North to expropriate a native uprising in the South.

The region seethed with trouble, and vexing problems festered next door in Laos and Cambodia. Unable to grasp simple truths about cultural and political differences, 'brass hats' in the Pentagon lumped together the very different interests of the Viet Cong, North Vietnam, China and the Soviet Union.

To recall key milestones of the Vietnam War – actually, a war fought in South and North Vietnam, Laos and Cambodia – and to understand the Phantom's role, this is a checklist of the important air campaigns.

5 August 1964: Operation Pierce Arrow – a one-day effort against targets in North Vietnam.

2 March 1965 to 31 October 1968: Operation Rolling Thunder – the first and longest campaign of air operations against North Vietnam.

Above: Surrounded by F-102A Delta Daggers, factory-new F-4C Phantoms of the 555th TFS 'Triple Nickel' assemble at Naha, Okinawa, during the McDonnell fighter's first Asian deployment. This show of force in the region failed to prevent Vietnam hostilities from escalating.

Right: The F-4B Phantoms of VMFA-531 'Gray Ghosts' were the first Marine aircraft to arrive at Da Nang in April 1965, as the American buildup gathered force. Marine ground troops arrived at the same time, dramatically increasing the US commitment to Saigon.

Unable to grasp anything foreign, Americans ignored difficult, hard-to-pronounce names like Xom Bong and Vinh Linh, hardly apt for radio chatter in the heat of combat, and divided North Vietnam into Route Packages, or RPs. Pilots talked of flying to RP One or to Pax Six. Roman numerals were supposed to be used (for example, Route Package VI) but rarely were. The region around Hanoi and Haiphong, where North Vietnam's heaviest defenses were concentrated, was Route Pack Six.

The US Navy kept aircraft carriers at Dixie Station in the South China Sea for operations over South Vietnam, and at Yankee Station in the Gulf of Tonkin for strikes against the North. Much of the air war was fought from land bases in adjacent Thailand, which allowed US Air Force aircraft to operate from its soil against targets in North Vietnam. The war was also supported by bases at Okinawa, Guam and in the Philippines.

For the F-4 Phantom, it began with Operation Pierce Arrow – the retaliation on 5 August 1964 for North Vietnamese torpedo boat attacks on US vessels in the Gulf of Tonkin. Supposedly a 'limited and fitting' response of air strikes against 'gun boats and certain facilities of North Vietnam', the strikes enjoyed top cover by Phantoms which saw no actual combat. For the next 11 years, warriors were to risk their lives in combat which, to one degree or another, was to remain 'limited' if almost never 'fitting'. In any normal conflict the Phantom would have been the war-winning airplane: in the Vietnam conflict, not won by the Americans, the Phantom prevailed in every campaign it fought.

The F-4B Phantoms from USS *Constellation* (CVA-64), which flew top cover for the Gulf of Tonkin air strikes on 5 August 1964, were a marvel of American technology. Every Navy carrier had two fighter squadrons on board, and the Phantom now made up just less than half of the US Navy's carrier-based fighter force. The other half comprised the Vought F-8 Crusader, which could operate from World War II 'Essex'-class warships. The F-4 flew from the postwar 'Midway' class (which in two instances put to sea with one squadron each of F-4s and F-8s) and the postwar 'Forrestal' class of later flat tops.

To single-seat, single-engine, cannon-armed F-8 Crusader jocks, the Phantom was an interceptor and *their* aircraft, loved by pilots in a way no Phantom ever was, was a *fighter*. In fact, the Phantom had better radar and Sparrow capability and sacrificed little in maneuverability.

The first US Air Force Phantoms in the region were gull-gray F-4Cs of the 555th TFS 'Triple Nickel', which deployed to Naha AB, Okinawa, between December 1964 and March 1965. In early 1965, the USAF also rotated squadrons through Ubon, Thailand. The Air Force flew the Phantom with two pilots, rather than a pilot and an RIO (radar intercept officer), and they too wanted to kill MiGs and become aces.

But the North Vietnamese rarely fought on any terms but their own. The North Vietnamese chose the time and place of any engagement. A chivalrous duel was the last thing a MiG pilot wanted. This was considered downright un-American! The North Vietnamese refused to fight *fair*. In the first air-to-air action of 4 April 1965, MiG-17s bushwhacked a pair of F-105 Thunderchiefs from behind, without warning, and escaped. This 'hit-and-run' tactic was to recur.

Many Americans in the air that day were veterans of the Korean air war. There, the biggest jet battles in history had been fought and, at times, 400 fighters grappled against each other. It was widely understood that in Korea American pilots had downed 15 MiGs for every fighter lost. The real figure was seven to one, which is still the best 'kill ratio' in history. And now North Vietnam's third-rate, Third World air force was defeating the Americans.

Marine air

Only the Marine Corps, up to the 1965 buildup, consistently flew the Phantom as an air-to-ground warplane to support its own troops. Two battalions of Marines came ashore at Da Nang on 10 April 1965 (the start of the buildup), and with them came the first Phantoms to fly from Vietnamese soil. The 'Gray Ghosts' of VMFA-531, under Colonel William C. McGraw Jr, arrived at Da Nang's airfield that day, and the Marines took up residence in tents – or under the wings of their planes – while Air Force personnel on the other side of the base lived in air-conditioned villas.

Warrant Officer John D. Cummings, who was to become a MiG killer seven years later, recalled, "At first, we just flew around and made a lot of black smoke. Our job was to help the ground guys with close air support. We flew a lot of missions with 2.75-in rockets and Zuni rocket projectiles. We had the newer low-drag bombs rather than the box-finned World War II stuff the stateside Marine units were equipped with, but we never had enough of the bombs. Our guys would go out with a six-bomb MER (multiple ejector rack) with only three bombs. We actually snitched ordnance from the Navy, some of which we didn't know how to use, like Snakeyes (fin-retarded bombs). We learned fast." Among other distinctions, VMFA-531 became the first squadron to use jet aircraft in support of helicopter-borne assault units. In July 1965, Cummings' squadron was replaced by VMFA-513 'Flying Nightmares', but the Marine aviation presence remained modest because the airfield facilities were inadequate.

The Marines' lot improved in late 1965 with construction of the base at Chu Lai and, in time, the Marines had as

many as four fighter squadrons 'in country' at a time. Some flew F-8 Crusaders (including the F-8E, the only version with significant air-to-ground capability) until about 1968, when the Phantom predominated and the F-4J joined the F-4B in Marine units.

In the Second Battle of Ia Drang Valley in October 1965, the US First Air Cavalry Division defeated a larger force of North Vietnamese regulars – and never again were Hanoi's forces to win any major battle on the ground. But in the air, even when the vaunted F-4 Phantom began arriving in large numbers, the Americans were getting their pants beat off.

In addition to North Vietnam's air force of Soviet-supplied MiGs, Hanoi was encircled by the largest number of AAA (anti-aircraft artillery) batteries ever implanted in one place. North Vietnam also introduced the SAM (surface-to-air missile). None of this weaponry was at the cutting edge of technology, nor were its users better-trained than the Americans, and when asked why a global super-power could not prevail over his countrymen, a North Vietnamese explained, "We live here."

The first American air-to-air kill of the war, in a bizarre sidelight to history, did not involve the North Vietnamese. On 9 April 1965, F-4B Phantoms from USS *Ranger* (CVA-61) battled Chinese MiG-17s near Hainan Island. The Phantom (BuNo. 151403), piloted by Lieutenant Junior Grade Terence M. Murphy of VF-96 'Fighting Falcons', shot down a MiG-17 but was then lost in action. The Chinese claimed that Murphy was shot down by an AIM-7 Sparrow missile fired by his wingmen.

In the final analysis, air-to-air combat was of secondary importance in a war where Phantoms were tasked to deliver ordnance. By early 1965, all three services were using the F-4 to deliver bombs. The dominant mission of American combat aircraft in the theater became interdiction – hitting targets behind the enemy's front line, sensing communications and supply routes, and harassing and destroying enemy surface forces. There was no front line in the accepted sense of the term, and some Phantom pilots were providing close air support to embattled soldiers throughout South Vietnam, while others were carrying bomb loads North. The RF-4B and RF-4C, with their multisensor reconnaissance capability, were as important as their ordnance-toting brethren.

On a mission North, a USAF F-4C Phantom typically carried four Sparrows, four Sidewinders and eight 750-lb

Above: One of the first RF-4C Phantoms (64-1051) to arrive at Tan Son Nhut airfield, Saigon, in October 1965. Though this is a nicely-posed night portrait (with a very real guard, much aware of the Viet Cong insurgent threat), the RF-4Cs flew mainly day missions in the early years of war, relinquishing the nocturnal hours to the RF-101C Voodoo.

Left: A VF-21 'Freelancers' F-4B Phantom (BuNo. 151485) makes a medium-altitude drop of bombs.

Left: A Phantom leaves wingtip vortex trails while hooking on to a KC-135 Stratotanker during a Southeast Asia combat mission. Even when air refueling was not essential (as during short-range missions), it permitted a heavier ordnance load. The latter purpose was often stymied by a 1966-67 'bomb shortage', which the Pentagon steadfastly denied but which sent Phantom crews into harm's way with less than a full bomb load.

Operation Bolo

Colonel Robin Olds took command of the USAF's 8th TFW at Ubon on 30 September 1966. Olds was a West Point graduate, football hero and air ace, with 24½ kills in P-38s and P-51s in World War II. Olds, a robust six-footer whose reddish-blond hair was beginning to turn gray, was 44 and he had not flown an aircraft in combat for 22 years. Olds had been a colonel for 16 years, longer than any of his men had been in the Air Force. His Phantom pilots were being defeated in battle and Olds intended to turn the tide.

Right: Phantom at war. An F-4C of the 497th TFS/8th TFW during the Operation Bolo era. The 497th TFS also flew black-bottomed F-4C and F-4D night-interdiction missions against the Ho Chi Minh Trail.

Above: Vietnam area camouflage came to be known as the TO 1-1-4 paint scheme, after the technical order which prescribed it.

Right: Colonel Robin Olds checks his Phantom's tailpipe under the watchful eye of his crew chief.

Below: 'Wolfpack' MiG killers: Capt. Francis M. Gullick, 1 Lt William D. Lafever, Capt. Richard M. Pascoe, Col. Robin Olds, Maj. Thomas M. Hirsch, Capt. Norman Wells, Maj. Everett J. Raspberry. Pascoe got two MiGs, rose to Major General, and only recently retired.

"In the last quarter of 1966, the MiGs began concentrated efforts to harass US strike forces. MiG attacks forced many strike flights to jettison bomb loads prior to reaching the target area, thus seriously degrading the strike effectiveness. The later model MiG-21s [had] the capability to carry radar-guided or heat-seeking missiles. This made the MiGs a real threat as well as a harassment to US fighters.

"En route to Ubon, I stopped in Saigon. We talked about mounting a major effort against the North Vietnamese MiG force. Then I took command of the 'Wolfpack'.

"When I joined that outfit, they were a sad-assed lot. They had taken their licks. They were losing people. I thought, man, this is just exactly why I came here because I'm going to change *that*.

"I stood up in front of them. I said, 'Okay, troops. I haven't fought for 22 years. You guys are here fighting this war. Pretty soon I'm going to be leading you. But *initially* I'm going to be flying 'Green Sixteen'. That means 'Tail End Charlie'. And you guys teach me, and teach me good, and teach me fast, because I learn fast. And just make sure you know more than I do, always. Otherwise, I'm going to come down on you like a ton of bricks. And when I get out front, you want to be damned sure you have a good leader out there – so teach me.'

"I flew Green Sixteen for about two weeks. We got shot at a lot. I saw stuff that absolutely horrified me – the tactics, the way they were going about it.

"I've heard this legend that North Vietnam's force of MiG-17s and MiG-21s was led by a wily and aggressive fighter wing commander known as Colonel Tomb. If so, he was my adversary in what we now called Operation Bolo. I thought it up. I planned it.

I carried it out. I approached the damned near unapproachable General Momyer, Seventh Air Force CO in Saigon. I gave my ideas. [Momyer] said go ahead.

"I went back to Ubon and got to work. I selected two smart youngsters to help me work out routes and timings. We 'dry ran' each scenario many times, one or the other of us taking the role of a North Vietnamese radar operator, the chief of the North Vietnamese defense net and the American strike force commander. We tried to figure North Vietnamese reaction time, communication delays, problem solving, decision making . . .

"D-day was set for 2 January. The only way to destroy MiGs was in air-to-air combat; the mission hinged on a method to get a sizeable number of MiGs airborne.

"The QRC-160 ECM pod – a barrage-type noise jammer – had been used by some American warplanes to partially neutralize Hanoi's defenses. But the F-4C Phantom had never before used the QRC-160, which arrived at Ubon on 27 December 1966. For Operation Bolo, our Phantoms were configured asymmetrically with a fuel tank under one wing and a QRC-160 under the other, a centerline fuel tank, four Sidewinders and four Sparrows.

"I commanded the strike force of 14 flights of F-4C Phantoms (56 aircraft), six flights of F-105 Wild Weasels configured for SAM suppression (24) and four flights of Lockheed F-104C Starfighters (16). Radio callsigns were a word-play on my name and the names of automobiles – OLDS, FORD and RAMBLER flights.

"Using the North Vietnamese MiG base at Phuc Yen as the primary target at H-hour, the arrival of the force into the battle area was set up on a careful schedule. Based on tanker requirements and the location of

our airfields, our force was divided into 'east' and 'west' components. The 'west' force of seven flights of F-4C Phantoms from the 8th Wing would get the MiGs airborne, sweep the suspected orbit areas and cover Phuc Yen and Gia Lam (Hanoi). The 'east' force, composed of five flights of F-4C Phantoms from the 366th Tactical Fighter Wing at Da Nang in Vietnam, was to cover Kep and Cat Bai and block egress and/or ingress at the Chinese airfield at Ning Ming, China.

"On 2 January 1967, the weather was not quite as good as I'd felt was the minimum for a successful fight. Over the battle area there was undercast up to 7,000 or 8,000 ft, with unknown bottoms.

"We launched. As lead of OLDS flight I was flying F-4C 63-7680 (FP), nicknamed 'Candy', with Lieutenant Charles A. Clifton. Chappie James was leading FORD flight and John Stone was leading RAMBLER flight. I attempted to lure MiGs into the air by feinting a strike by F-105 Thunderchiefs. Believing that bomb-laden and vulnerable Thuds were approaching, the Vietnamese ordered MiGs into the air. My flight was first into the area. To keep up the pretense that we were F-105s, aircraft radar and QRC-160 ECM pods remained on standby until we crossed the Red River near Phuc Yen.

"Into the imperfect weather came our entire armada – F-4s, F-104s, F-105s, EB-66s, supported by KC-135s and RC-121s. As the attack force got into North Vietnam, MiG-21s taxied out, guided by GCI operators who were directing the MiG pilots, they thought, towards easy pickings.

"We ingressed on a heading of 145°. Weather at the time was solid undercast, tops estimated 7,000 ft. I led OLDS flight past Phuc Yen for approximately 14–18 nm, then turned so as to cross Phuc Yen

again on a reciprocal heading. As the turn was completed, we picked up a radar contact low at 12 o'clock, high closure rate.

"Just as we neared the top of the undercast, the radar lock broke. The target was under or in the overcast and had passed beneath us on an opposite heading. I led the flight on past [Phuc Yen] airfield again. Just as we again crossed Phuc Yen, FORD flight arrived on time. Everything then happened at once. FORD called a MiG-21 closing on OLDs flight at their seven o'clock. OLDS 2 saw the MiG simultaneously. Additional MiGs were popping up through the clouds.

"After 90° of turn in a modified break, I sighted an aircraft at my 11 o'clock in a left turn, slightly low, about a mile and a quarter away. I closed on this target for positive identification.

"The target was positively identified as a MiG-21, silver in color, too distant for markings to be seen. I instructed the [backseat] pilot to go bore sight, put the pipper on target, and called for a lock-on and full-system operation.

"I was setting us up for an AIM-7 attack. Closure was enough to necessitate haste in establishing the proper attack parameter. We achieved a lock-on [and] went full system. I centered the steering dot (interlocks 'in') and pressed, released, pressed and held the trigger. I launched two AIM-7s and appeared to track. At that moment, we lost radar lock-on, having passed beyond minimum range, and the missiles had no chance to guide.

"I'd missed. My next act was to turn to the heat-seeking AIM-9 Sidewinder missile. I selected HEAT, put the pipper on the MiG as he was disappearing into the overcast, received an indistinct missile growl, and fired one AIM-9, knowing the missile had little chance to guide.

"During this encounter, OLDS 2 was busily engaged in pursuing the original MiG-21 that had closed behind my flight. In addition, as I closed on the MiG evaded in the cloud deck, I [found] another in my 10 o'clock, in a left turn, and just above the clouds. I then turned my attention to the second MiG.

"I was about to score a kill while upside down, rapidly checking cockpit functions and struggling to stay in shooting parameters.

"It was hairy. I pulled sharp left, turned inside him, pulled my nose up about 30° above the horizon, rechecked my missiles and ready panel, switched fuel to internal wing transfer, barrel-rolled to the right, held my position upside down and behind the MiG until the proper angular deflection and range parameters were satisfied, completed the rolling maneuver, and fell in behind and below the MiG-21 at his seven o'clock position at about 0.95 Mach.

"Range was 4,500 ft. Angle off was 15°. The MiG-21 obligingly pulled up well above the horizon and exactly down sun. I put the pipper on his tail pipe, received a perfect growl, squeezed the trigger once, hesitated, then squeezed again.

"The first Sidewinder leapt in front and within a split-second turned left in a definite and beautiful collision course direction. I did not take my eyes off the first Sidewinder and consequently did not see what the second missile did. It appeared, to my peripheral vision, to have guided also.

"Suddenly the MiG-21 erupted in a brilliant flash of orange flame. A complete wing separated and flew back into the airstream, together with a mass of smaller debris. The MiG swapped ends immediately, and tumbled forward for a few instants. It then fell, twisting, corkscrewing, tumbling lazily toward the top of the clouds.

"Our guys shot down no fewer than *seven* MiG-21s that day. RAMBLER flight, headed up by J. B. Stone, achieved the final kills.

"As for OLDS flight, after we'd done our part I gave the order to egress, knowing that OLDS 4, not having obtained fuel from his centerline tank, was then at Bingo [fuel minimum].

"We left the battle area as FORD flight broke off its engagement and as RAMBLER flight became engaged. We proceeded to home station as briefed. The score was seven to nothing. To mount Bolo, hundreds of men had worked grueling extra hours. When OLDS flight entered the pattern to return to base, hundreds were watching to see we all returned safely."

Baptism of Fire

Right: An F-4D Phantom (66-7661) of the 435th TFS/8th TFW at low level, late in the Vietnam War. The red star denotes a MiG-21 kill on 11 May 1972 by Captain Stephen E. Nichols and First Lieutenant James R. Bell. Busy '661 survived the war and later served with the District of Columbia Air National Guard, and is now on display at Andrews AFB, Maryland.

Below right: In Hollywood-style posed shots, fighter crews raced toward their aircraft to take off, or waved triumphantly when returning from a mission. In real life, outgoing Phantom jocks walked normally from a vehicle to their craft.

Below: 'Daisy Cutter' extended impact fuzes protrude from the inboard Mk 84 bombs being lugged, together with CBU-58 cluster units, by this F-4D Phantom (66-7730) of the 390th TFS/366th TFW 'Gunfighters', flying from Da Nang. The blue/white canopy rails and fin flash are also associated with this squadron.

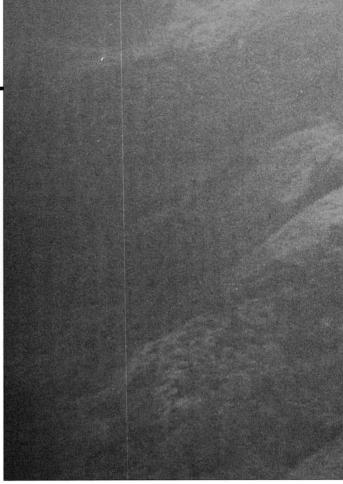

(340-kg) bombs. The Phantom flew to an 'anchor orbit', refueled from a KC-135 tanker, then punched into enemy air space at medium to high altitude, hauling its bomb load to a combat radius of 600 miles (960 km) or more. As SAMs proliferated, a shift was made to low altitude, the radius decreased and KC-135 anchors moved closer to the combat zone. Once at its target, the Phantom could drop its bombs from a dive or go in low to avoid SAMs, while risking small-arms fire.

Missiles

In air combat the Phantom relied upon its missiles. The AIM-7D Sparrow (144 in; 3.66 m long), powered by a Thiokol prepackaged liquid rocket motor, had been developed in 1960 and was accommodated in ventral trays, with target illumination by the Phantom's own radar. The radar-guided AIM-7 Sparrow gave the Americans a BVR (beyond visual range) capability at distances of up to 28 miles (45 km), but this was negated by the despised ROE (rules of engagement), which rarely permitted a 'missiles-free' BVR launch.

The AIM-9 Sidewinder had been blooded as early as the Taiwan Straits crisis (1958) by Chinese F-86F Sabres and became standard for USAF and US Navy fighters. The Sidewinder was 113 in (2.87 m) long and had a range of about 12 miles (19 km). Its infrared seeker head had to be cooled before it could lock on to a target, but this was a

straightforward process. Ultimately, the Sidewinder scored more aerial victories in the conflict than any other weapon.

A late entrant into the conflict, the F-4D was intended to employ the Hughes AIM-4D Falcon as a replacement for the AIM-9 Sidewinder. Of the three major air-to-air missiles of the war, the AIM-4 Falcon proved least suitable. Captain Thomas McInerney, who ferried the first Falcon-equipped F-4Ds to Southeast Asia, remembered, "The Falcon required all sorts of fancy setting up and had to be cooled before firing." The Falcon proved too temperamental for air-to-air combat with other fighters (a role for which *none* of the era's missiles had been designed) and took too long to spool up. Returning from a combat mission, Colonel Robin Olds told his mechanic line chief that he "didn't give a damn" if the Falcon was supposed to be the weapon of choice; it was "a piece of shit". Field modifications caused the Falcon to be replaced quickly by . . . the Sidewinder.

The first American crew to down a North Vietnamese MiG were Commander Thomas C. Page and Lieutenant John C. Smith Jr of VF-21 'Freelancers', flying an F-4B (BuNo. 151488) from USS *Midway* (CVA-41) near Haiphong, on 17 June 1965. Pilots of the USAF's 45th TFS operating from Ubon, Thailand, claimed two MiG-17s on 10 July 1965.

But the war was not going well. On 24 July 1965, an F-4C Phantom (63-7599) of the 47th TFS at Ubon became the first American warplane downed by a SAM. Eighteen months elapsed before the Phantom was configured to carry an ECM pod, which was at first the QRC-160. This offered limited protection from SAMs at the expense of one Sparrow missile (the pod was carried in a Sparrow bay). But, neither ECM pods nor imaginative tactics provided a full solution: SAMs claimed only 5.7 percent of all US aircraft shot down, but they forced the Americans to low altitudes where guns were lethal.

By late 1965, F-4B Phantoms were flying from carrier decks and Marine airfields in South Vietnam, and F-4C Phantoms were operating from USAF bases in Vietnam and Thailand. For close support, many believed slower airplanes like the prop-driven A-1 Skyraider were more accurate. Air-to-air action was going very poorly.

The RF-4C version of the Phantom made its debut in Southeast Asia on 30 October 1965, when the 16th TRS, Shaw AFB, South Carolina, arrived at Tan Son Nhut, near Saigon. The squadron became part of the 460th TRW, activated on 2 February 1966 under Colonel Edward H. Taylor. Within eyesight of the capital of the nation they were defending, RF-4C pilots were cautioned to turn quickly at the end of the runway when preparing to take off, lest they fall victim to Viet Cong mortar fire. Until 1972, the RF-4C flew day missions over South Vietnam and Laos, while hazardous night sorties up North were handled by the older, but faster, RF-101C Voodoo.

RF-4C Phantom

With the formation of the 432nd TRW at Ubon on 18 September 1966, the USAF's reconnaissance assets were now divided among two wings. The 432nd operated only a single RF-4C squadron, the 14th TRS, and acquired several squadrons of Phantom fighters while retaining its 'reconnaissance' designation. As for the RF-4C, a secret report (on 15 November 1966) for USAF Seventh Air Force

Above: This low-level bomber belongs to the 557th TFS/12th TFW at Cam Ranh Bay. The USAF's tailcode system evolved slowly: from 1967 to 1972, the first letter denoted a wing and the second a squadron. After 1972, all aircraft in a wing wore the same code.

Below: An F-4C of the 559th TFS, a constituent of the Da Nang-based 366th TFW 'Gunfighters'. Early in the war, every fighter wing flew every mission. Later, the 366th drew the air-to-ground role.

Dropping the Paul Doumer Bridge

On 10 May 1972, following a halt lasting more than 3½ years, US Air Force and Navy aircraft resumed large-scale attacks on North Vietnam. While Navy airplanes attacked targets at Haiphong and Hai Dong, Air Force F-4s struck at targets close to the enemy capital: the Paul Doumer Road/Rail Bridge and the Yen Vien Railyard. Each raiding force comprised 16 F-4s of the 8th TFW, with target support from a total of 28 F-4s (from the 13th, 336th and 555th TFSs, 432nd TRW) armed for air-to-air combat, eight F-4s (8th TFW) carrying chaff bombs, 12 F-105G Wild Weasels (from the 17th TFS, 388th TFW) for defense supression and four EB-66Es (from the 42nd TEWS, 388th TFW) providing stand-off radar jamming.

Soon after 0940, the 22-strong pre-strike support force crossed the Laos/North Vietnamese border and headed for the enemy capital. OYSTER and BALTER flights were in the lead, briefed to engage MiGs coming up to engage the raiders. Reduced to six aircraft after two had gone unserviceable, these fighters were to mount a barrier patrol northwest of Hanoi. 'Red Crown', the cruiser USS *Chicago* in the Gulf of Tonkin, reported approaching MiGs, and the four F-4s of OYSTER flight, flying at 2,000 ft, accelerated to supersonic speed and turned to meet the incoming enemy airplanes. These F-4s carried 'Combat Tree', a device which picked up and displayed signals from the MiGs' IFF transponders, and thus provided a positive hostile identification of the aircraft before they came within visual range. The four incoming MiGs were picked up at 15 miles.

In OYSTER 3, WSO Captain Chuck DeBellevue informed his pilot, Steve Ritchie, that the MiG in front was radiating enemy IFF code signals. "He's squawking MiG! . . . Stand by to shoot!" The F-4s eased into shallow climbs and, as the MiGs came within firing range, the three aircraft with serviceable radars launched a total of five AIM-7 Sparrows. Only two missiles functioned as advertized, but their effect was devastating. Captain Roger Locher, WSO in the leading F-4, saw two smoke puffs far away in front of him, and then he caught sight of two badly-damaged MiGs tumbling out of the sky.

The two surviving MiGs continued their headlong charge and passed close over the top of the Phantoms, as the latter turned and pulled into tight turns to get on their tails. Locher was about to launch a Sparrow at one of the enemy fighters when, suddenly, the tables turned. Appearing as if from nowhere, a pair of MiG-19s came up from below and swung behind the OYSTER leader. A burst of 30-mm cannon fire tore into the American fighter, starting a serious fire. Locher ejected, but the pilot, Major Robert Lodge, was still in the blazing fighter as it dived to the ground.

As this was happening, OYSTER 3 shot down another MiG-21 with an AIM-7. The survivors of BALTER flight then broke off the action and curved away to the southwest. By this time the rest of the pre-strike force was in position around Hanoi. Orbiting outside range of the capital's SAM batteries, the four EB-66s started jamming the enemy air defense radars. The four F-105Gs ran into the target area at low altitude, ready to engage active SAM sites with Shrike and Standard anti-radiation missiles.

The eight F-4s of DINGUS and HITEST flights then started to lay a trail of chaff along the final part of the route to the target. At 15-second intervals, each Phantom released an M-129 chaff bomb, which fell clear and opened to disgorge millions of thin metalized strips to confuse the enemy radar. The two flights headed towards Hanoi at 23,000 ft and 540 kt, with the four Phantoms in each flight maintaining 'jamming pod formation' (aircraft positioned in a line abreast, with a separation of 2,000 ft between them). The noise transmissions from the ALQ-87 pods carried by each airplane produced a combined wedge of jamming on the enemy radar screens, which prevented an accurate engagement of individual airplanes.

That morning, the SA-2 batteries around Hanoi launched scores of 'Guideline' missiles at the raiders. Flying as WSO in HITEST 4, Lieutenant Lanny Toups recalled: "All of a sudden I saw the RHAW gear light up. I told Mike [Captain Suhy, the pilot] I had a SAM at 10 o'clock. He said 'Oh shit, take it down!' And just about the time we started down, the missile detonated. It went off between us and [HITEST 3], the blast turned us upside down." Although this Phantom and others suffered near misses, thanks to the jamming

Although the glory went to the MiG killers (top, left to right) Capt. Stephen L. Eaves (WSO), 1 Lt D. Markle (pilot), Capt. Charles D. DeBellevue (WSO) and Capt. Richard S. Ritchie (pilot), 'smart' bombs (above) had more impact on Hanoi's ability to wage war.

none of the aircraft suffered serious damage.

The F-4s let go of their chaff bombs over Hanoi itself, and then turned west and withdrew. In the following six minutes the clouds of chaff-falling strips expanded and merged to form a chaff corridor, 2 miles wide and 18 miles long, leading to Hanoi. Flying through the chaff corridor, the Paul Doumer Bridge attack force closed on its target at 13,000 ft. The 16 Phantoms, led by Colonel Carl Miller, were divided up into four flights of four, all in jamming pod formation. The airplanes of GOATEE flight, heading the attack, each carried a pair of 2,000-lb electo-optical guided bombs (EOGBs). The aircraft of BILOXI, JINGLE and NAPKIN flights, coming up behind, each carried two 2,000-lb laser-guided bombs (LGBs). Four F-4s flew as close escort, and four F-105G Wild Weasels provided defense supression.

In the GOATEE flight airplanes, the WSO positioned the sighting reticle over the target on the TV screen in front of him, and pressed a button to lock the bomb on to the target. He then repeated the process with the second bomb. Five miles short of the target, the F-4s entered 30° dives, and shortly afterwards they released their bombs. Modern EOGBs are precise weapons, but these were not. Carl Miller recalled, "I pickled off my EOGBs. One made a 90° turn and went for downtown Hanoi – I think it impacted near the train station. I don't know where the other one went. The EOGB was a launch-and-leave weapon, they were supposed to stay locked on after release. But they didn't." The exploding EOGBs drenched

Above: *An F-4D Phantom (66-0234) of the 435th TFS/8th TFW hauls fuel, Sparrows and Paveway laser-guided bombs of the kind which dropped the Thanh Hoa and Paul Doumer Bridges.*

Mutual ECM cover

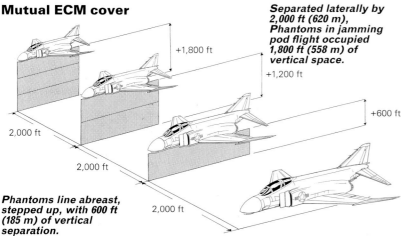

Separated laterally by 2,000 ft (620 m), Phantoms in jamming pod flight occupied 1,800 ft (558 m) of vertical space.

+1,800 ft

+1,200 ft

+600 ft

2,000 ft

2,000 ft

2,000 ft

Phantoms line abreast, stepped up, with 600 ft (185 m) of vertical separation.

Above: *'Smart' bombs, smart tactics, emphasis on the importance of electronic warfare and flight integrity all contributed to accurate delivery of ordnance on North Vietnam's vital bridges.*

Below: *During the 1972 Linebacker campaign, 8th TFW F-4D Phantoms keep a KC-135 boom operator busy en route to the target.*

the bridge in spray, but failed to inflict any damage on it.

As GOATEE flight left the target, the Phantoms of BILOXI, JINGLE and NAPKIN flights began their attacks with LGBs. One aircraft in each pair carried a laser designator pod to designate the target for its bombs and those dropped by its wing aircraft. Two by two, the raiders attacked in 45° dives, releasing their bombs at 12,000 ft and pulling out of the dives to remain above the worst of the anti-aircraft fire. Several bombs exploded against the bridge or in the water beside it, throwing spray and debris high into the air.

As the last of the Paul Doumer Bridge raiders left the target, the aircraft making for the Yen Vien Railyard followed them through the chaff corridor. The 16 F-4s of BERTHA, GIGOLO, GOPHER and ICEBURG flights dropped

their loads of eight 500-pounders and withdrew without loss.

Four flights of F-4s covered the raiders' withdrawal, and one of them, HARLOW flight patrolling near Hanoi, suffered another snap attack from a MiG-19. Attacking from below, the North Vietnamese fighter loosed off an accurate burst of cannon fire, which sent a Phantom down in flames.

During the action that day, US Air Force Phantoms shot down three MIG-21s, for the loss of two of their number. The Paul Doumer Bridge had suffered serious damage and was impassable to wheeled vehicles, but all of its spans were still in place. (During a follow-up attack the next day, LGBs dislodged a loosened span and it fell into the river.) The Yen Vien Railyard was cratered at its entrance and exit points, and many of the lines were cut.

Above: The high intensity of the Linebacker campaign often produced a 'mix' of squadrons flying together. An F-4D of the 13th TFS/432nd TRW ('OC' tailcode), an F-4E of the 469th TFS/388th TFW ('JV') and an RF-4C of the 14th TRS/432nd TRW top up from a KC-135.

Above right: In defiance of the rules, shark mouths were first painted on Phantoms by artist/fighter jock Captain Steve Steven. This 'JJ'-coded F-4E of the 34th TFS/388th TFW is on a mission from Korat, Thailand.

Right: Ground crews struggled to keep 'em flying. An RF-4C Phantom of the 14th TRS/432nd TRW fires the cartridge starter.

Below: In 1969, during the frustrating 'bombing halt' up North, an 'LA'-coded F-4E returns from battle, possibly in Laos.

headquarters in Saigon showed that the photo-Phantom's AN/APQ-102A SLAR (side-looking airborne radar) was having major teething problems and, after months of effort, was still not deemed reliable in combat. SLAR development problems were not fully 'fixed' for years. The US Marine Corps brought its reconnaissance variant of the Phantom into combat and, by March 1966, the RF-4B was operating from Da Nang.

The Phantom legend became serious starting in 1965, when the US mounted its Rolling Thunder campaign against the North. The brunt of these missions was borne by the F-105 Thunderchief protected by a CAP (combat air patrol) of Phantoms. Although, as the campaign dragged on into 1966, 1967 and 1968, the USAF inventory had no more F-105 airframes to offer up – nearly half of the production run was lost in Southeast Asia – and so the 'Thud' was gradually replaced in the air-to-ground role by the Phantom. (Most Navy and Marine Corps missions over the North were flown by Phantoms from the start.)

From the earliest days, USAF Phantom crews were also challenged by risky night missions into Laos and North Vietnam. The 497th TFS, part of the 8th TFW 'Wolfpack' at Ubon (which was soon to receive a new commander, Colonel Robin Olds), began nocturnal operations in 1966. Lieutenant Myron L. Donald recalls, "The 497th was a night truck-hunting squadron that flew over Laos and Route Package One in the southern part of North Vietnam. Usually, we had no assigned targets at the time of takeoff. We checked with the [C-130 Hercules] Airborne

Battlefield Command and Control Center (ABCCC) that would assign us an area. The lead aircraft carried flares, CBUs (cluster bomb units) and bombs. Lead would usually attack in the dark if he saw truck lights, or would drop flares in a likely area. Two would be in trail far enough back so that he could be over the areas as the flares lit. The number two aircraft usually had CBUs, rockets and bombs. Once on a target, we would fly a race track pattern over the target until we were out of ordnance or fuel. We flew out and back in radar trail and usually never saw each other during a mission."

As late as December 1966, North Vietnam's air arm had only 50 MiG-17 and 20 MiG-21 fighters (this total of 70 was to rise to 170), whereas US tactical warplanes in Southeast Asia numbered 400. The first 'kill' of a MiG-21 by a Phantom occurred on 23 April 1966 but, as of December 1966, the Americans had shot down only one MiG for every Phantom they had lost in aerial combat.

US Navy F-4G

A sidelight was the US Navy's F-4G Phantom, taken into battle by VF-213 'Black Lions' aboard USS *Kitty Hawk* (CVA-63). This Phantom looked little different from the F-4B, but it had a two-way datalink system installed behind the rear cockpit, which could relay information from the carrier concerning the status of a battle under way. This AN/ASW-21 datalink was complemented by a system which allowed the pilot to make a 'hands-off' approach to his carrier. Only 12 F-4Gs served, but the Navy was to use some of their features in a newer Phantom model, the F-4J.

Phantoms continued to fight in the North and South, from carriers and from land bases. When Colonel Robin Olds' 8th TFW mounted Operation Bolo on 2 January 1967, and shot down seven MiG-21s with no losses, it was an enormous triumph. But problems persisted. The Phantom's single most important item for air combat, its UHF radio, was located under the backseat: a radio change took hours and entailed removal of the entire seat. The F-4C radar, a pioneering innovation in its time, had a tendency to malfunction far too easily, and early F-4Cs sprang wing-tank leaks that required resealing after each flight. Eighty-five of them developed cracked ribs on outer wing panels, and the F-4C and RF-4C were at times grounded due to dripping potting compound. Early F-4Es had a high rate of engine stalls and flameouts, and unlike the spartan MiGs, the Phantom was complex and challenged maintenance personnel to the limit.

Once the first cohort of Americans in Vietnam had com-

Post-strike recce

When the F-4s of the 8th TFW withdrew after attacking the Paul Doumer Bridge and the Yen Vien Railyard, both targets were shrouded in so much smoke and dust that it was impossible to determine the extent of the damage. This was usually the case, and it was standard practice to send a couple of RF-4s through the target area a few minutes after an attack, when the dust had settled and most of the smoke had cleared, to take photographs for BDA (battle damage assessment).

On 10 May 1972, Major Sid Rogers led COUSIN flight, a pair of RF-4s of the 14th TRS, to take post-strike photographs. In their mad dash past Hanoi, the Phantoms flew at 650 kt, weaving from side to side and varying their altitude between 4,000 and 6,000 ft to present as difficult as targets as possible. The enemy gun batteries laid on their usual awe-inspiring greeting for the tailenders. Captain Don Pickard, flying in the wing Phantom, recalled: "After we passed the railyard we got everything in the world shot at us.

We started jinking, and as we approached Hanoi there was a trail of black puffs of bursting shells behind Sid. I said to my backseater Chuck Irwin, 'Good God, look at that stuff behind lead!' Chuck replied, 'It's a good thing you can't see the stuff behind us.'"

As he sped past the Paul Doumer Bridge Pickard glanced at the structure to his right; all of the spans appeared to be in place. A few seconds later he caught a glimpse of a MiG-17 about 500 yd behind and to the left of him in a vain attempt to maneuver into a firing position. The reconnaissance aircraft's panoramic camera snapped the slower enemy fighter before it was left far behind. South of Hanoi a SAM battery loosed off a missile at Pickard's aircraft. Again the panoramic camera observed the threat, but the pilot knew nothing of the missile's presence until it detonated. "I didn't see the SAM but I saw a whole bunch of red things, like tracer rounds but fanning out, come past my nose."

Miraculously, none of the fragments struck the aircraft.

In the heavy fighting of the 'longest day', 10 May 1972, Captain Donald S. Pickard (left) flew a two-ship RF-4C mission to Hanoi. Post-strike recce of North Vietnam's capital, including the Paul Doumer Bridge (below), meant dodging anti-aircraft fire, MiGs and the deadly SA-2 'Guideline' SAM (above).

pleted their tours, almost all Korean War experience was used up. (By 1966, no fewer than three of the Korean War's 39 air aces were POWs in Hanoi and none was still in the fight.) Thanks to a USAF policy that everybody would

McDonnell F-4E Phantom 67-0288 (JV) 469th TFS/388th TFW Korat RTAFB, Thailand, 1969–70

Pitot
The F-4E radome is capped by a 1-ft 1-in (0.3-m) pitot static probe which gathers air data from the undisturbed air ahead of the aircraft, to 'feed' the flight instruments.

have to go once before anybody would be sent twice, experienced pilots languished in the States while inexperienced men flew combat. The Navy and Marine Corps made a better effort to put the right people in cockpits, but not much better. Experienced or not, senior or junior, many Phantom crews had never actually fired a *real* missile. Many Phantom *airframes* had never fired a real missile. The USAF responded with a program called 'Charging Sparrow', sending crews on rotation to Clark Field to fire live AIM-7s: this remedy was a Band-Aid on a hemorrhage.

The politics of the Vietnam War defied comprehension. Fighters carried out the strategic bombing assault against North Vietnam while B-52s dropped bombs on the jungle in the South. Bombing was intended to draw the North Vietnamese to the negotiating table. *Not* bombing was intended to draw the North Vietnamese to the negotiating table. MiGs could be attacked in the air, but could not be bombed on the ground. Except that sometimes they could: for a brief period in April 1967, US warplanes *were* permitted to bomb North Vietnamese airfields. Also as part of this puzzle, separate fighting in Laos and Cambodia was concealed from the public.

24 April 1967 was typical of days of heavy fighting which cropped up from time to time. Lieutenant Charles E. (Ev) Southwick of VF-114 'Aardvarks' flew into battle in an F-4B Phantom (BuNo. 153000) and shot down a

Kill marks
Colonel Paul Douglas, commander of the 388th TFW at Korat, wore his World War II kills on 'Arkansas Traveler'.

Splitter plate
The intake splitter plate separates sluggish boundary layer airflow and provides optimum airflow to the engines at subsonic and supersonic speeds.

Dihedral
The Vietnam-era F-4E retains the standard Phantom wing with 3° of anhedral inboard. A 12° cant bends the wing upward outboard of all ordnance load stations, for improved stability.

Ordnance
This F-4E Phantom is armed for air-to-ground action against personnel or light targets (note the 'Daisy Cutter' extended impact fuzes). The Phantom carries two triple clusters of 1,000-lb Mk 84 bombs, two 370-US gal (308-Imp gal; 1400-liter) underwing fuel tanks and four AIM-7E-2 Sparrow missiles.

Radar
The black laminate radome, reshaped in the F-4E model to make room for the gun, covers the antenna for a Westinghouse APQ-120 solid-state radar fire control system with a smaller dish than that used by earlier Phantom radars.

Colonel Paul P. Douglas Jr, 388th TFW commander from January to December 1968, led the Takhli-based wing's efforts against North Vietnam before and after the bombing halt which ended the Rolling Thunder campaign. Beginning in October 1968, Douglas flew this F-4E Phantom, 'Arkansas Traveler' (67-0288). World War II ace Douglas previously flew a P-47 Thunderbolt and an F-105 Thunderchief with the same nickname.

Vietnam camouflage
Called TO 1-1-4 camouflage because of the technical order which prescribed it, the Vietnam-era paint scheme on US Air Force aircraft retained the gull-gray undersides found on Phantoms from the beginning but cloaked the top of the aircraft in a mix of greens and tan. Tailcodes, introduced in 1966, are 24 in (61 cm) high: until 1972, the first letter identified the wing and the second the squadron. Although camouflage was for concealment from an enemy, Vietnam-era F-4 Phantoms and other warplanes carried national insignia, individual markings and, in this squadron, even shark's teeth, all in full color.

The 388th TFW at war
The 388th TFW at Takhli, Thailand, began replacing its blooded F-105 Thunderchiefs with the first gun-equipped F-4E Phantoms to arrive in the war zone in October 1968, just as bombing of North Vietnam halted. Fighter pilots, like wing commander Colonel Douglas and part-time artist Captain Steve Steven, designer of the shark's teeth, found themselves carrying bombs into Laos on risky day and night missions that weren't acknowledged and didn't 'count' towards rotation home. Some pilots in the 388th TFW were aching for a shot at a MiG, especially since the F-4E's internal cannon had not been tried yet, but until 1972, when fighting resumed up North, they had to settle for tough soldiering in the air-to-ground role.

Anhedral tailplane
The downward-canted, all-moving horizontal tailplane offsets vortex wake from the Phantom's bent-up wingtips, helping to stabilize the aircraft in the pitch axis. This tail surface is completely clear of the jet exhaust, but has titanium skin on the segments closest to the engine outlets.

43

system available to the aircraft – Sparrow, Sidewinder and the gunpod – but the Americans were still shooting down less than two MiGs for every fighter they lost. This was, as they saw it, a dismal failure.

The F-4D Phantom, optimized for the USAF's air-to-ground needs, reached the combat zone in mid-1967 and began to supplant the F-4C. The first air-to-air kill for the F-4D was scored on 24 October 1967, when Major William L. (Bill) Kirk of the 433rd TFS/8th TFW claimed a MiG-21 using the externally-mounted gunpod. The US Navy introduced its own new version of the Phantom, the F-4J, with VF-33 'Tarsiers' and VF-102 'Diamondbacks' aboard USS *America* (CVA-66) in 1968.

On 1 October 1968, the bombing of North Vietnam (and the Rolling Thunder campaign) ended. Together with Lyndon Johnson's decision not to seek re-election came a 'bombing halt', which was to last for nearly four years. When the 469th TFS/388th TFW brought the cannon-armed F-4E Phantom to Korat, Thailand, in November 1968 – yet another new version of the McDonnell fighter introduced to combat – pilots were eager to battle MiGs. But the first major phase of the war was over; there was now to be an interregnum and battles with MiGs would not resume until 1972.

The bombing halt was a good time to tot up the results of the rivalry between the F-8 Crusader, which was near the end of its career, and the F-4 Phantom, which was not far from the beginning. In terms of numbers of aircraft deployed, the 'mix' of F-4s and F-8s was roughly 50:50 in 1965, but by 1968 had fallen to about 80:20 in favor of the Phantom. Carrier-based Crusaders flew almost no air-to-ground missions, so they could not be compared with the Phantom in the 'mud-moving' arena. In air combat, when the fighting up North ended in October 1968, and if only

Above: Wearing an experimental camouflage scheme which the US Navy tested in combat but did not adopt, an F-4G Phantom (BuNo. 150642) of VF-213 'Black Lions' catches the arresting wire on USS Kitty Hawk in the South China Sea.

Below: A VF-92 'Silver Kings' F-4J Phantom (BuNo. 153827, coded NG-201) takes off above 'the numbers' on USS Constellation (CVA-64) in the South China Sea.

MiG-17 using a Sidewinder, scoring the war's 48th MiG kill. Squadron mate Lieutenant H. Dennis Wisely (who had shot down an Antonov An-2 on 20 December 1966) maneuvered a second F-4B Phantom (BuNo. 153037) to the point where he was able to rack up MiG kill number 49 using a Sidewinder. Southwick, however, had been hit by AAA over Kep *before* downing his MiG, and had continued through the battle nursing an aircraft suffering from indeterminate damage. He was able to fly the F-4B eastward and so go 'feet wet' (get out over water) before it became abundantly clear that 153000 had fought its last battle. The AAA damage made it impossible for Southwick to transfer fuel and, therefore, impossible to get back to *Kitty Hawk*. He and his backseater ejected and were rescued.

Throughout spring and summer 1967, air-to-air action continued at a frenetic pace. The 366th TFW crew of Lieutenant Colonel Robert F. Titus and Lieutenant Milan Zimer, flying an F-4C Phantom (64-0776), achieved the unique feat of scoring three MiG kills, one with each

Navy victories are counted, the Crusader had bagged 19 MiGs compared with the Phantom's 13, an advantage of about 50 per cent. There were too many variables, however, for this to have much significance. Ironically, at a time when there was universal agreement that fighters needed guns, the Crusader had not managed a single kill with its cannon, although in two instances some shooting had occurred after a missile or rockets administered the *coup de grâce*: almost every F-8 kill belonged to the AIM-9 Sidewinder.

Phantoms continued to bomb North Vietnamese troops in Laos. These included Igloo White operations against the infiltration network known to Americans as the Ho Chi Minh Trail. Under limited circumstances, some missions could *still* be flown into North Vietnam. Reconnaissance missions were routine, and bombing missions were called 'Type III limited duration, protective reaction air strikes'. These strikes were ordered after North Vietnamese AAA shot down an 11th TRS/432nd TRW RF-4C Phantom (66-0388) on 5 June 1969. Further strikes by VF-92 'Silver Kings' and VF-96 'Fighting Falcons' F-4J Phantoms from USS *Constellation* (CVA-64) pounded North Vietnam in December 1971. Even though the Nixon administration was starting a measured withdrawal, the war was not over, as the five-day Proud Deep Alpha campaign demonstrated.

The difficulties of the Rolling Thunder period (1965-68), as well as the problems of operating sophisticated warplanes in a tropical backwater, did not escape American planners. US Navy Captain Frank Ault visited every combat unit in the fleet and came up with hundreds of suggestions in his Ault Report to improve performance in air-to-air combat. One of the recommendations called for DACT (dissimilar air combat training), which led to the creation of the US Navy's Fighter Weapons School, known as 'Top Gun'.

On 19 January 1972, the bombing halt was still in effect when a VF-96 Phantom crew, covering a reconnaissance mission codenamed Blue Tree, ran into a heavy barrage of SAMs, dodged them, and shot down a MiG-21 with a Sidewinder. Lieutenant Randall H. (Duke) Cunningham, frontseater of the F-4J Phantom, was a 'Top Gun' graduate. Cunningham and Lieutenant William Driscoll had racked up the 122nd MiG kill of the war, and the first in nearly two years.

New fighting

It did not take a clairvoyant to sense that another round of fighting was brewing. At Udorn, Thailand, Major Robert Lodge said as much to F-4D Phantom pilots of the 'Triple Nickel' 555th TFS/432nd TFW. Lodge was one of

Above and below: F-4Js of VF-96 in action. Lieutenants Randall ('Duke') Cunningham and his RIO, Willie Driscoll, of VF-96 became the Navy's only aces of the Vietnam War, sharing five kills. Early graduates of 'Top Gun', their success proved the truth of the Ault report, which pointed out the weaknesses of US fighter pilots and demonstrated the excellence of the training program designed to remedy these deficiencies. Even for Cunningham and Driscoll life was not all roses. After an epic mission in which they dispatched three MiGs, including Vietnam's 13-kill Colonel Tomb, they were forced to eject after being hit by a SAM.

Baptism of Fire

the leading air-to-air tacticians in the US Air Force. On 21 February 1972, in the first kill of a MiG in Laos, Bob Lodge and his backseater Captain Roger Locher in an F-4D Phantom (65-0784) chased a MiG-21 through a narrow valley at night and shot it down. If a new campaign were to open in the skies near Hanoi, Lodge seemed certain to become the first air ace of the war.

The bombing halt, years of diplomacy, plus every effort to find some solution in Vietnam, had all failed. The final offensive by Hanoi began on the night of 29/30 March 1972, when 12 divisions supported by armor and artillery invaded South Vietnam. The character of the war changed, abruptly. This was a *real* invasion, not a guerrilla war, and reinforcements were going to be needed. The first to respond were the F-4D Phantoms of the 3rd TFW at Kunsan AB, Korea, deployed to Da Nang and Ubon on 31 March.

On 2 April 1972, the invading North Vietnamese forces captured the provincial capital of Quang Tri and, on 6 April, President Nixon resumed limited bombing of North Vietnam under Operation Freedom Train. The two Phantom frontseaters with the 'right stuff' to become air

aces – the Navy's Duke Cunningham and the Air Force's Bob Lodge – both scored their second MiG kills soon after.

As North Vietnamese regular forces stormed southward, the US mounted a series of operations, called Constant Guard, which brought further aerial reinforcements. F-4E Phantoms from Eglin and Homestead AFBs, Florida, arrived at Udorn, which was already crowded, while F-4D Phantoms from Holloman AFB, New Mexico, deployed to Takhli, Thailand. On 8 May, President Nixon announced the mining of Haiphong Harbor, removed most restrictions on bombing up North, and replaced the limited Freedom Train effort with a new campaign called 'Linebacker'. The long years of the bombing halt were over.

The third day of the Linebacker campaign (10 May 1972) produced the largest air-to-air score of the war: 11 MiGs were shot down. At 0830 hours, Lieutenant Curt Dose launched in a two-aircraft F-4J Phantom division from *Constellation*. Meanwhile, heavy 'strike packages' from every F-4 wing in Southeast Asia were driving North towards targets in the Hanoi region. And from Udorn, Major Bob Lodge was leading a flight of four F-4D Phan-

toms, OYSTER flight, North. When another F-4D flight was delayed in approaching the Hanoi-Haiphong area, the aggressive Lodge took the assigned areas of both flights himself.

Curt Dose's flight 'beat up' Kep airfield and he used a Sidewinder to shoot down a MiG while at supersonic speed and treetop level. As the morning unfolded, Phantoms struck the Paul Doumer Bridge and other targets in the Hanoi-Haiphong region, and RF-4C Phantoms flew pre- and post-strike reconnaissance.

Cunningham's squadron mate, Lieutenant Michael J. Connelly, flying a VF-96 F-4J Phantom (BuNo. 155769), shot down two MiG-17s. Another Phantom crew from the same *Constellation* squadron, headed by Lieutenant Stephen C. Shoemaker, dispatched another MiG-17 with a Sidewinder. Cunningham and Driscoll claimed one MiG-17, then rescued a wingman by using a Sidewinder to bag another: their second kill of the day and fourth of the war. Their day was not over.

USAF ace

Major Bob Lodge led his four F-4Ds northwest from Hanoi at low altitude and high speed toward Yen Bai airfield. No US aircraft were north of Lodge, so he could fire his Sparrows head-on without visual confirmation of the

Above: Side number 201 was an F-4J Phantom of VF-74 'Be-devilers', one of numerous East Coast/Atlantic Fleet squadrons to deploy to Southeast Asia. This view is dated November 1974, during the cruise by USS Nimitz (CVN-68) between the end of the American combat role and the evacuation of Saigon.

Below: The 'Red Devils' of VMFA-232, here refueling from a KC-130 Hercules tanker, was the last Marine Corps squadron in combat in Southeast Asia, fighting through the cessation of hostilities in Vietnam on 27 January 1973 and in Cambodia on 15 August 1973.

Baptism of Fire

Above: CONUS-based squadrons frequently rotated 'in theater'. Here 'ED'-coded F-4Es of the 33rd TFW's 58th TFS from Eglin AFB, Florida, fly with the 13th TFS, 432nd TRW's 'OC'-coded F-4Ds from the latter unit's base at Udorn RTAFB. The two units participated in Operation Linebacker, where the gloves were off and there were fewer restrictions than had been applied during Rolling Thunder.

Above right: Steam from the last cat shot is still venting from the catapult track as a VF-114 F-4J is readied for launch from the Kitty Hawk. Two years after the end of the Vietnam War, the US Navy was still operating Phantoms in Southeast Asia.

Right: Laden with three fuel tanks and six Mk 82 bombs, an F-4J of VF-154 hurtles down a catapult, watched by a hovering Sea King plane guard helicopter. The F-4J proved popular and reliable.

MiGs. Warnings from 'Disco' (the EC-121 radar plane off the coast), from 'Red Crown' (the US Navy's radar picket ship) and from backseater Captain Roger Locher informed Lodge that plenty of MiGs were coming up to fight.

Lodge's OYSTER flight engaged a formation of MiG-21s and fired Sparrows from almost the limits of visual range. OYSTER 2, the F-4D Phantom (66-8734) piloted by Lieutenant John Markle, quickly brought down a MiG-21 using a Sparrow. The MiGs *still* lacked comparable head-on fighting capability – outside the range of their guns, at least – but they continued boring straight at Lodge's flight. One pilot with a clear view of the oncoming MiGs was in the OYSTER 3 slot, Captain Richard S. (Steve) Ritchie. Ritchie was an experienced Phantom frontseater, having completed an earlier tour as a 'Stormy FAC' (forward air controller), but he had not been in direct conflict with MiGs before. Although, his F-4D Phantom (66-7463) had already claimed three MiGs while being flown by others.

Bob Lodge wanted to prevent MiGs from reaching US strike forces in the Hanoi-Haiphong region. He succeeded, but OYSTER flight was suddenly engulfed in MiGs. Ritchie's backseater, Captain Charles B. DeBellevue, attained a radar lock-on enabling Ritchie to fire Sparrows. Their first missile missed. Their second Sparrow hit the MiG where its wingroots joined the fuselage. A brilliant explosion consumed the MiG, although the pilot managed to escape, with his parachute furling back into the slipstream.

Bob Lodge had blasted one MiG-21 out of the sky at the onset of the fight, the third aerial kill for the aggressive OYSTER flight leader who seemed certain to become an ace. Another MiG popped in front of him and would have been killed instantly, if only Lodge had had a gun. Then, four MiG-19s dropped out of the clouds and worked into Bob Lodge's six o'clock position. Lodge was still chasing a MiG-21 and may not have heard Markle's voice when the captain yelled at him that he was being tailed. Bob Lodge's F-4D Phantom (65-0784) was now an inviting target for the MiG-19s as they closed to within 1,500 ft (460 m) and opened fire with their cannon. "Break right!" boomed Markle's voice in Lodge's ears. *"Break right, now! They are firing at you!"*

Cannon shells pierced the Phantom's thin metal skin, rupturing its hydraulic and electrical lines, which exploded with a furious noise and set the F-4D on fire. Lodge's backseater, Locher, ejected. He was not rescued until 21 days later – the longest 'escape and evasion' of the conflict.

It is argued that Bob Lodge didn't eject because he wanted a few more seconds to bag the MiG-21 in front of him. Given Lodge's fighting abilities, that seems unlikely. Far more credible is that Lodge had been exposed to very

sensitive classified information on a previous tour of duty, and he made a personal decision that he would not fall into North Vietnamese captivity with this information. Lodge did not eject, and he was reported MIA (missing in action) until his death was confirmed. With three MiGs to his credit, and a record of leadership unmatched by any combat leader, Lodge would certainly have become the top MiG killer of the war. It therefore remains an outrage that the USAF did not put Lodge up for the Medal of Honor.

The 'longest day', 10 May 1972, continued to unfold. Randy Cunningham and William Driscoll fought a close-quarters battle with a MiG-17 and shot it down, their fifth kill – making them the first aces. Soon after, their F-4J Phantom (BuNo. 155800), callsign SHOWTIME 100, was tagged by a SAM and the pair ejected and were rescued at sea.

Heavy fighting

The Linebacker campaign was fought with far fewer restrictions than Rolling Thunder, and the fighting was hot and heavy. On 31 May 1972, USAF fighters claimed two more MiG kills in a continuing succession. One, Captain Steve Ritchie, flying an F-4D Phantom (65-0801), chalked up his second kill.

Most problems encountered by Phantom crews earlier in the war were being solved. Persistent minor changes to

Above: A final operational fling for the F-4 in Southeast Asia, 14 August 1973. A 58th TFS/33rd TFW F-4E (detached to the 8th TFW) lands back at Ubon after the last bombing mission over Cambodia, one day before fighting ceased.

improve internal systems had turned the F-4B, F-4C, F-4D, F-4E and F-4J of 1972 into exceedingly potent fighting machines. Maintenance techniques improved as a result of constant input by McDonnell field representatives, and the Linebacker campaign also brought to the fore a new generation of pilots who now could claim *recent* combat experience and who benefitted from realistic training. By mid-1972, the 'kill ratio' was beginning to tilt sharply and North Vietnam was losing five or six MiGs for every US fighter it claimed.

Captain Steve Ritchie used Sparrows to rack up his third and fourth kills in an F-4E Phantom (67-0362) on 8 July 1972. Ritchie's 432nd TRW also had other potent MiG killers in Lieutenant Colonel Carl G. Baily and Captain John A. Madden Jr, both of whom got three kills. All 'kill' claims of Air Force crews were reviewed by a board in Saigon, which examined all the evidence before awarding an aerial victory. The board disapproved two claimed MiG kills which would have made Madden an ace.

This honor went, instead, to Ritchie. On 28 August 1972, again flying the top-scoring F-4D Phantom (66-7463), Ritchie downed a MiG-21 over North Vietnam to become the first USAF ace of the conflict. On 9 September 1972, the team of Madden and Captain Charles B. DeBellevue, in an F-4D Phantom (66-0267), shot down two MiG-19s in a single fight. For DeBellevue, the kills were his fifth and sixth, making him the ranking ace of the war.

North Vietnam was now subjected to relentless daily bombing, much of it by Phantoms with new laser- and electro-optical guided bombs, or 'smart' bombs as the media dubbed them. US Marine aviators on land and US Navy air crews operating in the Gulf of Tonkin did their fair share of the pounding. On 11 September 1972, the crew of Major Thomas (Bear) Lasseter and Captain John D. Cummings, flying an F-4B Phantom (BuNo. 155226) of the VMFA-333 'Shamrocks', shot down a MiG-21 near Hanoi – the only time in the war a MiG was downed by a US Marine aircraft. It was a bittersweet victory: Lasseter and Cummings were downed by a SAM but rescued, and another 'Shamrock' F-4B was also lost in the battle. The

final ace of the war was USAF Phantom backseater Captain Jeffrey Feinstein, of the 13th TFS/432nd TRW at Udorn, who was credited with his fifth kill on 13 October 1972.

Now, the Linebacker campaign ended. The Nixon administration believed that Hanoi was ready for a settlement, and Secretary of State Kissinger proclaimed that "Peace is at hand." Linebacker had been very different from Rolling Thunder. On the enemy side, the SA-7 man-portable missile had been introduced and the MiG-19 had belatedly joined other members of the MiG stable. On the American side, Phantoms introduced laser-guided and electro-optical guided bombs, and a handful of F-4Cs were converted for the Wild Weasel mission against North Vietnamese SAM sites.

Very close to a settlement, Nixon finally decided that North Vietnam must be subjected to one final show of force. This was known as Linebacker II, or the 'Eleven Day War'. Between 18 and 29 December 1972, B-52 Stratofortresses finally went to Hanoi and Haiphong, flying 714 sorties and encountering a record 1,293 SAM firings. F-4 Phantoms and other allied warplanes supported this final spasm of fighting, which led to a truce agreement on 27 January 1973.

The 197th and last MiG kill of the war took place on 12 January 1973, when Lieutenant Victor T. Kovaleski of VF-161 'Chargers' aboard USS *Midway* (CV-41) used a Sidewinder to shoot down a MiG-17. Thus, *Midway* Phantoms scored the first and last kills of the war. Lieutenant Kovaleski also suffered the indignity of piloting the last aircraft to be lost over North Vietnam, when his Phantom was shot down two days later on 14 January. Both the pilot and backseater were rescued.

American forces started to trickle out of Southeast Asia. Although the Vietnam War ended on 27 January 1973, fighting persisted in Cambodia until 15 August 1973. Long after Marine ground combatants were withdrawn, the Marine presence ended when the F-4J Phantoms of VMFA-232 'Red Devils' came out of Nam Phong, Thailand, in August 1973.

The 1972 Linebacker campaigns against North Vietnam produced a six-to-one 'kill ratio', and had inflicted a sound defeat on North Vietnam's MiG force. The creation of the US Navy's 'Top Gun' school, followed in due course by the USAF's 'aggressor' squadrons, assured that future fighter pilots would be better prepared. The heavy, two-man, twin-engined F-4 Phantom reigned supreme as the best all-around fighter in the world. In the same year that the Vietnam War ended, the USAF flew the F-15 Eagle and the F-14 Tomcat, both sophisticated fighters ideally suited to American needs and with much better agility and handling. Until the F-14 and F-15 came along, the Phantom was to remain the dominant fighter in the world.

CHAPTER 3

PHANTOM SUPREME

By the end of the 1960s, the McDonnell Phantom could claim with some justification to be the defender of the free world. It formed the backbone of the USAF's fighter wings, the US Navy's carrier wings and the Marine's front–line air groups. It had also attracted export orders from the leading free world air arms, including Germany, Japan, Iran and Britain. Production continued apace, even after the 'Phabulous Phive Thousandth' F-4 rolled off the line.

Above: Projecting power far from Britain's shores, a Phantom FG.Mk 1 with the omega insignia of No. 892 Squadron launches from HMS Ark Royal.

In the past centuries, a nation wanting to project power to a distant trouble spot dispatched gunboats. In the 1960s and 1970s, the best way to mount a show of force was to send off a squadron of Phantoms. To the United States, the F-4 became, more than any other item of military equipment, a symbol of a nation's global reach.

In January 1968, North Korea launched a series of ground skirmishes, seized the US intelligence ship *Pueblo* (AGER-2) and threatened a full-scale invasion of South Korea – a crisis which would have thrust Americans into two major wars in Asia at the same time. The United States had failed to keep up a tactical air presence in South Korea and now was forced to act swiftly. A sudden deployment of 280 tactical warplanes was spearheaded by the F-4D Phantom-equipped 4th Tactical Fighter Wing, which moved abruptly to Korea under the 'bare base' concept. The wing's 334th, 335th and 336th Tactical Fighter Squadrons relocated halfway around the globe, exploiting air refueling, which was now an accepted tool in air warfare.

As a model for the worldwide contribution of the F-4 Phantom throughout its career, no other historic event is more illustrative than the 1968-69 confrontation in Korea,

In July 1965, this F-4B (152276) became the 1,000th Phantom to be delivered.

The 2,000th Phantom off the St Louis production line was a USAF F-4D (66-7489).

A USAF RF-4C and an Iranian F-4D mark progress with F-4J 155772.

F-4E 69-7294 plays 4,000th Phantom in February 1971, a slot really held by RF-4C 69-0381.

This F-4E for Turkey celebrates the 5,000th Phantom delivery in March 1978.

which flared to new heights when North Korean MiGs downed an EC-121 Super Constellation on 15 April 1969, killing 31 men aboard. The Korean situation gave vivid meaning to a term often used to describe the Phantom – 'multirole fighter'. It was happening at the very time when some officers in the Pentagon were arguing that the United States needed different warplanes for different missions. Badly burned by the failure of the 'multirole' TFX, which had led to widespread acceptance of the Phantom in the first place, Pentagon officers argued that one aircraft could not handle tactical nuclear duties, the conventional strike mission *and* – with its altogether different challenges – air-to-air combat.

The United States had been unprepared in Korea, because the only tactical aircraft in the theater were half a dozen F-4D Phantoms carrying 'special weapons'. All Phantoms, including reconnaissance variants, could carry

Phantom Supreme

one 2,170-lb (984-kg) B28 or one 2,060-lb (934-kg) B43 atomic bomb on a centerline stores station, and this much-overlooked capability made a vital contribution to Cold War readiness. With many tactical aircraft, including most Phantoms, this was merely a contingency, and one which fighter pilots disliked and rarely rehearsed. But the 'nuke'-equipped Phantoms at K-55 Osan, Korea, were kept on ramp alert, armed and ready, and were earmarked for nuclear strikes against Soviet or Chinese targets under the SIOP (Single Integrated Operations Plan). They could have been retargeted against North Korea in the event of a full-scale invasion followed by a decision to 'go nuclear', but because of command and control problems they could *not* be reprogrammed for conventional missions in time to save the *Pueblo*.

Missions

On a typical *nuclear strike mission*, an F-4 Phantom would have been configured with a centerline B28 bomb, two 370-US gal (308-Imp gal; 1400-liter) wing drop-tanks and

two AIM-9B Sidewinder missiles. The F-4 would take off on military power at a gross weight of 55,535 lb (25191 kg), refuel from a tanker immediately and cruise at 36,300 ft (11,064 m) to a combat radius of up to 1,000 miles (1600 km), and then descend toward the target using continuous evasive jinking before a dive-toss release which would enable the Phantom to clear the blast area quickly. Returning at the same cruising altitude, the Phantom would reach its base with a fuel reserve of 1,607 lb (729 kg). In tactical aviation, only certain crews were designated as 'nuclear-qualified' and opportunities to practice their Armageddon-style mission were few.

An *air defense intercept mission* would have been more likely at the outset of a Korean conflict, and remained a crucial function of the F-4 Phantom throughout its career. As an interceptor the F-4 Phantom could be configured with 600-US gal (500-Imp gal; 2270-liter) centerline tanks, two 370-US gal (308-Imp gal; 1400-liter) wing-tanks, four AIM-7E-2 Sparrow radar-homing missiles and four AIM-9B Sidewinder infrared, or heat-seeking, missiles. The F-4 would take off and climb out at maximum power at a gross weight of 49,263 lb (22346 kg) and cruise toward intercept at 39,000 ft (11900 m), adjusting altitude to gain optimum advantage against incoming 'bogies'. Flying to a maximum radius of 320 miles (515 km), or perhaps less depending on the use of the Phantom's hungry afterburner, the Phantom would carry out a successful interception and return to base with 1,990 lb (903 kg) of reserve fuel. In Korea, a high surge rate would have been essential to cope with a numerically superior enemy force. In later years, the Phantom took on air defense of the North American continent, where conditions permitted a greater combat radius.

The *air-to-ground strike mission* would also have been assigned to the Phantom in Korea, even before wresting air superiority – just as 'mud moving' remained the primary mission assigned to many Phantom squadrons. On a typical mission, the F-4 Phantom would be configured with six 750-lb (340-kg) general-purpose bombs, two

Left: All things to all people, the Phantom was not, alas, the ideal aircraft for a flight demonstration team. Maintainers did not enjoy long periods 'on the road' with it. In the US Navy's 'Blue Angels', the F-4J replaced the Grumman F-11A Tiger in the late 1960s and performed fairly well until economic and flight safety factors in the late 1970s resulted in the team converting to the A-4F Skyhawk.

Below: Early F-4Es in the 'Thunderbirds' livery at their home base, Nellis AFB, Nevada, on 22 November 1970. These patriotic Phantoms replaced the North American F-100D Super Sabre in the late 1960s, then in 1978 succumbed to the Northrop T-38 Talon in a change driven largely by the public perception of the team's operating costs.

Phantom Supreme

370-US gal (815-Imp gal; 3703-liter) wing-tanks, an AN/ALQ-101 ECM pod, three AIM-7E-2 Sparrows and four AIM-9B Sidewinders (replaced in the 1990s by AN/ALQ-131, AIM-7M and AIM-9M). On a strike interdiction mission, the F-4 would make a maximum power climb, cruise at 36,300 ft (11000 m) and fly out to a radius of 440 miles (708 km) for eight minutes of loiter in the target area before delivering bombs in a dive. There are, of course, an infinite variety of ordnance items which can hang under a Phantom's wings, hence dozens of mission profiles.

The Korean model, fortunately, did not become a real war with real bloodshed. In part, because of the rapid deployment of an impressive force of Phantoms, the Korean tensions of 1968-69 waned and no full-scale conflict broke out. It was no coincidence that the Republic of Korea air force was one of the earliest foreign recipients of the aircraft.

While the Phantom was being blooded in Vietnam and tested in Korea, it was becoming more numerous as the standard American fighter around the world. US Navy carriers making Mediterranean cruises typically included two Phantom squadrons per air wing. The US Air Force garrisoned no fewer than six Phantom wings in Europe. On Okinawa a Phantom wing deployed often to trouble-prone Korea, and Phantoms formed the backbone of the three US Marine Corps air wings. The standard tactical fighter in all three services was the Phantom.

A major change in the structure of the Air National Guard (ANG) and Air Force Reserve, in 1970, resulted in top-of-the-line Phantoms reaching the Reserve components. Foreign customers for the Phantom began to line up, starting with Britain and Israel.

Air National Guard Phantoms

The first ANG unit to convert to Phantoms was the 170th TFS/183rd TFG at Springfield, Illinois, which gave up the Republic F-84F Thunderstreak in favor of the F-4C on 31 January 1972. This squadron was assigned to an air-to-ground mission in the Phantom for many years before converting to the F-16 Fighting Falcon. Meanwhile, the first Air Force Reserve unit to use Phantoms was the 93rd TFS, or 'Florida Makos' at Homestead AFB, Florida, which took the unusual step of moving into the huge McDonnell fighter after flying EC-121 Super Constellations.

The ever-expanding presence of the Phantom meant different things to different people. The ANG and Air Force Reserve were still using the F-4 as a 'mud-mover' in the early 1970s (the air intercept mission was added to their duties later in the decade), but most of the attention devoted to the Phantom focused on the air-to-air role. The Phantom had done more than establish a standard for the world – it had launched a revolution. With grimly realistic training being provided by the Air Force's 'Red Flag' and the Navy's 'Top Gun' exercises, Phantom crews in the early to mid-1970s were probably the best-prepared fighter crews in the world.

"My most difficult mission"

During the first week of the Yom Kippur War, a formation of Phantoms went out to attack the air base at Mansura, in Egypt's Nile delta. Colonel R's aircraft was caught in an ambush by Egyptian MiGs. R and the navigator, the late Yitzhak Baram, were able to get out of the trap, but experienced one of the war's most difficult sorties.

"I have to tell the story of this flight very slowly and with a lot of concentration. It was a very difficult flight, and unique, the toughest sortie of my life.

"Its beginnings were on 11 October, when my squadron took part in an attack on the Benha airfield in the Nile delta. The aircraft were caught on the way back by MiGs. A tough dogfight ensued and a number of MiGs were shot down, as were two of our Phantoms.

"On the morning of the 14th a formation from the squadron went to Mansura, also in the Nile delta. It was clear that this was going to be a tough raid. Even very tough. The Mansura field was deep in the delta and was protected by batteries of SA-2 and -3 missiles. MiGs were expected in the target zone and the chances we would take them by surprise were slim.

"The first navigation leg was made over the sea. My navigator was the late Yitzhak Baram, who was killed a year later in an accident. We flew and strained our eyes in an effort to locate threats such as MiGs or missiles. So far, everything was quiet. But ground control came on even before we crossed the coastline. 'Watch out, there are MiGs above your target.' Okay; now there were both missiles and MiGs. The tension in every cockpit increased.

"The delta navigation leg was long. We were flying at very low altitude, so low that once or twice we had to pull up in order to pass over the great high-tension lines stretched across the area. We neared the target and the controller once more warned us about the MiGs. There was no doubt that there would be no element of surprise here. We would have to execute the raid as quickly as possible; if we remained at altitude for a few seconds too many the missile batteries would catch us. And if they couldn't, the MiGs would. Nor was there all that much fuel for roughing it up.

"We arrive and pull over Mansura. We take a good look around; there's still no visual contact with enemy aircraft, but we can see MiG drop-tanks spinning towards the ground – which is to say that MiGs are above us. They've seen our Phantoms and are now getting set up to come in on the formation.

"It's a tough decision: should you show your tail to the MiGs and dive on the target? Or should you emergency-dump all your ordnance and try to get away before it's too late? (But then, why bother to make this long and dangerous flight?)

"Number Two and I decide to go on. We hope the MiGs won't be able to launch any missiles until bomb release. Afterwards, we'll see. We go in and bomb the runway; another second and large mushrooms of smoke rise exactly from where they're supposed to. Phase one has been executed well. Now we have to go over to phase two: getting home safely!

"We exit with a hard break; we still don't see the MiGs but we know they're somewhere in our rear. And here Number Four begins to shout that he's on fire.

"I turn towards Number Four; the Phantom doesn't seem to be burning. But there are two MiGs closing in from behind.

"'Four, break hard left. They're sitting on you.'

"Four breaks left, with me following in on the threatening MiGs. It's hard to get out from an absolute disadvantage by yourself; that's why we talk so much about defense and mutual assistance.

Phantom at war – again. Although the camera distorts the size of the sun and the F-4E's low altitude, this image accurately conveys the low-level aspect of the fighting during the October War.

An F-4E closes in for the kill against an enemy MiG-17. The flame erupting from the MiG's tailpipe marks the first sign of what will be fatal damage.

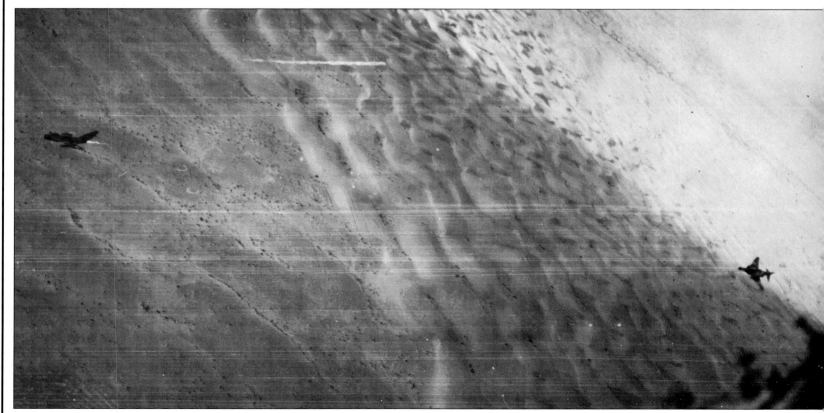

"I turn into the MiGs and drop some ordnance to clean up the aircraft. We're still not thinking in terms of a dogfight – more in terms of getting a partner out of a disadvantage. Indeed, the MiGs are giving up, and turning their attention to me while breaking away from Four, who straightens out and runs home.

"The MiGs' break doesn't look too nice. It seems as if they've received a warning from someone. Which means there are more MiGs around. And indeed, Baram soon shouts, 'Break! They're sitting on us!' I break and look back: two MiGs; range, 600 to 700 m. Two spumes of smoke suddenly depart the MiGs and run towards me. Air-to-air missiles!

"I pull back on the stick a little more. The missiles miss and the MiGs pull ahead. For a split second I hesitate on whether to do something about this pair of MiGs or break for home. And then Baram shouts for me to break once more, that another pair of MiGs is coming in. I don't know if this is the first pair, or if I'm up against six. At this point I've already broken hard twice; I'm low on speed and beginning to feel the pressure. I break a third time and my speed drops even more. And I don't have enough fuel to get into a dogfight.

"'Number Three in trouble with MiGs,' I radio. I hope someone will come and get me out of here.

I'm at very low altitude and see the MiGs behind me starting to set up. I maneuver sharply.

"'Are they still in the rear?' I ask Baram.

"'Affirmative,' he answers.

"'You sure?'

"'Yes,' he says, 'and now they're firing.'

"There are to be two especially difficult parts to this battle. The first will be when I realize that I'm alone above Mansura, in trouble with four and perhaps six MiGs, and that no one is about to come to my aid. No one; the rest of my formation is already far from the field. The second difficult part was the turn. The lessons of Benha were still fresh in my mind; here, I apparently had what I needed to get out of trouble – good speed and I was well set up in a turn – but there was nothing else in my favor.

"Okay, I've made up my mind, I'm going to try something else. Baram screams: 'Break! They're firing!' And here I pull up the nose sharply and look back to see what will happen. The MiGs pull up after me. If they make it I'm finished. Right now I'm climbing

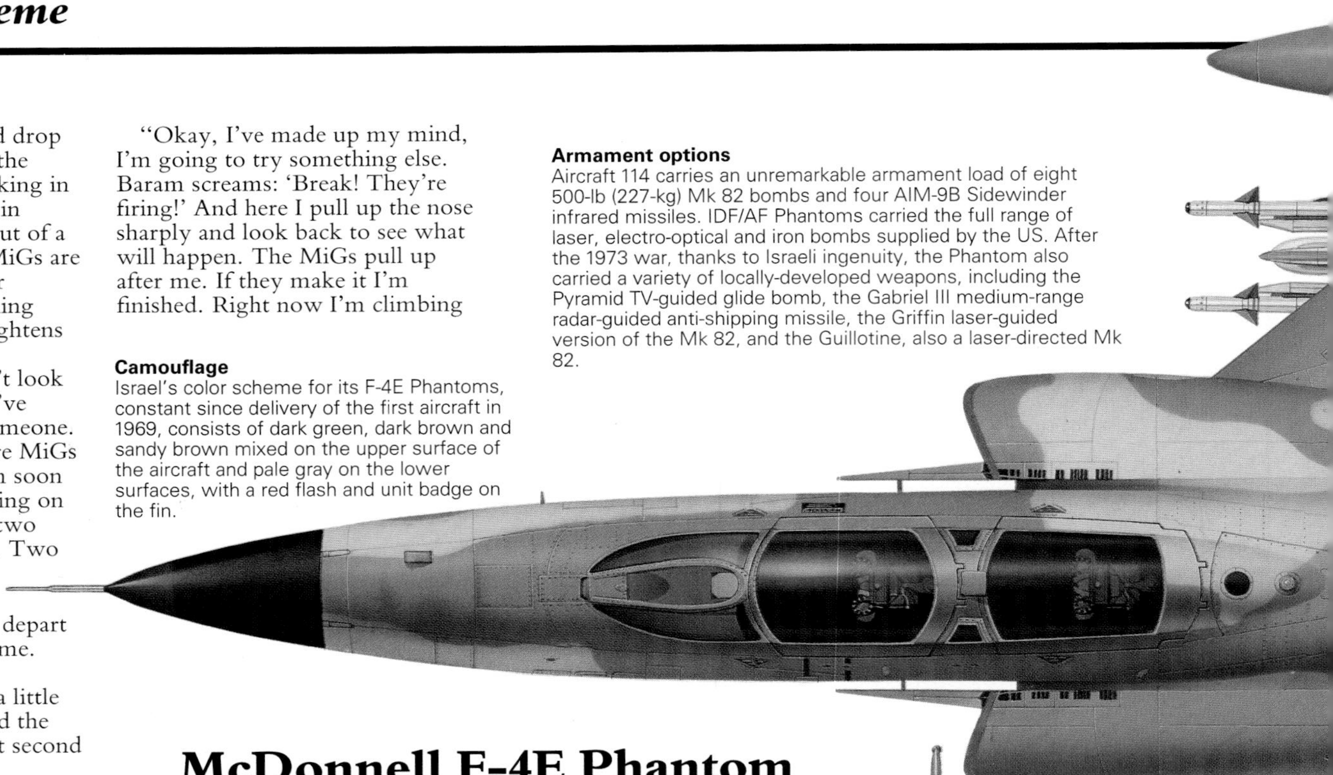

Camouflage

Israel's color scheme for its F-4E Phantoms, constant since delivery of the first aircraft in 1969, consists of dark green, dark brown and sandy brown mixed on the upper surface of the aircraft and pale gray on the lower surfaces, with a red flash and unit badge on the fin.

Armament options

Aircraft 114 carries an unremarkable armament load of eight 500-lb (227-kg) Mk 82 bombs and four AIM-9B Sidewinder infrared missiles. IDF/AF Phantoms carried the full range of laser, electro-optical and iron bombs supplied by the US. After the 1973 war, thanks to Israeli ingenuity, the Phantom also carried a variety of locally-developed weapons, including the Pyramid TV-guided glide bomb, the Gabriel III medium-range radar-guided anti-shipping missile, the Griffin laser-guided version of the Mk 82, and the Guillotine, also a laser-directed Mk 82.

McDonnell F-4E Phantom No. 119 Squadron, IDF/AF IDF Base Tel Nov *circa* 1973

The once-controversial F-4E Phantom became the backbone of the Israeli Defense Force/Air Force in the October 1973 war. The F-4E was first employed air-to-air during the 1969-70 War of Attrition, and later used as a multirole combatant with the emphasis on air-to-ground work as illustrated here. With the fuel and ordnance load shown, this F-4E would be able to bomb a target 480 miles (772 km) from its base and still have about 12 minutes of loiter to engage an enemy with its 20-mm cannon or four AIM-9 Sidewinders.

Drop tanks

The underwing 370-US gal (308-Imp gal; 1400-liter) Sargent Fletcher drop tanks shown are standard in Israeli use, whereas the 600-US gal (500-Imp gal; 2275-liter) centerline fuel tank is rarely observed in use. In recent years, Jerusalem's Phantoms have also carried beefed-up F-15 Eagle drop tanks which are stressed for higher *g*s.

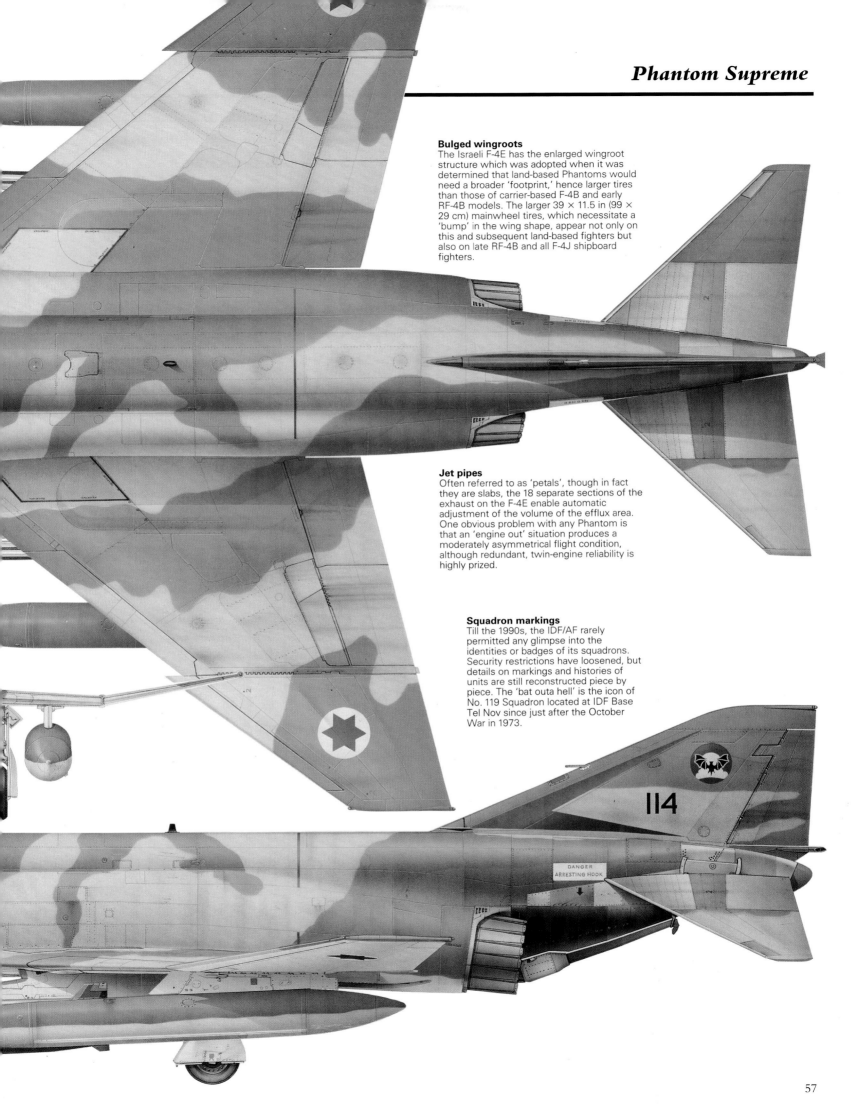

Bulged wingroots
The Israeli F-4E has the enlarged wingroot structure which was adopted when it was determined that land-based Phantoms would need a broader 'footprint,' hence larger tires than those of carrier-based F-4B and early RF-4B models. The larger 39 × 11.5 in (99 × 29 cm) mainwheel tires, which necessitate a 'bump' in the wing shape, appear not only on this and subsequent land-based fighters but also on late RF-4B and all F-4J shipboard fighters.

Jet pipes
Often referred to as 'petals', though in fact they are slabs, the 18 separate sections of the exhaust on the F-4E enable automatic adjustment of the volume of the efflux area. One obvious problem with any Phantom is that an 'engine out' situation produces a moderately asymmetrical flight condition, although redundant, twin-engine reliability is highly prized.

Squadron markings
Till the 1990s, the IDF/AF rarely permitted any glimpse into the identities or badges of its squadrons. Security restrictions have loosened, but details on markings and histories of units are still reconstructed piece by piece. The 'bat outa hell' is the icon of No. 119 Squadron located at IDF Base Tel Nov since just after the October War in 1973.

vertically, with the speed dropping off. The MiGs are behind but they can't keep up; they break contact in the middle of their pull-up and call it quits. Now I raise my head: up above is the second pair, just waiting for me to fall to one side so they can come in on me. And of course I have to fall because my speed is already just about gone. This is what they mean by 'out of the frying pan and into the fire'.

"The best pilot in the Air Force once said, 'When I'm at a total disadvantage, I pull maneuvers that would keep even me from shooting myself down – if I could only get in behind myself.' A pretty wise statement and something I'm going to do right now. I'm up fairly high and now lower my nose in a completely vertical dive towards the ground.

"At about the halfway point I know that if I don't pull out now I won't at all. I wait another second and pull on the stick with all my might, recovering at treetop height. The MiGs are right behind, range about 1000 m. They start setting up. Should I continue home at full power? The wheels in my head are spinning at top speed; my fuel is already well below the minimum required for a guaranteed return. I'll go on at full power, right on the deck; they'll have a very hard time aiming and hitting me. But a few miles ahead are the high-tension lines; I'll have to rise above them and then the MiGs will screw me.

"I turn hard. The two MiGs are behind, and Baram occasionally shouts for me to break as they launch missiles and fire their cannons. And then I go back to the move I pulled before, suddenly raising the nose to 90°, as hard as I can. Will they keep up? This time, too, the MiGs can't hold on and they fall away before I do.

"My fuel is already very low. While pulling out I decide I'll continue to attempt to break away till I hit half the amount I have now. If I can't break contact by then, I'll straighten out to the north and try to bail out over the sea at least. I already have my doubts about getting home with this amount of fuel.

"I go completely vertical. The MiGs have fallen away. We look around: none of them is in a threatening position. I choose a clear piece of sky and lower my nose towards it in a vertical dive like before. I begin to pull back and straighten out with the tree tops.

"We're approaching the power lines. Baram clears me and I pull up for a moment and then go back down and again stick close to the ground. Fuel's running out. I shut down the afterburners; speed drops off a bit and then stabilizes. Engines at full dry. The main problem right now, the principal enemy, is the fuel situation.

"We cross the coast towards home. Fuel's at a minimum. Start to climb. It's still impossible to take a homeward heading because we'll have to bypass the fortifications of Port Said, with their surface-to-air missiles. At any rate, a number of missile are fired at us as we pass north of Port Said; they fall into the sea in mid-flight.

"Where will we reach from here? Even Refidim is too far. I have 1000 lb of fuel and there's only one possible place: Baluza, the narrow and short strip close by the road, right at the edge of their missile umbrella. I go over the radio: 'Number Three coming down at Baluza. Prepare the runway for landing.'

"Number Four suddenly comes over the radio. 'I'm also going to land at Baluza.' Only one aircraft at a time can land at Baluza. Right now I'm down to 700 lb and I won't make it anywhere else. It's Baluza or bail out. I tell this to Number Four. 'Okay,' he answers, 'I don't have much either. Whoever gets to Baluza first lands.'

"He's got time to joke around. I inform him in the sternest terms to go to Refidim. He reconciles himself to this and makes it to Refidim for landing. I wouldn't have made it. I call Baluza control tower. Someone answers in a weak voice: 'Hear you; where are you coming in from?' It seems he's not used to speaking with aircraft. Barely hear him. Baram and I look for the runway and with great effort find it and move into final approach. People and a vehicle can be seen next to the runway. And here, in the middle of final, the controller tells me, 'Go round, you can't land.' I'm not sure I have enough fuel, but what can you do?

I open the throttles for five seconds and go round.

"'What's wrong?' I ask and, to myself, I add that another moment and I'll have to bail out.

'You can't land that way,' the man in the tower tells me, 'because the wind is the wrong way.'

"This is a bit much for my nerves right now. 'Imbecile!' I shout over the radio. 'For this you send me around? You just check and tell me whether the runway is clear for landing!'

"'The runway is clear,' he says, 'but the wind is still coming the wrong way.'

"My fuel right now is less than 300 lb and from time to time the indicator shows empty. I straighten out again according to the procedures for a forced landing and expect to hear the engines quit.

"Another five seconds; four, three and I'm down. Its width is like a narrow road. I feel I'm drifting and that I'm going to go off the runway; I shut down the engines and . . . catch the arresting cable while I'm still on the roadway. We did it."

An Israeli F-4E deploys its drag chute on approach. In the 1970s, Israel revealed little: the three-digit numerals had no meaning to anyone outside the IDF/AF. Details on squadrons, including markings, were sparse. This Phantom's shark mouth may have been part of a 'disinformation' scheme to convince adversaries that the IDF/AF possessed an extra F-4 unit, No. 113 Squadron.

Above: Spain's Ejercito del Aire came late to the universe of Phantom operators when it picked up 40 F-4Cs (designated C.12) and four RF-4Cs (CR.12s), all from the USAF inventory. The Spanish air arm assigned its Phantoms to Ala 12 ('Black Cats'), the fighter wing at Torrejon air base, near Madrid. Spanish Phantoms had local avionics upgrades.

Left: A 'clean' Israeli Defense Force/Air Force F-4E Phantom tucks in its wheels and heads skyward. Israel's 204 F-4E Phantoms were a 'mix' of new-build and ex-USAF warplanes, including those supplied rapidly in Operation Nickel Grass during the October War.

In air-to-air combat, Phantom crews made use of notions about power and energy maneuverability devised by Major John Boyd, of the USAF's Prototype Study Group. Boyd's emphasis on the importance of specific excess power, the standard of thrust-to-weight ratio reached at various conditions of speed, altitude and maneuver, had arrived too late for the Linebacker campaigns against North Vietnam, but were right on the mark.

Boyd said that the relationship between drag and thrust was what mattered most in a close encounter. Since energy is lost while climbing, increasing speed or banking, a point can be reached where drag exceeds thrust and the pilot is then at the mercy of aerodynamic forces rather than in control of his aircraft. By paying judicious attention to the airplane's attitude and through prudent fuel management and use of afterburner, a well-trained pilot could seize and hold the initiative. In certain maneuver situations the level flight thrust-to-weight ratio (0.73 to 1) of the F-4E Phantom could be increased to a more advantageous 0.9 to 1 or better, and by careful attention to energy maneuverability the big F-4E could prevail over the nimble MiG-21 even in a very close, protracted fight.

Phantom users

In addition to the first foreign users, the Naval Air Reserve and Marine Corps Air Reserve also began to operate the Phantom in the 1970s. The enormous power of the J79 engine, the long-range punch of the Sparrow and especially the middle- to close-range capability of the AIM-9 Sidewinder now reached full maturity for use in air-to-air action. The roster of ordnance items which could be carried by the Phantom in the air-to-ground role was truly en-

cyclopedic. For the most part the Vietnam-veteran Phantom in its years of maturity was to stay out of actual conflict while quietly helping to wrest victory in the Cold War. But even before the Vietnam fighting was finished, blood was to be shed in the Middle East.

The Israeli Defense Force/Air Force (IDF/AF), or Tsvah Haganah Le Israel/Heyl Ha'Avir, aggressively courted the F-4 Phantom. An announcement on 27 December 1968 disclosed that the Nixon administration had taken the controversial step of agreeing to an initial sale of 50 aircraft.

Israeli Phantoms

The first Phantoms arrived in Israel after a long ferry flight in September 1969, and went into action for the first time in the so-called 'War of Attrition', a period of undeclared hostilities marked by a series of Israeli attacks on terrorist concentrations and troublesome Egyptian and Jordanian SAM and artillery positions. The first operational F-4 mission was flown on 7 January 1970, under the leadership of Squadron Leader Samuel Chetz. On several occasions Israeli Phantoms clashed with Egyptian

Above: A Royal Navy F-4K Phantom with rocket pods and belly tank latches on to a No. 809 Squadron Buccaneer S.Mk 2 tanker. The RN Phantom was in many ways a new animal, with a new nose wheel, new engines and new avionics.

Right: The 'spook' on the tail of this Royal Navy Phantom, devised in 1962 by McDonnell technical artist Anthony 'Tony' Wong, adorns this Royal Navy No. 700(P) Squadron trials airframe to mark its appearance at Farnborough.

Main picture, far left: The 'Steel Chicken' badge on the fin of this Royal Navy Phantom (XT863) denoted No. 767 Squadron, the original RN training unit. The pure-white 'bone domes' of this RN crew recall an era before an item as innocuous as a helmet made a warplane easier for an enemy to detect.

Left: Unlike Phantom users who employed the front ladder for both crewmen, the Royal Navy devised a sensible ladder to get the backseater around the inlet and into the cockpit.

Below: As its nose-wheel bridle falls away, a Royal Navy F-4K Phantom points skyward with momentum from the Ark Royal's catapult.

MiG-21s, reportedly flown by Soviet pilots, downing several without loss to themselves. In February 1973, Israeli F-4Es scored probably the Phantom's most controversial kill, downing an unarmed off-course Libyan airliner which strayed over Israeli-occupied Sinai. One hundred and five of the 112 aboard died.

The October War, often called the Yom Kippur War because it was launched on the eve of the traditional Hebrew day of atonement, 6 October 1973, began with Egyptian Tupolev Tu-16 'Badger' bombers pressing attacks deep into Israeli territory; a Tu-16-launched 'Kelt' missile approaching Tel Aviv was shot down by an F-4E.

Using Mirage III fighters for air-to-air action, the Israelis employed the Phantom primarily in the air-to-ground role during the October War and faced a variety of new threats, including vehicle-mounted SA-6 'Gainful' missiles. The Israelis struck decisively against Syrian SAM sites on 7 October and acknowledged the loss of one Phantom. Some Phantoms bombed downtown Damascus. The war became a real slugfest which dragged on into October, and the United States found itself under strong pressure to support Israel.

The United States had been delivering Phantoms at a rate of two per month. Now, it was evident that Israel needed more warplanes immediately. The United States responded with Operation Nickel Grass, in which US Air Force F-4Es were ferried directly to Tel Aviv and were immediately thrown into battle once they had been modified with the Israeli-style probe refueling receptacle. One F-4E was 'turned around' and sent into battle still wearing the 'SJ' tailcode of the USAF's 4th TFW at Seymour Johnson AFB, North Carolina. Other Phantoms were delivered from the USAF's 401st TFW at Torrejon AB, Spain, and that wing's 614th TFS abruptly converted from the F-4E to the F-4D (not used by Israel) as a consequence. In addition to tons of other military supplies, a total of 34 F-4Es was rushed to Israel during Operation Nickel Grass.

During the 1973 Yom Kippur War, Israel claimed never to have lost an F-4 in air-to-air combat (it also claimed that Israeli infantrymen had downed large numbers of Su-7s

Phantom Supreme

Above: The first Phantom FGR.Mk 2s at RAF Coningsby, which had once been prepared as the first base for the abandoned TSR.Mk 2 strike aircraft.

Right: A brace of Phantom FG.Mk 1s refuels from a Victor K.Mk 1 three-point tanker. In July 1967, the RAF dispatched a Victor to the United States to carry out 'probe and drogue' compatibility trials.

Below: A No. 6 Squadron Phantom FGR.Mk 2 is shown carrying SNEB rocket pods, SUU-23 gunpod and AIM-7 Sparrow missiles, the latter subsequently being replaced by the further-reaching Sky Flash. Though not seen here, British Phantoms also carried AIM-9B Sidewinders, which were replaced in the 1980s with European-built AIM-9Ls.

with their Uzi submachine guns), perpetuating a myth that Israeli pilots are supermen incapable of losing in a fair fight, instead of the superbly trained and unequalled (but occasionally fallible) professionals they actually are. The sprinkling of air-to-air Phantom losses actually does more to enhance the Israeli Phantom's record, since it is more credible than a blanket denial of any loss to enemy air action (in the face of much evidence to the contrary).

Although the F-4E performed the bulk of Israeli ground attack and interdiction missions, losses were extremely light (35 is a widely accepted estimate, many of these falling to enemy SAMs and AAA), while kills of enemy aircraft were numerous (some estimates suggest 93 enemy aircraft were claimed by Israeli F-4Es between 1969 and 1985). In 18 days of fighting in 1973, Israeli F-4s are known to have downed many enemy aircraft, although Syrian MiG-17s and Su-7s flying ultra-low-level ground attack missions with Iraqi MiG-21s and Hunters flying top cover proved hard to stop. The Israelis did not have it all their own way, however; for example, on 10 October, independent eyewitnesses on the ground confirmed seven Israeli losses and only two Syrian. Among the Israeli losses were at least two (of five) F-4Es returning from a raid on northern Syria. A pair of MiG-21s intercepted the formation, downing at least two F-4s without loss to themselves. Other air-to-air F-4 losses undoubtedly occurred, and Egypt, Syria and Iraq have released the names of pilots who downed Phantoms in air combat, although the numbers of aircraft involved falls far short of the inflated claims issued during the war itself. Inflated claims were the norm on both sides in 1973.

Long after being replaced by F-15s and F-16s as its

primary fighter aircraft, F-4E and RF-4E Phantoms continue to serve the IDF/AF. Phantoms supported Israel's 1982 invasion of Lebanon, often in the defense suppression role, and have since been active in periodic air strikes on the country's border. Israel's program to upgrade the Phantom is perhaps the most ambitious of any user of the aircraft.

The 'big years'

The 1970s and early 1980s, the 'big years' for the Phantom in maturity, were a time when service life extension programs and other upgrades improved upon the basic F-4 design. These produced the USAF's F-4G Wild Weasel and the US Navy's F-4N and F-4S, none of which came from the manufacturer's production line. It was also a time when major programs were underway for continuing repair, update and improvement of existing Phantoms. An example was a program run by Boeing in Wichita for depot maintenance of F-4C Phantoms operated by the Air Force Reserve and the Air National Guard. In a typical year, the Wichita facility worked on 86 F-4C airframes, performing inspection for corrosion and metal fatigue and repairing and overhauling equipment, including ejection seats.

While USAF Phantoms stood alert in Germany and Korea and USN Phantoms waged the Cold War from aircraft carrier decks, the world provided plenty of examples of trouble for the Phantom to get involved in. In the United Kingdom, Phantoms flew from land and sea powered by the Rolls-Royce Spey 202/203, in a marriage of airframe and powerplant which was far from fully satisfactory. The Spey-powered Phantom was more costly but was inferior in speed at high altitude, range and ceiling to J79-powered variants. The Spey had been adapted from a civilian airliner powerplant for the subsonic Buccaneer strike aircraft and was never really satisfactorily matched to the F-4 airframe.

In the early/mid-1960s, British defense procurement was in turmoil. The bi-service Hawker P.1154 V/STOL and BAC TSR.Mk 2 deep interdiction aircraft had been canceled, and the RAF's purchase of the General Dynamics

Above: Three FGR.Mk 2s of Nos 6 and 54 Squadrons are seen with diverse loads.

Below: In the northern quick reaction alert (QRA) area, Phantoms were able to intercept aircraft like this 'Bear-D' at great range.

McDonnell F-4M Phantom FGR.Mk 2
No. 41 Squadron, Royal Air Force
RAF Coningsby
1974

The F-4M Phantom, known to the Royal Air Force as the Phantom FGR. Mk 2, was tailored for land-based operations and lacked the extended nose gear leg, carrier-deck catapult launch points and slotted stabilator found on the Royal Navy's F-4K Phantom FG.Mk 1. The RAF specified a new Ferranti navigation and weapons delivery system (NWDS), AN/AWG-12 fire control system, and radio and IFF (identification, friend or foe) tailored to British needs. In the early years following delivery of the 116th and last FGR.Mk 2, the camouflage scheme shown here was standard.

Enlarged intakes
To accommodate the Spey turbofan, the fuselage of British Phantoms was widened and air intakes were increased by 20 percent in frontal area to allow for the Spey's greater mass flow. These changes also required afterburner nozzles of increased size.

Radome
The Phantom FGR.Mk 2 has a 32-in (81-cm) quick-fold radome. Its APG-59 radar forms part of the package for the AWG-12 airborne multimode missile control system, which includes receiver, transmitter, RF oscillator, scan pattern generator, trackers and power supplies. The nose radome hinges to the right but, uniquely in the FGR.Mk 2, can also be run forward on extending rails.

RAF recce
With the Phantom FGR.Mk 2 equipped with the EMI reconnaissance pod, the RAF could gather reconnaissance imagery without investing in a dedicated RF-4. No. 41 Squadron used the pod for recce while retaining and practicing full ground-attack capability.

Ailerons
The Phantom FGR.Mk 2's leading-edge and trailing-edge flight surfaces, including ailerons, are of conventional all-metal construction. The aft 50 percent of the ailerons and trailing-edge flaps include use of honeycomb. The upward cant of the wing occurs outboard of ordnance stations and trailing-edge flight surfaces.

Radar
The Westinghouse APQ-59 pulse-Doppler radar, integrated with the ASW-25 weapon control computer, makes up the AN/AWG-12 airborne missile control system (MCS), unique to the Phantom FGR.Mk 2 but developed from the AN/AWG-10 system found on US Navy F-4J Phantoms and the AN/AWG-11 on the Royal Navy Phantom FG.Mk 1. The modular system lies at the heart of the Phantom's ability to strike from a distance with BVR missiles.

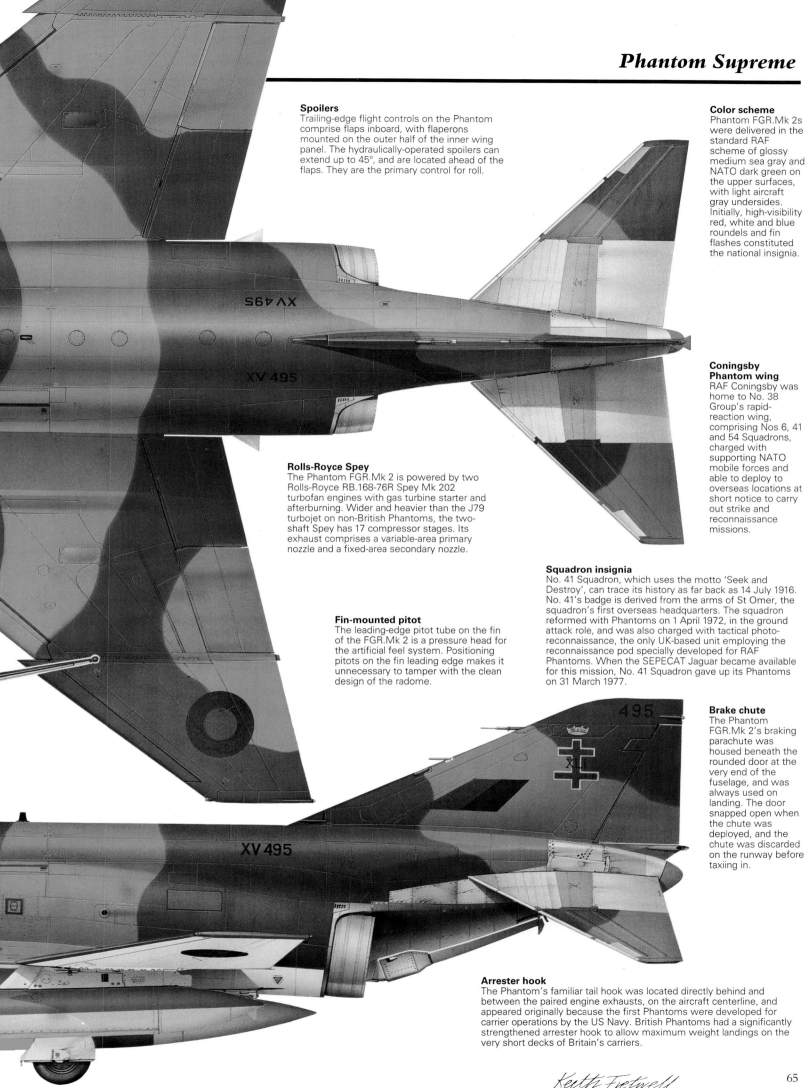

Spoilers
Trailing-edge flight controls on the Phantom comprise flaps inboard, with flaperons mounted on the outer half of the inner wing panel. The hydraulically-operated spoilers can extend up to 45°, and are located ahead of the flaps. They are the primary control for roll.

Color scheme
Phantom FGR.Mk 2s were delivered in the standard RAF scheme of glossy medium sea gray and NATO dark green on the upper surfaces, with light aircraft gray undersides. Initially, high-visibility red, white and blue roundels and fin flashes constituted the national insignia.

Coningsby Phantom wing
RAF Coningsby was home to No. 38 Group's rapid-reaction wing, comprising Nos 6, 41 and 54 Squadrons, charged with supporting NATO mobile forces and able to deploy to overseas locations at short notice to carry out strike and reconnaissance missions.

Rolls-Royce Spey
The Phantom FGR.Mk 2 is powered by two Rolls-Royce RB.168-76R Spey Mk 202 turbofan engines with gas turbine starter and afterburning. Wider and heavier than the J79 turbojet on non-British Phantoms, the two-shaft Spey has 17 compressor stages. Its exhaust comprises a variable-area primary nozzle and a fixed-area secondary nozzle.

Squadron insignia
No. 41 Squadron, which uses the motto 'Seek and Destroy', can trace its history as far back as 14 July 1916. No. 41's badge is derived from the arms of St Omer, the squadron's first overseas headquarters. The squadron reformed with Phantoms on 1 April 1972, in the ground attack role, and was also charged with tactical photo-reconnaissance, the only UK-based unit employing the reconnaissance pod specially developed for RAF Phantoms. When the SEPECAT Jaguar became available for this mission, No. 41 Squadron gave up its Phantoms on 31 March 1977.

Fin-mounted pitot
The leading-edge pitot tube on the fin of the FGR.Mk 2 is a pressure head for the artificial feel system. Positioning pitots on the fin leading edge makes it unnecessary to tamper with the clean design of the radome.

Brake chute
The Phantom FGR.Mk 2's braking parachute was housed beneath the rounded door at the very end of the fuselage, and was always used on landing. The door snapped open when the chute was deployed, and the chute was discarded on the runway before taxiing in.

Arrester hook
The Phantom's familiar tail hook was located directly behind and between the paired engine exhausts, on the aircraft centerline, and appeared originally because the first Phantoms were developed for carrier operations by the US Navy. British Phantoms had a significantly strengthened arrester hook to allow maximum weight landings on the very short decks of Britain's carriers.

Keith Fretwell

F-111K was also to founder. In place of the P.1154, the Harrier and Jaguar were being developed for the RAF strike attack role, but a stopgap was required until the latter could enter service. Thus, the primary RAF requirement was for a strike/attack and reconnaissance aircraft, answered by the Phantom FGR.Mk 2, which went into service mainly in Germany.

Royal Navy interest in the Phantom had begun even earlier, as the service had pulled out of the P.1154 program even before it was canceled. Owing to the small size of the United Kingdom carriers, numerous modifications were needed to operate the bulky fighter from the small decks. The FG.Mk 1 was primarily an air-to-air weapon, with secondary attack capability, and 54 were ordered for the 'Senior Service'. However, between placing the order and

Above: This is a Phantom FGR.Mk 2 of No. II (AC), or Army Cooperation, Squadron, a term which dates to the unit's interwar role. The badge is a 'wake knot' (as in Hereward, signifying cooperation with ground forces). The black and white triangles were replaced briefly by black and red to tone them down. Note the shark-mouthed reconnaissance pod.

Right: Symbolizing the commitment of RAF Germany to NATO's defense at the height of the Cold War, a Phantom FGR.Mk 2 of No. 14 Squadron makes a low-level pass in front of a typical Schloss. It did not happen often, but NATO exercises could bring British, German and American Phantoms together in the same formations.

RAF Phantom in Germany

The advent of the SEPECAT Jaguar for the strike/reconnaissance role relieved Phantoms of this mission.

Left: With a SEPECAT Jaguar of No. 14 Sqn. Below: A No. 19 Sqn Phantom and a Lightning F.Mk 2A.

delivery of the aircraft, the Royal Navy reduced its carrier force, resulting in a surplus of aircraft.

British Phantoms

This was to the advantage of the RAF, which adopted 14 of the FG.Mk 1s and immediately formed an interceptor squadron. When the Royal Navy finally ended its days as a conventional aircraft carrier operator in 1978, all surviving FG.Mk 1s were turned over to the light blue-suiters. By this time, the UK Phantoms were firmly entrenched in the air defense game. A considerable reshuffle had occurred in the mid-1970s when the FGR.Mk 2s were replaced by the Jaguar in the attack role, releasing the Phantoms for air-to-air duties, in which they began to supplant the Lightning. The extra burden of policing the Falklands later required

the RAF to acquire a further batch of F-4s. Together with USAF Phantoms in Iceland, British Phantoms seemed to enjoy generous pickings in the form of Soviet 'Bear' and 'Badger' reconnaissance aircraft sweeping down through the 'GIUK gap' (Greenland-Iceland-UK). RAF flight crews gained considerable experience intercepting the Russians, and credited their Phantoms with making the job practical. Though the Phantom was never to receive the love that was devoted to the British Lightning interceptor, it was to remain vital to the air defense of the United Kingdom.

A virtual standoff persisted on the Korean peninsula, where tensions were high in the late 1960s and moderated only slightly in the 1970s. On 4 December 1970, US Air Force Phantoms in South Korea raced all over the night

Left: Wearing the green frog's head emblem of the JASDF's (Japan Air Self-Defense Force) 301st Hikotai, commissioned at Hyakuri on 1 August 1972, a pair of F-4EJ Phantoms (57-8368 and 67-8378) prowls its home skies. This is the rather unremarkable color scheme in which Japan's Phantoms were delivered.

Below: The sole operator of the RF-4EJ reconnaissance Phantom was the 501st Tactical Reconnaissance Squadron at Hyakuri. The squadron operated RF-4EJs for nearly two decades, suffering its first loss of a recce Phantom only in 1992.

sky trying to intercept a MiG-15 which strayed south of the DMZ (DeMilitarized Zone) by accident, but never succeeded in catching up with the MiG before it crash-landed on a beach. On a reconnaissance mission over South Yemen in 1977, an Iranian RF-4E was shot down by a rebel shoulder-mounted missile and went down in one fathom of crystal-clear Gulf water, where it can be seen easily from boats and aircraft.

In terms of dollars, and to a lesser extent in numbers of aircraft, Iran was the Phantom's biggest foreign supporter. The Shah of Iran intended to dominate the Middle East and was building up his armed force with rapidly-acquired 'petrodollars'. Even after selecting more advanced aircraft types – orders were placed for the Grumman F-14 Tomcat and Northrop F-18L Hornet – the Imperial Iranian Air Force (IIAF) seemed eager and willing to buy up all the Phantoms it could get. Firm plans existed for at least 200 more Phantoms in addition to the 215 actually delivered.

The eight-year war between Iran and Iraq in the 1980s was a test for the F-4 Phantom in an unusual way. Having severed ties with revolutionary Iran (and, indeed, with 53 Americans held hostage in Tehran for 444 days, ending on 20 January 1981), the United States was no longer providing support to Iran's Phantom force, and UN sanctions also prevented other countries from giving

Above: An RF-4C Phantom (69-0369) of the 1st TRS/10th TRW at RAF Alconbury, England, commanded in the late 1980s by Vietnam veteran Lieutenant Colonel Don Pickard. These reconnaissance ships, together with others at Zweibrücken, Germany, had a key role within US Air Forces in Europe.

Left: VF-202 'Superheats' in Dallas, Texas, were typical of squadrons in the Naval Air Reserve which began to operate Phantoms while the McDonnell fighter was still in its heyday. The flag of the Lone Star State on the fin of this Phantom typifies the color scheme which adorned virtually every Navy and Marine Corps aircraft in the 1970s and early 1980s.

support – supposedly. Yet the Islamic Republic of Iran Air Force (IRIAF) seemed to find ways of keeping its aircraft aloft. Much later, it was discovered that Israel was providing covert assistance to Iran to keep its Phantoms flying. Surprisingly, it was not the radar or avionics which wore out first, but tires – and Israel supplied dozens of Phantom tires clandestinely. It was that most curious of alliances, based on the notion that the enemy of my enemy deserves my help.

Iran-Iraq War

When the Iran-Iraq War broke out on 23 September 1980, one Iranian F-4E was destroyed on the ground at Tehran by strafing Iraqi warplanes. It was a bizarre-looking way for an aircraft to be destroyed, the Phantom's nose broken off like a bottle stem. Both sides had difficulty reaching each other's capitals, but the IRIAF surprised everybody by putting F-4 Phantoms over Baghdad on a fairly regular basis. To complement the F-4E's secondary strike role, no fewer than 2,850 Hughes AGM-65 Maverick missiles had been purchased by Iran: these were used with mixed results. The IRIAF was less effective than it might have otherwise been because many of its best pilots and leaders, loyal to the Shah, escaped or were purged. Still, the IRIAF maintained an impressive sortie rate

against Iraq, and may have used inflight refueling by its tanker force comprising 12 Boeing 707-3J9 Cs and eight Boeing 747s.

Although the foreign customer list was not massive, this reflected more the cost, technical sophistication and capability of the Phantom rather than a measure of the world's desire to buy the big fighter. Australia flew its aircraft as 'fillers' pending the delivery of the F-111C, while NATO favourites Spain, Greece and Turkey received the F-4 to bolster Europe's southern flank. Far more crucial was the decision of two of the world's most influential nations – Japan and West Germany – to purchase the type. Japan was unique in building the F-4 under license, 125 out of the JASDF's 140 F-4EJs being wholly from Mitsubishi's Nagoya line. In fact, the last of these, delivered on 21 May 1981, was the aircraft which brought production of the 'Double Ugly' to a halt. West Germany accounted for a large batch of aircraft, split between the F-4F reduced-capability fighter and the RF-4E export tactical reconnaissance platform. Varying numbers of the latter were also supplied to Greece, Iran, Israel, Japan and Turkey, while Spain adopted a small batch of ex-USAF RF-4Cs.

Why were the Phantom's flaws – its less than optimum cockpit layout, the trouble-prone UHF radio, the smoke-belching engines, the atrocious high Alpha handling

characteristics and vicious departure – not corrected earlier? Why did production not commence of some of the improvements tested on the Phantom, such as beryllium and boron epoxy composite flight surfaces? Why, indeed, weren't more advanced Phantoms built as technology itself progressed? The reason was that the F-4 had fallen prey to its own perfection. It was in such demand and needed in such numbers that basic improvements such as elimination of Navy equipment (folding wing, arresting hook) from USAF aircraft was never undertaken because it was easier to keep going as before. The changes that were introduced slowly and gradually to the Phantom (maneuver slats, more powerful engines, improved avionics) occurred at modest tempo. In the late 1970s, McDonnell engineers could have produced a 'Super Phantom' with all solid-state digital equipment, improved radar, HUD and even fly-by-wire controls, but the company was still receiving orders for Phantoms

Above: The shape of things to come. This Patuxent Phantom served in the late 1970s as a 'chase' plane for refueling trials with the prototype McDonnell Douglas F/A-18A Hornet.

Right: Perhaps the most colorful Phantom that ever was, this F-4J (BuNo. 153088) of VX-4 'Evaluators' at Point Mugu, California, marked the 1976 American bicentennial.

without these innovations.

By 1978, when the 20th anniversary of the Phantom's first flight (and delivery of the 5,000th aircraft) was celebrated in lavish style, McDonnell was in the unenviable position of competing with itself. The successful record of the F-4D and F-4E in Iranian service made at least one of the Shah's key generals ask if it was really necessary to order the newer F-14 or the never-completed F-18L. The expected performance of the proposed RF-4(X) for Israel was utterly spectacular, and company executives feared it would undermine support for the controversial sale of the F-15 Eagle to that country. The price of the Phantom had also shot up much higher than the rate of inflation: flyaway cost was around $1.8 million in 1960, and close to $30 million in 1978.

'Phantoms Forever'

There were many in St Louis who wanted the production line to keep going. 'Phantoms Forever' was the motto of some McDonnell workers who knew they had a good thing and were not ready to quit. As late as 1978, McDonnell was almost certain of a major additional production order from Turkey and several other countries were seriously looking at new-build Phantoms. In the end, the decision to kill the Phantom was made by 'Mr Mac' himself. In a boardroom meeting, founder James S. McDonnell told executives that sales efforts on the F-4 would be discontinued. The company would concentrate on its newer products – the F-15, F/A-18 and AV-8B.

At the very juncture when revolution swept the Shah out of power, 31 more Iranian Phantoms (never assigned serials or constructor's numbers) were still scheduled to

begin their march down the production line. Closer to reality, but at the far end of the St Louis production line, were a handful of partially-completed Iranian RF-4Es (78-0751, 78-0745, 78-0788, 78-0854), never delivered, known to the company as the 'Iranian termination stores', which occupied 12,645 sq ft of the manufacturer's Building 82 for many years.

Above: Exploring new roles in its maturity, the Phantom used electronics to play the role of a mock enemy in the colors of VAQ-33 'Firebirds', as shown here on 12 August 1976. The EF-4B designation was assigned to the electronic aggressor in the foreground (BuNo. 153070), while the EF-4J designation for the other ship (BuNo. 153084) apparently never received official sanction.

Far left: An aircraft of the first fleet Phantom squadron, VF-74 'Bedevilers', is seen in 1976 bicentennial markings on the new carrier, USS Nimitz (CVN-68).

Left: When the Phantom first flew, the world-famous arch at St Louis did not exist. The Phantom had long and good years in which it dominated the world scene before moving aside to give way to newer fighters. Almost as if to symbolize a changing of the guard, a brace of five Phantoms passes over the arch, which would soon become a scenic backdrop for newer Eagles, Harriers and Hornets.

CHAPTER 4

PHANTOM TWILIGHT

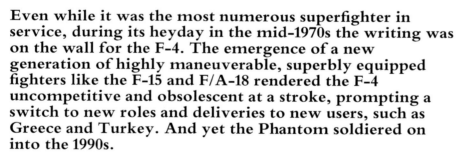

Even while it was the most numerous superfighter in service, during its heyday in the mid-1970s the writing was on the wall for the F-4. The emergence of a new generation of highly maneuverable, superbly equipped fighters like the F-15 and F/A-18 rendered the F-4 uncompetitive and obsolescent at a stroke, prompting a switch to new roles and deliveries to new users, such as Greece and Turkey. And yet the Phantom soldiered on into the 1990s.

Above: Fighter pilots, armorers and crew chiefs are supremely pragmatic men, not usually touched by artistry. But the silhouette of a McDonnell F-4 Phantom vaulting into the skies it came to command was, is and always will be – even near the final episode of the story – enough to bring tears to the eyes of even the least vulnerable in the profession of aerial arms.

At the very time the F-4 Phantom dominated the fighter business around the world, the new star in the sky foretold that the US Navy was undergoing change, and that 'Phantoms Forever' would no longer be the anthem of the American aircraft carrier. In the final spasm of a prolonged drama where Americans won every battle but lost the war, the evacuation of Saigon on 30 April 1975 was covered, in part, by the two fighter squadrons operating from USS *Enterprise*, the same warship which had taken the Phantom on its first shakedown cruise. The two squadrons were equipped with the Grumman F-14A Tomcat.

Even at that early stage, it was clear that the Phantom was aging. Rather like a human growing older, some

parts went faster than others. In the 1960s and 1970s, dramatic advances were made in air-to-air radars, and what had once been the Phantom's trump card, its radar, was the component which now fastest became out of date. The F-14 Tomcat, with its impressive AWG-9 radar and Hughes AIM-54 Phoenix long-range air-to-air missile, can reach out beyond 100 miles (160 km), or nearly twice as far as the Phantom, and can engage bombers or cruise missiles flying from altitudes of 50 to 80,000 ft (15 to 24,400 m) and at speeds of up to Mach 2.8. Other fighters, the F-15, F-16 and F/A-18, also took flight in the 1970s with newer and farther-reaching radars, offering lookdown/shootdown capability. Ironically, even though newer fighters could look an enemy 'in the face' at much greater BVR distances, there was still not a missile that was any better than the AIM-7 missiles carried by the Phantom – not until the AIM-120 AMRAAM, which only entered service in 1991.

Arrival of the Eagle

The McDonnell F-15 Eagle came along in 1972 and enlarged upon everything the Phantom had been – big, heavy, costly and, like most fighters for the remainder of the century, twin-engined. But unlike the Phantom, the Eagle was intended from the start to be armed with a gun and to be operated by a single pilot. With a huge wing and corresponding low wing loading, the Eagle was more

maneuverable. It also had a far better radar than the Phantom.

Because the Phantom was viewed by some as too big and complex, some US Air Force officers in the Pentagon pushed hard for a lightweight fighter – a 'hot-rod' like the MiG-21 or F-5 but incorporating newer technology. They got what they wanted in the shape of the F-16 Fighting Falcon. Initially intended not to have radar at all, it subsequently offered far better radar than the F-4. The F-16 introduced fly-by-wire controls and a very high degree of maneuverability. Even if planners wanted to fight beyond visual range, some close-quarters fighting was inevitable and it no longer made sense to spend more on F-4s which could not turn more than 10.5° per second, no matter what you did with new engines and fancy slats. This was espe-

Above: An early operational F-4G Advanced Wild Weasel (a converted F-4E) of the 35th TFW weaves through the mountains of southern California in the black tailcodes and wraparound camouflage of the immediate post-Vietnam era. The Weasel started out carrying AGM-45 Shrike and AGM-78 Standard ARM (shown) missiles to attack SAM-related radars.

Left: F-4J Phantoms wearing an experimental 'disruptive' camouflage scheme (devised by artist Keith Ferris) escort a Soviet Tupolev Tu-95RT 'Bear-D' reconnaissance aircraft over the western Pacific in March 1977. By this time, the Grumman F-14 Tomcat had reached its first carrier-based fighter squadrons, but the F-4N, F-4J and F-4S were to remain in the fleet for another decade.

Right: This F-4E Phantom was No. 5,000 on the production line and was painted in special markings for the Phantom's 20th anniversary in May 1978. Robert C. Little, who had made the first Phantom flight, took off his Vice President's hat to fly the 5,000th.

Below: On 21 June 1979, this Phantom FGR.Mk 2 flew the Atlantic to mark the 60th anniversary of the world's first nonstop transatlantic flight. XV424 and XV480 of No. 56 Squadron were painted in identical schemes for the flight from Goose Bay to Greenham Common by Squadron Leader A. J. Alcock (nephew of the original Alcock) and Flt Lt W. N. Browne.

cially true when the F-4 needed twice as many maintenance hours for every hour it spent aloft, and also had a higher price tag. As it became increasingly less suitable and inadequate in its traditional roles as MiG killer and mud-mover, the F-4 Phantom was chosen for new roles.

The Advanced Wild Weasel program of the mid-1970s, also known as Wild Weasel V, sought a replacement for the Republic F-105F/G Wild Weasel aircraft for the mission known today as active SEAD (suppression of enemy air defenses). The term embraces EW (electronic warfare) and SAM suppression by dedicated electronic warplanes hunting down hostile SAM installations (using radar for lock-on, tracking or missile guidance) and destroying them before or during an attack by other friendly aircraft on nearby targets. The F-105F/G had carried the fight to enemy SAM sites admirably, but was now long out of production, reduced to uneconomical numbers and increasingly difficult to maintain and support.

A handful of Phantoms had been introduced to this mission in Vietnam when the Wild Weasel IV program installed anti-SAM systems in a few F-4C aircraft. The 36 aircraft in this program have sometimes been referred to as EF-4C Phantoms, although there is no record that the designation had official status. When the newer Wild Weasel V effort was mounted in the mid-1970s, the USAF did not consider the F-4C. After pondering over several types, including the Grumman EA-6B Prowler, the USAF ran a 'fly-off' analysis to choose between the F-4D and F-4E.

Four F-4Ds (65-0657, 65-0660, 66-7635, 66-7647) were converted to the Weasel configuration, with enlarged ventral nose radome and EW fairing above the vertical fin, and these were tested at Edwards AFB, California, together with an F-4E (69-7254). The D models have been referred to as EF-4Ds, although the designation is unofficial. The USAF chose not to proceed with an F-4D derivative and instead chose a converted F-4E, redesignated F-4G, for the Advanced Wild Weasel mission.

Some 116 F-4E airframes were converted to the F-4G standard, by deletion of the 20-mm gun and the addition of the APR-38 system which provides comprehensive radar homing and warning. This employs no fewer than 52 special aerials, including those in the former gunpod and others in a new fairing at the top of the vertical tail. Ordnance carried by the F-4G Advanced Wild Weasel included AGM-45 Shrike, AGM-78 Standard ARM (no longer in service) and AGM-88 HARM (High-speed Anti-Radiation Missile). It is also capable of accommodating other weapons and carrying AIM-9 Sidewinders. The first example was delivered to the 35th TFW, George AFB, California, on 28 April 1978.

Final Phantom launch

It was the end of an era when HMS *Ark Royal* launched Phantom 010 in its final catapult shot on 27 November 1978. The Royal Navy, which had been the first export purchaser of the F-4 Phantom, was now shifting to smaller carriers bearing V/STOL Harriers (a move many recommended for the US as well), and surviving Phantoms in British naval service were now to take on new duties in the RAF. This historic launch was watched by many, who knew they were in attendance at a historic occasion.

Left: The Michigan Air National Guard took its F-4C Phantoms to the USAF's William Tell '82 competition sporting uncommonly colorful nose art from the paint brushes of Andrew Isola and Gary Bramble, civilian volunteers who worked hard to decorate the aircraft of the 191st Fighter Interceptor Group.

Phantom Twilight

While the USAF relegated its one-time MiG killer to Wild Weasel duties, the Royal Air Force's ground attack Phantom was withdrawn from the mud-moving role. Rapid advances in precision delivery of air-to-ground ordnance, coupled with the availability of the SEPECAT Jaguar optimized for this mission, allowed the RAF to re-role its Phantoms for air defense. The first attack squadrons to re-equip were those assigned to rapid response/out-of-area operations with No. 38 Group. In the Jaguar, Nos 6, 41 and 54 Squadrons at last gained an aircraft capable of operating from semi-prepared or austere airfields, which was easy to maintain and had a superb INAS. The three squadrons have clung to the little Anglo-French fighter ever since, long after other units have re-equipped with the Tornado. In 1974, Phantom FGR.Mk 2 reconnaissance aircraft serving with No. 2 Squadron, Laarbruch, RAF Germany, were also superseded by the SEPE-

Above: An F-4G in 1980s style 'lizard green' during a Bright Star exercise in Egypt. Phantom crews practiced rapid deployment to the Middle East for many years.

Right: Symbolizing the importance of the Phantom to the Naval Air Reserve in its declining years, an F-4N of VF-301 works the pattern at NAS Miramar, California.

Below: An F-4E Phantom of the 57th FIS lands with parabrake at NS Keflavik, Iceland.

CAT Jaguar. In due course, Jaguars became available to replace the Phantoms of Nos 14, 17 and 31 Squadrons in the strike/attack roles. The replaced Phantoms were moved to the air defense force in the UK to supplement the aging and shorter-ranged Lightning. In 1977, Phantoms were also moved to the air defense mission with RAF Germany, replacing the Lightnings with Nos 19 and 92 Squadrons at Wildenrath.

Air National Guard service

Ironically, the mission for which it had originally been built – the first Phantoms had been fleet defense interceptors – was now a job to which the Phantom could still be assigned when it was no longer useful for killing MiGs or dropping bombs. American forces followed the Royal Air Force's example. Numerous Air National Guard squadrons equipped with F-4D Phantoms, the variant which had once been intended for air-ground work, and were assigned to the air defense of North America. Here, the Phantom's belated duty as an interceptor continued into the late 1980s. One or two ANG squadrons retrofitted a few of their F-4Ds with infrared search-and-track devices, similar to those which had once been employed on the Convair F-102A Delta Dagger, although the fit was never widely adopted. Throughout the 1970s and 1980s, the missiles carried by the Phantom – and, indeed, by the fighters which replaced it – were constantly being improved, but no new missile was introduced into US service. In the UK, however, Hawker Siddeley Dynamics (which became BAe Dynamics during the program) produced a new SARH (semi-active radar-homing) missile based on the Sparrow airframe. Initially known as the XJ521, and later as Sky Flash, the new missile marked a considerable improvement over the AIM-7 and helped keep the F-4 viable until it was replaced by Tornados during the 1980s and early 1990s.

Phantoms against the Ayatollah

In a troubled new world where regional differences wrought greater peril than the Cold War, Phantoms were 'locked and loaded' for Operation Eagle Claw, the intrepid April 1980 attempt to rescue 53 American diplomats being held hostage in Iran. The battlegroup, headed up by USS *Coral Sea* (CV-43), included a rare deployment of two Marine fighter squadrons, VMFA-531 'Gray Ghosts' (below) and VMFA-323 'Death Rattlers' (bottom). Deck crews painted the Phantoms (note the wingtip of F-4N BuNo. 152975) with distinguishing red and black stripes for the rescue effort – as in most conflicts it became more important to make friendly aircraft visible to the good guys rather than to camouflage them from the enemy – and Phantoms from *Coral Sea* and *Nimitz* went on alert, ready to fight. The decision to withdraw was followed by a disastrous collision between an EC-130 and an RH-53D, resulting in a dismal curtailment of the rescue that might have been.

Inset above: A strong candidate for the most colorful Phantom that ever was, XT597 was the first production F-4K for the Royal Navy. XT597 donned this paint scheme to commemorate the type's 25th anniversary.

Right: VX-4 'Evaluators' at Point Mugu had their own contender for most colorful Phantom. Though not as colorful as the bicentennial ship which preceded it, this F-4S exuded real class, with its mix of blue and gold to mark the 75th anniversary of US naval aviation in 1987.

Phantom Twilight

In the 1980s, the Phantom approached the end of its heyday, and it managed to miss some of the important conflicts of the era – including the Falklands war, Grenada, the 'one-off' Lebanon air strike in December 1983 and the 1989 invasion of Panama. But Phantoms continued to be of critical importance to many front-line and secondary air force units.

RAF service

Even though the Phantom did not fight in the Falklands conflict, in its aftermath the RAF was tasked with keeping F-4s at Port Stanley. Because this added to the RAF's total commitment, including its NATO mission, Britain procured 15 used F-4Js from the US Navy. Known as F-4J(UK), these aircraft were delivered from Naval Air Rework Facility (NARF) at North Island, California, in late 1984 in a subdued gray color scheme. Features added to the F-4J(UK) included provisions for Sky Flash missiles and an SUU-23 centerline gunpod, the replacement of existing UHF radios and TACAN with two AN/ARC-159 radios and an AN/AR-118 TACAN, the replacement of the AN/AWG-10 with the -10B, and the addition of a telescopic sight in the rear cockpit.

Into the 1980s, the Iran-Iraq War persisted. We have already described how Iran's Phantoms were kept in the fight largely through Israeli assistance. On 30 August 1984, an Iranian F-4 landed at an Iraqi airport and its two pilots were granted political asylum. Still, by the late 1980s, the place to see an F-4 Phantom was not Iran, nor on American carrier decks, and no longer quite so much at the traditional air bases. The place to see a Phantom was in Arizona. There, basking in eternal sun, row after row, covered with spraylat and with vital parts removed, dead Phantoms were at rest. The Military Aircraft Storage and Disposition Center (MASDC) at Davis-Monthan AFB outside Tucson (and since renamed Aerospace Maintenance And Regeneration Center, AMARC) saw its Phantom population grow and grow as the F-4 became a creature of the boneyard.

Phantom upgrades

At the very moment the Phantom passed its zenith, numerous parties saw gain in the idea of putting new radar, engine and avionics into existing Phantoms and markedly increasing their capabilities. The Japanese plan for a Phantom upgrade resulted in the F-4EJ Kai, which is entering service only in the 1990s. The Israeli plan, at first very ambitious and later scaled down, failed to find foreign customers but it proved realistic for Israel's own F-4E force. Germany also embarked on an update plan (F-4F ICE) for its fleet.

Left: American RF-4C reconnaissance Phantoms were stationed on the European continent and in the UK, and others – like this 123rd TRW aircraft passing a German castle in June 1983 – deployed periodically to support the NATO commitment. After 'fighter' versions had been withdrawn, the RF-4C joined the F-4G Wild Weasel in finding one more war to fight, not against the Soviet Union as was once feared, but against Iraq in 1991's Operation Desert Storm.

Below: From the first days of its career to its last days of service, the Phantom flew from Edwards AFB, California, as a test ship with the USAF's 6510th Test Wing. This F-4D (66-7483), painted white with red trim and with 'ED' tailcode adopted in the mid-1980s, is carrying an AN/RMK-33A 38U-33 device on an evaluation hop.

The last trap

In a bittersweet instant that may have caused strong men to shed tears, the very last carrier landing – ever – by a Phantom was accomplished on 18 October 1986 by an F-4S of Naval Air Reserve squadron VF-202 'Superheats'. The deck is USS *America*'s (CV-66), which took the Phantoms on Mediterranean cruises and fought in Southeast Asian waters. With this 'grab' by a ready tailhook, the carrier-based Phantom became history.

Far right: A Royal Air Force Phantom FGR.Mk 2 of No. 228 Operational Conversion Unit (which, in wartime, would have assumed its shadow identity as No. 64 Squadron) blasts away from RAF Abingdon after an air show performance.

It was an American company that came up with the most ambitious 'Super Phantom' proposal of all, one with a ready market in the form of the 780 Phantoms serving (in 1984) with the ANG (to say nothing of the total 2,700 Phantoms in service worldwide). The Boeing Military Airplane Company (BMAC) in Wichita, Kansas, made a heavy investment into its plan for a 'Super Phantom'. The plan was to replace the J79 engines with 20,600-lb (91.6-kN) thrust afterburning Pratt & Whitney PW1120s, add 850-lb (385-kg) conformal fuel tanks for increased

range and replace the radar with the Hughes AN/APG-65 used on the F/A-18 Hornet, plus at least two dozen other changes. The US Department of Defense was interested in upgrading the ANG F-4 force and issued an RFP (request for proposals) to which Boeing and the engine maker responded.

For more than two years, BMAC pursued its Phantom upgrade, and a model of the proposed 'Super Phantom' with its guppy-like conformal fuel tank was displayed at Farnborough in 1984. Some reports indicate that Boeing actually completed a Phantom conversion and delivered it to Israel, although the Israelis have not acknowledged any help from BMAC. The Boeing Military Airplane Company's 'customer' however, as the company saw it, was the ANG, which in the mid-1980s still had hundreds of Phantoms. The plan remained active until early 1986 but was never adopted, because a commitment to a 'Super Phantom' program would have taken funding away from the newer F-15 and F-16 fighters, and no one was willing to do that.

In June 1987, Israeli Aircraft Industries (IAI) demonstrated *its* 'Super Phantom' (No. 229/4X-JPA/66-0327) at the Paris air show. This aircraft had been converted by IAI within Israel and was not connected to any activity by BMAC in the US. This upgraded F-4, known as the Phantom 2000, was powered by two Pratt & Whitney PW1120 engines, although an earlier test ship had flown with one J79 and one PW1120. Other improvements included an advanced multimode radar, wide field-of-view HUD (head-up display), multifunction displays for both pilot and WSO, computerized NWDS (Navigation and Weapons Delivery System) and improved radios. Israeli Aircraft Industries hoped, in 1987, to sell this updated Phantom to F-4 operators unable to afford a new aircraft, in addition to allowing Israel's own forces to extend the service life and mission capability of their Phantoms.

Although Israel never sold its 'Super Phantoms' abroad – and may have since dropped plans to retrofit the PW1120 engine, which depended upon it being installed in its own Lavi fighter (since canceled) – a more modest program to upgrade IDF/AF Phantoms is proceeding.

Right: A Taegu-based F-4D Phantom (66-7608) of the RoKAF (Republic of Korea Air Force) 11th Tactical Fighter Wing comes in for a landing with leading-edge flaps extended and brake chute dragging. This ship was delivered to the RoKAF in 1988, one of dozens of Phantoms which bolstered the South Korean air arm at the time their numbers were being reduced in the US inventory.

Top: An F-4E of Israel's No. 119 Squadron at Tel Nov. Note the refueling probe plumbed directly into the 'flying boom' receptacle behind the cockpit.

Above: Destined for South Korea, the 5,057th and last Phantom built by McDonnell (78-0744) poses at the St Louis plant which, at its peak, turned out 72 Phantoms per month.

By far the *least* ambitious program for upgrading the Phantom was proposed by the manufacturer itself. In 1984, defying company policy which was strongly against re-surrecting *any* Phantom effort, a few McDonnell employees put together a proposal 'for the 21st century'. The McDonnell experts were not prepared to invest in new engines and offered very minor changes, including one-piece windshield, improved smokeless J79 engines and ARN-118 TACAN. The company knew that a new radar had to be offered, but never specified which type. The program had little support in St Louis and died before any serious sales attempt was mounted.

About half-a-dozen one-piece windshields reached the USAF and the IDF/AF but, other than this, plans to upgrade the Phantom force proved disappointing. Mean-

while, as the 1980s progressed and the 1990s arrived, Phantoms began to bow out from some units.

'Phantom Farewells', or 'Phan-Outs', became routine as F-4s were replaced by other types. At Springfield, Illinois, where the very *first* ANG Phantoms had gone into service, the last one flew on 31 October 1989, replaced by the F-16 Fighting Falcon. A similar transition took place with the 184th TFG, Kansas ANG at McConnell AFB, Kansas, on 31 March 1990. The Marine Corps' sole RF-4B unit, VMFP-3, made its last flight on 13 August 1990 and was deactivated on 30 September 1990, leaving the Marines without a dedicated reconnaissance aircraft for the first time in 51 years. Despite this, it was clear that the RF-4C reconnaissance ship was likely to be the final Phantom in USAF and ANG service.

Desert Storm

As the 'Phantom Farewells' continued, Saddam Hussein's name gained sudden notoriety in the West, and there remained one more war for the Phantom to fight. Just after Iraq's invasion of Kuwait (2 August 1990), the 561st TFS, part of the 35th TFW at George AFB, California, under Colonel Ron Karp, deployed rapidly to the Middle East to form the nucleus of what became the 35th TFW (Provisional) at Sheikh Isa air base, Bahrain. Twenty-four F-4G Advanced Wild Weasels deployed on 15 August 1990, configured with three external fuel tanks, four chaff/flare dispensers, two AGM-88 HARMs on the inboard pylons, three AIM-7M Sparrow radar-guided missiles and an AN/ALQ-184 ECM pod in the fourth Sparrow well.

The 106th TRS, part of the Alabama ANG's 117th TRW at Birmingham, Alabama, under Colonel James F. (Jim) Brown, was asked to volunteer the instant Operation Desert Storm began, because it was the only recce unit equipped with KS-127 LOROP (long-range oblique photography). Using four RF-4Cs from their own unit plus two borrowed from the Mississippi ANG's 153rd TRS, the Alabama Guardsmen also deployed to Sheikh Isa, a.k.a. 'Shakey's Pizza' in the Southerners' slang.

Above: As the Phantom's time in Europe neared its end (and two-tone gray replaced lizard green), 'fighter' Phantoms were replaced largely by the F-16 Fighting Falcon, although F-4G Advanced Wild Weasels remained. Flying with the 52nd TFW from Spangdahlem, Germany, the Weasels made up half of a 'hunter/killer' team in which the F-16 was the other half, replacing retired F-4Es.

Left: Slime lights, more properly known as formation lights, glow on the tails of these F-4G Advanced Wild Weasels of the 561st Tactical Fighter Squadron, part of the 37th TFW, probably seen at their home, George AFB, California. The No. 2 F-4G, on the right, after hearing the tower's clearance for takeoff, watches for his leader's gear struts to flex. Then he will know that it is time to apply full afterburner and take off in formation.

To neutralize Saddam Hussein's SAM radars, the F-4G Advanced Wild Weasel was not merely the weapon of choice: it was the only choice. Thirty-four years after the first flight of the Phantom and 17 years after the development of the Phantom Wild Weasel, no SEAD version of the F-15, F-16 or F/A-18 existed. It was the Phantom or nothing. When Karp's F-4G crews kicked off the war on 17 January 1991, they began by fighting at higher altitudes than they had ever planned. In the NATO context, the F-4G had drilled to go in on its target at treetop level. In the Middle East deserts, Weasels flew against Iraqi radars at medium altitudes of 28,000 to 32,000 ft (8500 to 9700 m), because, with plenty of guns shooting, there was too much metal flying around.

Even before the photo-Phantoms got into the struggle against Saddam, one aircraft was lost. On 8 October 1990, an Alabama RF-4C Phantom (61-1044) was destroyed in a mishap, and Majors Barry Henderson and Stephen Schramm were killed.

The Alabama Guardsmen in Bahrain were relieved in December 1990 by the Nevada ANG's 192nd TRS, who continued to fly the same RF-4Cs plus an attrition replacement brought with them from Nevada. Soon after, the 12th TRS/67th TRW 'Blackbirds' at Bergstrom AFB, Texas, dispatched 12 RF-4Cs, which reached Sheikh Isa by 14 January 1991. Other Phantoms were sent to Incirlik AB, Turkey, to join the 7440th Composite Wing which mounted strikes against Iraq from the west. The 38th TRS/26th TRW from Zweibrücken AB, Germany, dispatched a dozen RF-4Cs, which were joined by four F-4E Phantoms from the 3rd TFS/3rd TFW, Clark AB, Philippines. The 23rd TFS/52nd TFW from Spangdahlem AB, Germany, also went to Incirlik with its F-4G Advanced Wild Weasels.

When war came with the launching of the first strikes on Baghdad on 17 January 1991, the RF-4C was limited to daytime operations but was given almost too many missions to handle. RF-4Cs were sent into Kuwait almost every day looking for the Republican Guard. RF-4Cs also flew to Baghdad, with air refueling, to reconnoiter Iraqi airfields around the capital. The recce Phantoms covered rocket fuel plants, chemical plants and communications and control centers, and they were repeatedly diverted from other photography missions to search for 'Scud' missile launchers.

As described by Major Steve Vonderheide, one of the Guardsmen from Reno, "We looked every day for 'Scuds', especially in western Iraq for those that threatened Israel. A mission in the KTO (Kuwait Theater of Operations) lasted 2½ hours, but we went into western Iraq on four- to seven-hour missions with multiple refuelings.

Far left: An F-4D Phantom of the 147th Fighter Interceptor Group, Texas Air National Guard, over the Gulf of Mexico on a 9 June 1988 mission. Phantoms employed in the air defense role were among the last to be replaced, but have now given way to ADF F-16A Fighting Falcons.

Left: In May 1988, an F-4E (68-0338) of the 131st Tactical Fighter Wing, Missouri Air National Guard, marks the Phantom's 30th anniversary. Based in St Louis, where it was built, this F-4E was also a double MiG killer.

Below left: Near the end of its career, an F-4J(UK) Phantom of No. 74 Squadron sits out a stormy night at RAF Wattisham. This aircraft (ZE363, coded 'W') was originally BuNo. 155868 and was one of 15 ex-US Navy F-4Js acquired by Britain in the early 1980s. The only J79-powered Phantom in British hands, the F-4J(UK) was more responsive to the throttle than the Spey-engined FGR.Mk 2.

Below: The USAF's 51st Fighter Wing never came home from the Korean War, where it flew F-86 Sabres against the MiG-15. This F-4E in the pattern at K-55 Osan AB, Korea, in 1986, got its MiG kill in Vietnam before moving north in Asia to join the wing's 36th TFS. Osan's 36th TFS/51st TFW was one of the last US operators of the F-4E abroad, and has now converted to the F-16C.

McDonnell F-4F ICE Phantom II ETD.61 (ex JBG 36), Luftwaffe NAS Point Mugu, California 1992

F-4F 38+43 (72-1253) is a Phantom reborn. The ICE (Improved Combat Efficiency), or KWS (Kampfwersteigerung), Phantom was conceived to bridge the gap before the introduction of Germany's EFA (European Fighter Aircraft) and may assume greater importance now that the future of a German EFA is unclear. This F-4F upgrade introduces new radar and BVR (beyond visual range) missiles, as well as a life expectancy until at least 2005. 38+43 is one of three developmental ships which deployed to Point Mugu for AMRAAM missile trials in mid-1992.

Avionics updates
Unremarkable on the outside, the ICE F-4F is completely 'rewired' on the inside. First-stage additions included the Honeywell H-423 laser inertial gyro autonomous navigation system, GEC CPU-143/A digital air computer, linked by Mil Std 1553R digital databus. For the interceptor mission, additional avionics changes accompany a new radome, radar and AMRAAM missiles.

Radar
Often viewed as the definitive fighter radar, the lightweight Hughes APG-65, designed for the F/A-18 Hornet, is compact and makes extensive use of plug-in LRI (line replaceable item) circuit and component packages while occupying a volume of just 4.45 cu ft (0.13 m³), including antenna. The radar weighs 340 lb (154 kg) excluding its rack, and can be pulled forward on rails when the radome is hinged through 180° for maintenance access. The APG-65 operates in an unprecedented number of modes to give pilot and navigator support in all phases of the mission, from terrain avoidance to missile shooting, and is deemed the ideal tool to work in partnership with the AIM-120A AMRAAM improved BVR missile.

Camouflage
The two-tone splinter gray worn by 38+43 has become the Luftwaffe standard and reflects Germany's reaching the same conclusion as other Phantom operators who turned to gray schemes in the final years of the fighter's operational life. The Luftwaffe experimented with several variations of its earlier forest-green paint scheme and with other variations in gray before arriving at the 'disruptive' camouflage pattern now employed.

Armament
The F-4F ICE is configured to carry four AIM-120A AMRAAMs and four AIM-9 Sidewinder IR missiles. The AMRAAMs employed in the German missile trials at Point Mugu are painted with red/white checkerboard sections and fin cap colors to aid in visual/photographic assessment of the BVR missiles' performance.

Gun
Internal armament is the General Electric M61A1 Vulcan ('Gatling') cannon with 820 rounds, as is found on the F-4E and F-4F, with a late MIDAS flash suppressor giving a blunt, canted appearance to the gun port.

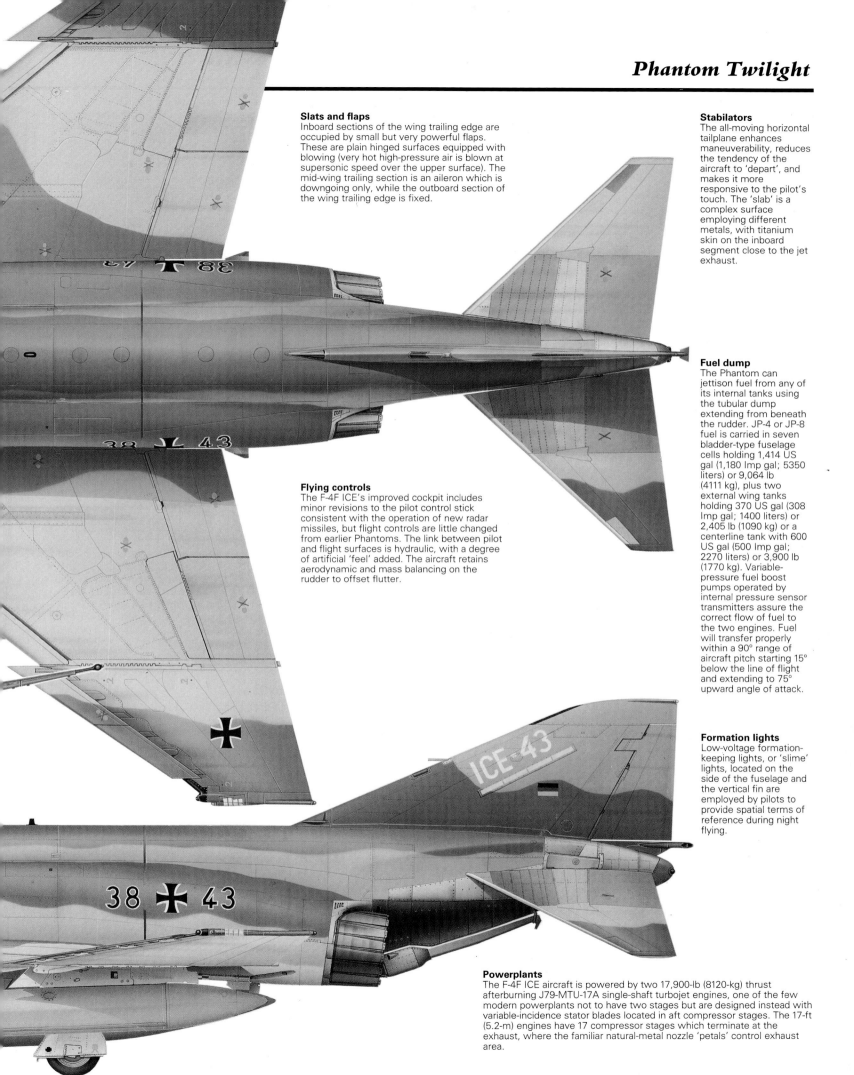

Slats and flaps
Inboard sections of the wing trailing edge are occupied by small but very powerful flaps. These are plain hinged surfaces equipped with blowing (very hot high-pressure air is blown at supersonic speed over the upper surface). The mid-wing trailing section is an aileron which is downgoing only, while the outboard section of the wing trailing edge is fixed.

Stabilators
The all-moving horizontal tailplane enhances maneuverability, reduces the tendency of the aircraft to 'depart', and makes it more responsive to the pilot's touch. The 'slab' is a complex surface employing different metals, with titanium skin on the inboard segment close to the jet exhaust.

Fuel dump
The Phantom can jettison fuel from any of its internal tanks using the tubular dump extending from beneath the rudder. JP-4 or JP-8 fuel is carried in seven bladder-type fuselage cells holding 1,414 US gal (1,180 Imp gal; 5350 liters) or 9,064 lb (4111 kg), plus two external wing tanks holding 370 US gal (308 Imp gal; 1400 liters) or 2,405 lb (1090 kg) or a centerline tank with 600 US gal (500 Imp gal; 2270 liters) or 3,900 lb (1770 kg). Variable-pressure fuel boost pumps operated by internal pressure sensor transmitters assure the correct flow of fuel to the two engines. Fuel will transfer properly within a 90° range of aircraft pitch starting 15° below the line of flight and extending to 75° upward angle of attack.

Flying controls
The F-4F ICE's improved cockpit includes minor revisions to the pilot control stick consistent with the operation of new radar missiles, but flight controls are little changed from earlier Phantoms. The link between pilot and flight surfaces is hydraulic, with a degree of artificial 'feel' added. The aircraft retains aerodynamic and mass balancing on the rudder to offset flutter.

Formation lights
Low-voltage formation-keeping lights, or 'slime' lights, located on the side of the fuselage and the vertical fin are employed by pilots to provide spatial terms of reference during night flying.

Powerplants
The F-4F ICE aircraft is powered by two 17,900-lb (8120-kg) thrust afterburning J79-MTU-17A single-shaft turbojet engines, one of the few modern powerplants not to have two stages but are designed instead with variable-incidence stator blades located in aft compressor stages. The 17-ft (5.2-m) engines have 17 compressor stages which terminate at the exhaust, where the familiar natural-metal nozzle 'petals' control exhaust area.

Above: An F-4C Phantom of the Oregon ANG banks sharply, baring Sparrows, Sidewinders and an SUU-23/A gunpod.

Above right: Dark clouds gather as an Idaho ANG RF-4C lands using its braking parachute.

Below: Two F-4Es in the two-tone gray scheme which was the final American color for the Phantom.

"We stood off with our long-range cameras and looked for places where a 'Scud' launcher could hide: under bridges, under bridge abutments, underneath hangars, inside hangar doors. They moved at night. We were trying to locate them, so they could be destroyed before they could cause more damage. Our film could be processed within 45 minutes of landing, and after the first few days of the war we had digital scanners which could transmit the photographs to Riyadh within moments of the time the film was processed."

As for the F-4G Wild Weasel, it was the key element in the USAF's EW operations against Iraq. Unlike the EF-111A Raven, which had a non-lethal SEAD function, jamming enemy radar screens to blank out the location of

incoming strike aircraft, the F-4G's mission was decidedly deadly. When the F-4G went in to launch its HARMs at a SAM site, the enemy naturally reacted by shutting down his radars, possibly unaware that HARM's strap-down inertial guidance system would continue to home in on the spot where the radar had been turned off. With no radar tracking them, the F-4G crew was unlikely to suffer a missile hit, but it had to attack through a veritable hail of gunfire. This could be distracting. At night, any pinprick of light could signify a tracer shell or a missile stalking the low-flying Weasel.

Still, only one F-4G (69-7571), belonging to the 81st TFS/52nd TFW, was lost. It happened on 18 January 1991 when enemy fire pierced the aircraft's fuel tank, causing a loss of fuel pressure. Returning from the mission running on empty, the Wild Weasel sought aerial refueling, but a dense fog scuttled the refueling and the F-4G was directed toward a friendly Saudi airstrip. Four landing attempts were unsuccessful and, during the fifth, the aircraft ran out of fuel. Both engines seized, but both crewmembers ejected safely. Many of the Phantoms which served in Operation Desert Storm were Vietnam veterans, the RF-4Cs under the same designation, the F-4Gs in their earlier identity as F-4Es.

'Gate guardians'

Despite the great job they'd done, Phantoms continued to retire to the boneyard. The 163rd TFS, Indiana ANG, occupying a cramped corner of Fort Wayne Municipal Airport, became the last Guard unit to operate the Phantom, retiring its final ship in 1991 and leaving an F-4E (67-0389) wearing the 'FW' tailcode on display in Fort Wayne – one of countless 'gate guardians' scattered among garrisons where, once, Phantoms flew and fought.

The 334th TFS/4th TFW at Seymour Johnson AFB, North Carolina, became the last active-duty USAF unit to bow out of the Phantom fighter business, giving up its F-4Es for F-15E Strike Eagles on 28 December 1990. The 38th TRS/26th TRW at Zweibrücken, Germany, waited until after Operation Desert Storm, and on 4/5 April 1991 gave up the last USAF recce Phantoms in Europe. The RAF No. 92 (East India) Squadron at Wildenrath flew its final mission on 27 June 1991 and stood down on 30 June, followed by No. 19 Squadron at Wildenrath, which flew its last QRA mission on 21 October 1991 in preparation for shutdown in December. The last 'fighter Phantom' in American service was retired by the US Marine Corps Air Reserve's VMFA-112 at NAS Dallas, Texas, in October 1991, although RF-4Cs and F-4Gs remain in service and various Phantoms also remain in service abroad.

With the USAF, the RF-4Cs are concentrated in the National Guard, but their days look numbered. Trends in tactical reconnaissance are leaning towards neat, podded

F-4 in Desert Storm

When the allied coalition launched its war to liberate Kuwait from Saddam Hussein on 17 January 1991, no warplane in the inventory was more essential than the aging but potent SAM killer, the F-4G Advanced Wild Weasel. F-4Gs from Spangdahlem, Germany, and George AFB, California, formed the 35th Tactical Fighter Wing (Provisional) at Sheikh Isa AB, Bahrain, and fired some of the earliest shots of the war to take down Iraqi air defense sites. RF-4Cs were also part of the 35th TFW (P) and flew daylight oblique-photography missions, including part of the 'Great 'Scud' Hunt'. Some F-4Gs, RF-4Cs and a handful of Pave Tack-capable F-4Es also operated with the 7440th Composite Wing at Incirlik AB, Turkey, working against targets in northwestern Iraq. Combat success of the soon-to-be-retired Phantom caused the US Air Force to rethink its plans, not only about phasing out the F-4G and RF-4C, but about facing the end of the 1990s without a dedicated platform for the SEAD and reconnaissance roles.

Below: An F-4G Advanced Wild Weasel lugs three fuel tanks and HARM missiles over the desert.

Right: One F-4G in each flight carried an ECM pod, either the ALQ-119 or, as here, the ALQ-184.

Phantom Twilight

Right: When the Missouri Air National Guard shifted to the F-15 Eagle, many of its F-4E Phantoms joined a spurt of exports to overseas operators. The St Louis F-4Es appeared in Turkey, many still wearing their distinctive shark mouths. In the late 1980s and early 1990s, other F-4D and F-4E Phantoms from Air National Guard squadrons went to Greece and South Korea.

Below: En route to the USA for AIM-120 AMRAAM missile trials, this F-4F Phantom (38+43, alias 72-1253) is a prototype for the MBB/Hughes ICE program, an ambitious upgrade with APG-65 lookdown/shootdown radar, Honeywell gyro inertial navigation system, GEC Marconi digital air data computer and other improvements, plus AMRAAM.

Latest exports

While other Phantom operators phased out or reduced their F-4 fleets, Greece, South Korea and Turkey dramatically increased theirs. Greece, which added 27 F-4Es (like those below) from the USAF inventory after Operation Desert Storm, was expected to receive 11 more in 1992, and has shown some interest in surplus RAF Phantoms. South Korea added 23 surplus F-4Ds and six RF-4Cs in 1988-89, and is expected to add a further dozen F-4Es to its existing fleet. Turkey has received at least 50, and possibly 70, additional F-4Es in the late 1980s and early 1990s.

systems to be carried by regular tactical aircraft – in the USAF's case the F-16. Advances in infrared equipment have largely negated the need for bulky film camera systems, allowing current reconnaissance systems to be video-based and much smaller. NATO forces such as the RAF and Luftwaffe have already adopted non-film reconnaissance systems. Similarly eroding the need for dedicated tactical reconnaissance platforms has been the acquisition of stand off radar systems such as J-STARS and the U-2R/ASARS-2. Adequate coverage can be achieved by a mix of these high-value surveillance aircraft and by regular F-16s carrying podded infrared systems.

Wild Weasel assets are also in the process of being transferred to ANG units, the first state to receive the F-4G being Idaho. Like the RF-4s, replacements for the active-duty force will very likely come in the shape of a current tactical type, the F-15E and F-16 being candidates to adopt the SEAD mission as an additional capability to the ground attack role.

More than 10,000 men have logged a thousand hours in the Phantom; one-third that number are thought to have flown 2,000 hours. About half a dozen US pilots and a handful of other nationalities have exceeded the 5,000-hour mark – the high-hour man apparently being the US Marine Corps Brigadier General Michael Sullivan, who flew the Phantom for nearly 30 years.

But anyone who really expected 'Phantoms Forever' should have known that nothing is eternal. While some operators have increased the size of their Phantom fleets in the 1990s (Greece, South Korea, Turkey), the Phantom is increasingly a high-cost option in addition to its obvious age handicap.

It has been said that by 2008, the 50th anniversary of the F-4, an estimated 1,000 Phantoms may still be flying. It would be folly to predict anything that far ahead, but 100 would be more likely, and it is certain that anyone flying Phantoms at that time will be a second-rank operator, if not a Third World user. The F-4's day is drawing to a close. Slowly and majestically, the Phantom is coming to earth from a sky it once commanded, and its era is coming to an end.

Above left: The very last American naval unit to fly the Phantom was VMFA-321 'Hell's Angels', the Marine Air Reserve squadron at Andrews AFB, Maryland, which flew these F-4Ss until July 1991. Like the US Air Force and Navy, the Marines finally had to say "so long" to the Phantom as new types like the F/A-18 Hornet came into service.

Inset left: Still sexy after all these years, older now but virile as ever, this F-4E Phantom of the 163rd TFS/122nd TFW, Indiana Air National Guard at Fort Wayne, is still able to cast a spell and woo its admirers.

WEAPONS & WARLOADS

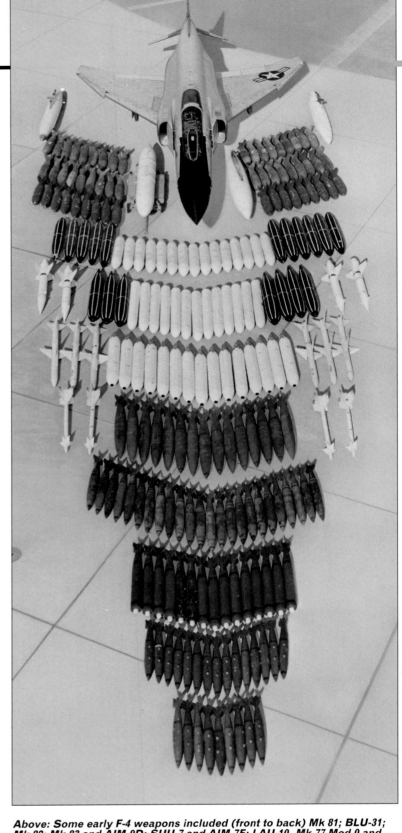

This article simplifies weapons designations as much as possible. Most of the prefixes and suffixes which append them have been omitted. For instance, the prefix 'AF/' indicates an item used only by the Air Force, while 'AN/' means one used by both the Air Force and Navy. Using the current weapon designation system, an '/A' indicates the device remains attached to the exterior of the aircraft, and a '/B' suffix that it is released from the aircraft to do whatever it is designed to do. While the original design has just a numerical designation, subsequent models are indicated by a letter following the number (eg. GBU-12/B, -12A/B, etc.). This article uses only enough of a designation to visually distinguish between versions. For example, while a new explosive filler may result in a new bomb version, since the bomb's external appearance is unchanged, it is ignored.

GENERAL-PURPOSE BOMBS

General-purpose (**GP**) bombs are the most commonly used weapons of aerial warfare. They are inexpensive, easy to produce and have numerous applications, including providing the warhead for most precision-guided munitions (**PGM**s). All have suspension lugs spaced at 14 in (36 cm), except for the Mk 84 and M118, which use 30-in (76-cm) spacing.

The Mk 80 series bombs, with an explosive content of roughly 50 percent, are based on studies done by Douglas Aircraft in 1946. Production began during the Korean War, although they did not actually see service until Vietnam. The Mk 81 250-lb (113-kg) bomb was found to be ineffective during Vietnam and its use was discontinued. A number of different fins can be fitted to these bombs. The most common is the low-drag, general-purpose (**LDGP**) conical fin. Bombs fitted with this kind of fin are commonly called 'slicks', a slang term also used to describe inexperienced fighter pilots. High-drag fins include both the new Goodyear Aerospace air inflatable retard (**AIR**) series as well as the Vietnam-era Snakeye (**SE**). (The 'eye' suffix identifies a weapon developed by the Naval Air Warfare Center Weapons Division , until recently known as the Naval Weapons Center, at China Lake, California.) The Snakeye was developed to allow a bomb to be delivered from low altitude and descend slowly enough that it would be well behind the aircraft before exploding. To illustrate the black humor of the profession, during Vietnam, when Snakeye was used with napalm, the pair was referred to as 'Snake and Nape', or 'Shake and Bake' (a product to aid in frying chicken), the dropping of which resulted in 'Crispy Critters' (a popular children's breakfast cereal). While the Snakeye could only be used with the Mk 82 (and forced many aircraft to slow down to deliver them), AIRs exist for all major bombs and can be released at much higher airspeeds. They are often referred to by their canister designations, munition stabilizing and retarding unit (**BSU**): -49 and -50 for the Mk 82 and Mk 84, respectively. It is interesting to note how the Navy developed the BSU-86 Snakeye-type fin for their Mk 82s to replace the Mk 15 Snakeye, ignoring the Air Force's BSU-49 AIR.

While the Vietnam-era Mk 80-series bombs have US Navy designations, the Korean-vintage M117 and M118 used US Army Air Force designations. They were originally classed as demolition bombs because their explosive content was about 65 percent. Widely used in Vietnam, the 750-lb (340-kg) **M117** was afterward used only by the B-52. Low-drag versions were originally fitted with M131 conical fins, which were eventually replaced with the miscellaneous munitions unit (MAU) -103 conical fin with strakes. The high-drag **M117R** used the MAU-91 Snakeye-type fin. The **MC-1** was an M117 case filled with 24 US gal (20 Imp gal; 90 liters) of the lethal nerve gas Sarin (GB); bursters would rupture it on impact to disperse its contents. Unlike normal bombs, this chemical bomb would have been painted medium gray with a green nose band. The 3,000-lb (1360-kg) **M118** was used extensively by the F-105D during Vietnam, and was the basis for the GBU-9 and GBU-11 PGMs used by the F-4D. (Although the F-4 was authorized to drop the unguided M118, there is no evidence it actually did so in combat.)

The visually distinguishing characteristic of naval GP bombs is their very rough ablative coating, developed after several tragic shipboard fires during the Vietnam War. This coating causes the bombs to burn in a fire, instead of exploding. Instead of the single 3-in (7.6-cm) yellow band found on Air Force bombs, the Navy bombs have two, spaced 3 in (7.6 cm) apart, to reaffirm from a distance that the bombs have the ablative coating. The increased weight of otherwise identical Navy bombs is due to this coating (applied only to the warhead, not the fins).

Above: Some early F-4 weapons included (front to back) Mk 81; BLU-31; Mk 82; Mk 83 and AIM-9D; SUU-7 and AIM-7E; LAU-10, Mk 77 Mod 0 and AGM-12B; LAU-3 and BLU-1; and M117.

Below: Mk 82 LDGP 500-lb bombs were the prime weapon of the Phantom during Vietnam. These were fitted with 'Daisy Cutter' fuze extenders.

Below: When 'Daisy Cutters' were carried on the inboard pylons, Mk 82 LDGP bombs with normal M904 nose fuzing were usually carried on the centerline from a MER.

Above: A 469th TFS F-4E heads for North Vietnam during 1972 carrying a mixed load of Mk 82 LDGPs on the centerline, 'Daisy Cutters' on the inboards, AIM-7E-2s, an ALQ-87 and a KB-18.

US bombs

The Phantom has carried almost the full range of US bombs, slick and retarded, and used most in anger during the long involvement in Vietnam. Minor differences often exist between US Air Force and US Navy versions of the same weapon.

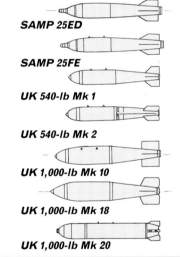

Above: A 497th TFS F-4D and two deployed 4th TFW F-4Es drop Mk 82 LDGPs during a 1972 Skyspot mission.

Left: This black-bellied 12th TFW F-4D is ready to deliver some Christmas bombs near Phu Cat in 1970. Visible are inboard Mk 82 LDGPs, outboard Mk 84 LDGPs, AIM-7E-2s and a KB-18.

Foreign bombs

The F-4 has carried a variety of non-US weapons, especially in British and Israeli hands. Spain also used a variety of indigenous bombs.

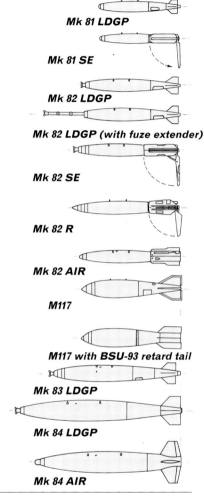

US GENERAL-PURPOSE BOMBS

BOMB	WARHEAD	WEIGHT	FIN KIT	REMARKS
Mk 81 LDGP	Mk 81	260 lb	Mk 81	conical fin
Mk 81 SE	Mk 81	280 lb	Mk 14	Snakeye retard fin
Mk 82 LDGP	Mk 82	510 lb	Mk 82	conical fin – USAF
Mk 82 LDGP	Mk 82	540 lb	Mk 82	conical fin – USN
Mk 82 SE	Mk 82	540 lb	Mk 15	Snakeye retard fin – USAF
Mk 82 SE	Mk 82	570 lb	Mk 15	Snakeye retard fin – USN
Mk 82 R	Mk 82	565 lb	BSU-86	Snakeye-type retard fin – USN
Mk 82 AIR	Mk 82	550 lb	BSU-49	air inflatable retard – USAF
M117	M117	820 lb	M131	original conical fin
M117	M117	806 lb	MAU-103A	conical fin w/strakes
M117 AIR	M117	870 lb	BSU-93	air inflatable retard
MC-1	M117	720 lb	M131	chemical bomb (GB)
Mk 83 LDGP	Mk 83	1,040 lb	Mk 83	conical fin – USN
Mk 84 LDGP	Mk 84	1,972 lb	Mk 84	conical fin – USAF
Mk 84 LDGP	Mk 84	2,020 lb	Mk 84	conical fin – USN
Mk 84 AIR	Mk 84	2,020 lb	BSU-50	air inflatable retard – USAF
M118 LDGP	M118	3,020 lb	M118	conical fin – USAF

In all probability, Spanish air force aircraft used indigenously-built bombs, in lieu of the US Mk 80 series which they resemble. The International Technology **ALD** series of bombs are basically clones of the Mk 80 series, named for their nominal weight in kilograms. The **ASH** bombs are ALDs equipped with cross-shaped retarding parachutes. The Expal BR, BRF, BRP and BRP.S bombs are sheet steel bombs with forged steel, pointed nose plugs welded to them. The **BR** bombs have a high-explosive warhead and conical fins. The externally identical **BRF** bombs have a layer of thousands of tiny steel balls between the outer shell and explosive interior to create a fragmentation effect four times greater than that of a BR bomb. When these bombs are fitted with retard fins, they become **BRP** and **BRFP**. When the basic warheads are fitted with the 'super' series of retard fins, which allow delivery from very low altitudes, they become

BRP.S and **BRFP.S**.
The standard **British GP** bombs weigh 540 and 1,000 lb (245 and 454 kg). There are several versions of these warheads, the 1,000-lb (454-kg) Mk 13, with its heat-resistant explosive filler, is commonly used for external carriage. Although the table matches warheads against fin types, it is believed that all warhead/fin combinations are compatible. With an explosive content of about 50 percent, they fall into the British category of medium case (**MC**) bombs.
MATRA 250-kg (550-lb) bombs, built by Société des Ateliers Mécanique de Port-sur-Sambre (SAMP), were certified only for contingency rearming of USAF A-7Ds and F-4D/Es at NATO bases. There were two versions so qualified: the German **25 ED**, with external arming wires, and the French **25 FE**, with internal arming wires. The fins of both bombs are equipped with parachutes giving a high-drag delivery option.

FOREIGN GENERAL-PURPOSE BOMBS

BOMB	WARHEAD	WEIGHT	FIN KIT	REMARKS
ALD-250	HE	540 lb	conical	Spanish Mk 82
ASH-250	HE	578 lb	retard	Spanish
BR 250	HE	551 lb	conical	Spanish
BRP 250	HE	551 lb	retard	Spanish
BRP.S 250	HE		retard	Spanish, low altitude
BRF 250	Frag		conical	Spanish
BRFP 250	Frag		retard	Spanish
BRFP.S 250	Frag		retard	Spanish, low altitude
BR 375	HE	827 lb	conical	Spanish
BRP 375	HE		retard	Spanish
BRP.S 375	HE		retard	Spanish, low altitude
ALD-500	HE	992 lb	conical	Spanish Mk 83
ASH-500	HE	1,036 lb	retard	Spanish
BR 500	HE	1,102 lb	conical	Spanish
BRP 500	HE		retard	Spanish
BRP.S 500	HE		retard	Spanish, low altitude
BRF 500	Frag	1,102 lb	conical	Spanish
BRFP 500	Frag		retard	Spanish
BRFP.S 500	Frag		retard	Spanish, low altitude
BR 1000	HE	2,205 lb	conical	Spanish
SAMP 25ED	25E	575 lb	25D	German
SAMP 25FE	25F	590 lb	25E	French
UK 540 lb	Mk 1	562 lb	No. 116	conical fin
UK 540 lb	Mk 2	640 lb	No. 118	retard fin
UK 540 lb	Mk 2	650 lb	No. 118	retard fin w/No. 960 fuze
UK 1,000 lb	Mk 10	1,040 lb	No. 114	conical fin
UK 1,000 lb	Mk 18	1,150 lb	No. 117	retard fin
UK 1,000 lb	Mk 20	1,160 lb	No. 117	retard fin w/No. 960 fuze

General-purpose bombs

Often overlooked, the different fuzes used with GP bombs are absolutely crucial to inflicting the desired damage to a given target. The most easily identified of all nose fuzes was the M904 mounted on a fuze extender, commonly known by the term **'Daisy Cutter'**. Developed during the Vietnam War as a kind of poor man's proximity fuze, it is nothing more than a length of pipe (usually 36 in/91 cm,

but also available 18 in/46 cm and 24 in/61 cm) with the fuze on the end. This allowed the bomb to explode before it buried itself in the soft soil of Vietnam, thus increasing its blast effect.

While nose fuzes are usually identifiable visually, most tail fuzes are hidden by the fin assembly – except for the M905 which uses the ATU-35 anemometer for spin arming.

GENERAL-PURPOSE BOMB FUZE OPTIONS

FUZE	LOCATION	TYPE	REMARKS
M904	nose	instantaneous/short delay	
M905/ATU-35	tail	instantaneous/short delay	USAF
Mk 43	nose	proximity	high-drag bombs only
Mk 344	tail	impact	electrical – USN
Mk 346	tail	impact	electrical – USN
Mk 347	nose	impact	mechanical – USN
Mk 376	tail	impact	electrical – USN
FMU-26	nose or tail	instantaneous/short delay	USAF
FMU-54	tail	instantaneous	high-drag bombs only – USAF
FMU-72	nose or tail	long delay	USAF
FMU-113	nose	proximity	modern 'Daisy Cutter' – USAF
FMU-117	tail	proximity	USN
FMU-139	nose or tail	instantaneous/short delay	w/nose plug for penetration – USN
No. 947	tail	impact	UK bombs
No. 951	tail	impact	UK retard bombs
No. 952	nose	proximity	UK bombs
No. 960	nose	proximity	UK retard bombs
TF-4000E	nose	electronic time delay	ASH bombs only
TF-5000	tail	mechanical	ASH bombs only

PENETRATION BOMB

The bomb live unit (**BLU**) **-31** was a 750-lb (340-kg) class penetration bomb, with a strong case making it suitable for use against reinforced concrete structures. Intended for low-level deliveries, it could be used as a skip bomb or land mine, depending on fuzing. At one time it actually had two designations: **MLU-10** penetration bomb and **BLU-14** skip bomb. The BLU-31's

distinctive blunt nose prevented it from ricocheting off the target. It was qualified for use by USAF aircraft, including the A-1, F-84, F-86, F-100, F-105 and F-4.

BLU-31

FUEL-AIR EXPLOSIVES

Fuel-air explosives (**FAE**) were developed for use against underground bunker complexes during Vietnam. The first FAEs were actually called explosive fuel munitions (**EFM**). Two very similar 2,500-lb (1134-kg) class weapons were developed by the **Pave Pat** program: the BLU-72, designed for use with the A-1 Skyraider, and the BLU-76, for use with the F-4. They contained a fuel-air mixture which vaporized as the bomb case ruptured. The overpressure that resulted when the cloud was ignited was an effective antipersonnel weapon when used against bunkers, foxholes, tunnels and similar targets.

BLU-76

Right: A BLU-72 Pave Pat explosive fuel munition displayed at the old USAF Armament Museum at Eglin AFB, FL. This display item lacked the additional side fins shown in the drawing.

LASER DESIGNATION SYSTEMS

Delivery of LGBs requires laser designation of the target. While ground-based designation is an option, it is an extremely problematical one requiring extensive coordination to ensure that the proper laser codes are used and that the target is illuminated at the right time, and from the right direction. The preferred method is aerial designation from the delivery aircraft, if at all possible. Methods used by the F-4 for laser designation have included virtually every pod-type designation system employed by the USAF, except LANTIRN.

The earliest operational designator, known as the **'Zot Box'**, was mounted on the left side of the rear canopy frame of F-4Ds. It probably had the formal designation of airborne, visual, special purpose (**AVQ**) **-9 Pave Light**. It was also exported for use with Iranian F-4Ds. Tested at Eglin AFB on F-4C 63-7407, it required the aircraft to be flown in a left turn around the target while other aircraft delivered the LGBs. If ejection became necessary, the WSO had to demount and store the Zot Box before ejecting! USAF F-4s equipped with the Zot Box were assigned to the 8th TFW, based at Ubon RTAFB, and included 65-0597, 0609, 0612, 0642, 0677, 0705, 0786; 66-7505, 8814, 8815, 8817 and 8823. All survived the war except for 8814, which was lost on 28 February 1969.

The next designation system was the **AVQ-10 Pave Knife**. Six of these droop-nosed, 1,188-lb (539-kg) pods were built for the USAF. They were mounted to the left inboard pylon and contained a stabilized optics system comprised of a Westinghouse laser designator and a Dalmo-Victor low-light-level television (**LLLTV**), which made night deliveries theoretically possible, although there is no evidence this was actually done. Attempts were made to cue the pod's optics to the aircraft radar, but there is no evidence they were successful. Target

acquisition was accomplished by having the pod look in the same direction as the pilot's bomb sight, with the WSO then finding the target as the pilot pointed the aircraft at it. In addition to 'buddy lasing', self designation was also possible. Best known of all the Vietnam-era designators, it was first tested on F-4C 64-0875 at Eglin AFB, then fitted to 12 F-4Ds modified by TO (technical order) 1F-4D-560. These were 66-7652, 7674, 7675, 7679, 7680, 7681, 7707, 7709, 7743, 7760, 7766 and 7773. Two of these aircraft (and their pods) were lost during the war, 7680 on 5 July 1972 and 7707 on 10 July 1972 (on the runway at Ubon). All Pave Knife aircraft were assigned to the 433rd TFS, 8th TFW (FG).

The **AVQ-11 Pave Sword** was an outgrowth of the earlier AVQ-14 Pave Arrow program (used by 12 F-100Ds between January 1968 and March 1969). It used a modified AIM-9 seeker head as a laser spot tracker to detect targets designated by AVQ-12 Pave Spot laser-equipped O-2As. The target was then attacked using either LGBs or 'dumb' bombs. Contained in a modified SUU-11 gun pod, suspended from the right-forward Sparrow well or right inboard pylon, Pave Sword was only used by two aircraft, 66-8738 and 8812, which were also fitted with the Pave Phantom airborne radio navigation aid (**ARN**) -92 'Towel Rack' long-range aid to navigation (**LORAN**) antennas. They were assigned to the 497th TFS 'Night Owls' of the 8th TFW (FP), based at Ubon RTAFB, whose aircraft bellies were painted black.

Below: An 8th TFW F-4D heads for North Vietnam in October 1971 carrying GBU-10A/B 2,000-lb El outboard, an ALQ-101 Pave Knife designator pod on the left inboard pylon, AIM-7E-2 Sparrows and an ALQ-87 ECM pod in the fuselage bays.

Right: Contained in the modified shell of a SUU-11 gunpod, the ALQ-119 Pave Sword laser spot tracker pod was used to help get the pilot's eyes on the target his forward air controller wanted him to bomb. This technique was refined and miniaturized into the AAS-35 Pave Penny pod.

Right: This ADTC RF-4C was testing the Pave Tack pod at El Toro MCAS when it was zapped by VMFP-3 in 1976.

Left: This view reveals the back of the Pave Tack pod head in a stowed position, used to reduce drag.

PAVEWAY LASER-GUIDED BOMBS

Aircraft 8738 was lost on 5 October 1972. This basic concept was developed into the AAS-35 Pave Penny, which became standard equipment on both the A-7D and A-10A.

A less than successful experiment conducted during 1969-70 was called **Pave Fire**. Its objective was to use LLLTV and laser ranging to enable its aircraft to perform the Dive-Toss maneuver at night. During this delivery, the aircraft dived from a medium altitude, acquired and designated the target, then pulled up before releasing its unguided bombs, 'tossing' them from beyond the range of the target area defenses. The trick was in designating the target, which told the weapon delivery computers the distance to the target, enabling them to know when to release the bombs. Because radar ranging was not terribly accurate, Dive-Toss was never very successful when used by the Phantom. Pave Fire was only used by F-4D 66-8700, mounted to the centerline pylon.

The most commonly used F-4 laser designation system was the 425-lb (193-kg) Westinghouse **AVQ-23 Pave Spike** pod. Basically a miniaturized Pave Knife, Spike used TV optics, making it daylight capable only. Its greatest advantage was its small size, which allowed it to be suspended from the left-front Sparrow well by a standard ECM pod adapter. A total of 327 USAF F-4D/Es was modified to accept the overall Pave Spike system, known as ASQ-153. Some of the 156 pods are known to have been exported to Turkey for use with their F-4Es and to the United Kingdom for use with their Buccaneers. Several F-4Ds were modified by TO 1F-4D-566 to equip them with Pave Spike and employed during the Vietnam War. These included 66-7509, 7531, 7547, 7634, 7661, 7722, 7746, 8804, 8819 and 8821. They are believed to have equipped the 497th TFS, 8th TFW, at Ubon RTAFB. Blocks 36 through 45 F-4Es (67-0342 through 69-7589) incorporated TO 1F-4E-588, and were also capable of using this system. These were the last F-4Es retired by the USAF.

The **AVQ-26 Pave Tack** pod was the first laser designation system to provide the capability to autonomously deliver LGBs at night. It was originally planned to equip 180 F-4Es and 60 RF-4Cs with this system. However, because of a protracted and difficult development program, the actual number was substantially lower. A practical drawback to using the 1,385-lb (629-kg) pod with the F-4E was its large size, which required carriage on the centerline station, replacing the 600-US gal (500-Imp gal; 2270-liter) external fuel tank. In the end, Phantom crews referred to the AVQ-26 as 'Pave Drag'. A total of about 150 pods was built.

Precision avionics vectoring equipment (**PAVE**) was an Air Force effort begun during the Vietnam War which resulted in a number of programs, the most successful of which was Texas Instrument's Paveway laser-guidance kit for 'dumb' bombs. The formal designation for this class of weapon is guided bomb unit (**GBU**). All operational laser-guided bombs (**LGB**s) have 1-in (2.5-cm) wide identification stripes on the right side of their wings and canards (the front fins are called canards, while the rear ones are wings). Long-winged versions of Paveway I bombs had different colored stripes on the high- and low-speed portion of the fins.

The earliest LGB was the **KMU-342**. Based on the M117 750-lb (340-kg) bomb, it experimented with several configurations and was tested in the war zone with F-4Ds. As far as is known, no GBU designation was ever assigned to it. Unlike later LGBs, the control fins were located at the rear of the bomb, behind the wings.

Paveway I LGBs were developed and used during Vietnam. They had two kinds of canards and wings. The so-called 'short-wing' (originally called 'high-speed') versions were developed for delivery from medium altitude using the 'buddy lasing' techniques dictated by early designator systems. 'Long-wing' (originally called 'low-speed') versions were developed later for use in high-threat areas where toss deliveries from low altitude would be required. Of all the Paveway I LGBs, only the Mk 82-based **GBU-12**, Mk 83-based **GBU-16** and Mk 84-based **GBU-10** were retained and improved. The impressive-looking M118-based **GBU-11** was rejected after it proved less effective than the GBU-10 because its relatively thin case tended to break up before exploding.

Several laser-guided cluster bombs were tested by F-4s, but none were procured. These included the **GBU-1**, a modified Mk 7 dispenser with 247 Mk 118 'Rockeye II' anti-tank bomblets; **GBU-2**, a modified SUU-54 dispenser with 1,825 BLU-63 fragmentation

A 497th TFS F-4D refuels. To maximize range while carrying the Pave Knife pod, it carried centerline and right outboard fuel tanks.

bomblets; **GBU-3**, a modified SUU-51 dispenser with 48 BLU-87 'Ringtail' fragmentation bomblets; and **GBU-13**, again a SUU-51, but with 790 BLU-63 fragmentation bomblets. The **GBU-17** was a test weapon for something called a hard structure munition (**HSM**), perhaps a precursor of the BLU-109.

Paveway II bombs are externally distinguishable from Paveway Is by their 'pop-out' wings, which make handling and carriage easier. Like the earlier bombs, they have 'bang-bang' computer control and guidance (**CCG**) sections which use full control deflection to alter the bombs' path, thus shortening their range. For this reason, Paveway I and II bombs are dropped ballistically, with the laser only being turned on during the last few seconds to refine the impact point.

Paveway III CCGs use proportional guidance, which increases bomb range and accuracy. They are also known as low-level, laser-guided bombs (**LLLGB**). LLLGB kits were developed for both 500-lb (227-kg) **GBU-22** and 2,000-lb (907-kg) **GBU-24** bombs but, at four times the price of Paveway IIs, only the latter generated a performance increase warranting production.

Above: The GBU-3 laser-guided cluster bomb was never bought.

Below: A close-up shot reveals the GBU-10A/B 2,000-lb Paveway I.

Laser-guided bombs

During the Vietnam War, USAF F-4s used a variety of laser-guided bombs and designation systems. Development of such weapons continued throughout the aircraft's career, and the last F-4Es in service carried the latest weapons.

Below: The AVQ-23 Pave Spike laser designator pod first saw service in Vietnam. They were used by the US until 1991, and exported.

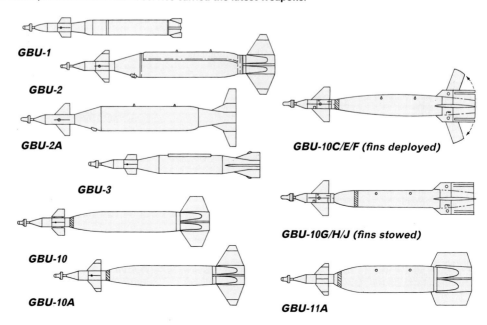

GBU-1

GBU-2

GBU-2A

GBU-3

GBU-10

GBU-10A

GBU-10C/E/F (fins deployed)

GBU-10G/H/J (fins stowed)

GBU-11A

Paveway laser-guided bombs

Above: Seen at Nakhon Phanom RTAFB (aka 'Naked Fanny') in January 1972, this Da Nang-based 390th TFS F-4D carried GBU-10A/B 2,000-lb Els on the outboard pylons, a 'two canister' ALQ-87 ECM pod on the right inboard pylon and a centerline fuel tank.

Even as recently as the Gulf War, USAF F-4Es equipped with Pave Tack were deployed operationally, intended as designators for Incirlik-based F-111Es but also capable of dropping laser-guided bombs themselves.

GBU-12

GBU-12A

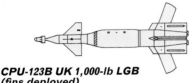

CPU-123B UK 1,000-lb LGB (fins deployed)

GBU-12B/C/D (fins deployed)

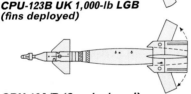

GBU-16A/B (fins deployed)

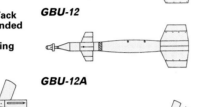

GBU-13

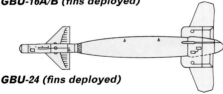

GBU-24 (fins deployed)

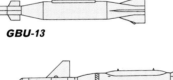

GBU-24A

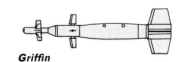

Griffin

US PAVEWAY LASER-GUIDED BOMBS

BOMB	WARHEAD	CLASS	FIN KIT	REMARKS
M117 LGB	M117	750 lb	KMU-342	operational test
GBU-1	Mk 20	555 lb	KMU-420	Rockeye II LGB
GBU-2	CBU-75A	2,400 lb	KMU-421	Pave Storm short wing
GBU-2A	CBU-75A	2,400 lb	KMU-421	Pave Storm long wing
GBU-2B	CBU-75A	2,400 lb	KMU-421	Paveway II wings
GBU-3	CBU-74	860 lb	KMU-422	Paveway II
GBU-10	Mk 84	2,055 lb	MXU-600	Paveway I short wing – yellow ID stripes
GBU-10A	Mk 84	2,062 lb	MXU-600A	Paveway I long wing – yellow & brown ID stripes
GBU-10C-D-E-F	Mk 84	2,083 lb	MXU-651	Paveway II – yellow ID stripes
GBU-10G-H-J	BLU-109	2,103 lb	MXU-651	Paveway II 'GBU-10I' – yellow ID stripes
GBU-11-A	M118	3,066 lb	KMU-370	Paveway I short wing – white ID stripes
GBU-12	Mk 82	614 lb	MXU-602	Paveway I short wing – orange ID stripes
GBU-12A	Mk 82	619 lb	MXU-602A	Paveway I long wing – orange & green ID stripes
GBU-12B-C-D	Mk 82	611 lb	MXU-650	Paveway II – orange ID stripes
GBU-13	CBU-77	1,000 lb	KMU-422	Paveway II
1,000-lb LGB	Mk 83	1,100 lb	MXU-641	Paveway I long wing
GBU-16A-B	Mk 83	1,110 lb	MXU-667	Paveway II
GBU-17	HSM			test only
GBU-22	Mk 82	500 lb		Paveway III
GBU-24	Mk 84	2,315 lb	BSU-84	Paveway III – gray ID stripes
GBU-24A	BLU-109	2,335 lb	BSU-84	Paveway III – gray ID stripes

PAVEWAY FUZE OPTIONS

FUZE	LOCATION	TYPE	REMARKS
M905/ATU-35	tail	short delay	Paveway I
FMU-26	nose or tail	short delay	Paveway I
FMU-81	nose or tail	short delay	Paveway II/III
FMU-124	tail	impact	Paveway II – USN
FMU-139	nose or tail	instantaneous/short delay	Paveway II/III
FMU-143	tail	instantaneous/short delay	penetration warheads

The Israeli Aircraft Industries (IAI) **Griffin** is very similar to the American Paveway I LGBs. Their most identifiable feature is the gimbaled seeker head which replaces the US 'ring-wing' with 10 fins. These bombs are operational with Israel and have been exported to five other countries. The follow-on to Griffin is called **Guillotine**, also built by IAI. Its seeker resembles that of a Paveway III weapon, with a tail section similar to those found on Paveway IIs. It is under development.

OTHER LASER-GUIDED BOMBS

BOMB	WARHEAD CLASS		FIN KIT	REMARKS
Griffin	Mk 82	500 lb		Israel – fixed wing
Griffin	Mk 83	1,000 lb		Israel – fixed wing
Griffin	Mk 84	2,000 lb		Israel – fixed wing
Guillotine	Mk 82	500 lb		Israel – pop-out wing
Guillotine	Mk 83	1,000 lb		Israel – pop-out wing

ELECTRO-OPTICAL AND IMAGING INFRARED BOMBS

In addition to LGBs, another approach to PGMs explored during Vietnam was Rockwell's homing bomb (**HOBO**), more formally known as electro-optical guided bomb (**EOGB**). The **GBU-4** and **GBU-5** were not produced, and may have been cluster bombs rather than unitary munitions. The only HOBOs used operationally were the **GBU-8** and **GBU-9**, fitted to the Mk 84 and M118 warheads, respectively. HOBO guidance kits allowed the WSO to acquire and lock-on to the target as the pilot dived the aircraft towards it. Once locked on, the bomb would use a contrast seeker to guide itself to the target, allowing the launching aircraft to exit the target area without having to guide the bomb. This type of guidance is called lock-on before launch (**LOBL**). These bombs were used successfully during the Vietnam War by F-4Ds (66-7505 and later) of the 8th TFW, from Ubon RTAFB. The GBU-8 was also exported to Israel and used by F-4Es and A-4Hs.

The **KMU-359** resembled a GBU-8 with an AIM-9 seeker head mounted to its nose. Its guidance scheme is unknown. Apparently not given a GBU designation, it was never procured.

The **GBU-15** modular guided weapon system (**MGWS**) bomb family was initially called EOGB-II. Basically, Maverick missile seekers are mated to Mk 84 warheads fitted with large wings so they can be launched from beyond the range of enemy defenses. They also have datalink capability, making it possible to guide bombs from well away from the combat zone, allowing the launching aircraft to escape. The program initially suffered from abysmal reliability problems, and the long-range, planar-wing (**PW**) version, known as modular guided glide bomb (**MGGB-II**), was canceled. The bomb is normally guided all the way to impact, but can also be locked on at any point during its flight, known as lock-on after launch (**LOAL**). Datalink control is exercised through the

Above: A TISEO-equipped F-4E drops a long-chord GBU-15. On the centerline is the AXQ-14 datalink pod used to control the bomb. The 3rd TFS was the only GBU-15 qualified F-4 unit.

airborne television, special-type (**AXQ**) **-14** pod, originally called electronic datalink pod (**MGGB EDLP**). At about $150,000 each, GBU-15s are used sparingly against well-defended, high-value targets. The only USAF F-4E unit known to have employed the GBU-15 was PACAF's 3rd TFS. Both clear-windowed electro-optical (**EO**) and yellowish-orange windowed imaging infrared (**IIR**) seeker heads are used. There are also two types of fin groups, the original 'long-chord' cruciform wing (CW) and the newer 'short-chord'. Both give the same glide performance and are compatible with both warheads. GBU-15s utilize the FMU-124 instantaneous or short-delay impact fuze.

The Rafael **Pyramid** is an Israeli-developed, TV-guided bomb based on the Mk 82 warhead. It resembles the AGM-62 Walleye, but is only about half as long, and has the same guidance options as the GBU-15. It is uncertain if this weapon has actually entered production.

The Elbit Computers Ltd **Opher** is an Israeli-developed passive IR-guided bomb based on the Mk 82 and Mk 83 warheads. Externally, they look like the short-winged GBU-12 and 1,000-lb LGB, but with a larger, gimbaled seeker head. Released from the aircraft like an ordinary bomb, an Opher senses the heat generated by a hot target (like a tank), and guides itself. The obvious advantage over an LGB is that it is a launch-and-leave weapon. This system has been operational with the Israeli air force since 1988.

Electro-optical guided bombs

Another precision-guided munition first used operationally in Vietnam was the electro-optical guided bomb, using contrast difference or imaging infrared for lock-on. Because such weapons guide themselves to the target once locked-on, the launch aircraft can make an escape maneuver immediately, and does not have to designate the target with a laser.

US EO/IIR GUIDED BOMBS

BOMB	SEEKER	WARHEAD	FIN GROUP	WEIGHT	REMARKS
GBU-4	KMU-353	BLU-89			GP bomblet?
GBU-5	KMU-353	BLU-90			shaped-charge bomblet?
GBU-8	KMU-353	Mk 84		2,247 lb	HOBO
	KMU-359	Mk 84		2,123 lb	HOBO w/AIM-9 GCS
GBU-9	KMU-390	M118		3,420 lb	HOBO
GBU-15(V)-1	DSU-27	Mk 84	MXU-724	2,510 lb	long-chord EO
GBU-15(V)-2	WGU-10	Mk 84	MXU-724	2,560 lb	long-chord IIR
GBU-15(V)-21	DSU-27	Mk 84	MXU-787		short-chord EO
GBU-15(V)-22	WGU-10	Mk 84	MXU-787		short-chord IIR
GBU-15(V)-31	DSU-27	BLU-109	MXU-787		'GBU-15I' EO
GBU-15(V)-32	WGU-10	BLU-109	MXU-787		'GBU-15I' IIR

Left: This right side view of a GBU-8 HOBO, predecessor of the GBU-15 and AGM-130 guided weapons, reveals the conduit running along the side of the bomb connecting the seeker at the front with the datalink antenna in the tail.

Right: The KMU-359 probably used passive IR guidance to home in on 'hot' targets (like power plant generators).

Right: While promising a truly impressive stand-off capability, the planar-winged version of the GBU-15 suffered repeated failures during testing and was ultimately canceled.

Left: Another view of the GBU-8.

GBU-8

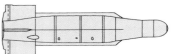

GBU-9

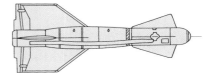

GBU-15(V)-1

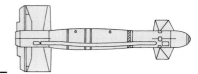

GBU-15(V)-21

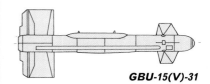

GBU-15(V)-31

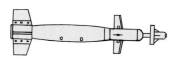

Rafael Pyramid

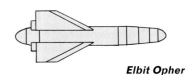

Elbit Opher

FIRE BOMBS

Commonly known as napalm, these bombs were widely used during the Vietnam War but have since almost completely disappeared from the US inventory. They were filled with a thickened fuel mixture which scattered and ignited on impact, sticking to and burning whatever it landed on. The BLU-52 was a tear gas (**CS**) bomb conversion of the BLU-1C/B. Unlike other BLU-1s, it was painted olive drab with ½-in (1.2-cm) red bands centered on 3-in (7.6-cm) gray bands around the nose, center and aft sections of the bomb. While BLU-27s were also olive drab, they only had a single 3-in (7.6-cm) red band on the nose section. Virtually all remaining BLU-1 and BLU-27 shells have been converted for use as MXU-648 travel pods. The Spanish firm Expal still builds three varieties of fire bombs, which are generally similar to BLU-series bombs.

Above: A mix of Mk 82 Snakeyes on the centerline and 750-lb class BLU-27 napalm-filled fire bombs was seen on this 497th TFS 'Wolfpack' F-4D in September 1971.

The original Mk 77 was a streamlined weapon, dating from 1951. The blunt, unpainted **Mk 77 Mod 5** bomb body is delivered with 43 lb (20 kg) of imbiber beads which, when filled with 63 US gal (52 Imp gal; 238 liters) of fuel, forms napalm.

US FIRE BOMBS

BOMB	WEIGHT	FINS	REMARKS
BLU-1-B-C	874 lb	optional	unpainted, flange seam
BLU-27	868 lb	optional	unpainted, welded seam
BLU-27A-B-C	750 lb	optional	olive drab, welded seam
BLU-52	375 lb	yes	olive drab, flange seam
Mk 77 Mod 0	750 lb	none	unpainted or olive drab, similar to M116
Mk 77 Mod 1	500 lb	none	unpainted, shortened Mod 0
Mk 77 Mod 2	500 lb	none	unpainted, exposed rear fuze
Mk 77 Mod 4-5	500 lb	none	unpainted, blunt ends, filler caps offset left

OTHER FIRE BOMBS

BOMB	WEIGHT	FINS	REMARKS
BIN-100	220 lb	none	Spanish, similar to BLU-10
BIN-250	550 lb	none	Spanish, similar to BLU-11
BIN-375	825 lb	none	Spanish, similar to BLU-27
N-Container	750 lb	none	NATO BLU-1 designation

CLUSTER BOMBS

While structures and other 'hard' targets are best dealt with by classical 'bombs', area targets such as troop and armor concentrations, truck parks and artillery batteries are more susceptible to cluster munitions. Many early cluster munitions were dispersed from containers retained by the aircraft. This had two major drawbacks: first, it increased aircraft drag, thus decreasing range; and second, the dispersion pattern of the bomblets was very dependent on speed and altitude, forcing the aircraft to maintain a predictable flight path during delivery – never a wise move in combat! For these reasons, only dispensers released from the delivery aircraft are used today. Once these are released from the aircraft, the dispenser shell breaks apart, scattering the bomblets. Most cluster bomb dispensers have 14-in (36-cm) suspension lug spacing.

CBU-41

The **CBU-41** was a 520-lb (235-kg) incendiary cluster bomb developed during the Vietnam War for use with the F-105 and F-4. Although similar in size and shape to the Mk 7, no reference associates it with a dispenser. It contained 18 BLU-53 fire bomblets, each containing napalm and weighing about 20 lb (9 kg). It was not produced.

M30 cluster bomb

The M30 dispenser had a blunt nose, but could be easily distinguished from the BLU-31 by its obvious longitudinal seam. After it had cleared the aircraft, the dispenser would split along its seam and release its load.

The **M30E2** was an 880-lb (400-kg) chaff bomb based on the M30. Painted olive drab, it was used by F-4s to create relatively safe corridors for the following bomber aircraft to fly through en route to their targets.

The **M36E2** was a 975-lb (442-kg) incendiary cluster bomb based on the M30. It contained 182 3.6-lb (1.6-kg) M126 bomblets, which created an intensive fire by burning magnesium for about five minutes. This bomb could be distinguished from the M30E2 by the thick red and thin yellow bands around its nose. These Vietnam War-era bombs were carried internally by B-52s and B-57s, and externally by F-4s.

M129 cluster bomb

The **M129** cluster bomb is used to deliver propaganda leaflets. Shaped generally like the M117 750-lb (340-kg) class bomb, but constructed of fiberglass-reinforced plastic, its empty weight is only about 92 lb (41 kg). Painted

overall olive drab, the M129 contains about 30,000 5-in × 7-in (13-cm × 18-cm) leaflets, giving it a loaded weight of about 200 lb (90 kg). It splits longitudinally to dispense the leaflets. The M129 has been qualified for use with the A-1, A-26, A-37, B-52, B-57, F-84, F-86, F-100, F-104, F-105, F-4, F-5 and T-28.

Below: A 435th TFS F-4D carries SUU-42 flare pods on the outboard and pairs of M36E2 incendiary cluster bombs on the inboard pylons. Also visible are an ALQ-87 ECM pod and the ARN-92 'towel rack' LORAN antenna.

Mk 7 cluster bomb

All versions of ISC Technologies **Mk 7** dispenser use the Mk 339 time-delay nose fuze, which is set before take-off and requires bomb release at a specific altitude and airspeed to produce optimum bomblet dispersion. Mods (versions) prior to Mod 6 had a single yellow band, while Mods 6 and later have two yellow bands to indicate their thermal protective coating.

The **Mk 20 Rockeye II** is the most widely used version of the Mk 7 dispenser. This anti-armor weapon, developed by the Naval Air Warfare Center Weapons Division at China Lake (and adopted by the Air Force), first entered service in 1968 and was used

extensively in both Vietnam and Iraq. Its shaped-charge bomblets look very much like throwing darts and are effective against both tanks and ships. This is the *only* cluster bomb to bear the title Rockeye II. The Mk 12 Rockeye I was a 1960s development program which resulted in a 750-lb (340-kg) dispenser containing 96 anti-armor bomblets, and was not produced. Often mistakenly identified as Rockeye II, the USAF's CBU-87 is a completely different cluster bomb. The International Technology **ABL-250** is essentially a Spanish clone of the Mk 20.

The **CBU-59** anti-material, anti-personnel (**APAM**) weapon is effective against concentrations of thin-skinned vehicles and personnel. It can be

distinguished from other Mk 7 versions by stenciling on the side of the dispenser stating, 'Contents: (Live loaded) BLU-77/B'.

Right: Mk 20 Rockeye IIs were used in Vietnam, and 20 years later during Desert Storm. The same Mk 7 dispenser was used by the Navy for its CBU-59 'APAM' and CBU-78 'Gator' cluster bombs.

Mk 7 CLUSTER BOMB SUMMARY

BOMB	DISPENSER	SUBMUNITIONS	TYPE	WEIGHT
Mk 20	Mk 7	247 Mk 118	Rockeye II anti-armor – USAF	490 lb
Mk 20	Mk 7	247 Mk 118	Rockeye II anti-armor – USN	511 lb
CBU-59	Mk 7	717 BLU-77	APAM	760 lb

Mk 23 Padeye

The **Mk 23 Padeye** was a 1,000-lb (454-kg) class dispenser developed during the mid-1960s for use by the A-4, A-7, F-105 and F-4. With an empty weight of about 360 lb (163 kg), it would have been filled with 210 3-lb (1.4-kg) chemical bomblets containing the lethal nerve agent Sarin (GB). Padeye was designed to remain intact until reaching the ground, when impact would set off a detonator to eject the bomblets from the rear of the dispenser. The delivery of tear gas (CS) was also contemplated. It was not produced.

SUU-7 dispensers

The suspension, underwing unit (**SUU**) -7 family was a series of rearward-ejecting dispensers developed during the Vietnam War and used by the A-4, A-6, A-7, F-84, F-100, F-105 and F-4. The dispensers weighed about 150 lb (70 kg) when empty, but as much as 900 lb (410 kg) when loaded. They consisted of 19 tubes, with a rounded nose fairing and a conical tail from which the tubes protruded. When the pilot wanted to commence dispensing, the tube selected would be unblocked and the bomblets ejected by a combination of a spring and

ram-air pressure from a 4.4-in (11-cm) hole in the nose of the dispenser. The main difference between the dispensers was in the number of tubes which could be selected for simultaneous dispensing. The **SUU-7A/A** allowed selection of one, two or three tubes; the **SUU-7B/A** two, four or six; and the **SUU-7C/A** added a salvo option. Also, the C model featured internal ballast, while the others all needed an external ballast ring bolted on in front of the ejection tubes.

The **BLU-3** family were 1.75-lb (0.8-kg) cylindrical, fragmentation bomblets which required delivery from altitudes between 100 and 300 ft (30 and 90 m). The bomb dummy unit (**BDU**) -27 was its ballistic trainer and contained a spotting charge. The **BDU-28** was a 1.5-lb (0.7-kg) drill device used to train ground crews in loading the BLU-3, BLU-4 and BLU-17. The **BDU-40** was similar to the BDU-27 except that it used a shotgun shell for the spotting charge.

The **BLU-4** and **BLU-4A** were anti-personnel fragmentation bomblets which

Left: An early TAC F-4C carries six M117 GP bombs on the centerline and a total of six SUU-7 dispensers on the inboard pylons.

weighed about 1 lb (0.5 kg). The **BLU-16** was a 4-lb (1.8-kg) cylindrical smoke bomblet developed from the M54 white phosphorus incendiary bomblet used in World War II. The **BLU-17** only weighed about 2.3 lb (1 kg), and was also cylindrical in shape. It would detonate about five seconds after release, generating dense, white smoke.

The **BLU-24 'Jungle Bomb'** was a 1.6-lb (0.7-kg), anti-personnel bomblet designed to penetrate jungle foliage. The basic bomblet was about the size of a tennis ball, with a nine-bladed tail designed to impart a 3,500-rpm spin rate which armed the bomb. When the bomblet penetrated the foliage, it would ricochet about until its spin rate decreased to about 2,000 rpm, when it exploded into cast-iron fragments. The **BLU-66** was similar, except that its outer surface was scored to improve its fragmentation characteristics, and coated in plastic to reduce the resulting drag increase.

SUU-13 dispensers

The **SUU-13** family was a series of downward-ejecting dispensers developed during the Vietnam War and qualified for use by the A-1, A-7, A-37, F-105, F-111 and F-4. The dispensers weighed about 185 lb (84 kg) when empty, but as much as 830 lb (375 kg) when loaded. They consisted of two 1-ft (0.3-m) deep bays, with 20 4.6-in (11.7-cm) diameter tubes per bay. On each end of the main body of the dispenser were streamlined aerodynamic fairings, although there was an alternate 'bobtail' rear fairing used when the normal one would interfere with the aircraft. When the pilot depressed the 'pickle' button, the bomblets were ejected one tube at a time, at a rate selected before take-off. The main differences between the dispensers were in the method of removing the safety pallet prior to flight and the rate of bomblet dispensing. The **XM56** was developed from the SUU-13 for use by Army UH-1B/D helicopters. Except as noted, SUU-13s were painted olive drab with a 3-in (7.6-cm) yellow band around the front of the dispenser body.

The **BLU-18/B** was a very small anti-personnel bomblet (sometimes called T57E2), which weighed less than 0.5 lb (0.3 kg). Thirty of them, or the **BDU-34/B** dummy trainer, could be carried in each SUU-13 tube. The **BLU-25/B** was similar, but small enough that 32 could be carried in each tube. The **BLU-49/B 'Ringtail'** was a 10-in (25-cm) long, anti-material bomblet. Only one of these 13-lb (6-kg) bomblets was carried per SUU-13 tube. While it required over five seconds after release to arm, the **BLU-49A/B** cut this to only three seconds. The **BLU-60/B 'Ringtooth'** was a BLU-49/B with modified impact fuzing. The related **BLU-67/B** was used for cratering, and was fuzed so to penetrate the ground prior to exploding.

The **BLU-43/B 'Dragontooth'** was a 0.3-oz (8.5-g) anti-personnel mine (**APM**),

SUU-7 DISPENSER SUMMARY

BOMB	DISPENSER	SUBMUNITIONS	TYPE	WEIGHT
CBU-1	SUU-7	509 BLU-4A	anti-personnel	779 lb
CBU-1A	SUU-7A	509 BLU-4A	anti-personnel	779 lb
CBU-1B	SUU-7A	509 BLU-4	anti-personnel	
CBU-6	SUU-7A	406 BLU-16	smoke (test)	
CBU-8	SUU-7A	406 BDU-27	dummy	
CBU-9	SUU-7A	409 BDU-28	drill	688 lb
CBU-11	SUU-7A	261 BLU-16	smoke (test)	
CBU-13	SUU-7A	130 BLU-16	smoke	
		131 BLU-17	smoke (test)	
CBU-2	SUU-7B	409 BLU-3	fragmentation	858 lb
CBU-2A	SUU-7B	409 BLU-3	fragmentation	858 lb
CBU-2B	SUU-7B	409 BLU-3	fragmentation	870 lb
CBU-8A	SUU-7B	409 BDU-40	dummy	
CBU-9A	SUU-7B	409 BDU-28	drill	688 lb
CBU-12	SUU-7B	261 BLU-17	smoke	650 lb
CBU-2C	SUU-7C	409 BLU-3	fragmentation	870 lb
CBU-9B	SUU-7C	409 BDU-28	drill	
CBU-12A	SUU-7C	213 BLU-17	smoke	650 lb
CBU-46	SUU-7C	444 BLU-24	anti-personnel, Jungle Bomb	890 lb
CBU-46A	SUU-7C	444 BLU-66A	anti-personnel, Jungle Bomb	
CBU-46B	SUU-7C	444 BLU-66B	anti-personnel, Jungle Bomb	

SUU-13 DISPENSER SUMMARY

BOMB	DISPENSER	SUBMUNITIONS	TYPE	WEIGHT
CBU-7	SUU-13	1,200 BLU-18	anti-personnel	810 lb
CBU-15	SUU-13	40 BLU-19	chemical (GB) (test)	
CBU-16	SUU-13	40 BLU-18	chemical (BZ) (test)	
CBU-17	SUU-13	1,200 BDU-34	dummy (test)	
CBU-18	SUU-13	1,280 BLU-25	anti-personnel (test)	
CBU-28	SUU-13	40 CDU-2	Dragontooth APM	450 lb
CBU-28A	SUU-13	40 CDU-2A	Dragontooth APM (test)	
CBU-30	SUU-13	40 CDU-12	tear gas (CS)	385 lb
CBU-37	SUU-13	40 CDU-3	Dragontooth APM (test)	
CBU-37A	SUU-13	40 CDU-3A	Dragontooth APM (test)	
CBU-38	SUU-13	40 BLU-49	Ringtail fragmentation bomb	702 lb
CBU-47	SUU-13	40 CDU-8?	Dragontooth APM (test)	
CBU-50	SUU-13	40 BLU-60	Ringtooth fragmentation bomb	
CBU-51	SUU-13	40 BLU-67	cratering bomb (test)	
CBU-61	SUU-13	40 CDU-23	tear gas (CS) (test)	
CBU-7A	SUU-13A	1,200 BLU-18	anti-personnel	810 lb
CBU-17A	SUU-13A	1,200 BDU-34	dummy	
CBU-7B	SUU-13B	1,200 BLU-18	anti-personnel (test)	
CBU-16A	SUU-13B	40 CDU-8	chemical (BZ) (test)	
CBU-38A	SUU-13B	40 BLU-49	Ringtail fragmentation bomb	
CBU-38B	SUU-13C	40 BLU-49A	Ringtail fragmentation bomb	
CBU-38C	SUU-13C	40 BLU-49B	Ringtail fragmentation bomb	

used as an area denial weapon. It was about 2 in (5 cm) across, with a profile much the shape its name implied. They were loaded in groups of 120 into **CDU-2** containers, which were then loaded into the tubes of the SUU-13. Both the BLU-43/B and BLU-43A/B were designed to become safe relatively soon after being dispensed, while the BLU-44/B, which was loaded in like-sized groups into the **CDU-3**, remained active for a longer period. The BLU-55/B was yet another version; it was loaded into the CDU-8. The Soviet Union was impressed enough with 'Dragontooth' to copy it, using it in great quantities in Afghanistan.

Several chemical bomblets were designed for use with the SUU-13. These included the **BLU-19/B23**, which was loaded into **CDU-9** (for a total weight of 8.6 lb/3.9 kg), and contained the lethal nerve gas Sarin (GB). The **BLU-20/B23** contained the non-lethal incapacitating agent BZ. The **BLU-30/B23** was a bomblet which contained tear gas (CS)

Dispenser weapons

The Phantom has used a wide variety of cluster bombs and dispenser weapons, with anti-personnel, anti-armor, chemical and incendiary bomblets. RAF and Luftwaffe Phantoms have used the British Hunting BL-755 and Israel has used indigenous CBUs. Phantoms have also been used extensively to test dispenser weapons designed for other aircraft types, including the German VBW and MW-1 systems.

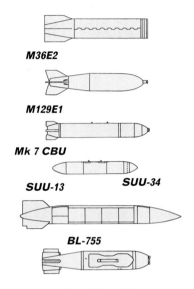

M36E2

M129E1

Mk 7 CBU

SUU-13   *SUU-34*

BL-755

Below: A 13th TFS F-4D from Udorn in July 1971 displays a pair of SUU-13 dispensers suspended from TERs. Use of these dispensers by F-4s is believed to have been fairly rare.

carried in the 22-lb (10-kg) **CDU-23**. The **BLU-39/B23** (sometimes called E49), was a 2-oz (57-g) bomblet of tear gas (CS), 32 of which were loaded into the **CDU-12** container for dispensing. The BLU-50/B was similar to the BLU-39,

except that it was loaded into the **CDU-8** and dispensed BZ. Any dispenser loaded with these agents would have been identifiable by a gray (instead of yellow) band, with a ¾-in (2-cm) red band for CS or BZ, or three green bands for GB.

SUU-30 cluster bomb

Developed during the Vietnam War, the SUU-30 family has been qualified for use by the A-1, A-4, A-6, A-7, A-10, A-26, A-37, B-52, B-57, FB-111, F-100, F-105, F-111, F-4, F-5, F-15E, F-16 and OV-10, and exported to Israel for use on the Kfir. A total of nine different versions of the dispenser has existed, but only five were

actually produced. The original **SUU-30/B** was a redesign of the Mk 5 'Sadeye' dispenser to reduce the size of its fins enough to permit carriage on MERs and TERs. The **SUU-30A/B** featured a modified fin assembly, with fintip fences aligned with the air flow. The **SUU-30B/B** was a complete redesign which resulted in a blunter dispenser. The **SUU-30C/B** was

externally identical to the SUU-30A/B, but featured some internal structural modifications. The **SUU-30D/B** through **SUU-30G/B** were used to test various fin configurations. The resulting **SUU-30H/B**, with drag plates attached to the trailing edges of the fins, was the final configuration produced.

Most SUU-30 cluster bombs utilized spherical bomblets with sharp-edged

ridges, called 'flutes', on their exteriors. These caused the bomblets to spin-arm and self-disperse. The BLU-26 family were orange-sized bomblets which weighed about 1 lb (0.5 kg). The **BLU-26** had an instantaneous impact fuze; the **BLU-36** a long, random-delay fuze; the **BLU-41** armed as its spin rate increased but did not explode until it had decreased again, thereby allowing it to penetrate the deep jungles of Southeast Asia before exploding at ground level; the **BLU-59** had a short random-delay fuze; the **BLU-63** was functionally identical to the BLU-26, with the **BLU-63A** adding an incendiary capability; and the **BLU-86** was functionally identical to the BLU-36. The **BDU-42** was a dummy trainer version for these bomblets.

The XM38 family were golf ball-sized, anti-personnel bomblets which each weighed about 0.3 lb (0.1 kg). The **XM38** and **BLU-48 'Jungle Bomb'** were probably the same thing, functioning like the BLU-41. The **XM40** and **BLU-75** were also probably the same thing, functioning like the **BLU-26**. The **BLU-61** and **BLU-61A** were grapefruit-sized bomblets which each weighed about 3 lb (1.4 kg) and functioned like the BLU-26. The **BLU-84** was probably a modification of the BLU-61. The **BLU-68** and **BLU-70** were modifications of the BLU-26 with incendiary material replacing the steel balls. They were developed and

Above: Note the small tabs on the fintips of these three SUU-30B/B dispensers with FMU-56 proximity fuzes. On the later SUU-30H/B, the tabs were moved to the trailing edge of the fins.

tested by the **'Pave Road'** program. The **BLU-85** was a 6-lb (2.7-kg) linear shaped-charge, anti-material fragmentation bomblet.

SUU-30 CLUSTER BOMB SUMMARY

BOMB	DISPENSER	SUBMUNITIONS	TYPE	WEIGHT
CBU-20 (original designation of CBU-24)				
CBU-21 (original designation of CBU-23)				
CBU-23	SUU-30	670 BLU-26	fragmentation (test)	
CBU-24	SUU-30	670 BLU-26	fragmentation	811 lb
CBU-29	SUU-30	670 BLU-36	fragmentation mine	811 lb
CBU-49	SUU-30	670 BLU-59	fragmentation mine	818 lb
CBU-62	SUU-30	2,000 XM38	anti-personnel frag (test)	
CBU-63	SUU-30	2,000 XM40	anti-personnel frag (test)	
CBU-24A	SUU-30A	670 BLU-26	fragmentation (test)	
CBU-29A	SUU-30A	670 BLU-36	fragmentation mine	825 lb
CBU-49A	SUU-30A	670 BLU-59	fragmentation mine	818 lb
CBU-24B	SUU-30B	670 BLU-26	fragmentation	832 lb
CBU-29B	SUU-30B	670 BLU-36	fragmentation mine	832 lb
CBU-49B	SUU-30B	670 BLU-59	fragmentation mine	839 lb
CBU-52	SUU-30B	217 BLU-61	fragmentation	692 lb
CBU-52A	SUU-30B	217 BLU-61A	fragmentation	777 lb
CBU-53	SUU-30B	670 BLU-70	incendiary	839 lb
CBU-54	SUU-30B	670 BLU-68	incendiary	839 lb
CBU-56	SUU-30B	2,000 BLU-75	anti-personnel frag (test)	
CBU-58	SUU-30B	650 BLU-63	fragmentation	810 lb
CBU-67	SUU-30B	670 BDU-42	dummy (test)	
CBU-68	SUU-30B	2,000 BLU-48A	anti-personnel frag (test)	
CBU-69	SUU-30B	217 BLU-84	fragmentation (test)	
CBU-70	SUU-30B	79 BLU-85	fragmentation	718 lb
CBU-24C	SUU-30C	670 BLU-26	fragmentation	802 lb
CBU-29C	SUU-30C	670 BLU-36	fragmentation mine (test)	
CBU-49C	SUU-30C	670 BLU-59	fragmentation mine	810 lb
CBU-67A	SUU-30C	670 BDU-42	dummy (test)	
CBU-24D	SUU-30D	670 BLU-26	fragmentation (test)	
CBU-49D	SUU-30D	670 BLU-59	fragmentation mine (test)	
CBU-24E	SUU-30E	670 BLU-26	fragmentation (test)	
CBU-49E	SUU-30E	670 BLU-59	fragmentation mine (test)	
CBU-24F	SUU-30F	670 BLU-26	fragmentation (test)	
CBU-49F	SUU-30F	670 BLU-59	fragmentation mine (test)	
CBU-24G	SUU-30G	670 BLU-26	fragmentation (test)	
CBU-49G	SUU-30G	670 BLU-59	fragmentation mine (test)	
CBU-24H	SUU-30H	670 BLU-26	fragmentation (test)	
CBU-49H	SUU-30H	670 BLU-59	fragmentation mine (test)	
CBU-52B	SUU-30H	217 BLU-61A	fragmentation	790 lb
CBU-58A-B	SUU-30H	650 BLU-63A	frag/incendiary	820 lb
CBU-71	SUU-30H	650 BLU-86	frag/incendiary mine	810 lb
CBU-71A	SUU-30H	650 BLU-68A	frag/incendiary mine	820 lb
CBU-71B	SUU-30H	650 BLU-68B	frag/incendiary mine (test)	

A black-bellied, LORAN-equipped F-4D of the 497th TFS/8th TFW 'Wolfpack' at Ubon RTAFB is shown with a full load of SUU-41 'Gravel' pods and a pair of AIM-7E-2s.

Above: The LORAN-equipped 433rd TFS F-4D is shown employing three SUU-38 dispensers in February 1972, with CDU bomblet containers clearly visible dropping away from the aircraft.

Left: These SUU-41 'Gravel' pods are distinguishable by their yellow bands.

(36 cm) long (with its fins folded for carriage in the dispenser), and designed to bury itself in the ground so as to be hard to detect. The BLU-46/B was a small anti-personnel mine, which would have been loaded into the **CDU-6**. The BLU-47 was a small anti-personnel bomblet which would have been loaded into the **CDU-7**. The BLU-48 'Jungle Bomb' was a golf ball-sized, anti-personnel bomblet, weighing about 0.3 lb (0.1 kg), which would have been loaded into the **CDU-13**.

The most interesting of these dispensers was the **SUU-41 'Gravel Pod'**. Although never produced in large quantities, they were used in combat. Only specially-modified F-4Ds had the monitoring equipment necessary to use this weapon; examples included 66-7555 of the 435th TFS (FO), 66-8730 of the black-bellied 497th TFS (FP), and 66-8788 of the 25th TFS (FA), all with the 8th TFW, based at Ubon RTAFB. The dispensers could be reused about five times and were painted with a distinctive yellow band aligned with the back of the front weapons bay. The bomblets were packed in containers of liquid freon and, when they thawed out, became live — even if still in the dispenser! For this reason, the WSO monitored their

temperature; reportedly there was a red light which would come on to serve as a 'five minute warning'. Once dispensed, the bomblets were detonated by pressures of 35 to 40 psi (241 to 275 kPa) until, after a period of time, they became safe. Although the bomblets would not kill, they would ruin one's foot.

The XM40E5 **'Sandwich Button Bomb'** (and its dummy trainer, the XM39) was used as a warning device. It weighed about 2 oz (60 g) and looked like a 1-in (2.5-cm) square throw-pillow. Very similar in size and function was the XM45 **'Micro Gravel Mine'** (and its dummy trainer, the XM46). While similar in appearance to these bomblets, the XM44 electronic anti-intrusion device (**EAID**) was unique in that it was set off by vibration. Its dummy was the XM44(D). The XM48 was called the **'Mechanical Button Bomb'**. The **'Gravel Mines'** were larger and weighed about 5 oz (140 g). The XM41 (and its dummy, the XM42), were pie shaped. However, the XM41E1 (and its dummy, the XM42E1), resembled 3-in (7.6-cm) square throw-pillows, as did the XM65. The XM41 or XM42 were contained in the **CDU-4**; the XM40E5, or a combination of the XM46 and XM44(D), could be carried in the **CDU-5**; combinations of the XM40E5 and XM44, or their dummies, were contained in the **CDU-10**; and combinations of the XM40E5 and XM48, or their dummies, were contained in the **CDU-11**. The XM65 was probably dispensed from the **CDU-14**. A similar scheme was used with the A-1 Skyraider's XM3 dispenser.

SUU-34/36/37/38 and 41 dispensers

This family of downward-ejecting dispensers was developed during the Vietnam War. They were authorized for use with the F-105, F-111 and F-4D, but only used operationally by the latter. The dispensers' subtle differences were externally indistinguishable. The **SUU-36** (originally called **SUU-34**) weighed 247 lb (112 kg) when empty and 848 lb (384 kg) when loaded; the **SUU-37**, 188 lb (85 kg) and 835 lb (378 kg); the **SUU-38**, 210 lb (95 kg) and 905 lb (410 kg); and the **SUU-41**, 188 lb (85 kg) and 700 lb (315 kg). All had 10 weapons bays of slightly varying dimensions. The

most significant difference was the time it took for them to dispense their loads. For the SUU-36, this took between one and nine seconds; the SUU-37, 0.4 to three seconds; the SUU-38, two to 44 seconds; and the SUU-41, 0.4 to 30 seconds. When used with F-4Ds, these pods were fitted with optional fins.

The wide area anti-personnel mine (**WAAPM**) family included several versions of a 1.3-lb (0.6 kg) fragmentation mine: the **BLU-42/B**, **BLU-42A/B** and **BLU-54/B**. The 20-lb (9-kg) **BLU-45/B** was an anti-vehicle land mine. It was about 4 in (10 cm) square and 14 in

SUU-36/37/38/41 DISPENSER SUMMARY

BOMB	DISPENSER	SUBMUNITIONS	TYPE	WEIGHT
CBU-33	SUU-36	30 BLU-45	anti-vehicle mine	848 lb
CBU-43	SUU-37	10 CDU-13	fragmentation (test)	
CBU-44	SUU-37	80 CDU-6	fragmentation mine (test)	
CBU-45	SUU-37	80 CDU-7	fragmentation (test)	
CBU-34	SUU-38	540 BLU-42	anti-personnel mine	919 lb
CBU-34A	SUU-38	540 BLU-42A	anti-personnel mine	919 lb
CBU-42	SUU-38	540 BLU-54	anti-personnel mine	919 lb
CBU-39	SUU-41	10 CDU-4	Gravel mines	700 lb
CBU-40	SUU-41	10 CDU-5	Button bombs	700 lb
CBU-40 Mod	SUU-41	10 CDU-10	Button bombs	700 lb
CBU-?	SUU-41	10 CDU-11	Button bombs	700 lb
CBU-?	SUU-41	10 CDU-14	Gravel mines	700 lb

SUU-51 cluster bombs

The **SUU-51** was an experimental, clamshell-shaped dispenser which weighed about 200 lb (90 kg) empty and 900 lb (400 kg) when loaded. It was developed during the Vietnam War for use with the A-7D, F-105, F-111 and F-4. Equipped with 'pop-out' fins, its main consequence was to be used as the warhead for the unsuccessful GBU-3 and GBU-13 laser-guided cluster bombs.

The **BLU-61A** was a 3-lb (1.4-kg) fragmentation bomblet, primarily used with the SUU-30 dispenser (under which it is described). The **BLU-63** was a 1-lb (0.5-kg) fragmentation bomblet, primarily used with the SUU-30 dispenser (under which it is described). The BLU-81 **'Grasshopper'** was an anti-vehicle mine. Twelve of these bomblets were carried in each **CDU-24**. The **BLU-87** was a **'Ringtail'** bomblet, probably a modification of the 13-lb (6-kg) BLU-49 described under the SUU-13 entry.

SUU-51 CLUSTER BOMB SUMMARY

BOMB	DISPENSER	SUBMUNITIONS	TYPE
CBU-66	SUU-51	?? CDU-24	Grasshopper mine container
CBU-74	SUU-51A	48 BLU-87	Ringtail fragmentation bomb
CBU-74A	SUU-51B	48 BLU-87	Ringtail fragmentation bomb
CBU-76	SUU-51B	290 BLU-61A	fragmentation
CBU-77	SUU-51B	790 BLU-63	fragmentation

SUU-54 cluster bomb

The **SUU-54** was an experimental, clamshell-shaped dispenser which weighed about 300 lb (135 kg) empty and 2,000 lb (900 kg) when loaded. Developed during the Vietnam War for use with the A-7D, A-10A, F-105, F-111 and F-4, it was unique in being the only cluster bomb with 30-in (76-cm) suspension lug spacing. Its main consequence was to be used as the warhead for the unsuccessful GBU-2 LGB, as well as both cruciform- and planar-winged versions of the GBU-15.

The **BLU-61A** was a 3-lb (1.4-kg) fragmentation bomblet, primarily used with the SUU-30 dispenser (under which it is described). The **BLU-63** was a 1-lb (0.5-kg) fragmentation bomblet, primarily used with the SUU-30 dispenser (under which it is described). The **BLU-86** was a 1-lb (0.5-kg) fragmentation/incendiary mine, primarily used with the SUU-30 dispenser (under which it is described). The **BLU-87** was a **'Ringtail'** bomblet, probably a modification of the 13-lb (6-kg) BLU-49 described under the SUU-13 entry. The 4-lb (1.8-kg) **BLU-91** anti-personnel and **BLU-92** anti-tank **'Gator'** mines became operational with the SUU-64 dispenser and are described there.

SUU-54 CLUSTER BOMB SUMMARY

BOMB	DISPENSER	SUBMUNITIONS	TYPE
CBU-75	SUU-54	1,780 BLU-63	fragmentation
CBU-75A	SUU-54A	1,440 BLU-63	fragmentation
		360 BLU-86	frag/incendiary mine
CBU-79	SUU-54	650 BLU-61A	fragmentation
CBU-80	SUU-54	90 BLU-87	Ringtail fragmentation bomb
CBU-84	SUU-54	135 BLU-91	Gator anti-personnel mine
		45 BLU-92	Gator anti-tank mine
CBU-85	SUU-54A	180 BLU-91	Gator anti-personnel mine
CBU-86	SUU-54A	180 BLU-92	Gator anti-tank mine

SUU-58 dispenser

The **SUU-58** was an experimental downward-ejecting dispenser developed towards the end of the Vietnam War for the delivery of the Gator mine system. It was intended for use with the A-7D, F-105, F-111 and F-4. However, it was canceled in favor of the SUU-64. The 4-lb (1.8-kg) **BLU-91** anti-personnel and **BLU-92** anti-tank Gator mines became operational with the SUU-64 dispenser and are described there.

SUU-58 DISPENSER SUMMARY

BOMB	DISPENSER	SUBMUNITIONS	TYPE
CBU-78	SUU-54	26 BLU-91	Gator anti-personnel mine
		38 BLU-92	Gator anti-tank mine
CBU-82	SUU-54A	54 BLU-91	Gator anti-personnel mine
CBU-83	SUU-54A	54 BLU-92	Gator anti-tank mine

SUU-64/65 cluster bomb

One dispenser with an 'added twist' is the **SUU-65** version of the Alliant Techsystems tactical munitions dispenser (**TMD**). After release, its fins unfold and cant to spin the dispenser to a preselected rate before opening. This permits ideal bomblet dispersion, even when released from very low altitudes. The **SUU-65** can be distinguished from the very similar **SUU-64** by the large crossbar at the back of the fin assembly. At present, it is only used with the **CBU-87** combined effects munition (**CEM**). The 3-lb (1.4-kg) **BLU-97** CEM bomblets, similar in size and shape to a beer can, are stabilized by a tail-mounted ballute, have an anti-material shape charge in the nose, and a body that explodes into anti-personnel and incendiary fragments.

The **CBU-89 Gator** uses the SUU-64 to deliver a combination of 4-lb (1.8-kg) **BLU-91** anti-personnel and **BLU-92** anti-tank mines (the Army designations are XM74 and XM75, respectively). The former deploy tripwires and detonate when the wires are disturbed; the latter sense magnetic disturbances and fire self-forging warheads at passing tanks. Both eventually self destruct.

TMD CLUSTER BOMB SUMMARY

BOMB	DISPENSER	SUBMUNITIONS	TYPE	WEIGHT
CBU-87	SUU-65	202 BLU-97	combined effects	960 lb
CBU-89	SUU-64	72 BLU-91	anti-personnel	
		22 BLU-92	anti-tank	700 lb

Cluster bomb fuzing

Once again, fuzing is of critical importance. Two types can be used: time delay and proximity. A time delay fuze is set on the ground, and requires bomb release at a specific altitude and airspeed to produce optimum bomblet dispersion. Proximity fuzing uses a radar in the fuze to sense height above the ground, providing much greater latitude in delivery parameters. Of course, they are more expensive.

US CLUSTER BOMB FUZES

FUZE	LOCATION	TYPE	REMARKS
M907	nose	time delay	SUU-30
Mk 339	nose	time delay	SUU-30 and Mk 7
FMU-26	nose	time delay	SUU-30
FMU-56	nose	proximity	SUU-30
FMU-110	nose	proximity	SUU-30
FZU-39	nose	proximity	SUU-30, -64 and -65

TAL cluster bomb

The 550-lb (250-kg) Rafael **TAL** cluster bomb is very similar in appearance, size and function to the SUU-30. It dispenses two kinds of bomblets: the **TAL-1**, which weighs about 17 oz (480 g), and the **TAL-2**, which weighs about 14 oz (400 g). Loads of 279 of the former, or 315 of the latter, can be carried. The dispenser is believed to be operational, and probably used by Israeli F-4s.

An F-4M banks over RAF Coningsby with a 'publicity shot' load of Sky Flash missiles, an EMI recce pod and BL755 cluster bombs. Designed for low-altitude deliveries, BL755s were used successfully in the Falklands by Harrier GR.Mk 3s.

BL755 cluster bomb

The 611-lb (277-kg) Hunting Engineering **BL755** cluster bomb dispenses a total of 147 bomblets from seven compartments. Designed primarily as an anti-armor weapon, the bomblets have shaped-charged warheads which also have a secondary fragmentation function. The original weapon became operational in 1972 with the Royal Air Force and has been exported to several countries. The **Improved BL755**, with better anti-armor bomblets, became operational in 1987. BL755 was designed for delivery from the very low altitudes expected in a European war. It was successfully used in the 1982 Falklands War, but proved ineffective during the 1991 Gulf War, which was fought from medium altitudes.

Cluster bombs

Vertical ballistic weapon (VBW)

This 770-lb (350-kg) anti-tank dispenser was developed by Messerschmitt-Bölkow-Blohm (MBB) for the Luftwaffe. It required the delivery aircraft to overfly tank formations at 250 ft (75 m) while sensors in the dispenser pod automatically detected and classified potential targets, then determined when to dispense the submunitions. In theory, the reduced number of bomblets carried was made up for by precise delivery. Extensive testing was conducted on the F-4F, Alpha Jet and Tornado.

Below: Another weapon tested on the F-4 was the VBW. The target detection and classification technology developed in this program is being incorporated into stand-off weapons.

Multi-purpose weapon (MW-1)

Development of this 8,000-lb (3620-kg) class, Raketen Technik GmbH (RTG)-developed weapon dates from 1966, with deliveries beginning in 1984. Each version dispenses about 6,000 lb (2720 kg) of submunitions, optimized for attacking different main target groups (MTG). **MTG-1** units are for attacking armored and mechanical units; **MTG-2** for airfields. The modular dispenser comes in four sections and contains 112 transverse tubes (224 openings) into which the submunitions are loaded. The area covered by the munitions can be adjusted in flight. There are five types of submunitions: the **KB-44** is a 1.3-lb (0.6-kg) armor-piercing bomblet, only used with the MTG-1; the **MIFF** is a 7.5-lb (3.4-kg) anti-tank bomblet, used with both dispensers; the **MUSA** is a 9.2-lb (4.2-kg) fragmentation weapon useful against trucks and aircraft, used with both dispensers; the **MUSPA** is a 9.2-lb (4.2-kg) airfield denial weapon with acoustic fuzing, only used with the MTG-2; and the **STABO** is a 35-lb (16-kg) penetrator designed to crater and heave a runway, only used with the MTG-2. While some testing was carried out using F-4Fs, the only operational use of this weapon is on German and Italian Tornado IDS.

A Flight Systems F-4C is shown flying MBB's modular dispenser system (above), while (below) a Luftwaffe F-4F dispenses bomblets from the related MW-1.

UNDERWATER MINES

The Mks 36, 40 and 41 **Destructors (DST)** are Mk 80 series GP bombs with Mk 75 DST acoustic/magnetic influence fuzing. The USAF's M117D uses this kit also. Since they differ only in fuzing, they can be delivered by any aircraft that can drop the basic bomb being used. Developed during the Vietnam War, they are primarily used as shallow underwater mines against surface ships, but also have capabilities against overland targets.

Although the Mk 80 series-based mines are technically cleared for use with standard conical fins, given their propensity for exploding when they hit the water at high speeds it is doubtful that they would ever be used with anything but Snakeye-type fins. The Mk 84-based Mk 41 was not deployed. Except for the B-52G, which could carry the Mk 40, USAF aircraft were only cleared to use the Mk 36 and M117D.

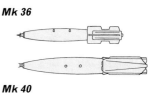

Mk 36

Mk 40

UNDERWATER MINES

MINE	WARHEAD	WEIGHT	FIN KIT	REMARKS
M117D	M117	857 lb	MAU-91	acoustic/magnetic, 300 ft
Mk 36	Mk 82	560 lb	Mk 15	acoustic/magnetic, 300 ft
Mk 40	Mk 83	1,060 lb	MAU-91	acoustic/magnetic, 300 ft
Mk 41	Mk 84	2,000 lb	unknown	acoustic/magnetic, 300 ft

ROCKETS

2.75-in rockets

Developed under the **'Mighty Mouse'** program, 2.75-in (7-cm) rockets were widely used during the Vietnam War. The **Mk 4** (high-speed) folding-fin aircraft rocket (**FFAR**) motors are 39.4 in (100 cm) long and weigh 11.4 lb (5.2 kg).

Warhead types include high-explosive (**HE**); high-explosive anti-tank (**HEAT**) with a shaped-charge; target practice (**TP**) and warhead training units (**WTU**); high-explosive fragmentation (**HE Frag**), sometimes called pearlite malleable iron (**PMI**); and white phosphorus (**WP**) for target marking. Combat warheads are olive drab with yellow nose bands; WP and smoke are green with white letters; and TP heads are blue with white lettering. Most warheads use impact fuzes (except for the WDU-4, with a built-in fuze which senses deceleration before firing its flechettes).

Rocket pods are made of treated paper with a thin aluminum outer skin. They have optional paper front fairings which shatter on rocket impact. While some older pods used paper aft fairings which shattered to form a funnel protecting the underside of the launching aircraft's wing from rocket debris, many now have metal funnels – if they bother with such niceties at all. All of the pods are retained by the aircraft, most having at least some reusable components. All use 14-in (36-cm) suspension lug spacing.

There have been numerous launcher units (**LAU**) over the years, varying little in external appearance. Loaded 19-tube launchers weigh about 500 lb (227 kg), and have included (current pods underlined) the LAU-3, -50, -51, -60, -61, -69, -91, -94, and -130. Loaded seven-tube launchers weigh about 250 lb (113 kg), and have included (current pods underlined) the LAU-32, -49, -54, -56, -59, -68, -90, and -131. Although the **SUU-20** training dispenser was designed to fire four FFARs, this option was seldom exercised.

The **Pave Mack** project during the Vietnam War explored a concept called laser aided rocket system (LARS). A few rockets were fitted with laser seeker heads, but the effort was soon abandoned.

The chart matches fuzes, warheads and motors. Fuze and warhead lengths are exposed lengths and do not include the screw-in connections. Warhead details do not include the fuze unless specifically stated. FFAR details are for the fuze specified in the remarks.

Left: Preflight inspection of LAU-61 19-tube, 2.75-in FFAR pods. After Vietnam this class of weapon was seldom used by the USAF.

Below: A 35th TFS F-4C from Yokota is seen in Korea during January 1969, with LAU-61 rocket pods mounted on the inboard pylons and three more mounted on the front stations of the centerline MER.

2.75-in WARHEAD/ROCKET COMBINATIONS

WARHEAD	TYPE	WARHEAD		FFARs		REMARKS
		length	weight	length	weight	
Mk 1	HE	6.0 in	5.8 lb	48.5 in	17.8 lb	1a, 2a/b/d/e/f/g
Mk 5	HEAT	6.5 in	5.8 lb	48.0 in	18.0 lb	2c
Mk 61	TP (Mk 1)	8.1 in	6.5 lb	47.5 in	17.9 lb	3a
Mk 64	HE Frag	10.5 in	8.6 lb	53.0 in	20.6 lb	1a, 2d/e/f/g
Mk 67	WP	10.5 in	4.5 lb	53.0 in	16.5 lb	1a, 2d/e/f/g
M151	HE Frag	10.5 in	8.6 lb	53.0 in	20.6 lb	1a, 2d/e/f/g/h
M156	WP	10.5 in	10.4 lb	53.0 in	22.4 lb	1a, 2d/e/f/g
M229	HE	23.2 in	15.9 lb	65.4 in	27.9 lb	1a, 2f/g (Mk 40 only)
M230	TP (M151)	10.5 in	8.7 lb	53.0 in	20.7 lb	2k, 3b
WDU-4	Flechette	15.5 in	9.1 lb	54.9 in	20.5 lb	2,200 flechettes
WTU-1	TP (M151)	13.6 in	9.4 lb	53.0 in	20.8 lb	3c
WTU-10	TP (Mk 1)	10.5 in	10.1 lb	49.9 in	21.5 lb	3d
WTU-14	TP (Mk 1)	11.9 in	10.1 lb	51.3 in	21.5 lb	3e

Remarks:
1a) Lengths and weights computed for M427 fuze.
1b) Lengths and weights computed for Mk 176 fuze.
2a) Mk 176 fuze extends 2.1 in (5.3 cm) from the warhead and has a slight delay between impact and detonation. It weighs 0.7 lb (0.3 kg).
2b) Mk 178 is physically identical to the Mk 176, but explodes on impact.
2c) Mk 181 fuze extends 2.1 in (5.3 cm) from the warhead and explodes on impact. It weighs 0.8 lb (0.4 kg).
2d) Mk 352 fuze extends 2.2 in (5.6 cm) from the warhead and explodes on impact. It weighs 0.4 lb (0.2 kg).
2e) FMU-90 is physically identical to the Mk 352, but has a slight delay between impact and detonation.
2f) M423 fuze is used with helicopters. It extends 3.1 in (7.9 cm) from the warhead and explodes on impact. It weighs 0.6 lb (0.3 kg) and is only used with the Mk 40 FFAR motor.
2g) M427 fuze is used with fixed-wing aircraft. Identical to the M423 in appearance and function, but it can also be used with the Mk 4 FFAR motor.
2h) M429 fuze extends 5 in (13 cm) from the warhead and is a proximity (VT) fuze. It weighs 0.9 lb (0.4 kg) and is only used with the Mk 40 FFAR motor and the M151 warhead.
3a) Mk 61 is an inert, cast shape simulating the Mk 1 warhead with a Mk 176 fuze.
3b) M230 is an inert, cast shape simulating the M151 warhead. It is used with the M435 inert fuze.
3c) WTU-1 is an inert, cast shape simulating the M151 warhead with an M423 fuze.
3d) WTU-10 dummy warhead is a Mk 1 casing with a cylindrical, inert plug inserted in it, increasing length by 4.5 in (11.4 cm).
3e) WTU-14 dummy warhead is a Mk 1 casing with a streamlined, inert plug inserted in it, increasing length by 5.9 in (15 cm).

This F-4 (above) displays typical carriage of Zuni pods and (below) a Vietnam-era 'Pukin' Dog' F-4B unleashes a volley of 5-in Zunis.

5-in Zuni unguided rockets

Zuni 5-in (13-cm) unguided rockets were widely used during the Vietnam War by both the Navy and Marines. There have been three types of 5-in (13-cm) rocket motors, nine warheads and two rocket pods. The older **Mk 16** FFAR motors are 76.3 in (194 cm) long and weigh about 65 lb (30 kg). The **Mk 71 Mod 0** WAFAR motors are 69.7 in

(177 cm) long and weigh about 68 lb (30 kg), while the **Mk 71 Mod 1**s are 76.4 in (194 cm) long and weigh about 80 lb (35 kg). The Mod 0 WAFARs use the same basic rocket motor, but are shorter because of their fin configuration; the Mod 1s use this more efficient design feature to increase the amount of propellant in the same motor length as the FFAR.

Warheads include the general-purpose (**GP**), anti-tank/anti-personnel (**AT/APers**), practice (sometimes called **WTU**), HE Frag, flare for target illumination, and smoke for target marking and incendiary missions. Combat warheads are olive drab with yellow nose bands, smoke are green with white letters, and practice warheads are blue with white lettering. All warheads use impact fuzes, except for the flare head which uses an integral mechanical time delay fuze.

The reusable **LAU-10** rocket pods are made of treated paper with a thin aluminum outer skin. They also have optional (and seldom used) paper front and rear fairings which are interchangable and shatter upon rocket impact. When used, the aft fairing forms a funnel which protects the underside of the launching aircraft's wing from debris during rocket firing. All versions use 14-in (36-cm) suspension lug spacing and hold four Zuni rockets. The basic pod is 94.9 in (241 cm) long; with fairings this increases to 128.9 in (327 cm). Loaded LAU-10s weigh about 650 lb (295 kg).

The chart matches fuzes, warheads and motors. Fuze and warhead lengths are exposed lengths and do not include the screw-in connections. Warhead details do not include the fuze unless specifically stated. FFAR details are for the complete round with the fuze specified in the remarks. For Mk 71 Mod 0, subtract 6.6 in (17 cm) and add 3 lb (1.4 kg); for Mk 71 Mod 1 add 0.1 in (0.25 cm) and 15 lb (7 kg). Source data is very inconsistent – all weights and lengths are approximate.

5-in WARHEAD/ROCKET COMBINATIONS

WARHEAD	TYPE	WARHEAD		Mk 16 FFARs		REMARKS
		length	weight	length	weight	
Mk 6	Practice	16.0 in	47.1 lb	96.2 in	113.1 lb	1a, 2f/g, 3a
Mk 24/0	GP	16.0 in	44.1 lb	96.1 in	109.5 lb	1b, 2a/b/c/d/f/g
Mk 24/1	GP	15.9 in	45.0 lb	96.0 in	110.4 lb	1b, 2a/b/c/d/f/g
Mk 32	AT/APers	24.0 in	43.3 lb	102.6 in	108.7 lb	1c, 2b/c/d
Mk 33	Flare	33.0 in	45.9 lb	109.3 in	110.9 lb	
Mk 34	Smoke	33.5 in	50.9 lb	112.1 in	116.3 lb	1d, 2b/c/d
Mk 34	Incendiary	32.9 in	50.9 lb	115.4 in	118.5 lb	1e, 2a
Mk 62	Practice	18.8 in	46.8 lb	95.1 in	111.8 lb	3b
Mk 63	HE/Frag	28.2 in	56.4 lb	110.7 in	124.0 lb	1f, 2a/b/c/d/e
WTU-11	Practice	28.7 in	56.4 lb	111.2 in	124.0 lb	1f, 2a/e, 3c

Remarks:
1a) Lengths and weights computed for ogive nose.
1b) Lengths and weights computed for Mk 352 fuze with BBU-15 adapter and 1.5-in (3.8-cm) fuze adapter collar, also used with FMU-90 and Mk 188.
1c) Lengths and weights computed for Mk 352 fuze with BBU-15 adapter.
1d) Lengths and weights computed for Mk 352 fuze with BBU-15 adapter and 2.9-in (7.4-cm) fuze adapter collar.
1e) Lengths and weights computed for Mk 93 nose and 2.3-in (5.8-cm) fuze adapter collar.
1f) Lengths and weights computed for Mk 93 nose.
2a) Mk 93 ogive nose extends 6.2 in (15.7 cm) from the warhead and weighs 2.6 lb (1.2 kg). Used to penetrate targets, it depends on the integral M191 fuze at back of warhead for detonation.
2b) Mk 188 fuze extends 2.5 in (6.3 cm) from the warhead and explodes on impact. It weighs 0.8 lb (0.4 kg).
2c) Mk 352 fuze with the BBU-15 adapter extends 2.3 in (5.8 cm) from the warhead and explodes on impact. It weighs 0.4 lb (0.2 kg).
2d) FMU-90 fuze with the BBU-15 adapter is physically identical to the Mk 352/BBU-15, but has a slight delay between impact and detonation.
2e) M414 is identical to the Mk 93 in appearance and function.
2f) Ogive nose extends 3.9 in (9.9 cm) from the warhead and weighs about 1 lb (0.5 kg).
2g) Plug nose extends about 2 in (5 cm) from the warhead and weighs about 3 oz (85 g).
3a) Mk 6 is a cement-filled inert version of the Mk 24 warhead.
3b) Mk 62 is an inert, cast shape simulating the Mk 24 warhead with an ogive nose.
3c) WTU-11 is a cement-filled inert version of the Mk 63 warhead.

TBA 68-mm rockets

The Thomson Brandt Armaments (TBA) 68-mm rocket family has been widely used by European air arms since first being introduced in 1955. The 'first-generation' rockets were employed by Royal Air Force/Navy (RAF/RN) Phantoms with the **MATRA F4 Type 155** 19-tube launcher. The rockets used were both the Type 25 and 68F18, with a range of about 6,400 ft (4000 m).

The TBA-designed Type 155 (French designation was F4) had a pointed nose which negated the need for the frangible nose used on American-style pods.

68-mm WARHEAD/ROCKET COMBINATIONS

WARHEAD	TYPE	ROCKET		REMARKS
		length	weight	
252.5XF3	Practice	35.8 in	11.0 lb	marking practice
253.3XF2	Practice	35.8 in	11.0 lb	inert practice
253ECC	HEAT	35.8 in	11.0 lb	shaped-charge
256P.EAP	HE/Frag	35.8 in	13.7 lb	GP with 440 fragments
259L.LEM	ECM	46.1 in	13.7 lb	chaff screening

Above: A Royal Navy No. 892 Sqn F-4K launches from HMS Ark Royal with a load of MATRA 155 rocket pods, a common NATO weapon.

Nuclear bombs

USAF and US Navy Phantoms carried a variety of nuclear weapons during their career. Some RAF Phantoms also carried US nuclear weapons, and it is believed that some Israeli Phantoms may have had a nuclear capability.

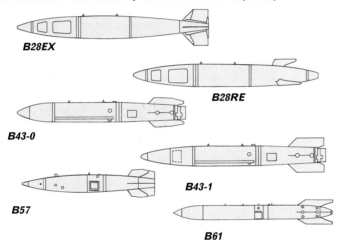

B28EX

B28RE

B43-0

B43-1

B57

B61

Left: This early F-4B carries a Mk 104, the training shape used to simulate the ballistics of the B28 nuclear weapon. The AIM-9Ds and AIM-7Es shown here would not be required, or normally seen, on an aircraft configured for this mission.

NUCLEAR BOMBS

All US nuclear bombs are thermonuclear (i.e. hydrogen bombs). Delivery options are dependent on the bomb/aircraft combination and the type of target destruction required. All bombs incorporate parachutes as a standard feature to assist in level weapon delivery (and aircraft escape!). While there may be several variants of a given weapon, only the basic designations are presented here. (The term 'Mk' is sometimes used instead of 'B'.)

Design work on the **B28** family of nuclear weapons began in 1954, and they remained in service until about 1990. It was a modular design, produced as five different types of bombs, and was also used as a warhead on the MGM-13 'Mace' and AGM-28 'Hound Dog' missiles. Five yields were available, ranging from 70 kT to 1.45 mT, the tactical versions having the lower values. The yield of these weapons could not be adjusted in the field. The **B28EX** (for 'external' carriage) had a streamlined shape and four tail fins, but was not equipped with a retarding parachute; it had ground and airburst options. Several training versions existed, including the BDU-10 and Mk 104 ballistic shapes, as well as the MD-6 and BDU-26 load trainers. The **B28RE** (for 'retarded, external' carriage) also had a streamlined shape, but it only had three fins, which were mounted well forward of the tail. It also had ground and airburst options, but could be delivered from low altitude. These weapons were used by the A-6, F-100, F-105 and F-4.

The **B43** program began in 1955, with the weapons remaining in service until about 1990. A total of five yields were available, the largest being about 1 mT; the yields of these could not be adjusted in the field. There were two versions designed for external carriage: the B43-0 and B43-1. The **B43-0** could only be used for parachute-retarded laydown deliveries, and it had a steel nose spike covered by an aerodynamic nose cone. After the bomb separated from the

aircraft, the nose cone was jettisoned and the spike helped the bomb to penetrate hard targets and held it in place for several seconds (to allow the aircraft to escape), before detonating. The **B43-1** was a multipurpose weapon with a longer nose, which contained a fuzing radar. It could be used with free-fall airburst, retarded airburst (with or without a ground burst back-up) or retarded laydown. Several training versions existed, including the BDU-18 (free-fall) and BDU-8 (retarded) ballistic shapes, as well as the BDU-6 and BDU-35 load trainers. External carriage B43s were carried by the A-6, B-58, FB-111, F-100, F-104, F-105, F-111 and F-4.

The **B57** was designed as a nuclear depth charge, but was later adopted for used as a low-yield tactical nuclear weapon. Nicknamed the 'Dr Pepper' bomb (after the American soft drink), its delivery options included laydown and toss (sometimes called loft) with either air or surface burst. Several training versions existed, including the BDU-12 ballistic shape, as well as the BDU-11, BDU-19 and BDU-20 load trainers. External carriage B57s were carried by the A-4, A-6, A-7, FB-111, F-104, F-105, F-111, F-4, F-16 and F/A-18.

The **B61** was the most commonly used weapon by tactical fighters, and was nicknamed the 'Silver Bullet' because of its shape and color. Delivery options included free-fall or retarded airburst, laydown and toss (with either air or surface burst). Several training versions existed, including the BDU-38 ballistic shape, as well as the BDU-36 and BDU-39 load trainers. External carriage B61s were carried by the A-4, A-6, A-7, FB-111, F-104, F-105, F-111, F-4, F-16 and F/A-18.

All US F-4s were built with a nuclear capability, including the reconnaissance versions. Only the right outboard station could not carry these weapons. Because it was too long for carriage on the inboard pylons, only a single B26 could be carried, using either the left outboard or centerline stations. However, two of the B43, B57, or B61 could be carried by using the inboard stations. Any F-4s which were exported had the nuclear wiring and controls removed beforehand.

Typically, the ballistic shapes were painted white, while the actual weapons were unpainted, or painted silver.

US NUCLEAR BOMBS

BOMB	WEIGHT	YIELD	INVENTORY	SHAPE	USE
B28EX	2,030 lb	70-350 kT	4,500 total	BDU-10	free-fall tactical
B28RE	2,170 lb	70-350 kT	for five types	BDU-4	retarded tactical
B43-0	2,060 lb	1 mT max	about 1,000	BDU-8	retarded tactical
B43-1	2,120 lb	1 mT max	for two types	BDU-18	free-fall tactical
B57	500 lb	520 kT	about 1,000	BDU-12	tactical and maritime
B61	710 lb	10500 kT	over 3,000	BDU-38	tactical and strategic

TRAINING WEAPONS AND OTHER STORES

Training missiles

Dropping and firing live bombs occurs infrequently during training, and most of the time training ordnance is used. For missiles this means rounds with working seekers, but no rocket motors, warheads or guidance sections. Where a live missile would display black (guidance), yellow (warhead) or brown (rocket motor) bands, training rounds either display blue bands or the entire section is painted blue. The designation of air-to-ground training missiles is **ATM** rather than

AGM, and air-to-air missiles are normally referred to as 'captive', e.g. AIM-9P-**CAP**.

Full-size practice bombs

Full-scale USAF training bombs are normally referred to as 'inert Mk 82' rather than the formal title of bomb, dummy unit (**BDU**) -50. There are also **inert Mk 84s** (but without a BDU designation). These bombs are usually painted overall blue and are filled with concrete instead of explosives. USN full-scale LDGP training bombs include the

wet sand-filled **Mk 86** (Mk 81), **Mk 87** (Mk 82) and **Mk 88** (Mk 83). The Navy designation for the BDU-50 is **Mk 124**.

Subscale training bombs

The most commonly carried training bombs are referred to as 'blue bombs' and 'beer cans'. Both of these bombs were developed by the Navy and adopted by the Air Force. The 'blue bombs' are streamlined 25-lb (11-kg) bombs and are called **Mk 76** by the Navy and **BDU-33** by the Air Force. They simulate the ballistics of a Mk 82 SE. 'Beer cans'

are painted Dayglo orange, weigh 10 lb (4.5 kg) and are shaped like a beer can with fins. Called by their naval designation of **Mk 106** for years, the Air Force has only recently been given a slightly altered version the designation **BDU-48**. Its ballistics most closely resemble a retarded nuclear weapon. Both of these bombs can be mounted on specially modified multiple and triple ejector racks (**MER** and **TER**), or in SUU-20 and SUU-21 dispensers. The Navy also uses another subscale bomb, the 50-lb (23-kg) **Mk 89**, for practicing Mk 80 series LDGP deliveries.

Training bomb dispensers

The **SUU-20** dispenser holds six practice bombs and four 2.75-in (7-cm) rockets (the latter option is rarely used). The explosively ejected bombs are exposed on the bottom of the dispenser, and a mix of Mk 106s and BDU-33s is common. The SUU-21 was developed because aircraft based in Europe overfly populated areas more frequently than those based elsewhere. The SUU-21's bombs are contained within enclosed bomb bays and are ejected by springs. No rocket capability exists with the SUU-21. The **Aero 8A** practice bomb container (**PBC**) was used by USN A-4s and F-4s for dropping Mk 76 and Mk 106 practice bombs.

Air-to-air gunnery targets

The F-4 has been used to tow and launch targets for air-to-air gun and missile training. The aeronautical system/non-mission expendable, electromechanical, miscellaneous model 15 (**A/A 37U-15**) tow-target system (**TTS**) was used by the F-84, F-86, F-100, F-104, F-105 and F-4 (from the left outboard pylon). It comprised the 482-lb (219-kg) RMU-10 tow reel pod and 195-lb (88-kg) TDU-10 'Dart' gunnery target. The 16-ft (5-m) long Dart was reeled out 2,300 ft (700 m) behind the towing aircraft, and scoring was accomplished by counting the bullet holes in the recovered dart, with different aircraft using bullets dyed different colors. The **A/A 37U-33** aerial gunnery target system (**AGTS**) replaced the TTS and was used by USAF F-4s. It comprised the 357-lb (162-kg) RMK-33 tow set and 107-lb (49-kg) TDK-36 target set, which was towed 1,640 ft (500 m) behind the aircraft and deployed a Dart-sized tetraplane target. Real-time acoustic scoring was used. The 900-lb (408-kg) **A/A 37U-36** AGTS was designed for carriage on the left outboard station on F-4s, on the centerline on F-15s, and on the center wing stations on F-16s. It consisted of the RMK-35 reeling machine and TDK-39 target group, which was towed about 2,000 ft (600 m) behind the aircraft. A real-time RF scoring system was used.

Air-to-air missile targets

The **RMU-2** was a 900-lb (408-kg) reel launcher authorized for use by USAF F-4s. The 1,866-lb (846-kg) RMU-8 was used by the F-101 and F-4 (from the centerline) to tow targets for both IR and SAR missile practice. Targets included three versions of the 100-lb (45-kg) TDU-9, which served as both IR and radar targets for AIM-4 Falcon missiles; the 43-lb (20-kg) TDU-22, which also existed in three versions with various degrees of radar and IR augmentation; and TDU-25, which was primarily an IR missile target, although it did feature radar augmentation to assist in initial radar acquisition. The **RMK-19** tow system evaluated by the Navy for use with F-4s was a modified RMU-8 with a very large target replacing the TDU-9/22/25s.

The **TDU-11** was a World War II-vintage, high-velocity aircraft rocket (**HVAR**), modified with tail flares and launched from AIM-9 launcher rails to serve as a target for early USAF Sidewinders. Aircraft authorized to use this target included the F-100, F-105, F-4 and F-5. The **AQM-37** (originally designated both Q-12 and KD2B-1) was a 575-lb (261-kg) liquid-fueled rocket used for air-to-air missile evaluation and aircrew training. It could be launched by the A-4, F-4 and F-8 from the LAU-24 trapeze ejector and featured both radar

An MN ANG F-4D (above) carries the A/A 37U-15 gunnery target tow system comprised of the RMU-10 reel and TDU-10 dart, and (right) an NATC F-4J carries a RMK-19 tow system.

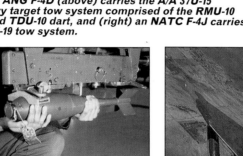

Above: A BDU-33 25-lb practice bomb is loaded on a practice bomb dispenser.

Right: A 434th TFS F-4E from George AFB seen over southern California in May 1974. It carries open-bottomed SUU-20 dispensers, each capable of holding six BDU-33 and/or Mk 106 practice bombs and four 2.75-in FFARs.

Above: AIS pods can be mounted on any aircraft station that can carry an AIM-9.

Below: A 496th TFS F-4D carries SUU-21s, which featured bomb bays for increased safety over crowded Europe. On the centerline is a SUU-23 gunpod with a long tailcone.

and IR augmentation. During the early 1970s, the AQM-37 was evaluated as a defense-suppression missile by the Air Force under the surface attack guided missile (**SAGMI**) program. This Navy target utilized a preset guidance program and was non-recoverable. The **AQM-81 Sandpiper** was designed as a supersonic follow-on to the AQM-37 and used a modified LAU-24 for launch from F-4s. It was propelled by a hybrid rocket motor.

Cargo pods and delivery containers

The miscellaneous unit (**MXU**) **-648** is a baggage pod made from old BLU-1/27 firebomb shells, whose original designation may have been CNU-169. While a few have removable tailcones, most have a small door on the left side of the pod. Virtually all fighter and attack aircraft carry these on flights away from their home base, except for non-Pave Tack F-111s, which use their large weapons bay instead. The 215-lb (98-kg) **CTU-1** was a USN low-altitude delivery container intended to deliver up to 500 lb (227 kg) of supplies to ground troops from the A-1, A-6 and both USN and USAF F-4s. If used with F-4s, a maximum of three could be carried, suspended from the aft-outboard station of MERs carried on the outboard pylons, plus one on either forward MER station on the centerline pylon. The **CTU-2** was probably a USAF version of the CTU-1, authorized for use with the F-4C/D/E. Its original destination was probably M4A, which was used by the A-4 and F-100.

Instrumentation system pods

The aircraft instrumentation system (**AIS**) pods are used as part of the air combat

maneuvering instrumentation (**ACMI**) and related systems, which allow real-time and post-mission evaluation of training exercises. The film *Top Gun* used ACMI in one scene. These systems allow the battle to be viewed from any angle, even from the 'cockpits' of opposing aircraft. Some recent versions, such as the Red Flag mission debriefing system (**RFMDS**), allow the evaluation of surface-to-air and air-to-air engagements, as well as bombing accuracy. AIS pods resemble unfinned Sidewinder missiles with pitot tubes and are mounted to AIM-9 launchers. There are several versions, including the airborne, special type (**ASQ**) T-11, 13, 17, 20, 21 and 25. Except for the T-11, which has a ram-air scoop on its side, all pod differences are internal. The airborne, telemetering, special type (**AKQ**) **-T1** resembles the AIM-7, but serves the same function as the AIS pods.

Photographic pods

Several photo pods and related systems were associated with the F-4. The one most often used operationally was the **KB-18** bomb damage assessment (**BDA**) pod, which could be carried in

either forward missile bay – although in practice they always seem to have been carried in the right one. This camera system took nose-to-tail panoramic photos at a rate of two or four frames per second. The negatives were 2.75 in (7 cm) wide and 9.4 in (24 cm) long. With 250 ft (76 m) of film, the KB-18 had a running time of 40 or 80 seconds, depending on the exposure rate. Selected RAF F-4Ms carried the centerline fuel tank-sized **EMI reconnaissance pod**, which incorporated radar, photographic and infrared linescan sensors. The **AAVS Type 4**, or 'Nellis Pod', could be mounted from pylons, MERs or TERs, and was probably used to document weapon release tests. The **LM-119** was a Navy film delivery container authorized for use by the A-4, A-6 and F-4.

Miscellaneous pods

The **APX-95** was a 90-lb (41-kg) transponder pod authorized for use on the A-7D and F-4C/D/E; on F-4s, it was carried on either of the inboard pylons. The Hughes **AVB-1** was a laser ranging pod evaluated on two F-4Cs between 1965 and 1970. Housed in an AIM-7-

shaped pod (without fins, but with a window for the laser) in the front right missile bay, it fired a laser at the target (defined by the pilot's bombsight) to solve the ranging part of the ballistic equation for dropping 'dumb' bombs. Although this technique has been used by other aircraft since, the AVB-1 was not adopted. The **D-704** is a USN buddy refueling store and resembles a 300-US gal (250-Imp gal; 1135-liter) fuel tank. It can be carried by the A-6E (on the centerline) and the S-3A/B (under the left wing). Although qualified for use with the F-4, in practice this was seldom, if ever, done. The **RCPP-105** was a podded auxiliary power unit which could be carried by USN F-4s.

Spray tanks

Several biological and chemical agent spray tanks were qualified for use with the F-4, but none was ever known to have been used operationally. The aeronautical system/mission expendable, biological dissemination model 1 **A/B 45Y-1** weighed 230 lb (104 kg), and was carried on the outboard pylons and used to dispense 530 lb (240 kg) of a wet agent called UL-1 at a rate of 20 US gal (17 Imp gal; 76 liters) per minute. It was also used as a pesticide disseminator and was redesignated as the external dispensing device (**PAU**) **-10**. The 480-lb (218-kg) **A/B 45Y-2** was carried on the centerline and/or outboard pylons and used to dispense two dry biological anticrop agents: TX (320 lb; 145 kg) and LX (70 lb; 32 kg). The 570-lb (259-kg) **A/B 45Y-3** was carried on the outboard pylons and used to dispense 1,340 lb (608 kg) of defoliant. For use as a pesticide disseminator it was redesignated **PAU-7**, and for dispensing the lethal nerve agent VX it was called a miscellaneous tank unit (**TMU**) **-28**. The 535-lb (243-kg) **A/B 45Y-4** was carried on the centerline and/or outboard pylons and used to dispense 215 lb (98 kg) of a dry chemical agent. The **TMU-66** was a one-, two-, three- or four-module defoliant spray tank for use with Agents Orange, Blue or White. Each module weighed about 235 lb (107 kg) and could carry about 540 lb (245 kg) of agent. The 761-lb (345-kg) **A/B 45Y-7** was carried on the centerline and/or outboard wing stations.

Flare and sonobuoy dispensers

The **SUU-25** was an LAU-10 5-in (13-cm) rocket pod modified to dispense 25-lb (11-kg) class flares. The SUU-25 weighed about 500 lb (225 kg) when loaded, and carried eight Mk 24, Mk 45 or LUU-2 flares, which burned at two million candlepower for 3, 3½ and 5 minutes, respectively. The **SUU-40** was similar to the SUU-25, but only weighed about 350 lb (160 kg) when loaded. The **SUU-43** was an SUU-25 modified to deliver Class A sonobuoys, including the 16-lb (7-kg) passive SSQ-23, 20-lb (9-kg) bathythermograph SSQ-36, 19-lb (8.6-kg) passive SSQ-38, 20-lb (9-kg) passive SSQ-41, 30-lb (13.5-kg) active SSQ-47, the classified SSQ-48, 40-lb (18-kg) active SSQ-50, 29-lb (13-kg) passive SSQ-53, 20-lb (9-kg) active SSQ-57 and 39-lb (17.7-kg) active SSQ-62. The **SUU-44** is a purpose-built flare dispenser, similar to the SUU-40, but the only store it presently dispenses is the Mk 45 flare. These dispensers have been carried externally by the A-1, A-6, A-7, A-10, A-26, A-37, F-100, F-105, F-4, F-5, AH-1/1T/W, P-3C, S-3A/B, AV-8 and OV-10A/D.

The **SUU-42** was a large, bullet-shaped dispenser for 25-lb (11-kg) class flares and seismic sensors. When loaded,

it weighed about 850 lb (385 kg) and held 16 LUU-1 (red) target markers, LUU-2 flares, LUU-5 (fuchsia) target markers or MJU-3 (modified LUU-2) IRCM flares. Target markers differed from flares in that they burned for 30 minutes at 1,000 candlepower. The SUU-42 was authorized for carriage on the A-7D, AC-130 and F-4D. During Vietnam the **SUU-42A** was used by ARN-92 (LORAN) equipped F-4Ds to deploy groups of eight 'Igloo White' sensors, camouflaged to look like dead trees, on to the Ho Chi Minh trail to help locate convoys for attack. The sensors were a mix of GSQ-117 and GSQ-141 acoustic sensors, or acoubuoys, and air-delivered seismic intrusion devices (**ADSID**) 1, 3 and TC-425, which could also be carried on MERs and TERs. Using their very accurate LORAN navigation system, the F-4Ds could implant the sensors in precisely known locations. They would then be monitored by EC-121s or, later in the war, unmanned QU-22B 'Pave Eagle II' relay drones, which transmitted the data back to an infiltration surveillance center for evaluation.

The 172-lb (78-kg) **LAU-55** dispenser could carry six 150-lb (68-kg) MLU-32/B99 'Briteye' flares, which had a five-minute burn time at 5 million candlepower. It is not known if this program ever progressed beyond the test stage, but it was associated with the A-1, A-7D, A-26A, B-57, B-66, F-84, F-100, F-104, F-105, F-4 and T-28.

Chaff dispenser pods

Chaff dispenser pods were used during the Vietnam War to generate 'chaff corridors' to help hide bomber formations from enemy radars. The chaff was normally contained in cartridges about 6

SUU-20 practice bomb dispenser

MXU-648 baggage pod

SUU-21 practice bomb dispenser

in (15 cm) long and 1 in (2.5 cm) in diameter, which were ejected from the dispenser and dispersed by the slipstream. The 186-lb (84-kg) **ALE-37** carried 100 lb (45 kg) of chaff and was used by the Navy's A-6, AV-8A, F-4 and SH-3. The 205-lb (93-kg) **ALE-38** carried 320 lb (145 kg) of chaff and was used by the USAF's A-7D, B-52, F-105, F-4C/D/E/F and RF-4C. The 210-lb (95-kg) **ALE-41** carried 320 lb (145 kg) of chaff and was used by the Navy's ERA-3B, A-4M, A-6E, EA-6A/B, A-7E and F-4S. The 225-lb (102-kg) **ALE-43** carried 300 lb (136 kg) of chaff and was used by the Navy. The ALE-38, ALE-41 and ALE-43 all used the shell of the earlier ALE-2.

Fuel tanks

F-4s used 370-US gal (308-Imp gal; 1400-liter) wing tanks that were built by Sargent Fletcher. Centerline tanks of 600-US gal (500-Imp gal; 2270-liter) capacity were also built by Sargent Fletcher and Royal Jet. However, in the early 1980s, USAF F-4s started to be equipped with McDonnell Douglas F-15 600-US gal (500-Imp gal; 2270-liter) centerline tanks, beginning with F-4Gs. This change was made after a series of tank failures during low-level, high-speed flight, at least one of which led to the loss of the aircraft.

Above: A well-used MXU-648 travel pod. Those used by wing commanders are brightly marked.

Bomb racks

The F-4 made extensive use of both six-store multiple ejector racks (**MER**) and three-store triple ejector racks (**TER**). The different rack versions were visually indistinguishable from one another, but had varying capabilities and internal features. The release sequence from MERs was bottom back, then front; rear left, then right; front left, then right. USAF F-4 MERs included the MER-3, MER-9, MER-10 and MER-101, and USN F-4 MERs included the MER-4 and MER-7. The release sequence for TERs was bottom, left, then right. USAF F-4 TERs included the TER-3 and TER-9, and USN F-4 TERs included the TER-1 and TER-7.

ELECTRONIC COUNTERMEASURES (ECM) PODS

ECM pods were introduced during the Vietnam War to counter SAMs. Over the years they have been refined and updated to cope with new threats. Although some pods look very similar to earlier ones, many have completely new electronics. While noise jamming was used initially, newer pods use deception techniques to make radar think an aircraft is in a slightly different location to where it actually is, causing radar-guided SAMs to detonate just far enough away to allow the aircraft to escape.

Most Air Force pods began as quick-reaction capability (**QRC**) programs before being assigned airborne, countermeasures, special purpose (ALQ) designations. These earlier designations

Above: An ALQ-119(V)-15 is shown on a 16th TRS RF-4C.

Below: A pair of 'two can' versions of the ALQ-87 is shown on an AIM-7E-2-armed 388th TFW F-4E.

included QRC-160A-1 for ALQ-71(Y)-1, QRC-160A-8 for one- and two-can ALQ-87s, QRC-513 for three- and four-can ALQ-87s, QRC-335A/101-1 for ALQ-101(V)-1, QRC-522 for ALQ-119, and QRC-559 for ALQ-131. Current USAF ECM pods include the ALQ-119, -131 and -184, as well as the QRC 80-01. All pods use 30-in (76-cm) suspension lug spacing. Over the years the Navy has generally preferred internal ECM systems, although the ALQ-81, -88 and -120 pods were developed for F-4s, using the A/A 37U shell.

Above: This LORAN-equipped 13th TFS F-4D at Udorn RTAFB in 1972 carries an ALQ-101(V)-1 ECM pod in its right-forward Sparrow well.

Left: Most ALQ-87s were 'two canister' versions, with different combinations of five canisters also being used.

Above: At their last appearance at Red Flag, 334th TFS TISEO-equipped F-4Es carried three-band, 'deep' versions of the ALQ-131. Also of note is the F-15 fuel tank and AIM-9P-3.

ECM POD SUMMARY

POD	WEIGHT	LENGTH	HEIGHT	COVERAGE	REMARKS
ALQ-71(V)-1	200 lb	91 in	10 in	two band	QRC-160A-1
-2	238 lb	79 in *	10 in	two band	
-3	243 lb	102 in *	10 in	three band	ALQ-Mk IIIA
-4	483 lb	124 in *	10 in	four band	
ALQ-72	224 lb	99 in	10 in	I/J bands	
ALQ-81	420 lb	150 in	10 in	A/A 37U shell	(RF -4B)
ALQ-87(V)-1	180 lb	74 in	10 in	one band	
-2	300 lb	110 in	10 in	two band	
ALQ-B7(V)-3	525 lb	152 in	10 in	three band	
ALQ-B7(V)-4	640 lb	188 in	10 in	four band	
ALQ-88	420 lb	150 in	10 in	A/A 37U shell	(RF -4B)
ALQ-101(V)-1	249 lb	100 in	10 in	one can; E/F and G/H bands; 155 built	
ALQ-101(V)-3	400 lb	156 in	10 in	two can; E/F and G/H bands; 71 built	
ALQ-101(V)-4	470 lb	156 in	10 in	two can; E/F, G/H and I/J bands; 324 built	
ALQ-101(V)-6	490 lb	156 in	10 in	two can; 58 built	
ALQ-101(V)-8	520 lb	157 in	15 in	'gondola' upgrade of -3/4/6 pods; 300+ built	
ALQ-101(V)-9	320 lb	112 in	15 in	'gondola' upgrade of -1 pods	
ALQ-101(V)-10	520 lb	157 in	15 in	-8 upgraded to ALQ-119(V)-12 capability	
ALQ-119(V)-long	575 lb	143 in	21 in	low/med/hi	(V)-1/4/7/10/12/15
QRC 80-01(V)-3	575 lb	143 in	21 in	low/med/hi	
ALQ-119(V)-short	319 lb	105 in	15 in	low	(V)-2/5/8/13/16
ALQ-119(V)-medium	400 lb	115 in	21 in	med/hi	(V)-3/6/9/11/14/17
QRC 80-01(V)-4	400 lb	115 in	21 in	med/hi	
ALQ-120	420 lb	150 in	10 in	A/A 37U shell	(USN F-4s)
ALQ-131-deep	680 lb	111 in	24.5 in	bands 3/4/5	
ALQ-131-shallow	585 lb	111 in	20 in	bands 4/5	
ALQ-184(V)-1	680 lb	156 in	20 in	bands 4/5	
ALQ-184(V)-2	510 lb	116 in	20 in	bands 4/5	

* Alternate tailcone added 12 in (30 cm) to length.

ECM pods

Experience in the Vietnam War demonstrated the need for ECM jamming pods on tactical aircraft. Phantoms were among the first to be so equipped. Since then rapid advances in technology have led to the use of a succession of ECM pods.

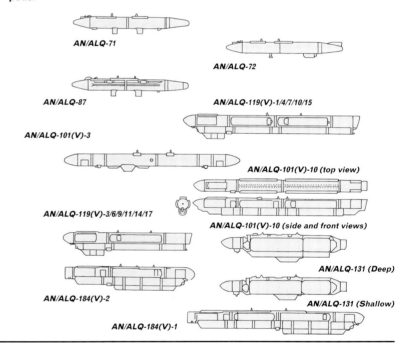

AN/ALQ-71

AN/ALQ-72

AN/ALQ-87

AN/ALQ-119(V)-1/4/7/10/15

AN/ALQ-101(V)-3

AN/ALQ-101(V)-10 (top view)

AN/ALQ-119(V)-3/6/9/11/14/17

AN/ALQ-101(V)-10 (side and front views)

AN/ALQ-131 (Deep)

AN/ALQ-184(V)-2

AN/ALQ-131 (Shallow)

AN/ALQ-184(V)-1

INFRARED COUNTER-MEASURES (IRCM)

IRCM pods use sophisticated techniques to defeat infrared missiles. Although still used with large, unmaneuverable aircraft, fighters now rely on a combination of expendable flares and maneuverability. Neither of the pods described here is believed to have reached operational status. The 250-lb (113-kg) **AAQ-8** was based on the shell of the ALQ-71 and authorized for carriage on either inboard or the right, outboard pylon of USAF F-4s. The 380-lb (172-kg) **ALQ-123** was authorized for carriage on the A-3B, A-4M, A-6E, A-7E, C-130, USN F-4s and P-3C.

GUNS

The 265-lb (120-kg) General Electric **M61** 'Vulcan' 20-mm six-barreled Gatling gun was developed in the 1950s. Its uses a linkless feed system and is externally powered from the aircraft's hydraulic or electrical system. The self-powered aircraft gun unit (**GAU**) -4, used in the **SUU-23** gun pod, was virtually identical, except it was driven by gun gas. The 1,739-lb (789-kg) SUU-23 and earlier 1,702-lb (772-kg) **SUU-16** (which used the M61) could be distinguished by the former's air inlet just above and behind the muzzle, while the latter deployed a ram-air turbine (**RAT**), from a large hatch located towards the middle of the pod, prior to being fired. This restricted its use to a maximum of 350 kias (knots indicated air speed). Both pods held 1,200 rounds and used a linkless feed mechanism. The SUU-16 was originally called the M12, while the SUU-23 was the XM25. Both the M61 and GAU-4 fire

Right: The SUU-23 20-mm Vulcan gunpod can be distinguished from the very similar SUU-16 by the small ram air inlet located just above and behind the gun barrels.

Below: A Michigan 'Six Pack' F-4C, from Selfridge ANGB, has an air show load of wall-to-wall SUU-23s; two was the maximum legal load.

Above: F-4B 149406, on loan to the USAF as 62-12169, tests SUU-16 gunpods. SUU-16s used a ram-air turbine (RAT) for power, while SUU-23s used the gun gas.

Right: A 414th FWS F-4E at Nellis AFB in November 1979 is seen with a pair of Pave Claw GPU-5 30-mm gunpods. Derived from the GAU-8 Avenger developed for the A-10A, it was designed to give other aircraft an anti-tank gun.

at up to 6,000 rpm with a muzzle velocity of 3,400 ft per second (fps) (1036 m per second – m/s). At the maximum rate of fire, prolonged bursts can generate nearly 4,000 lb (1814 kg) of reverse thrust! Active aircraft equipped with internal M61s include the A-7D/E, B-52H, AC-130A/H, F-4E, F-14, F-15, F-16 and F/A-18 (**GAU-11**). The F-22 will also probably be equipped with it. F-111s can carry the M61 in their weapons bay, but haven't since the 1970s. The F-4C/D/Es were the only users of the SUU-16, while the SUU-23 was also used by the F-4K/M.

The **GAU-13 Pave Claw** 30-mm four-barreled Gatling gun is the basis of the gun pod unit (**GPU**) **-5** anti-tank cannon pod. It uses a closed loop feed and storage system, is pneumatically driven, and fires at 2,400 rpm with a muzzle velocity of 3,200 fps (95 m/s). When loaded with 353 rounds of ammunition, the gun pod weighs 1,865 lb (846 kg). F-16As of the 174th TFW (NY ANG) are known to operate it, and some F-4 units during the late 1980s carried the GPU-5 as a centerline store.

AIR-TO-AIR MISSILES

AIM-4 Falcon

The Hughes Falcon dates from about 1949, when it first received the F-98 fighter designation from the USAF. In 1950 this was changed to guided aircraft rocket (**GAR**) -1 and given the name Falcon. The basic aerodynamic shape of this missile can still be seen in the AIM-54 Phoenix and AGM-65 Maverick.

The 110-lb (50-kg) **GAR-1 Falcon** had a semi-active radar-homing seeker (**SARH**). It had a speed of about Mach 2.5 and a range of 5 nm (5.7 miles; 9 km). About 4,000 were produced, entering service in 1954 with the F-89H and later with the F-102A. It was redesignated air intercept missile (**AIM**) -4 in 1962, when it was no longer in service.

The 130-lb (60-kg) **GAR-1D** had larger, redesigned control surfaces, which gave it improved maneuverability. About 12,000 were produced, entering service in 1956 with the F-89H, F-101 and F-102A. This version was redesignated the AIM-4A in 1962, after most had already been converted to AIM-4Ds.

The 120-lb (54-kg) **GAR-2** was an IR-guided version of the GAR-1 and entered service in 1956. About 16,000 were produced, and it was probably redesignated AIM-4B in 1962, when it was no longer in service.

The 130-lb (60-kg) **GAR-2A** was an IR-guided version of the GAR-1D. About 9,500 were produced, entering service in 1956 with the F-101, F-102A and later with the F-106A. This version was redesignated the AIM-4C in 1962, and most were converted to AIM-4Ds.

The 135-lb (61-kg) **GAR-2B** was converted from earlier GAR-1Ds and -2As. It featured an improved IR seeker, and USAF use included the F-89, F-101, F-102 and F-4D/E. Redesignated **AIM-4D** in 1962, it was also built in Sweden as the Rb 28 for use with the J35 Draken and AJ37 Viggen. (A 123-lb/56-kg trainer was designated A/B 37A-T1.) When employed by F-4s it required dedicated use of the inboard pylons and had a tendency to cause engine flameouts when fired. These were not qualities that endeared it to fighter pilots in combat. It was used for a short time in Vietnam by F-4Ds, but it was replaced by the AIM-9 after much frustration and the killing of only four MiG-17s and one

MiG-21 between 26 October 1967 and 5 February 1968.

The 140-lb (64-kg) **GAR-3** featured improved SARH guidance and was introduced in 1958 for use with the F-106. Only 300 were produced, and it was redesignated AIM-4E in 1962, probably after it went out of service.

The 152-lb (70-kg) **GAR-3A Super Falcon** was an SARH-guided version featuring improved accuracy and ECCM features. Its rocket motor had a high initial thrust, followed by a lower, sustaining thrust, and the missile could be distinguished by a 4-in (10-cm) aerodynamic nose probe. It entered service with the F-106A in 1960 and was redesignated the **AIM-4F** in 1962.

The 149-lb (68-kg) **GAR-4A** was an IR-guided version of the GAR-3A, which lacked the nose probe. It also entered service with the F-106A in 1960 and was redesignated the **AIM-4G** in 1962.

The **AIM-4H** was an improvement program for the AIM-4D, which would have incorporated a new warhead with laser proximity fuzing, as well as increased maneuverability and possibly dual-mode IR/SAR guidance. However, the program was not pursued.

AIM-7 Sparrow, XJ 521 Sky Flash and Aspide

The original Navy air-to-air missile (**AAM-N**) **-2 Sparrow I** was a Douglas missile which began as Project Hot Shot in May 1946. It featured beam-rider guidance, which simply attempted to keep the missile within the center of the firing aircraft's radar beam that was (hopefully) pointing at the target. It entered fleet service in 1956 – 10 years after the program began – and was used with the F3D-1M and -2M Skyknight and F7U-3M Cutlass. It was redesignated AIM-7A in 1962, after it went out of service, with only about 1,000 having been produced.

The **AAM-N-3** was another Douglas project which had a completely new guidance system featuring an active radar seeker. It was designed originally for the F5D Skylancer, but when that program was canceled in 1956, it was taken over by the Canadian government for their CF-105 Arrow, which was also canceled

in 1959. The missile was belatedly redesignated AIM-7B in 1962.

The genesis of the ultimate Raytheon 500-lb (227-kg) class AIM-7 Sparrow began in 1951 with their **AAM-N-6 Sparrow III**. In reality, this was a completely new missile which featured SARH guidance, a 65-lb (29-kg) continuous-rod warhead and a solid-fuel rocket motor. The first guided launch occurred in 1953. It replaced the Sparrow I in production in 1956, and reached the fleet in August 1958, with about 2,000 being produced to arm the F3H-2M Demon. The USAF had designated the Sparrow III the AIM-101, but in 1962, the joint designation system redesignated the missile the AIM-7C. An infrared-guided system version of this missile was successfully tested in 1957, but was canceled.

The **AAM-N-6A** replaced the AAM-N-6 in production during 1959. Its performance was increased by a limited proximity-fuzing capability, enabling head-on intercepts, and a storable liquid-fuel rocket motor which permitted supersonic launches. It was redesignated the AIM-7D in 1962, with 7,500 being produced to arm the F4H-1 and F-110A Phantom II.

The **AIM-7E Sparrow IIIB** entered production in 1963 and incorporated a new solid-fuel rocket motor which resulted in a 75 percent increase in range. However, experience in Vietnam proved that it was virtually useless against maneuvering, fighter-sized targets, especially at low level.

The **AIM-7E-2** 'dogfight' modification, identifiable by the 'L' markings on its wings, was introduced in 1969 to

Above: A 1972-vintage F-4E of the 36th TFW from Bitburg AB, Germany, takes off on a Zulu Alert scramble with a full load of AIM-4D Falcons and AIM-7E-2 Sparrows.

improve the AIM-7E's performance. It featured a shorter minimum range, as well as maneuverability and fuzing improvements. The **AIM-7E-3** featured additional fuzing and reliability improvements, while the **AIM-7E-4** was an E-3 modifications to allow it to be used with early F-14A Tomcats. The final 'E' was the **AIM-7E-6**. Over a period of 10 years, 25,000 AIM-7Es of various versions were produced, but none remain operational with the USAF or USN. Up to this point, the configuration of AIM-7s had been guidance and control section, wing, warhead and rocket section.

Work on the British **XJ 521 Sky Flash** began in 1973. It was essentially an AIM-7E-2 with an indigenous monopulse seeker, which gave it performance similar to the AIM-7M's seeker against low-flying targets, but it had the lower aerodynamic performance of the older missile. It also incorporated a new fuze and other internal modifications, with an improved rocket motor being fitted to later versions. It entered service with the RAF in 1978 on the F-4K/M and was basic equipment for the Tornado F.Mk 2/3. Sky Flash was exported to Sweden and entered service with JA37 Viggens in 1981 as the Rb 71.

Development of the **AIM-7F** began in 1966, although it did not enter service until 1975. Avionics improvements enabled a new 88-lb (40-kg) high-explosive, blast-fragmentation warhead

AIM-9 SIDEWINDER VARIANTS

VERSION	REMARKS
AIM-9A	Also known as XAAM-N-7. Sidewinder 1. About 300 produced for USN.
AIM-9B	Original designations were AAM-N-7 Sidewinder 1A (USN) and GAR-8 (USAF). About 71,700 built
	24.5 in (62 cm) long guidance control section (GCS) had an uncooled, lead-sulfide (PbS) IR seeker, covered by a glass dome; 15-in (38-cm) span fins.
	13.5 in (34 cm) long, 10 lb, Mk 8 blast-fragmentation warhead.
	3 in (7.6 cm) long Mk 303 (contact) and Mk 304 (influence) fuze section.
	75 in (190 cm) long Mk 17 rocket motor (2.3 nm; 2.6 miles; 4.3 km range) with 22 in (56 cm) span wings.
FGW Mod 2	European-built AIM-9B. Swedish designation Rb 324. 9,200 built
	GCS had improved electronics, carbon-dioxide (CO$_2$) cooled seeker and silicon (Si) dome.
AIM-9B-2	AIM-9B with 75 in (191 cm) long improved-performance SR116 rocket motor.
AIM-9C	Original designation Sidewinder 1B. 1,000 built for USN.
	25.5 in (65 cm) long USN-developed SARH variant, similar in appearance to the AIM-9B, with 16 in (41 cm) span BSU-14 fins.
	6.5 in (16.5 cm) long Mk 15 target detection device (TDD). Positioning of warhead and fuze reversed from AIM-9B.
	11.5 in (29 cm) long, 22.4 lb (10 kg), Mk 48 continuous-rod warhead.
	71 in (180 cm) long Mk 36 rocket motor (11 nm; 12.5 miles; 20 km max range) with 25 in (63.5 cm) span Mk 1 wings.
AIM-9D	Same as AIM-9C except with an IR seeker. Original designation Sidewinder 1C. 1,000 built for USN.
	24 in (61 cm) long Mk 18 GCS had an ogive-shaped, anodized nose.
	PbS seeker, covered by a magnesium-fluoride (MgF$_2$) dome.
	GCS was nitrogen (N$_2$) cooled from a bottle contained within the LAU-7 launcher rail.
AIM-9E	Total of about 5,000 modified AIM-9Bs for USAF.
	26.5 in (67 cm) long GCS had ogive nose and a Peltier thermo-electric cooler.
AIM-9E-2	AIM-9E with SR116 rocket motor.
AIM-9F	Designation reserved for possible USAF purchase of FGW Mod 2 variant known as the Mod 14K.
AIM-9G	AIM-9D with improved GCS. 2,120 built for USN.
	Incorporated the off-boresight, Sidewinder expanded acquisition mode (SEAM).
AIM-9H	AIM-9G with solid-state GCS. 7,720 built for USN.
AIM-9I	Designation not assigned.
AIM-9J	About 13,000 built, both AIM-9B/E/J modifications and new-builds.
	30.5 in (77.5 cm) long GCS with modified servo, electronics and 130211 double-delta fins.
	3 in (7.5 cm) long Mk 303/304 TDD or Mk 303 Mod 4 with combined functions.
	75 in (191 cm) long Mk 17 motor.
AIM-9J-1	Modified AIM-9J with 25.5 in (65 cm) long GCS which incorporates rate bias and solid state electronics. Over 7,000 produced.
	3 in (7.5 cm) long target detecting device unit (DSU) -21/B active optical target detector (AOTD) which utilizes gallium-arsenide (GaAs) lasers.
AIM-9J-2	AIM-9J with 75 in (191 cm) long SR116 rocket motor.
AIM-9J-3	AIM-9J-1 with SR116 rocket motor.
AIM-9K	China Lake developed alternative to AIM-9L. Not produced.
AIM-9L	About 16,000 built for USN and USAF, 3,500 for Europe. Swedish designation Rb 74.
	25.5 in (65 cm) long AN/DSQ-29 GCS has an indium-antimony (InSb) seeker which gives it an all-aspect capability. BSU-32/B 22-in span 'pointy' fins.
	USAF versions are argon (A) cooled from a bottle contained in the missile while USN versions are nitrogen (N$_2$) cooled from a launcher rail bottle.
	6.5 in (16.5 cm) long DSU-15/B AOTD.
	11.5 in (29 cm) long WDU-17 annular blast-fragmentation (ABF) warhead.
	71 in (180 cm) long Mk 36 rocket motor with Mk 1 wings.
AIM-9M	Originally AIM-9L product improvement program (PIP). Over 7,000 built.
	Modified with closed cycle cooling, IRCM and background discrimination.
	Reduced-smoke version of Mk 36 rocket motor.
AIM-9N	About 23,000 AIM-9B/Es modified for foreign military sales (FMS). Swedish designation Rb324J.
	30.5 in (77.5 cm) long GCS with same features as AIM-9J-1 GCS.
	Same TDD options as AIM-9J.
	13.5 in (34 cm) long Mk 54 blast-fragmentation warhead.
	Mk 17 rocket motor.
AIM-9N-1	AIM-9N with DSU-21/B fuze.
AIM-9N-2	AIM-9N with SR116 rocket motor.
AIM-9N-3	AIM-9N-1 with SR116 rocket motor.
AIM-9O	Designation not assigned.
AIM-9P	Redesignation of AIM-J-1.
AIM-9P-1	AIM-9P with DSU-21/B TDD.
AIM-9P-2	AIM-9P with SR116 rocket motor.
AIM-9P-3	AIM-9P-1 with SR116 rocket motor.
AIM-9P-4	AIM-9P GCS modified to be all-aspect capable, DSU-21/B TDD, Mk 8 warhead and an improved SR116 rocket motor. FMS version.
AIM-9JULI	German program to upgrade AIM-9J/N/Ps to AIM-9L performance standards.

to be located in front of the wing, allowing the rocket motor to be enlarged, thus improving range. This virtually new missile introduced a Doppler seeker and improved virtually all other components to make it more capable against maneuvering, low-altitude targets. Production of the AIM-7F ended in 1980. Both the AIM-7F and the later AIM-7M have been used to arm the F-4E/G/S, as well as the F-14, F-15, F-16ADF and F/A-18.

Above: An RAF F-4M banks away to show its fuselage-mounted Sky Flash, wing-mounted AIM-9L Sidewinders and SUU-23 gunpod.

The final front-line air-to-air version is the **AIM-7M**, which has a monopulse seeker, active radar fuze, focused blast fragmentation warhead and numerous other evolutionary improvements to increase reliability and decrease cost. It entered service in 1982, with production ending in 1992.

AIM-9 Sidewinder

Development of the 200-lb (91-kg) class Sidewinder missile family began in 1951 at the Naval Ordnance Test Station (**NOTS**). Forty years and nearly 30 versions later, it is by far the most successful and deadly air-to-air missile in the world, and has been copied by friend and foe alike. Produced mainly by Ford Aerospace and Raytheon, the AIM-9 has evolved from a missile which could only be launched at close range from directly behind a non-maneuvering target to an all-aspect weapon with up to five times the range of the original. It also served as the basis for the MIM-72 Chaparral and AGM-122 Sidearm. Beginning as a Navy missile adopted by the Air Force, requirements soon drove the two services along separate development paths. This persisted throughout the Vietnam War, until costs forced common development of the AIM-9L and subsequent versions.

Modifications of the original **Aero 3B** launcher rails to accept the AIM-9L/M/R missiles resulted in the **LAU-105**, while the newest launcher for Sidewinders is the **LAU-114**.

AIM-82

This proposed USAF replacement for the AIM-9 (canceled in favor of the AIM-95), would have been used on the A-6B/E, A-7D/E, F-4E/J, F-14A and F-15A.

AIM-95 Agile

This was a Hughes missile developed for the USN in competition with the AIM-82 and intended as an AIM-9 replacement. It was canceled in development, but was tested on F-4Js during 1972.

This 555th TFS F-4D in late 1972 at Udorn RTAFB (top) carries AIM-9J/7E-2s, and ALQ-87/101 ECM pods. The AIM-9E (above) was used extensively during Vietnam.

AGM-97 Seekbat

This was a canceled air-to-air version of the AGM-78, designed for use by the F-4E as a counter to the MiG-25 'Foxbat' until the F-15 became operational.

AIM-120 Advanced, Medium-Range Air-to-Air Missile (AMRAAM)

The Hughes AIM-120 is the replacement for the AIM-7 Sparrow. An extremely controversial weapon, it has had a long and difficult gestation, emerging as a missile far more lethal than the one it replaces.

AMRAAM's most important improvement is the incorporation of an active-radar seeker. Although done before with the AIM-54 Phoenix, putting this feature into a Sparrow-sized airframe is a significant achievement. It allows the launching aircraft to simultaneously engage several targets and maneuver 'out of the fight' before the missiles hit their targets. The Sparrow, by comparison, requires the launching aircraft to maintain radar contact with a single target until the missile hits it. The

disadvantage of this was dramatically demonstrated during the famous Aimval/Aceval tests during the mid-1970s. In one engagement, which became known as 'The Towering Inferno', four F-15s engaged four F-5s with simulated AIM-7s. Before they were all 'shot down' by the Sparrows, the F-5s were able to launch simulated AIM-9s which 'destroyed' all the F-15s. AMRAAM would have allowed a single F-15 to target all four F-5s before withdrawing beyond the range of their AIM-9s.

The other main area of emphasis with AMRAAM has been reliability and maintainability. Sparrow was infamous

during the Vietnam War for its unreliability. Getting this feature right was one of the main reasons it took so long to get the AIM-120 into full-rate production, which finally happened in early 1992. Virtually all areas of performance have been improved over the AIM-7, including reducing motor smoke, increasing speed and range, improving warhead fuzing and lethality, and better ECCM performance.

The proposed **AIM-120B** will incorporate technology developed for the canceled AIM-54 replacement – the advanced air-to-air missile (AAAM). Plans are to fund advanced seeker technology demonstration contracts with the two

AAAM teams – Hughes/Raytheon and General Dynamics/Westinghouse. Consideration is also being given to the possibility of incorporating ramjet, multipulse rocket, variable-flow ducted rocket or a booster rocket on advanced AIM-120s to increase range.

With a weight of only 350 lb (159 kg), the AIM-120 can be rail-launched from stations previously associated only with AIM-9 Sidewinders. This was done during the Gulf War, when the F-15Cs of the

33rd TFW were the first unit to take AMRAAM into combat. Unfortunately, by the time the aircraft software was set up to allow carriage of AIM-7s, -9s and -120s, the Iraqi air force was hiding in their shelters or fleeing to Iran, and there was no opportunity to actually use the new missile in combat. AIM-120 will eventually replace the AIM-7 on all F-14Ds, F-15s, F-16s, F/A-18s, F-22As and German F-4Fs.

Air-to-air missiles

The original F4H-1 Phantom was designed as a dedicated interceptor, armed with the AIM-7 Sparrow missile. Many other AAMs have been carried since.

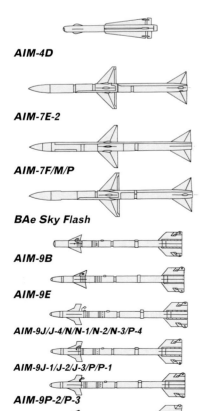

AIM-4D

AIM-7E-2

AIM-7F/M/P

BAe Sky Flash

AIM-9B

AIM-9E

AIM-9J/J-4/N/N-1/N-2/N-3/P-4

AIM-9J-1/J-2/J-3/P/P-1

AIM-9P-2/P-3

AIM-9D/G/H

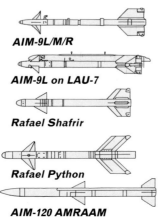

AIM-9L/M/R

AIM-9L on LAU-7

Rafael Shafrir

Rafael Python

AIM-120 AMRAAM

Shafrir

The Rafael **Shafrir** was developed from the AIM-9 beginning in 1961, entered service in 1969 and was used successfully in the 1973 Yom Kippur War. It was superseded in 1978 by the **Shafrir 2**, which was used in 1982 over the Bekaa Valley. This missile has a 6.3-in (16 cm) diameter body, compared with 5 in (13 cm) for the similar AIM-9. It weighs about 210 lb (95 kg), with a 20-lb, (9-kg) HE Frag warhead, and is limited to rear hemisphere attacks. It has been carried by the Mirage III, Kfir, A-4, F-4E, F-15A/B and F-16A/B, and was exported.

Python 3

The Rafael **Python 3** is a 265-lb (120-kg) infrared-guided air-to-air missile. Its development began in 1978, driven by the desire for a larger warhead to increase missile lethality. Developed from the earlier Shafrir 2, it can be easily distinguished by its large, swept-back tail. It has a 24-lb (11-kg) HE warhead, detonated by an active laser fuze. The all-aspect seeker can be slaved to the aircraft radar, or used in boresight and scan modes. Authorized for use by the Kfir, F-4E, F-15 and F-16, the Python 3 was credited with about 50 kills over the Bekaa Valley soon after its introduction in 1982. The Python 3 has been exported, and a Python 4 version may be in production.

AIR-TO-SURFACE MISSILES (ASMs)

AGM-12 Bullpup

Studies leading to the development of the Navy air-to-surface missile (**ASM-N) -7 Bullpup** began in 1951, with the first successful launch occurring in 1955. This missile had a 250-lb (113-kg) warhead and was propelled at Mach 1.8 by a solid-fuel rocket motor. It was guided by the pilot, who used a joystick controller and watched flares mounted to the missile tail fins. The USAF designated the Bullpup initially the B-83, and then the ground attack missile (**GAM**) -83. It was jointly redesignated the air-to-ground missile (**AGM**) -12A in 1962.

The 577-lb (262-kg) **ASM-N-7A Bullpup A** entered Navy service in 1960. It had an increased range of 8 nm (9 miles; 15 km) and speed of Mach 2.5, thanks to the use of a storable liquid-fuel motor. Initially called the GAM-83A by the USAF, it was redesignated **AGM-12B** in 1962. The 600-lb (272-kg) AGM-12B-2 and -3 featured fragmentation warheads. About 40,000 Bullpup As, including 8,000 in Europe, were built. AGM-12B was qualified for use by the A-4, A-5, A-6, A-7, F-100, F-104, F-105, F-4, F-5, F-8 and P-3 in US service, and up to four could be carried by F-4s (one per wing station) using LAU-34 launchers. They were also used by Royal Navy Buccaneers and Sea Vixens, as well as by Denmark, Norway and Turkey.

The 1,800-lb (816-kg) ASM-N-7B was redesignated the **AGM-12C Bullpup B** before becoming operational in 1964. This much larger missile featured a 1,000-lb (454-kg) semi-armor piercing (SAP) warhead and an aerodynamic range of 10 nm (11 miles; 18 km), although its effective range was limited to the range at which its flares could be seen by the pilot. A total of 4,600 of these was produced and used extensively by the A-4 and F-105D. Two could be carried by F-4s, from the inboard wing pylons.

The **AGM-12D** was initially known as the GAM-83B by the Air Force. It was basically an AGM-12B armed with an H45 nuclear warhead. About 100 were built and deployed between 1962 and 1978 with the F-100D and F-105D.

The **AGM-12E**, another Air Force version, was an AGM-12C with an anti-personnel cluster bomb warhead. Only 840 of these were produced. Two could be carried by F-4s, from the inboard wing pylons.

AGM-45 Shrike

The 400-lb (180-kg) **AGM-45 Shrike** was developed by the Naval Weapons Center during the Vietnam War as the first anti-radiation missile (**ARM**). Produced by Texas Instruments, the **AGM-45A** (original designation: ASM-N-10) had a single-burn motor and became operational in 1965. The **AGM-45B** introduced a dual-burn motor, with the initial acceleration thrust followed by a second, sustaining thrust. Altogether, 12 guidance, eight warhead, three control and seven motor sections were developed by the time production of over 13,000 Shrikes ceased in 1978. All versions maintained the same external configuration. The AGM-45 can be launched from the USN **Aero 5**, USAF **LAU-34** or the newer **LAU-118**, which can also be used to launch the AGM-88. The Shrike in USAF service has been carried by EF-105Fs, F-105Gs, F-4C (Wild Weasel), F-4Gs and Wild Weasel F-16Cs, while USN carriers have included the A-4, A-7, A-6E and F/A-18. Foreign use has included Israeli F-4Es and Kfirs, as well as the British Vulcan B.Mk 2.

AGM-53 Condor

A requirement for the ASM-N-11 was issued in 1962. A development contract was awarded to Rockwell in 1966 and the first launch of the 2,130-lb (966-kg) **AGM-53 Condor** occurred in 1970 from an F-4. It had a 630-lb (286-kg) linear shaped-charge warhead and a range of about 60 nm (68 miles; 110 km). It featured TV guidance via a secure datalink housed in a 675-lb (306-kg) pod. Although a technical success, it was a financial disaster, costing nearly four times as much as the AGM-54 Phoenix at the time of its cancelation in 1976. It would have been carried by the A-4, A-7, F-4, P-3 and S-3.

AGM-62 Walleye

Walleye is an unpowered guided missile developed for the Navy beginning in 1962. Although it has been allocated the designation AGM-62, it is usually referred to as 'Walleye'.

Over 4,500 **Walleye Is** were produced between 1966 and 1970 by Martin Marietta. Equipped with TV seekers which required lock-on before launch (**LOBL**), they had 845-lb (383-kg) linear shaped-charge warheads. Built by Martin, the 1,120-lb (508-kg) **Mk 1** missiles entered service in 1967 and were used in combat during the Vietnam War by Navy A-4Fs, A-6Es and A-7Es. They also saw limited use by Air Force F-4Ds modified by TO 1F-4D-559 (66-7505 and later) and were exported to Israel. The **Mk 2** was a trainer version with an inert warhead; the **Mk 4** was a load trainer.

Walleye I ER/DL resulted from a Navy requirement for increased stand-off range. One thousand four hundred of the extended-range/datalink (**ER/DL**) versions were converted from Walleye Is beginning in late 1972. The 1,200-lb (544-kg) missiles featured larger wings and incorporated a lock-on after launch capability (**LOAL**) which used the 168-lb (76-kg) airborne armament fire-control (**AWG**) -16 datalink pod. Although the missile could be guided by the launching aircraft, usually a different aircraft would carry the datalink pod and provide guidance. A 1 kT-yield W72 nuclear warhead was fitted to the USAF's Walleye I **Mk 6** for use with F-4Ds. These were the only USAF AGM-62s to use the AWG-16, with the missile on the left and pod on the right inboard pylons. A total of 300 W72s was produced between 1970 and 1972; they were retired in 1979.

Walleye II featured a 2,060-lb (934-kg) linear shaped-charge warhead. Initially known as 'Fat Albert', 529 of the 2,455-lb (1114-kg) **Mk 5** missiles were built for the Navy by Hughes, and an additional 1,481 were converted from Walleye Is. 'Conversion' is perhaps too mild a term, the only external similarity being the nose section.

Walleye II ER/DL was developed towards the end of the Vietnam War, with three being used in combat. Weighing 2,490-lb (1130-kg), a total of 2,400 was converted from earlier missiles to the **Mk 23** standard for the Navy. While externally similar to the Walleye II, they had larger wings. Also, the AWG-16 was superseded by the 645-lb (292-kg) airborne remote-control (**AWW**) -7 and the externally identical, 690-lb (313-kg) **AWW-9** Walleye datalink pods. In 1977, Hughes was given a contract to develop an imaging infrared (**IIR**) seeker head which is now used by the AGM-62, AGM-65 and GBU-15.

AGM-63 Brazo/Pave Arm

This was a joint USAF/USN program during the Vietnam War to develop an anti-radiation missile based on the AIM-7. It was tested from F-4Ds before being canceled in favor of the AGM-88 HARM.

A very early test version of the AGM-65A Maverick is seen mounted to an LAU-88. LAU-88s were widely used by F-4s, but most aircraft found the single-rail LAU-117 easier to manage.

AGM-65 Maverick

Developed during the Vietnam War as a subsonic, launch-and-leave replacement for the AGM-12 Bullpup, the Hughes Maverick has evolved over the years and remains in production. While all the same size, AGM-65s utilize a variety of guidance and warhead sections. The original 125-lb (57-kg) high-explosive, shaped-charge warheads have been replaced in later AGM-65s by 300-lb (136-kg) blast-penetration warheads. All versions use the same rocket motor, with maximum launch range dependent on target size and seeker performance. While maximum aerodynamic range is about 12.5 nm (14 miles; 23 km), a more realistic range is nearer 8 nm (9 miles; 15 km). Launchers include the three-rail **LAU-88** (for A, B and D versions –

authorized for A-7D/E, A-10A, F-111F, F-4D/E/G and F-16), and single-rail **LAU-117** (which can be used with any version, and is authorized for LAU-88 aircraft as well as the A-4M, F-5E, F/A-18, P-3 and S-3). Maverick has been exported to Greece, Iran, Israel, Korea and Turkey for use with their F-4Es; Saudi Arabia for use with its F-5Es; Sweden for use with its AJ37 Viggens; and Switzerland for use with its Hunters. Only F-4Ds from 66-7505 onwards were Maverick-capable.

AGM-65A has an electro-optical (TV) seeker, which the pilot uses to acquire the target. After designating the target and ensuring the missile is locked on, he fires it and can either select another target or commence escape maneuvering. The **AGM-65B** has the advantage of 'scene magnification', which enables it to be locked on to the same target as an AGM-65A from twice the range. Both missiles are white, with clear seeker domes. The AGM-65B has 'SCENE MAG' stenciled on its side.

AGM-65C was a semi-active laser (SAL) version developed in the late 1970s, although in 1979 both the USAF and USN decided to forego this seeker in favor of IIR guidance. The USMC became the only user of SAL guidance, in the form of the **AGM-65E**, which features the larger warhead. SAL permits ground troops to designate targets for close air support.

AGM-65D was the first IIR version produced. The advantage of IIR over EO guidance is its ability to be used at night and in conditions of smoke and haze. For the **AGM-65F**, the Navy modified the IIR seeker's tracking function for anti-ship attacks and incorporated the larger warhead. The **AGM-65G** combines the guidance features of both the 'D' and 'F' with the latter's warhead. The USAF IIR missiles are olive drab, while the USN's are gray. IIR training missiles have yellowish seeker domes, while on the actual missiles they are silverish.

AGM-65 MAVERICK VARIANTS

VERSION	GUIDANCE	WEIGHT	WARHEAD	REMARKS
AGM-65A	EO	465 lb	125 lb	
AGM-65B	EO (Scene Mag)	465 lb	125 lb	
AGM-65C	SAL	465 lb	125 lb	not produced
AGM-65D	IIR	485 lb	125 lb*	USAF only
AGM-65E	SAL	645 lb	300 lb	USMC only
AGM-65F	IIR (anti-ship)	675 lb	300 lb	USN only
AGM-65G	IIR	675 lb	300 lb	USAF/USN

AGM-78 Standard ARM

The 1,390-lb (630-kg) General Dynamics **AGM-78 Standard ARM** was developed by mating AGM-45 guidance sections to the Navy's RIM-66 Standard SAM to increase the stand-off range of Wild Weasels. It attacked SAM sites by homing in on their radar emissions. With a 215-lb (97-kg) warhead, it had a range of about 15 nm (17 miles; 28 km) at Mach 2, and used the LAU-77 (A-6B/E, EF-105F and F-105G) and LAU-80 (F-105G and F-4G) launchers. The **AGM-78A** was produced from 1968 to 1970. The AGM-78A-1 had no BDA unit, but the AGM-78A-2 did. The AGM-78A-4 was an A-1 with a completely new guidance section. The **AGM-78B** was an A-4 with a BDA unit – it usually had a brown radome and was produced in 1971. The **AGM-78C** was produced for the USAF in 1971 and 1972. It had a new guidance section with a full-band radome, a WP smoke signal and memory circuits to counter radar shutdown tactics. The **AGM-78D** was the final production version which was introduced in 1974 and developed to the D-2 standard by the time production ended in 1976. USAF

phase-out of the AGM-78 was completed by about 1990. About 300 were exported to Israel under the 'Purple Fist' program and used successfully in the Bekaa Valley in 1982. It was also exported to South Korea.

An Israeli F-4E with a pair of Rafael 'Popeye' guided weapons, along with their datalink pod. The refueling probe will definitely be needed!

AGM-142 Popeye

Popeye is a 3,300-lb (1497-kg) conventional stand-off missile armed with a 1,975-lb (896-kg) high-explosive warhead (probably the Mk 84). It was developed by Israel's Rafael Armament Development Authority in the early 1980s and was procured by the US Air Force under the 'Have Nap' program. Co-produced by Martin Marietta, it features inertial guidance coupled with EO terminal homing. Believed to have been influenced by Rafael's earlier Pyramid program, as well as Israeli experience with the Maverick missile, its similarities in guidance, datalink and warhead to the shorter-ranged GBU-15 are notable. It serves in the Israeli air force on the F-4E, with the F-16 being another logical candidate. Evaluated on the F-111F and F-15E, the 50-nm (57-mile; 92-km) range missile entered USAF service with conventionally dedicated B-52Gs in the early 1990s. Popeye was not used during the Gulf War, reportedly because of the concerns about the effects of using an Israeli-developed weapon on the coalition.

Gabriel

The Israeli Gabriel radar-guided anti-ship missile exists in several versions – none of which are known to have been exported. The **Gabriel 1** was a ship-launched missile developed during the 1960s; the improved **Gabriel 2** was introduced in the 1970s; and the **Gabriel 3** in about 1980. The **Gabriel 3AS** was the first air-launched version, weighing 1,234 lb (560 kg) with a range of about 18 nm (21 miles; 33 km). Powered by a solid-fuel rocket motor, it is inertially guided at a radar altimeter-controlled altitude of about 65 ft (20 m), with the option of a midcourse update from the launching aircraft. In its terminal phase, the missile descends to strike its target at the waterline with a 330-lb (150-kg) semi-armor piercing warhead. It entered service in about 1985 and has been authorized for carriage by A-4, F-4, Kfir and Sea Scan aircraft. The **Gabriel 4LR** will be a new missile, weighing 2,116 lb (960 kg), with a 529-lb (240-kg) warhead. Its range will be about 100 nm (115 miles; 185 km), using a solid rocket booster followed by a turbojet sustainer. It will probably be ship-launched and may enter service as early as 1993.

ASM

Developed for the Japanese Self-Defense Force by Mitsubishi Heavy Industries as the Type 80, the **ASM-1** is a 1,345-lb (610-kg) anti-ship missile with a 330-lb (150-kg) semi-armor piercing warhead. Development began in 1973, with service entry 10 years later. Originally tested with the Mitsubishi F-1, it has also been cleared for use with the P-3C and F-4EJ. Slightly heavier than the AGM-84, with a warhead only two-thirds as large, it is not known to have been exported. Performance and guidance are similar to the Harpoon, with a range of 49 nm (56 miles; 91 km), radar altimeter altitude control, inertial midcourse and active

radar terminal guidance. Unlike Harpoon, ASM-1 uses a solid rocket motor instead of a turbojet for propulsion.

Development of the follow-on **ASM-2** began in the early 1980s as the Type 88. This missile, based on the SSM-1 coastal defense missile, is expected to enter service in 1995 and generally equates to the AGM-84D. Use of turbojet propulsion will more than double its range over the ASM-1 to 93 nm (107 miles; 172 km), and its guidance program will incorporate a multiple turnpoint capability. Both IIR and passive radar terminal guidance have been mentioned. It is expected to be cleared for carriage on the F-1, P-3C, FS-X, F-15J and F-4EJ.

AGM-88 High-speed Anti-Radiation Missile (HARM)

Based on lessons learned in Vietnam, the 800-lb (363-kg) class AGM-88 is fast enough to give SAM operators minimum opportunity to shut down their radar before the HARM does it for them. HARM has three methods of employment: **1** In the pre-briefed mode the missile is programmed on the ground for up to three specific missile sites. Upon detecting those sites, it is launched on a ballistic trajectory. (Although HARM can be launched in the direction of a target, it guides in azimuth only, not range, thus relying on the target to emit and identify itself.) **2** The self-protection mode launches the missile against threats detected by the launching aircraft's radar warning receiver. **3** The target of opportunity mode uses the HARM's seeker to help determine when

to launch against a previously unknown threat. One interesting technique used during the opening stages of the Gulf War was to use multiply-launched drone missile (**BQM**) **-74C** targets as decoys, thus enticing the SAM sites into turning on their radars for the incoming barrage of HARMs.

There are three versions of the AGM-88, differing mainly in the features of the guidance section electronics. The **AGM-88A** requires the seeker to be sent back to a depot in the US to be reprogrammed. The **AGM-88B** allows the seeker to be reprogrammed on the flight line. This version, with Block-3 software, was the main one used during the Gulf War. The **AGM-88C** will incorporate further seeker improvements and replace the steel cubes in the

warhead with considerably more lethal tungsten alloy ones. HARMs are launched from the **LAU-118** launch rail, which can also accommodate the older AGM-45.

USN/USMC HARMS are carried by ICAP II EA-6Bs, SWIP A-6Es and F/A-18s, while the USAF only employs them from F-4Gs and F-16C Wild Weasels. The F-4G is by far the HARM's most effective launch platform, because its airborne radar-receiving, passive-detecting (**APR**) -47 system allows it to detect, identify and precisely locate threat radars and then attack them or direct other aircraft to attack them. No other aircraft has this capability and the Air Force elected to retain two squadrons (at Spangdahlem AB, Germany, and Boise IAP, Idaho), until a Wild Weasel version of the F-15E can be developed.

PHANTOM VARIANTS

The McDonnell Phantom was built in greater numbers than any other Western jet fighter, over a period of nearly 20 years. During this time, the basic design was continually refined and modernized, and adapted to meet new roles and differing requirements. This led to a bewildering succession of production variants, which were augmented by variants produced by the conversion of old airframes. Here the Phantom family is described in detail.

Above: The 'Top Flight' YF4H-1 screams into the air for an attempt on the world altitude record. The aircraft succeeded, reaching 98,650 ft (30041 m).

Below: An F-4B of the 'Sundowners' of VF-111 dumps a stick of 500-lb bombs on 'suspected VC' positions during the long involvement in Vietnam. The Phantom performed miracles routinely in Vietnam, but in the end it was the right airplane being used in the wrong way, in the wrong war.

For 20 years, from 1960 to 1980, the F-4 Phantom II was accepted, at least in what might still be called 'the West', as the standard against which lesser fighters were judged. It had the best radar and the best supersonic engine installation of its day, as well as two seats, two engines, exceptional range and endurance, and inflight refueling by either the probe/drogue or flying boom method. Despite the supposed penalties of carrier equipment, it had an all-round flight performance in terms of speed and climb that no contemporary warplane could fully equal. Not least, while the British Lightning carried two AAMs and the French Mirage IIIA carried just one, it could enter battle with eight AAMs, four of them IR-homing dogfight Sidewinders and the other four large radar-guided medium-range Sparrows.

It is not surprising that the total number built was 5,195, almost all (5,057) being built at MCAIR (McDonnell Aircraft Company) at St Louis, Missouri. Except for the F-86 Sabre, no other Western warplane since 1945 can equal this total, which is even more impressive considering that the F-4 was more expensive than any other production fighter of its day.

Left: Britain's ambitious plans to transform the F-4 by installing the Rolls-Royce Spey backfired somewhat, producing an aircraft with performance characteristics that were inferior in many vital respects.

Committee for Aeronautics) came up with the Area Rule for minimum transonic drag, and this was reflected by a slight 'Coke-bottling' of the project's very broad fuselage.

The primary mission of the F3H-C was long-range attack, and for this purpose it was planned to have nine external stores stations plus all-weather radar. Initially a single-seater, it was clearly capable of flying so many missions that in November 1953 MCAIR proposed the novel concept of an aircraft which, in about eight hours, could be fitted with any of seven different front ends. These were for single-seat fighting with four 20-mm Colt Mk 12 cannon (as in the rival Vought F8U), two-seat all-weather interception with guided missiles, surface attack, multisensor reconnaissance, electronic warfare, Elint, EW jamming, and various forms of training. The multinose concept was not accepted, but MCAIR's obvious commitment led to a series of formal proposals from August 1954. As a result, in September 1954 the company was asked to submit a refined and more specific proposal, and a month later it re-

Yet few could call this paragon of virtues a thing of beauty. One of the first comments by the US Navy, the original customer, was, "When you watch her take off, you see her arched nose and downswept stabilator separated by a bulky midriff that looks as awkward as a goose with drooping tail feathers and middle-aged spread." And a US Air Force major countered with, "When I first saw a Phantom I thought it so ugly I wondered if it had been delivered upside down."

The project began in May 1952, when MCAIR had a good track record with the FH-1 Phantom, the first carrier jet in service in the world, and the vastly superior F2H Banshee, in action off Korea. MCAIR's Model 58, the XF3H Demon, first flown in August 1951, was a much more advanced design that was crippled by a bad engine, but the land-based XF-88 Voodoo was developing well into the XF-101 Voodoo, then the most powerful fighter in the world, and which was flown in 1954. MCAIR was determined to win the US Navy's first supersonic fighter contract but, in May 1953, the winner was Vought, with the single-engined XF8U-1 Crusader that incorporated a high wing pivoted to the fuselage.

MCAIR's losing design had a conventional low wing and two engines, but the project team, led by Herman D. Barkey, was convinced it was a sound basis for a superior fighter. Indeed, it had to produce such an aircraft to stay in business. From August 1953, the study called Model 98A involved more than half the available engineering staff. The designation F3H-C reflected the fact that the design was to a large extent based on the F3H Demon. This Navy fighter was gradually being reborn as the F3H-2, redesigned with the Allison J71 engine, and was eventually to take its place in two versions in the Navy carrier air wings. The F3H-C differed in having a more powerful engine, the Wright J67 (license-built Bristol Olympus) being suggested, and it was designed for a high supersonic Mach number. Just in time, Richard Whitcomb at the NACA (National Advisory

Above: A USAF-style star and bar camouflage the fact that this slatted F-4E, seen with everything 'hanging out', is destined for the air force of Israel.

Right: Certainly the most capable Phantom variant, the F-4F ICE integrates the F/A-18's benchmark APG-65 radar and the AIM-120 AMRAAM with the aging airframe of the F-4F. It makes the Phantom a great BVR bomber destroyer, but agility and acceleration cannot match modern fighters.

Above: The AH-1 in mock-up form. This design represented a midway point in the evolution from the F3H Demon to the F4H Phantom. It was a single-seater, and lacked the distinctive anhedral tail and upturned wingtips of the Phantom proper, but was otherwise a recognizable F-4 forerunner.

Below: The first of the breed in flight. Both YF4H-1 prototypes featured a long pitot-static boom on the nose. The two aircraft differed in detail, with the second having an operable radar and a rear cockpit which could be occupied.

Above: The first prototype was lost on 21 October 1959, after the failure of an access door led to a succession of more serious failures. It had already demonstrated a dazzling performance, and shown the potential of the production Phantom.

Right: The initial front-line service version of the Phantom was the F4H-1, later redesignated F-4B. An F-4B of VF-102 'Diamondbacks' is seen here. Many early F-4Bs had long and productive service careers, some being refurbished and upgraded to F-4N standards. These aircraft served into the 1990s.

ceived a contract for two flight articles and one static test airframe. The designation AH-1 reflected the fact that the mission selected was that of surface attack. Armament comprised four 20-mm cannon plus any Navy attack store, carried on no fewer than 11 pylons.

In early 1955, while the Navy was having doubts about the entire project, critical decisions were taken to change the design. The most important was to switch to the General Electric J79 engine, which at one stroke put this obviously big aircraft into the Mach 2 class. This in turn demanded a major design effort on the nozzles and, particularly, on the inlets,

which had to be more complex than anything seen on earlier fighters. A rear cockpit was added, and the loss of the 150-US gal (125-Imp gal; 568-liter) front fuselage fuel cell was made up by enlarging the planned centerline drop-tank from 450 to 600 US gal (375 to 500 Imp gal; 1705 to 2273 liters). This change moved the CG (center of gravity) aft, which in turn countered the forward shift caused by incessant growth in the mass of equipment in the nose.

Other changes altered the appearance considerably. Exhaustive tunnel testing showed the need for enhanced stability, especially directional (yaw) stability at high AOA (angle of attack). The wing, whose 45° sweepback was caused mainly by sharp taper on the leading edge, was originally a plain surface with 2° dihedral and a straight leading edge. To fit carrier lifts the outer sections folded upward, and in 1955 these were redesigned so that when hinged downward they still had 12° of dihedral. They were also extended in chord by 10 percent, with a down-cambered leading edge ending in an abrupt 'dogtooth' discontinuity to cause a powerful upper-surface vortex at high AOA and thus preserve lateral control and avoid pitch up. Yaw stability also required more fin area. MCAIR was concerned at the size of fin needed, and in order to fit within hangar clearance height the fin had already been made exceptionally long. The only alternative was to use acute dihedral or anhedral on the horizontal tail, and these surfaces were accordingly sloped down at 15°. Even this proved insufficient, and the anhedral finally chosen was no less than 23.25°.

In April 1955, two officers from the Navy BuAer (Bureau of Aeronautics) and two from CNO (Chief of Naval Operations) visited St Louis, and a single meeting enabled the design to be completed and the prototypes to be built. MCAIR was told that what the Navy wanted was not the AH-1 but the F4H-1, a long-range fleet defense interceptor. Among other things it had to fly a two-hour CAP at a radius of 250 nm (287 miles; 462 km) from the carrier. This was the basis of MCAIR's Model 98.

Almost overnight MCAIR threw out the 11 stores pylons and replaced them by missile armament. The main armament was to comprise four of the as-yet untested Sparrow III missiles, recessed in tandem pairs along each side of the broad and almost flat underside. After discussion, the four 20-mm guns were deleted.

Prototype construction began later in 1955, and the first of two F4H-1s (sometimes incorrectly called XF4H-1) was flown at Lambert-St Louis Municipal Airport, adjacent to the MCAIR plant, on 27 May 1958. The pilot was chief engineering test pilot Robert C. 'Bob' Little, with the rear cockpit housing instrumentation.

The F4H-1 Phantom was a remarkably advanced aircraft by the standards of the day, combining the most modern innovations in structure, control systems, avionics, armament, propulsion and aerodynamics. Together the whole package made the Phantom unbeatable, and the excitement generated by the rollout and first few flights of the prototype was widely and deeply felt. The F4H-1 was in every sense an aircraft at the cutting edge of every aerospace technology and, as the years went by, this helped it to adapt to changing requirements and new roles. So advanced was the Phantom that even at the end of its service life its outright performance remained impressive, with a high absolute top speed and excellent acceleration and rate of climb.

A brief technical description of the F4H-1 follows, as a baseline for the differences described in the listing of variants.

Aerodynamics

In many respects the shape of the F4H was a direct extrapolation of the preceding F3H Demon. The wing was originally almost identical, though without fences. The aerofoil profile selected was NACA 0006.4-64 at the root, this

being a symmetric section with round leading edge. The thickness/chord ratio of 6.4 percent at the root was thinned down to only 4 percent at the fold and 3 percent at the tip, the average being 5.1 percent. The aspect ratio was low at 2.82, and the net area was 530 sq ft (49 m²). Sweepback, which was almost 50° on the leading edge, was exactly 45° when measured along the standard 25-percent chord line (one-quarter of the way back from the leading edge). Care was taken to achieve the best fuselage shape. The tandem cockpits were covered by a single canopy that was flush with the top of the fuselage downstream. A crucial feature was that the two engines were installed far apart, with room for a large fuel capacity between the ducts, which in turn gave the fuselage a distinctive cross-section, modified by the Area Rule across

Above: Some F-4Bs (and F-4Ns) ended their days as unmanned target drones, designed to be blasted from the sky in missile trials.

the top of the wings. At the rear, however, the two nozzles had to be close together, so the engines were inclined in plan view. The design of the rear fuselage was the most difficult part of all, despite MCAIR's prior experience with the F3H and, especially, the twin-engined supersonic F-101. The body cross-section was suddenly reduced by approximately half at the engine nozzles, which varied greatly in profile and area. Downstream the tail end tapered quite sharply, the stabilators being very close behind the nozzles and thus mounted as high above the jets as possible. Another unusual feature was that there was no portion of fuselage below the wing, i.e. the belly of the aircraft was entirely wing, although the natural curvature of the aerofoil did raise the

Below: The F-4B in its element, operating from the deck of a US Navy carrier. The introduction of the Phantom transformed the capabilities of the carrier air wing.

leading and trailing edges an inch or two above the fuselage bottom line.

Flight control

MCAIR never had any doubt that all flight controls should be fully powered, each surface being driven by a power unit fed by two independent hydraulic systems. There was still plenty of scope for design choices, and those finally adopted had several unusual features. This was especially the case with lateral control. The outer panels, with 12° dihedral, contained no movable surfaces except for a hinged (drooping) leading edge. The trailing edge of the horizontal main wing was divided into two, the inboard surface being a flap and the outboard an aileron. The latter moved down only, not up, and immediately ahead of

each a large spoiler was recessed into the upper wing surface. Thus, to roll to the left the right aileron would go down and the left spoiler would go up. Pitch control was entirely governed by the stabilators, or slab tailplanes, sloping down at 23.25°, which were driven in unison through a total angle which at low speeds could reach 40°. The simple rudder was interconnected with the ailerons at low speeds to cancel any yaw input. There were no tabs anywhere. The entire leading edge was arranged to hinge down (droop) at low speeds. Following research by John D. Attinello and the Navy, the leading edges, as well as the flaps, were all blown by high-pressure air bled from the engine compressors. The resulting supersonic sheet of air served to keep airflow attached at high AOA. A hydraulically-powered

airbrake was added under the wing, hinged on two arms to the near spar behind the MLG bay.

At the outset the F-4 Phantom II was the outstanding combat aircraft of its generation. Able to fly from a runway or a carrier deck, it was one of the very few aircraft able to fly both fighter and attack missions with equal success. It was designed by a team with outstanding experience and capability, and its combination of tremendous propulsive power and almost unlimited flight performance – demonstrated by 15 world records – made the F-4 driver an object of envy, and of immediate attention whenever he entered a club or mess populated by pilots of lesser aircraft.

In its early years, flying with the Navy and Marines as a night and all-weather interceptor, the F-4 matched these unrivaled abilities with unprecedented safety. This is very important to the young pilot converting to his first front-line type. The Phantom might appear awesomely large and powerful, and incredibly sophisticated, but the knowledge that not one pilot had been killed on conversion helped dispel fear. So did the knowledge that squadron after squadron was clocking up 10,000 hours with no accident, previously an exceedingly rare accomplishment. Even in the rather more varied and demanding missions flown by the USAF only one major accident was recorded in the first 20,000 hours, compared with eight for the F-111, 24 for the F-104 and 26 for the F-100.

This all changed when the F-4 went to war in Vietnam in the late spring of 1965. In the first two years, casualties among the first F-4C squadrons reached almost 40 percent, a total of 54 aircraft. By 1971, the Navy and Marines had lost 79 F-4s in combat, and the USAF no fewer than 283. Some were shot down, in most cases by AAA. Others were either abandoned or lost in a stall/spin departure at low level, when it was rare for the crew to escape. The Phantom proved it could bite the unwary.

In a combat situation, the F-4 quickly lost its reputation for viceless handling, proving it needed to be treated with a great deal of respect. Before the war, the art of close-in dogfighting had

Above: A shortage of F-105s led to the conversion of surplus USAF F-4Cs for a new role – defense suppression. These so-called Wild Weasel F-4Cs led eventually to the F-4G.

Below: The USAF's F-4C was essentially little more than an F-4B, although a host of minor equipment changes justified the new designation.

Having begun its USAF career in the same gray and white colour scheme as the USN Phantom, USAF F-4s picked up warpaint during the involvement in Vietnam, as seen on this well-armed F-4D.

virtually been lost. Few fighters even carried a gun, and high *g* maneuvering was rarely practiced. Few pilots had therefore taken the F-4 into the corners of the envelope where it was likely to depart. Close-in dogfights with agile little Vietnamese MiG-17s and MiG-21s quickly changed all that. In such engagements, when pulling high *g*, or when at high angles of attack, it was all too easy to lose control of the F-4, especially if a centerline store was being carried (or worse still, if there was an asymmetric underwing load). Although the Phantom had an angle of attack limitation of 19.2 units of Alpha, well before this was reached the pilot had to ensure that the stick was kept centered, since the tiniest application of aileron would cause a vicious departure and spin.

The F-4 flight manual is succinct: "Loss of lateral roll control can occur at angles of attack well below [those at which you experience] . . . buffet and stall. Use of excessive lateral control [aileron] will produce adverse yaw. . . . Above 15 units angle of attack . . . attempts to roll the airplane with lateral stick deflections [aileron] will result in yaw opposite to the direction of the intended turn. This becomes more severe at high angles of attack. At very high angles of attack aileron inputs generate almost pure airplane yaw response. The natural tendency to raise the wing with aileron must be avoided. Aileron deflection at the point of departure from controlled flight will cause a rapid spin entry."

Roll had to be initiated using rudder in such circumstances, an unnatural process and easy to forget at the height of an engagement when watching the angle of attack meter might not be the top priority. In any case, using excessive rudder at high angles of attack caused its own problems. "Attempts to yaw the airplane with rudder will produce roll in the same direction as yaw. The use of rudder inputs to produce yaw and in turn generate roll will provide the highest attainable roll rates at high angles of attack. The rudder must be used judiciously, however, since excessive rudder inputs will induce excessive yaw."

Spinning the F-4, even at medium altitude, has always been regarded as a game for fools. With a height loss of well over 2,000 ft (600 m) per revolution, such a spin is effectively unrecoverable below 10,000 ft (3000 m). The flight manual puts it plainly: "Total altitude loss from the point of out-of-control to level-flight recovery can be as little as 10,000 ft, but will be more like 15,000 ft . . . If the AC [aircraft commander] considers that there is insufficient altitude for recovery, the crew should eject at the earliest possible moment." Spin recovery is difficult, even from a normal erect spin, since the aircraft will easily reverse into a spin in the opposite direction, if the recovery has not been perfect. From a flat spin the only chance

Right: Stripped of paint during a major overhaul, this F-4D has a patchwork appearance, showing clearly the different materials from which the aircraft was constructed.

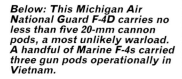

Below: This Michigan Air National Guard F-4D carries no less than five 20-mm cannon pods, a most unlikely warload. A handful of Marine F-4s carried three gun pods operationally in Vietnam.

The USAF's F-4E was tailored to that service's requirements for a multirole fighter, and for the first time incorporated a built-in cannon in a totally reconfigured nose. This aircraft carries a load of 'Daisy-Cutter' bombs with prominent fuse extenders.

Above: One of the newest service Phantom variants is the F-4EJ Kai, a Japanese upgrade which features new avionics, defensive systems and radar. These two are from the 306th Squadron.

Below: An F-4E of the Spangdahlem-based 52nd TFW demonstrates the awesome bomb load that could be carried by the Phantom. These F-4Es operated as the 'killer' half of Wild Weasel 'hunter/killer' pairs.

of survival is offered by ejection. And yet many Phantom pilots will not criticize the handling characteristics of their beloved F-4.

In his assessment written for *Flying Combat Aircraft* (Iowa State), the man with more F-4 hours than anyone else (over 4,000 by 1980), Major Alexander Harwick, declared, "The Phantom is an honest airplane that gives more than ample warning when it is being pushed too hard. When it is accelerated properly, the pilot feels both the seat belt across his lap and the seat cushion beneath him. A very mild rumble is felt in the seat when the aircraft is in an optimum turn, a turn that tends to conserve energy. In a maximum turn the aircraft gives a distinctive buffet. Beyond this rate of turn it goes into hard wing-rock before it lets go and chases its tail. All that is required to stop the fuss is to release back-pressure on the stick. To spin a Phantom takes an asymmetrical load, an out-of-trim aircraft, a bent airframe or a ham hand. Should one meet any of these conditions, one need only break the angle of attack by putting the stick forward and/or using the drag chute."

Harwick's comments referred mainly to the slick-winged F-4 versions. Of the slatted E model he enthused mainly on "the beautifully redesigned cockpit, made to be used by a fighter pilot to bring ordnance to bear on the enemy rather than by some human engineer who mans a mahogany bomber for a living. The slats were added to improve the turning performance. They do this,

but at the price of higher drag, with resulting high energy decay. Because the amount of energy available defines the options open to any pilot in an air-to-air engagement, it is imperative to manage energy extremely carefully in the slatted Phantom."

Today's fighters

There is little point in comparing the Phantom with fighters designed 20 or more years later. These later fighters have flight controls and even wing lift systems of a different order, and enjoy structure stressed for sustained 9*g*; lower wing loading, either by being lighter or by having a larger wing; advanced electronic flight-control computers, often with fly-by-wire linkages and always with sophisticated aileron/rudder interconnects; full-span leading-edge flaps (or, as proposed for McDonnell's own F-15XX, camber-changing slats); powerful control surfaces; and the ability to routinely reach AOA up to 90° and still aim guns accurately or fire missiles, and retain good engine response. Quite apart from these advances, not imagined as attainable in the mid-1950s when the Phantom II was designed, developments such as low-observable 'stealth' and supercruise capability (sustained supersonic flight without afterburner) have today relegated most F-4s to electronic warfare, reconnaissance and training missions, at least in major air forces. Tens of thousands of pilots all over the world learned their trade in the F-4, however, and have the highest regard for it. For them, as for a million enthusiasts, a maximum-performance F-4 takeoff will be an exciting event well into the next century.

In general, the airframe was wholly conventional, the ruling materials being high-strength fracture-tough aluminum alloys, assembled by precision bolts, screws, various rivets and

Left: The F-4G remains in front-line USAF service, and made an invaluable contribution to the Gulf War, clearing a path through hostile air defenses for packages of other coalition strike aircraft.

Below: Israel has refurbished and upgraded its F-4Es, adding new avionics but not the new engine once proposed. These aircraft have already seen extensive service, and look set to continue to fulfill a vital role in Israel's defense for years to come.

patented fasteners. The wing skins began as flattened slabs 2.5 in (6.4 cm) thick, subsequently machined in skin mills to leave integral stiffening. The front spar at 15 percent chord and the main spar at 40 percent were machined from single forgings, the space between them being sealed to form an integral tank in each wing. The space between the main and rear spars was occupied largely by the retracted main landing gear. Aft of the forged rear spar, four forged ribs carried the flaps and ailerons. Three complete ribs, at the centerline and wing folds, were also forgings.

Steel and titanium

Much of the structure, including leading edges, spoilers, flaps, ailerons and fixed trailing edges, were light alloy bonded honeycomb. The fuselage frames were forged and the skin mainly flush riveted, though the entire underskin aft of the engine nozzles was stainless steel (part welded) and titanium. The main keel structure was steel and titanium, and the area under the fuel tanks was double-skinned. To cool the fuselage bay housing the engine afterburners, air was rammed in at the base of the fin leading edge and discharged through left and right apertures under the stabilators. To facilitate the assembly of wiring and equipment, each fuselage was built as left and right halves, joined later at the centerline. The fin had multiple light alloy spars and sheet or honeycomb skin, the rudder being entirely honeycomb. Each stabilator had steel ribs and stringers, titanium skins and a trailing edge (aft of 60 percent chord) of steel honeycomb to withstand intense noise and high temperature.

Landing gear

Outstandingly tough, the tricycle landing gear was designed to hit the deck at a sink rate of 22 ft per sec (6.7 m/sec) at a weight of 33,000 lb (15000 kg). The three tricycle units each had a single leg, retracted hydraulically. The main units had plate brakes, initially with no antiskid system, and retracted inwards. The twin-wheel nose gear was hydraulically steerable and self-centering, pneumatically extended for catapult launches, and retracted rearwards. All wheels were automatically braked during the retraction cycle. A braking parachute was housed in a drum compartment in the extreme tail end of the fuselage.

Propulsion

A winner from the start, the General Electric J79 turbojet had only a single shaft (one turbine driving one compressor), but thanks to the use of multiple variable-incidence stator vanes it had a very high pressure ratio compared with rival engines. The stator vanes in front of the first seven stages of rotating blades in the J79 compressor

*Above: The Phantom has also been adapted to fulfill the tactical reconnaissance role. Recce Phantoms have a new camera nose, with a smaller radar, but **USAF RF-4Cs** retained a nuclear strike capability.*

*Left: The nose of the **RF-4C** incorporated three camera stations, with cleverly designed drop-down access hatches which also acted as camera mounts. This allowed film to be loaded and unloaded extremely rapidly.*

*Below: An **F-4D** with its radome open to show the entirely conventional antenna for its **AN/ APG-109A** radar. Also clearly visible are the huge variable intake ramps, which act as splitter plates, removing sluggish boundary layer air.*

were mounted on pivots and linked via external rings and levers to dual rams driven by engine fuel to rotate all the vanes to the best angle for each engine speed. Thus the J79 was able to compress the incoming air much more than engines with fixed stator vanes. This meant more power for a given weight and, in particular, reduced fuel consumption. The engines fitted to the F4H-1 prototype were essentially of the YJ79-GE-3 sub-type, weighing 3,680 lb (1670 kg) each and rated at 10,050 lb (45 kN) thrust dry (MIL) and 15,600 lb (70 kN) with maximum afterburner. The installation featured the only fully variable supersonic inlets actually built in the world at that time, apart from the prototype B-58. The outer edges were cut well back from top to bottom, with a fixed lip of very small radius. The inner wall was extended forward in the form of a large ramp, terminating at the front in a nearly vertical sharp lip some 2 in (5 cm) from the side of the fuselage to avoid ingesting turbulent boundary-layer air. In the absence of actual knowledge, MCAIR guessed that the ramp angle should be between 5 and 10°. Ideally the inlet was to have hinged inner walls driven in and out to vary throat area, but the first F4H-1 had simple fixed ramps, set at 5° for the first flight and later, briefly, at 4°. All subsequent aircraft had variable inlets. Fuel was housed in six flexible bladder-type cells in the fuselage, with a total capacity of 1,343 US gal (1,118 Imp gal; 5082 liters), and two integral wing-tanks adding a further 630 US gal (525 Imp gal; 2387 liters). Provision was made for three drop-tanks, 600 US gal (500 Imp gal; 2273 liters) on the centerline and 370 US gal (309 Imp gal; 1402 liters) in a McDonnell or (shorter and fatter) Sargent Fletcher drop-tank on each outboard wing pylon (Nos 1 and 9). The resulting total capacity of 3,315 US gal (2,760 Imp gal; 12547 liters) is even today exceptional for a fighter. The only remarkable feature of the fuel system is that no attempt was made to make the bladder-type fuselage cells self-sealing, and this dangerous design persisted until well into the production of the final sub type, the F-4E.

Systems

The fuel system was from the start designed for single-point pressure fueling only. A socket under the belly can refuel or defuel at a nominal rate of 252 US gal/min (210 Imp gal/min; 955 liters/min). The first aircraft had no provision for inflight refueling, but did include the three vents that were later often prominent: one at the aft end of each fixed wing outer (hinge) rib to serve the associated wing-tank and one projecting beyond the base of the rudder to serve the fuselage cells. Fuel collects in a tank under fuselage cell No. 2, from where individual pumps feed each engine. Of course, either engine can draw fuel from any tank. Engine lubricating oil was housed in a 5.2-US gal (4.3-Imp gal; 19.5-liter) tank strapped to each engine. High-pressure engine bleed air is used to blow the flaps and inboard droop leading edges, and also to drive the separate air-conditioning systems for the cockpits and avionics. The latter (few of which were in the No. 1 aircraft) were air-cooled except for the main radar. The three hydraulic systems were filled with Skydrol 500 and operated at 3,000 lb/sq in (20685 kPa). Two systems, one driven by a pump on the left engine and the other by the right, drive the ailerons, spoilers and stabilator – the surfaces essential for continued flight. Different pumps on both engines energize the utility (No. 3) system, for leading- and trailing-edge flaps, landing gear, airbrakes, rudder, nosewheel steering, wing fold and arrester hook. Each engine also was arranged

to drive a 20-kV alternator via a CSD (constant speed drive) to feed current at 200 V at a constant 400 Hz (cycles per second) for the avionics and other services. Transformer/rectifier units (TRUs) convert AC to DC at 28 V. An internal battery was not thought necessary, as the engines were started by high-pressure air from a pneumatic starter cart impinging on the turbine blades. The only emergency provision was an RAT (ram-air turbine) driving a hydraulic pump for the flight controls, providing full-control power at speeds above 130 kt (148 mph; 238 km/h).

Fuel capacity

There has been a great deal of muddled reportage on the internal fuel capacities of the various models of the Phantom. The integral

Right: The General Electric J79 turbojet, versions of which power all but the British Phantom variants. Like the basic Phantom airframe, this superb engine has been updated and upgraded to produce more thrust, better reliability, longer life, and even less smoke.

Below: F-4Ds on the line at St Louis, the Phantom's birthplace. Eventually 5,057 Phantoms were to roll off this production line, with further aircraft being constructed by Mitsubishi in Japan. Other factories, in the USA, Britain and Germany, built sub-componenets and sub-assemblies.

tanks in the wings of most versions have a combined capacity of 630 US gal (525 Imp gal; 2385 liters), and the external fuel usually comprises 600 US gal (500 Imp gal; 2273 liters) on the centerline and 741 US gal (617 Imp gal; 2805 liters) in two wing-tanks. The following are the capacities of the flexible cells in the fuselage: F-4B 1,357 US gal (1,130 Imp gal; 5137 liters), N model is similar; F-4C 1,343 US gal (1,118 Imp gal; 5082 liters); RF-4C to Block 40 1,260 US gal (1,049 Imp gal; 4769 liters), from Block 41 1142 US gal (951 Imp gal; 4323 liters); F-4D 1,260 US gal (1,049 Imp gal; 4769 liters); F-4E to Block 40 1,364 US gal (1,136 Imp gal; 5164 liters), from Block 41 1,225 US gal (1,020 Imp gal; 4637 liters); F-4G 1,226 US gal (1,021 Imp gal; 4641 liters); F-4J 1,347 US gal (1,122 Imp gal; 5101 liters), K, M and S models are similar.

Phantom
Variant by Variant

F3H-(C)

Not built

The first proposal which led to the Phantom was a single-engine 'Super Demon' of 1953, known in the design stages as F3H-(C). This was to have been an enlarged version of the F3H-2 Demon fighter then serving in the Fleet and was one of several American fighters of the era planned for the Wright J67-W-1, the American version of the Bristol Olympus. This powerplant did not materialize as a realistic choice for American aircraft.

Herman D. Barkey's engineering team, which in time produced the Phantom, saw the F3H-(C) as having almost exactly the same dimensions as the fighter they finally produced. Although purely a preliminary design, never ordered or built, the F3H-(C) is the first of several Demon variants which fully and properly deserve to be considered as the first versions of the Phantom.

F3H-(E)
(Model 98A)

Not built

The F3H-(E) was one of six studies dated 25 August 1953, each of which was a carrier-based, all-weather, single-seat attack fighter based on the Demon. It dispensed with the Demon's nose-high attitude, standing level on a normal tricycle undercarriage, albeit with an extendable nosewheel leg for catapult launches. It retained the Wright J67 turbojet (itself a license-built afterburning Bristol Olympus), and had a 45° swept wing of 450 sq ft (42 m²) and an internal fuel capacity of 1,703 US gal (1,418 Imp gal; 6446 liters).

F3H-G/H
(Model 98B)

Not built

The contemporary Model 98B was slightly larger than the F3H-(E), with a 530-sq ft (49-m²) wing and internal fuel capacity of 1,972 US gal (1,642 Imp gal; 7465 liters). It retained four internal 20-mm cannon, and was the last of the Phantom forerunners to be so armed. Multiple exchangeable nose sections were planned for the recce, fighter and two-seat interceptor roles. The aircraft was initially intended to be powered by a pair of Wright J65-W-4 engines (a license-built Armstrong Siddeley Saphire) and featured an Aero 11B fire-control system. Since the J65 was causing huge problems in the FJ-3 Fury, McDonnell engineers installed a mismatched pair of engines in the mock-up, with a J65 and an example of the new J79-2 engine intended for the B-58 Hustler. An AN/APQ-150 radar was proposed. McDonnell made an unsolicited proposal to the US Navy on 18 September 1953, but the F8U Crusader was selected instead.

AH-1

Not built

The AH-1 was closely based on the F3H-G and was designed to meet the US Navy's requirement for a multirole, next-generation fighter capable of meeting the latest MiG threat at all speeds and all altitudes. As originally designed, it retained twin engines, four internal cannon and 11 external hardpoints. On 18 November 1954, the US Navy issued a letter of intent for two prototypes and a static test airframe, but only a month later (on 14 December) the multirole nature of the aircraft was axed, and McDonnell were instructed to remove cannon and hardpoints (except for a centerline pylon for a 600-US gal/500-Imp gal/2270-liter fuel tank) and add troughs for four Raytheon Sparrow AAMs. A Raytheon-modified APQ-50 radar was also added. J79 engines were formally adopted on 15 April 1955, in a letter from the BuAer to the CNO. On 23 June 1955, the design was redesignated F4H-1, losing the attack designator for ever.

Right: The AH-1 design progressed from being a multirole fighter-bomber to being a missile-armed interceptor. The aircraft, shown in mock-up form, displayed evidence of its Demon parentage.

YF4H-1
(Model 98S)

First flight: 27 May 1958; St Louis
Pilot: Robert C. Little
Number built: two
Identities: 142259 and 142260

One day after the AH-1 was redesignated F4H-1, McDonnell issued a new model number for the aircraft, which became the Model 98Q. This was short-lived, since when a contract for 18 airframes (beginning with two flight test articles and a static test airframe) was signed on 24 June 1955, it was for the APQ-72-equipped Model 98R. The two models were then redesignated Model 98S, the changed designation indicating the provision of Sidewinder capability on the two rear stations, and the provision of two inboard wing pylons, which could each carry either a single Sparrow or two Sidewinder 1Bs or 1Cs.

The prototypes were powered by two J79-2 afterburning turbojets, and featured a 56 ft (17 m) long area-ruled fuselage. The outer wing panels were canted up by 12° and the stabilators had a 23° 15' anhedral. Unusually, the aircraft had no ailerons, with spoilers and downward flaperons only.

Having lost out to the original F8U Crusader in its original form, the as-yet unnamed Phantom was selected in preference to the advanced F8U-3 Crusader derivative.

The first aircraft had the rear cockpit filled with instrumentation. Painted glossy Navy gray and white, it had, in addition to normal service and warning markings, a bright red arrow stripe along the top of the fuselage on each side, 'F4H-1' in 26-in black letters on each side of the nose, and red and white barber pole stripes on the nose instrument boom which replaced the radar. Four dummy Sparrow missiles were carried in their ventral recesses. A single Stanley Aviation ejection seat was fitted, and other features included 5° inlet ramps, flush NACA-type inlets on the lower sides of the forward fuselage to feed ram air to the air-conditioning system and a complex pattern of large perforations on the spoilers. As already noted, Robert Little made the first flight at St Louis, on 27 May 1958. Soon after this, No. 142259 went to Edwards AFB, California, where it convincingly demonstrated its superiority over the first Vought F8U-3. It returned to St Louis in October 1958, continuing in various test programs until, on flight 296, on 21 October 1959, it suffered failure of the aft access door of the right engine, which led to successive further failures and the loss of both aircraft and pilot (Gerald 'Zeke' Huelsbeck).

The No. 2 aircraft, 142260, was completed with operable APQ-50 radar, fully equipped rear cockpit, variable inlet ramps set at 5° for the fixed portion and 10° for the variable panel downstream, and feeding J79-2 engines, which by 1958 had established MIL (maximum dry) and maximum (afterburner) thrust ratings of 10,350 and 16,500 lb (46 and 73.4 kN), respectively. Other features included imperforate spoilers; a ram-air turbine, which could be extended upward by a pneumatic ram from a compartment with

F4H-1 Prototype

Labels: Stanley ejection seat · Small radome for AN/APG-50 radar · Early streamlined rear cockpit · No seat in rear cockpit · High-intensity strobe light · Engine bay cool air inlet · Fuel dump pipe · Recessed NACA-style cooling scoop · Test instrumentation pitot – static probe · Dummy AIM-7 air-to-air missiles · Early cutback intakes and original fixed intake ramps · Hinged leading-edge flaps · Early-style arrester hook · General Electric J79-GE-3A turbojet engines twin doors above the left intake duct to drive an emergency hydraulic pump for the flight controls; an ASA-32 autopilot; and, from 1960, wiring for missiles. It was finished in Navy gray and white, with Dayglo red fin, outer wings and stabilator tips, and with upper-fuselage stripes terminating at the front in a second 'V', surrounding the inlet warning notice on each side of the nose.

The first flight was in October 1958. Aircraft 142260 was then retrofitted with Martin-Baker Mk H5 seats and set a world altitude record at 98,560 ft (30041 m) during Project Top Flight on 6 December 1959, flown by Commander L. E. Flint, Jr. It also set a world 15/25-km speed record at 1,606.342 mph (2585.086 km/h) in Operation Skyburner on 22 November 1961, flown by Lieutenant Colonel R. B. Robinson, USMC, fitted with crude PCC (pre-compressor cooling) water injection into the inlet ducts. This speed equated to about Mach 2.43. A major assignment of 142260 was to gain time on Dash-8 and 68A engines.

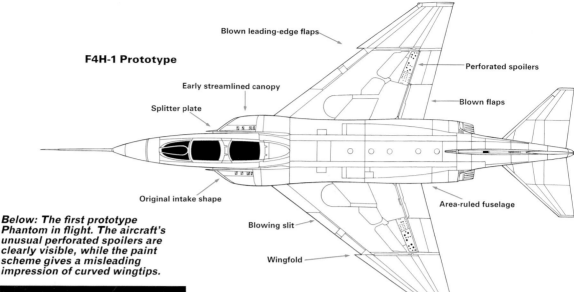

F4H-1 Prototype

Blown leading-edge flaps
Perforated spoilers
Early streamlined canopy
Blown flaps
Splitter plate
Original intake shape
Area-ruled fuselage
Blowing slit
Wingfold

Below: The first prototype Phantom in flight. The aircraft's unusual perforated spoilers are clearly visible, while the paint scheme gives a misleading impression of curved wingtips.

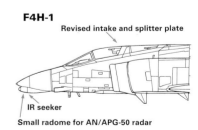

Above: Seen before its maiden flight, the first Phantom prototype had its rear cockpit filled with test instrumentation and its nose filled with ballast to compensate for the lack of radar.

F4H-1 (Later F4H-1F, then F-4A)
(Model 98AM)

First flight: not known
Pilot: not known
Number built: 45
Identities:
Block 1: 143388 to 143392 (5)
Block 2: 145307 to 145317 (11)
Block 3: 146817 to 146821 (5)
Block 4: 148252 to 148261 (10)
Block 5: 148262 to 148275 (14)

The next 45 Phantoms were built as F4H-1s, but inevitably the standard of build changed considerably during their manufacture. On 1 May 1961, the Navy decided to redesignate the first 47 aircraft (including the surviving prototype) as F4H-1Fs, the designation F4H-1 being continued for aircraft 48 onwards. On 18 September 1962, the survivors of these 47 aircraft were again redesignated as F-4As. Excluding the two prototypes they were built in five blocks.

Blocks 2 and 3 were regarded as preproduction and the remaining 24 as production aircraft. Hardly any two were identical, though the standard engine was the Dash-2 or -2A, fed by the definitive supersonic inlet. The latter had a much larger inner splitter plate, standing 3 in (7.5 cm) away from the wall of the fuselage, with 12,500 small perforations through which boundary-layer air was

sucked by aft-facing ejectors projecting above and below. The outer lip of the inlet was completely altered, and appeared straight from the side view, although it sloped forwards from bottom to top. The inner ramp walls were hinged and positioned by actuators according to airflow demand signals from a computer. After further tests the angle limits were fixed at 10° and 14°. The ram-air inlets to the liquid-refrigerant cooling for the avionics and cockpit on the lower sides of the forward fuselage, previously of the NACA flush type, were replaced by plain pitot inlets standing away from the fuselage skin, the increased pressure recovery being worth the extra drag. From Block 2 (145307) onward, the high-pressure blowing system along the wing leading edge and flaps was made operative, and it was retrofitted to two earlier aircraft. The radar was still the APQ-72, though initially still with the 24-in (61-cm) reflector. Attachments for five (and later nine) of the original 11 pylons were restored, with the inboard wing pylons equipped to carry and fire an extra Sparrow missile or two Sidewinders, one on each side.

Other changes included the provision of a Lear AJB-3/3A bombing system and a General Electric ASA-32 autopilot. As improvements were introduced on the production line, they were also retrofitted to some earlier aircraft, so that very early F4H-1s were seen with late standard

intakes (without the faired upper lip) and late standard splitter plates. The J79-GE-2A engine (with 1,000 lb st/44 kN more thrust) was often fitted to earlier aircraft.

An inflight-refueling probe was added on the right of the cockpit, normally flush and almost invisible, but it extended hydraulically, so that during contact the drogue was clearly visible about 4 ft (1.2 m) to the right of the windscreen. This required the elimination of the right console in the rear cockpit, and the controls from that panel were redistributed. Other additions included the 360° steering capability for the nose gear and AJB-3 and ASQ-19. These aircraft were not capable of reaching operational standard but carried out numerous test and development programs.

From Aircraft No. 19 (Block 3, BuNo. 146817) several major improvements were introduced, two of which were externally obvious. Crews had

F4H-1
Streamlined low-slung canopy
Original intake shape
Flush cooling inlet
Small radome for AN/APG-50 radar

F4H-1
Revised intake and splitter plate
IR seeker
Small radome for AN/APG-50 radar

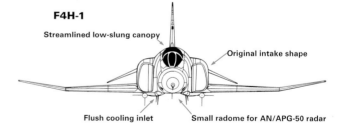

complained of poor field of view, and MCAIR responded by raising the seats (the front cockpit floor being repositioned 23 in/58 cm higher) and fitting new and more capacious canopies above the top line of the fuselage. The other obvious change was the 32-in (81-cm) antenna reflector fitted to the AN/APQ-72 radar, which demanded a much larger radome. A hydraulic drive was added to drive this scanner.

Phantom Variants: F4H-1 (F-4A)

The AN/APQ-72 radar incorporated an APA-157 illuminator to provide Sparrow compatibility. Under the radome the AAA-4, in a distinctive pod, was added; this had been fitted (or retrofitted) to F4H-1Fs from No. 5 onward. An invisible upgrade in several Block 5 aircraft was the Dash-8 engine, rated at 10,900 lb (48.45 kN) dry and 17,000 lb (75.65 kN) with maximum afterburner. The new inlets had been tailored to the higher airflow demanded by this more powerful engine, though even the first Phantom had a thrust/weight ratio that had never before been enjoyed by any fighter pilot (a figure of unity was quite attainable). The increased thrust more than offset the slight extra drag of the higher canopy. Despite the intrusion of the refueling probe installation, the rear cockpit was modified to permit subsequent installation of dual flight controls, although this was not required by the Navy.

On 3 July 1959, MCAIR celebrated its 20th anniversary. With the acquiescence of the Navy, it announced the name Phantom II as its latest and most important aircraft – its first successful design, the FH-1 Phantom, no longer being in service. It was soon common to omit the suffix II. Meanwhile, production of the Phantom continued, and the designation changed from F4H-1F to F4H-1 from aircraft No. 48 (Block 6). Under the 1962 designation scheme these aircraft were redesignated F-4B, and all previous Phantom II aircraft became F-4As. The F4H-1F/F-4A fleet, which in 1962 numbered 40 active aircraft, proved ideal testbeds in many trials and research programs at numerous Navy establishments. Aircraft from Block 3 onwards served in the East Coast and West Coast RAGs to train crews and perfect operational techniques. Only a handful of F-4As remain in existence, with 143388 (the third built) at the USMC museum and 148275 (the last) at the US Naval Academy.

Phantom No. 7 after the 100th F4H-1 flight. This aircraft has a tail-mounted anti-spin chute, and features the enlarged 'scoop-type' cooling inlet on the forward fuselage.

F4H-1F (F-4A) 19th aircraft onwards

Martin-Baker Mk H5 ejection seats
Window added
Retractable IFR probe on starboard side
High canopy line
Twin pitots on leading edge
Enlarged radome for AN/APQ-72 radar
Enlarged cooling inlet
Revised intakes
Enlarged intake ramps
General Electric J79-GE-2 or -2A turbojet engine (some aircraft re-engined with J79-GE-8)
AAA-4 IR sensor

Seen in side view, the early Phantoms looked very different to the aircraft we know today. The small nose radome, low rear canopy line and different engine intakes all disappeared during the production life of the F4H-1/F-4A.

Right: Phantom No. 6 is hoisted off the deck of the USS Independence. The flush NACA-type cooling intakes fitted to the first few Phantoms are clearly visible here. This view also gives an excellent impression of the original engine intakes.

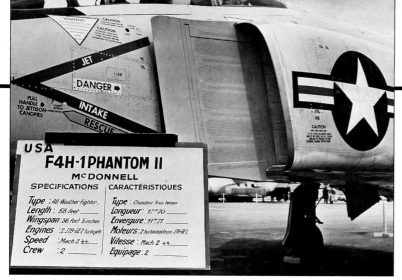

Above: Close-up view of the intake of aircraft No. 21 (145819), which visited the Paris air show. The splitter plate was to undergo one more major redesign, but this was the definitive shape of the intake.

145819 lands at Le Bourget for the type's first major overseas public engagement. The Phantom generated a storm of interest, though few nations could operate such a sophisticated fighter.

F4H-1 (later F-4B)
(Model 98AM)

First flight: 25 March 1961; St Louis
Pilot: Thomas Harris
Number built: 649
Identities:
Blocks 6-8: 148363 to 148434 (72)
Blocks 9-11: 149403 to 149474 (72)
Blocks 12-28: 150406 to 150493 (88)
150624 to 150653 (30)
150993 to 151021 (29)
151397 to 151519 (123)
152207 to 152331 (125)
152965 to 153070 (106)
153912 to 153915 (4)
153916 to 153950 (35-canceled)

The F4H-1 was the first definitive production version of the Phantom and was optimized for use as a fleet defense interceptor, while retaining some ground-to-air capability. To differentiate Block 6 F4H-1s from earlier aircraft, the latter were assigned the new F4H-1F designation. Fortunately, in 1962, the new designation system removed the confusion and early aircraft were redesignated F-4A, and Block 6 aircraft onward were redesignated F-4B. There was virtually no difference between Block 6 and late Block 5 aircraft. Officially, the F4H-1/F-4B was distinguished by having full operational equipment (AN/APQ-72 with a 32-in/81-cm dish and APA-157 illuminator, AJB-3 nuclear bombing system, AN/

ASA-32 AFCS and the full set of hardpoints) and by being powered by the same 17,900-lb st (80-kN) General Electric J79-GE-8A or -8B engines as the last five F-4As and tested on the second aircraft, 142260. The APR-30 was fitted to all F-4Bs (the first 18 by retrofit).

All aircraft were fitted with the Aero-27A centerline ejector rack, plumbed for a 600-US gal (500-Imp gal; 2273-liter) fuel tank, LAU-17A inboard pylons, wired for a Sparrow or two Sidewinders, and two MAU-12 outerwing pylons plumbed for 370-US gal (308-Imp gal; 1400-liter) fuel tanks.

In the air-to-ground role, the F-4B could carry a variety of ordnance, with a typical maximum bombload of around 16,000 lb (7250 kg). Depending on the mission and combat radius, the F-4B could carry up to eight 1,000-lb (450-kg) Mk 83 iron bombs, four AGM-12C Bullpup B AAMs, or 15 packs of 2.75-in (70-mm) FFAR (folding-fin aircraft rockets).

F-4Bs were delivered first to the RAG squadrons charged with training fleet aircrews. VF-121 'Pacemakers' at Miramar received its first Phantom on 30 June 1960 (an F4H-1F) and was operating the F4H-1 (F-4B) by early 1961. VF-101 'Grim Reapers' at Oceana followed. The first operational training squadron, as distinct from training unit, was VF-74 'Bedevilers' in the Atlantic Fleet. Its combat operational debut came on 6 August 1964, when F-4Bs from VF-142 'Ghostriders' and VF-143 'Pukin' Dogs'

Above: The only way of telling a very late F-4A from an F-4B was by its serial number. A few F-4As were used for training, but the F-4B was the first real service variant.

Below: An early F-4B of VF-74, the first fleet fighter squadron operational with the Phantom. Squadron markings got progressively more colorful.

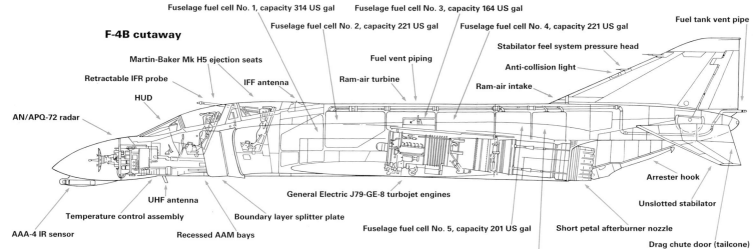

125

F-4B

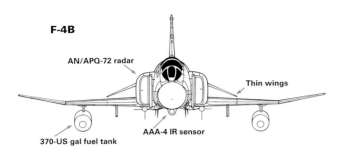

AN/APQ-72 radar

Thin wings

370-US gal fuel tank

AAA-4 IR sensor

Right: Typifying a 'late' F-4B, this VF-111 aircraft is fitted with various new antennas, including the distinctive APR-30 RHAW aerials on the tailfin. Shark mouth and sunburst rudder were typical of the US Navy's gaudy squadron markings.

aboard USS *Constellation* (CVA-64) provided cover to warplanes that struck North Vietnamese torpedo boat bases following the Gulf of Tonkin Incident. An F-4B scored the Navy's first MiG kill of the Vietnam War in 1965.

The 649 F-4Bs included one converted to F-4B, two to NF-4B, 228 to F-4N and 44 to QF-4B standards. In addition, two aircraft (149405 and 149406) were evaluated by the USAF, pending delivery of their own F-4C. Many F-4Bs were retrofitted with APR-30 RHAW gear, with one or both fin-top antennas, and some had the F-4J's slotted stabilator to cure 'Mach tuck'. The last F-4B in service was 152217, which was retired from VMFA-321 'Hell's Angels' at Andrews in January 1978. Two F-4Bs were modified on the production line to become YRF-4C prototypes.

F-4B (early configuration)

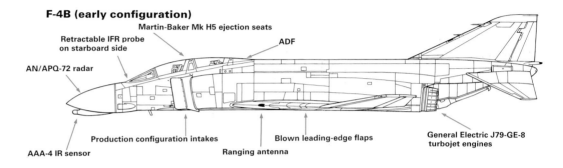

Retractable IFR probe on starboard side

Martin-Baker Mk H5 ejection seats

ADF

AN/APQ-72 radar

AAA-4 IR sensor

Production configuration intakes

Ranging antenna

Blown leading-edge flaps

General Electric J79-GE-8 turbojet engines

F-4B (late configuration)

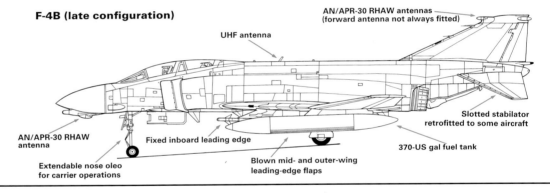

AN/APR-30 RHAW antennas (forward antenna not always fitted)

UHF antenna

AN/APR-30 RHAW antenna

Extendable nose oleo for carrier operations

Fixed inboard leading edge

Blown mid- and outer-wing leading-edge flaps

370-US gal fuel tank

Slotted stabilator retrofitted to some aircraft

EF-4B

First flight: unknown
Pilot: unknown
Number converted: one
Identity: 153070

In December 1976, the US Navy approved the EF-4B designation for F-4Bs then serving with VAQ-33 'Firebirds', who were supporting the US Navy's FEWSG (Fleet Electronic Warfare Support Group) at NAS Norfolk, Virginia. Five Phantoms served with VAQ-33 as high-speed targets and as threat simulators to train air defense radar operators and to test defensive systems. Three remained in service when the designation was approved, apparently one F-4B (BuNo. 153070) and two F-4Js, which were redesignated EF-4J. These aircraft were not extensively modified, but were equipped with some unique items of electrical equipment.

Above: The sole EF-4B was used as a high-speed electronic aggressor by VAQ-33. The aircraft was fitted with some unique equipment items and operated alongside two similarly modernized F-4Js.

NF-4B

First flight: not known
Pilot: not known
Number converted: two
Identities: not known

The NF-4B appellation was applied to two F-4Bs employed in test work at the NADC (Naval Air Development Center), Warminster, Pennsylvania, in the 1970s. The 'N' prefix indicates structural modifications which bar the aircraft from returning to full operational status.

QF-4B

First flight: not known
Pilot: not known
Number converted: 25
Identities: 148365, 148378, 148383, 148386, 148393, 148414, 148415, 148424, 148431, 149409, 149414, 149420, 149423, 149428, 149431, 149432, 149433, 149434, 149441, 149446, 149451, 149452, 149461, 149466, 149471

The increasing inadequacy of the Navy's existing target drones prompted a major program in 1970 to fund a completely new NAT (Navy Agile Target). In the meantime it was agreed to convert available examples of the subsonic F-86H Sabre and supersonic F-4B Phantom into remotely-piloted targets for use in testing anti-aircraft defense systems, including live firings by missiles. The F-4B program took much longer than expected. The first aircraft, F-4B 148365, was gutted at NADC, Warminster, beginning in mid-1970. No attempt was made to remove the carrier equipment, but the radar and all armament systems were stripped out, together with communications, navigation and autopilot boxes. In their place ballast was fitted in the nose to preserve center of gravity position, and a UHF command/control link added, with prominent blade antennas above and below the nose. Though the whole purpose of the exercise was to simulate a maneuvering target, the converted QF-4B was limited to 5g. From late 1971, the first conversion was subjected to prolonged testing in basic

remote-control research, using a DF-8L Crusader as director. This work then went on to include switching to/from the human safety pilot(s), air-combat maneuvering, air-to-air and surface-to-air weapon trials, air-to-surface missions and ECM-aided penetration of hostile airspace. A high-visibility Dayglo red paint scheme was adopted, with black upper surface walkways and black Modex 40 on the sides of the nose. This aircraft was

Still wearing the markings of its old unit, VMFAT-201, the prototype QF-4B makes a post-conversion test flight at the Naval Air Development Center at Warminster, Pennsylvania.

delivered to the NMC (Naval Missile Center) at Point Mugu, California, in April 1972, for further prolonged testing. Six further UHF conversions (148378, 148386, 149409, 149423, 149428 and 149466) were subsequently delivered to the NMC, and a further six were converted at the NARF (Naval Air Rework Facility), Cherry Point, North Carolina. These incorporated photographic and electronic scoring sensors, together with various ECM jammer and IRCM (IR countermeasure) payloads. Several were transferred to the Army at White Sands and other ranges for live testing of the Patriot SAM system. Altogether, 44 QF-4Bs were converted, with differing command, datalink and scoring systems, later conversions being of the QF-4N.

Above: Most QF-4B sorties are flown manned, chasing cheaper unmanned drones. Even a surplus F-4B represents a major investment after drone conversion.

QF-4B

Ballast in nose

UHF command/control link antennas

Radar, communication, navigation and autopilot equipment removed

Most QF-4Bs initially wore a garish and highly conspicuous overall Dayglo orange color scheme. This one also wears the badge of the Pacific Missile Test Center at Point Mugu, California.

RF-4B (known as F4H-1P before 1962)
(Model 98DH)

First flight: 12 March 1965; St Louis
Pilot: Irving S. Burrows
Number built: 46
Identities:
151975 to 151983 (9)
153089 to 153115 (27)
157342 to 157351 (10)

The RF-4B for the US Marine Corps actually emerged after the Air Force's RF-4C, and is externally similar in appearance. While the Navy considered that its carrierborne strategic and tactical reconnaissance needs were met by the

RA-5C and RF-8G, respectively, the Marines had an urgent need for a modern reconnaissance platform. Some sources suggest that the Navy was keen to obtain its own RF-4 variant, but was prevented from doing so by the plentiful supply of RF-8s. Authority was granted in February 1963 for the acquisition of a reconnaissance Phantom for the Marines based on the airframe of the F-4B, but with the recce nose of the RF-4C.

It was agreed at the July 1963 mock-up review that the rear cockpit should be configured for a reconnaissance systems operator, with no flight controls. As in the RF-4C, the LS-58A camera mount in the nose usually carries KS-56 and KS-87

cameras, although provision is made for the much larger KS-91 or KS-127A. Two ALE-29A/B chaff/flare dispensers were installed, one on each side above the rear fuselage. Major avionic items included APQ-99, ASN-48 with CAINS (Carrier Alignment INS), ARC-105, ASN-48 or -58, APQ-102A, AAA-4, APR-25/27 and ASW-25B. ALQ-126 was installed to obviate the need to carry external jammer pods, but ALR-17 (on the RF-4C) was omitted.

The final 12 aircraft (153114, 153115 and 157342 to 157351) were built with the wide wheels and 'thick' wing of the F-4J. The final three aircraft (157349 to 157351) were completed with the smoothly-rounded undernose bulge of the kind seen on many RF-4Cs; this reduced drag and turbulence and increased interior space. Surprisingly, on

these three aircraft the pilot no longer had control of the angle of a KS-87 camera at Station 2, which was fixed.

Deliveries were made to VMCJ-2 at Cherry Point, North Carolina, and VMCJ-3 at El Toro, California, both units providing aircraft for VMCJ-1 in Vietnam in 1966. In 1975, all surviving aircraft were combined in a single unit, VMFP-3, at El Toro, to provide dispersed detachments ashore and afloat. From 1978, all surviving aircraft underwent an SURE (Sensor Update and Refurbishment Effort) at NARF, North Island.

One kit was used for factory verification, and another 28 were used by North Island to upgrade the surviving aircraft. The upgrade included the provision of slotted stabilizers, AN/ASN-92 Carrier Alignment INS (replacing ASN-48), AN/ASW-25B datalink, AN/

Phantom Variants: RF-4B

APD-10B SLAR (replacing APQ-102A), AN/AAD-5 IR reconnaissance set (replacing AN/AAD-4) and AN/ALR-45 and -50 (in place of APR-25). Various external ECM fits were replaced by ALQ-126 or -126B, allowing the RF-4B to remain in front-line use until 10 August 1990.

Below: Seen at North Island in 1975, this RF-4B of VMCJ-3 was typical of the many which served the Marine Corps. In addition to their normal shore assignments, the aircraft were occasionally deployed on carriers.

Below right: The first of the last three RF-4Bs built wears the markings of VMCJ-2. This trio differed from other RF-4Bs by having a rounded undernose fairing, which improved aerodynamics and increased internal volume.

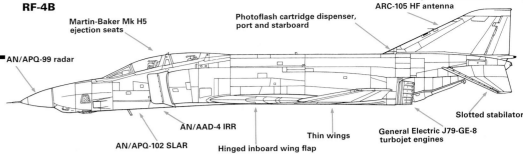

RF-4B

Martin-Baker Mk H5 ejection seats — AN/APQ-99 radar — Photoflash cartridge dispenser, port and starboard — Revised fin panel with built-in ARC-105 HF antenna — Slotted stabilator — General Electric J79-GE-8 turbojet engines — Thin wings — Hinged inboard wing flap — AN/AAD-4 IRR — AN/APQ-102 SLAR

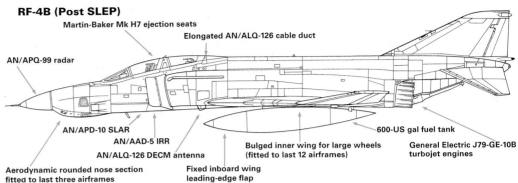

RF-4B (Post SLEP)

Martin-Baker Mk H7 ejection seats — Elongated AN/ALQ-126 cable duct — AN/APQ-99 radar — AN/APD-10 SLAR — AN/AAD-5 IRR — AN/ALQ-126 DECM antenna — Aerodynamic rounded nose section fitted to last three airframes — Fixed inboard wing leading-edge flap — Bulged inner wing for large wheels (fitted to last 12 airframes) — 600-US gal fuel tank — General Electric J79-GE-10B turbojet engines

F-110 (F-4C from 18 September 1962)
(Model 98DE/DJ)

First flight: 27 May 1963 (production F-4C); St Louis
Pilot: not known
Number built: 583
Identities:
62-12199 (1)
63-7407 to 63-7713 (307)
64-0654 to 64-0928 (275)
Plus 62-12168 to 62-12196 (29)
borrowed F-4Bs from US Navy

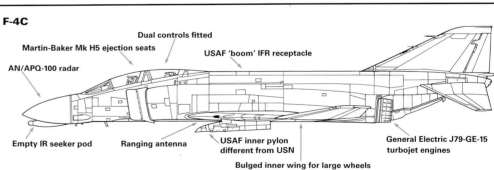

F-4C

Martin-Baker Mk H5 ejection seats — AN/APQ-100 radar — Dual controls fitted — USAF 'boom' IFR receptacle — Empty IR seeker pod — Ranging antenna — USAF inner pylon different from USN — Bulged inner wing for large wheels — General Electric J79-GE-15 turbojet engines

The adoption of the F-4 by the USAF was made inevitable by the dramatic results of Operation Highspeed, a flyoff between the US Navy's F-4B and the USAF's then best fighter, the F-106. The F-4 demonstrated 70 percent better maintenance man-hours per flying hour, and better speed, altitude, range and radar range, together with the ability to lug 22,500-lb (10206-kg) of bombs. Two US Navy F-4Bs were loaned to the USAF for 120 days for more serious evaluation, being painted in 'US Air Force' markings with a TAC badge on the fin and the designation F-110A on the nose.

The USAF's Specific Operational Requirement 200 requested an aircraft based on the F-4B, but with added ground attack capability and dual controls for a second pilot in the back seat. These

minimal changes each had to be justified. This standard had been agreed with MCAIR as the DE model on 13 November 1961. Folding wings, cat hooks and arrester hook were retained, and Dash-15 engines were specified, similar to the Navy Dash-8 but with self-contained cartridge starting. Martin-Baker Mk H7 seats were fitted, and the rear cockpit was to be equipped with full dual controls for a PSO (pilot systems operator). The high tire pressure of the F-4B was unacceptable for USAF operations, and the wheel/tire assembly was redesigned with lower pressure and the width increased from 7.7 in (19.5 cm) to 11.5 in (29 cm). In turn, this enabled a Hydro-Aire anti-skid braking system to be installed, considered by the Air Force to be essential even with an emergency hook. The larger wheels required shallow bulges in the upper and lower wing skins. The inflight-refueling probe was replaced

by a standard USAF retractable socket in the dorsal spine.

The backseat PSO had new consoles, a lowered panel for improved forward visibility, and a relocated radar tracking handle, attack switches and other refinements. To add enhanced ground attack potential, the AN/APQ-72 radar was modified to APQ-100 standard for ground mapping and came with a range strobe for manual bombing. The AN/AJB-3 nuclear bombing system was replaced by the newer AJB-7 all-altitude nuclear bombing system, for the release of atomic weapons on a timed basis from target or offset aimpoint in level and loft modes at various established angles. The Litton AN/ASN-48 (LN12A/B) inertial navigation system (INS) was later introduced to the F-4. Some F-4Cs were equipped with the SST-181X Combat Skyspot radar bombing system.

Other major equipment items included

ASN-39 (later -46), ASN-48 (later -92), ALR-17, APR-25/-26, APA-157, APN-141 (later -159), A24G, ASA-32A, ASQ-19 and ARW-77. Later in the aircraft's career the lack of an internal gun was compensated for by the adoption of a centerline SUU-16/A cannon pod.

Provision was made for all USAF tactical stores, including AGM-12 (GAM-83) Bullpup and the Mk 28 Special (i.e. nuclear) weapon. Other armament could include one or three SUU-16/A (later -23/A) pods, housing an M61A1 gun and 1,200 rounds of 20-mm ammunition.

In the first week of 1962, Tactical Air Command began serious evaluation of the two F4H-1s (14905 and 14906) borrowed for 120 days from the Navy. They were still officially F4H-1s but were painted with the designation F-110A, the intended USAF designation. Subsequently a further 27 F4H-1s were borrowed, the total (with the first two)

This is one of a pair of F4H-1s borrowed from the US Navy and assigned the F-110A designation. The serial was a contraction of the BuAer number (149405).

Following the evaluation of two F4H-1s, a further 27 were borrowed from the Navy, four being shown here. The aircraft were not fitted with boom receptacles.

being as follows: 62-12168, formerly 149405; 62-12169, formerly 149406; 62-12170, formerly 150480; 62-12171, formerly 150486; 62-12172, formerly 150493; 62-12173, formerly 150630; 62-12174, formerly 150634; 62-12175, formerly 150643; 62-12176, formerly 150649; 62-12177, formerly 150650; 62-12178, formerly 150652; 62-12179, formerly 150653; 62-12180, formerly 150994; 62-12181, formerly 150995; 62-12182, formerly 150997; 62-12183, formerly 150999; 62-12184, formerly 151000; 62-12185, formerly 151002; 62-12186, formerly 151003; 62-12187, formerly 151004; 62-12188, formerly 151006; 62-12189, formerly 151007; 62-12190, formerly 151009; 62-12191, formerly 151011; 62-12192, formerly

151014; 62-12193, formerly 151016; 62-12194, formerly 151017; 62-12195, formerly 151020; 62-12196, formerly 151021.

These aircraft were delivered mainly to the 4453rd CCTW (Combat Crew Training Wing) at MacDill AFB, Florida, and some (as F-4Cs) went to the 12th TFW, the first combat unit to be equipped with the F-4C. This was soon followed by the 15th TFW at the same base in 1964. The latter unit deployed its 45th TFS to Thailand, where two F-4C crews scored the USAF's first two MiG kills of the Vietnam War on 10 July 1965. In time, F-4Cs took over the bulk of heavy fighting in South and North Vietnam.

The F-4Cs were originally delivered in

An early F-4C in standard delivery scheme of gull gray and white, with 'FJ' buzz-code. USAF F-4Cs were designed for operation by two pilots, but this practice was phased out in the late 1960s.

the same gull gray and white color scheme as the US Navy's F-4B, although the involvement in Vietnam soon prompted a change to green and brown tactical camouflage. Humidity caused major serviceability problems in Vietnam, and the fix cost was $41,667 per aircraft.

The last F-4C rolled off the line on 4 May 1966 and, by 1969, the USAF had decided that its two-pilot policy was in error, and flight controls were removed from rear cockpits, the backseater becoming a Wizzo (weapon systems

The F-4C was heavily involved in the Vietnam fighting, this being a napalm-toting example of the 557th TFS, 12th TFW at Cam Ranh Bay. Such aircraft were used primarily for ground-pounding.

officer). The last F-4C was delivered in May 1966 and, the only F-4C export was of ex-USAF (mainly 81st TFW) aircraft, which were shipped to Spain in 1971-72. Refurbished by CASA and designated C.12s, they were used to provide two 18-aircraft squadrons, Nos 121 and 122, in Ala de Caza 12 at Torrejon. Each squadron also operated two ex-USAF RF-4Cs. The Phantoms were withdrawn from front-line use by 121/122 Squadron when re-equipment with the MCAIR EF-18A was complete in July 1990.

EF-4C

First flight: not known
Pilot: not known
Number converted: 36
Identities: 63-7423, 63-7433, 63-7437, 63-7440, 63-7443, 63-7447, 63-7452, 63-7459, 63-7462, 63-7467, 63-7470, 63-7474, 63-7478, 63-7481, 63-7508, 63-7512, 63-7513, 63-7565, 63-7567, 63-7568, 63-7574, 63-7594, 63-7596, 63-7607, 63-7615, 64-0675, 64-0741, 64-0757, 64-0781, 64-0787, 64-0790, 64-0791, 64-0815, 64-0840, 64-0844, 64-0847

On TDY deployment to Korat from its base at Kadena, this 67th TFS, 18th TFW Wild Weasel F-4C carries a pair of Shrike anti-radiation missiles. The date was 28 December 1972.

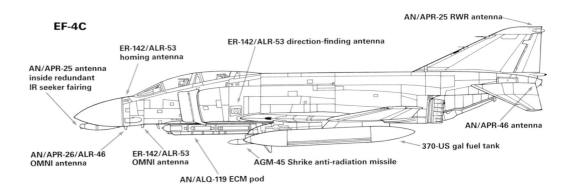

EF-4C

AN/APR-25 RWR antenna

ER-142/ALR-53 direction-finding antenna

ER-142/ALR-53 homing antenna

AN/APR-25 antenna inside redundant IR seeker fairing

AN/APR-26/ALR-46 OMNI antenna

ER-142/ALR-53 OMNI antenna

AN/ALQ-119 ECM pod

AGM-45 Shrike anti-radiation missile

AN/APR-46 antenna

370-US gal fuel tank

The EF-4C designation was an informal one applied to 36 F-4Cs which, in 1968, were temporarily converted into Wild Weasel IV defense suppression aircraft. It had always been appreciated that the original Weasel aircraft, the F-100F and F-105G, were mere stopgaps pending the development of a definitive aircraft, fully able to detect, locate and silence hostile air defense radars. The F-4 was the obvious aircraft to choose as a basis, but the F-4C conversion still suffered from significant deficiencies, some caused by the difficulty of running in additional cable looms. For example, the big AGM-78 Standard ARM could not be carried.

The modification included the provision of an AN/APR-25 RHAWS, with small spiral antennas on the empty AAA-4 pod and brake-chute door. An AN/APR-26 SAM launch warning system was also fitted. EF-4Cs also employed AN/ALQ-119 noise and deception ECM pods and were retrofitted in 1973 with the AN/ALR-46 receiver and AN/ALR-53 long-range homing receiver. For its mission of

neutralizing the Fan Song radars associated with Soviet-designed SA-2 missile batteries, the EF-4C carried AGM-45 Shrike ARMs, as well as conventional ordnance.

Deployment began in 1969 at Kadena

AB, Okinawa, with the 67th TFS, followed by the 52nd TFW's 81st TFS at Spangdahlem. Relocated to Thailand, the 67th TFS used its 'EF' aircraft on Linebacker raids. The main problem encountered was the unreliability of the

Shrike missile, which had to be preset before takeoff to hit a particular radio frequency. From 1973, surviving 'EFs' received ALR-46 and -53, and they were then returned to F-4C status for the ANG. (See F-4G, second entry.)

Taxiing at Kadena in October 1972, this EF-4C carries a training round for the Shrike missile. The Wild Weasel IV was slightly hampered by not being able to launch the AGM-78 Standard ARM.

Following their active-duty service, the EF-4Cs were largely handed over to the Guard for service as regular fighters. This machine flew with the Indiana ANG, but still sports its characteristic antenna fairings.

YRF-4C
(Model 98DF)

First flight: 8 August 1963; St Louis
Pilot: William S. Ross
Number built: two (converted on the line from F-4B)
Identities: 62-12200 and 62-12201

MCAIR had studied reconnaissance variants from the start of the Model 98 project, offering the 98F unarmed photographic version as early as 25 August 1953. Numerous variations followed, including the concept of a single aircraft with multiple quick-fit noses for different missions. Eventually the USAF Model 98AX (September 1958) and 98DF (January 1961) led to the definition of Specific Operational Requirement 196 (antedating that for the F-110A), approved on the last day of 1962. In parallel, MCAIR developed the Model 98DH for the Marines, as noted under the RF-4B entry. The two reconnaissance versions differed only in the previously permitted changes between the F4H-1 and F-110A.

The Air Force had an urgent need for an upgraded aircraft to replace the RB-66 variants and RF-84F, and the Phantom promised a quantum advance in speed, range, endurance, precision track and navigation and, above all, in sensor installations. Initial trials were carried out at Holloman AFB, New Mexico, in 1961 using sensor pods carried by F-4A No. 145310. The Air Force then purchased two F-4Bs already on the production line and had these completed as YRF-4Cs (AF 62-12200 and 12201).

Aerodynamically similar to the

production RF, with the length extended by the camera bays in the nose from 58 ft 3 in (17.75 m) to 62 ft 5 in (19 m), the first aircraft was flown by William S. 'Bill' Ross on 8 August 1963. Later, APQ-99, ASN-56 and ARC-105 were added, but not the reconnaissance sensors. Aircraft 62-12200 later served as the first YF-4E, testing the undernose gun installation, followed by the first tests of slatted wings in Project Agile Eagle (1969), FBW 'fly-by-wire' flight controls and other modifications in the PACT (Precision Aircraft Control Technology) program. It finally went to the USAF Museum. The second YRF-4C became a gate guardian at Chanute AFB, Illinois.

Exhibiting the redesigned nose, 62-12200 was the first of the reconnaissance Phantoms (the RF-4C preceded the RF-4B).

Above: A head-on view of the first YRF-4C highlights the window for the forward-facing camera. Other features are the alignment of the auxiliary intakes and the instrumentation boom for flight test.

RF-4C
(Model 98DF)

First flight: 18 May 1964; St Louis
Pilots: Jack Krings and B. A. McIntyre
Number built: 503
Identities:
63-7440 to 63-7463 (24)
64-0997 to 64-1085 (89)
65-0818 to 65-0945 (128)
66-0383 to 66-0478 (96)
67-0428 to 67-0469 (42)
68-0548 to 68-0611 (64)
69-0349 to 69-0384 (36)
71-0248 to 71-0259 (12)
72-0145 to 72-0156 (12)

The RF-4C was based on the airframe of the F-4C, although extra equipment reduced the internal fuel capacity. All offensive armament and provision for armament was removed, although an RF-4C was tested with 12 Mk 82 bombs, and all aircraft retained the capability of carrying a single nuclear weapon on the centerline (aircraft from the European-based 10th TRW were eventually fitted with AJB-7 LABS (low-altitude bombing system) gear for nuclear delivery). In connection with the SCAR (strike control and reconnaissance) role, 39 RF-4Cs were made compatible with AN/AVQ-26 Pave Tack to allow them to designate for smart weapons carried by other 'Fast Movers'. Under the SCAR concept, an RF-4C could lead attacking aircraft into the target area, acting as a 'Fast FAC'. In recent years RF-4Cs have also been armed with AIM-9 Sidewinder AAMs for self-defense.

The F-4Cs AN/APQ-72 radar was replaced by the much smaller Texas Instruments AN/APQ-99 for mapping, and terrain and collision avoidance. This was eventually replaced by the Texas Instruments APQ-172 in all surviving RF-4Cs with the USAF and ANG. Since it was intended for day and night photographic reconnaissance, the RF-4C is fitted with one or two pairs of photoflash ejectors on the upper rear fuselage, behind hydraulically-actuated doors. Up to and including aircraft 71-0259, pairs of ejectors were fitted on each side, one with 26 M112 photoflash cartridges (peak illumination 260 million candlepower), and one with 10 M123 cartridges. From 72-0145 a single LA-249A ejector was carried, with 20 M185 cartridges (peak illumination 1 billion candlepower). Immediately behind the radar, in Station 1 (the Forward Station), the RF-4C could carry a single forward oblique (23.5° or 43.5° depression) or vertical KS-87 camera with a 3-in (7.6-cm) or 6-in (15-cm) focal length lens.

Behind that, in Station 2 (the Low Altitude Station), a KA-56 low-altitude panoramic camera with a 3-in (7.6-cm) lens was usually carried, though this could be replaced by a trio of vertical, left and right oblique (37.6° depression) KS-87s with a 3-in (7.6-cm) or 6-in (15-cm) lens. Alternatively, a left or right oblique KS-87 could be carried with a 12-in (30-cm) or 18-in (46-cm) lens, with 5°, 15° or 30° depression. A vertical KA-1 with 24-in (61-cm) or 36-in (91-cm) lens could be carried instead, or a KS-72 with 6-in (15-cm) lens could replace a KS-87 in the 30° oblique position. An optical sight can be installed in the cockpit, showing the area being photographed by the oblique cameras, which is additional to the recce system viewfinder on the cockpit coaming, which views the ground forward of and below the aircraft. This has either a 30° or 60° field of view.

Immediately ahead of the cockpit is Station 3 (the High Altitude Station), which normally accommodates a single KA-55A or KA-91 high-altitude panoramic camera in a stabilized mount. Various mapping cameras were an alternative option, or the station could be used by two split vertical KS-87s with 6-in (15-cm) or 12-in (30-cm) lenses. This station was also used to house the AN/AVD-2 Laser Reconnaissance Set, which has now been withdrawn from use.

From aircraft 69-0375, the low altitude panoramic camera could be used in conjunction with an ejectable film cassette. This is ejected when the bomb button is actuated. The door is pneumatically actuated, then the film is cut and rewound. The cassette is sealed and ejected, deploying a parachute two seconds later. A transmitter is provided to aid cassette recovery. Without inflight film processing the panoramic camera can take 1,000 ft (305 m) of film, but

when such processing is available the non-ejectable cassette takes 500 ft (152 m) and the ejectable cassette 250 ft (76 m).

The RF-4C has employed a number of other cameras, including the giant General Dynamics HIAC-1 LOROP camera in a G-139 pod. The camera (originally developed for the Martin/General Dynamics RB-57F) gave an incredible stand-off capability, one photo showing every detail of

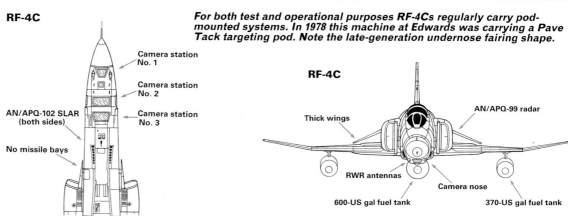

For both test and operational purposes RF-4Cs regularly carry pod-mounted systems. In 1978 this machine at Edwards was carrying a Pave Tack targeting pod. Note the late-generation undernose fairing shape.

RF-4C

Camera station No. 1
Camera station No. 2
AN/APQ-102 SLAR (both sides)
Camera station No. 3
No missile bays

RF-4C

Thick wings
AN/APQ-99 radar
RWR antennas
Camera nose
600-US gal fuel tank
370-US gal fuel tank

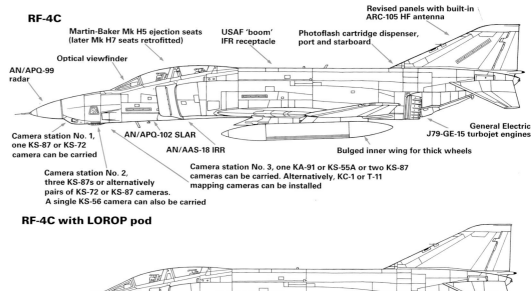

RF-4C

Martin-Baker Mk H5 ejection seats (later Mk H7 seats retrofitted)
USAF 'boom' IFR receptacle
Revised panels with built-in ARC-105 HF antenna
Photoflash cartridge dispenser, port and starboard
Optical viewfinder
AN/APQ-99 radar
Camera station No. 1, one KS-87 or KS-72 camera can be carried
AN/APQ-102 SLAR
AN/AAS-18 IRR
Camera station No. 2, three KS-87s or alternatively pairs of KS-72 or KS-87 cameras. A single KS-56 camera can also be carried
Camera station No. 3, one KA-91 or KS-55A or two KS-87 cameras can be carried. Alternatively, KC-1 or T-11 mapping cameras can be installed
General Electric J79-GE-15 turbojet engines
Bulged inner wing for thick wheels

RF-4C with LOROP pod

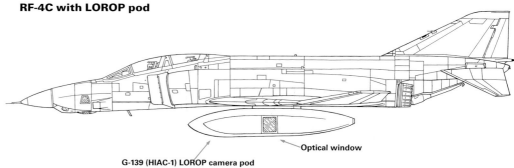

Optical window
G-139 (HIAC-1) LOROP camera pod

Dallas/Fort Worth International having been taken from 95 miles (153 km) away, at an altitude of 60,000 ft (18000 m) and a speed of Mach 1.8! The podded camera was originally tested on RF-4C 66-0419 of the 16th TRS, 363rd TRW, before attention switched to the RF-4X and F-4E(S) projects, described separately. Despite very high drag, the pod was adopted for operational use by the USAF when the PCC-equipped aircraft was canceled, and was used by Korean-based RF-4Cs (including ZZ/60-440) under the codename Operation Peace Eagle.

In 1977 tests of the Chicago Aerial Industries EWACS (Electronic Wide Angle Camera System) began, which gave 140° coverage with the image being stored on magnetic tape. The 60-lb (27-kg) unit took up only one cubic foot of space.

The RF-4C does not rely solely on optical sensors. The AN/AVD-2 laser reconnaissance set has already been mentioned, and RF-4Cs have been noted carrying a podded AN/UXD-1 laser recce pod. Other non-optical sensors include the AN/AAD-5 or AN/AAS-18 IR detecting set, installed just aft of the nose-wheel bay, and the AN/APQ-102 radar mapping set, which produces high-resolution radar mapping and can provide moving target indication, scanning a 20° sector below the flight path. This was later replaced by the AN/APD-10 on some aircraft, with a podded extended range antenna in a modified 600-US gal (500-Imp gal; 2271-liter) tank (the aircraft still contained 214 US gal/178 Imp gal/810 liters in its nose and tail!) and a UPD-8 datalink assembly replacing the No. 2 Station door. This had a steerable antenna which allowed radar 'pictures' to be transmitted to a ground station, and replaced the UPD-4 which had flush antennas on each side of the nose. Many of the aircraft so modified were converted by MBB at Manching. The AN/AVQ-9 IR detecting set and laser target designator has been used by some RF-4Cs to provide slant range for weapons aiming and high-resolution thermal imaging for navigation and terrain avoidance.

For electronic reconnaissance (plotting the position of hostile emitters), a handful of RF-4Cs were retrofitted with Litton Industries AN/ALQ-125 Terec (originally known as Pave Onyx), which is optimized for detecting, identifying and locating hostile AAA and SAM radars. The equipment is programmed to recognize 10 types of threat radar, and to continuously search for the five highest

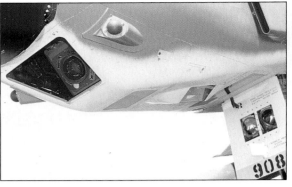

The original nose shape featured a flat underside, and an angled window projection for the High Altitude Station. The forward-facing camera is clearly visible.

An aerodynamic refinement applied to many RF-4Cs was a bulging to the camera housing, also allowing the carriage of larger cameras. The two antennas either side are for the radar warning receiver.

priority emitters. The returns were processed into a hostile electronic order of battle, which was displayed in the rear cockpit. Twenty-three kits were supplied, with six for each of three TAC squadrons and the rest for aircraft undergoing maintenance, etc.

Precise navigation is essential for any tactical reconnaissance aircraft, which may spend much of its time working 'alone, unarmed and unafraid'. In 1970, 20 aircraft were retrofitted with ARN-92 LORAN to give an all-weather blind navigation capability. The aircraft involved were all 18 Block 40 RF-4Cs (68-0594 to 68-0611) and two from Block 41 (69-0349 and 69-0350). These initially served with the 67th TRW's 12th and 91st TRSs. The Lear Siegler AN/ARN-101 Digital Modular Avionics System was added to all surviving RF-4Cs (beginning with USAFE's 1st and 17th TRSs) and the enhanced navigation accuracy this conferred allowed the adoption of the SCAR role. To give precise air-to-ground distance (to feed the velocity-to-height ratio to the camera controls) the radar altimeter used was the APN-203(V)2.

Warning systems included ALR-17, -31, -46, -50 or -126, navigation was by ASN-46A and 56, and the HF radio (ARC-105) required a giant shunt antenna recessed into both sides of the fin. Seventy-five RF-4Cs in USAFE were given ECM pods between 1969 and 1970, the work being undertaken at RAF Alconbury. Under an overlapping program between July 1968 and January 1969,

Dynalectron provided better emergency egress by modifying canopies and seats at Alconbury, Bentwaters, Hahn and Spangdahlem.

Initial plans called for the RF-4C to equip 14 TAC squadrons, with the first activated in 1965. The first production RF-4Cs went to the 33rd TRTS, a training squadron, at Shaw AFB, South Carolina, starting on 24 September 1964. The first operational RF-4C squadron, the 16th TRS at Shaw AFB, was deemed combat-ready in August 1965 and deployed to Tan Son Nhut, South Vietnam, in October 1965. The second squadron in combat with the RF-4C was the 15th TRS in

February 1967. In later years, the RF-4C became an important part of the ANG force. A small number of USAF and ANG RF-4Cs participated in Operation Desert Storm, and the RF-4C is expected to remain in service until at least 1995.

The RF-4C was in production longer than any variant except the F-4E, and the last RF-4C was delivered in December 1973. Two foreign users employed the RF-4C: Spain (six aircraft) which assigned the designation CR.12, and South Korea (18 aircraft). Two more were loaned to the Israeli air force under Project Night Light, pending delivery of Israel's own RF-4Es.

For night illumination of targets the RF-4C carries a photoflash cartridge. Seen on a 26th TRW machine are two launchers for the M112 cartridge, each with 26 rounds.

The ALQ-125 Terec equipment allowed the plotting of hostile radars. The antenna is shown here, occupying the Low Altitude Station.

RF-4C cutaway

Nose landing gear emergency air bottles

Optical viewfinder installation

AN/APQ-99 radar

Radar antenna

Pitot tube

AN/AAS-18 IRR

AN/APQ-102 SLAR

Camera station No. 3, one KA-91 high-altitude camera

Camera station No. 2, three KS-87 low-altitude vertical and starboard/oblique and starboard oblique cameras

RWR antenna, port and starboard

Camera station No. 1, one KS-87 forward/oblique camera

Martin-Baker Mk H7 ejection seats

Fuel vent piping

IFR receptacle

Fuselage fuel cell No. 1, capacity 231 US gal

Fuselage fuel cell No. 2, capacity 207 US gal

Fuselage fuel cell No. 3, capacity 184 US gal

Fuel tank vent pipe

ARC-105 HF radio antenna, recessed into both sides of fin
Upper pitot head deleted

Tail navigation light

Photoflash cartridge ejector, port and starboard

Fuselage fuel cell No. 4, capacity 221 US gal

Formation-keeping strip lights

General Electric J79-GE-15 turbojet engines

Fuselage fuel cell No. 5, capacity 201 US gal

Fuselage fuel cell No. 6, capacity 235 US gal

Arrester hook

Unslotted stabilator

Short petal afterburner nozzle

F-4D
(Model 98EN)

First flight: 9 December 1965; St Louis
Pilot: Raymond D. Hunt
Number built: 825
Identities:
64-0929 to 64-0980 (52)
65-0580 to 65-0801 (222)
66-0226 to 66-0283 (58)
66-7455 to 66-7774 (320)
66-8685 to 66-8825 (141)
67-14869 to 67-14884 (16) to Iran
68-6904 to 68-6919 (16) to Iran

Although externally almost identical to the F-4C which preceded it in USAF service, the F-4D was a very different aircraft under the skin. It was the first purpose-designed USAF Phantom variant, incorporating all the modifications the USAF really wanted. It was foreshadowed by a plethora of studies, some of which included manual terrain-following, TF30 turbofans, and even the nose-mounted gun, which later reappeared on the F-4E. These were considered too expensive and too ambitious. Authorized in March 1964, the F-4D marked the first Phantom variant optimized for air-to-ground operations.

Retaining the basic airframe and engines of the F-4C, the F-4D has the same internal fuel tankage as the RF-4C. The major differences concerned the avionics. The APQ-100 was replaced by the smaller, lighter, partly solid-state AN/APQ-109 as part of the AN/APA-65 radar set, which introduced an air-to-ground ranging mode using movable cursors.

Externally the nose appeared unchanged, except for the removal of the AAA-4 pod. The ASQ-19 miniaturized CNI (communication/navigation/identification) suite became standard, ASN-48 was replaced by ASN-63, AJB-7 was connected to ASQ-91 for delivery of LGBs and other 'smart' weapons, and, often as a retrofit, the backseater was given a TV display fed from the seeker of a HOBOS (homing bomb system), initially GBU-8 and later GBU-15. For unguided stores, the ASG-22 lead computing optical sight was fed from the A24G. In the course of Block 27, the IRST (IR search and track) pod under the radome was replaced, but not to house AAA-4; instead, it carried the forward pre-amplifier and antennas of the APR-25/26. Later, as a retrofit, this RHAW (radar warning and homing system) installation was replaced by APS-107A, with fin antennas, and ALR-69(V)2, with antennas in the chin pod. Externally-hung jammers included ALQ-87, ALQ-101 and ALQ-119. A multiple ejector rack (MER) was provided for the centerline pylon (originally intended for a fuel tank) and triple ejector racks (TERs) for the inboard underwing pylon.

Delivery of F-4Ds began in March 1966, initially to the 36th TFW at Bitburg, Germany, followed by the 4th TFW at Seymour Johnson AFB, North Carolina, in January 1967. The F-4D gradually began to replace the earlier F-4C in Vietnam from the spring of 1967, initially with Lieutenant Colonel Robin Olds' 8th TFW, the 'Wolfpack'. The first F-4D MiG kill was scored on 5 June 1967, when Major Everett T. Raspberry and Captain Francis Gullick shot down a MiG-17 near Hanoi. The F-4D eventually scored 45 air-to-air kills in Vietnam, more than any other aircraft type, and the USAF's three aces all scored their fifth kills in F-4Ds during the 1972 Linebacker campaign.

To supply the greater electrical power needed for the F-4D's larger number of automated (rather than manual) systems, the alternators were uprated to 30 kVA.

The F-4D retained the AIM-7 Sparrow capability of earlier Phantoms and introduced capability for the Hughes AIM-4D Falcon IR missile. Provision for AIM-9 Sidewinders was deleted initially, and then restored when the Falcon proved unsuccessful in air-to-air combat in Vietnam. The cylindrical Pave Spike laser designator pod for 'smart' bombs occupied one of the fuselage wells on many F-4Ds, thereby reducing the number of Sparrows by a quarter. The Pave Spike aircraft which had AGM-65 Maverick capability were 66-7509, 66-7531, 66-7547, 66-7634, 66-7661, 66-7722, 66-7746, 66-8819 and 66-8821.

The fatter, drooped Pave Knife laser designator pod could be fitted on an inboard pylon instead of Falcons/Sidewinders, as could the Westinghouse ALQ-101 combination noise and deception jamming pod, the General Electric ALQ-87 barrage noise jammer pod and other ECM items. Many of these items found their way onto the earlier F-4C, which had not been equipped for an ECM pod and had employed the QRC-160 pod on a jerry-rigged basis in the field.

Pave Knife aircraft were 66-7652, 66-

Another Reserve F-4D, this time from Tinker AFB. The 465th TFS sported the 'SH' tailcode, said to stand for the fighter pilot's favorite saying: 'Shit Hot'.

One of the principal improvements introduced by the F-4D was the solid-state APQ-109 radar. This enhanced air-to-ground capability and was lighter.

7674, 66-7675, 66-7679 to 66-7681, 66-7707, 66-7709, 66-7743, 66-7760, 66-7766 and 66-7773. Combat missions with Pave Knife began on 23 May 1968, initially in conjunction with the GBU-10/B, the 'smart' version of the Mk 84 bomb. On 10 May 1972, using Pave Knife to guide an M118 3,000-lb (1360-kg) bomb, an F-4D severed a span of the great Paul Doumer Bridge near Hanoi, which had survived hundreds of previous attacks.

Two F-4Ds, 66-8738 and 66-8812,

Right: Close-up detail of an F-4D's undernose pod reveals the antennas for the ALR-69(V)2 radar warning system.

Many F-4Ds ended their days with Reserve units, this example flying with the 301st TFW of the Air Force Reserve. It wears an experimental disruptive camouflage which was not adopted fleet-wide.

F-4D

AN/APS-107A RHAW antenna
AN/ARN-92 LORAN (not fitted to all aircraft)
Martin-Baker Mk H7 ejection seats
IFF antenna
AN/APG-109A radar
RHAW sensors
Ranging antenna
General Electric J79-GE-15B turbojet engines
AN/ALR-69(V)2 RHAW
Blown leading-edge flaps
Formation-keeping strip lights
Mk 82 500-lb Snakeye bombs

133

were fitted with Pave Sword (AVQ-11), another precision attack sensor, while 66-8700 received Pave Fire. AVQ-9, the laser designator, was fitted to 65-0597, 65-0609, 65-0612, 65-0642, 65-0677, 65-0705, 65-0786, 66-8814, 66-8815, 66-8817 and 66-8823. This installation was tested on F-4C 63-7407. The F-4D also introduced the associated 'smart' weapons to actual warfare, as well as the improved SUU-23/A gun pod.

Under Pave Phantom, from late 1967, 72 aircraft from Blocks 32 and 33 were equipped with ARN-92, with 'towel rail' antenna. These were 66-8708 to 66-8714, 66-8719, 66-8722, 66-8726 to 66-8728, 66-8730 to 66-8735, 66-8737 to 66-8739, 66-8741 to 66-8745, 66-8747 to 66-8750, 66-8755, 66-8756, 66-8758, 66-8759, 66-8761, 66-8762, 66-8765, 66-

Devoid of paint apart from safety markings and unit fin-stripe, this F-4D graphically displays the paneled construction. Also obvious are the locations of the LVF strip lights for low-light formation-keeping.

8768 to 66-8770, 66-8772, 66-8774, 66-8776, 66-8777, 66-8779, 66-8782, 66-8784 to 66-8799, 66-8802, 66-8803, 66-8805, 66-8806, 66-8810, 66-8812, 66-8816, 66-8818 and 66-8825. This LORAN navaid, together with a precision intervalometer, was required for precision navigation at night, principally for seeding ADSID (Air-Dropped Seismic Intruder Device) and other Igloo White sensors for detecting activity on the Ho Chi Minh

trail. These relatively cheap and expendable sensors were dropped in showers, some detecting noise and others vibration, even that caused by pedestrians. The chief operators of 'towel rail' F-4Ds in Southeast Asia were the 25th and 497th TFSs of Robin Olds' 8th TFW and the 555th TFS of the 432nd TFW. Subsequently, these aircraft were passed onto the 457th TFS, 301st TFW; 23rd TFS, 52nd TFW; and 704th TFS, 924th TFG (AFRES).

A further F-4D modification, codenamed Combat Tree, in 1968-69 permitted retention of a full missile load while carrying ECM gear, and added a location for an ECM pod on the inboard pylon, which now carried two more AIM-9J Sidewinders on each side. An aft-facing combat camera could only be carried at the expense of a Sparrow. Two F-4Ds were field-converted in Vietnam under the Pave Arrow program, in which a Sidewinder IR heat seeker was mounted on a fixed pod for locating heat sources from ground targets.

Aircraft 66-7635 and 66-7647 were stripped of weapons and tested at Edwards AFB, California, as the interim Improved Wild Weasel IV with upgraded APS-107. A few D models served in the Wild Weasel role (see EF-4D entry).

Of the 793 F-4Ds which reached the USAF, 18 were immediately (1968) transferred to the RoK (South Korean) AF, under Operation Peace Spectator, followed in 1969 by a further 18, all from early Blocks 24 to 26, the second batch

having been previously used by the USAF's 3rd TFW. These were transferred to the RoKAF in return for the transfer of F-5s to Vietnam under Operation Enhance Plus. At least 59 surplus F-4Ds have been transferred to Korea.

In the RoKAF, the F-4Ds were properly maintained and proved a great success, leading to subsequent orders for two batches of F-4Es. A few F-4Ds still fly from Taegu AB, Korea. A second customer was the Shah's kingdom of Iran, which placed its own orders for new aircraft: these were supplied as Blocks 35, 36, 37 and 39. The Imperial Iranian Air Force aircraft incorporated numerous minor improvements, mostly introduced to the USAF aircraft in the F-4E, but they lacked AJB-7 and all nuclear capability. They were numbered 3-601 to 3-632, and they initially equipped 306 Squadron. After the Islamic revolution, the force was increasingly cannibalized, and all surviving D models have been used to help keep 45 (of 177) F-4Es flying. By 1992, all F-4Ds had been withdrawn from the fighter interceptor groups of the Air National Guard.

One Block 28 aircraft, 65-0713, was retained by MCAIR for test programs, and on one occasion flew with a rudder made of boron fiber composite and had the nose completely rebuilt to serve as one of the prototype YF-4Es (see YF-4E entry). After 1971, surviving D models were invariably retrofitted with low-voltage formation strip lights on the fin, fuselage sides and nose.

EF-4D

First flight: not known
Pilot: not known
Number converted: four
Identities: 65-0657, 65-0660, 66-7635, 66-7647

The EF-4D designation was applied to four aircraft impressed as prototypes for the Wild Weasel (Wild Weasel IV/V) program. Two (65-0657 and 65-0660) were retrofitted with AN/ANS-107 RHAWS and a target acquisition system for the AGM-78 Standard ARM. Two others served as testbeds for the AN/APS-38 warning and attack system.

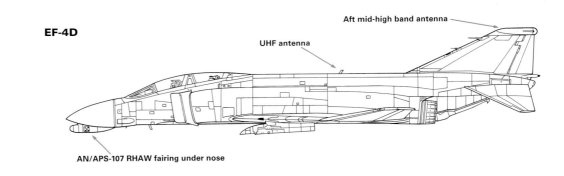

EF-4D

Aft mid-high band antenna
UHF antenna
AN/APS-107 RHAW fairing under nose

YF-4E
(Model 98HN/HO)

First flight: 7 August 1965; St Louis (62-12200)
Pilots: Joe Dobronski and Ed Rosenmyer
Number converted: three
Identities: 62-12200 (former YRF-4C), 63-7445 (former F-4C), 65-0713 (former F-4D)

The original F3H-E was designed around four internal 20-mm cannon, but by the time the F-4 reached hardware stage, Naval philosophy had changed and the aircraft emerged as a 'Missileer'; the gun was widely regarded as an outdated anachronism with no place aboard a modern fighter. The Air Force was slower than it might have been in adopting the Phantom, with many officers resenting what they saw as political interference and unreasonable pressure to accept a Navy fighter in the interests of commonality. However, once the F-4C entered squadron service, the Phantom was quickly embraced, and the Air Force started to pressure for a variant optimized for their own needs. The first step along this road was the F-4D, which proved to

YF-4E 62-12200

Martin-Baker Mk H7 ejection seats
Gun bay scavenge inlet
UHF antenna
TACAN antenna
AN/APG-30 radar
Fixed inboard wing flap
Early M61A1 20-mm cannon fitted in RF-4C nose
Blown mid- and outer-wing leading-edge flaps
Unslotted stabilator
General Electric J79-GE-J1B turbojet engines
Unslotted 'thin' wing

be an interim aircraft, while Air Force generals drooled over proposals of Phantoms with TF30 turbofans, Phantoms with swing wings and Phantoms with internal cannon. Combat deployment of the F-4C and F-4D in Southeast Asia from 1965 and May 1967, respectively, revealed shortcomings in these variants and in the very concept of the gunless fighter, and reinforced Air Force desires for a new variant.

In Vietnam, all air-to-air missiles proved expensive, unreliable, vulnerable to countermeasures and rendered almost unnecessary by the ROE, which

demanded visual acquisition. Radar-guided weapons also placed the launch aircraft in a position of unnecessary vulnerability. As an interim step, the AIM-9 Sidewinder replaced the useless AIM-4, and podded 20-mm cannon were carried on the centerline. The latter proved relatively inaccurate, however, and used up a valuable ordnance/fuel station.

An initial F-4 variant with internal M61 cannon was proposed to the Air Force in March 1961, but was met with little success. Further work on cannon-armed F-4s continued, and proposals for F-4s with cannon packs in a Sparrow recess

(which gave better rigidity and accuracy than a pylon-mounted pod) and for F-4s with nose-mounted guns were drawn up. Both were sensible and practical, but premature.

The gun-armed F-4E TSF (tactical strike fighter) was finally funded in June 1965, and it was decided to use the YRF-4C (originally built as a Navy F-4B) as a testbed. The aircraft had lost its forward Sparrow recesses, but retained early 'thin' wingroots, and was quickly modified to be able to carry a six-barrelled General Electric M61A1 rotary cannon in what had been its recce nose, with an

After having served as the aerodynamic prototype for the RF-4C, hard-working 62-12200 was reworked with a cannon installation in the reconnaissance equipment area.

The second YF-4E (seen here with target towing equipment) was the first to feature the definitive cannon installation. No radar was fitted, although the new radome shape was carried.

F-105 barrel stabilizer. An AN/APG-30 radar was installed, along with a lead computing gunsight cannibalized from an Air National Guard F-100D. Flight test instrumentation was carried in a centerline pod.

After only 50 flights the aircraft, by then redesignated YF-4E, was re-engined with J79-GE-J1B engines (these being the prototypes of the J79-10 and J79-17 series). The success of the initial flight test program led to an Air Force commitment to proceed with the new variant, and it was decided to modify two

more F-4s to F-4E standards, this time with the definitive nose-mounted cannon installation. The second YF-4E had the gun and no radar, but the third YF-4E had both gun and radar. Both aircraft were initially powered by J79-GE-J1B engines, but were later re-engined with the definitive J79-GE-17, which required new mounts and additional titanium sheeting in the engine bays to accommodate the increased temperatures. The third YF-4E later flew with a boron rudder and the prototype TISEO pod.

The smooth progress of the F-4E

belied the tremendous difficulties inherent in the project. Lack of space meant that a new ammunition feed system had to be designed, and this task was complicated by the fact that the system had to be capable of continuing to fire even when dud, missing or fired rounds were in the feed system. The proximity of the radar to the gun demanded extremely effective vibration damping and noise/blast elimination. The McDonnell engineers successfully solved the problems.

Development of the proposed

Coherent On Receive Doppler Subsystem (CORDS), a component of the Hughes Airborne Missile Control Subsystem (AMCS) progressed much less smoothly. Designed to offer better detection of low-flying targets, CORDS had been test flown in February 1965, and was intended to be fitted to the 35th and subsequent F-4Es. It quickly proved so unreliable that the target slipped to the 120th F-4E before the system was canceled.

F-4E
(Model 98HO)

First flight: 30 June 1967 (66-0284)
Pilots: R. D. Hunt and Wayne Wight
Number built: 1,389
Identities:
Blocks 31-33 (part): 66-0284 to 66-0382 (99); 35 later to Egypt
Blocks 33 (remainder)-36: 67-0208 to 67-0398 (91); 26 later to Turkey
Blocks 37-41: 68-0303 to 68-0547 (245); many for Israel
Blocks 42-43 (part): 69-0236 to 69-0307 (72); many to Israel, last four loaned to RAAF
Blocks 43 (remainder)-44 (part): 69-7201 to 69-7273 (73); 20 loaned to RAAF
Blocks 44 (part): 69-7286 to 69-7303 (18)
Blocks 44 (remainder)-45: 69-7546 to 69-7589 (44); some to Israel (see F-4ES entry)
Block 45; see F-4EJ entry
Blocks 46-47: 69-7711 to 69-7742 (32); to Iran
Block 48: 71-0224 to 71-0247 (24)
Block 49: 71-1070 to 71-1093 (24)
Blocks 51-56: 71-1094 to 71-1166 (73); to Iran
Block 50: 71-1391 to 71-1402 (12)
Blocks 51-53 (repeated): 71-1779 to 71-1796 (18); to Israel
Blocks 50-51 (repeated, part): 72-0121 to 72-0144 (24)
Blocks 51 (remainder)-53 (part): 72-0157 to 72-0168 (12)
Block 52: see F-4F entry
Block 53 (remainder): 72-1407 (1)
Blocks 54-56 (repeated, part): 72-1476 to 72-1499 (24)
Blocks 54-56 (part): 72-1500 to 72-1535 (36); to Greece
Blocks 56 (remainder)-58: 73-1016 to 73-1055 (40); to Turkey
Blocks 57 (part)-59 (part): 73-1157 to 73-1204 (48)
Blocks 57-59 (completed): 73-1519 to 73-1554 (36); to Iran
Blocks 60-61: 74-0643 to 74-0666' (24)

Blocks 60 (repeated)-62: 74-1014 to 74-1037 (24); to Israel
Blocks 60-61 (repeated): 74-1038 to 74-1061 (24)
Block 60 (completed): 74-1618 to 74-1619 (2); to Greece
Blocks 61-62; 74-1620 to 74-1653 (34)
Block 63 (part): 75-0222 to 75-0257 (36); to Iran
Block 63 (remainder): 75-0268 to 75-0637 (10); to Luftwaffe
Block 64 (part): 75-0638 to 75-0655, renumbered 77-1743 to 77-1760 (18); to Greece
Block 64 (remainder): 76-0493 to 76-0511 (19); to South Korea
Blocks 65-66: 77-0277 to 77-0308 (32); to Turkey
Block 67: 78-0727 to 78-0744 (18); to South Korea

The production version of the F-4E was originally to have been designated F-4E Plus, the 'Plus' standing for 'Plus gun', but this designation was dropped. Operational experience in Vietnam, which had underlined the need for an internal gun, also dictated some of the equipment carried by the new variant. The AN/APS-107A proved unreliable, and its replacement, the AN/APS-107B (experimentally installed on the first F-4E), was little better. The first 67 aircraft were thus delivered with no RHAW gear at all, although they were retrofitted with AN/APR-36/-37 by Applied Technology Industries at Lincoln, Nebraska. AN/APR-36 and -37 have now been superseded by AN/ALR-46. The first 26 aircraft (some sources say 30) were delivered without the AN/APQ-120 radar (which was the replacement for the canceled CORDS), although this was soon retrofitted.

By comparison with previous variants, the gun-armed F-4E introduced a seventh fuel tank, and one of the two fin-mounted pitots (the upper) was relocated to the nose. The emergency ram-air turbine was deleted, together with the powered wing-folding mechanism: these two changes

Above: 66-0285 was the first true representative F-4E, and was used for spin trials. The cameras, markings and huge chute fairing were connected with this.

F-4E

Early gun blast diffuser, as fitted to 66-0284 in June 1967

alone saved a substantial amount of weight. The Sky Spot radar beacon was incorporated, allowing the F-4E to blind bomb from above cloud without a Sky Spot-equipped B-66 or A-3.

The second production F-4E, 66-0285, introduced the long 'turkey-feather' afterburner and a slotted stabilator, and was flown for the first time on 11 September 1967. The slotted stabilator was added to give greater tailplane authority, counteracting the increased

A McDonnell test-ship launching from St Louis highlights the early gun blast deflector configuration.

weight in the nose imposed by the cannon installation. The slotted stabilator was a direct result of work carried out on the F-4J development program. As the first fully aerodynamic representative F-4E, 66-0285 was earmarked for spin testing, and featured a test camera on the spine, an enormous drag/spin chute fairing added to the tailcone and prominent red and white camera tracking marks on the wingtips. The third aircraft, 66-0286, was delivered to TAC at Nellis AFB, Nevada, on 2 October 1967 for service testing and training.

The F-4E was produced in greater numbers than any other Phantom (even discounting the similar F-4F for Germany and Japan's F-4EJ), and major improvements and changes were added throughout the production run. At Block 39 a stall-warning system was added. The first aircraft in Block 40, 68-0452, introduced an APU under the stabilator, which was needed to replace the emergency ram-air turbine which, together with the powered wing-fold, had been deleted to save weight. One of the major changes concerned the fuselage fuel cells. Tank Nos 1 to 6 were unchanged, while cell No. 7 added a further 104 US gal (87 Imp gal; 394 liters). The fact that aircraft could be lost by not having self-sealing tanks was finally realized at Block 41, where the omission was rectified. This reduced fuselage fuel capacity from 1,364 to 1,225 US gal (1,136 to 1,020 Imp gal; 5164 to 4636 liters), less than any previous fighter version (while most published descriptions assumed that fuel capacity was greater).

Another important series of upgrades concerned the RHAW system. The first production blocks of the F-4E retained the APS-107, but at Block 42 this was replaced by the APR-36/37. This was a more comprehensive set, served by four flat, circular, spiral receiver antennas, one on each side of the extreme tail end of the fuselage, facing aft, and one on the front of each wingtip, facing ahead. At Block 54, high-performance antennas and coaxial cables were fitted, and at Block 56, the system was replaced by ALR-46. This was virtually a digital edition of -36/37, but with the addition of a DSA-20 processor. As well as covering all threats from 2-18 GHz, the processor can be reprogrammed on the flightline to respond to any new threat. It provides the expected visual and aural cues in the cockpit, and can also control jamming assets directly. At about the same time, all aircraft were wired for two jammer pods (which increasingly were ALQ-131), and fitted with an AN/APX-80 IFF transponder and an optional removable strike camera in one of the Sparrow bays (usually left, front).

Further major changes were introduced at 71-0237, in Block 48. The main wingbox was given thicker lower skins, the steel reinforcing strap previously required being deleted. ASX-1 TISEO was fitted to the left leading edge and the ailerons were arranged to droop at low speeds (with gear extended) by 16.5° (see F-4J). Perhaps surprisingly, ASN-63, ASQ-91 and ASN-46A were deleted, though the ASG-26 (LCOSS) was improved, and to make it easier to read the various weapon-control switches and displays, these were all relocated at top center, close to the sight.

The most significant change at 71-0237 was to replace the blown leading-edge droops by powerful slats. The provision of leading-edge slats to enhance the Phantom's combat maneuverability had first been considered as early as 1958, but a suitable slat was not designed and tunnel tested for another 10 years. Serious consideration of slats began in 1969, with the Agile Eagle project, which was originally intended to enhance F-15 agility. When it became apparent that the

F-15 did not need slats, the F-4 became the beneficiary of the project. The first YF-4E was the first Agile Eagle F-4, and was fitted with fixed inboard and outboard slats. To provide a comparison, YF-4J 151497 was flown with outer wing slats only.

It was found that the addition of slats delayed the onset of prestall buffet by some 3 to 5 units of α and maneuvering performance was much improved. However, longitudinal stability was degraded, as was performance in level flight, and more work was clearly

needed. The outer slats-only configuration improved longitudinal stability, but high α lateral stability was degraded. In October 1970, stronger inboard and outboard slats were fitted to a bailed Israeli F-4E (68-0544) and the slat envelope was expanded to 30 units α,

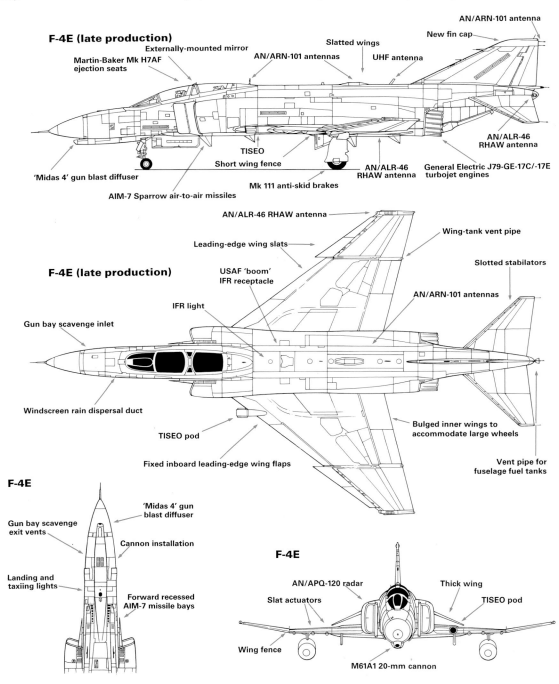

F-4E
- AN/APS-107 RHAW antenna
- USAF 'boom' IFR receptacle
- Formation-keeping strip lights
- Martin-Baker Mk H7 ejection seats
- Ram-air turbine not fitted
- IFF antenna
- TACAN antenna
- Gun bay scavenge inlet
- AN/APQ-120 radar
- Slotted stabilator
- General Electric J79-GE-17 turbojet engines
- Ranging antenna
- M61A1 20-mm cannon
- Blown mid- and outer-wing leading-edge flaps
- Automatic wingfold mechanism removed
- Early gun blast diffuser
- Bulged inner wing for large wheels

F-4E (late production)
- AN/ARN-101 antenna
- New fin cap
- Externally-mounted mirror
- Slatted wings
- Martin-Baker Mk H7AF ejection seats
- AN/ARN-101 antennas
- UHF antenna
- AN/ALR-46 RHAW antenna
- TISEO
- Short wing fence
- AN/ALR-46 RHAW antenna
- General Electric J79-GE-17C/-17E turbojet engines
- 'Midas 4' gun blast diffuser
- Mk 111 anti-skid brakes
- AIM-7 Sparrow air-to-air missiles

F-4E (late production)
- AN/ALR-46 RHAW antenna
- Wing-tank vent pipe
- Leading-edge wing slats
- Slotted stabilators
- USAF 'boom' IFR receptacle
- AN/ARN-101 antennas
- IFR light
- Gun bay scavenge inlet
- Windscreen rain dispersal duct
- Bulged inner wings to accommodate large wheels
- TISEO pod
- Fixed inboard leading-edge wing flaps
- Vent pipe for fuselage fuel tanks

F-4E
- 'Midas 4' gun blast diffuser
- Gun bay scavenge exit vents
- Cannon installation
- Landing and taxiing lights
- Forward recessed AIM-7 missile bays

F-4E
- AN/APQ-120 radar
- Thick wing
- Slat actuators
- TISEO pod
- Wing fence
- M61A1 20-mm cannon

750 kt or Mach 2, and from −1*g* to + 8.6*g*. This aircraft was flown in actual combat, and Israeli pilots' enthusiasm for the modification convinced the USAF to continue the evaluation.

Under Agile Eagle I 10 different slat configurations were tested, and efforts were made to find a compromise solution which would be aerodynamically efficient, possible to actuate without using actuators of excessive drag and did not use more hydraulic power than was available. Eventually the McDonnell engineers were successful and under Agile Eagle II the fourth F-4E, 66-0287, was used to validate the slat modification kit. Aircraft 71-0237, the 756th production F-4E, was the first with slats fitted as built, and many earlier aircraft were retrofitted. 71-0237 was not the first production aircraft to fly with slats, as it was grounded by a fuel leak, and was beaten into the air by the next aircraft, 71-0238, which made its maiden flight on 11 February 1972.

The Air Force ordered its first slat modification kits in April 1972, and the first retrofit was completed at the Ogden Air Logistics Center at Hill AFB, Utah. 69-7524 made its first flight with slats on 28 September 1972. Three hundred and four early USAF F-4Es were eventually retrofitted with slats, comprising virtually all those aircraft used by the 'Thunderbirds' team. The modification included the addition of a reinforcing strap to the underside of the wing center section, replacement of the outer wing panels and provision of a wingtip antenna for AN/ALR-46.

The slats were a tremendous achievement. Too thin for normal lever-mounted retracting slats, the Agile Eagles had tested fixed slats, or simple hinging devices, before the production configuration was worked out. In this the outer panels were developed with exceedingly powerful 'maneuver slats' driven by a hydraulic jack on the main space and terminating in a large dogtooth at the inboard end, whether open or closed. Immediately downstream of the dogtooth was a small fence. The inboard wing was likewise fitted with a powered slat carried on parallel links and was driven by a hydraulic jack under the slat itself, ahead of the front spar. This slat terminated 3 ft (91 cm) from the root, the innermost leading edge remaining fixed. It was said that if two F-4Es both began a maximum-rate turn at medium height at Mach 0.9, the slatted aircraft would

complete a 180° turn in 14 seconds, and the unslatted aircraft would then be 0.4 nm behind and 0.2 nm outside the turn radius of the slatted aircraft.

Further improvements, from Blocks 53 or 56 and beyond, were the Mk III anti-skid brake system, a gunsight camera, Maverick capability and the Dash-17C or E engine, with low-smoke combustor and low- or high-energy ignition. Perhaps at least as important was a redesign of the gun installation. Midas, one of several modifications studied by the DoD Batelle Institute, eventually cured what proved to be a major problem. The M61A1 six-barreled gun is of modest calibre (20 mm), but because of its firing rate of up to 6,000 rpm its muzzle horsepower is colossal, much higher than the F-4's main engines. The sheer power of the muzzle blast and the volume of highly explosive (when mixed with air) gun gas meant that careful attention had to be paid to the installation design. In addition, the gun had to function reliably, powered by the aircraft hydraulics but fired electrically, even when the gun was fed with live rounds, missing rounds or even previously fired rounds. General Electric achieved this objective, with at least 630 of the available rounds usable.

With the original muzzle design the F-4E experienced flameout problems, and a loud whistle, which could be heard before an approaching aircraft. Several different muzzle configurations were tested before Midas 4 added a long blast diffuser on each of the six barrels, joined to the barrel by a stripper diffuser, which both ejects most gas sideways and also decelerates and cools the blast. To blast fresh air through the gun compartments, a ram inlet was fitted above the forward fuselage, which opened during gun firing

and for 30 seconds after. Another division of General Electric then produced the T-4 reset, a 'derichment system' triggered by the gun-firing circuit which enabled either engine to dump gas-enriched air overboard before it entered the compressor. These modifications were incorporated from Block 48, and retrofitted to existing inventory aircraft. Production continued to Block 67.

Further modifications added during production of the F-4E included the provision of low-voltage formation-keeping lights, and a host of navigation and other avionics systems. Two aircraft from the Missouri ANG (68-0345 and 68-0351) received a new wraparound windscreen of polycarbonate/acrylic sandwich, which offered both an enhanced view and better birdstrike protection. Jointly developed by McDonnell and Goodyear Aerospace, the windscreens were fitted in 1985 for a one-year evaluation at the behest of the Air Force Flight Dynamics Laboratory. They proved remarkably successful but funding was not forthcoming, so, apart from a handful of RF-4Cs, only the St Louis-based Guard aircraft used for the evaluation ever received the modification.

When the USAF's formation display team, the 'Thunderbirds', re-equipped with the F-4E, it received modified early F-4Es. These aircraft were among the few not to be retrofitted with slats. The aircraft were stripped to bare metal (all previous 'Thunderbirds' types having flown in polished bare metal finish), but the Phantom's patchwork appearance forced the adoption of a white gloss base color for the red, white and blue team markings. The gun and APQ-120 were removed and replaced by storage for tools, chocks, covers, baggage, starter

From Block 48 production, the Midas 4 update revised the contours of the gun, adding a blast diffuser to each barrel and a distinct projection forward under the radome. This was retrofitted to existing aircraft.

cartridges, spare drag chutes and ballast. Gun vents were faired over, and a strip navigation antenna was provided, along with glidescope and VHF. Engine modifications allowed afterburner to be selected at 89 percent power. Four Sparrow shapes were permanently fitted, serving as oil (forward) and dye (aft) tanks. Perhaps the most unusual modification was the replacement of the kick-in entry steps. The originals were hinged at the top, the replacements at the bottom. This prevented the spring-loaded covers from scuffing the highly polished boots of pilots and groundcrew!

The F-4E was widely exported, with Germany and Japan taking their own sub-variants, and other operators taking stock F-4Es with very few changes. Israel, as always, was an exception. Its F-4Es were delivered in stock USAF configuration, but have since undergone many unique modifications. Many early aircraft have been retrofitted with slats and TISEO, while others have received modifications to give compatibility with the AGM-78 Standard ARM. Israel has always been keen on EW equipment, perhaps because during the 1973 Yom Kippur War Israeli aircraft were defenseless against the CW-guided 9M9 (NATO SA-6) SAM, and 43 F-4s were written off. This both spurred hasty development of CW countermeasures and also resulted in the urgent transfer of 118 F-4Es from USAF stocks (see subsequent entry on Israel for serials). Israel's own answer was the

F-4E cutaway

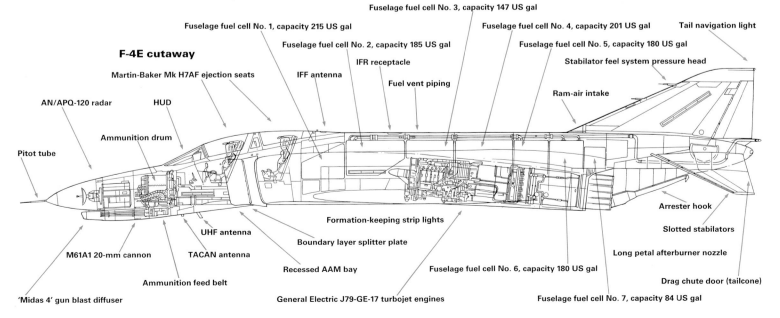

Fuselage fuel cell No. 3, capacity 147 US gal
Fuselage fuel cell No. 1, capacity 215 US gal
Fuselage fuel cell No. 2, capacity 185 US gal
Fuselage fuel cell No. 4, capacity 201 US gal
Fuselage fuel cell No. 5, capacity 180 US gal
Tail navigation light
IFR receptacle
IFF antenna
Stabilator feel system pressure head
Martin-Baker Mk H7AF ejection seats
Fuel vent piping
Ram-air intake
AN/APQ-120 radar
HUD
Ammunition drum
Pitot tube
Formation-keeping strip lights
Arrester hook
UHF antenna
Boundary layer splitter plate
Slotted stabilators
M61A1 20-mm cannon
TACAN antenna
Recessed AAM bay
Long petal afterburner nozzle
Ammunition feed belt
Fuselage fuel cell No. 6, capacity 180 US gal
Drag chute door (tailcone)
'Midas 4' gun blast diffuser
General Electric J79-GE-17 turbojet engines
Fuselage fuel cell No. 7, capacity 84 US gal

Elta EL/L-8202 jammer. Elta also produced the EL/M-2021 radar and an advanced HUD. Other updates fitted in Israel include a crude fixed inflight-refueling probe, with an external pipe leading to the front of No. 3 tank, and LW-33 INS. New weapons tested or adopted include twin 30-mm DEFA 554 guns, and Shafrir, Python, Luz and Gabriel missiles. Prototypes have been flown of three FLIR sensors, a 14.5-in (37-cm) pod on the TISEO fairing, a 16.5-in (42-cm) pod under the left front Sparrow bay and a 20-in (51-cm) turret replacing the M61 gun. See also F-4ES.

Excluding the F-4EJ, 1,387 F-4Es were built, of which 993 were for the USAF, 394 were delivered new to foreign customers, 24 were taken from store and loaned, and 191 were passed on to foreign customers from USAF stocks.

The Target Identification Sensor – Electro Optical (TISEO) fairing was located on the inboard leading edge of the port wing of later production F-4Es, including many export aircraft.

In foreign hands, the F-4E remains a vital front-line airplane, especially with Israel. This one carries indigenous antiship missiles.

Appropriately enough, among the last F-4Es in USAF service were these operated by the Missouri ANG at St Louis, birthplace and spiritual home of the Phantom.

A frameless, wraparound windscreen was experimentally fitted to a number of Phantoms, including at least three Missouri F-4Es and an unknown number of RF-4Cs.

F-4 Agile Eagle

First flight: not known
Pilot: not known
Number converted: not known
Identities: not known

The first studies for a maneuverability-enhancing slat system began in 1958, but proceeded slowly. Such slats were built and tunnel tested until 1968, and then only as an offshoot of the Agile Eagle program designed to enhance the turn performance of the F-15 Eagle. Studies soon showed that the F-15 would not need slats, but there would be advantages if they were fitted to the F-4. The YF-4E (previously YRF-4C) prototype, 62-12200, was used to establish baseline performance parameters without slats, and was then flown with fixed slats. These improved turn performance and high Alpha handling. The YF-4J, 151497, was flown with outboard slats only, but this configuration proved unsatisfactory, with poor directional stability at high angles of attack. Both configurations imposed unacceptable speed (500 kt; 570 mph; 917 km/h; or Mach 1.2) and *g* (5.2) limitations, and McDonnell fitted a new set of stronger slats cleared to 750 kt (855 mph; 1376 km/h) and 8.6*g* to an Israeli F-4.

Under Agile Eagle I the first F-4E, 66-0284, flew with 10 different fixed slat configurations during the summer of 1971, and explored methods of actuation which would not increase drag when retracted and which would not require too much hydraulic power. The eventual production configuration contained 150 joints and the most complex machinings ever attempted by McDonnell. Under Agile Eagle II, which lasted from August 1971 to March 1972, the fourth F-4E, 66-0287, was used to validate the

production slat modification kit, while the 756th F-4E, 71-0237, became the first F-4 built with slats.

Above: The YRF-4C in flight with fixed leading-edge slats during the Agile Eagle project, originally intended to enhance the agility of the new F-15. Several different slat configurations were flown, and many more were tunnel tested.

Below: A rear view of 62-12200 with one of the full-span slat configurations tested.

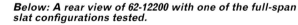

Below: When it became clear that the F-15 did not need slats, they were applied to the F-4E.

F-4E(F)
(Model 98MZ)

Not built

The F-4E(F) was designed for the Luftwaffe, who originally specified a stripped, lightened, simplified and, above all, low-cost Phantom when they ordered the aircraft. Derived from the single-seat IFX contender, the F-4E(F) had modified slats but was otherwise externally similar to the F-4E.

A retouched picture of an Israeli F-4E on a predelivery test flight, with rear cockpit faired over, gives an impression of what the F-4E(F) might have looked like.

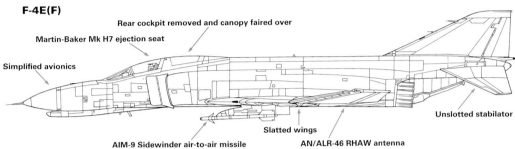

F-4E(F)

Rear cockpit removed and canopy faired over

Martin-Baker Mk H7 ejection seat

Simplified avionics

AIM-9 Sidewinder air-to-air missile

Slatted wings

AN/ALR-46 RHAW antenna

Unslotted stabilator

F-4EJ
(Model 98)

First flight: 14 January 1971; St Louis (17-8301)
Pilots: not known
Number built: 140
Identities:
17-8301 to 17-8302 (2); built by MCAIR
27-8303 to 27-8306 (4); manufactured by MCAIR but
27-8305 and 27-8306 assembled by Mitsubishi
37-8307 to 37-8323 (17); 37-8307 to 37-8313 manufactured by MCAIR and assembled by Mitsubishi; remainder by Mitsubishi
47-8324 to 47-8352 (29); from here all by Mitsubishi; 47-8324 to 47-8331 renumbered with prefix 37
57-8353 to 57-8376 (24)
67-8377 to 67-8391 (15)
77-8392 to 77-8403 (12)
87-8404 to 87-8415 (12)
97-8416 to 97-8427 (12)
07-8428 to 07-8436 (9)
17-8437 to 17-8440 (4)

The F-4EJ is the Japanese version of the F-4E, optimized for the fighter interceptor role. The F-4EJ dispenses with the AN/AJB-7 bombing system and provision for air-to-ground conventional and nuclear weapons.

In the Nihon Koku Jietai (Japan Air Self-Defense Force), six interceptor squadrons (or *hikotai*) have operated the F-4EJ, in addition to the JASDF Air Proving Wing at Gifu AB. Two of these squadrons have since converted to the F-15J/DJ Eagle. The F-4EJ differs from the F-4E in the deletion of the bombing computer and substitution of non-slatted wings and stabilators. Because of the defensive role required by Japan's constitution, these aircraft were delivered without air-refueling capability, although the hardware needed for air refueling was purchased and stored. Subsequently, the standard F-4E boom receptacle was added for training with USAF KC-135s.

Like the F-4E, the Japanese interceptor has the Westinghouse AN/APQ-120 solid-state radar fire-control system, 20-mm M61A1 Vulcan cannon with 640 rounds, and AIM-7/9 missile capability, but many of the simpler avionic items, including the CNI suite, were Japanese. A datalink system, gun camera and Japanese-designed RHAW were added to the F-4EJ.

Above: The prototype F-4EJ was entirely US built, as was the second. Later aircraft were assembled by Mitsubishi, who eventually manufactured the type under license.

In Japanese serial numbers, the first digit is the final digit of the year of delivery (37-8316 having been delivered in 1973) using the Western calendar, and the second digit identifies the aircraft type, 7 having been assigned to the Phantom.

The JASDF received 140 F-4EJ Phantoms, including four assembled by McDonnell in St Louis, 13 delivered by the American manufacturer in the form of knockdown kits assembled by Mitsubishi in Nagoya (two of which were not assembled), and the remaining 125 aircraft manufactured by Japan. The first aircraft, 17-8301, was built by MCAIR and flew at St Louis on 14 January 1971; MCAIR also flew 17-8302, 27-8303 and 27-8304. MCAIR also manufactured 27-8305, 27-8306 and 37-8307 to 37-8313 for assembly by the licensee Mitsubishi at Nagoya-Komaki. The next two, 37-8314 and 37-8315, were delivered as forward-fuselage trial kits (and not assigned MCAIR construction numbers) and were built into complete aircraft in Japan.

Aircraft 17-8440, delivered on 20 May 1981, was the last Phantom built. Throughout the 1980s the force of 140 F-4EJs gradually dwindled and has reached 125 in 1992. Since July 1984 a major SLEP (Service Life Extension Program) has been converting surviving aircraft to F-4EJ Kai standard.

Japanese Phantom squadrons tend to provide their own target facilities, so the sight of an F-4EJ in target tug configuration is relatively common. This one wears the markings of 305th Hikotai.

Above: Part camouflage, part special scheme, this 306th Hikotai Phantom's livery includes the unit's insignia.

Below: Japanese Phantom units have decorated their F-4EJs with special color schemes at the drop of a hat.

EF-4EJ

First flight: unknown
Pilot: unknown
Number built: unknown
Identities: include 37-8316, 47-8339, 47-8341, 87-8359

The (possibly informal) designation EF-4EJ was applied to a small number of F-4EJs in the Japanese aviation press during the early 1980s. The aircraft seemed to carry a modified centreline fuel tank, with dielectric antennas in the nose and a pair of AN/ALQ-6 ECM pods underwing. They were reportedly used to provide jamming support for friendly fighters, perhaps only during exercises.

The aircraft noted flew with several different squadrons.

F-4EJ Kai
(Model 98)

First flight (after conversion): 17 July 1984; Komaki (07-8431)
Pilot: not known
Number to be converted: 96
Known identities: 37-8313, 37-8314, 37-8315, 37-8321, 37-8322, 37-8323, 47-8324, 47-8328, 47-8329, 47-8330, 47-8331, 47-8332, 47-8334, 47-8342, 47-8345, 47-8346, 47-8348, 47-8369, 57-8335, 57-8357, 67-8378, 67-8379, 67-8388, 67-8390, 77-8394, 77-8398, 77-8402, 77-8404, 87-8407, 87-8414, 97-8423, 97-8425, 97-8426, 97-8427, 07-8428, 07-8431, 07-8434, 17-8436, 17-8437, 17-8440

The F-4EJ Kai Phantom is the result of a long-discussed and ambitious SLEP to bring Japan's fighter interceptor up to standard for the 1990s. This modernization effort began in July 1984 with the first flight of a 'partial' F-4EJ Kai (the suffix Kai means 'extra' or 'augmented'). The first operational F-4EJ Kai was delivered on 24 November 1990 to the JASDF's 6th Air Wing at Komatsu.

Intended to extend individual airframe lives from 3,000 to 5,000 hours, the F-4EJ Kai program has the provision of lookdown capability with Westinghouse AN/APG-66J pulse-Doppler radar as its key component. Although this is much smaller and lighter than APQ-120, it has generally higher performance and more operating modes, with better lookdown, shootdown capability. Externally, the installation of the new radar can be detected by the presence of a new radome, which incorporates tiny fore and aft strengthening strips.

Also included among 47 new items aboard the upgraded Phantom are a new central computer, Kaiser HUD, Hazeltine AN/APZ-79A IFF system and license-built Litton LN-39 INS. Other external changes include the provision of twin RWR antenna fairings for the new J/APR-6 (or J/APR-4 Kai?) RHAWS on the trailing edge of the fintip and on the wingtips, and a new, much taller UHF blade antenna on the spine. Like the last USAF F-4Es in service, the aircraft also often carry an F-15 fuel tank, which is stressed to higher *g* loadings than the original F-4 unit. The same tank has also started to make an appearance on 'ordinary' F-4EJs. The F-4EJ Kai will be capable of launching AIM-7E/F Sparrow, AIM-9L/P Sidewinder and Mitsubishi ASM-1 antiship missiles, as well as the AN/ALQ-131 ECM pods. Plans to fit slatted wings (which many in the JASDF wanted on the original F-4EJ) were ruled out because of cost.

Of 125 surviving Japanese F-4EJs, only 96 are planned to be upgraded to F-4EJ Kai standard, rather than the initial proposal of 110. Seventeen of the remaining 29 will be adapted for the reconnaissance role under the designation RF-4EJ Kai and 12 will be retired. The number of Japanese Phantom squadrons will be reduced to three, each squadron increasing its number of aircraft from 18 to 22, and these will remain in service well past the year 2000. It is expected that some of

the upgraded aircraft will be allocated to close air support missions and the F-4EJ Kai aircraft already in service have been seen wearing a variety of experimental camouflage color schemes. At least two of the 301st Hikotai aircraft (37-8398 and 97-8427) wear a tan and two-tone green color scheme, marginally less gaudy than the scheme applied to Japanese RF-4EJs and similar to that worn by attack-dedicated Mitsubishi F1s.

F-4EJ Kai

Twin aft-facing radomes for J/APR-6 RWR
Wingtip antenna for J/APR-6 RWR
Tall AN/AC-164 UHF blade antenna
AN/APG-66J pulse-Doppler radar
Strengthening ribs on radome
AN/ALQ-131 ECM pod
Increased-size lower UHF antenna
ASM-1 air-to-surface missile
610-US gal F-15 fuel tank, stressed to higher *g*
Slotted stabilator
Unslatted wing
Unidentified antenna on tailcone

Above: Wearing the markings of the Air Proving Wing at Gifu, 07-8431 was the prototype F-4EJ Kai conversion. External changes are subtle, but represent a major upgrade in capability.

Above: Seen shortly after conversion, this F-4EJ Kai wears no unit markings at all. So far two Hikotai have re-equipped with the new aircraft, with one more to follow.

Right: 306th Hikotai was the first unit to convert to the F-4EJ Kai, and quickly discovered that the new APG-66J radar brought a welcome improvement in capability. The aircraft are also structurally refurbished and incorporate a host of avionics improvements.

Right: A 301st Hikotai F-4EJ Kai shows off its new radome, which covers the APG-66J radar. This is externally identifiable by the tiny strengthening strips which reinforce the radome, although these cannot be seen from any distance.

Right: A pair of 306th Hikotai F-4EJ Kais blasts off. The rearmost aircraft carries the Kanji (character) 'Kai' on its intake splitter plate. Recently, F-4EJ Kai aircraft have begun to receive a green and brown color scheme similar to that worn by the Mitsubishi F-1, and indicating the growing importance of the air-to-ground role. Apart from the changes to the radome, the F-4EJ has changed RWR antenna on the tailfin and wingtips, and has new UHF aerials above the fuselage and on the undercarriage door.

F-4E(S)
(Model 98)

First flight: 20 December 1975; Carswell AFB, Texas (69-7576)
Pilot: Jerry Singleton (USAF)
Number converted: three
Identities: 69-7567, 69-7570, 69-7576 (subsequent IDF/AF identities unknown)

The F-4E(Special), almost always known simply as the F-4E(S), was designed and produced (by conversion of three Block 44 unslatted IDF/AF F-4Es by General Dynamics as part of the ambitious Peace Jack program. The Peace Jack project actually covered three quite separate Phantom subvariants. The first covered a standard RF-4C with an underfuselage HIAC-1 pod. These pods significantly reduced flight performance, but some were later delivered to the USAF, apparently primarily for use in Korea. The inadequacy of the HIAC-1/RF-4C combination prompted General Dynamics to examine a modified aircraft, designated F-4X, with a boosted high-Mach propulsion system, using water injection to provide precompressor cooling (PCC).

The podded HIAC-1 still imposed an unacceptable drag penalty, and the original configuration was refined to include the HIAC-1 camera in a recontoured nose, picking up the new designation RF-4X. When the USAF finally pulled out of the RF-4X and the project was canceled in mid-1975, this new nose section was retained to form the basis of a more straightforward F-4E conversion for Israel alone, powered by standard J79 engines. This new aircraft was designated F-4E(S).

Three Israeli F-4Es were delivered to General Dynamics' own 'Skunk Works' in Building 30 at Fort Worth for conversion, the first keeping the original RF-4X mock-up, which had its cardboard PCC tanks and intakes removed. The new nose increased aircraft length by some 12 in (30 cm) and provided 70 cu ft (2 m³) of space, although it followed standard F-4E contours quite closely. One useful element of the F-4E(S) was that it did resemble a standard F-4E, and to heighten this illusion even had a false black radome painted on. Under the skin, the new nose was very different, however, with a super-accurate Environmental Control System to keep the HIAC-1 camera at an optimum temperature, minimizing barrel and lens distortion.

The camera was mounted horizontally along the aircraft centerline on rotary bearings, with a drive motor at the front which rotated the lens to look through three specially-made oblique and vertical/oblique windows. Behind the HIAC-1 a vertical KS-87 camera was installed, and the three aircraft were also fitted with datalink, Elta IFF and UHF, and formation-keeping strip lights. The HIAC-1 is aimed using a special sight on the canopy sill.

The flight test program commenced on 20 December 1975 and was shrouded in secrecy, using Air Force test pilots at adjacent Carswell AFB, Texas. The three aircraft flew with US civil registrations based on their military serials (N97576, N97570 and N97567) and were redelivered to Israel in 1978. Rumors suggest that at least one of the three aircraft has been lost in action.

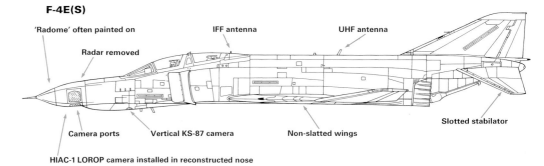

F-4E(S)

'Radome' often painted on — IFF antenna — UHF antenna
Radar removed
Camera ports — Vertical KS-87 camera — Non-slatted wings
HIAC-1 LOROP camera installed in reconstructed nose
Slotted stabilator

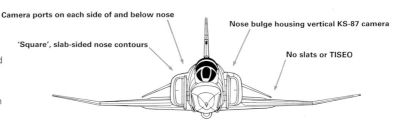

Camera ports on each side of and below nose
'Square', slab-sided nose contours
Nose bulge housing vertical KS-87 camera
No slats or TISEO

Below: The first of three F-4E(S) airframes converted for high-speed reconnaissance duties, using the enormous HIAC-1 LOROP camera. This was carried pod-mounted by some USAF RF-4Cs, with a very high drag penalty. A false radome is painted on the nose.

RF-4E
(Model 98LG)

First flight: 15 September 1970; St Louis (69-7448)
Pilot: not known
Number built: 150
Identities:
69-7448 to 69-7535 (88); for Germany, reserialed 35+01 to 35+88
69-7590 to 69-7595 (6); for Iran
72-0266 to 72-0269 (4); for Iran
74-1725 to 74-1736 (12); for Iran
75-0418 to 75-0423 (6); for Israel
77-0309 to 77-0316 (8); for Turkey
77-1761 to 77-1766 (6); for Greece
78-0751 to 78-0754 (4); for Iran
78-0788 (1); for Iran
78-0854 (1); for Iran Not delivered
78-0855 to 78-0864 (10); for Iran Not delivered

An obvious development, this essentially joined the airframe and engines of the original (unslatted) F-4E with the nose of the RF-4C. The RF-4E has a slatted stabilator but not slatted wings and is powered by J79-GE-17 engines, which have in recent years been brought up to J79-GE-17C standard and have been made smokeless. The improvement in specific fuel consumption of the Dash-17 engine was important in the RF model as it extended its mission radius by some five percent.

The German purchase, valued at DM2,052 million, required offset participation by German industry. Incorporating German equipment in lieu of some US items which were considered too sensitive for export at the time, the Luftwaffe RF-4Es use Fairchild KS-87B and KS-56D cameras in the forward oblique position and in the three panoramic locations, the latter capable of covering 180° on each side of the aircraft's path of travel. For the night photography mission the RF-4E employs photoflash cartridges, which are fired upward from locations in the rear fuselage.

Sensors included an AAS-18A IRLS, improved UPD-4 SLAR and, for Luftwaffe aircraft, an advanced Goodyear UPD-4 SLAR packaged into a pod carried on the centerline. This is capable of giving a high-definition picture of the target along the flight path. Luftwaffe RF-4Es are equipped with an air-to-ground digital datalink for all systems and can develop film from all sensors in flight and eject it for real-time assessment by battlefield commanders.

The first flight (69-7448) took place on 15 September 1970. German industry participated in production, as with the F-4, and some German equipment was incorporated. Luftwaffe service began on 20 January 1971 with AKG 51 at Bremgarten, which received 42 aircraft. Other aircraft equipped AKG 52 at Leck from 17 September 1971. Luftwaffe codes ran from 35+01 to 35+88. In 1974, under Peace Trout, E-Systems developed a prototype Elint installation based on APR-39, with a 13-antenna direction-finding array forming a distinctive bulge under the forward camera access door. This aircraft is one of several which stayed with ESt 61 for special test and development.

In 1978, it was decided that ground attack missions might be more important than recce in some war scenarios (for instance in the face of a mass breakthrough by Soviet forces), and it was decided to give the Luftwaffe RF-4Es ground attack capability. MBB at Ottobrunn and Manching were contracted to provide hardpoints and

RF-4E (Standard)

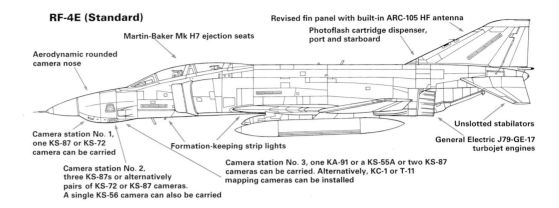

Revised fin panel with built-in ARC-105 HF antenna
Photoflash cartridge dispenser, port and starboard
Martin-Baker Mk H7 ejection seats
Aerodynamic rounded camera nose
Camera station No. 1, one KS-87 or KS-72 camera can be carried
Formation-keeping strip lights
Camera station No. 2, three KS-87s or alternatively pairs of KS-72 or KS-87 cameras. A single KS-56 camera can also be carried
Camera station No. 3, one KA-91 or a KS-55A or two KS-87 cameras can be carried. Alternatively, KC-1 or T-11 mapping cameras can be installed
Unslotted stabilators
General Electric J79-GE-17 turbojet engines

RF-4E (Luftwaffe with SLAR)

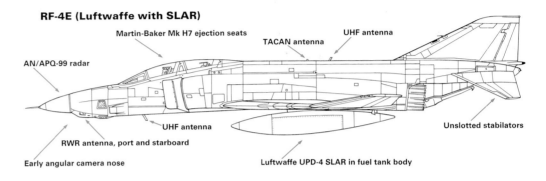

Martin-Baker Mk H7 ejection seats
UHF antenna
TACAN antenna
AN/APQ-99 radar
UHF antenna
RWR antenna, port and starboard
Early angular camera nose
Luftwaffe UPD-4 SLAR in fuel tank body
Unslotted stabilators

Above: The prototype RF-4E in flight. The RF-4E essentially mated the airframe of the F-4E with the camera nose of the RF-4C. Germany's RF-4Es were finally retired in 1992, and sold on to NATO ally Turkey.

Below: Israel was another customer for the RF-4E, its aircraft having the rounded nose shape associated with later RF-4Cs, while Luftwaffe aircraft had the earlier 'squared-off' nose shape. Israeli RF-4 operations are shrouded in secrecy.

wiring for underwing weapons pylons, which were able to carry up to six Hunting BL755 CBUs or 5,000 lb (2270 kg) of other ordnance. A weapons aiming site was fitted for the pilot, with weapons selection switches in both the front and rear cockpits. The opportunity was also taken to upgrade the aircraft's cameras and linescan, and to add Tracor AN/ALE-40 chaff dispensers. Work began in November 1979, with converted aircraft emerging in a new wraparound, two-tone green and gray 'lizard' camouflage, and the secondary attack commitment was held until 1988.

RF-4Es have been delivered with both recce nose shapes, the German aircraft, for example, with the angular nose associated with the RF-4B and early RF-4C, and Greek, Israeli and South Korean aircraft with the more streamlined nose associated with later RF-4Cs.

The final 11 aircraft for Iran were canceled for political reasons while the parts were on the production line. These aircraft were accorded MCAIR line numbers, bringing the total number of F-4s manufactured at St Louis up to 5,068; but the company has not announced the sale of the components as spares. After Germany, Iran remains the largest customer, but evidence shows that the RFs have been cannibalized to keep the few remaining serviceable F-4Es flying. The Greek aircraft replaced the RF-84F in Mira 348, and Turkish aircraft were delivered from November 1978, equipping No. 113 Squadron at Eskisehir. Israeli RFs, first delivered in February 1971, have been repeatedly upgraded both structurally and with avionics and equipment, although the Super Phantom/Kurnass 2000 described later refers to the F-4C upgrade. All Israeli Phantoms, including RFs, can carry Python, Shafrir or Sidewinder missiles and they have indigenous reconnaissance and avionics equipment installed. Repeated rumors that Israeli RFs have been sold to South Korea remain unconfirmed.

RF-4EJ
(Model 98)

First flight: 26 November 1974; St Louis
Pilot: not known
Number built: 14
Identities:
47-6901 to 47-6905 (5)
57-6906 to 57-6914 (9)

The JASDF purchased 14 reconnaissance Phantoms, all manufactured by MCAIR as Block 56, numbered 47-6901 to 47-4905 and 57-6906 to 57-6914. The initial build standard was almost identical to that of the RF-4C; the only differences are deletions, for example the RHAW suite. This omission was rectified by fitting APR-3 on delivery. The original pale (gull) gray and white camouflage was replaced by a green and brown color scheme.

From the start, all RFs have equipped the 501st Hikotai at Hyakuri, and by the summer of 1992 not one aircraft had been lost. The JASDF has established a need for more RFs and is at present upgrading the original 14 aircraft and also converting 17 fighters to RF-4EJ Kai standard. The RF-4EJs are scheduled to have their AN/APQ-99 radar replaced with a new Texas Instruments AN/APQ-172 radar, receive a new INS, an IR reconnaissance system, digital cockpit displays and a VHF radio to replace the existing UHF radio.

Above: Japan's 14 RF-4EJs were all built by McDonnell at St Louis, and differed from the RF-4C in detail only. This aircraft wears the original light gray color scheme, with stylized squadron markings.

Right: In service, Japan's RF-4EJs received a brown and two-tone green camouflage scheme, and the operating unit, 501st Hikotai, has adopted a unit badge consisting of the head of 'Woody Woodpecker'. All have survived, and are presently being upgraded to RF-4EJ Kai standards.

RF-4EJ Kai
(Model 98)

First flight (after conversion): February 1992
Pilot: not known
Number to be converted: 17
Known identities: 37-6404 (prototype, ex 87-6406)

In addition to upgrading the RF-4Es, the JASDF has contracted Mitsubishi Electric to convert 17 F-4EJs to RF-4EJ Kai standard. In addition to the SLEP work, these are being equipped with digital avionics, including APQ-172 radar, a HUD, a podded Thomson-CSF Raphael SKAR and a large Elint pod derived by Mitsubishi-Melco from the Thomson-CSF Astac (as fitted to the Mirage F1CR). They also hope to fit LOROP and Terec pods. At least three pods have been fitted to the prototype, 37-6406. The converted aircraft will retain combat capability, including the gun, and will have no structural modifications.

Above: The designation RF-4EJ Kai is actually applied to two quite different aircraft. These two RF-4EJ Kais are simply refurbished and upgraded RF-4EJs, incorporating many of the same modifications as the F-4EJ Kai, and with an APQ-172 radar.

Right: A similar RF-4EJ Kai, identifiable mainly by its new RWR antennas.

RF-4EJ Kai

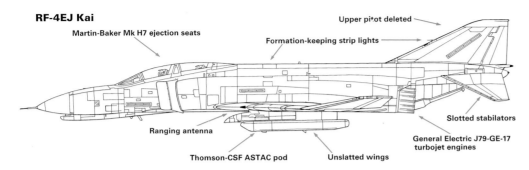

Martin-Baker Mk H7 ejection seats
Upper pi⁺ot deleted
Formation-keeping strip lights
Ranging antenna
Thomson-CSF ASTAC pod
Unslatted wings
Slotted stabilators
General Electric J79-GE-17 turbojet engines

LOROP pod

Raphael-based SLAR 2000 pod

Left: The second Phantom variant to bear the RF-4EJ Kai designation are the F-4EJs, which are not being upgraded to F-4EJ Kai standards but which are instead being upgraded for the reconnaisance role. The prototype, seen here, changed serial from 87-8406 to 87-6406, the third digit being a role designator. It carries a LOROP pod on the centerline.

Below left and below: The same aircraft carries two alternative reconnaissance pods, the ASTAC (left) and SLAR 2000 (right). The unique three-tone blue-gray camouflage scheme is unlikely to be adopted by 'production' conversions.

F-4F
(Model 98NQ)

First flight: 18 May 1973; St Louis
Pilot: not known
Number built: 175
Identities: 72-1111 to 72-1285, reserialed 37+01 to 38+75

The F-4F evolved from the single-seat Phantom variant developed for the 1960 IFX competition for a single-seat export fighter. This eventually lost out to the Northrop F-5E Tiger II, and the idea of a single-seat Phantom was quietly killed, until Germany selected such an aircraft in 1971 under the designation F-4E(F). Intended as an interceptor, the new aircraft had no AIM-7 Sparrow capability and a simplified avionics suite. Before the F-4E(F) could enter production, the Germans changed their minds and opted for a two-seat derivative of the F-4E, influenced by the success of their new two-seat RF-4E reconnaissance aircraft and by the capability of USAFE F-4Es. Flight tests of an F-4E confirmed the German decision.

The new German Phantom emerged as a lightweight, simplified F-4E, which was cheaper and incorporated significant participation by German industry. The F-4F emerged 3,300 lb (1497 kg) lighter than the stock F-4E, the weight reduction

being achieved by removing the No. 7 fuselage fuel tank and all Sparrow equipment, including missile ejector launchers and internal wiring. The AN/APQ-120 radar was simplified, with no beacon search or constant wave illuminator for Sparrow missiles. Interestingly, a Sparrow illuminator and the appropriate wiring was added to the German Phantoms in 1981. Although no inflight refueling receptacle was initially fitted (it has since been retrofitted), internal piping for such a receptacle was installed. Other changes included the provision of an unslotted tailplane as an economy and weight-saving measure.

One hundred and seventy-five F-4Fs were ordered under the DM 3,900 million Pace Rhone program. The first was built entirely by McDonnell, but further F-4Fs included substantial airframe components built by MBB. MTU at Munich built 488 J79-17A turbojets for the German F-4Fs, having previously built similar J79 engines for the German F-104 Starfighters.

Some eight F-4Fs were initially retained in the USA for training, but seven of these were later flown to Germany as attrition replacements and were themselves replaced by a batch of 10 new F-4Es (72-628 to 72-637). The remaining US-based F-4F was passed to the USAF's Systems Command as an NTF-4F until it, too, returned to Germany in 1982.

The delivery of F-4Fs began on 5 September 1973, and ended with the delivery of 38+75 'Spirit of Cooperation' in April 1976. The aircraft equipped two interceptor wings and two ground attack wings, all previously operating the F-104 Starfighter. The F-4Fs received an upgrade between November 1980 and late 1983, gaining a digital weapons computer and improved ECM, cockpit displays and all-weather systems. These modifications conferred the ability to operate with a greater range of weapons,

including the AGM-65 Maverick and the new AIM-9L Sidewinder. This allowed all German Phantom units to be dual-tasked, with the air defense wings gaining a secondary ground attack commitment, and vice versa. Dual tasking was abandoned in 1988.

Further modifications are being incorporated under the Kampfwehrsteigerung (KWS), or Improved Combat Efficiency, program, but this will result in a change of designation to F-4F/ICE.

Below: Phantom tail units take shape at MBB's Augsburg plant. The F-4F incorporated a high level of German-built equipment and even sub-assemblies like the tail units seen here.

F-4F ICE

First flight: July 1989 (37+15); not known
Pilot: not known
Number to be converted: 110 (+40)
Identities: 37+13, 37+15, 38+43

To serve as an interim fighter pending the introduction of the quadrinational EFA (European Fighter Aircraft), Germany decided to upgrade its fleet of Phantoms, extending their lives for service until the year 2005. While little could be done to give the F-4 any real measure of close-in dogfighting capability (especially by comparison with modern lightweights like the F-16 and F/A-18, to say nothing of the MiG-29), it was felt that better BVR combat capability would be a welcome addition. Forbidden from policing its own airspace in peacetime under the terms of the surrender (but unlike Finland and Austria not explicitly barred from having air-to-air missiles), German F-4s were previously very austerely equipped, and the ICE (Improved Combat Efficiency) program (the initials KWS, for Kampfwehrsteigerung, are used in German) radically changed this. By taking two of the best examples of the most crucial equipment items of the 1990s fighter, the remarkable Hughes AIM-120 AMRAAM and the highly regarded Hughes APG-65 radar (often thought of as the definitive fighter radar), the humble F-4F was to be transformed.

The heart of the F-4F ICE is provided by the APG-65 radar. Originally used by the F/A-18 Hornet (itself in service with or selected by the USN, USMC, Australia, Canada, Finland, Kuwait, Spain and Switzerland) and since fitted to the AV-8B+, the APG-65 has often been considered for combat aircraft upgrades, and despite the introduction of the much improved APG-73 it remains the standard against which other fighter radars are judged. Hughes can be equally proud of the other main element of the ICE upgrade – the AIM-120 AMRAAM missile. Although the AIM-120 relies on a form of semi-active radar homing for the initial part of its flight, the target must be illuminated by the launch aircraft, autonomous mid-course inertial guidance and active terminal homing do allow a real measure of fire-and-forget capability. In shorter range engagements, the missile's own active radar seeker can be used on its own, negating the need for inertial homing (with or without guidance updates from the launch aircraft). Other elements of the ICE program include a new Litef digital fire-control computer, a TST radar-control console, the provision of four Frazer-Nash ejectors (similar to those used by the Tornado ADV) for the belly-mounted Hughes AIM-120 AMRAAMs, new IFF, a new air data computer and a new inertial platform, as well as a new nose radome and some auxiliary black boxes.

The ICE upgrade for the F-4F was initiated during late 1983 and initially called for the upgrade of 75 Phantoms serving with JG 71 and JG 74, with a more modest avionics update for the 75 remaining Phantom fighter bombers of JBG 35 and JBG 36. There was to be the option of a full ICE upgrade for these aircraft at a later date. It was soon decided that the program should have two stages, with all F-4Fs receiving the Honeywell H-423 laser inertial gyro autonomous navigation system and a GEC Avionics CPU-143/A digital air data computer, linked by a Mil Std 1553R digital databus and with 110 interceptor aircraft receiving the full package of ICE

modifications. The increase in numbers of full ICE-modified aircraft marked the switch of one of the fighter-bomber wings to the fighter interceptor role (JBG 36 becoming JG 72) and a favorable exchange rate. This left only 40 partly-modified F-4Fs, which may still be brought up to full ICE standards, since they too are likely to switch to the fighter role when JBG 35 becomes JG 73. The flight test program for the fighter-bomber version (which also acted as Phase 1 of the interceptor upgrade) began in October 1988, with fleet aircraft retrofits commencing in March 1990. The program is now complete.

The incorporation of a Litton ALR-68(V)-2 radar warning receiver was added to the upgrade program during 1989, and this was applied to all modified F-4Fs. There was the option of converting the F-4F's J79 engines to a 'smokeless' model at a cost of between DM150 and 200 million.

The F-4F ICE flight test program began in July 1989, using F-4F 37+15 (ex 72-1125), which was equipped to launch, but not guide, the AIM-120 AMRAAM. The second test aircraft was 37+13 (72-1123), which was equipped with the full F-4F ICE avionics suite and which began flight tests in April 1990. Aircraft 37+15 rejoined the test program in March 1991, having been brought up to the same standard. This first phase of the flight test program was led by MBB and aimed to prove the attack system's full functional integrity up to and including simulated AMRAAM firings, and was completed in August 1991.

The program to retrofit fleet F-4Fs began in July 1991, and is scheduled to be completed by the end of 1995. The original target of achieving IOC by 1990 had long before been replaced by the more realistic target of redelivery of production conversions from May 1990, but this had been delayed by the late first flight (originally scheduled for late 1987). By mid-1991 the first two aircraft had been joined by an IGT/OpEval aircraft, 38+43 (72-1253), for phase two of the test program. Led by the BWB (Bundesamt für Wehrtechnik und Beschaffung, or Federal Office for Military Technology and Procurement), this phase is being carried out by a joint BWB/MBB test team, supported by on-site teams from MBB and TST (Telefunken Systemtechnik).

In September 1991, the trio of aircraft were deployed to the NAWC Weapons Division at Point Mugu (previously known as the Pacific Missile Test Center, or PMTC) for performance and operational system evaluation, which was scheduled to include the launch of six instrumented AMRAAMs. The first of these was conducted on 22 November 1991, and a direct hit resulted in the destruction of

F-4F ICE

Martin-Baker Mk H7 ejection seats
Ammunition drum
AN/APG-65 radar
Pitot probe
AIM-120 AMRAAM in 'Sparrow' recess
M61A1 20-mm cannon
Frazer-Nash gas-powered missile ejector launchers

Above: An F-4F ICE with radome unfolded shows off the Hughes AN/APG-65 radar, which forms the core of this ambitious and expensive upgrade.

the BQM-34S target drone. This marked the first AMRAAM launch by a foreign aircraft. The three aircraft were accompanied by a group of about 85 German civil servants, Luftwaffe personnel and contractor support teams from both MBB and TST. The deployment was due to end with a double AMRAAM firing in September 1992, having successfully validated the integration of the APG-65 radar and AIM-120 AMRAAM with the F-4F ICE airframe.

By July 1992, six 'production' ICE conversions had been redelivered to JG 71 'Richthofen'. Now that the EFA has been effectively canceled by the German government, the F-4F ICE is left as an interim aircraft with no chosen replacement. While the upgrade has transformed the Phantom's BVR capabilities, such a replacement is urgently required. In June 1992, it was revealed that Deutsche Aerospace (parent organization of MBB) had launched a late bid to upgrade 38 RoKAF F-4Es to similar standards. MBB was originally part of a team offering an APG-65-equipped F-4, which included

McDonnell Douglas and Hughes, but which withdrew from the Korean Phantom Upgrade (KPU) program after Korea reversed its decision to procure the F/A-18. This left a General Dynamics/Rockwell proposal for an upgrade based around the Westinghouse APG-68 radar fitted to RoKAF F-16s. Deutsche Aerospace is now understood to be offering an F-4F ICE-style upgrade without direct US participation, subject to the granting of a license to transfer APG-65 technology. The radar is already being manufactured under license by TST. A contract is due to be awarded in October 1992.

An F-4F ICE test aircraft is laden with AIM-120 AMRAAM missiles and test camera pods (in rebuilt underwing fuel tanks). These are used to film missile separations and firings.

F-4(FBW), F-4 PACT, F-4 CCV

First flights: not known (PACT), not known (CCV)
Pilot: not known
Number converted: one
Identity: 62-12200

The long-serving YRF-4C prototype, 62-12200 (which had gone on to become the first YF-4E), gained a new lease of life when it was selected for use as a fly-by-wire (FBW) control system testbed, conducting basic research into survivable flight control systems. Known as the PACT (Precision Aircraft Control Technology) demonstrator, the aircraft made its first flight in its new guise on 29 April 1972. Mechanical reversion was eventually removed and an all-FBW flight (lasting 70 minutes) was made on 22 January 1973. With its FBW control system, the aircraft was a natural choice for CCV (Control Configured Vehicle) research. Rebuilt with 40-sq ft (3.7-m^3) canard foreplanes (which had 20° of movement) and with outboard flap sections modified as flaperons, the aircraft flew a total of 30 test flights, first flying in its new configuration on 29 April 1974. Lead ballast was added to the rear fuselage to move the center of gravity aft and to destabilize the aircraft in pitch. Its working life ended on 5 December 1978, when it was donated to the US Air Force Museum.

The fourth major episode in the life of 62-12200 began in 1972 when it first flew as a fly-by-wire control aircraft. In 1974 it flew with canard foreplanes added as the F-4 CCV. No mechanical reversion was incorporated, and the aircraft was destabilized by lead ballast.

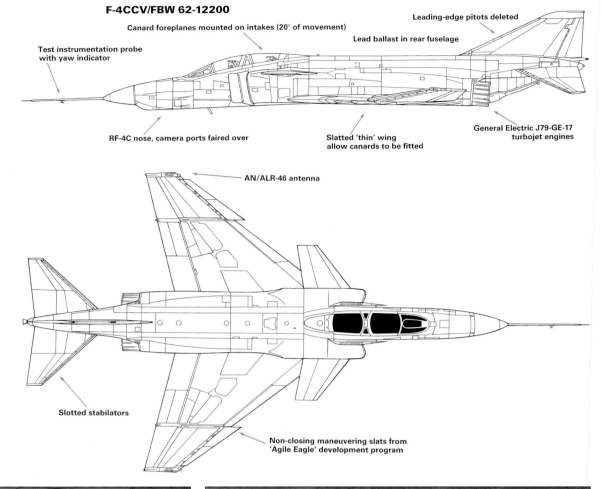

F-4CCV/FBW 62-12200

Canard foreplanes mounted on intakes (20° of movement)

Test instrumentation probe with yaw indicator

Leading-edge pitots deleted

Lead ballast in rear fuselage

RF-4C nose, camera ports faired over

Slatted 'thin' wing allow canards to be fitted

General Electric J79-GE-17 turbojet engines

AN/ALR-46 antenna

Slotted stabilators

Non-closing maneuvering slats from 'Agile Eagle' development program

F-4G

First flight: 20 March 1963 (150481)
Pilots: Thomas S. Harris and John J. Kiely
Number converted: 12
Identities: 150481, 150484, 150487, 150489, 150492, 150625, 150629, 150633, 150636, 150639, 150642

One of the least known and most confusingly designated Phantom variants was the US Navy's little-known F-4G, which predated the similarly designated USAF Wild Weasel variant by some 12 years!

Influenced by the success of the Air Force's SAGE (Semi-Automatic Ground Environment), which pioneered the control of interceptors without voice commands, the US Navy decided to institute a similar system for fleet air defense. Under its system, the Navy hoped to link its fighters, surface ships and AEW aircraft, notably the new W2F-1 (later E-2) Hawkeye, by datalink. This, it was hoped, would allow fighters to be controlled through a non-voice link, coupling their autopilots to a ship or aircraft-based controller. The same system was also designed to allow a night/all-weather hands-off landing capability.

To test this ambitious idea, a single F-4B (148254) was fitted with an AN/ASW-13 datalink set which, coupled with a shipborne AN/SPN-10 radar and AN/USC-2 datalink, allowed hands-off landings to be achieved. The next step was the fitting of the AN/ASW-21 in place of the ASW-13, which allowed weapons, oxygen and fuel status to be relayed to the controller.

To allow the SPN-10 radar to track the F-4 to touch down, a radar reflector had to be bolted to the nose of 148254, but on production conversions this was given a retractable installation immediately ahead of the nose-wheel bay. Other changes included the reconfiguration of the No. 1 fuel tank, which lost 600 lb (270 kg) of fuel to make room for datalink black boxes, and the provision of a datalink status panel, yards to touch down display and an approach power compensator system (APCS) in the front cockpit, and various control boxes in the 'pit'. The APCS automatically added or reduced power, based on the angle of attack, responding to stick movements.

Twelve F-4Bs were converted on the production line, two going to the NATC at Patuxent River in early 1963 and the rest to VF-96 in the summer of 1963 for testing. The 10 VF-96 aircraft were transferred to VF-213 between January and March 1964. On 31 March 1964, in recognition of the datalink Phantom's unique capabilities, the NATC aircraft were redesignated F-4G, and the VF-213 aircraft followed on 6 April.

The reassignment of the squadron from CVW-21 to CVW-11 was originally to have been accompanied by a squadron

The F-4G designation was first applied to the datalink version of the F-4B, which featured an automatic intercept communications function, and full automatic carrier landing capability. For the latter, the aircraft carried a retractable radar reflector, as seen on both the NATC example above, and the VF-213 aircraft above left. The reflector allowed the ship-based SPN-10 radar to accurately track the position of the incoming aircraft.

redesignation (to VF-116), but while the aircraft were being repainted the change was canceled before the combat cruise aboard the USS *Kitty Hawk*, which began on 19 October 1965. During this cruise, VF-213 also evaluated a matt dark green upper-surface camouflage scheme, but this did not prevent them from losing an F-4G (and an F-4B) to AAA.

The surviving F-4Gs were stripped of AN/ASW-21 and reworked as F-4Bs from 1966, seven surviving to be converted to F-4Ns. The automatic landing and remote-controlled intercept capabilities of the F-4G were incorporated in the F-4B by addition of the AN/ASW-25, which lacked the two-way features of AN/ASW-21, however.

In 1966 half of Kitty Hawk's Air Wing 11 (along with aircraft on Constellation and Enterprise) received an experimental dark green scheme, including the F-4Gs of VF-213. This was an attempt to render the aircraft less visible to MiGs, but the results were inconclusive and the aircraft reverted to light gray.

F-4G
(Model 98)

First flight: 6 December 1975 (69-7254)
Pilot: not known
Number converted: 116
Identities: 69-0236 to 69-0243, 69-0245 to 69-0248, 69-0250 to 69-0255, 69-0257 to 69-0259, 69-0261, 69-0263, 69-0265, 69-0267, 69-0269 to 69-0275, 69-0277, 69-0279, 69-0280, 69-0281, 69-0283 to 69-0286, 69-0292, 69-0293, 69-0297, 69-0304, 69-0306, 69-7201, 69-7202, 69-7204 to 72-7220, 69-7223, 69-7228, 69-7231 to 69-7236, 69-7251, 69-7253, 69-7254, 69-7256 to 69-7260, 69-7262, 69-7263, 69-7270, 69-7272, 69-7286 to 69-7291, 69-7293, 69-7295, 69-7298, 69-7300 to 69-7303, 69-7546, 69,7550, 69-7556, 69-7558, 69-7560, 69-7561, 69-7566, 69-7571, 69-7572, 69-7574, 69-7579 to 69-7584, 69-7586 to 69-7588

The very last datalink F-4G had been redesignated F-4B by August 1970, leaving the F-4G designation as a little-known historical anachronism. Mindful of the success and popularity of the F-105G

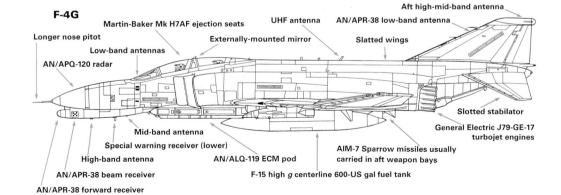

in the Wild Weasel role, the USAF decided to allocate their latest SAM killer the 'vacant' -G suffix, despite the fact that it had been used already.

By 1970, the need for an F-105 replacement in the Wild Weasel, or defense suppression role, was obvious and urgent. The F-105 airframe was no longer in production, and attrition in Vietnam had made it a scarce resource. Any F-105G lost simply could not be

replaced. It was also judged to be deficient in performance. The Phantom was quickly judged to be a suitable alternative Weasel platform, with its twin-engined safety, excellent performance, agility and production status. The F-4C formed the basis of the Wild Weasel IV program, the converted aircraft gaining the unofficial designation EF-4C (see EF-4C entry). These operated successfully enough during Linebacker II

but were always regarded as interim aircraft, with insufficient new wiring looms for much necessary equipment and unable to launch the new AGM-78 Standard ARM.

Various studies were initiated for an Advanced Wild Weasel, based on the airframes of the F-4C, F-4D and F-4E. The F-4E (which was still in production) was soon selected. The slaughter of Israeli F-4s by Soviet-supplied SAMs in 1973

gave added impetus to the Wild Weasel V program, and a number of converted F-4Ds (see EF-4D) and F-4Es were used for trials at Edwards AFB, California. F-4E 69-7254 served as the YF-4G prototype, although it was originally known simply as the F-4E Advanced Wild Weasel. EF-4Ds included 66-7647 and 66-7635 (which had the definitive AN/APR-38 fin-tip fairing and a nonstandard nose antenna). The designation EF-4E was mooted for the new variant, but never seriously considered, since this would have indicated a passive jamming platform, whereas the Wild Weasel V was always intended to have a more offensive defense suppression role.

The heart of the F-4G is provided by the AN/APR-38 radar and missile detection and launch homing system. This is reprogrammable at squadron level and is being updated to identify all currently known air defense radar systems and to display their locations in a predetermined order of priority to the F-4G crew.

The central sensor installation, APR-38, was developed under MCAIR management, using many subcontractors, such as IBM for the radar warning system, Texas Instruments for the radar warning computer, Loral for the control indicator subsystem, Lear Siegler for the ARN-101 nav/attack system and Tracor for ALE-40 dispensers.

Many possible configurations for antennas were finally reduced to an optimum arrangement in which the 52 receiver and emitter antennas were found all over the aircraft. The main mid-high-band receivers are in the front of the glassfiber chin gondola, replacing the unwanted gun, and in a sheet-metal pod above the fin. Eight of the blade antennas provide low-band signals, while five others are directional blades giving the threat bearing on the rear cockpit displays. The forward antennas were modified early in F-4G production by adding five small spiral antennas on each side to receive from each beam. These antennas form a distinctive 'four-leaf clover' pattern. The backseater, called 'the Bear', has three main displays: a PPI (plan-position indicator), a panoramic analysis display and a homing indicator. The PPI is duplicated in the front cockpit and gives threat range and bearing, guns being denoted by an A and SAMs by the number of their NATO designation (thus, 6 threats are an 'SA-6'). The top 15 threats are prioritized, the most dangerous having a bright triangle superimposed. The Bear can override this and choose his own threat.

An F-4E was converted to serve as a prototype for the F-4G Wild Weasel V program, this featuring the prominent fairings on the fintip and undernose area.

In the front cockpit the LCOSS indicates the chosen threat by its red reticle and the aircraft ground track by a green cross. By maneuvering to put the cross on the red reticle and depressing the bomb release button, the computer does the rest. It is not necessary to be able to see the ground. Of course the F-4G carries more than 'iron bombs'; standard stores have included AGM-45 Shrike, AGM-78 Standard ARM, AGM-88 HARM, AGM-65A, B or D Maverick precision-guided missiles carried in triple groups, the Mk 84 EOGB (electro-optical glide bomb), HOBOS (homing bomb system) and cluster weapons such as Rockeyes, CBU-52 and CBU-58. Other external stores include ALQ-119 or ALQ-131 jammer pods in the left front Sparrow bay, leaving room, if necessary, for three AIM-7 Sparrows. Four Sidewinders can also be carried in the usual way on the sides of the inboard pylons. Apart from the totally new avionics, the only significant change between the F-4E and F-4G is that the J79-17 engines are modified to minimize smoke, the nose pitot boom is longer and the centerline pylon is upgraded to carry the F-15-type tank which is cleared for 5g maneuvers even with 600 US gal (500 Imp gal; 2273 liters) of fuel (compared with 3.5g for other F-4 versions).

All the F-4Gs, a total of 116 aircraft, were rebuilds of existing F-4Es from Blocks 42 to 45. The work was carried out at the USAF Ogden (Utah) Air Logistic Center, from 1975 to June 1981. The first to be completed, 69-7254, made its first flight as an F-4G on 6 December 1975, when the APR-38 was not fully developed. Twenty were retained for training and attrition, the other 96 going to the 37th (now 35th) TFW at George AFB, California, followed by the 52nd at Spangdahlem AB, Germany, and the 3rd TFW at Clark AB, Philippines. The one-time suggestion that the F-4G would "soon be replaced by the EF-111A Raven" is erroneous, if only for the reason that

After a series of programs involving F-100F, F-105F, F-105G, F-4C and F-4D, the USAF finally had received its definitive defense suppression platform with the F-4G Wild Weasel V.

Above: F-4Gs went to the 37th TFW at George AFB, which adopted the 'WW' tailcode, standing for Wild Weasel. Subsequently, aircraft went to theater forces in Europe and the Pacific.

the latter is unarmed and cannot eliminate or suppress the threats it discovers. Accordingly, as well as SLEP airframe work to ensure a life into the 21st century, the F-4Gs are being improved in a PUP (performance upgrade program) for Wild Weasel VI, which began in 1986 and will certainly cost more than the estimated $600 million. The chief task in this work is to strip out almost all the APR-38 and replace it by the even more capable APR-47. This wholly new sensor system is being managed by MCAIR and includes a directional receiver subsystem by E-Systems and the Sperry CP-1674 signal processor. The latter offers five times faster signal processing, eight times the memory, 20 times the display capability and 10 times the data-processing rate of APR-38. The new system also makes better use of the stand-off capability of HARM and Maverick missiles, and other later anti-radar weapons.

Meanwhile, the unmodified aircraft played a literally leading part in the Gulf War of 1991, with aircraft from the 35th TFW scything a path through Iraqi air defenses with HARM missiles ahead of the massive initial strike of 17 January

Above: The APR-38 RHAWS combines data from 52 antennas located around the F-4G airframe. Several of the important receivers are grouped in the nose fairing, as detailed here. Another major grouping is in the fintip bullet fairing.

1991. Though it was originally the intention in 1990 to withdraw all F-4G aircraft in favor of a definitive version of the F-16, this was reversed in 1992. It is now the intention to keep the F-4G in service until about 2000, equipping one ANG squadron and the 81st TFS of the 52nd TFW. The replacement now envisaged is a HARM-equipped F-15E. All F-4Gs will be US-based, the 52nd moving from Germany to a location yet to be announced. The Idaho ANG squadron has replaced the two squadrons of the 35th FW at George AFB, which deactivated during 1992.

Above: Fully loaded to hunt and kill radars, this F-4G displays the three main early-generation weapons, namely AGM-45 Shrike (outboard pylons), AGM-65 Maverick (starboard inner pylon) and AGM-78 Standard (port inner pylon). An ALQ-119 ECM pod is carried.

Below: AGM-88 HARM has virtually replaced all former weapons, this offering greatly enhanced kill capability and greater launch versatility. The aircraft of the 35th TFW have now been transferred to the Idaho ANG.

F-4(HL)

Not built

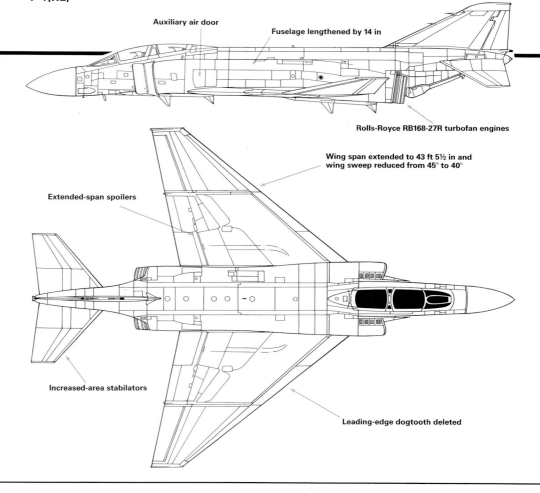

The F-4(HL) was proposed to Britain in a document published in March 1966. Based on the F-4M airframe, it featured an extended span wing (43 ft 5½ in; 13.25 m) with slightly less sweep (40° instead of 45°) and extended span spoilers. Powered by the 20,514-lb st (91-kN) Rolls-Royce RB-168-27R, the aircraft also had a 14-in (36-cm) fuselage plug added just aft of the wing leading edge, increasing the overall length to 61 ft 7½ in (18.78 m), and wheel base to 23 ft 5½ in (7.15 m). Catapult performance (based on HMS *Eagle*'s catapults) was much improved, while approach speed was reduced by some 12 kt (14 mph; 22 km/h) even by comparison with the F-4K. There was a general improvement in performance, although maximum speed and acceleration both suffered slightly. Radius of action and CAP times were increased by between 30 and 50 percent, depending on the sortie profile. A first flight was scheduled for early 1968, working on a go-ahead in July/August 1966. McDonnell envisaged a production run of 500, 200 of these for the Royal Navy.

Labels on diagram: Auxiliary air door; Fuselage lengthened by 14 in; Rolls-Royce RB168-27R turbofan engines; Wing span extended to 43 ft 5½ in and wing sweep reduced from 45° to 40°; Extended-span spoilers; Increased-area stabilators; Leading-edge dogtooth deleted

F-4J
(Model 98EV)

First flight: 27 May 1966 (153072); St Louis
Pilot: not known
Number built: 522
Identities:
Blocks 26-27: 153071 to 153088 (18)
Blocks 28-32: (part): 153768 to 153911 (144)
Blocks 32 (remainder)-33 (part): 154781 to 154788 (8)
Blocks 33 (remainder)-34 (part): 155504 to 155580 (77)
Blocks 34 (remainder)-39: 155731 to 155902 (172)
Block 42: 155903 (1)
Blocks 40-44: 157242 to 157309 (68)
Blocks 45-47: 158346 to 158379 (34)

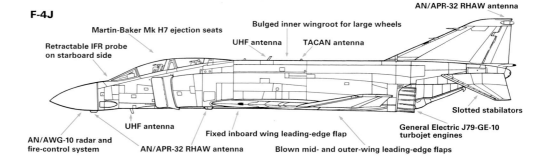

Labels on diagram: AN/APR-32 RHAW antenna; Martin-Baker Mk H7 ejection seats; Bulged inner wingroot for large wheels; Retractable IFR probe on starboard side; UHF antenna; TACAN antenna; UHF antenna; Slotted stabilators; AN/AWG-10 radar and fire-control system; AN/APR-32 RHAW antenna; Fixed inboard wing leading-edge flap; General Electric J79-GE-10 turbojet engines; Blown mid- and outer-wing leading-edge flaps

BuNo. 151473 was one of three F-4B-19-MCs converted to YF-4J standard. Seen at El Centro in 1977, the aircraft is configured for ejection seat trials.

The F-4J was designed as the follow-on to the original F-4B, correcting some of the deficiencies which had become apparent in service. Increased weight and more demanding sink rate requirements (38,000 lb at 23.5 fps/17250 kg at 7.2 m/sec, by comparison with 33,000 lb at 22 fps/15000 kg at 6.7 m/sec for the F-4B) necessitated the use of a beefed-up landing gear with strengthened main legs of vacuum-melted steel and fitted with the wide tires previously associated with Air Force Phantom variants. Consequently, the upper and lower surfaces of the inner wing were bulged like those introduced on the F-4C. One reason for the increase in weight was the addition of the No. 7 fuselage fuel cell, even though there was no gun in the nose to balance it. The No. 1 fuel cell was actually slightly reduced in size to accommodate the computer and other items like the AN/AWG-10 fire-control system, whose APG-59 radar was heavier and bulkier than the earlier APQ-72, and which had the same 32-in (81-cm) dish. It allowed both high and low altitude targets to be tracked.

More importantly, the Navy demanded improved takeoff and landing performance. With speed, climb and range requirements ruling out the use of the high drag slatted wing, McDonnell was forced to examine other ways of improving approach characteristics.

On its first flight over St Louis, BuNo. 153072 displays the much cleaner lines of the F-4J. Further noticeable differences included the wing bulges to accommodate larger wheels.

Left: Hooked up to the bridle, an F-4J of VMFA-333 readies for launch. 'Triple Trey' was deployed on board Nimitz for a 1976 cruise. Note the intake-side ALQ-126 DECM fairing.

Above: This was the fourth true F-4J, seen in the service of the Pacific Missile Test Center. Although the radome remained unchanged from the F-4B, the 'J' had a new APG-59 radar.

Working in partnership with engineers from Britain's Hawker Siddeley (whose blown tailplane had transformed the Buccaneer's carrier approach characteristics), McDonnell added a slot to the stabilator leading edge, effectively turning the stabilator into a miniature inverted slatted wing, able to provide tremendous down force at low speeds, and allowing huge leading edge down deflection without stalling. This rotated the aircraft powerfully nose-up on launch or recovery. It was also found that stabilator power and effectiveness were improved by locking the inboard leading-edge flap in the up position. The combination of fixed inboard leading edge and slotted tailplane featured in almost all subsequent F-4 variants, with the notable exception of the F-4K (and the alphabetically earlier F-4F and F-4EJ). It was even retrofitted to surviving F-4Bs, and to the F-4N.

Lift at low speeds was further enhanced by provision of 16.5° drooped ailerons (i.e with gear and flaps down, 16.5° deflection downward became the new 'ailerons neutral' position). As a result of these improvements, approach speed was reduced from 137 kt (157 mph; 253 km/h) to 125 kt (144 mph; 231 km/h) although the ultimate slow-approach speed modifications were reserved for the derived F-4K (which

see), intended to operate from Britain's tiny aircraft carriers.

The new variant was given a new powerplant, the 17,900-lb st (80 kN) J79-GE-10, similar to the USAF's -17 but with a turbine air impingement starter instead of a cartridge starter. The new engines were externally distinguishable by their longer afterburner 'turkey feathers'. Engine-driven alternators were uprated from 20 kVA to 30 kVA. Other changes included the removal of the IRST pod below the nose, and the provision of an AN/ASW-25A one-way datalink, AJB-7 nuclear bombing system and an RAT, which extended from a compartment above the port engine duct.

The F-4J's maiden flight was made by the second aircraft, the first being used for various ground tests. The first F-4J deliveries began on 1 October 1966, and VF-101 began re-equipping from 27 December. F-4Js were used extensively during Operation Rolling Thunder and then returned to Vietnam during Linebacker. The F-4J was the last US aircraft in operation in Southeast Asia, with Marine F-4Js finally departing Nam Phong in August 1973.

Further changes were introduced during the course of production. From 1969, Sidewinder Expanded Acquisition Mode (SEAM) was provided, and the cockpit was made compatible with a

VTAS helmet-mounted sight. An AN/AYK-14 or other dogfight computer was added, and AN/APX-76 or AN/APX-80 was also provided. During production, Sanders AN/ALQ-126 DECM was added, with prominent slender fore and aft canoe fairings on each intake, which had a hemispherical dielectric antenna at the leading edge. These were significantly shorter than the similar antennas added to the F-4N. Two more antennas were added below the engine intakes. An AN/APR-32 RWR was added, this also being retrofitted to some F-4Bs. Seven aircraft were slightly modified for use by the Navy's 'Blue Angels' flight demonstration team. These aircraft had oil and smoke injectors added, and were beautifully

painted in the team's attractive blue and gold livery. The surviving aircraft were returned to standard configuration following the heavy losses which prompted the team to re-equip with the smaller A-4F Skyhawk.

Two hundred and forty-eight F-4Js were upgraded to F-4S standard, 15 more to F-4J(UK) configuration; and a handful to other marks, including the DF-4J and EF-4J (see separate entries).

Below: While in the employ of the NATC, F-4J BuNo. 157286 was fitted with wing slats, as evidenced by the underwing actuator/slat guide fairings.

F-4J(UK)
'Phantom FGR.Mk 3'

First delivery to UK: 30 August 1984
Number built: 15
Serial numbers: ZE350 to ZE364

Britain's procurement of the F-4J(UK), provisionally dubbed the Phantom FGR. Mk 3 before it entered service, was prompted by a perceived shortage of air defense aircraft following the Falklands War, when a flight of Phantoms was stationed in the Falklands, and when it had become obvious that the service introduction of the Tornado F.Mk 3 would be slower than had originally been anticipated. The solution to the RAF's 'fighter shortage' came in the shape of 15 surplus USN/USMC F-4Js, reworked at NAS North Island, California, at a cost of £33 million. The F-4J was chosen since it had initially formed the basis of the original British Phantom variants, and since its AWG-10 radar was broadly compatible with that fitted to the RAF's other F-4s. Only a very limited amount of UK equipment was installed (including Sky Flash missiles) and aircrew had to wear USN flying equipment until shortly

F-4J(UK)

Externally-mounted rearview mirror

Martin-Baker Mk H7 ejection seats
British harnesses added later

Periscope

Empty ALQ-126 fairing

Formation-keeping strip lights

BAe Sky Flash air-to-air missile

AIM-9L Sidewinder air-to-air missile

SUU-23/A gun pod on centreline

370-US gal fuel tank

before the type's retirement. Prominent DECM antennas on the intake shoulders were actually empty!

The F-4J(UK)s were delivered in August 1984, following crew training at El Toro and Yuma. They equipped a newly reformed No. 74 Squadron at RAF Wattisham, giving the RAF a fighter-

The F-4J(UK) remained the official designation during the type's RAF career, the 'Phantom FGR.Mk 3' never being adopted, principally on account of confusion with the Tornado F.Mk 3.

equipped 'Tiger Squadron' for the first time in many years. The aircraft were painted in the USA, applying a bluer than normal gray over a particularly gaudy yellow primer. This gave the aircraft an unusual greenish or turquoise tinge until they were subsequently repainted in standard RAF air defense colors.

The aircraft were eventually retired when the disbandment of No. 228 OCU freed up relatively low-time FGR.MK 2 airframes to re-equip No. 74 Squadron. The retirement of the F-4J(UK)s was greeted with dismay in some quarters,

since the aircraft had recently been extensively refurbished and fitted with British ejection seats (scavenged from retired F-4Ks), and also their better performance had been highly prized.

F-4J(UK) and F-4S in formation highlight the individual differences between the marks. Painting in the US resulted in the strange color, although this was later rectified. The F-4J(UK)s were retired in favor of FGR.Mk 2s when surplus aircraft became available.

F-4J(FV)S and F-4M(FV)S

Not built

Had it been built, the F-4(FV)S would have marked the most radically modified Phantom variant ever. It was intended as a follow-on to the F-4J in US Navy service, avoiding the large amount of time inherent in the development of an all-new aircraft by using the proven F-4 airframe as a basis. It also offered 59 percent parts commonality with the existing aircraft (57 percent by weight). The USN could foresee a need for greater fleet defense capability and improved ground attack performance in a new fleet defense fighter, with a probable need to thwart saturation attacks by enemy aircraft coming in at all altitudes, some releasing long-range cruise missiles. This necessitated an ability to simultaneously launch missiles against look-up, look-down and same-altitude targets, including very fast missiles. The F-4(FV)S was thus a *de facto* alternative to the F-14 Tomcat. Since it was designed to meet the same broad requirement as the F-14, it was not surprising that the F-4(FV)S shared some common features.

In order to reconcile the conflicting demands of speed, low-level ride, range and approach speed, McDonnell Douglas adopted a variable geometry wing. Since the existing inner wing was too thin to accept pivots for 'swinging' outer panels, an entirely new, shoulder-mounted wing was designed, and the undercarriage was redesigned and relocated in the lower fuselage. The wing was fully variable between sweep angles of 19° and 70°, giving spans between 37.8 and 60 ft (11.5 and 18.3 m). Takeoff weight rose to 54,670 lb (24798 kg), while landing weight rose to 45,510 lb (20643 kg); larger wheels and tires were offered as a consequence. The horizontal stabiliser was also redesigned, losing its anhedral, and internal fuel capacity was increased from the F-4J's 2,000 US gal (1,665 Imp gal; 5571 liters) to 2,601 US gal (2,166 Imp gal; 9846 liters). Performance was significantly improved, with better ceiling, speed, acceleration time and radius. Approach speed was reduced by 10 kt (11 mph; 18 km/h) and the landing roll was reduced by about 100 ft (30 m).

McDonnell hoped to sell a very similar aircraft to the RAF, drawing up a comprehensive brochure on an F-4M(FV)S, which it published in October 1967. It was hoped that this aircraft would be selected instead of the Anglo-French AFVG. The new type bore the same relationship to the standard F-4M as the F-4J(FV)S bore to the standard F-4J, although it was powered by a pair of 20,514-lb st (91-kN) Rolls-Royce RB-168-27R turbofans, which offered a marginal increase in thrust and a more creditable reduction in specific fuel consumption. This allowed a 115 percent increase in CAP time, and 73 percent better lo-lo-lo and hi-lo-lo-hi radius. A first flight was scheduled for January 1970,

with a first production aircraft following 11 months later.

A further improved F-4(FV)S was proposed to both the US Navy and the RAF, powered by the General Electric GE1/10S092B. The first flight was anticipated in March 1971. McDonnell proposed building 200 F-4M(FV)Ss, quickly followed by 400 F-4(FV)S GE1/10s (total cost given as $3.242 billion), or 35 Spey-engined aircraft followed by 565 GE-engined machines (total cost given as $3.209 billion). Both plans were aimed at giving Britain 200 of the more advanced aircraft, with McDonnell buying back the Spey Phantoms for resale. Costs were given as $927 million or $1,027 million.

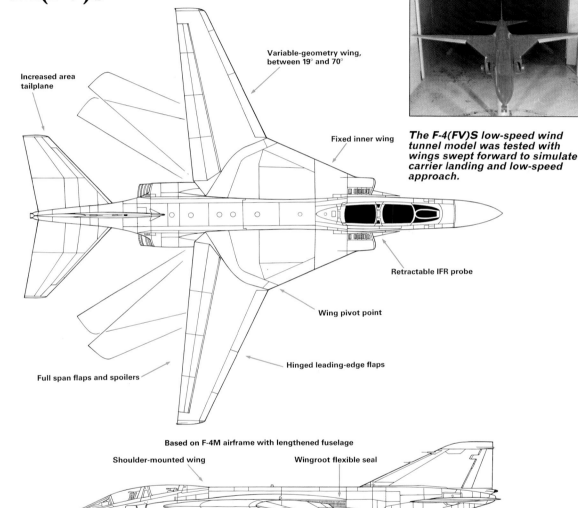

Variable-geometry wing, between 19° and 70°

Increased area tailplane

Fixed inner wing

Retractable IFR probe

Wing pivot point

Hinged leading-edge flaps

Full span flaps and spoilers

The F-4(FV)S low-speed wind tunnel model was tested with wings swept forward to simulate carrier landing and low-speed approach.

Based on F-4M airframe with lengthened fuselage

Shoulder-mounted wing

Wingroot flexible seal

Increased area tailplane with no anhedral

Auxiliary inlet doors

Larger wheels and tires

Rolls-Royce RB-168-27R turbofan engines

The polysonic wind tunnel model (below) better displays the configuration of the aircraft. The principal differences compared to the Phantom were (1) variable-geometry shoulder-mounted wings with large glove section, (2) increased vertical fin size, and (3) zero anhedral tailplane.

DF-4J
(Model 98)

First flight: not known
Pilot: not known
Number converted: unknown
Identities: includes 153084

At least one F-4J, formerly an EF-4J, was converted to serve as a drone-director with controls and transmitter in the rear cockpit which allowed it to guide RPVs.

The DF-4J closely resembles the QF-4 variants which it directed, with the same distinctive blade aerial above the nose. The aircraft also guided other drones, and was operated by the US Navy's Pacific Missile Test Center at Point Mugu. The aircraft was previously an EF-4J with VAQ-33.

EF-4J
(Model 98)

First flight: not known
Pilot: not known
Number converted: two
Identities: 153076 and 153084

In December 1976, the US Navy approved the EF-4 designation for F-4 Phantoms then serving with VAQ-33 'Firebirds', supporting the US Navy's FEWSG at NAS Norfolk, Virginia. Five Phantoms served with VAQ-33 as high-speed targets and as threat simulators to train air defense radar operators and test defensive systems. Three remained in service when the designation was approved, apparently one F-4B Phantom (see EF-4B) and two F-4Js, which were redesignated EF-4J. These aircraft were not extensively modified, but were equipped with some items of unique electrical equipment.

VAQ-33 operated a number of specially-equipped F-4Bs and F-4Js as electronic aggressors. In 1976 these were redesignated with an 'EF-' prefix, by which time two F-4Js were on charge.

YF-4K Phantom FG.Mk 1

First flight: 27 June 1966
Pilot: not known
Number built: two
Identities: XT595 and XT596

British acquisition of the Phantom followed the cancelation of the indigenous Hawker Siddeley P.1154 (RN) in February 1964, leaving the Royal Navy without a replacement for its ageing Sea Vixens. The P.1154 was an ambitious supersonic V/STOL strike fighter, which was to have been built in two versions; one for the Royal Navy and one for the Royal Air Force. Replacing this homegrown aircraft with an American product was a bitter blow, and Britain demanded a high British parts content to ease the impact on employment in the UK aircraft industry.

McDonnell had little previous overseas sales experience, but realized that their new aircraft had considerable overseas sales potential. While their Phantom was still regarded as primarily a carrier-based fighter, McDonnell targeted Argentina, Australia, Brazil, Canada, the Netherlands and the United Kingdom, all of whom had aircraft carriers in service. A British marketing effort was launched on 9 December 1959, with the publication of a report entitled 'The Carrier Suitability of the F4H-1 Airplane on British Carriers'. A delegation visited London in April 1960, meeting the MoD, Royal Navy, Royal Air Force and Rolls-Royce. Britain's Director of Naval Warfare made a reciprocal visit in July 1960, and, during this, Commander P. C. S. Chilton became the first Briton (and the 73rd pilot overall) to fly the Phantom.

It soon became apparent that an RN Phantom variant would require a higher attitude on launch, slower approach speed and greater power. A nose-wheel

dolly was originally proposed, before McDonnell designed a nose oleo with double extension (to 40 in/102 cm instead of the F-4B's 20 in/51 cm). This was tested on a US Navy F-4B aboard the USS *Forrestal* on 11 April 1963.

An 'F-4B for Great Britain' memo followed in September, and a Royal Navy order materialized in July 1964. The new aircraft was based heavily on the F-4J and not on the F-4B as had originally been planned (the aircraft was originally referred to as the F-4B(RN) or F-4RN). To allow a landing weight of 36,000 lb (16500 kg) (reflecting the Royal Navy's unwillingness to jettison unused ordnance before landing) and to allow steeper approaches and a 24 fps (7.3 m/sec) sink rate and an 8 percent slower approach speed, the British Phantom was given a strengthened undercarriage, 16½° drooped ailerons, enlarged leading-edge flaps (both with BLC), stabilator slots and reduced stabilator anhedral. These improvements were also incorporated into the F-4J. Unique improvements included a folding radar and radome to allow the aircraft to use

small British carrier lifts, the extra nose-wheel extension previously mentioned and a strengthened (4.8g) arrester hook, as well as the Rolls-Royce Spey engine.

Short Brothers, BAC and Rolls-Royce British parts, sub-assemblies and the Rolls-Royce engines were shipped to St Louis for assembly by McDonnell Douglas. Unfortunately, the complex offset agreements increased the unit price, caused delays and had an unfortunate effect on performance.

Maiden flight of the Royal Navy's YF-4K, developed for use on the Royal Navy's tiny aircraft carriers, with aerodynamic improvements and Spey engines.

Britain also had to shoulder all the development costs of the Spey Phantom, resulting in a very high unit cost.

The adoption of the Rolls-Royce Spey 202/203 for the RN Phantom was decided at an early stage, even though it

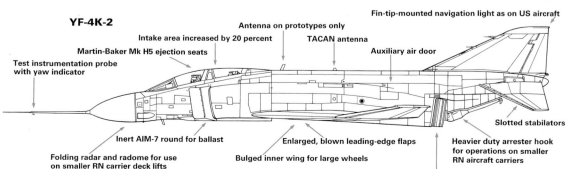

YF-4K-2

- Test instrumentation probe with yaw indicator
- Martin-Baker Mk H5 ejection seats
- Intake area increased by 20 percent
- Antenna on prototypes only
- Fin-tip-mounted navigation light as on US aircraft
- TACAN antenna
- Auxiliary air door
- Inert AIM-7 round for ballast
- Folding radar and radome for use on smaller RN carrier deck lifts
- Enlarged, blown leading-edge flaps
- Bulged inner wing for large wheels
- Slotted stabilators
- Heavier duty arrester hook for operations on smaller RN aircraft carriers
- Rolls-Royce Spey 201 turbofan engines

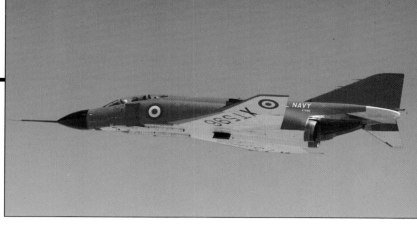

The incorporation of the untried Rolls-Royce Spey turbofan led to huge extra cost, a slower maximum speed, a lower ceiling and slower 'burner light-up times. On the other hand, range was dramatically increased.

The second YF-4K in flight. Both prototypes initially carried a long 'jousting lance' pitot static boom. The aircraft carries dummy Sparrows forward for center of gravity reasons.

necessitated major changes, including new inlet ducts (at least 6 in/15 cm wider) to handle the greater mass flow (240 lb/sec; 109 kg/sec) instead of 169 lb/sec (77 kg/sec), new engine intakes, new intake ramps and a redesigned engine bay. In fact, McDonnell Douglas had considered submitting a Spey-powered Phantom to meet the USAF's TFX requirement (eventually filled by the F-111) and completed Spey/Phantom studies in 1962 in anticipation of an RN order. Royal Navy interest had grown steadily since the announcement that the P.1154(RN) would not be Spey-powered. The Spey was at the time viewed with great favor, not least because a non-afterburning version of the engine was being used to power the Mk 2 Buccaneer. The Spey was thought to be essential in order to provide sufficient power to operate the Phantom safely from Britain's short-decked carriers, and to provide more bleed air for BLC, which would in turn allow slower approach speeds.

As it turned out, the Spey gave a 10 percent increase in operational radius, a 15 percent increase in ferry range, and better take-off, initial climb and low-level acceleration figures. On the other side of the coin, the maximum speed dropped from Mach 2.1 to Mach 1.9, and ceiling, performance at altitude and afterburner light-up time deteriorated.

The first two Phantoms ordered by the Royal Navy were development test aircraft, with British engines but US equipment, and these bore the US designation YF-4K. To the Royal Navy they were merely the first two Phantom FG.Mk 1s, and they were initially equipped with a nose-mounted test pitot probe.

F-4K Phantom FG.Mk 1

First flight: 2 November 1966
Pilot: not known
Number built: 50
Identities:
XT597 to XT598 (2)
XT857 to XT876 (20)
XV565 to XV592 (28)

With the rapid rundown of the UK carrier force, prompted by the early retirement of *Victorious* after a fire in the CPO's mess and the prohibitively high cost of refitting and refurbishing HMS *Eagle* to suit her for Phantom operations, only *Ark Royal* was left as a Phantom 'platform'. Therefore half of the RN F-4Ks were diverted immediately to the RAF, equipping No. 43 Squadron at RAF Leuchars, Scotland. Aircraft transferred to the RAF were later made compatible with the underfuselage SUU-23/A.

The F-4K can be recognised by the quadrant on the rear fuselage, which allowed deck crew to check that the correct stabilator angle was set for a catapult launch, and by the presence of a row of three vertical approach lights on the nose-wheel door.

Uniquely, British equipment on the F-4K included a Ferranti AN/AWG-11 radar (a license-built version of the AN/

F-4K Phantom FG.Mk 1 (late RN configuration)

Marconi ARI 18228 RWR fairing
UHF/VHF antenna
Martin-Baker Mk H5 ejection seats
AN/AWG-11 radar and fire-control system
Slotted stabilator
Approach lights – three in a vertical strip on leg door
UHF antenna
Anti-skid brakes
Rolls-Royce Spey 203 turbofan engines
40-in extra-extensible nose leg
No provision for gun pod
600-US gal fuel tank on centerline

Right: After service with the Royal Navy, the RAF took over many Phantom FG.Mk 1s for service in the air defense role at Leuchars in Scotland, augmenting the small batch which were delivered directly. This aircraft wears unusual enlarged national insignia over its air defense gray color scheme, along with the markings of No. 111 Squadron.

An early Royal Navy Phantom FG.Mk 1 lands aboard the HMS Eagle. Refitting this ship for Phantom operations was judged 'prohibitively expensive', leaving the Navy with only one carrier.

A heavily-laden No. 892 Squadron Phantom FG.Mk 1 blasts off from the Ark Royal. Eight 500-lb bombs was a significant warload for a catapult launch.

McDonnell Douglas F-4K Phantom FG.Mk 1
No. 892 Squadron
HMS *Ark Royal*
1977

This aircraft (XT872) first flew on 17 June 1968, and was delivered to NASU at RAF Yeovilton on 27 September. After trials at the Royal Aircraft Establishment at Bedford, the aircraft joined No. 892 Squadron as '007' on 2 April 1969. The aircraft continued to serve with No. 892 until the Phantom was withdrawn from Royal Navy service in September 1978. The aircraft then went to No. 4 Squadron of the Aircraft Engineering Wing at RAF St Athan for storage and modifications (including removal of nuclear strike equipment).

No. 892 Squadron
No. 892 Squadron had a long and proud history, dating back to its 1942 foundation as a Martlet-equipped fighter squadron. Postwar the unit flew a succession of Sea Venoms, Sea Vixens and, finally, Phantoms. The squadron reformed for the last time on 31 March 1969, from a nucleus provided by No. 700 P Squadron, the Phantom IFTU. The unit made frequent deployments aboard the HMS *Ark Royal*, and deployed to the USS *Saratoga* for cross-deck operations, and to Schleswig, Leuchars, Cecil Field, Lossiemouth, Oceana, Ramstein and Roosevelt Roads. The unit's official badge consisted of a winged eye below a flash of Lightning, floating above the waves, against a black background. This badge replaced the crowned '77' logo on the nose of No. 892's Phantoms.

Engine intakes
The need to operate from the Royal Navy's short-decked aircraft carriers meant that more power and more bleed air (for boundary layer control) would be needed. It was decided to power the aircraft by an afterburning version of the Rolls-Royce Spey, the greater mass flow of which demanded the provision of enlarged intakes. These imposed a significant drag penalty, and also gave the Spey Phantom its distinctively 'muscular' appearance when viewed from the front. The huge jetpipes drooped much more than those of J79-engined F-4s.

Color scheme
Like other postwar Royal Navy carrier aircraft, the Phantom wore a color scheme of dark sea gray top surfaces with white undersides. Gloss paint was used, with high-visibility red, white and blue roundels.

Armament
The Royal Navy's Phantoms were not compatible with the SUU-23 gun pod, although aircraft transferred to the RAF were later made compatible with this inaccurate but morale-boosting weapon. This aircraft carries a mixture of 12-round rocket pods and 500-lb bombs, with Sargent Fletcher fuel tanks outboard. The British Phantoms all had strengthened pylons, which allowed them to carry 1,000-lb bombs on all stations.

Radar
The fire control system fitted to the F-4K was designated AN/AWG-11, and built under license by Ferranti. It differed in detail only to the AN/AWG-10 of the F-4J. The radar and radome folded to allow the aircraft to use a small British carrier lift. Later in their careers, British Phantoms received a three-stage radar upgrade, including a Sidewinder Expanded Acquisition Mode.

Extra extendable nose oleo
To give a higher attitude on launch, McDonnell designed a nose oleo with extra extension (by 40 in). This was tested on an otherwise standard F-4B during trials on the USS *Forrestal*, and proved successful enough to be incorporated on the production F-4K (initially known as the 'F-4B for Great Britain').

Slotted stabilator
The F-4K was fitted with redesigned, slotted stabilators. These were effectively fitted with an inverted slat, allowing greater tailplane authority and making it easier to rotate the nose by generating extra downforce. These had slightly reduced anhedral and had an adjacent incidence indicator on the rear fuselage. This allowed the deck crew to visually check that the correct angle was set on launch.

Squadron markings
No. 892 Squadron decorated its aircraft with a huge red chevron on the tailfin, with a white diamond superimposed, containing a black Omega. This last proved prophetic, since the unit proved to be the Fleet Air Arm's last carrierborne fixed-wing (non-V/STOL) squadron. In 1977 a red, white and blue nose flash was applied to the noses of the squadron's Phantoms for the Queen's Silver Jubilee review of the fleet. The crown and '77' logo were later replaced by the squadron badge, but the flash remained. All squadron aircraft carried the 'R' tailcode (for *Ark Royal*), with a three-digit deck code on the nose, commencing with 0.

Fintip RWR fairing
Relatively late in their career, the Royal Navy's Phantoms were fitted with Marconi ARI 18228 radar warning receivers, this necessitating the fitting of a box-like antenna fairing atop the tailfin to house forward and rear hemisphere receivers.

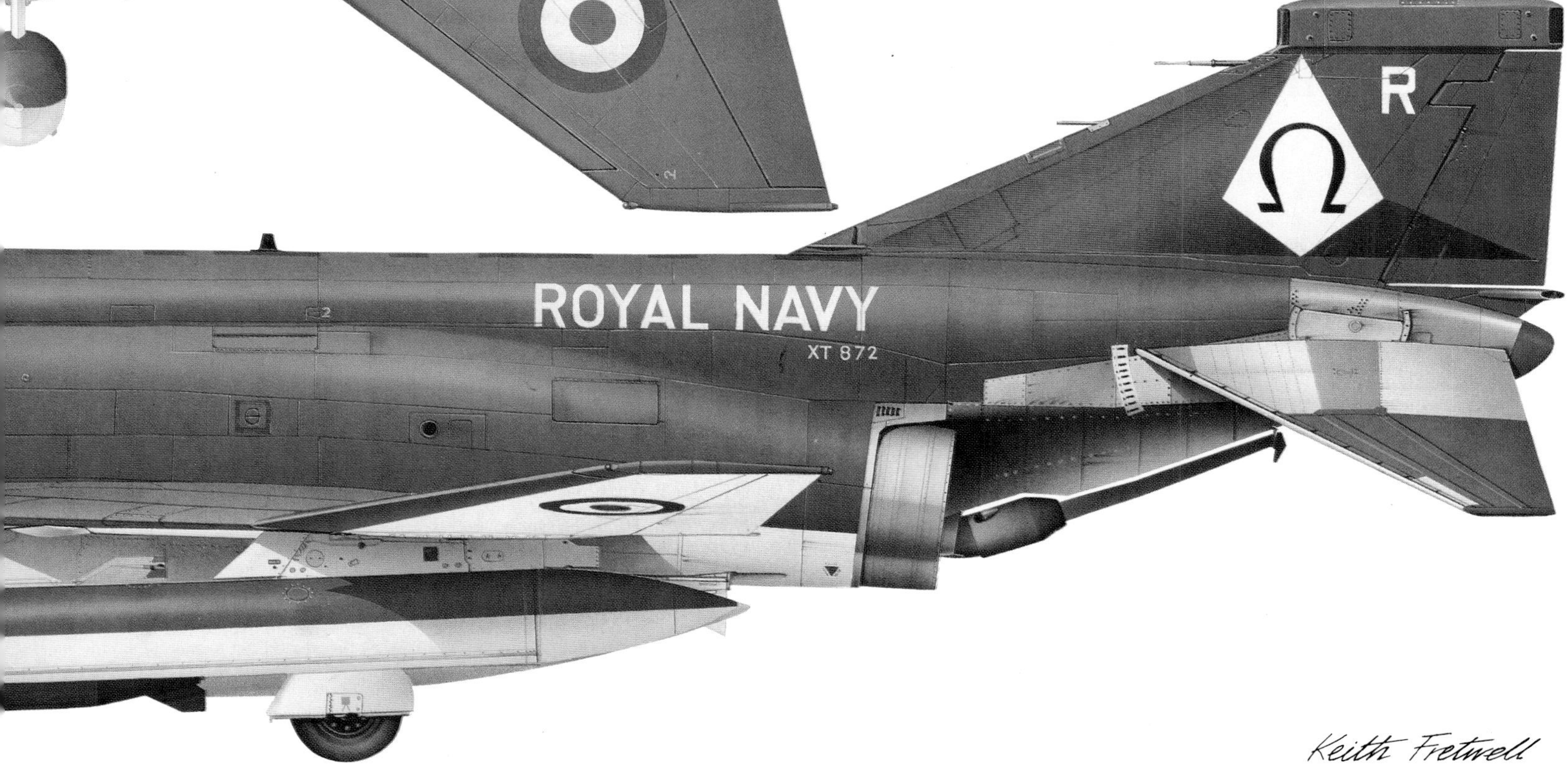

ROYAL NAVY
XT 872

ROYAL NAVY
XT 872

Keith Fretwell

AWG-10), a Plessey PTR-373 receiver and transmitter, a Dowty Electronics UHF standby receiver amplifier and a PTR-374 D403P UHF airborne emergency transmitter/receiver.

The Martin-Baker Mk H5 ejection seats were originally supplied with US harnesses, but these were replaced, and the seats were later upgraded to the same H7 standard as those in the US Navy F-4J, which had zero-zero capability. All British Phantoms were given strengthened pylons, which conferred the ability to carry a 1,000-lb (454-kg) bomb and still be able to land aboard a carrier. These pylons were fitted with three piston ejector release units, but were later up-gunned.

By the late 1980s, the best way of telling a fully-modified RAF FG.Mk 1 from an FGR.Mk 2 was by the serial number, or the tiny 'traffic lights' on the nose-wheel door.

An FG.Mk 1 of No. 111 Squadron in gray and green camouflage. This sometimes peeled away in places to show the colors of No. 892, which had been hastily overpainted when the aircraft swapped service.

Below left: This aircraft, operated by the A&AEE, may be the RAF's last Phantom.

F-4K Phantom FG.Mk 1 (Mod)

Modified nose radome shape

F-4L

Not built

The F-4L designation was applied to an unbuilt Spey-engined variant intended for the US Navy. Adoption of the more powerful Spey would have allowed US Navy Phantoms to operate from the smaller carriers, which otherwise relied on F-8 Crusaders to provide air defense. The advantages offered by the more powerful British engine were felt to be outweighed by considerations of cost and commonality.

YF-4M Phantom FGR.Mk 2

First flight: 17 February 1967
Pilot: not known
Number built: two
Identities: XT582 and XT583

Whereas the Royal Navy's procurement of the F-4K represented the sensible choice of the best aircraft to meet the requirement, the RAF Phantom procurement owed little to military requirements and a great deal to party politics. When a Labour government was elected in October 1964, it was implacably hostile to Britain's aircraft industry, which it described as a 'featherbed' and a 'retarded child', and resented for absorbing too large a proportion of research funding. The Air Staff were told that two of the industry's three most vital programs would have to go. These were the Hawker Siddeley P.1154 and the HS.681. Remarkably, the BAC TSR.2 escaped this initial axe. The P.1154 was replaced by an order for the Phantom, on the basis that the P.1154 would not ''be in service in time to serve as a Hunter replacement . . . there is a time gap of some years which no

government can ask either its service chiefs or servicemen to accept.'' At the same time, the HS.681 was replaced by the C-130. By April 1965, the TSR.2 had been replaced by the F-111, depriving Britain's aircraft industry of its three most crucial projects in one fell swoop, and condemning the RAF to operate what it saw as inferior and less ambitious equipment.

The US government had been prepared to offset the dollar cost of these procurement programs with generous orders for British aircraft (including one for VC-10s for the USAF), but the Wilson government failed to follow through. They fortunately continued to push for a high UK equipment content in Britain's Phantoms, but, stupidly, specified the Spey (which the RAF did not want) in place of the cheaper, proven J79.

The Phantom was never a wholly McDonnell aircraft, and suppliers such as Aeronca, Beech, Cessna, Douglas, Fairchild Republic, Goodyear and Northrop were all involved in producing parts and sub-assemblies. For the British

The prototype YF-4M takes off from St Louis. The RAF was not an entirely willing Phantom user, having had the aircraft forced upon them instead of the favored P.1154.

Phantom program, a number of British companies submitted bids, and many were successful. Some 'places' were guaranteed but, in many cases, British

manufacturers undercut their American rivals. BAC's Strand Road, Preston factory built aft fuselages, fins, rudders and tailcones, stabilators and inboard leading-edges at a rate of 10 per month, completing the work by 1969.

Short Brothers built outer wing panels and leading-edge flaps, while Delaney Gallay produced heat exchangers and titanium insulation blankets. Goodyear UK

produced brakes, subcontracting the anti-skid system to Dunlop. Ferranti produced a new INAS, based on that developed for the TSR.2, and built the AN/AWG-10 under license as the AWG-12 (interfaced with the INAS on the F-4M). Marconi produced new fuel flow meters, an ASN-46 navigation computer under license from Bendix, the General Electric autopilot and a Honeywell fuel gauge. Government-furnished equipment included the Cossor SSR 1500 IFF Mk

10A transponder and SSR 1503 controller. Finally, Hawker Siddeley (now BAe) at Brough became the aircraft weapons system sister design firm, responsible for in-service support and modifications, as though the aircraft had been built at Brough itself.

The first two RAF Phantoms were delivered as development test airframes under the US designation YF-4M. They differed only in detail to the production F-4M Phantom FGR.Mk 2.

*The RAF's Phantoms incorporated a significant amount of British equipment, and whole sub-assemblies were built by **BAC** (tail units) and **Shorts** (outer wings).*

F-4M Phantom FGR.Mk 2

First flight: 26 December 1967
Pilot: not known
Number built: 116
Identities:
XT891 to XT914 (24)
XV393 to XV442 (50)
XV460 to XV501 (42)

The production Royal Air Force Phantom was the F-4M. Externally almost identical to the F-4K, the F-4M lacked the Royal Navy aircraft's extendable nose-wheel unit (using a standard F-4C nose oleo) and had a standard non-slatted stabilator. It differed from RN aircraft in being compatible with the SUU-16/A and SUU-23/A gun pods, and in having a Ferranti INAS based on that developed for the TSR.2, HF radio and a radar altimeter. The RAF's F-4Ms entered service in the interdiction/strike role, and were equipped to carry the SNEB rocket pod, the 1,000-lb (454-kg) bomb, the BL755 CBU and American-supplied B28, B43, B57 or B61 nuclear weapons. The B28 would have been carried singly on station five, while the other weapons could have been carried in threes.

A proportion of RAF F-4Ms were equipped with dual controls, and some were compatible with a new reconnaissance pod developed by EMI. This contained a roll-stabilized Texas Instruments RS-700 infrared linescan unit and a high-definition Q-band sideways-looking radar, which had mapping and moving target indication capabilities. It also contained five optical cameras, with one forward, one vertical and two oblique F.95s and a single vertical F.135 whose twin lenses gave a stereo picture. An electronic flash unit could be accommodated in a special underwing tank. The pod could also accommodate an oblique F.95 with a 12-in (30-cm) lens or an F.126 medium-altitude vertical camera.

When the RAF's Phantom FGR.Mk 2s were replaced by the Jaguar during the

F-4M Phantom FGR.Mk 2 (early RAF configuration)

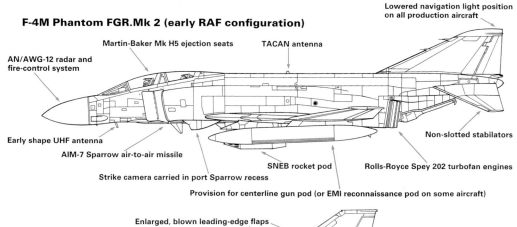

Martin-Baker Mk H5 ejection seats
TACAN antenna
AN/AWG-12 radar and fire-control system
Lowered navigation light position on all production aircraft
Non-slotted stabilators
Early shape UHF antenna
AIM-7 Sparrow air-to-air missile
SNEB rocket pod
Rolls-Royce Spey 202 turbofan engines
Strike camera carried in port Sparrow recess
Provision for centerline gun pod (or EMI reconnaissance pod on some aircraft)

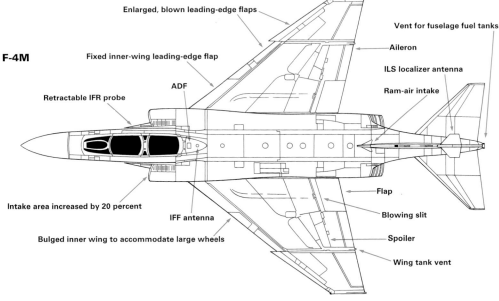

F-4M

Enlarged, blown leading-edge flaps
Vent for fuselage fuel tanks
Aileron
ILS localizer antenna
Ram-air intake
Fixed inner-wing leading-edge flap
ADF
Retractable IFR probe
Flap
Blowing slit
Intake area increased by 20 percent
IFF antenna
Spoiler
Bulged inner wing to accommodate large wheels
Wing tank vent

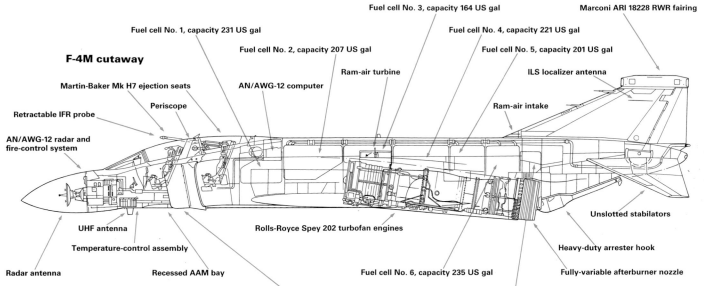

F-4M cutaway

Fuel cell No. 3, capacity 164 US gal
Marconi ARI 18228 RWR fairing
Fuel cell No. 1, capacity 231 US gal
Fuel cell No. 4, capacity 221 US gal
Fuel cell No. 2, capacity 207 US gal
Fuel cell No. 5, capacity 201 US gal
Ram-air turbine
Martin-Baker Mk H7 ejection seats
AN/AWG-12 computer
ILS localizer antenna
Periscope
Ram-air intake
Retractable IFR probe
AN/AWG-12 radar and fire-control system
UHF antenna
Temperature-control assembly
Rolls-Royce Spey 202 turbofan engines
Unslotted stabilators
Heavy-duty arrester hook
Radar antenna
Recessed AAM bay
Fully-variable afterburner nozzle
Boundary-layer splitter plate
Fuel cell No. 6, capacity 235 US gal
Fuel cell No. 7, capacity 104 US gal

Phantom Variants: F-4M Phantom FGR.Mk 2

mid-1970s, they in turn replaced Lightnings in the air defense role. They were initially armed with AIM-9 Sidewinders and AIM-7 Sparrows. The January 1972 Air Staff Target for a new medium-range AAM resulted in a January 1973 Air Staff Requirement for an updated AIM-7 with repackaged control and power sections and incorporating the newly developed Marconi monopulse seeker head and EMI radar proximity fuse. The new missile was originally known as the XJ521, and was built by Hawker Siddeley (later BAe) Dynamics as the Sky Flash. Firings were conducted at the Naval Weapons Center at China Lake and the Pacific Missile Test Center at Point Mugu by two F-4Js leased from the US Navy. The missile quickly replaced the AIM-7 in RAF service, on both the Phantom and the Tornado ADV.

F-4M Phantom FGR.Mk 2 (late RAF configuration)

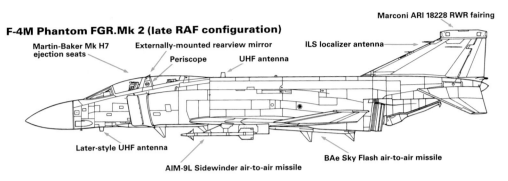

F-4M

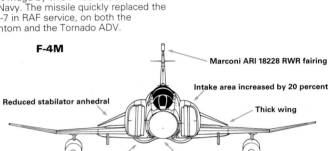

- Reduced stabilator anhedral
- Marconi ARI 18228 RWR fairing
- Intake area increased by 20 percent
- Thick wing
- Jet pipes and nozzles 'hang' below level of wing
- AWG-12 radar and fire-control system

Below: *No. 74 Squadron was the RAF's last front-line Phantom unit, flying its FGR.Mk 2s until October 1992.*

Above: *This No. 54 Squadron aircraft is armed with four SNEB rocket pods and carries a centerline EMI reconnaissance pod.*

The prototype Project Bee Line F-4B flies over the Naval Air Research Facility, North Island, which converted 228 F-4Bs to F-4N configuration.

F-4N
(Model 98)

First flight: 4 June 1972 (153034)
Pilot: not known
Number converted: 228
Identities: (in conversion sequence)
153034, 150430, 150652, 150491,
150452, 150635, 150444, 151398,
150460, 151424, 150407, 150634,
150441, 151016, 151451, 150422,
151491, 150996, 151015, 150445,
150472, 151433, 151442, 151434,
151006, 151400, 150425, 150479,
150640, 150627, 150450, 150485,
150625, 152235, 152267, 150466,
151439, 152241, 151480, 150412,
151004, 152291, 151431, 150630,
152280, 150411, 152230, 150651,
150468, 151513, 151468, 151435,
150648, 150429, 151417, 151476,
151463, 150492, 152278, 151519,
150482, 150475, 151484, 150476,
152277, 150465, 151430, 151469,
150642, 151456, 151436, 152306,
151000, 151444, 151448, 150436,
152259, 152258, 152272, 152253,
151489, 152229, 150419, 152288,
150643, 150438, 151413, 150456,
150448, 150632, 150423, 151406,
152254, 152236, 150415, 150489,
151003, 152294, 152302, 151471,
152991, 152223, 152275, 150442,
151487, 150426, 150638, 152969,
153024, 152967, 152227, 151502,
151498, 151422, 150478, 152237,
152210, 153059, 153047, 151464,
150432, 150481, 153026, 151401,
153045, 153065, 150464, 152977,
151475, 152318, 152281, 153053,
152295, 153039, 153050, 153023,
152975, 153914, 152981, 153017,
152252, 152313, 152323, 151514,
151452, 151477, 150480, 150440,
153008, 152982, 151446, 153016,
152293, 150639, 151008, 152243,
153915, 152226, 151510, 152221,
151440, 152222, 152326, 153058,
153012, 152968, 152965, 151504,
153067, 152225, 152310, 152214,

152317, 152970, 153010, 152212,
152250, 150435, 152208, 153056,
152269, 152996, 152282, 151415,
150993, 151465, 152307, 152300,
152283, 152983, 153036, 153057,
152270, 152990, 152298, 152244,
153019, 153027, 152986, 153062,

153030, 153011, 151503, 151461,
152321, 151002, 152290, 152246,
151449, 151455, 152971, 153064,
150490, 152992, 152303, 152279,
150628, 151007, 152217, 151011,
150484, 153006, 151482, 152327,
151511, 152284, 153034

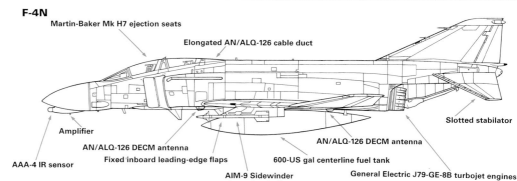

F-4N
Martin-Baker Mk H7 ejection seats
Elongated AN/ALQ-126 cable duct
Amplifier
AAA-4 IR sensor
AN/ALQ-126 DECM antenna
Fixed inboard leading-edge flaps
AIM-9 Sidewinder air-to-air missile
600-US gal centerline fuel tank
AN/ALQ-126 DECM antenna
Slotted stabilator
General Electric J79-GE-8B turbojet engines

Below: A VF-302 F-4N approaches the deck. The F-4N had a long career with the Reserve squadrons of the US Navy and Marine Corps, after a relatively short active-duty life.

Phantom Variants: F-4N

By 1970, both the US Navy and McDonnell Douglas were expressing concern over the age and condition of the F-4Bs, many of which were over 10 years old, and some of which were in active service in Vietnam. A program was thus initiated to refurbish and modernize the surviving F-4Bs, and this was given the codename Bee Line. Aircraft selected for conversion (those in the best condition) were sent to the Naval Air Rework Facility at NAS North Island, California, where they were stripped and inspected for any signs of fatigue or damage. The aircraft were then rebuilt using new parts wherever this would extend service life (an extension of between 3,500 and 5,000 hours was hoped for). The aircraft were totally rewired, and new or inspected avionics were added. The F-4N also incorporated a lot of new equipment and many new features.

By 1971, many F-4Bs had been fitted with F-4J-style slotted stabilators, which helped solve 'Mach tuck' problems when decelerating from supersonic speed and which reduced approach speeds. All F-4Ns received the new stabilator. Similarly, all F-4Ns had their inboard leading-edge flaps locked shut. New equipment included Sanders AN/ALQ-126 or -126B Deceptive ECM, with intake-mounted antennas fitted to most F-4Ns (to early examples by retrofit), although the latter were in longer fairings than those used by the same equipment on the F-4J, extending back one frame further because of difficulties in routing cables. This was to be the main identification feature between the F-4N and the older F-4B, since the aircraft retained thin wings and tires, the F-4B's main radar and undernose IRST. Dash-8 engines also remained. Radar-homing and warning antennas for the ALQ-126 were fitted to the undersides of the intakes and wings (just aft of the undercarriage bays), these being tied in to the antennas on the trailing edge (and sometimes also the leading edge) of the tail fin.

Other additions to the F-4N included a

Right: An F-4N serving with the Pacific Missile Test Center carries an AQM-81N drone under the centerline plyon. A notable feature of some F-4Ns was the addition of RWR antenna to the leading edge of the fintip.

helmet sight Visual Target Acquisition System (VTAS) and a Sidewinder Expanded Acquisition Mode (SEAM). A new mission computer was provided, together with auto altitude reporting, APX-76 or APX-80 air-to-air IFF and an AN/ASW-25B one-way datalink. The electrical generating system was upgraded with 30-kVA constant speed alternators. The first renovated F-4Ns joined the fleet in February 1973, and examples served with the Marine Corps Reserve into the 1980s.

Right: The Marine Corps made extensive use of the F-4N, these colorful examples serving VMFA-321 at Andrews AFB. The unit flew the variant from 1977 to 1984, when the F-4S arrived. These survived until July 1991.

Below: Without doubt one of the smartest-looking Phantoms ever, this was VF-202's F-4N CAG-bird in 1977. VF-202 was one of two F-4 fighter units within CVWR-20, the East Coast Reserve Air Wing.

Above: Marked for the commander of VF-111, this 'Sundowners' F-4N also has bicentennial marks. The key identification feature of the 'N' was the very long DECM fairing on the upper intake sides.

QF-4N
(Model 98)

First flight: not known
Pilot: not known
Number converted:
not known
Identities: 150412, 150415, 150419,
150423, 150432, 150456, 150464,
150475, 150489, 150630, 150993,
151000, 151002, 151004, 151007,
151406, 151415, 151430, 151435,
151440, 151449, 151455, 151461,
151463, 151465, 151469, 151471,
151475, 151476, 151484, 151503,
151504, 152214, 152217, 152221,
152222, 152223, 152226, 152229,
152230, 152235, 152243, 152253,
152258, 152269, 152272, 152277,
152279, 152281, 152282, 152303,
152310, 152321, 152323, 152326,
152968, 152972, 153011, 153024,
153030, 153034, 153053, 153056,
153058, 153059, 153064, 153065,
153067, 153074, 153076, 153084?,
153812?, 153914

The original Phantom drone, the QF-4B,
was severely limited in maneuver
capability, despite the fact that it had
been originally intended to simulate agile
targets. The QF-4N was similarly
intended to simulate the most agile
targets, in order to test AAM systems to
the utmost, and the Navy thus
determined that the new FSAT (full-scale
aircraft target) should not be handicapped
by an artificially low *g* limit.

Everything that was not essential to
the target mission was removed (a
weight saving of more than a ton was
achieved) and the rear cockpit was
stripped to accommodate command
receivers for the AN/ASA-32 system. The
front cockpit, however, remained, and
the QF-4N is 'man-rated'.

The first QF-4N was unveiled in February
1983 and delivered to China Lake for
trials (manned and in 'NOLO', or no live
operator configuration) on 1 May 1986.
The NARF at Cherry Point subsequently
produced some 60 QF-4N conversions,
most of these going to the PMTC.

*Right: In current gray scheme, a
QF-4N lands with a supersonic
aerial target suspended beneath
the centerline. Two crew members
are on board for the mission.*

*Above: A remarkable inflight photo depicts a QF-4N in 'NOLO' configuration, control being effected completely
by remote control. The QF-4N introduced greater agility compared to the QF-4B model, mainly due to drastic
weight-saving and a relaxing of g limits.*

*Above: One of the more unusual paint scheme/aircraft
combinations was provided by this QF-4N of the
PMTC, which was redecorated to represent a Vietnam-
era F-4B for the film Flight of the Intruder.*

*Above: The US Navy standardized on the QF-4N for its
drone program, these being operated chiefly by the
Pacific Missile Test Center at Point Mugu (now the
Naval Air Warfare Center, Weapons Division). This
aircraft carries a camera for recording missile attacks.*

*Above: This QF-4N wears the
'NAWC' titles adopted by the
former PMTC on 1 January 1992,
when this unit and the Naval
Weapons Center at China Lake
joined together as the NAWC/WD.*

*Left: Shark's mouth markings
adorned this QF-4N in the early
1990s. The drone Phantoms will be
around for some years, as the
ultimate expenditure of airframes is
limited by the use of purpose-built
drones and towed targets.*

F-4P
(Model 98)

Not built

The F-4P designation was at one time
thought to have been applied to the
single HIAC/PCC mock-up, which is now
better known as the F-4X.

The slat actuators under the inboard wing leading edge are clearly visible in this head-on view of a VMFAT-101 F-4S as it plugs into the refueling drogue.

The prototype F-4S is seen here before installation of leading-edge slats. The first 47 conversions were delivered without slats, which were retrofitted.

F-4S
(Model 98)

First flight: 22 July 1977; NARF North Island, California (158360)
Pilot: not known
Number converted: 248 (some sources state 265); 302 originally planned
Identities: 153779, 153780, 153784, 153787, 153791, 153792, 153798, 153800, 153805, 153808 to 153810, 153814, 153818 to 153821, 153823 to 153828, 153832, 153833, 153835, 153840, 153842, 153843, 153845, 1253847, 153851, 153853, 153855 to 153860, 153862, 153864, 153868, 153869, 153872 to 153874, 153877, 153879 to 153882, 153884, 153887, 153889 to 153891, 153893, 153896, 153898 to 153900, 153902 to 153904, 153907, 153909 to 153911, 154781, 154782, 154786, 154788, 155515, 155517 to 155519, 155521, 155522, 155524, 155525, 155527, 155528, 155530 to 155532, 155539, 155541 to 155545, 155547, 155549, 155550, 155552, 155555, 155558 to 155562, 155565 to 155568, 155570, 155572, 155573, 155575, 155579, 155731 to 155733, 155735, 155736, 155739 to 155741, 155743, 155745 to 155747, 155749, 155753, 155754, 155757, 155759, 155761, 155764 to 155767, 155769, 155772, 155773, 155779, 155781, 155783, 155784, 155786, 155787, 155792, 155794, 155801, 155805 to 155808, 155810, 155812, 155813, 155818, 155820 to 155823, 155825, 155827 to 155830, 155833, 155834, 155836, 155838 to 155840, 155845, 155847 to 155849, 155851, 155854, 155855, 155858, 155859, 155862 to 155864, 155869, 155871, 155872, 155874, 155876, 155878, 155879, 155881, 155883, 155887,

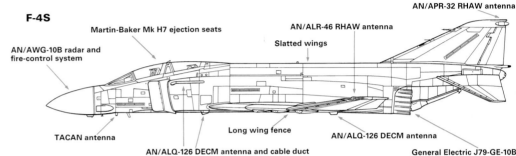

F-4S

AN/AWG-10B radar and fire-control system

Martin-Baker Mk H7 ejection seats

Slatted wings

AN/ALR-46 RHAW antenna

AN/APR-32 RHAW antenna

TACAN antenna

Long wing fence

AN/ALQ-126 DECM antenna and cable duct

AN/ALQ-126 DECM antenna

General Electric J79-GE-10B turbojet engines

The F-4S was essentially an updated, refurbished and slatted F-4J, and had a very short career with active-duty fighter squadrons, soon being replaced by F-14s.

155888, 155890 to 155893, 155896 to 155901, 157242, 157243, 157245, 157246, 157248 to 157250, 157254, 157255, 157257, 157259, 157260, 157267 to 157269, 157272, 157276, 157278, 157279, 157281 to 157283, 157287, 157290 to 157293, 157296 to 157298, 157301, 157304, 157305, 157307 to 157309, 158346, 158348, 158350, 158352 to 158354, 158362, 158370, 158372, 158374, 158376

The success of the Bee Line project (which had upgraded F-4Bs to F-4N standard) prompted the Navy to rework surviving F-4Js to a similar standard, with structural modifications and improved avionics.

The aim of the program was to extend F-4J service life to allow the aircraft to fill the gap until the Phantom could be replaced by the F/A-18 (in Marines service) and by the F-14 (in US Navy service). The NARF at North Island, California, was warned to prepare for the upgrade program, officially the Airframe Change 599 Service Life Extension Program, as soon as the Bee Line project was complete. The first prototype F-4S (158360) made its first post-conversion flight at North Island on 22 July 1977.

Because the Vietnam War had seen the Phantom move away from the traditional long-range BVR intercept role and into close-in dogfighting and ground attack, it was decided to introduce two-

position leading-edge maneuver slats on the F-4S. Such slats gave a 50 percent improvement in combat turning capability in comparison with an unslatted F-4J, and operated automatically as a function of AoA, extending at 11.5 units of Alpha and retracting at 10.5 units; they can be overridden from the cockpit. The slats used on the F-4S consisted of two sections: one on the outboard part of the fixed inner wing and the other on the folding outer-wing panel. (The first few S conversions also had the inboard inner-wing flap, but this was rendered inoperable under a later modification.) The Navy conducted its own research into the effects of slats at Patuxent River during the early 1970s, using a variety of fixed slat configurations on F-4J 153088. The Navy eventually selected a very similar slat to that used on the Air Force F-4E, albeit with a much longer fore-and-aft fence outboard on the wingfold. The actuator fairings for the inboard slat sections were especially prominent.

Delays meant that the first 47 F-4Ss were delivered without slats, and survivors had them retrofitted at North Island or Cherry Point. The first F-4S conversion delivered with slats from the start was 155899, which was delivered to VMFA-251 in late November 1979. All F-4S conversions incorporated a host of other modifications and improvements. The aircraft were stripped and minutely inspected, receiving a plethora of landing

gear and wing/fuselage structural improvements, including visible external straps on the wing spar. Electrical systems were rewired using lighter, more reliable Kapton wire, and the hydraulic systems were replumbed using stainless steel tubing.

Another change that was visually apparent was the installation of 'smokeless' J79-GE-10B engines, with low smoke combustor and low energy ignition, which got rid of the Phantom's distinctive sooty black smoke trail, leaving only a wisp of white smoke coming out of burner. The same engine was fitted to some F-4Js.

A digital AN/AWG-10B weapon control system was provided, with new AN/ARC-159 dual UHF radios and an ARN-118 TACAN. The new AWG-10B required the retraining of RIOs. Low voltage formation-keeping strip lights were fitted on the sides of the nose, mid-fuselage and tailfin, their vivid green color earning them the soubriquet of 'slime lights'. The ALQ-126 or 126A of the F-4J was retained, with the same short intake fairings.

The F-4S served with a number of second-line units, including the PMTC. The last such aircraft were retired during 1991.

The F-4S was the last major Phantom variant, but served with a relatively large number of units, albeit for a short time. First deliveries were to the Marine Corps, with VMFA-451 'Warlords' receiving unslatted F-4Ss in June 1978. This was followed by VMFA-212 'Lancers' at Kaneohe Bay, Hawaii. The first Navy unit was VF-21 'Freelancers' at NAS Miramar, California. Thirteen US Marine Corps and 12 US Navy fighter squadrons eventually received the F-4S, several of them Reserve units. The last Navy F-4Ss were those of VF-202 'Superheats' at NAS Dalla, Texas, who retired their aircraft in May 1985. The last Marine F-4Ss (and the last naval aviation Phantoms, apart from drones) were retired from VMF-112 in early 1992.

The last F-4S served with the squadrons of the US Marine Corps Reserve. This aircraft, wearing an unusual 'Ferris'-style camouflage scheme, served with VMF-321 'Hell's Angels' at NAF Washington. Sister squadron VMF-112 'Cowboys' at NAS Dallas retired their final aircraft at the beginning of 1992.

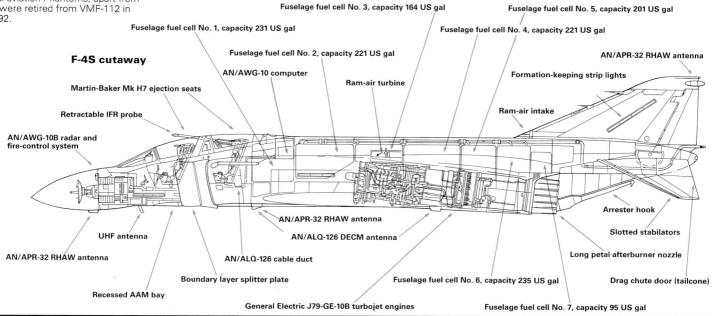

F-4S cutaway

Fuselage fuel cell No. 1, capacity 231 US gal
Fuselage fuel cell No. 2, capacity 221 US gal
Fuselage fuel cell No. 3, capacity 164 US gal
Fuselage fuel cell No. 4, capacity 221 US gal
Fuselage fuel cell No. 5, capacity 201 US gal
AN/AWG-10 computer
Ram-air turbine
AN/APR-32 RHAW antenna
Formation-keeping strip lights
Ram-air intake
Martin-Baker Mk H7 ejection seats
Retractable IFR probe
AN/AWG-10B radar and fire-control system
UHF antenna
AN/APR-32 RHAW antenna
AN/APR-32 RHAW antenna
AN/ALQ-126 DECM antenna
AN/ALQ-126 cable duct
Boundary layer splitter plate
Recessed AAM bay
General Electric J79-GE-10B turbojet engines
Fuselage fuel cell No. 6, capacity 235 US gal
Fuselage fuel cell No. 7, capacity 95 US gal
Arrester hook
Slotted stabilators
Long petal-afterburner nozzle
Drag chute door (tailcone)

QF-4S
(Model 98)

First flight: not known
Pilot: not known
Number converted: not known
Identities: 158358

The prototype QF-4S was 158358, previously VX-4's 'Black Bunny', which was sent to NARF Cherry Point, North Carolina, for drone conversion in late 1988. Funds have not been forthcoming for the conversion of further F-4S airframes to FSAT drones.

F-4T

Not built

In a vain attempt to keep the F-4 production line open during the late 1970s, McDonnell Douglas proposed a stripped-down F-4E derivative optimized for the air superiority role. Since the F-4E was clearly vastly inferior to the new generation of agile fighters already being developed, this represented a very forlorn hope indeed. The aircraft was to have been stripped of all non air-to-air related systems, retaining only the built-in M61 cannon, the four AIM-7s and four AIM-9s for its armament. A digital computer was to have managed the weapons system.

No customers materialized for this outmoded dinosaur, and it became increasingly apparent that in its original primary role the F-4 had finally had its day.

F-4X and RF-4X
(Model 98)

Not built (but F-4E 69-7576 served as mock-up for RF-4X)

The F-4X and RF-4X were advanced F-4E derivatives designed by General Dynamics to carry the company's HIAC-1 ultra-long focal length LOROP camera as part of Project Peace Jack (see also RF-4C and F-4E(S) entries). The camera offered unrivaled resolution (240 lines per milimetre, or 12 in at 20 nm range, or 38 in at 68 nm). The HIAC-1 featured a 66-in (168-cm) focal length f4 lens with shutter speeds from 1/60 to 1/3000 of a second. Film capacity was 1,000 ft (305 m) and exposure rate was four per second. The heavyweight HIAC-1 had originally been carried only by the big-winged, four-engined Martin/General Dynamics RB-57F, but was progressively improved and lightened from 3,500 lb (1588 kg) to 1,228 lb (557 kg) in later production models. Such a light HIAC-1 made carriage by other aircraft types a distinct possibility.

Israel had long been interested in acquiring the HIAC-1 and RB-57F, but its requests were never approved. Eventually, in 1971, US attitudes to the export of the HIAC-1 changed, and General Dynamics was authorized to develop what became the G-139 pod, containing an HIAC-1 and other sensors. It was intended from the start to be applied primarily to the F-4 Phantom. Twenty-two feet (6.7 m) long and weighing over 4,000 lb (1800 kg), the prototype pod was tested on an RF-4C in October 1971, and soon proved to restrict speed, maneuverability, altitude and range to an unacceptable degree. The first solution proposed was to increase the power of the J79 engine; proposals to re-engine the F-4 with TF30 or PW1120s were rejected on the grounds of cost.

The J79's thrust had already been successfully increased by using water injection for pre-compressor cooling (PCC) in various F-4 record attempts, and it was decided to use a similar system, combined with new intakes and splitter plates, on the Peace Jack Phantom. Water for the PCC system was to be contained in a pair of three-compartment 2,500-US gal (2,082-Imp gal; 9463-liter)

F-4X

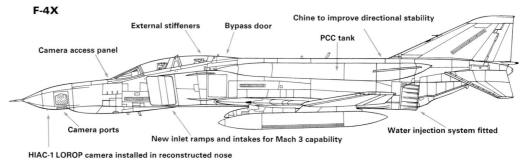

Chine to improve directional stability
External stiffeners
Bypass door
PCC tank
Camera access panel
Camera ports
New inlet ramps and intakes for Mach 3 capability
HIAC-1 LOROP camera installed in reconstructed nose
Water injection system fitted

tanks, which also contained pumps and regulators, bolted to the intersection joints of the fuselage spine and engine nacelles. The system promised to give a 150 percent increase in thrust at altitude. The new intakes, which allowed speeds of up to Mach 3.2 and which gave cruise performance of Mach 2.7, were much larger, with a sophisticated system of internal cowls, splitter plates, vortex generators and bleeds to allow airflow and shock-wave formation to be tightly controlled. By this time, the new Phantom was known as the F-4X, and was attracting strong interest and financial support from Israel.

The promised performance of the F-4X soon led to problems, at least insofar as exports were concerned. Without a recce pod the aircraft clearly had enormous potential as an interceptor. This threatened the infant F-15 program and promised to give Israel a more capable potential interceptor than anything in US service, and which might one day pose a

threat to the SR-71. Fortunately for Israel, continued concern over the drag imposed by the podded HIAC-1 led to a new configuration (which was soon designated RF-4X), which dispensed with the F-4E's AN/APQ-120 AI radar and accommodated the camera in its nose. Removal of interceptor capability reassured the State Department and Israel was back in the program. Aircraft 69-7576 (its previous IDF/AF identity is unknown) was delivered to General Dynamics in December 1974 and was

used as the RF-4X mock-up. Meanwhile, the US Air Force began to withdraw from the project, afraid of the impact the RF-4X flight test results might have on the F-15 program, and unconvinced by the safety and reliability of PCC. They demanded further in-depth testing, which simply could not be funded. The Israelis could not support the program alone, and the RF-4X died. It would have had the capability of cruising at Mach 2.7 for 10 minutes, at 78,000 ft (23800 m) (the endurance limit being set by water

Above: This F-4E (later delivered to Israel as an F-4E(S) recce platform) served as the RF-4X mock-up. The nose was recontoured on the starboard side only, and the huge coolant tank (made of cardboard) was fitted on one side only.

consumption). The nose-mounted HIAC-1 installation, however, lived on to form the basis of the F-4E(S).

Boeing Military Airplane Company Modernized ('Super') F-4 Phantom

Boeing Enhanced Phantom

Not built

Boeing announced details of an F-4 modernization scheme (in association with Pratt & Whitney) during early 1984, aimed mainly at export customers. McDonnell themselves had declined to participate in the project, perhaps realizing that the F-4 had reached the sensible peak of its development, or maybe worried that an upgraded Phantom might compete with F-15 or F/A-18 sales.

As an initial step, a single F-4 was converted into a demonstrator for Israel, with a single PW1120 in place of one of its J79 turbojets. An approval by US Deputy Defense Secretary William H. Taft IV for USAF flight demonstrations of a re-engined F-4 and second demonstrator, with two PW1120s, was planned. The PW1120 was a twin-shaft turbojet, derived from the F100 used by the F-15 and F-16 (with about 70 percent commonality), some 40 in (102 cm) shorter than the J79, of similar diameter, compatible with the F-4's existing intake, and with 25 percent greater dry thrust and 30 percent more augmented thrust. It was 25 percent lighter than the J79-GE-19. Improved specific fuel consumption would increase the F-4's

range by up to 18 percent. The new powerplant gave a massive increase in performance, improving sustained turn rate from 9° to 10½° per second, boosting the thrust-to-weight ratio from 0.76 to 0.92, and improving the sea level climb rate from 41,300 to 51,000 ft per minute (12600 to 15550 m/min). The acceleration time from Mach 0.9 to 1.6 at 36,000 ft (11000 m) was cut by 18 percent.

This aircraft was also planned to have had a 1,100-US gal (916-Imp gal; 4164-liter) conformal fuel tank on the belly,

with hardpoints on it for four bombs or two Sparrow missiles. This offered nearly twice the fuel of a standard centerline tank, was stressed to the same limits as the airframe and generated 29 percent of the drag. An avionics update was also planned, with various options to meet individual customer requirements. A typical configuration would include an MIL-STD-1553B databus, with APG-65

radar, a GEC HUD (as used by the F-16), a Honeywell 423 ring laser gyro INS and Sperry MFDs. 'Production' conversions were envisaged to be completed in the customer's own country in a cooperative program between Boeing and an indigenous aircraft company. In February 1986, the USAF's Aeronautical Systems Division suspended development of Boeing's Phantom upgrade.

GEC HUD

AN/APG-66 radar

Pratt & Whitney PW1120 turbofan engines

BMAC 1,100-US gal conformal fuel tank with hardpoints

AN/ALE-40 chaff/flare dispenser

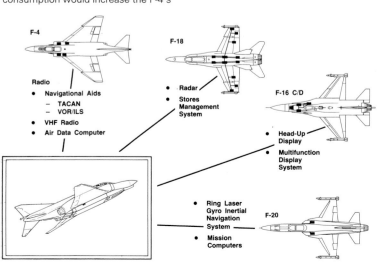

F-4

Radio
- Navigational Aids
  - TACAN
  - VOR/ILS
- VHF Radio
- Air Data Computer

F-18
- Radar
- Stores Management System

F-16 C/D
- Head-Up Display
- Multifunction Display System

F-20
- Ring Laser Gyro Inertial Navigation System
- Mission Computers

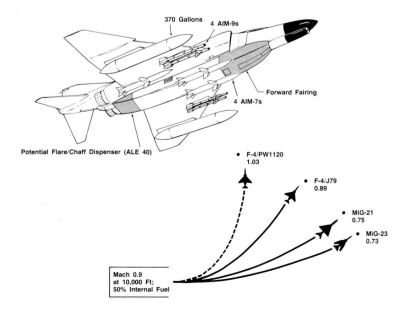

370 Gallons

4 AIM-9s

4 AIM-7s

Forward Fairing

Potential Flare/Chaff Dispenser (ALE 40)

Mach 0.9 at 10,000 Ft; 50% Internal Fuel

F-4/PW1120 1.03

F-4/J79 0.89

MiG-21 0.75

MiG-23 0.73

Super Phantom/ Kurnass 2000

First flight: 15 July 1987
Pilot: not known
Number converted: not known
Identities: not known

Israel's ambitious Phantom upgrade program was initiated in 1980, after the decision to procure the indigenous Lavi as an A-4/Kfir replacement. It was decided that an F-4 replacement (the F/A-18 was reportedly preferred) would be prohibitively expensive, and since IAI already had much experience in updating and improving the basic F-4, an upgrade of the Phantom was launched. The F-4 was already known as the Kurnass (Heavy Hammer) in IDF/AF service, and the upgrade project was dubbed Kurnass 2000. The project had five main aims, which were to incorporate new technologies, improve maintainability, eliminate known weaknesses, enhance handling and performance, and extend service life by 15 years. The extent of the cooperation between IAI and Boeing is unknown, although it is a fact that Boeing's own very similar upgraded F-4 was launched with Israel in mind, and one of the two uncompleted prototypes was said to have been destined for Israel.

The ambitious upgrade includes a new Kaiser wide-angle HUD, an Elbit mission computer (derived from the F-16C's ACE 3), a display computer controlling new multifunction displays, a HUD video camera, new radios and intercom, and major improvements to the EW and defensive avionics suite. The aircraft are totally rewired and the hydraulic system is replaced. Fuel tank leaks have been cured and various parts of the structure have been strengthened, including the wing/fuselage attachments, wing lower skins, main spar, hardpoints, engine supports, horizontal stabilator and lower fuselage skins. Outer wing panels have been replaced.

Work on the first of two prototypes began in July 1984, at the IDF/AF's Central Maintenance Unit. The first aircraft, recoded 001, made its maiden flight on 15 July 1987 and was formally accepted on 11 August 1987. Further conversions are undertaken by Bedek as aircraft become due for D-level overhauls, and cost more than $8 million each. Series deliveries of the Kurnass 2000 began in April 1989.

The Kurnass 2000 was originally to have received a new Norden Synthetic Aperture Multi-Mission Radar System, derived from that developed for the A-6F upgrade and using technologies developed for the A-12. Cancelation of these two programs led to delays and problems. A few test sets were delivered to Israel in 1992. It is intended to retrofit the Norden radar in all Kurnass 2000 aircraft in the coming years.

Another intended element of the Kurnass 2000 upgrade was scrapped due to cost. The Pratt & Whitney PW1120 turbofan was fitted to an Israeli Phantom (No. 334, and awaiting repairs at Bedek) to explore the airframe/engine combination's possibilities, and to act as an engine testbed for the Lavi. Initially flown on 30 July 1986 with a single PW1120 in the starboard nacelle only, the aircraft was soon flying with two turbofans (from 24 April 1987). The engine proved extremely successful, allowing the Phantom to exceed Mach 1 without recourse to afterburner, and endowing a combat thrust-to-weight ratio of 1.04:1 (17 percent better than the F-4E). This improved sustained turn rate by 15 percent, climb rate by 36 percent, medium-level acceleration by 27 percent and low-level speed with 18 bombs was increased from 565 to 605 kt (650 to 695 mph; 1046 to 1120 km/h). The aircraft received the civil registration 4X-JPA and was displayed at the 1987 Paris air show.

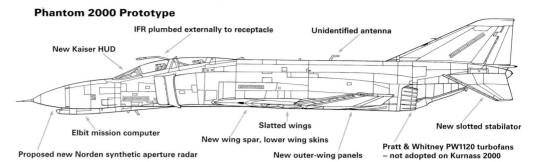

Phantom 2000 Prototype

IFR plumbed externally to receptacle · Unidentified antenna · New Kaiser HUD · Elbit mission computer · Slatted wings · New slotted stabilator · Proposed new Norden synthetic aperture radar · New wing spar, lower wing skins · New outer-wing panels · Pratt & Whitney PW1120 turbofans – not adopted on Kurnass 2000

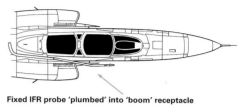

Fixed IFR probe 'plumbed' into 'boom' receptacle

The re-engined Kurnass 2000 takes off during the Paris air show at Le Bourget during 1987. Plans to fit all Kurnass 2000s with the PW1120 were abandoned.

A dummy PW1120 is offered up to 334 during fit checks by the Bedek division of IAI. The aircraft flew first with one PW1120 (in the starboard nacelle).

Right: 334 takes off for the first time with PW1120 power alone. The aircraft made its first flight with two PW1120s on 24 April 1987.

Below: A production Kurnass 2000, wearing the markings of No. 201 Squadron. The aircraft is fitted with TISEO and slats, and carries a fixed inflight-refueling probe. It retains J79 power, like all 'production' conversions.

FLYING THE
PHANTOM

Above: Julian Lake at the controls of 'his' F-4B. As commander of VF-74, Lake was assigned Modex 101, 100 being reserved for the CAG (Carrier Air Group commander).

Right: A few years later Julian Lake was the skipper of the USS John F. Kennedy, which naturally embarked two F-4 squadrons, like virtually every US supercarrier of the period.

Below: The Project LANA Phantoms line up. Among the 'AD'-coded aircraft from East Coast RAG VF-101 is a single 'NJ'-coded F-4B, from West Coast rival RAG, VF-121. Lake's own part in LANA proved frustrating, refueling problems robbing him of the chance of setting the fastest time.

Rear Admiral Julian Lake, the first Phantom squadron commander and later the commander of Air Wing Eight and skipper of the aircraft carrier USS *John F. Kennedy*, describes his experiences of McDonnell's F-4 Phantom. John Roberts, former USAF fighter pilot, describes in intimate detail the Phantom's cockpit, his former 'office'.

Julian Lake was a career naval aviator, retiring from the service as a Rear Admiral and Commander Naval Electronic Systems Command in September 1976, having clocked up 34 years of active duty and having won a Distinguished Service Medal and Bronze Star. Lake flew as a night-fighter pilot in World War II and in Korea, and has flown 40 aircraft types, most of them all-weather fighters, including the F4U Corsair, F6F Hellcat, F7F Tigercat, F-84 Thunderstreak, F-86 Sabre, F-100 Super Sabre, F3H Demon, F4D Skyray, F8U Crusader, F11F Tiger, F-102 Delta Dagger, F-106 Delta Dart, F-14 Tomcat and F-15 Eagle. Perhaps the proudest moment of his career came in 1960, when he was appointed to command the 'Be-devilers' of VF-74, the US Navy's first F4H Phantom squadron. During his tenure the squadron participated in the Bendix Trophy race (Project LANA), and many tests and trials against other fighter types. Much of the Phantom's success can be attributed to VF-74's pioneering work and, here, their first commander tells his story.

"I joined the Navy in October 1942. I was a student at VPI – Virginia Polytechnic Institute – in Blacksburg, Virginia. I was in the ROTC (Reserve Officers Training Corps) there and I was very keen on getting into the war, which had begun for the US in December 1941. I had long wanted to be a naval aviator. The authorities at the school encouraged us to stay on and get our degrees and our commissions, however.

"I used the war as an excuse, though, and left school to join the Navy to become a naval aviation cadet. It turned out to be a good decision because all my college classmates wound up as sergeants in the Army and had to go back to school after the war to complete their degrees. I never regretted the decision to leave school early. I selected the Navy over the Army Air Corps because, having been in the Army ROTC program, I knew I wanted no part of the Army.

Hellcats by moonlight

"I grew up in Newport News, Virginia, where I watched the aircraft carriers being built (they're still being built there), and the Norfolk Naval Base was an active military area nearby. I got to see Navy airplanes as a kid.

"I trained at Glenview, Illinois, in Yellow Perils (naval N3N trainers), and then went to Corpus Christi, Texas, for advanced training, and I got my wings in 1944. I went off to operational flight training, where I built up time in operational combat-type aircraft. I was in fighters – the older ones like the F4F Wildcat. I was keen on getting into the newer F6F Hellcat. My colleagues told me I had 'sold my soul' to get into the Hellcats because, in order to fly the newer airplanes, I opted for night-fighter training. The Hellcats were used for night-fighter work and, therefore, I got into them that way. The night fighter mission wasn't popular. Anyway, I never regretted this decision either. I thus began my career in all-weather/night-fighter aircraft, a field in which, for the most part, I remained for the remainder of my career.

"I was a fighter training officer in the late 1950s at Naval Air Forces Atlantic Fleet in Norfolk. We were watching, with great interest, the developing competition between the Chance-Vought F8U-3 and the McDonnell F4H-1. The first was a single-engined, single-pilot fighter. The McDonnell was a twin-engined, dual-crew (pilot and RIO) machine. By this time I had done a stint with the US Air Force flying two-place interceptors, the F-94C and F-89D, and also the single-place F-86. I had also flown the two-place F3D Skyknight, a Navy aircraft. This experience in the two-place aircraft convinced me of the viability of having two crewmen in modern fighters. The 1,000 lb of fuel that had to be sacrificed in order to put the

Above: The LANA aircraft were conspicuously marked with broad colored bands on their wings and fuselage. Lake's aircraft (coded 'AD'/183, far right) wore broad red stripes.

Below: Lake's VF-74 gained the honor of being the first unit to take the Phantom aboard a carrier, the USS Forrestal.

second person in the cockpit was, in my view, well worth the price. As a result, with respect to the competition, I was betting on the Phantom to win.

"I went off to the Naval War College in Newport, Rhode Island, in 1959. By this time my background included night-fighter experience in World War II and in Korea, and I had attended the Navy Test Pilot School at Patuxent River, Maryland, and had duty at the Test Center.

"Fortunately, the Raytheon Company was nearby in Bedford, Massachusetts, and I went up to Bedford to log 'proficiency flight time' at the facility there. They had a Phantom there, and I got into the backseat and flew hops with them. I had already become quite familiar with radar and knew how to operate the equipment. I kept working on a program to get into the front seat. I went to McDonnell's main plant in St Louis and spent my Christmas holidays in Phantom ground school, then returned to Newport.

In the driving seat

"I finally got into the front seat and began flying the aircraft in both positions, building up Phantom time – a kind of 'masterpiece of sniveling', I suppose, the way I garnered the flight time. I was persistent and pulled it off.

"After I got out of the War College I transferred to Naval Air Station Oceana, Virginia, slated to become CO of the first operational F-4 Phantom squadron (1960 to 1962) and continued my conniving, scheming and politicking to get the testers to free up the Phantom for fleet duty. The testers seemed to want to test the F-4H until the wings fell off.

"This was a stressful time because every time we turned around, something went wrong with the aircraft. This meant delays, sometimes of up to six months. If the delays kept up I would probably be transferred elsewhere and miss my opportunity to be the first CO of a Phantom squadron. There was a lot of wheeling and dealing and pleading going on, urging people to stop their 'nitpicking' ways.

Phantom champion

"There was great competition for the job as the first Phantom CO, but that's not what occupied my attention as much as trying to keep the program moving. My motives were suspect, of course, as I traveled to Washington, DC, to sit in on the conferences where decisions were made on the progress of getting the Phantom ready. I think they got pretty tired of my presence, however. The aircraft finally was ready on time and I got off their backs. In the meantime, the F-4 program had started in San Diego at NAS Miramar, and the first Pacific Fleet crews were going through their RAG.

"VF-101 was the Atlantic Fleet Training Squadron. Pilots from this squadron would check out in the Phantom, then train the pilots assigned to my squadron, VF-74.

I'd already flown the airplane, of course, but nobody seemed to pay any attention to that. So VF-101 completed their check-outs. I had taken command of VF-74 when it still had the F4D Skyray, an all-weather interceptor, although not a very good one. Anyway, we began training the squadron in earnest now.

"We began our workups with the airplane, familiarization first, before starting to work with the weapons system. The airplane was terrific. It was unusual in that it arrived with the fire-control system in place. In the past, we would usually get the airplane and we would have a lot of railroad rails bolted into the nose to take the place of the missing radar. It was always several months after we had a new airplane before we'd finally get the radars installed. Not so with the Phantom. The radar was not only there but it was working! It was stupendous! Compared with the other all-weather aircraft I had flown, this was an order of magnitude better. And I had extensive experience in radar-equipped fighters, such as the F6F-5N, F4U-5N, F3D Skyknight and several Banshee models, including the F2H. I was the project pilot at Patuxent River, assigned to evaluate a Hughes and a Westinghouse radar in the same model airplane, which was very interesting. Then I did that tour with the Air Force, flying the three interceptors current at the time – the F-94C, F-89D and F-86. Then I was XO of a Skyray squadron before I went up to a staff job at Norfolk, before going to the War College.

In a league of its own

"The other all-weather interceptor around at the time was the F3H Demon, which I had checked out in and got to fly quite a bit when I was on the staff. I was a different kind of staff officer, in that I got out to the squadrons and tried to fly all the time. So, I had a considerable background of experience and knowledge in fighter-type radars. I can say without qualification that the Westinghouse Aero 1A radar in the Phantom was just mind-boggling. The air controllers loved us, because all they had to do was point us in the general direction of the target and we would detect it, lock it up and take over the intercept.

"It took a while for the fleet to respond to all of this 'sudden' capability which was before them in the form of the Phantom. Not only was the aircraft's performance outstanding, the radar and missile armament was far ahead of anything we had before. The Sparrow missile had been in the fleet for a while, but ours was an improved model of the Sparrow and, combined with the radar performance, was stupendous. We began to get into the idea of 'all-aspect intercepts', or attack from the forward as well as the rear 'hemisphere'.

Thinking ahead

"The Navy Phantom didn't have any guns, only missiles: Sparrows and Sidewinders. Up until that time, the fleet had been thinking in terms of rear hemisphere attacks with guns and Sidewinders. All of a sudden we got into the forward hemisphere world with a vengeance.

"We had to do some things to make up for lapses in the total system, however. We didn't have any kind of a scope recorder to retain information in order to be able to critique it – or to evaluate what the pilot and the RIO had done in a given intercept – whether they had gotten their lock-on properly, executed the intercept properly, and whether the pilot had steered the circle and dot accurately up until the point of the trigger squeeze of the missile.

"So we got into some homegrown R&D and got lots of cooperation from the Bureau of Aeronautics and the McDonnell (later McDonnell Douglas) people. We came up with a reasonable kind of a scope cap. This had to be 'walked around' all the bureaucrats and safety people, but we got the thing done.

"At the same time we didn't have anything to shoot at but drone targets, which were too expensive and which could not be used in a routine training environment. So, we got a DELMAR target reel and DELMAR targets and

loaded them under the airplane. We suddenly found we could put out a tow line two to three miles long, and by adjusting the parameters properly we could engage in our own live-firing exercises with the Phantom and its missiles. This meant a major increase in fleet capabilities of this weapons systems and in our readiness posture, because now we could go out and exercise the whole system.

Flying the Phantom

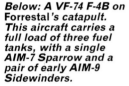

Right: Early F-4Bs often carried their Sparrows underwing, rather than in the underfuselage missile recesses. Exercises with Air Force F-106s were an early highlight for VF-74, with the confidence inspired by having an indisputably better aircraft and the excitement of closing speeds of up to Mach 4.

"You could have the best radar maintenance in the world and the best aircraft maintenance in the world; still, when you got ready to employ the missile you also had to have a whole list of things to be concerned about that involved precise actions. The missile had to be properly mounted on the airplane and properly safed and armed with reliable safing and arming devices. Everything had to be checked out, so that when the pilot squeezed the trigger the missile responded by launching. There were many hurdles that had to be negotiated, and the only way we could do it was go out and shoot the missiles and solve any problems that came up. The same was true of any kind of ordnance with fuzes and things of that nature in modern warfare. You must go through the whole cycle to prove it would work. Your maintenance personnel had to be carefully and thoroughly trained. But this was all part of the excitement of having that squadron and being able to see that we got the proper target and the proper scoring mechanism to determine how we were doing.

The LANA experience

"There was tremendous interest in the airplane. The Air Force was most interested. I took the Commanding General of Tactical Air Command out and ran him around at Mach 2.2 and put him in the landing pattern at 135 kt, which was pretty scary to those guys because they liked extra speed on their approaches to landings. Then we had Project LANA, which was the Bendix Race. 'L' stood for the roman numeral denoting 50 (or 50th) and the other letters stood for the Anniversary of Naval Aviation.

Below: A VF-74 F-4B on Forrestal's catapult. This aircraft carries a full load of three fuel tanks, with a single AIM-7 Sparrow and a pair of early AIM-9 Sidewinders.

"The race came very close to becoming a disaster because of the A3D tankers – one over New Mexico, one over Kansas City and one over Fort Wayne, Indiana. Over Kansas City we damn near ran out of gas. When we arrived at the refueling point we had little of our own gas left: we had to refuel or land. There were landing fields available along the route, but the idea was to fly all the way across the US nonstop if we were to have any chance of beating the competition, which was the West Coast unit flying the Phantom.

"We had problems with refueling over Kansas City and this decided the winner of the race. The first and second airplanes, myself and Lamoreaux, came very close to running out of fuel before we hooked up with the tanker. It was a problem we hadn't encountered during preparation for the flight. Tankers would get up to the refueling altitude of 35,000 ft just about the time we were ready for them. But on the day of the race, they were on station early. The JP-5 (fuel) had moisture in it and it would freeze up in the small metering lines and foul the refueling package. Anyway, we got through it safely, although we lost to the West Coast guys.

"It was a frantic but fun evolution. Right after that, they concocted a flyoff with the F-106, which was pretty new at the time. I relished this because I had recognized the lack of any electronic counter-countermeasures (ECCM) provisions in our fire-control system. The main thrust of

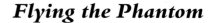

Project High Speed, as this flyoff was called, was electronic warfare (EW). We started working out some ECCM 'fixes' for the airplane. We installed them in VF-74's airplanes and they became authorized, fleet-wide changes.

Counting on the RIO

"The RIO could retain control of the antenna and do 'manual' intercepts, rather than having the system go into automatic track which would allow the 'enemy' to break lock. A half-action switch allowed the RIO to defeat that by making sure the antenna did not break the lock-on, and so we had some EW guys about ready to fall on their swords because they didn't know we had this ability of making them look bad.

"At any rate, we had a lot of exercises with the F-106, including head-on intercepts. Pretty exciting because the closing velocities were tremendous: Mach 4 in some cases. We created a lot of sonic booms in the area. We thus gained new knowledge in areas of the EW field that had never been explored before.

"I guess we were ready to go (in VF-74) in about a year after we started training with the new plane. Our primary mission was anti-air warfare, to defend the fleet and to

escort attack aircraft into their targets. Our nuclear mission would have been the same. A lot of our training involved creating as we went along. We were leading the way, so to speak. We had EW capabilities that the rest of the fleet didn't possess and we had our missile shoots, using our scope cameras to grade our exercises. They didn't have any Red Flag exercises in those days. We were doing a lot of things that the Navy eventually did integrate into the training scenarios.

Twin-engined security

"The Phantom more than met my expectations, although we had more than a few problems. Unlike the Air Force's F-104, we didn't have to eject when we lost an engine because we had two of them. We got to be rather expert in making single-engine carrier landings. When an engine (fuel) pump failed – if you kept the engine going it would burn up – we would shut the engine down to save it, and make it back to the runway or the carrier with one engine. The fact that the Phantom had two engines paid off almost

The Phantom was not without its teething troubles. Precautionary engine shutdowns were routine, and the aircraft was more popular with pilots than with the maintenance crew.

Below: Handling in the circuit was surprisingly benign, and approach speeds were low by the standards of the day.

Above: Two VF-74 Phantoms are readied for a dusk launch from Forrestal. The Phantom's excellent radar made it "an order of magnitude better than any previous fighter interceptor," recalled Lake.

immediately. We worked very hard to get 'maintenance manhours per flight hour' down to the lowest possible number.

"We were getting ahead of the system, using a lot of the data ourselves before it could be absorbed into the system. But this was one of the expectations of working with a brand-new airplane. One aspect that we enjoyed particularly was that we seemed to be more motivated than our counterparts on the West Coast. They would stop and scratch their heads when a problem came up, whereas our philosophy was to get right at the dilemma and get on with solving it. There was a certain amount of satisfaction in showing those other guys up. I always thought part of the reason for this was that the Pacific Fleet had too many engineers in their headquarters and we didn't have as many. This allowed us to be a bit more practical.

"We had pretty good luck with the accident rate. I don't think we had any, except the nose strut oleo failed when I landed once and that was charged as an accident. But we didn't lose any airplanes until after I left. Then we had a problem and we had a crew who had to eject from an airplane. It was only a matter of time before the accidents began to happen. The rate wasn't any worse than any other aircraft, however, with respect to its time in service.

"The Phantom was not a pre-eminent dogfighting airplane. We could hold our own against the Crusaders, but when it came down to mixing it up close in, the Crusaders had the better turning aircraft. There were no bones about

that. They had machine guns, we did not. I didn't encourage a lot of mixing it up with the Crusaders, although it went on. You can't take a squadron of feisty pilots and not expect them to want to 'hassle'. We could disengage at any time we wanted to, however. Just light the burners and go!

"We loved to bug 'opponents' at the Officer's Club by asking them if they had been through Mach lately. When they answered 'yeah', we would then ask 'which one?' (Meaning Mach 1 or Mach 2 – only the Phantom could do Mach 2.) We were proud of our Mach 2 aircraft.

Fighter interceptor

"The Phantom was primarily an interceptor. It would be a long time before it took on the fighter-bomber role. What the Navy needed at the time was a fighter-interceptor, not a fighter-bomber. It was when the Vietnam War got started and the Air Force got hold of it that the mission changed. Of course, the Air Force would take any airplane, hang bombs on it, and call it a fighter.

"The ability of the Phantom to get aboard was very good. It was a very smooth airplane with lots of power. If you got too slow, it quickly told you because you would have a hard time seeing the deck and the landing signal mirror. The one (negative) feature was that it felt just as comfortable at 160 kt as it did at 140. So you had to make sure you didn't get too fast. As I said, when you started to get too slow, the nose started getting in the way of where

The other side of the coin . . .

"I entered the Phantom world after a tour on the Lightning and training on the Chipmunk, JP, Gnat and Hunter. I had to be dragged, kicking and screaming, from the Lightning, away from the joys of what felt like unlimited thrust and the cachet of being 'single-seat'. The benefits of improved radar performance and a more viable weapon load were obvious, but increased endurance was a mixed blessing for a chap with a bladder used to 45-minute Lightning sorties, and the presence of a navigator initially seemed very strange. I guess that as F-4 crew we consoled ourselves with the thought that dogfighting agility was irrelevant, and that the only way to win in the modern air battle would be to smack the other guy in the teeth from a million miles out with a long-range missile. I suppose the Gulf War proved that to be correct, although close-combat hassles are, and always will be, great fun in peacetime. At the time, however, it felt depressing to be regularly 'waxed' by the Lightning mates who had once been my colleagues.

"The Phantom's weaknesses as far as I was concerned were inadequate thrust when 'loaded for bear' – with underwing jugs, Sparrows, 'Winders and a gun on the centerline – poor acceleration, slow burner light-up and some nasty handling at low speeds. You just had to watch that AOA indicator all the time, since at high Alpha you could experience some vicious departures. There were tricks. At high Alpha you stopped using aileron and used bootfuls of rudder instead, but when the phrase 'carefree handling' came into common usage it was clear that the Phantom lacked such an attribute.

"Perhaps I'm biased. After all, the Phantom came closer than any aircraft to killing me. I remember the occasion, vividly. We were returning to base after a particularly fruitless CAP, hours on station with no trade, and had suffered the ignominy of being bounced by a brace of Binbrook Lightnings. I'm a modest sort of chap, and certainly don't like being a film star, so you can imagine what I felt like knowing that these guys probably had yards of gun-camera film of my Phantom. The only consolation was that our humiliation had been short-lived, the Lightnings mercifully reaching bingo fuel after only a few minutes.

"In those days, they still used Hawker Hunters for advanced pilot training, and there were two squadrons at Wittering that were used to train up a pool of young 'mud-movers' for the Jaguar force. Occasionally, detachments of these boys would arrive at an air defense base, especially during 'Priory' or other exercises, to practice their war role of low-level point defense. Knowing that our airfield was being 'defended' by such a Hunter detachment, we made a diligent radar and visual search before setting up for a straight-in approach to the active. Some way into the descent, Steve, the nav, called that he had a Hunter in our eight o'clock. I glanced around and, sure enough, there was this prehistoric Hunter nine with tanks going hell-for-leather for my six.

"No way was I going to be a film star twice in one day, and I was certainly not going to end up bettered by some refugee airplane from the 1950s, piloted by a super-annuated has-been TWU instructor or, worse, by a young trainee 'mud' waiting for a Jaguar OCU slot. I had my pride. So I rolled on about 90° of port bank, selected full burner and pulled sharply back on the stick. The F-4 began to turn smartly towards our assailant, but then, with the pedal shaker doing its thing and with enough buffet to shake out fillings, the aircraft flicked on its back. With nothing but grass and mud filling the canopy, which seemed like inches from my head, and Mr Mac's mighty fighter suddenly transformed into 23 tons of potential death, as devoid of energy as I was of ideas, my life flashed before my eyes. Suddenly, finally, the burners ignited. 'Thank you Rolls-Royce. Thank you SENGO. Thank you God.' With death still staring me in the face, but with some thrust to get out of his clutches, I pushed on the stick as hard as possible and we climbed away inverted. In the bar that evening the Hunter pilot wandered over.

"'Great defensive maneuver. I just couldn't follow that, not that close to the ground!'"

Three air defense RAF Phantoms overfly a Royal Navy warship. Not every pilot loved the Phantom. The tiny proportion of doubters are represented here by an anonymous RAF pilot (a dyed-in-the-wool single-seat fighter man), who missed the cachet of being 'single-seat, fast-jet', who resented being posted away from his beloved Lightning and who found one aspect of the Phantom's handling not quite to his liking.

you intended to land. It was a very easy airplane to bring aboard and all the pilots liked it. We had a good boarding record (landing rate/quality of approach and landing).

"There were a lot of things to check for on preflight, a few bottle pressures, for instance. During the walkaround, you checked the general appearance of the aircraft, looking for hydraulic or oil or fuel leaks, scuffed tires, any loose cabling, or anything like that.

"On catapult launches, it was no problem. After we had been operating the airplane for a while we developed the procedure of keeping the stick full aft on the cat shot. This was a safety precaution, although it wasn't that necessary. But like a lot of things, once it got to be the standard operating procedure, you kept on doing it, like it or not.

"The Phantom's takeoff performance was spectacular. One of our favorite maneuvers was to call for a high-performance takeoff, get it off the ground, clean it up (raise gear and flaps), hold the nose down briefly, then pull the stick back and go straight up out of sight. It had a fantastic rate of climb. It was a lot of fun to show off in. The afterburner was used for land-based takeoffs as a matter of standard procedure for increased safety.

"Landing and flap limit speed was 250 kt. The aircraft didn't have any nuclear capabilities. The plane's mission

Above: VF-74 was an elite unit, crammed with handpicked pilots and RIOs and first to operate the Navy's only Mach 2 fighter. Morale was sky high. Lake continued his association with the Phantom and VF-74 as CAG of Air Wing Eight.

was to defend the fleet, to defend the air wing. The wing 'attack' aircraft would make their penetrating missions into hostile territory.

"The whole program was a lot of fun and very competitive. There was a lot of competition with the West Coast. It was kind of galling that they got invited to our Bendix Race party and took home the door prize. But those things happen.

"When we went aboard ship we found we had problems with, of all things, the running lights. The landing signal officers and the CO of the ship were very stuffy about this. They wouldn't take us aboard unless we had at least one wing light and an approach light working. For some reason the damn lights were failing regularly. It took us a while to get 'ruggedized' light bulbs to withstand the particular vibrations on the airplane. Still, we managed to finish our carrier qualifications on schedule and, again, it took a lot of skulduggery, persuasion and all that to make it happen. But that just made it more fun. And the competition with the Air Force was great, as was the competition with the BuAer engineers, keeping them properly motivated to

keep our ECCM program going – this was a real struggle.

"Being the skipper of VF-74 was easy because I had been assigned guys with so much talent. The Navy had really handpicked just about everybody in the squadron and it was a real pleasure to be in charge of it. The airplane, once we got it out of the hands of the testers and the bureaucrats, was a fantastic machine and had very few problems. It had no shortcomings at that time that I could see, although I knew it was a mistake that we did not have a machine gun and I could see the day coming when we would get the bomb racks out and start lugging bombs around. The need for all that blinding speed was getting kind of lost.

"I could also see that it probably was going to be one of the last 'ultrasonic' airplanes in the inventory. The F-15 and the F-14 are not quite as fast as the Phantom (although there will be some argument about that) and I don't know anyone who bothers to take airplanes out to those speeds anymore. The F/A-18 has got a fixed duct and it's not going to get much over Mach 1.6 or 1.7. Up until the more modern machines, like the YF-22 and -23, it was an absolute necessity to have a movable ramp to keep the shock

The F-4 cockpit: A pilot's view

The F-4E cockpit is the halfway point between the steam-gauge cockpits of early jets and the glass, multifunction cockpits of today. John Roberts flew 1,000 hours in the Phantom, including two Vietnam combat tours, one in the F-4E. He was the operations officer and air combat tactics instructor pilot in a NATO fighter squadron.

Ergonomics is the art and science of fitting people to their environment, with such objectives as comfort and efficiency, and such examples as the 'QWERTY' typewriter keyboard and the modern kitchen. The fighter cockpit is the most challenging and complicated of all environments. No astronaut, Formula One driver or computer operator faces a more daunting combination of mental and physical effort in order to perform at top level. The design of the fighter cockpit has only recently caught up with the tech-

nology and demands of high performance. There is a beautiful and functional simplicity to a Spitfire cockpit; but, as aircraft improved and as technology allowed new systems in old airframes, the engineers tended to stick new items wherever they could find room, and the cockpit became a crowded clutter of random glass and metal projections. By the time we reached the F-4 in the early 1960s, the need to cram ever more instruments and controls for its many different missions into the same limited space carried us to the high point on the difficulty curve: cockpit tasks in faster, more demanding aircraft were growing beyond the capability of the pilot. The flow of diverse, erratic information that had to be absorbed and processed, and the many different, often simultaneous, responses that had to result, were exceeding human performance limitations. Accidents were being attributed to this single cause of cockpit overload. Therefore, by necessity, the engineers had to get serious about cockpit design. They had to simplify information and combine controls in concentrated, upfront locations, so

Aircraft Commander John Roberts (right) and WSO Ron Daskevich (left) trained as a team, learning crew coordination, before going to Vietnam. Due to an early shortage of navigators, Ron was a pilot on his first tour.

wave positioned on the lip of the duct to get much past 1.6. Of course, the F-16 fits into the same category as the F/A-18. These are both highly successful airplanes, and they don't need to go over Mach 2.

"It was quite an experience to devise the competitive exercises for the airplane and we certainly had to modify them because of the capabilities of the Phantom and its fantastic radar. Of course it wasn't long before they were working on improvements to the radar. When we saw the AWG-10 radar on the drawing boards we saw even more capability coming.

"I kept up my association with VF-74 when I was Air Wing Eight commander (VF-74 was in Air Wing Eight). I continued to fly the airplane. I also took advantage – one of the last air wing commanders to do so – of flying all the different types of aircraft in the wing. It was rapidly becoming passé for the CAG to fly all the aircraft on the ship. It was a good thing, because the airplanes were getting to be complicated and it was a handful to keep 'qualified' and current in all of them, especially with respect to carrier landings. I got away with it, but it was not a good idea."

Below: VF-74's F-4Bs were distinguished by a jagged red lightning flash along the fuselage, and a stylised 'AJ' tailcode. Later, the squadron's distinctive devil's head badge began to make an appearance on engine intakes.

An F-4E of the 47th TFS from MacDill AFB, during 1969, carried a rocket pod on the left inboard pylon, and on the right inboard a practice bomb dispenser, with six smoke bombs for range scoring.

that the pilot had more time to think and fewer tasks to perform, especially if the backseater was to be eliminated to allow greater aircraft performance.

The early F-4 was not all bad: it had the new Flight Director System which combined many flight/navigation instruments into two central multifunction units; the stick and throttles incorporated a few different switches to help the pilot reduce hand movements; and the radar and missile-firing systems were a big improvement. But, it aimed guns and bombs about the same as a P-47, and there were too many controls behind the pilot's normal hand position or far down in the cockpit, which required dangerous head movements that led to disorientation accidents or mission degradation. One of my worst flying experiences was trying to change the weapon switches down in front of the stick in a darkened cockpit on night control missions close to the ground in the F-4C. Sticking your head down in the black barrel while still flying the aircraft, and then coming up and trying to

Flying the Phantom

re-orient to the real world, also mostly black, was downright dangerous. We lost people that way. The all-time classic, which occurred frequently in Vietnam, was selecting 'Centerline' instead of 'Wings' on the obscure little dial with the worn letters down under your knees, and pickling off the external gun pod on a dive-bomb pass – a short, expensive dud which undoubtedly gave the Viet Cong some humorous relief. In another example, a friend of mine dropped a couple of fuel tanks on Fort Myers, Florida, because the jettison switch was located very close to the air refueling door switchback underneath the canopy rail, where you could not see it while trying to move into position behind a tanker.

A significant step

The E version of the F-4 was a big step forward; not so radical that you could not jump around from model to model (I was current in the C, D, E and RF versions at the same time in Vietnam), but it was enough of an improvement that there was a totally different feeling of comfort and modernity. It wasn't really HOTAS (hands on throttle and stick) or 'heads up' for almost everything you do, like an F-16, but it was a big move in that direction. Of course, the transitional D model had a weapons release computer and an earlier lead-computing sight, but the main advantage of the E was the way that it tied all the new systems together in a better cockpit and incorporated the internal gun. The weapons computer and multifunction sight (the first, partial head-up display) allowed the pilot to drop bombs and shoot bullets using computer and radar parameters. Eventually, they repositioned things in the cockpit and concentrated the weapons controls on the front panel, where they could be handled without turning your head through three dimensions. The E model, of course, was designed as a comprehensive fighter by the USAF, as opposed to the fleet interceptor envisioned by the Navy a decade earlier and borrowed pretty much as is for the F-4C, so it is not surprising there was room for refinement. After the 100 and the 'Deuce' and the 104 and the 'Thud', fighter pilots finally felt that they were in a modern, thoughtfully-designed

The worst part of a combat mission was taking gas at night in a thunderstorm, with a full load. Lights under the tanker's nose gave the receiver pilot an accurate indication of up/down and fore/aft corrections.

cockpit instead of something left over from the propeller era and thrown together by some guy who had never flown an airplane. It was still steam gauges and large knobs instead of today's colored glass and multifunction buttons at your fingertips, but it was a hell of an improvement. I flew my second combat tour with the 388th TFW at Korat, the first operational F-4E wing, and we were allowed to use the computerized bombing system going North, whereas the D could not do so in South Vietnam because of the fear of faulty system releases on friendlies. And the gun was a comfort on a MiG CAP.

Computer age

The F-4E was a great success: the testimony is the fact that, more than 30 years later, there are still around 1,500 of the 5,201 Phantoms still operational, most of them F-4Es and little changed from the 1980 version described below. One of the major events that also helped was the computer and micro-electronic revolution that allowed many kinds of information to be stored and processed for display in the cockpit, and which provided electronic control of aircraft/weapon performance. Navigation,

weapons delivery, flight director, autopilot, inertial navigation, air data and other computers were integrated to do things far more advanced than the capabilities of the old individual instruments and controls.

The main instrument panel

If you look at almost any fighter from the 1960s to the early 1980s you will see the standard **Flight Director System**, two large instruments mounted one above the other in the center of the cockpit. It was the first big improvement in cockpit design after World War II – the first intelligent combination of numerous functions into single instruments. It effectively combines a variety of three-dimensional information onto two central locations, allowing the pilot to perform various functions and determine the aircraft's position, in space and in relation to the Earth's surface, at a glance. It cuts down the 'cross check' – the technique whereby the pilot reviews various control, performance and navigation instruments and then makes corrective movements on throttle and stick – the essence of instrument flying. Instead of searching the cockpit for scattered bits of information while trying simultaneously to think and respond to earlier information flow, the pilot can now use the flight director to organize and simplify that information.

The **attitude director indicator (ADI)** incorporates a modern, electric attitude sphere that rotates in both directions through 360°, giving a constant pitch and heading reference. If you do a loop or 360° turn it goes right on around without flipping. You can always see your aircraft attitude and magnetic heading on the same ball, instead of having to look at two different instruments. This reduces both cockpit clutter and eye movement. In the same vein, they added further information systems, such as the old turn-and-slip indicator (needle and ball), ILS glide slope and steering bars, and various warning flags. Now you have almost everything you need to fly a precision GCA or ILS on just one instrument, instead of several. As a back-up for ADI failure, a separate and simple standby attitude indicator is situated on the right of the HSI.

The **horizontal situation indicator (HSI)**, just below the ADI, shows the pilot his position on the Earth relative to various navigational aids, courses or ground points that may be selected. The little airplane sits in the center

The E was an improvement over earlier models, big gain being moving the weapons panels up to the front. With the internal gun, plus the improved sight and weapons computer from the D model, it was a long way from the original C model. Compared to today's fighters, the pilot had to put his eyes and hands in the cockpit far too often. Add-ons clutter the windscreen and too many controls are located under the arms.

F-4E front cockpit

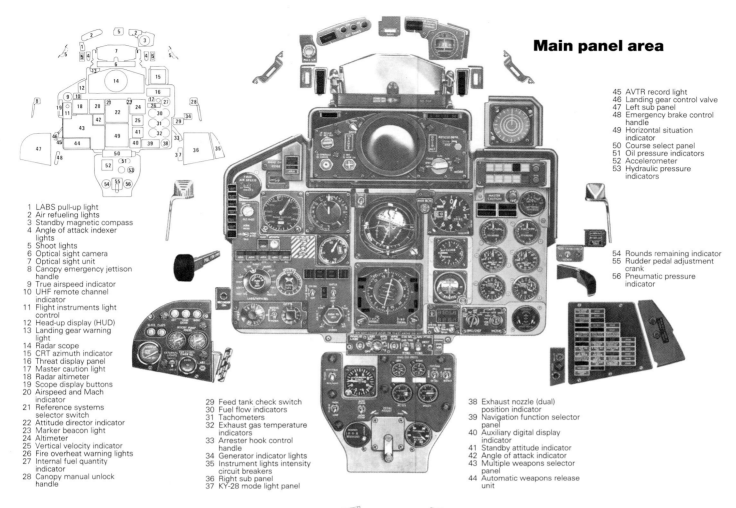

Main panel area

45 AVTR record light
46 Landing gear control valve
47 Left sub panel
48 Emergency brake control handle
49 Horizontal situation indicator
50 Course select panel
51 Oil pressure indicators
52 Accelerometer
53 Hydraulic pressure indicators

54 Rounds remaining indicator
55 Rudder pedal adjustment crank
56 Pneumatic pressure indicator

1 LABS pull-up light
2 Air refueling lights
3 Standby magnetic compass
4 Angle of attack indexer lights
5 Shoot lights
6 Optical sight camera
7 Optical sight unit
8 Canopy emergency jettison handle
9 True airspeed indicator
10 UHF remote channel indicator
11 Flight instruments light control
12 Head-up display (HUD)
13 Landing gear warning light
14 Radar scope
15 CRT azimuth indicator
16 Threat display panel
17 Master caution light
18 Radar altimeter
19 Scope display buttons
20 Airspeed and Mach indicator
21 Reference systems selector switch
22 Attitude director indicator
23 Marker beacon light
24 Altimeter
25 Vertical velocity indicator
26 Fire overheat warning lights
27 Internal fuel quantity indicator
28 Canopy manual unlock handle

29 Feed tank check switch
30 Fuel flow indicators
31 Tachometers
32 Exhaust gas temperature indicators
33 Arrester hook control handle
34 Generator indicator lights
35 Instrument lights intensity circuit breakers
36 Right sub panel
37 KY-28 mode light panel

38 Exhaust nozzle (dual) position indicator
39 Navigation function selector panel
40 Auxiliary digital display indicator
41 Standby attitude indicator
42 Angle of attack indicator
43 Multiple weapons selector panel
44 Automatic weapons release unit

Left console area

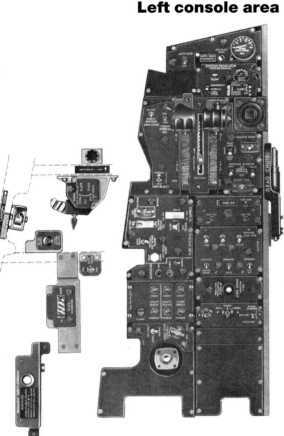

1 Utility panel (left)
2 Oxygen control panel
3 AGM control handle
4 Engine control panel (inboard)
5 Throttles
6 Engine control panel (outboard)
7 Eject light/switch
8 Flaps/slats control panel
9 Canopy selector
10 Extra picture switch
11 Gun camera switch
12 Fuel control panel
13 VOR/ILS control panel
14 Drag chute control handle
15 AFCS control panel
16 Boarding steps position indicator
17 Intercom system control panel
18 AN/ALE-40 programmer
19 Slats override switch
20 Armament safety override switch
21 Anti g control valve
22 Blank panel
23 Blank panel

Right console area

1 Master caution reset
2 Communication control panel
3 CNI equipment cooling reset button
4 Emergency vent handle
5 Utility panel (right)
6 Defog/foot heat control handle
7 Navigation control panel
8 Eight-day clock
9 Generator control switches
10 IFF control panel
11 DCU-94A bomb control-monitor panel
12 Compass control panel
13 Exterior lights control panel
14 Temperature control panel
15 Cockpits light control panel
16 Space for AVTR
17 Standby attitude circuit breaker and intensity control panel
18 Emergency floodlights panel
19 Circuit breaker panel
20 Formation lights control panel
21 Instrument lights intensity control panel

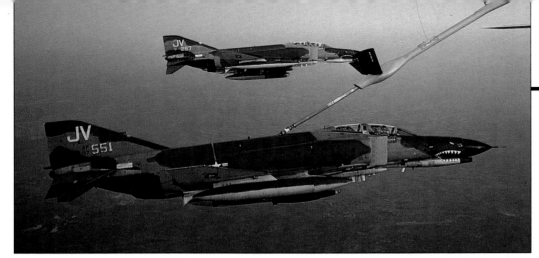

of a compass rose that rotates to keep aircraft heading at the top. A bearing pointer and mileage readout show the relative location of a station, waypoint or target. A **course deviation indicator (CDI)** moves back and forth over the airplane to show the relationship to the course selected, allowing easy intercepts. Together with a few other warning flags and indicators, it becomes a comprehensive view of position in a variety of situations. This is a great improvement on the old navigation needles (like those in the backseat) that required greater pilot interpretation to determine or establish position, with less accurate results. Although, of course, there is still much more information required, so clustered around the flight director are several other important items.

The **airspeed/Mach indicator** reads from 0 to 1,500 kt, and displays the Mach number at all altitudes. High-speed navigation and weapons delivery require more accurate airspeed, taking account of air pressure and temperature and various aircraft conditions. In addition, the inertial navigation system provides a separate digital readout of ground speed, compensating for wind.

The **altimeter** is a counter-pointer, with only one needle covering 1,000 ft around the dial, and rotating counters showing total thousands and hundreds. Thus, the pilot can both read and visualize his exact altitude within a few feet. In addition, a radar altimeter measures exact altitude above the ground from 0 to 5,000 ft, for display on a separate gauge to the left of airspeed. This is used primarily for low-

The first E wing in the war, the 388th TFW, included the 34th ('JJ') TFS and 469th ('JV') TFS. Note the color coding on the sliding refueling boom which shows perfect position. Korat F-4Es attacked supply trails in Laos from 1969 until 1972.

level flight and accurate weapons laydown deliveries, as it does not function beyond 30° of pitch and bank. A light warns of flight below a selected altitude.

Airspeed and altitude are positioned on the left and right of the ADI, so that everything the pilot needs for basic flight and navigation control form a 'T' for efficient cross check.

Other instruments

Two other important gauges are found just below this group. The **vertical velocity indicator** is electrically and flight data computer operated, but is still the same old lagging indication of rate of climb and descent that all pilots find useful in combination with the rate of change of the altimeter. The **angle of attack (AOA) indicator** is extremely important in the F-4, because many things, from high-performance maneuvering to landing, are carried out at the ideal angle of attack of 19 units on the gauge, providing maximum turn performance. If you exceed that, you can get into trouble, high airspeed or not. This is so important that it is backed up by audio and light systems. On final approach, you don't even have to watch airspeed or the AOA gauge, just fly 19 units with the familiar tone and red lights above the instrument panel and you will be at

the correct airspeed for your weight. In a high-AOA dogfight, you can cause the aircraft to depart from normal flight, go out of control, by using aileron at high AOA, so you roll the aircraft with rudder in that situation, which you get well-trained to recognize without looking at the gauge.

The **standard engine instruments** are arrayed down the right side below the fuel counter and fire warning lights. The usual fuel pressure, RPM and tailpipe temperature gauges are supplemented on afterburner aircraft by a nozzle position indicator showing the opening of the nozzle during reheat. Other instruments like oil and hydraulic pressure are located in front of the stick with the *g* meter, gun controls and counter.

The **warning and indicator lights** are primarily located on the lower right corner of the front panel. A 'Master Caution' light high on the front panel illuminates most of these lights, telling the pilot to check the panel. The advantage of this improved system is that everything is positioned together where you can see it, and the pilot is no longer required to spot faulty readings or performance on a number of instruments or on unseen systems. When the oil pressure drops below a certain level, you can't miss the warning.

Magic systems

The **inertial navigation system (INS)** is the most incredible of all the F-4 black boxes. It has three high-speed gyros in three planes that can measure the slightest motion and, in conjunction, compute the new location of the air-

Right: After landing from the final flight, the tradition in Vietnam was to parade the base and then get dunked. Korat had a pool, but some bases had to make do with something smaller.

Below: A Korat-based E model from the 469th TFS flies in formation with an 'OZ'-coded bird from the 432nd TRW at Udorn, which had both fighter and recce Phantoms. Large missions often involved coordinated packages and escorts of recce and bomber aircraft with MiG-CAP Phantoms.

craft despite any combination of high-speed, three-dimensional maneuvers. Imagine this. The Phantom takes off, flies 100 miles and engages in a supersonic, high-g dogfight. The INS, which was told exactly where it started from, will sense every minute change and acceleration during that time and compute a new latitude and longitude for display in the rear cockpit. Since it knows where the aircraft is at any time, the INS will tell you the direction and distance to any other point on the Earth that the navigator dials in, such as home base. It even senses wind, giving the accurate ground speed readout in the rear cockpit. After an hour or two of flight, the INS coordinates will drift off a few miles, but they are accurate enough to get you to where you are going. Of course, it can be used in many ways, for example for finding waypoints and targets, and it provides a back-up or replacement for TACAN and radar navigation. The new ring laser gyros on the latest inertials are extremely accurate, perhaps only a few hundred feet out after a long flight. I

still can't believe that thing can sense an acceleration from 599 to 600 kt, compensate for all the changes in a loop, feel a tiny crosswind, every movement of the aircraft, and come up with a new position. Absolute magic.

Bomb aiming

The C model of the F-4 had a fixed sight and a simple glass on which it was projected. You simply went to a chart and found the correct mil setting to dial in for the ballistics of the weapon to be fired or dropped. After that, it was up to the pilot. In a dive-bomb pass, for example, he had to visually read altitude, dive angle, back angle and airspeed, then move the sight pipper toward the target, and manually pickle off the bomb when all the ideal parameters came together as close as he could fly them. Any deviation of one or more parameters would cause an error. If you didn't establish, for example, your 45° dive at 500 kt at 5,000 ft, the bomb was long or short. So, it became a challenge to note slow airspeed or too much dive angle, or whatever combination was developing during the pass, and compensate by adjusting other parameters or moving the sight picture. The human brain isn't fast enough to compute all the permutations as they occurred, and accurate bombing was very difficult. The F-4D/E moved halfway to the F-16 technology by incorporating the **weapons release computer system (WRCS)**. In the commonly-used dive-toss mode, this simply measures various aircraft parameters, takes in the slant range to the target from the radar, feeds in the crosswind from the INS, and tells the bomb when to fall off the aircraft. All you have to do is put the pipper on the target, hold the pickle button and then pull up until bomb release. The only problems are controlling the pipper in a strong crosswind (or heavy ground

Below: John Roberts, a flight commander in the 34th TFS, takes a final look at Korat after returning from an attack on the trail. Missions to Laos were totally different from his first tour at Cam Ranh Bay in the D model and his year in Saigon flying the RF-4 while a general's aide.

fire), and the radar has some trouble with rough terrain. But, the main thing is that the computer takes care of all the computations, and you don't have to fly the ideal pattern, as it will compensate for large errors. The system has a variety of useful release modes for various weapons and conditions.

The **lead-computing optical sight (LCOS)** is a tremendous advance over the fixed sight and one of the great accomplishments in air combat technology, akin to Tony Fokker's forward-firing machine gun, the Gatling gun and the air-to-air missile. Previously, the pilot had to size up the situation and figure out where to aim his bullets based on his judgment of the flight conditions of two different airplanes in space. The only solution was to get in close, and high-speed flight made that difficult. The LCOS combines information about your aircraft, like airspeed, air density and AOA, and then your radar combines data about the target, such as distance, relative velocity and direction. The computer takes all this and then says, 'OK, I know where I am heading and I know where he is heading, so we have to point our nose here in order for our bullets to reach a point in space at the same time he does.' When both aircraft are traveling at 1,500 ft per second, with a constantly changing angle and relative speed, that is not easy. With your missiles and gun armed, you select 'Air-to-Air' next to the radar display, put the pipper on the target and flick the auto-acquisition switch on the outboard throttle, which locks up the radar; the pipper drops to the bottom of your HUD and oscillates as everything changes, asking you to pull your nose way out in front, leading the target. The difficult part is setting up so that you have time to put it on the target and fire. You must keep him in front of you and avoid Fox Four, using your F-4 as the last bullet. If the gyrations are too extreme, you can disengage the radar and the pipper will freeze for a range of 1,000 ft.

The **radar homing and warning (RHAW)** indicator is on the top of the right instrument panel, above a row of lights for various threat

The lovely supersonic lines and swept angles of the Phantom against a beautiful background will always be remembered by those who flew it. The aircraft crew and other flight members learned to share responsibilities and cover each other in search of safe and effective performance. No other fighter had been so versatile and so powerful in combat. Now, even the F-16 can do it all.

warnings. When radars of various frequencies strike the receiver, a distinctive strobe appears in the direction of the source, with intensity indicating signal strength, but not distance. The result is an indication of a specific enemy radar scan or missile lock-on from a preprogrammed dictionary of frequency bands, so that you can see exactly what is coming. A red light warns of a missile launch. This is a crucial indicator in modern air combat.

The side panels

The long panels under your arms contain a bewildering clutter of switches for various systems which cannot be listed here. Apart from the usual engine starting, landing gear, autopilot, air conditioning, radio, lighting and many other familiar controls, a few of the more important system are as follows.

The **identification friend or foe (IFF)** allows you to dial in numbers in several different modes. When interrogated by another aircraft or ground radar, this transmits a code which appears on the other radar's scope, clearly identifying you amid other traffic. An emergency position highlights your return on all scopes. The latest IFFs contain a new mode, classified in detail, which allows specific callsigns to be displayed on friendly scopes such as AWACS and other fighters, enabling accurate control of an air battle.

There are two modern systems that permit radio transmissions with security and prevent jamming. The KY-28 system encrypts transmissions so that they cannot be read by enemy intercept. In addition, the Have Quick system causes the transmitter and receiver to jump around together on a preset series of frequencies, many per second, so that frequency jamming can not interfere.

Nuclear weapons require some additional controls and safety measures for bomb arming and release. The **stick and throttle** contain a few items not found on earlier jets. The auto-

acquisition radar switch on the left throttle allows the pilot to bypass the navigator and lock the radar on targets under the pipper for quick shooting.

The rear cockpit

USAF F-4s can be flown from the rear, in contrast to most Navy and RAF birds. Sufficient flight and navigation instruments run across the top of the panel. Below this panel is the radar scope, with the majority of controls next to the throttles and the hand controller on

the right console for arms-down operation. The side panels contain various controls, such as the INS, weapons and duplicates of the front cockpit switches. Much thought was put into these cockpits designed for crew coordination, enabling the navigator to assist the pilot in various ways. Again, this was an interim step between the old F-94 and F-101 two-man aircraft and the new, third-generation F-15E. The 'pit' is a crowded, busy, poorly-designed place, with poor forward visibility, cramped movement and awkward operation. As an IP, I was glad I could get back up front most of the time, but I give credit to the many great navigators, the GIBs, who mastered the Wizzo Wizardry and helped make the Phantom the greatest fighter aircraft in history. The F-4E was the big stepping stone into the miraculous cockpits of today's fighters.

There were few changes in the rear cockpit. Here the RHAW scope is centered, compared to the more typical upper-right location shown on the opposite page. There were a number of variations in cockpit arrangement as specialized weapons and missions, such as Wild Weasel, called for new equipment. All USAF rear cockpits had sticks, and some navigators became proficient at basic flying, even refueling. It was important to develop good crew coordination because some information was displayed in only one cockpit. Flying from the rear was not easy.

F-4E rear cockpit

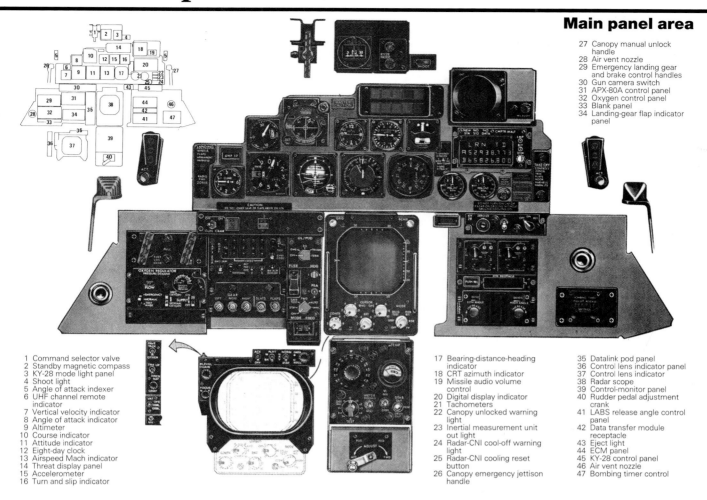

Main panel area

27 Canopy manual unlock handle
28 Air vent nozzle
29 Emergency landing gear and brake control handles
30 Gun camera switch
31 APX-80A control panel
32 Oxygen control panel
33 Blank panel
34 Landing-gear flap indicator panel

1 Command selector valve
2 Standby magnetic compass
3 KY-28 mode light panel
4 Shoot light
5 Angle of attack indexer
6 UHF channel remote indicator
7 Vertical velocity indicator
8 Angle of attack indicator
9 Altimeter
10 Course indicator
11 Attitude indicator
12 Eight-day clock
13 Airspeed Mach indicator
14 Threat display panel
15 Accelerometer
16 Turn and slip indicator

17 Bearing-distance-heading indicator
18 CRT azimuth indicator
19 Missile audio volume control
20 Digital display indicator
21 Tachometers
22 Canopy unlocked warning light
23 Inertial measurement unit out light
24 Radar-CNI cool-off warning light
25 Radar-CNI cooling reset button
26 Canopy emergency jettison handle

35 Datalink pod panel
36 Control lens indicator panel
37 Control lens indicator
38 Radar scope
39 Control-monitor panel
40 Rudder pedal adjustment crank
41 LABS release angle control panel
42 Data transfer module receptacle
43 Eject light
44 ECM panel
45 KY-28 control panel
46 Air vent nozzle
47 Bombing timer control

Left console area

1 Blank panel
2 Sensor select panel
3 Radar control panel
4 Target insertion controller
5 Navigation computer set control
6 Communications control panel
7 Marker beacon VOR/ILS audio control
8 Oxygen quantity gauge
9 Cabin altimeter
10 Anti g suit control valve
11 Pull-up tone cutout switch
12 Emergency flap control panel
13 Canopy selector
14 AN/ALE-40 panel
15 Throttles
16 Blank panel

Right console area

1 Coder control
2 Pave Tack control panel
3 Antenna control panel
4 Stall warning tone control panel
5 Extra picture switch
6 SST-181X pulse selector switch
7 Nuclear store consent switch
8 Cockpit lights control panel
9 Blank panel
10 Keyer control
11 Navigation control panel
12 Intercom control panel
13 Blank panel

PHANTOM USERS

UNITED STATES OF AMERICA

US Air Force

Although originally designed and built as a naval carrierborne interceptor, the McDonnell Phantom eventually saw service in greater numbers, for a longer time, as a land-based multirole tactical fighter with the US Air Force. Early evaluations of Navy aircraft conclusively proved the superiority of the F-4 over all air force fighters and, swallowing its pride, the USAF ordered its own Phantoms. The air force designation F-110 was soon forgotten, and successive variants were procured, introducing more and more modifications to meet specific air force requirements, culminating in the F-4E.

At the height of its USAF career, the F-4 equipped units in Vietnam, Europe and the continental USA, serving in the fighter, fighter-bomber, reconnaissance and defense suppression roles. Even in 1992, the USAF and Air National Guard still operated around 200 F-4Gs and RF-4Cs, but though these represent only a fraction of even the 1980s Phantom fleet, they represent one of the world's largest collections of F-4s and are likely to serve into the new millenium.

1st Tactical Fighter Wing

The 1st Fighter Wing (Air Defense) operated F-106 Delta Darts from Hamilton AFB prior to redesignation as the 1st Tactical Fighter Wing and assignment to MacDill AFB, Florida, to operate the F-4E. The wing had previously been the first to operate the F-86 Sabre in 1949 at George AFB, California. The move to MacDill AFB on 1 October 1970 was a retitling process in which the 15th TFW inactivated. The squadrons passed on to the 1st TFW were the 45th TFS, 46th TFS, 47th TFS, 4530th TFTS equipped with the F-4E (tailcoded 'FB' with a red and white tail stripe; 'FD', yellow; 'FE', green; and 'FF', white). In addition, the 4424th CCTS operated the B-57 ('FS', black). The 4501st TFRS was replaced by the 4530th TFTS but maintained the same markings. On 1 July 1971, the 45th TFS, 46th TFS and 47th TFS were replaced by the 71st TFS, 27th TFS and 94th TFS, again maintaining the former markings. B-57

operations ceased on 30 June 1972. The common wing tailcode of 'FF' was implemented in mid-1975 on the F-4Es of all assigned squadrons.

On 10 June 1975, the 1st TFW and all three squadron titles were reassigned to Langley AFB, Virginia, and converted to the F-15 Eagle. The F-4E operations at MacDill AFB were taken over by the 56th TFW and the new wing adopted the 'MC' tailcode.

The 1st TFW flew the F-4E Phantom from MacDill during 1970-75, with the 'FD' code successively used by the 46th and 27th TFSs.

3rd Tactical Fighter Wing

The 3rd Tactical Fighter Wing previously parented A-37 Dragonfly- and F-100 Super Sabre-equipped squadrons from Bien Hoa AB, RSVN, prior to moving to Kunsan AB, Republic of Korea, without its personnel or equipment on 15 March 1971. The 475th TFW based at Misawa AB, Japan, transferred its existing resources to the 3rd TFW. The wing then operated the F-4D with the 35th TFS ('UP', light blue), 36th TFS ('UK', red) and 80th TFS ('UD', yellow). Two squadrons, the 44th TFS ('ZL', orange) and the 67th TFS ('ZG', white/red), were attached during 1972 from the 18th TFW, based at Kadena AB, Okinawa. All three assigned squadrons were upgraded to the F-4E by late 1974. The 3rd TFW did not fully implement the tailcode of 'UP'.

The 3rd TFW moved to Clark AB, Philippines, on 16 September 1974 to replace the 405th FW, although the three former component squadrons remained at Kunsan AB under the newly established 8th TFW. The former 405th FW components, the 1st Test Squadron and the 90th TFS, with the 'PN' tailcode, were also assigned to the 3rd TFW on its transfer date. The 1st TS flew both the F-4C and F-4D, while the 90th TFS flew the F-4D (blue). The 90th TFS re-equipped with the F-4E in 1973 and the 3rd TFS, previously flying the A-7D at Korat RTAFB, arrived in December 1975 as a further 'PN'-tailcoded (red) F-4E operator. From 1976, the wing also operated the T-38A (and later just the F-5E), with an

The definitive F-4E version of the Phantom equipped elements of the 3rd TFW between 1973 and 1991.

aggressor squadron, the 26th AS. The 1st TS inactivated in October 1978.

In 1979, the first F-4G arrived for use within the 90th TFS. The 90th TFS 'Pair O' Dice' carried just that on the fin caps of its F-4Es and F-4Gs. Top cover missions were flown during the abortive December 1989 coup against President Aquino, and although no armament was expended the aircraft contributed to the government's survival.

With the continued run-down of forces within the Pacific, the closure of Clark AB was accelerated. Six days after the last F-4 departure, Mount Pinatubo erupted, ending

the usefulness of Clark AB. The F-4E and F-4G were noted at several locations after the 3rd TFW was reassigned as the 3rd Wing at Elmendorf AFB, Alaska, on 16 December 1991. The F-4Es mainly went to AMARC, while six of the F-4Gs were assigned to the 7440th Composite Wing at Incirlik AB, Turkey, during the Gulf War. Several went to the Idaho ANG, while more were earmarked for conversion to drones. Many were temporarily stored at George AFB, California, until they were redistributed among the units there or disposed of to AMARC.

4th Tactical Fighter Wing

The 4th Tactical Fighter Wing is probably best known as one of the two F-86 Sabre interceptor wings that operated in Korea between 1951 and 1953. The 4th TFW's F-4 era began at Seymour Johnson AFB, North Carolina, in 1967. The 334th TFS, 335th TFS and 336th TFS started F-4D operations after flying the F-86 Sabre, F-100 Super Sabre and F-105 Thunderchief. The wing's aircraft were not camouflaged until 1968. In line with other TAC-operated types, toned-down paint schemes required some identification, 50 tailcodes in the 'S' range were implemented: 'SA' (blue), 'SB' (green) and 'SC' (yellow) to the F-4Ds of the 334th TFS, 335th TFS and 336th TFS during July 1968.

The 4th TFW deployed to Kunsan AB, Republic of Korea, following the seizure of the USS *Pueblo* in early 1968. The 334th TFS moved to Kwang-ju AB, RoK, in March 1968 and then returned to Seymour Johnson AFB at the end of July 1968. The 335th TFS and 336th TFS returned in June and July 1968. Colonel Charles E. Yeager, of X-1 fame, was the commander of the 4th TFW between 23 March 1968 and 30 May 1969.

The wing started to re-equip with the F-4E during 1970 while at Seymour Johnson AFB, and maintained F-4E deployments within the 8th TFW in Southeast Asia between April

1972 and September 1973 under Constant Guard. The object was to bolster air power during peak periods of need. The 334th TFS and 336th TFS went to Ubon RTAFB in April 1972 to begin a complex rotation of 4th TFW fighter assets. The known deployments are:

334th TFS	4th TFW	'SA'	F-4E	11 Apr 72 – 8 Jul 72
336th TFS	4th TFW	'SC'-'SJ'*	F-4E	12 Apr 72 – 15 Sep 72
335th TFS	4th TFW	'SJ'	F-4E	8 Jul 72 – Dec 72
334th TFS	4th TFW	'SJ'	F-4E	25 Sep 72 – 12 Mar 73
336th TFS	4th TFW	'SJ'	F-4E	9 Mar 73 – 7 Sep 73

*336th TFS recoded during deployment

The 4th TFW adopted the 'SJ' common tailcode under the AFM66-1 concept in 1972. Actual dates are unknown, but the changeover may have been implemented during deployments. The 337th TFS, activated in 1982, also flew 'SJ'-coded F-4Es, inactivating three years later. The first F-15E arrived in 1989, and by the end of 1990 the wing had fully re-equipped.

The 4th TFW at Seymour Johnson AFB was one of the longest-lived users of the F-4E derivative.

8th Tactical Fighter Wing

The 8th Tactical Fighter Wing replaced the 32nd TFW as an F-4 operator at George AFB, California, on 10 July 1964. The initial assigned squadrons were the 68th TFS, 431st TFS, 433rd TFS and 497th TFS operating gray F-4Cs. In December 1965, the 8th TFW was reassigned to Ubon RTAFB, taking with it the 433rd TFS and 497th TFS to engage in the Southeast Asian conflict. The 555th TFS was added in February 1966, when wing-wide camouflage was also adopted. By January 1967, the 8th TFW inaugurated the application of tailcodes and squadron colors on assigned F-4Cs, and the three initial F-4C operators started coding with 'F' range tailcodes in early 1967. They were the 433rd TFS 'Satan's Angels' ('FG', blue/orange, later green/black), 497th TFS 'Night Owls' ('FP', blue/orange, later black) and the 555th TFS 'Triple Nickel' ('FY').

In addition to the F-4, the 8th TFW operated the F-104C with the 435th TFS, which re-equipped with 'FO'-tailcoded F-4Ds

in July 1967. Several other units were assigned to the 8th TFW, including the 13th BS, the 16th SOS and the 25th TFS, flying B-57s, AC-130s and F-4Ds ('FK/FS', 'FT' and 'FA'). The 555th TFS was reassigned to the 432nd TFW at Udorn RTAFB in May 1968. During 1967, the 433rd TFS, 497th TFS and the 555th TFS upgraded to the F-4D from the F-4C.

The 8th TFW was assigned the combat air patrol mission, which resulted in the 'MiG Killer' title, and also participated in Operation Bolo, under its commander Colonel Robin Olds. Later, the units were assigned specialized attack roles, with the 497th TFS and the 13th BS adopting the night-attack role. These aircraft were noteworthy for their black undersides rather than the standard light gray. The wing common tailcode 'WP' ('Wolf Pack') was applied to all components (16th SOS, 25th TFS, 433rd TFS, 435th TFS and 497th TFS) by January 1973. Several F-4 units attached from CONUS-based wings during 1972-1973, while maintaining CONUS tailcodes. Known deployments include:

334th TFS	4th TFW	'SA'	F-4E	11 Apr 72 – 8 Jul 72
336th TFS	4th TFW	'SC'–'SJ'*	F-4E	12 Apr 72 – 15 Sep 72
335th TFS	4th TFW	'SJ'	F-4E	8 Jul 72 – Dec 72
334th TFS	4th TFW	'SJ'	F-4E	25 Sep 72 – 12 Mar 73
308th TFS	31st TFW	'ZF'	F-4E	11 Dec 72 – 11 Jan 73
336th TFS	4th TFW	'SJ'	F-4E	9 Mar 73 – 7 Sep 73
58th TFS	33rd TFW	'ED'	F-4E	8 Jun 73 – 14 Sep 73

*336th TFS recoded from 'SC' to 'SJ' during its deployment.

As Ubon RTAFB operations phased down in 1974, the 8th TFW replaced the 3rd TFW at Kunsan AB, RoK, on 16 September 1974. The F-4D-equipped 35th TFS and 80th TFS were the assigned units after the move, and the F-4D-equipped 497th TFS rejoined the 8th TFW in 1978, until they were reassigned to the 51st CW on 1 January 1982. The 35th TFS and 80th TFS started re-equipping with the F-16A/B on 15 May 1981, with the arrival of the first training example.

While at Ubon, the 8th TFW flew a number of F-4Ds with black under-surfaces on night attack tasks.

10th Tactical Reconnaissance Wing

The 10th Tactical Reconnaissance Wing moved from Spangdahlem AB, Germany, during 1959 to RAF Alconbury, UK, while flying the B-66 Destroyer. The 10th TRW was assigned the 1st TRS and 30th TRS and converted to the RF-4C starting on 12 April 1965, with the 32nd TRS added on 15 August 1966. The assigned RF-4Cs were initially flown in the gray/white color scheme and later changed to the standard tactical camouflage. The three RF-4C squadrons, the 1st TRS, 30th TRS and 32nd TRS adopted 'AR' (blue), 'AS' (red) and 'AT' (yellow)

tailcodes and colors, respectively, in January 1970. Under the wing common tailcode concept introduced in 1972, all three units recoded to 'AR'. The 30th TRS and 32nd TRS inactivated in 1976, followed by the 1st TRS in 1987. The wing also operated the F-5E of the 527th TFTAS until mid-1988. The 10th TRW was redesignated the 10th Tactical Fighter Wing on 20 August 1987, in preparation for flying the A-10 Thunderbolt II.

USAFE's first Phantom operator was the 10th TRW at Alconbury. It flew the RF-4C on reconnaissance duties from 1965 until 1987.

12th Tactical Fighter Wing

The 12th Tactical Fighter Wing was one of the two initial USAF F-4 wings, having previously flown F-84 variants at MacDill AFB, Florida. Both wings used borrowed USN F-4Bs and the USAF-purchased F-4Cs in working up to operational readiness. The wing was reassigned from MacDill AFB to the Cam Ranh Bay AB complex, RSVN, on 8 November 1965 with the 555th TFS and 558th TFS; the 557th TFS and 559th TFS followed. The 12th TFW operated in various roles in support of US and allied forces in Southeast Asia. The 555th TFS was reassigned to the 8th TFW at the start of 1966 and was replaced shortly after by the 391st TFS. The wing's F-4Cs were flown initially in the gray/white color scheme, but switched to camouflage in 1966. In late 1966, 'XT' (yellow), 'XC' (red), 'XD' (green) and 'XN' (blue) tailcodes and squadron colors were applied to the 391st TFS, 557th TFS, 558th TFS and 559th TFS.

In response to the seizure of USS *Pueblo*, the 391st TFS moved to the 475th TFW at Misawa AB, Japan, in July 1968, taking with

it the 'XD'-tailcoded F-4Cs of 558th TFS. In return, the 558th TFS received the 'XT'-tailcoded F-4Cs, formerly operated by the 391st TFS.

During 1970 and 1971, the 557th TFS, 558th TFS and 559th TFS inactivated, while the 12th TFW was reassigned, in name only, to Phu Cat AB, RSVN, on 31 March 1970. The wing assumed control of the former 37th TFW's F-4D assets flown by the 389th TFS ('HB', red) and 480th TFS ('HK', green). The wing inactivated on 17 November 1971 until being redesignated the 12th Flying Training Wing on 22 March 1972 at Randolph AFB, Texas, with T-37 and T-38 trainers.

Both the F-4C and F-4D were used by the 12th TFW during operations from Cam Ranh Bay and Phu Cat.

15th Tactical Fighter Wing

The 15th Tactical Fighter Wing was activated at MacDill AFB, Florida, in 1962, and initially flew the F-84. The wing then transitioned to the new F-4C, with the 45th TFS, 46th TFS and 47th TFS, and subsequently also the 43rd TFS. The wing quickly progressed through to the F-4E model and, in 1968, tailcodes were assigned to the 43rd TFS ('FB', blue/white), 45th TFS ('FC'), 46th TFS ('FD', yellow), 47th TFS ('FE', green) and 4501st TFRS ('FF' allocated, but no assigned aircraft). The B-57 was also operated within the 13th BS and the 4424th CCTS, and both

carried the 'FK' tailcode. The 13th BS was later reassigned to the 8th TFW at Ubon RTAFB. The 43rd TFS was reassigned to the 21st Composite Wing at Elmendorf AFB, Alaska, on 1 April 1970, taking the former 45th TFS, 'FC'-tailcoded F-4E. The 45th TFS then switched codes from 'FC' to 'FB' and used the former 43rd TFS's F-4Es. The 15th TFW inactivated on 1 October 1970, with the remaining 45th TFS, 46th TFS and 47th TFS and the 4424th CCTS reassigned to the 1st TFW, maintaining tailcodes and squadron colors.

Early production F-4Cs of the 15th TFW are portrayed on the ramp at MacDill AFB, Florida, soon after deliveries got under way.

18th Tactical Fighter Wing

The 18th Tactical Fighter Wing had been stationed at Kadena AB, Okinawa, since 1954, flying the F-86 Sabre, T-33 Shooting Star, F-100 Super Sabre and F-105 Thunderchief. The F-4 arrived in 1967, with the 15th TRS forming as an RF-4C unit, having formerly flown the RF-101 Voodoo. In addition, the 18th TFW also operated the F-105 and EB-66 Destroyer. In late 1967, the wing was assigned 'Z' ranged tailcodes, and the 15th TRS adopted the 'ZZ' tailcode on RF-4Cs. On 15 March 1971, the 44th TFS ('ZL', orange/black) and 67th TFS ('ZG', white/red) were assigned with F-4Cs. The 67th TFS also operated the F-4C Wild Weasel in the SAM suppression role, and several detachments were made to Korat RTAFB, making the type's combat debut. Other assigned units were the F-105 Thunderchief-equipped 12th TFS ('ZA', 'ZB'),

44th TFS ('ZL', orange/black), 67th TFS ('ZG', white/red) as well as the 19th TEWS with EB-66 Destroyers; the 19th TEWS inactivated in October 1970. The 1st SOS was also assigned during the 1972-1973 period with 'GT'-coded EB-57E Canberras.

The 18th TFW recoded 'ZZ' after June 1972, and the 25th TFS was added in late 1975 with further F-4Ds. Starting in 1979, the 12th TFS, 44th TFS and 67th TFS converted to the F-15 Eagle at Eglin AFB, Florida, interrupting the 33rd TFW's own conversion. The 25th TFS inactivated on 22 August 1980 without converting to the F-15 Eagle. The 15th TRS, still equipped with the RF-4C, transferred to the newly established 460th TRG in 1989 and recoded 'GU', thus drawing an end to the F-4's history with the 18th TFW.

In addition to the F-4D, the 18th TFW also operated RF-4Cs from its base at Kadena for many years.

21st Composite Wing
21st Tactical Fighter Wing

The 21st Composite Wing was activated at Elmendorf AFB, Alaska, on 8 June 1966 and maintained control over several air defense associated units flying the C-130, F-102 Delta Dagger and T-33A Shooting Star. The F-4's association with the 21st CW began with the reassignment of the 43rd TFS from the 15th TFW at Langley AFB, Virginia, on 23 June 1970 with 'FC'-tailcoded F-4Es. The F-4E assumed the air defense role from the F-102 Delta Dagger, and this role was carried out from a number of forward operating locations including Eielson, King Salmon and Galena. On 1 January 1980, the 18th TFS, also flying the F-4E, was assigned to the 21st CW upon the inactivation of the 343rd TFG.

The 21st CW redesignated as the 21st Tactical Fighter Wing on 1 October 1979, and the 43rd TFS began conversion to the F-15 Eagle in March 1982, completing in October 1982.

Responsibility for air defense of Alaska was entrusted to two F-4E squadrons of the 21st Composite Wing throughout the 1970s.

26th Tactical Reconnaissance Wing

The RF-101-equipped 26th Tactical Reconnaissance Wing arrived at Ramstein AB, Germany, from Toul-Rosières AB, France, in late 1966. The wing operated a variety of other aircraft, including the EB-57 Canberra, C-47 Dakota, C-130 Hercules, RF-4C, F-102 Delta Dagger and UH-1N Twin-Huey. The F-4 units comprised the 38th TRS, flying the RF-4C since 1965, and the 526th TFS with the F-4E, which converted from the F-102 Delta Dagger in 1970.

In 1970, tailcodes in the 'R' range were introduced to the 26th TRW, with 'RR' being assigned to the RF-4Cs of the 38th TRS and 'RS' to the 526th TFS's F-4Es. Under the AFM66-1 concept, the 26th TRW recoded to 'RS', although only two RF-4Cs were recoded due to the knowledge that the squadron was soon to be moved to Zweibrücken AB, Germany.

The 26th TRW moved to Zweibrücken AB under the 'Battle Creek' title, as part of a series of base and wing switches which

Non-standard serial presentation identifies this RF-4C as assigned to the 26th TRW commander.

inverted the bases of the 26th TRW and 86th TFW on 31 January 1973. The 38th TRS moved with the 26th TRW to Zweibrücken and adopted the 'ZR' tailcode for its RF-4Cs. The 525th TFS with F-4Es remained at Ramstein AB, Germany, and was absorbed by the 86th TFW. The 26th TRW absorbed the RF-4C-equipped 17th TRS at Zweibrücken. The 417th TFS, with a single F-4D, activated with the 26th TRW, which lasted one month before inactivating due to 'poor munitions storage' in late 1978.

The 17th TRS inactivated on 13 December 1978, leaving the 38th TRS as the wing's sole component. The 38th TRS deployed its assets to Incirlik AB, Turkey, in February 1991, for assignments over Iraq during Operation Desert Storm. On their return, most RF-4Cs were transferred to AMARC for storage, as the 38th TRS inactivated on 4 April 1991 and the 26th TRW followed on 5 April 1991.

31st Tactical Fighter Wing

The 31st Tactical Fighter Wing activated at Homestead AFB, Florida, in May 1962. The wing was assigned to Tuy Hoa AB, RSVN, during December 1966 to control F-100 Super Sabre operations, and then returned to Homestead AFB on 15 October 1970 and assumed the assets of the tenant 4531st TFW. The initial F-4E units within the wing were the 436th TFS ('ZD', red), 478th TFS ('ZE', white/blue), 560th TFS ('ZF', green) and 68th TFS ('ZG'). The 478th TFS and 560th TFS inactivated on 31 October 1970, while the 68th TFS was reassigned to the 4403rd TFW at England AFB, Louisiana, and the 436th TFS to the 479th TFW at George AFB, California. The 306th TFS, 309th TFS and 308th TFS were reassigned from the 4403rd TFW at England AFB to the 31st TFW at Homestead AFB, Florida, and assumed the 'ZD', 'ZE' and 'ZF' tailcoded F-4Es from the 436th TFS, 478th TFS and 560th TFS. All three were formerly assigned to the 31st TFW at Tuy Hoa AB, while flying the F-100 Super Sabre. The 307th TFS transferred from the 401st TFW on 14 July 1971, replacing the 306th TFS and assuming the 'ZD' tailcode and the latter squadron's F-4Es.

Under the wing common tailcode concept introduced in 1972, all the 31st TFW-

assigned F-4Es adopted the 'ZF' tailcodes. The inactive 306th TFS redesignated to the 306th TFTS on 5 June 1978, and reactivated on 1 July 1978 to complete a four-squadron F-4E wing. The wing designation changed to 31st Tactical Training Wing on 30 March 1981, while the 306th TFS, 307th TFS and 309th TFS redesignated as TFTS on 1 July 1983, 9 October 1980 and 1 July 1982, respectively. All units began conversion to the F-4D during 1981-1982. In late 1985, the 31st TTW began to re-equip with the F-16A/B, and the last 31st TTW-assigned F-4 left Homestead AFB in 1987. In late 1986, just prior to F-16A/B conversion, the wing changed its tailcode to 'HS', and hence F-4Ds from all three squadrons were noted with both 'HS' and 'ZF' tailcodes.

Replacement of F-4Es by F-4Ds like this accompanied the 31st Wing's redesignation as a training unit.

32nd Tactical Fighter Wing

The 32nd Tactical Fighter Wing operated the F-4C for a very short period between April and July 1964 at George AFB, California. The F-4C operations were reassigned to 8th

TFW control on 10 July 1964, with the 32nd TFW inactivating on 15 July 1964. The established units included the 68th FIS, 433rd FIS and 497th FIS, while the 782nd TFS, 783rd TFS, 784th TFS and 785th TFS were still on strength. This mix of units was sorted by the 8th TFW, which assumed control on 10 July 1964.

32nd Tactical Fighter Squadron

The 32nd FIS was redesignated 32nd Tactical Fighter Squadron on conversion from the F-102 Delta Dagger to the F-4E in July 1969. The F-4Es were operated in standard camouflage until May 1970, when the 'CR' tailcode was used. ('C' represented

'Camp Amsterdam' and 'R' was in line with and the second digit sequence of the USAFE of 'R', 'S', 'T', 'U' and 'V' being used in order). The assigned F-4Es were primarily used in the air defense role until being replaced by the F-15 Eagle in late 1978.

Although designated as a tactical unit, the 32nd TFS F-4Es operated in the air defense role.

33rd Tactical Fighter Wing

The 33rd Tactical Fighter Wing reactivated at Eglin AFB, Florida, on 1 April 1965 after a period of inactivation. The wing was initially established with the 4th TFS, 16th TFS, 25th TFS and 40th TFS with F-4Ds on 20 June 1965. The 31st TFW provided F-4Ds and later F-4Es in large numbers to the conflict in Southeast Asia. Typically, a squadron would form up under a 31st TFW designation, and then transfer to Southeast Asia, assuming the designation of a unit due for re-equipment. The 31st TFW-assigned TFS would then start working up again for the next squadron. In addition to deployments to the Southeast Asia conflict, the 33rd TFW provided F-4 formation assets for six squadrons in Southeast Asia.

4th TFS	F-4D assets	to 433rd TFS	8th TFW	'FG'	Jul 67
40th TFS	F-4D assets	to 555th TFS	8th TFW	'FY'	May 67
16th TFS	F-4D assets	to 13th TFS	366th TFW	'OC'	Oct 67
25th TFS	F-4D assets		8th TFW	'FA'	May 68
40th TFS	F-4E assets	to 469th TFS	388th TFW	'JV'	Nov 68
16th TFS	F-4E assets	to 421st TFS	366th TFW	'LC'	Apr 69
4th TFS	F-4E self		366th TFW	'LA'	Apr 69
40th TFS	F-4E assets	to 34th TFS	388th TFW	'JJ'	May 69

Initial units in 1968 comprised the 4th TFS, 16th TFS, 40th TFS and the 4533rd TTS(T), later coded 'EB', 'ED', 'EE' and 'EG'. The 4th TFS left for Southeast Asia and the 40th TFS inactivated in mid-1969. In 1970, the 58th TFS replaced the 16th TFS. The 4533rd TTS(T) inactivated on 12 April 1971, and was replaced by the TAWC-assigned 4485th TS. F-4 usage continued after the wing common tailcode 'ED' was assigned to the F-4Es of the remaining squadron, the 16th TFS. The 59th TFS became operational in July 1973 with further 'ED'-tailcoded F-4Es, The 'ED' tailcode changed to 'EG' during October 1978. In 1979, the F-4E replacement started arriving in the form of the F-15 Eagle, which finally replaced the F-4E during that year.

Assigned to the 33rd TFW, the F-4E seen here displays the code/letter combination of the 4533rd Tactical Training Squadron (Test), also assigned F-4Ds and RF-4Cs.

35th Tactical Fighter Wing 35th Tactical Training Wing

The 35th Tactical Fighter Wing activated at Phan Rang AB, RSVN, and replaced the 366th TFW in controlling the 352nd TFS, 614th TFS and 615th TFS, which flew the camouflaged F-100 Super Sabre. Before the wing inactivated on 31 July 1971, it operated the A-37 Dragonfly and the B-57 Canberra. The 35th TFW reactivated on 1 October 1971 at George AFB, California, to replace the inactivating 479th TFW. As the switch of wings took place prior to the common wing tailcode, each squadron had its own individual code: initial units were the 4535th CCTS ('GC'), the 4452nd CCTS ('GC', blue), the 434th TFS ('GD', light blue) and the 35th OMS ('GE') with the UH-1. The 35th TFW became the major F-4 training wing, and under the AFM66-1 common wing tailcode concept, all the wing squadrons recoded to 'GA'. The 4535th CCTS and 4452nd CCTS inactivated on 1 December 1972, and were replaced by the 20th TFTS and 21st TFTS.

The Wild Weasel role was first assigned to the 35th TFW with the F-105. The 561st TFS, 562nd TFS and the 563rd TFTS were added in 1973, 1974 and 1975, respectively, and the three eventually transitioned to the F-4G as the conversion production line permitted, starting on 28 April 1978. The Weasel squadrons also operated the 'GA'-tailcoded F-4E, and by June 1979 the wing started recoding with the 'WW' tailcode, thus becoming a two-tailcode wing, although only two 'GA'-tailcoded F-4Gs were noted. Non-Weasel related assets maintained the 'GA' tailcode. The switch to F-4Gs was completed on 12 July 1980.

The 39th TFTS was also assigned in July 1977 with F-4Cs and F-4Cs (Wild Weasel modified), and was later redesignated the 563rd TFS. The 434th TFS redesignated to the 434th TFTS while flying the F-4D and F-4E, and in 1977 the squadron's status changed to non-operational until it was reassigned elsewhere.

Luftwaffe-type camouflage helps to identify this Phantom as an F-4F which was used for training German pilots from George AFB, California, as part of the 35th TFW.

The Wild Weasel operations of the 561st TFS, 563rd TFS and 562nd TFTS were passed to the co-based 37th TFW on 30 March 1981, and the wing was redesignated the 35th Tactical Training Wing on 1 July 1984. The wing status returned to the 35th TFW designation on 5 October 1989, when F-4E/G Wild Weasel operations were returned from the 37th TFW. The co-based 37th TFW designation was reassigned to cover F-117 operations at Tonopah. The 561st TFS and the 562nd TFTS returned to 35th TFW control with 'WW' codes.

As part of the 20th TFTS, the German Luftwaffe undertook its F-4 training at George AFB. This started with the F-4F in standard Luftwaffe camouflage with USAF markings and codes, and later with specially purchased 1975 block F-4Es in full USAF camouflage and markings, all under the designation of the 1st GAFTS.

As part of the USAF's effort in the Gulf War, the 561st TFS deployed as part of the 35th TFW (Provisional) to Sheik Isa AB, Bahrain, in the SAM suppression role. The 35th TFW was the only wing to follow wartime aircraft painting instructions, and all squadron color stripes were removed and the aircraft arrived back in the USA without these, nose art or 'kill' markings.

In 1991 the wing was redesignated the 35th Fighter Wing. This designation was short-lived as George AFB was due for closure in 1993 and the 35th FW inactivated. All components have inactivated or transferred, and the Weasel role has passed to ANG units, with Idaho ANG being the first. The 1st GAFTS has moved as the 9th FS to Holloman AFB, New Mexico.

36th Tactical Fighter Wing

The 36th Tactical Fighter Wing previously flew the F-84, F-86 Sabre, F-100 Super Sabre, F-105 Thunderchief and F-102 Delta Dagger from Bitburg, Germany, before the F-4 was introduced. In mid-1970, the wing components were the 22nd TFS, 23rd TFS and 53rd TFS, which converted to the camouflaged F-4Ds from the F-105 Thunderchief starting in 1966, as the demand for the F-105D Thunderchief increased in Southeast Asia. The F-102 Delta Dagger-equipped 525th TFS transitioned to the F-4E in October 1969 in the air defense role and, in addition, the wing also controlled

Elements of Bitburg's 36th TFW had F-4Ds between 1966 and 1973. This example is from the 53rd TFS.

the B-66 Destroyers of the 39th TEWS.

The 36th TFW assigned 'B' range codes and with second letters 'R', 'S', 'T', 'U' and 'V', respectively, to the 22nd TFS, 23rd TFS, 53rd TFS, 525th TFS and 39th TEWS. Both the 23rd TFS and 39th TEWS were based at nearby Spangdahlem AB, Germany, until they were reassigned to the newly established 52nd TFW on 31 December 1971. The remaining F-4 units adopted the 'BT' tailcode under the AFM66-1 common tailcode concept during 1972. The 22nd TFS and 53rd TFS converted to the F-4E during 1972-1973, and all three squadrons further re-equipped with the F-15A/B in 1977, with the last F-4E leaving on 9 March 1977.

37th Tactical Fighter Wing

The 37th Tactical Fighter Wing was activated at Phu Cat AB, RSVN, on 1 March 1967 to control F-100 Super Sabre assets. On 15 June 1969, two F-4D units, the 389th TFS ('HB', red) and 480th TFS ('HK', green), were transferred from the 366th TFW at Da Nang AB, RSVN. The F-100 Super Sabre assets were reassigned in 1969. The 37th TFW inactivated on 31 March 1970 and was replaced by the 12th TFW.

The 37th TFW was reactivated on 30

March 1981 at George AFB, California, taking control of the Wild Weasel assets from the co-based 35th TFW. The F-4Es and F-4Gs of the 561st TFS, 563rd TFS and the 562nd TFTS were tailcoded 'WW'. On 5 October 1989, the 37th TFW moved to Tonopah to control F-117 operations, and control of Wild Weasel assets was returned to the 35th TFW on that date, while the 563rd TFS inactivated.

The specialist Wild Weasel unit at George operated numerous F-4Es alongside the F-4G version.

48th Tactical Fighter Wing

Formerly based at Chaumont AB, France, the 48th Tactical Fighter Wing moved to RAF Lakenheath, UK, in January 1960 with the F-100 Super Sabre. The conversion

period to the F-4D was very lengthy, commencing during October 1971 and being completed by August 1974. As the conversion began close to the wing common tailcode date, the assigned F-4Ds adopted the 'LK' tailcode for the 492nd TFS (blue), 493rd TFS (yellow) and 494th TFS (red). This tailcode was used from early 1972 until July/August 1972, when the 48th TFW recoded to 'LN'. Under Operation Ready Switch the F-4D assets were reassigned to the 474th TFW at Nellis AFB, Nevada. The 48th Tactical Fighter Wing is the only wing within the USAF to have a non-numerical title – it is known as 'The Liberty Wing'.

F-4Ds assigned to the Lakenheath-based 48th TFW eventually joined the 474th TFW at Nellis AFB.

49th Tactical Fighter Wing

The 49th Tactical Fighter Wing moved from Pacific operations to France to operate the F-100 Super Sabre. The wing moved to Spangdahlem AB, Germany, in 1959, converting from the F-105 to the F-4 in March 1967, and was reassigned to Holloman AFB, New Mexico, in July 1968 as part of the 'dual-based' concept. The 49th TFW remained NATO-committed, and its

components returned to Germany during Reforger rapid deployment exercises. In mid-1968 the 49th TFW assigned F-4D-applied tailcodes in the 'H' range to the 7th TFS ('HB', blue), 8th TFS ('HC', yellow) and 9th TFS ('HD', red). The 417th TFS was added with further F-4Ds in late 1970. The 417th TFS started using the 'HA' tailcode before switching to 'HE' by the year's end. The wing adopted the 'HO' tailcode in 1972.

The 49th TFW deployed from Holloman AFB, New Mexico, to Takhli RTAFB on 13 May 1972, bolstering air power in Southeast Asia. The 49th TFW deployed until 27 October 1972. The 417th inactivated within the 49th TFW on 31 March 1977. The wing started re-equipping with the F-15. F-4Es were assigned again in 1992 when the 9th FS received the Luftwaffe training role from the 35th FW.

Equipped with the F-4D while based in Germany, the 49th TFW retained them on moving to the USA in 1968.

50th Tactical Fighter Wing

The 50th Tactical Fighter Wing moved from Toul-Rosières, France, to Hahn AB, Germany, in late 1959 while operating the F-100 Super Sabre. The wing re-equipped with the F-4 in 1966. The two F-4D components were the 10th TFS ('HR', blue) and 496th TFS ('HS', black/yellow). The 496th TFS converted to the F-4E in late 1970. In 1972, the 50th TFW adopted the code 'HR' under the AFM66-1 common wing tailcode concept. The 10th TFS converted to the F-4E in July 1976 and a third squadron, the 313th TFS (white), was added with further F-4Es in November. Operations continued with F-4Es until the 50th TFW converted to the F-16A/B during early 1982. The last assigned F-4E left Hahn AB in mid-1982.

Non-standard markings on this 50th TFW F-4E are associated with the unit's participation in a tactical weapons meeting held by NATO.

51st Fighter Interceptor Wing
51st Air Base Wing
51st Composite Wing

The 51st Fighter Interceptor Wing was assigned to Naha AB, Okinawa, during 1950. The wing moved to Osan AB, RoK, in November 1971, becoming the 51st Air Base Wing after being primarily an air defense unit with F-102 Delta Dagger. The wing redesignated as the 51st Composite Wing (Tactical) on 30 September 1974, controlling the 19th TASS, switching between the OV-10 and the OA-37, and the F-4E equipped the 36th TFS with 'OS' tailcodes. The wing further redesignated as the 51st TFW on 1 January 1982, with the addition of the 497th TFS ('OS', blue). In addition, the

51st TFW controlled the A-10A-equipped 25th TFS. The 497th TFS recoded to 'GU' when the unit moved to Taegu AB, also in Korea, but still under 51st TFW control.

Two squadrons of F-4Es served with the 51st Wing from its base at Osan, South Korea.

52nd Tactical Fighter Wing

The 52nd Tactical Fighter Wing activated within USAFE to control the former 36th TFW units based at Spangdahlem AB, Germany, on 31 December 1971. The two assigned squadrons, the 23rd TFS ('BS', blue/red) with F-4Ds and 39th TEWS ('BV', green/white) with B-66 Destroyers used the 'B' range tailcodes of the 36th TFW. Eight months later, the 52nd TFW adopted its own wing common tailcode of 'SP'. This was an odd occurrence, as each squadron *should* have adopted the 'S' range tailcodes prior to the wing common 'SP'. The 'ZS'-tailcoded Wild Weasel F-4C arrived to replace the B-66 Destroyer operations, which ceased in late 1972 (movement achieved through Operation Battle Creek, a reshuffling of USAFE units on and around 15 January 1973). The Wild Weasel maintained their odd 'ZS' tailcode until the start of 1973 when the 'SP' code became wing wide. The

480th TFS activated with the F-4D on 15 November 1976. Both the 23rd TFS and 480th TFS converted to F-4Es during March and April 1980. In 1979, the 81st TFS converted from the Wild Weasel F-4C to the much more capable F-4G. A change of policy resulted in all three 52nd TFW squadrons flying both F-4Es and F-4Gs, rather than one variant, in December 1983. This equipment remained until 1987, when the wing took on the F-16C/D.

The 52nd TFW contributed F-4G assets from the 23rd TFS to the 35th TFW (Provisional) at Sheik Isa AB, Bahrain, and to the 7440th CW based at Incirlik AB in Turkey. Several F-4Gs deployed had previously seen combat in Southeast Asia prior to conversion from F-4E standards. Subsequently, all F-4Gs were concentrated in the 81st FS.

Full-color unit insignia may be clearly seen on this F-4G Weasel of Spangdahlem's 52nd TFW.

54th Tactical Fighter Wing

The 54th Tactical Fighter Wing activated on 15 June 1970, at Kunsan AB, RoK, taking the place of the reassigned 354th TFW. The 354th TFW and the 54th TFW controlled CONUS F-4 units, which were deployed following the seizure of USS *Pueblo* by

North Korea. Two F-4E units were attached during 54th TFW control, the 16th TFS from Eglin AFB, Florida, 33rd TFW ('ED') and the 478th TFS from Homestead AFB, New Mexico, 4531st TFW ('ZE') between June and September 1970. The 54th TFW inactivated on 31 October 1970, after a rather short life span.

56th Tactical Fighter Wing, 56th Tactical Training Wing

The 56th Tactical Fighter Wing was reassigned to MacDill AFB, Florida, on 30 June 1975 to operate 'MC'-tailcoded F-4Es. Prior to operating the F-4E, the 56th Special Operations Wing had flown the OV-10A, CH-53 and A-1 from Nakhon Phanom RTAFB in the Southeast Asia conflict. The previous operator of the F-4Es had been the 'FF'-coded 1st TFW, which re-equipped with the F-15 Eagle on moving to Langley AFB.

The 56th TFW controlled the 61st TFS (yellow), 62nd TFS (blue), 63rd TFS (red) and 4501st TFRS (white), and all were equipped with the F-4E. The 4501st TFRS inactivated during early 1976 with its functions being taken over by the activated 13th TFTS. In 1978, the 56th TFW started converting from the F-4E to the less capable F-4D. All four squadrons further re-equipped with the F-16A/B starting in 1980, and the conversion was completed in 1981.

In the final period of the Phantom era, the MacDill-based 56th Wing transitioned from the F-4E to the F-4D during the course of 1978.

57th Fighter Weapons Wing, 57th Tactical Training Wing

The 57th Fighter Weapons Wing activated on 15 October 1969, assuming control of the former 4525th FWW units at Nellis AFB, Nevada. The sole F-4 flying unit, the 4538th CCTS, was redesignated the 414th Fighter Weapons Squadron on the same date. The assigned F-4Cs and F-4Ds carried the 'WD' tailcode, together with a yellow and black checkered tail stripe. A second unit, the 66th Fighter Weapons Squadron, activated in September 1971 to develop the Wild

Weasel role with the F-4C. The 'WA' tailcode appeared as a wing standard, prior to the June 1972 formal adoption of common tailcodes by TAC wings. The 66th FWS became non-operational in July 1975, and the 414th FWS traded its F-4Cs and F-4Ds for the F-4E in late 1971. It was replaced by the F-4 division of the Fighter Weapons School on 1 June 1981. The F-4Es stayed with the wing until August 1985.

The wing underwent two redesignations, the first to the 57th Tactical Training Wing, on 1 April 1977, and then redesignating back to 57th Fighter Weapons Wing on 1 March 1980.

Most versions of the Phantom were flown by the 57th from Nellis on a variety of tasks. F-4Es like this were used from 1971 to 1985.

57th Fighter Interceptor Squadron

The 57th Fighter Interceptor Squadron operated the F-102 Delta Dagger when conversion to the F-4C began in 1973 at NAS Keflavik, Iceland. The squadron operated in the air defense role, and as such was one of only two F-4 operation squadrons to operate without wing control. The F-4Cs were operated in tactical camouflage until changing to air defense gray just prior to the conversion to the F-4E. This started on

21 March 1978. The F-4Es of the 57th FIS also operated in the gray air defense scheme, with a variety of black and white checkered markings. In 1985, the squadron began to re-equip with the infinitely more capable F-15 Eagle.

Air Defense Command operation of the Phantom was limited, to say the least, but the Keflavik-based 57th FIS flew both the F-4C and F-4E.

58th Tactical Fighter Training Wing, 58th Tactical Training Wing

Luke AFB, Arizona, and its assigned wings have, for many years, been associated with the advanced pilot training of various current fighter aircraft. Up until 1970, the wing operated mainly the F-100 Super Sabre. Transition to the A-7D Corsair began when the decision was made to swap training roles with the 4453rd CCTW/355th TFW based at Davis-Monthan AFB, Arizona, then operating the F-4C. The wing was one of three exceptions in adopting a common wing tailcode prior to 1972, with 'LA' being used from the start of application.

The 550th TFTS was the first squadron to be equipped with the F-4C in January 1970. Other units followed with the F-4C, applying colored tail stripes. The F-4 users were the 310th TFTS (green) transitioning in May

1971, the 311th TFTS (yellow) transitioning in August 1971, and the 426th TFTS (blue) transitioning in August 1971. The 58th Tactical Fighter Training Wing was redesignated the 58th Tactical Fighter Wing on 1 April 1977. In addition, the wing controlled the Williams AFB-assigned 425th TFTS, which operated 'LA'-tailcoded F-5s of various types.

The wing started converting to the F-15 Eagle in much the same replacement training unit role in 1977, with the newly established 461st TFTS. The 550th TFTS transitioned to the new aircraft in August 1977, followed by the 426th TFTS in January 1981. The 310th TFTS and 311th TFTS inactivated as F-4C users on 4 November 1982, bringing to an end the 58th Tactical Training Wing's F-4 association.

Red and white stripes on this F-4C of the 58th TTW were designed to enhance visibility during ACM.

66th Tactical Reconnaissance Wing

The 66th Tactical Reconnaissance Wing moved from Laon AB, France, to RAF Upper Heyford, England, on 1 September 1966. Its components, the 17th TRS and 18th TRS, flew the RF-101C. The 17th TRS started to

re-equip with the RF-4C on 27 March 1969, with aircraft in the early white/gray scheme. The 17th TRS was reassigned to the 86th TFW, and was then moved to Ramstein AB, Germany, on 24 January 1970. The 18th TRS was reassigned prior to the 66th TRW inactivating on 1 April 1970.

67th Tactical Reconnaissance Wing

Prior to its activation as an F-4 user at Mountain Home AFB, Idaho, on 1 January 1966, the 67th Tactical Reconnaissance Wing had flown the B-66 and RF-101 from Yokota AB, Japan, until 8 December 1960. The 10th TRS was assigned on the wing activation date, followed by the 22nd TRS on 20 September 1966 and the 7th TRS on 15 December 1967, all flying the RF-4C. The 11th TRS was assigned between 1 April and 25 October 1966 while working up for assignment in Southeast Asia. In July 1968, the RF-4C of the 7th TRS, 10th TRS and 22nd TRS received 'KT' (green), 'KR' (yellow) and 'KS' (blue) tailcodes, respectively. The 417th TFS arrived from USAFE at about the same time and applied the 'KB' tailcode to its F-4Ds. The 417th TFS reassigned to Holloman AFB, New Mexico, late in 1970; the 10th TRS inactivated on 30 June 1971.

On 15 July 1971, the 67th TRW was reassigned to Bergstrom AFB, Texas, replacing the inactivating 75th TFW. The 22nd TRS inactivated on the transfer date.

The former 75th TRW units, the 4th TRS, 9th TRS and 91st TRS, were maintained from the 75th TRW, with the tailcodes 'BB', 'BC' and 'BA'. The 7th TRS moved with the wing and maintained the 'KT' tailcode until the squadron inactivated during October 1971, together with the 4th TRS. During August and October 1971, the 12th TRS and 45th TRS replaced the 9th TRS and 4th TRS, but maintained 'BC' and 'BB' tailcodes. All the remaining squadrons, the 12th TRS, 45th TRS and 91st TRS, recoded to 'BA' under the common wing tailcode concept in 1972. The 45th TRS inactivated on 31 October 1975. The 62nd TRTS was assigned from the 363rd TRW, at Shaw AFB, South Carolina, on 1 July 1982. With defense cuts, Bergstrom AFB and the 67th TRW were targeted for inactivation.

During the Gulf War the 67th TRW furnished RF-4Cs as part of the 35th TFW (P) at Sheikh Isa AB, Bahrain. The 91st TRS inactivated in September 1991, with the 12th TRS and wing due to follow by 1994.

RF-4Cs of the Bergstrom-based 67th TRW should be retired by 1994.

75th Tactical Reconnaissance Wing

The 75th Tactical Reconnaissance Wing activated at Bergstrom AFB, Texas, on 17 May 1966 to control RF-4C squadrons. The 4th TRS activated in November 1966, the 9th TRS in September 1969, the 14th TRS on 3 April 1967 and the 91st TRS on 1 July 1967.

The 14th TRS inactivated on 6 November 1967, leaving three component units in July 1968, when tailcodes were applied. The 4th TRS, 9th TRS and 91st TRS tailcoded their RF-4Cs 'BB' (light blue), 'BC' (yellow) and 'BA' (red), respectively. The 75th TRW inactivated on 15 July 1971, with the 67th TRW assuming control of and maintaining the former squadrons and markings.

81st Tactical Fighter Wing

The 81st Tactical Fighter Wing flew the F-101A/C Voodoo in the tactical fighter-bomber role between 1958 and 1966. In late 1965, the wing began to replace its former mounts with the F-4C within the 78th TFS, 91st TFS and 92nd TFS. The conversion process was completed in April 1966. The 78th TFS replaced its F-4Cs with F-4Ds, with the early aircraft going to the Spanish air force during 1966. In January 1970, the 81st TFW tailcoded its resident F-4s in the 'W' range at RAF Bentwaters and RAF

Woodbridge. The 78th TFS flew 'WR'-tailcoded F-4Ds while the 91st TFS and 92nd TFS flew F-4Cs tailcoded 'WS' and 'WT'. The 81st TFW adopted the 'WR' code as the common wing tailcode in 1972. In October 1973, the 91st TFS and the 92nd TFS upgraded from the F-4C to the F-4D. The 81st TFW started converting to the A-10A on 24 August 1978, with bulk deliveries starting during January 1979.

The fin code on the F-4C seen here indicates assignment to the 92nd TFS, 81st TFW, at RAF Bentwaters.

and the 36th TFS inactivated on 15 May 1971.

The wing moved to Mountain Home AFB, Idaho, on 15 May 1971, to equip with the F-111F. The 366th TFW replaced the 347th Tactical Fighter Wing at Mountain Home AFB on 30 October 1972. The wing activated in Southeast Asia to continue flying the F-111 until inactivating on 30 June 1975. Three months later, the 347th TFW activated at Moody AFB, Georgia, as an F-4E wing

carrying the 'MY' tailcode. Initially assigned units were the 68th TFS and 70th TFS. The 339th TFS joined on 4 May 1976, inactivating on 1 September 1983, when replaced by the 69th TFS. The 347th TFW had converted to the F-16 Falcon by April 1988.

The 347th TFW's second period of duty as a Phantom operator saw it flying the F-4E version from Moody AFB, Georgia, during 1975-88.

86th Tactical Fighter Wing

The 86th Tactical Fighter Wing operated from Landstuhl AB, Germany (later known as Ramstein-Landstuhl), until 1968, flying various types such as the F-100 Super Sabre and the F-102 Delta Dagger. The 86th TFW was then reassigned to Zweibrücken AB, Germany, in November 1969. The 17th TRS was activated flying the RF-4C on 12 January 1970 and the 81st TFS flying the F-4C on 12 June 1971. The RF-4Cs and F-4Cs carried the 'ZR' and 'ZS' tailcodes, respectively. The wing adopted 'ZR' as their tailcode under the wing common tailcode concept in 1972. The 81st TFS did not recode due to knowledge of a transfer to the 52nd TFW in January 1973 under Battle Creek. This shift

in the units included a base and unit shuffle between the 26th TRW and the 86th TFW. The 17th TRS remained at Zweibrucken AB, Germany, while the 86th TFW absorbed the 526th TFS ('RS', 'Black Knights', red) at Ramstein AB, Germany. This remained the only tailcoded component until the 512th TFS 'Dragons' activated with 'RS'-coded (yellow) F-4Es in early 1977. All 86th Tactical Fighter Wing F-4Es were exchanged for examples of the F-16C/D during 1985 and 1986, drawing to a close the 86th TFW's association with the F-4.

Activated in 1977, the 512th TFS flew F-4Es from Ramstein under the parentage of the 86th TFW until it re-equipped with the F-16 during the course of 1985-86.

354th Tactical Fighter Wing

The 354th Tactical Fighter Wing was activated at Kunsan AB, South Korea, to control deployed units replacing the 4th TFW on 2 July 1968. Personnel were primarily activated from ANG units. The wing's tactical components comprised units rotated from CONUS. Known F-4 deployments include:

| 'ZF' | 560th TFS | 4531st TFW | F-4D | 23 Jun 69 – 17 Dec 69 |

'SA'	334th TFS	4th TFW	F-4D	16 Dec 69 – 31 May 70
'SB'	335th TFS	4th TFW	F-4D	8 Dec 69 – 23 May 70
'ED'	16th TFS	4531st TFW	F-4E	29 May 70 – 14 Jun 70
'ZE'	478th TFS	4531st TFW	F-4E	21 May 70 – 14 Jun 70

The wing's assets were passed on to the 54th TFW on 14 June 1970, when the wing transferred to Myrtle Beach AFB, South Carolina, on 15 June 1970, with A-7D Corsairs.

355th Tactical Fighter Wing

The 355th Tactical Fighter Wing had a very limited association with the F-4. The wing assumed control of its component units from the 4453rd CCTW on 30 September

1971 at Davis-Monthan AFB, Arizona. At that time the 4453rd CCTW/355th TFW was switching from the F-4C to the A-7D with the 58th TFTW at Luke AFB, Arizona. On the change date, one unit, the 4455th CCTS, still had 'DM'-tailcoded F-4Cs, but was inactivated eight days later on 8 October 1971.

343rd Tactical Fighter Group

On 15 November 1977 the 343rd Tactical Fighter Group activated as a 21st TFW component to control the 'FC'-tailcoded F-4Es of the 18th TFS. The control

arrangement lasted until the 18th TFS was directly assigned to the 21st Composite Wing on 1 January 1980. The group was later activated as a wing controlling Alaskan A-10A operations, while the squadron was later re-assigned to the wing as an F-16C/D unit.

347th Tactical Fighter Wing

The 347th Tactical Fighter Wing activated at Yokota AB, Japan, to control operations on 15 January 1971. The wing controlled a diverse variety of types, including the EB-57, RB-57, C-130 and F-105. Three F-105D Thunderchief squadrons, the 35th TFS, 36th TFS and 80th TFS, transitioned to the F-4C

in early 1968. These squadrons carried the tailcodes 'GG', 'GL' (red) and 'GR' (blue/yellow). The 35th TFS and 80th TFS were reassigned to the 3rd TFW on 15 March 1971

Carrying a dummy Shrike anti-radar missile, the EF-4C depicted here is carrying fin code letters used by the 35th TFS at Yokota.

363rd Tactical Reconnaissance Wing
363rd Tactical Fighter Wing

Shaw AFB, South Carolina, had been the hub of reconnaissance activity within Tactical Air Command for many years. The assigned 363rd Tactical Reconnaissance Wing was equipped with RF-101 Voodoos and RB-66 Destroyers when the first RF-4C was first assigned to the 16th TRS in June 1965. The squadron later deployed to Southeast Asia as part of the 460th TRW. The training component, the 4415th CCTS, activated on 1 February 1967 with further RF-4Cs. In July 1968, tailcodes were assigned to all components within the 363rd Tactical Reconnaissance Wing in the 'J' range. The 4415th CCTS applied 'JL' (white) as a tailcode before being redesignated as the 33rd TRTS on 15 October 1969. The former RF-101 Voodoo-equipped 18th TRS received the RF-4C in late 1970, applying the 'JP' (blue) tailcode. The 16th TRS returned to the wing from Southeast Asia on 15 February 1971, with 'JM'-tailcoded (blue/

white) RF-4Cs. The 22nd TRS was assigned with the RF-4C and the B-57E on 15 July 1971, before being replaced by the 62nd TRS on 15 October 1971.

Under the wing common tailcode concept in 1972, the 16th TRS, 18th TRS, 62nd TRS and 33rd TRTS, adopted the 'JO' tailcode. The 18th TRS and 33rd TRTS inactivated on 30 September 1979 and 1 October 1982. The wing redesignated to 363rd TFW on 1 October 1981. The 62nd TRS was reassigned to the 67th TRW on 1 July 1982. The only remaining RF-4C unit, the 16th TRS, recoded to 'SW' as the wing common tailcode changed officially to this on 1 October 1982, although RF-4Cs were noted with the 'JO' tailcodes as late as 2 February 1983. The first four 'SW'-coded F-16As arrived for wing maintenance training on 26 March 1982, in the company of a single 'SW'-tailcoded RF-4C, with bulk deliveries beginning in June 1982. The last RF-4C left Shaw AFB on 16 December 1989.

RF-4Cs flew with the 363rd TRW/TFW for just over 24 years, ending in mid-December 1989 when the last photo-Phantom left Shaw AFB. This is a typical lizard-painted RF-4C.

366th Tactical Fighter Wing

The 366th Tactical Fighter Wing operated the F-100 Super Sabre at Holloman AFB, New Mexico, prior to its conversion to the F-4. In 1965, the F-4C was introduced to the 389th TFS, 391st TFS and 480th TFS. The wing deployed to Phan Rang AB, RSVN, on 20 March 1966 with the 389th TFS. Shortly thereafter, on 10 October 1966, the wing moved to Da Nang AB, RSVN, where it was joined by the 390th and 480th TFS. Initially, the assigned F-4Cs were deployed in the gray/white scheme, and were painted in tactical camouflage after their arrival in Southeast Asia during late 1965 and 1966. The wing, known as the 'Gunslingers', was a major participant in both air-to-ground and air-to-air roles during its tenure in Southeast Asia.

The wing adopted a separate tailcode system rather than the later standard PACAF system. The three F-4C squadrons, the 389th TFS, 390th TFS and 480th TFS, started applying tailcodes to their F-4Cs, in January 1967. The first of two letters ('A', 'B' and 'C') represented the squadron, the second the individual aircraft. Thus, possible tailcodes were:

Following transition from the F-4C to the F-4D, the 366th TFW's 390th TFS adopted the tailcode 'LF'.

389th TFS	'AA' to 'AZ'	F-4C (red/white)
390th TFS	'BA' to 'BZ'	F-4C (blue/white)
480th TFS	'CA' to 'CZ'	F-4C

This system continued throughout the F-4D conversion process during early 1968. Late in 1969, the 390th TFS recoded 'LF', while the 480th TFS and 389th TFS transferred to Phu Cat AB, RSVN, and adopted the 37th TFW tailcodes 'HB' and 'HK', thus ending this unique system. The 4th TFS and 421st TFS arrived from CONUS in April 1969 with F-4Es and coded their mounts 'LA' (yellow/orange) and 'LC' (red). Both left in May 1972, joining the 432nd TRW at Takhli RTAFB. The 35th TFS attached for the period between 3 April and 12 June 1972, flying 'UP'-tailcoded F-4Ds from the 3rd TFW. The remaining F-4 user, the 390th TFS, inactivated on 30 June 1972. The wing was reassigned to Takhli RTAFB on 27 June 1972 without any F-4 components and was then reassigned to Mountain Home AFB, Idaho, on 31 October 1972 as an F-111 operator.

388th Tactical Fighter Wing

The F-105-equipped 388th Tactical Fighter Wing was assigned to Korat RTAFB from McConnell AFB, Kansas, on 8 April 1966 with the 35th TFS, 44th TFS and 469th TFS. The first F-4 assignment to the wing was to the 35th TFS, which attached from the 3rd TFW flying 'UP'-tailcoded F-4Ds between 12 June and 10 October 1972. In addition to the F-105 Thunderchief, the wing operated A-7D Corsairs, EB-66 Destroyers and AC-130 Hercules gunships. 'JJ'-tailcoded (black) F-4Es arrived with a deployment of the 40th TFS in May 1969, with assets assigned immediately to the 34th TFS, known as the 'Rams'. This process was repeated in December 1969 with the 469th TFS bringing 'JV'-tailcoded F-4Es. The F-105 remained only in the Wild Weasel role.

The wing was heavily involved throughout the Southeast Asian conflict, with most missions flown 'Up North' and over Laos. As

the US commitment drew to a close, the number of assigned units were reduced. The 469th TFS inactivated at the end of October 1972 and the 34th TFS downgraded to the F-4D in October 1974. In 1975, the wing was involved in the rescue attempts of the SS *Mayaguez*. The 34th TFS and the 388th TFW were reassigned in title to Hill AFB, Utah, on 23 December 1975 to operate 'HL'-tailcoded F-4Ds. The 388th TFW's three new squadrons, 4th TFS (yellow), 34th TFS (red) and 421st TFS (blue), continued to use the 'HL' tailcode. The wing converted to the F-16A/B Falcon starting on 6 January 1979 as the first operational wing to do so, with the last F-4D leaving before the end of 1979.

This ferocious-looking F-4E bears the code combination of the 34th TFS, which formed part of the 388th TFW at Korat, Thailand.

401st Tactical Fighter Wing

The 401st Tactical Fighter Wing transferred to Torrejon AB, Spain, from England AFB, Louisiana, while flying the F-100 Super Sabre. The assigned squadrons, the 307th TFS, 353rd TFS and 613th TFS, re-equipped with the F-4E in 1970 using 'TJ', 'TK' and 'TL' tailcodes. This wing was one of two exceptions to the USAFE standard practice of using 'R', 'S', 'T', 'U' and 'V' as second letters. On 15 July 1971, the 307th TFS and 353rd TFS were replaced by the

612th TFS and 614 TFS, maintaining the same assets and markings. In mid-1972, the 401st TFW adopted 'TJ' as the wing common tailcode, and in a shuffle of F-4 assets within USAFE the wing downgraded to the less capable F-4C model in late 1973 and then upgraded to the F-4D during 1978/79. The assigned F-4 squadrons changed markings frequently from a solid color to the same color checkered with white; the 307th TFS carried both black/white checks and solid blue fin caps as their squadron markings. The 613th TFS started with a yellow fin cap with black stars, and later changed the stars to lightning flashes, while the 353rd/614th TFS F-4s carried a red fin cap with black diamonds, and later dropped the diamonds. At one stage, all the wing-assigned aircraft carried black and white checkered stripes. The wing again re-equipped, this time with the F-16A/B Falcon, starting on 3 February 1983.

When the time came for the 401st TFW to convert to F-4Cs, it picked up aircraft from the 81st TFW.

405th Fighter Wing

The 405th Fighter Wing replaced the 6200th Air Base Wing, at Clark AB, Philippines, on 9 April 1959. The wing was unusually titled, as it did not contain the word 'Tactical'. The wing operated the F-102 Delta Dagger, F-100 Super Sabre and B-57 Canberra. The first F-4 user within the 405th FW was the 1st Test Squadron, which activated in April 1970 using 'DS' and 'PA' tailcodes on a few F-4Cs and F-4Ds. The unit was involved in testing overhauled F-4s before these were returned to their units. The former F-100-equipped 523rd TFS received the F-4C/D in 1970 and applied the 'PN' tailcode, and this unit deployed to the conflict in Southeast Asia without being reassigned in 1972. In 1972, both squadrons adopted the 'PN' tailcode under the common wing tailcode concept. The 90th TFS activated within the 405th FW in late 1972 and achieved operational status in August 1973 with the F-4D. In 1973, these were exchanged for F-4Es which were

released from their commitment in Thailand. The 523rd TFS inactivated in August 1973. On 16 September 1974, the 3rd TFW replaced the 405th FW, assuming the then-current 'PN' tailcode with the 1st TS and 90th TFS.

In August 1979, the redesignated 405th Tactical Fighter Training Wing activated at Luke AFB, Arizona, and assumed some of the 58th TFTW's assets. This included the 310th TFTS (green), 311th TFTS (yellow) and 426th TFTS (blue), and all flew 'LA'-tailcoded F-4Cs. The 426th TFTS completed converting to the F-15 Eagle by the end of 1980. As the need for advanced pilot training in the F-4C diminished, the assigned assets were reduced. The 310th TFTS and 311th TFTS inactivated on 11 April 1982, ending the 405th TFTW's association with the F-4.

Elements of the 405th Fighter Wing were equipped with the F-4D model during 1972-73.

432nd Tactical Reconnaissance Wing 432nd Tactical Fighter Wing

The 432nd Tactical Reconnaissance Wing activated at Udorn RTAFB on 18 September 1966 to control F-4 operations, primarily against North Vietnam and Laos. The 11th TRS (black), flying the RF-4C, arrived from Mountain Home AFB, Idaho, on 25 October 1966, while the 14th TRS (red) arrived on 28 October 1967. The fighter-bomber role was added to the wing's tasks with the arrival of the 13th TFS (blue), flying F-4Ds, in October 1967. In May 1968, the 13th TFS, 11th TRS and 14th TRS, respectively, tailcoded their F-4s 'OC', 'OO' and 'OZ'. The 555th TFS 'Triple Nickel', was reassigned from the 8th TFW, adopting the 'OY' tailcode on its arrival in May 1968. The 11th TRS inactivated in November 1970. The 432nd TRW hosted numerous deployments to boost USAF airpower during peak periods of need during 1972. The following tactical fighter units were attached:

58th TFS	33rd TFW	'ED'	F-4E	29 Apr 72 – 14 Oct 72
307th TFS	31st TFW	'ZF'	F-4E	29 Jul 72 – 28 Oct 72
308th TFS	31st TFW	'ZF'	F-4E	9 May 72 – 29 Jul 72
414th TFS	57th FWW	'WZ'	F-4D	Jun 72 – Fall 72
523rd TFS	405th FW	'PN'	F-4E	9 Apr 72 – 25 Oct 72

The 414th TFS's deployment is not mentioned in the 432nd TRW's official history, and is believed to be classified.

The 'LA'- and 'LC'-tailcoded F-4Es of the 4th TFS and 421st TFS were assigned in May 1972, even though they were based at Takhli RTAFB, before joining the wing on 31 October 1972. The 4th TFS, 13th TFS, 421st TFS, 555th TFS and 14th TRS all received the 'UD' tailcode starting in August 1973, although many aircraft were not recoded before unit inactivations and transfers. As with many Southeast Asian wings, the application of a common wing tailcode was not accorded a high priority. The 25th TFS replaced the 555th TFS on 14 November 1974, the latter being reassigned to the 405th TTW at Luke AFB, Arizona, to fly the first F-15 Eagles.

The wing designation was changed to the 432nd Tactical Fighter Wing on 15 November 1974, reflecting the reduced importance of the reconnaissance role compared with the wing's tactical fighter function. With the reduction of the USAF commitment in Southeast Asia, units began to inactivate. The 13th TRS and 14th TRS inactivated on 30 June 1975, while the 25th TFS was reassigned to the 3rd TFW. The 4th TFS and 421st TFS were reassigned as F-16 Falcon units within the 366th TFW at Hill AFB, Utah, on 23 December 1975, after having had a non-operational status at Udorn RTAFB. Wing operations ceased on 30 November 1975 and the 432nd TFW inactivated and redesignated as the 432nd Tactical Drone Group on 23 December 1975, activating on 1 July 1976 at Davis-Monthan AFB, Arizona, controlling DC-130- and CH-3E-equipped units.

The red fin stripe and code letter combination on this RF-4C confirm it as being assigned to the 432nd TRW at Udorn in Thailand.

460th Tactical Reconnaissance Wing, 406th Tactical Reconnaissance Group

The 460th Tactical Reconnaissance Wing was assigned to Tan Son Nhut AB, RSVN, on 18 February 1966. Most of the assigned units were previously assigned directly to the 2nd Air Division. The wing controlled various RF-101 Voodoo, RB-57 Canberra and AC-47 gunship units. The RF-4C-equipped 16th TRS arrived on 31 October 1965, while the 12th TRS arrived on 2 September 1966. When tailcodes were applied during 1967 in the 'A' range, the two RF-4C units adopted 'AE' and 'AC' tailcodes.

Another PACAF unit that flew RF-4C Phantoms was the 460th TRW at Tan Son Nhut.

The phase-down of wing operations began in 1970, with completion on 31 August 1971. The 16th TRS was reassigned to the 475th TFW at Misawa AB, Japan, on 15 March 1970, and the 12th TRS was reassigned to the 67th TRW at Bergstrom AFB, Texas, on 31 August 1971. The wing inactivated on 31 August 1971, with the remaining non-F-4-equipped units being assigned to the 483rd TAW.

The 460th TRG consolidated with the 460th TRW on 31 January 1984 and, as such, reactivated on 19 September 1989 at Taegu AB, Korea. The group controlled the 15th TRS, which activated on 1 October 1989, controlling the 'GU'-tailcoded RF-4Cs until it inactivated in late 1990. The aircraft were then mostly turned over to the RoKAF.

474th Tactical Fighter Wing

The 474th Tactical Fighter Wing at Nellis AFB, Nevada, was equipped with the F-111 before converting to the F-4D under Operation Ready Switch during August 1977. This movement involved three wings passing equipment to each other. The 474th TFW's assigned F-111As were transferred to Mountain Home AFB, Idaho, where the assigned F-111Fs were transferred to RAF

Lakenheath's 48th TFW. In turn, the Lakenheath F-4Ds were reassigned to the 474th TFW. The three assigned squadrons, the 428th TFS ('Buccaneers', light blue), 429th TFS ('Black Falcons', yellow) and 430th TFS ('Tigers', red), flew the F-4D until converting to the F-16 Falcon in 1982.

Acquiring F-4Ds from the UK-based 48th TFW in 1977, the 474th TFW at Nellis eventually received F-16s.

475th Tactical Fighter Wing

The 475th Tactical Fighter Wing was assigned to Misawa AB, Japan, on 15 January 1968. The initial assigned units, the 67th TFS, 356th TFS and 391st TFS, with tailcodes 'UP', 'UK' and 'UD', respectively, flew the F-4C and F-4D. The 16th TRS with the RF-4C was then added. The 'LC'-tailcoded F-4Es of the 421st TFS were delayed on their delivery flight to the 366th TFW at Da Nang AB, RSVN, and were attached to the 475th TFW between 23 April and 25 June 1969. The wing's assets were

Misawa's 475th TFW operated a mix of F-4Cs and F-4Ds with three TFSs during the late 1960s.

used to reform the 3rd TFW at Kunsan AB, RoK, on 15 March 1971, with the 475th TFW inactivating.

479th Tactical Fighter Wing

The 479th Tactical Fighter Wing started flying the F-4 in 1965, at George AFB, California, working up on the F-4C and F-4D. The components of the 479th TFW made a complex arrangement of assignments and transfers. Initial deliveries of F-4Cs were made to the 434th TFS and 476th TFS in early 1965. Two further squadrons, the 68th TFS and 431st TFS, were activated on 6 December 1965, and the 4452nd CCTS activated on 16 January 1968.

On the initial assignment of tailcodes, the 68th TFS, 431st TFS, 434th TFS, 476th TFS and 4452nd CCTS were assigned 'GA', 'GB', 'GC', 'GD' and 'GE' tailcodes, respectively. However, the 'GA' tailcode was not taken up by the 68th TFS, as the squadron was reassigned before the application date, so the 4535th CCTS (activated in October 1968) applied it instead. The 476th TFS did not carry the assigned 'GD' tailcode, as the squadron inactivated during September 1968. The now vacated 'GD' tailcode was assumed by the 434th TFS after the 'GC'

Resident at George AFB during 1965-71, the 479th TFW was eventually equipped with F-4Es.

tailcode had been used for a short period. The 4452nd CCTS applied the 'GC' code, while the base flight's UH-1s took up the 'GE' tailcode.

The 4546th TTS was also assigned to the 479th TFW, flying F-4s with a red and white checkered fin cap, together with the 'GB' tailcode. The 4546th TTS is not listed by official sources, but was assigned between 1970 and 1971. On 1 October 1971, the 35th TFW replaced the 479th TFW, at George AFB, and all remaining coded units were reassigned to the 35th TFW, while the 479th TFW inactivated.

3247th Test Squadron

The 3247th Test Squadron operated a large variety of 'AD' tailcoded aircraft, including F-4C, F-4D, F-4E and RF-4C Phantoms, as part of the 3246th Test Wing, at Eglin AFB, Florida. These were commonly non-standard paint schemes, several being noted in overall air defense gray with test markings. The unit started adding the 'AD' tailcode in

late 1982 to a white tail stripe containing a row of red diamonds. The abbreviation for the 3247th TS changed from TS to TESTS on 30 June 1986. The 3247th TESTS recoded to 'ET' starting on 1 October 1989, but by this time only the F-4E remained on charge.

Eglin's 3247th Test Squadron flew examples of all major Phantom sub-types, including this F-4C.

4453rd Combat Crew Training Wing

The 4453rd Combat Training Wing operated as the main F-4C training unit at Davis-Monthan AFB, Arizona, after moving from MacDill AFB, Florida, where both F-4Bs and F-4Cs were operated. It incorporated the 4454th CCTS, 4455th CCTS and 4456th CCTS and used the 'DM' tailcode long before common wing tailcodes became standard. The wing also controlled DC-130 drone operations.

The F-4 operations were reassigned to the 58th TFTW at Luke AFB, Arizona, the switch bringing A-7D Corsairs to Davis-Monthan AFB. The 4453rd CCTW's F-4Cs were used to form the 310th TFTS, 426th TFTS and 550th TFTS at Luke AFB, forming the 355th TFW (with the same personnel), which activated on 1 July 1971. The 4453rd CCTW formally inactivated on 30 September 1971.

Responsibility for the training of Phantom crewmen was entrusted to the 4453rd CCTW until late 1971.

4485th Test Squadron

The 4485th Test Squadron replaced the 4453rd TTS (T), 33rd TFW on 12 April 1971 and was assigned to the Tactical Air Warfare Center at Eglin AFB, Florida. The squadron operated a pair of 'EG'-tailcoded F-4Ds, an RF-4C and a loaned F-4E in late 1977. A yellow fin cap was noted as the squadron's marking on some aircraft. The 'ED' tailcode was used between late 1978 and early 1982, when the 4485th TS recoded to 'OT', and received a new black and white checkered

fin stripe. Several aircraft of various types were operated together with RF-4C and F-4E. Detachment 5, which was based at George AFB, California, equipped with the F-4G, initially carried the 35th TFW code of 'WW' before switching to 'OT' with a gray checkered pattern on the fin cap, representing a toned-down version of the black and white checkers.

Another test outfit located at the Eglin complex was the 4485th TS. This F-4G is from Det. 5 at George.

4525th Fighter Weapons Wing

The 4525th Fighter Weapons Wing activated on 1 September 1966 to control four Nellis AFB assigned combat crew training squadrons, each operating a different type.

The 4538th CCTS operated the F-4C, F-4D and F-4E. During the initial coding of units on 10 July 1968, the 4538th CCTS adopted the 'WD' tailcode, with F-4s carrying a black and yellow checkered tail stripe. The squadron and wing were replaced on 10 October 1969 by the 414th FWS, 57th FWW.

189

4531st Tactical Fighter Wing

During the 31st TFW's tenure in Southeast Asia in 1966, the 4531st Tactical Fighter Wing was assigned as the tenant unit at Homestead AFB, Florida. The wing started converting from the F-4C to the F-4D on 8 February 1967 and to the F-4E on 13 November 1968. The wing's components were the 68th TFS, 436th TFS, 478th TFS and 560th TFS and the tailcodes 'ZG', 'ZD', 'ZE' and 'ZF' were applied in mid-1968. The wing provided several deployments to Southeast Asia to bolster units based there in times of need. F-4 deployments to locations in Southeast Asia included:

Filling the gap left by deployment of the 31st TFW, the 4531st TFW flew from Homestead in 1966-70.

68th TFS	354th TFW	'ZG'	F-4E	20 Jun 69 – 9 Dec 69
560th TFS	354th TFW	'ZF'	F-4D	23 Jun 69 – 17 Dec 69
478th TFS	354th TFW	'ZE'	F-4E	21 May 70 – 15 Jun 70
478th TFS	54th TFW	'ZE'	F-4E	15 Jun 70 – 2 Sep 70

The 31st TFW returned to Homestead AFB from Tuy Hoa AB, RSVN, on 15 October 1970, replacing the 4531st TFW.

6512th Test Squadron

The 6512th Test Squadron operated a fleet of F-4C, F-4D, F-4E and RF-4C Phantoms from Edwards AFB, California, from 1972 as part of the 6510th Test Wing. Other high-numbered test squadrons flew F-4s in limited roles at Edwards AFB. The 6512th TS's F-4s were used in various test roles and by the USAF Test Pilot School. The aircraft were flown in a variety of different paint schemes, such as air defense gray and overall white.

Carrying a non-standard air data probe, this garishly-marked F-4C is one of many Phantoms that have been assigned to the Air Force Flight Test Center at Edwards.

During 1983, the 'ED' tailcode was applied to the assigned aircraft. The markings of a white-outlined blue tail stripe containing white 'X's was standard on 6512th TS operated aircraft.

'Thunderbirds'

The 'Thunderbirds' Aerial Demonstration Team converted to the F-4E in June 1969 at Nellis AFB, Nevada. The initial aircraft were delivered in camouflage with the various display markings applied on top. In time for

Taking over from the Super Sabre in 1969, several early production F-4Es flew with the 'Thunderbirds' team until replaced by the lightweight T-38A Talon in 1974.

the first performance, the aircraft received an overall white scheme with red and blue patterns, after natural metal was found to look 'tatty' because of the Phantom's use of many different types of alloy. Each aircraft carried the position number on the tail. Although looking stock in appearance, the Thunderbird aircraft were modified for the role. The gun and radar packages were removed and 421 lb (190 kg) of lead ballast were inserted for balance. There were also various antenna changes, and smoke-generating equipment was installed. The F-4E remained in this role until being replaced by the T-38A in 1974, because of economic and flight safety considerations.

Other units

As one of the most numerous USAF aircraft types ever produced, the Phantoms saw service with a plethora of second-line units, in ones and twos and sometimes in larger numbers, often fulfilling vital but unsung test duties. While most of the Phantoms at Edwards AFB were operated by the 6512th Test Squadron, the parent 6510th Test Wing did operate a number of other F-4s. Organizations like the Air Defense Weapons Center at Tyndall AFB and the Air Force Special Weapons Center at Kirtland were also Phantom operators. Phantoms also were used as ground instructional airframes for technical training at a number of locations, including Chanute, Lowry and Shepherd. A further front-line operator was the 6252nd TFW, which briefly parented two F-4C units during 1965-1966. The Ogden Air Logistics Center was responsible for fleet maintenance, and generated sufficient of its own trials work to merit permanent assignment of airframes.

Above: Another Eglin test unit was the 3246th Test Wing (ADTC), which tested armament on various aircraft. Shown here are F-4Ds.

Right: A modest number of F-4Cs were used by the Air Defense Weapons Center from Tyndall AFB during the early part of the 1980s.

As the main Phantom rework center, the Ogden ALC at Hill AFB, Utah, was assigned at least one F-4D for use on test projects.

Air Force Reserve

As a result of the implementation of the Total Force Policy, giving a greater role in the national defense to reserve components, the Air Force Reserve again organized fighter squadrons in 1972. Initial equipment consisted of F-105D/Fs and A-37Bs. Phantoms were first assigned to the AFRES in 1978 when the 93rd Tactical Fighter Squadron was activated at Homestead AFB, Florida, with F-4Cs.

Four other AFRES squadrons were equipped with Phantoms during the 1980s, with the last two retaining their F-4Es until 1991 when they converted to Fighting Falcons.

	F-4C	F-4D	F-4E
89th TFS, 906th TFG		82-89	
93rd TFS, 915th TFG	78-81		
93rd TFS, 482nd TFW	81-83	83-90	
457th TFS, 301st TFW		80-87	87-91
465th TFS, 507th TFG		80-88	
704th TFS, 924th TFG		81-89	89-91

89th Tactical Fighter Squadron, 906th Tactical Fighter Group

Activated on 1 July 1982 as the flying unit of the 906th TFG at Wright-Patterson AFB, Ohio, the 89th TFS flew 'DO'-coded (for 'Dayton, Ohio') F-4Ds until its conversion to F-16A/Bs was initiated in October 1989.

A Maverick air-to-surface missile is carried beneath the wing of the 89th TFS F-4D depicted here. This unit flew F-4Ds during 1982-89.

93rd Tactical Fighter Squadron, 915th Tactical Fighter Group

93rd Tactical Fighter Squadron, 482nd Tactical Fighter Wing

The first AFRES squadron to fly Phantoms, the 93rd TFS came into being in February 1978 when the 915th Airborne Early Warning and Control Squadron, the parent group of the 79th AEWCS flying EC-121s from Homestead AFB, Florida, was reorganized into the 915th TFG. The 93rd TFS received its 'FM'-coded (for 'Florida Makos') F-4Cs in October 1978. Less than three years later, on 1 April 1981, the parent group was inactivated and the 93rd TFS began reporting directly to the co-located 482nd TFW. The squadron converted to F-4Ds in the fall of 1983, subsequently converting to F-16A/Bs in November 1989.

Homestead's 93rd TFS was the first AFRES Phantom unit and initially had F-4Cs, which gave way to F-4Ds in the course of 1983.

465th Tactical Fighter Squadron, 507th Tactical Fighter Group

Activated at Tinker AFB, Oklahoma, in May 1972, the 465th TFS was initially equipped with 'UC'-coded F-105D/Fs. Its parent group was reassigned the 301st TFW from the 442nd TAW in July 1972, and during the spring of the following year the squadron began reporting directly to the co-located 301st TFW and changed its tailcode to 'SH' (for 'Sierra Hotel', phonetic for 'Shit Hot').

Still flying F-105D/Fs, the 465th TFS came under the 507th TFG beginning in October 1975. The 465th converted to 'SH'-coded F-4Ds in the fall of 1980 and switched to F-16A/Bs during the spring of 1989.

Pictured during transition from the F-4D to the F-16A, the 465th TFS used the tailcode 'SH'.

457th Tactical Fighter Squadron, 301st Tactical Fighter Wing

Having previously flown C-123Bs as a tactical airlift squadron, the 457th was activated as a tactical fighter squadron on 8 July 1972. Reporting directly to the 301st TFW, with which it was co-located at Carswell AFB, Texas, the 457th TFS was initially equipped with the Thunderchief variant of the F-105D. The enlarged dorsal fairing of its aircraft resulting in the squadron being assigned the tailcode 'TH', for 'Texas Humpbacks'. The 457th TFS converted to Pave Phantom F-4Ds in 1981 and to F-4Es in 1987. The Phantom era ended for the 457th TFS during spring 1991, when it converted to 'TF'-coded (for 'Texas Falcons') F-16A/Bs.

The F-4E version of the Phantom was flown by the 457th TFS between 1987 and 1991, when this unit was assigned F-16s.

704th Tactical Fighter Squadron, 924th Tactical Fighter Group

The 704th Tactical Airlift Squadron was redesignated the 704th TFS on 1 July 1981 after completing its conversion from 'ER'-coded C-130Bs to 'TX'-coded F-4Ds. Based at Bergstrom AFB, Texas, and coming under the 924th TFG, the 704th TFS exchanged its LORAN-equipped Pave Phantom F-4Ds for F-4Es upgraded with DMAS (Digital Modular Avionics System) in 1988. In July 1991, the 704th TFS re-equipped with F-16A/Bs.

The first Phantom version flown by the 704th TFS was the F-4D, represented here by one of the LORAN-configured machines.

Tracor Flight Systems

Tracor Flight Systems, Inc. (TFSI), headquartered at Austin, Texas, but with flying operations at Mojave, California, operates one of the world's largest private flying fleets of high-performance jet aircraft and has been, so far, the only significant civil operator of the F-4 Phantom. TFSI's initial plan was to lease four F-4Cs from the USAF to use on company projects. These aircraft aged to the point that no more extensions were forthcoming from the USAF for completion of their depot maintenance requirements. Therefore, the F-4Cs were returned to the USAF (AMARC, Davis-Monthan AFB, New Mexico) and were replaced by four F-4D Phantoms currently on lease from the USAF. In addition, TFSI has a February 1992 contract from the USAF to convert USAF F-4 aircraft of various models into QF-4 target drones. The drones will be converted from several variants (RF-4C, F-4E, F-4G); the number to be converted is understood to be about a dozen.

On 7 February 1986, TSFI received two F-4Cs (63-7567/N402FS and 64-0741/N403FS) from the Indiana ANG. Both arrived with PDM (periodic depot maintenance) inspections overdue; additionally, 64-0741 was due a 600-hour inspection and had engine problems. Aircraft 63-7567 flew company projects for its short tenure and departed on 11 June 1987 to be placed on museum display at Travis AFB, California. Phantom 64-0741 flew only one hour at Mojave and was down for major maintenance, which was never completed; the Air Force museum took responsibility for the aircraft. Because the USAF museum wanted an F-100A aircraft then on display at Mojave (which it now displays at Edwards AFB, California), a trade was made which left F-4C 64-0741 displayed on a pedestal in front of the tower at Mojave Airport.

In the late 1980s, TFSI acquired two more F-4Cs (63-7889/N420FS and 63-7545/N421FS) which flew various company projects before running out of allowed time for PDM inspection. Both apparently remained at Mojave in non-flying status for some time, but 63-7889 departed on 27 April 1992 and 63-7545 on 19 November 1991, both for AMARC.

Two further F-4Cs (63-7564/N422FS and 63-7606/N423FS) arrived at TFSI Mojave on 11 September 1987 from the Indiana ANG. Phantom 63-7564, which traces its history to Colonel Robin Olds' 8th TFW 'Wolfpack' in Southeast Asia, flew 237 hours in support of programs, including the AQM-37 supersonic target, Patriot missile, McDonnell Douglas AIWS (glide bomb) and Teledyne Ryan parachute programs, before departing on 6 April 1992 for Eglin AFB, Florida, where it was destroyed in an explosion, apparently on the ground, in a planned test of the destruct package selected for use on drones. Aircraft 63-7606 departed Mojave on 14 August 1991 for AMARC.

TFSI now operates four F-4D Phantoms: 64-0965/N424FS arrived on 28 March 1991; 65-0763/N426FS on 19 March 1991; 66-7505/N427FS on 14 August 1991; and 66-7483/N430FS on 24 September 1991.

Few details are available about approximately one dozen USAF drones (so far, designated only QF-4) that are to be converted by TFSI. The company acknowledges being in possession of F-4Gs 69-7261, 69-7301 and 69-7263, which have been denuded of Advanced Wild Weasel capability and will be converted to drones. It is understood that RF-4Cs and F-4Es also will be converted.

One of several Phantoms which have seen service with the Mojave-based Tracor Flight Systems concern, the civil-registered F-4D seen here is part of a four-strong fleet that is assigned to test projects.

Air National Guard

'Phabulous' Phantoms entered ANG service in February 1971 when the 106th TRS, 117th TRW, Alabama ANG, commenced its conversion from Republic RF-84Fs to RF-4Cs. Thereafter, recce Phantoms equipped nine tactical reconnaissance squadrons in the Alabama, California, Kentucky, Minnesota, Missouri, Nebraska and Nevada Guards. In 1992, only four ANG squadrons still flew RF-4Cs, and the last of these aircraft are currently expected to remain in service until 1996.

The first ANG squadron to fly F-4s in the tactical fighter role was the 170th TFS, 183rd TFG, Illinois ANG, which received its first F-4Cs in January 1972. Thereafter, F-4Cs, F-4Ds, F-4Es and F-4Gs were flown by 17 tactical fighter squadrons in the Alabama, Arkansas, California, District of Columbia, Georgia, Hawaii, Idaho, Illinois, Indiana, Kansas, Louisiana, Missouri, New Jersey, Texas and Vermont Guards. The F-4G is the only version remaining in Guard service, and in 1992 Wild Weasels equipped the 124th Fighter Group, Idaho ANG.

Between 1978 and 1990, F-4Cs and F-4Ds were also flown in the air defense role by seven fighter interceptor squadrons and an air defense training squadron (the 114th TFTS) in the California, Michigan, Minnesota, North Dakota, New York, Oregon and Texas Guards. All of these squadrons have now converted to F-16A/B ADFs or F-15A/Bs.

	F-4C	RF-4C	F-4D	F-4E	F-4G
106th TRS, 117th TRW, AL ANG		71-Crt			
110th TFS, 131st TFW, MO ANG	79-85			85-91	
111th FIS, 147th FIG, TX ANG	82-87		87-89		
113th TFS, 181st TFG, IN ANG	79-88			88-91	
114th TFTS, 142nd FIG, OR ANG	84-89				
121st TFS, 113th TFW, DC ANG			81-89		
122nd TFS, 159th TFG, LA ANG	79-86				
123rd FIS, 142nd FIG, OR ANG	81-89				
127th TFS, 184th TFG, KS ANG			79-87		
128th TFS, 116th TFW, GA ANG			83-86		
134th TFS, 158th TFG, VT ANG			82-87		
136th FIS, 107th FIG, NY ANG	82-87		87-90		
141st TFS, 108th TFW, NJ ANG			81-85	85-91	
153rd TRS, 186th TRG, MS ANG		79-91			
160th TRS, 187th TRG, AL ANG		71-83			
160th TFS, 187th TFG, AL ANG			83-88		
163rd TFS, 122nd TFW, IN ANG	79-86			86-91	
165th TRS, 123rd TRW, KY ANG		76-89			
170th TFS, 183rd TFG, IL ANG	72-81		81-89		
171st FIS, 191st FIG, MI ANG	78-87		87-88		
173rd TRS, 155th TRG, NE ANG		72-Crt			
177th TFTS, 184th TFG, KS ANG			84-90		
178th FIS, 119th FIG, ND ANG			77-90		
179th TRS, 148th TRG, MN ANG		76-83			
179th FIS, 148th FIG, MN ANG			83-90		
182nd TFS, 149th TFG, TX ANG	79-86				
184th TFS, 188th TFG, AR ANG	79-88				
189th TRTF, 124th TRG, ID ANG			84-Crt		91-Crt
190th TRS, 124th TRG, ID ANG		75-91			
190th FS, 124th FG, ID ANG					91-Crt
192nd TRS, 152nd TRG, NV ANG		75-Crt			
194th FIS, 144th FIW, CA ANG			84-89		
196th TFS, 163rd TFG, CA ANG	82-87			87-90	
196th TRS, 163rd TRG, CA ANG		90-Crt			
199th TFS, 154th CG, HI ANG	76-87				

160th Tactical Reconnaissance Squadron, 187th Tactical Reconnaissance Group

160th Tactical Fighter Squadron, 187th Tactical Fighter Group

From its base at Dannelly Field ANGS on the edge of the Montgomery MAP, the second Alabama ANG unit has flown Phantoms both in the recce and tactical fighter roles. The 160th TFS, 187th TFG, officially completed its conversion from F-4Ds to Fighting Falcons on 1 October 1988.

Designated a fighter squadron and equipped with P-51Ds when extended federal recognition in October 1947, this Alabama unit was redesignated the 160th TRS in September 1950. In the tactical reconnaissance role, the 160th briefly flew RF-51Ds, but was re-equipped with RF-80As shortly after being activated during the Korean call-up. It deployed to Europe in

January 1952 and flew RF-80As in Germany and France before being returned to state control and temporarily switching back to RF-51Ds. Thereafter, the 160th TRS successively flew RF-80As (from June 1955) and RF-84Fs (from May 1956).

The 160th TRS received RF-4Cs during the first half of 1971 and first deployed abroad in May/June 1980 when it went to Germany to take part in Best Focus. After flying RF-4Cs for 12 years, the unit switched to F-4Ds and became the 160th TFS on 1 July 1983. It deployed to Germany in August 1985 for Coronet Meteor, but a little over two years later it began preparations to convert from F-4Ds to F-16A/Bs.

Alabama Air National Guard

106th Reconnaissance Squadron, 117th Reconnaissance Wing

Based at Sumpter Smith ANGB, Birmingham MAP, the 106th TRS became the first ANG unit to be assigned Phantom IIs when it received RF-4Cs on 25 February 1971. Twenty-one years later, the unit still flies recce Phantoms with no replacements in sight. Organized in the Alabama National Guard in January 1922 as the 135th Squadron, this unit was given its current numerical designation in 1924. Mobilized during World War II, it flew ASW missions in the United States and bombing missions (as the 100th Bombardment Squadron) in the Southwest Pacific theater. Reorganized postwar as the 106th Bombardment Squadron, the unit became the 106th TRS in February 1951. Prior to receiving its RF-4Cs it had been equipped with RB-26Cs and RF-84Fs. With Thunderflashes, it served at Chaumont AB, France, during the Berlin Crisis.

While equipped with RF-4Cs, the 106th TRS first deployed overseas in March 1976 when it sent aircraft, crews and support personnel to Ramstein AB, Germany. It deployed to the UK in June/July 1983 (Coronet Joust) and September 1986 (Coronet Mobile). At the start of Operation Desert Shield in August 1990, three years after becoming the first ANG unit to be equipped with the KS-127A LOROP (Long-Range Oblique Photography) system, the 106th TRS deployed six LOROP-equipped aircraft and personnel to the United Arab Emirates on a voluntary basis. Later relocating to Bahrain, the Alabama volunteers were relieved in the Gulf in December 1990 but left their aircraft (minus one lost with its crew in a crash on 8 October 1990) in the theater to be flown and maintained by Nevada Guardsmen during Operation Desert Storm. On 16 March 1992, the Birmingham units dropped 'Tactical' from their designation to become the 106th RS, 117th RW.

Displaying special markings for the parent 117th Wing, an RF-4C of the 106th Reconnaissance Squadron climbs almost vertically.

Below left: Alabama's 160th used reconnaissance and fighter models of the F-4. This is an RF-4C from the 1980 period.

Above: After using RF-4Cs for more than a decade, the F-4D was acquired by the 160th TFS in 1983 and remained in service until 1988.

Arkansas Air National Guard

184th Tactical Fighter Squadron, 188th Tactical Fighter Group

Operating from facilities at the Fort Smith MAP, the 184th TFS flew F-4Cs for 10 years and deployed to Panama in February 1981 and twice to Turkey (Coronet Crown in September/October 1983 and Coronet Cherokee in September/October 1986).

Organized after the end of the Korean War, the 184th TRS received federal recognition in October 1953 and was initially equipped with Douglas RB-26Cs. Based at Fort Smith, it converted to jets in 1956, and was equipped successively with Lockheed

RF-80As (from June 1956), Republic RF-84Fs (from January 1957) and McDonnell RF-101Cs (from December 1970). Reorganized as a fighter unit in 1972, the 184th converted to North American F-100Ds during the summer of that year, and it was redesignated 184th TFS in June 1972. F-4Cs replaced F-100Ds during the summer of

The F-4C version was flown by the Arkansas ANG's 184th TFS for close to a decade, starting in 1979.

1979 and these Phantoms were retained until April 1989, when the 184th TFS completed its conversion to F-16A/Bs.

Fin markings on these rather drab F-4Cs (above) identify them as being assigned to the 196th TFS which later flew RF-4Cs (right).

196th RS, 163rd RG, in March 1992, is expected to take on the air refueling mission in 1994 and to trade its RF-4Cs for KC-135Rs.

California Air National Guard

194th Fighter Interceptor Squadron, 144th Fighter Interceptor Wing

The 194th FIS was equipped with F-4Ds for six years starting in late 1983. Based at the Fresno ANGS, Fresno Air Terminal, the unit also maintained an alert detachment at George AFB, California. Between April 1986 and April 1987, the 194th FIS and its parent, 144th FIW, provided F-4Ds and personnel to Operation Creek Klaxon, the ANG's assumption of air defense commitment at Ramstein AB, Germany, while the 86th TFW, USAFE, was converting to Fighting Falcons.

The 194th Fighter Squadron (SE) was federally recognized in March 1949 and was equipped with F-51Ds and F-51Hs until the summer of 1953, when it converted to F-86As. The switch to jets led to the relocation of the 194th from Hayward to Fresno in November 1954. Since then, the 194th FIS has remained in central California and has not been called to active duty. It has successively converted to F-86Ls (April 1958), to F-102A/TF-102As (July 1964), to F-106A/Bs (summer 1963), to F-4Ds (winter 1983) and to F-16A/B ADFs (summer 1989). Still retaining air defense as its primary role, the Fresno units were redesignated 194th FS, 144th FW, on 16 March 1992.

Above: Replacing the F-106 in late 1983, the F-4D was used on air defense tasks by the 194th FIS from Fresno until it gave way to the F-16 in the summer of 1989.

Below: A mixture of tactical camouflage and gray-painted aircraft formed the initial equipment of the 194th FIS when it acquired the F-4D; both schemes are depicted here.

196th Tactical Fighter Squadron, 163rd Tactical Fighter Group

196th Reconnaissance Squadron, 163rd Reconnaissance Group

After flying P-51Ds since its organization in November 1946, the 196th FS became the first Guard unit to convert to jets when it received F-80Cs directly from the Lockheed assembly line in June 1948. Called to active duty in October 1950, the 196th Fighter-Bomber Squadron converted to F-84Es prior to deployment to Japan and subsequent combat operations in Korea. Following its return to state control in July 1952, the squadron was re-equipped with F-51Hs and redesignated 196th Fighter Interceptor Squadron in January 1953. The 196th FIS converted to F-86As in March 1954, to F-86Ls in February 1961 and to F-102A/TF-102As in March 1971.

A victim of increased environmental awareness and post-Vietnam War anti-military attitude, the California ANG unit based at the Ontario IAP lost its jets when it converted from Convair F-102A/TF-102As to Cessna O-2As in 1983. After flying the Cessna push-pull light aircraft for nearly six years, the squadron was redesignated 196th TFS from 196th TASS on 1 October 1982 and moved from Ontario to March AFB to convert to F-4Cs. While flying F-4Cs, the squadron deployed to Spain in May/June 1986 for Coronet Laguna. The unit converted to F-4Es during the spring of 1987 and, switching to the recce role and converting to RF-4Cs, it was redesignated 196th TRS, 163rd TRG from 196th TFS, 163rd TFG, on 1 July 1990. The unit, which was redesignated

District of Columbia Air National Guard

121st Tactical Fighter Squadron, 113th Tactical Fighter Wing

Based at Andrews AFB, the 121st TFS, 113th TFW flew its first F-4D sorties in July 1981, received its first F-16As in September 1989, and completed its conversion from Phantoms to Fighting Falcons during the fall of 1990. While equipped with F-4Ds, the 121st TFS deployed to the UK in June 1983 (Coronet Shield) and to Iceland in April/May 1986 (Coronet Kiowa). In 1984, it became the first Guard unit to be trained with the Pave Spike system and LGBs.

Unlike other Guard units which have a dual state/federal status, with the governors of their state as their commanders-in-chief in peacetime, the District of Columbia ANG comes directly under the Commanding General of the District of Columbia. When placed on federal active duty, all Guard units have the President of the United States as their commander-in-chief. The flying unit of the District of Columbia was organized on 10 April 1941 as the 121st Observation Squadron and, redesignated 121st Liaison Squadron, took part in combat operations in Algeria, Italy and France during World War II. Since the end of the war, the squadron has successively flown F-47Ds, F-84Cs, F-94Bs (on active duty during the Korean War), F-51Hs, F-86Es, F-86Hs, F-100Cs (with which it was activated during both the 1961-62 Berlin Crisis and the 1968-69 *Pueblo* Crisis), F-105D/Fs, F-4Ds and F-16A/Bs.

The 121st TFS tailcode 'DC' was first applied to the F-4D, which was operated during 1981-90.

Georgia Air National Guard

128th Tactical Fighter Squadron, 116th Tactical Fighter Wing

Although it flew Phantoms for only 4½ years, the 128th TFS did manage to deploy overseas in August 1985, when its F-4Ds went to Germany (Coronet Meteor). Remaining based at Dobbins AFB and continuing to operate in the tactical fighter role, the Georgia ANG unit officially completed its conversion to F-15A/Bs on 31 March 1987.

Organized in May 1941 as the 128th Observation Squadron, the first flying unit in the Georgia Guard was almost immediately placed on active duty. It went on to fly ASW missions over the Gulf of Mexico and bombing missions from Italy as the 840th Bombardment Squadron equipped with B-17Gs. Postwar, it was reorganized as a fighter squadron and flew P-47Ns, F-51Hs, F-84Ds, F-84Fs and F-86Ls, before converting to C-97Fs and becoming the 128th Air Transport Squadron. As a transport unit, it flew C-124Cs between 1966 and 1973, but in April of that year it once again became a fighter squadron and was re-equipped with F-100Ds. The Super Sabres were replaced by F-105Gs in 1979. The 128th TFS began its conversion from Wild Weasel F-105Gs to F-4Ds in January 1983 and completed the process in less than nine months.

A yellow fin stripe adds a splash of color to this otherwise drab F-4D of Georgia's 128th TFS.

Hawaii Air National Guard

199th Tactical Fighter Squadron, 154th Composite Group

Based at Hickam AFB, the Hawaii ANG has had sole responsibility for the air defense of the 50th State since 1957. Organized in September 1946 as the 199th FS, its flying unit first received P-47Ns in July 1947, was redesignated the 199th FIS in 1952 and converted to F-86Es in 1954. To provide all-weather air defense, the 199th FIS received F-86Ls in 1958 and F-102As in 1961. The 'Deuces' were replaced by F-4Cs in 1976, and in June of that year the squadron became the 199th TFS, even though air defense was still its primary mission.

While flying F-4Cs, the 199th TFS made three overseas deployments, going to Japan in June 1980 (Cope North) and twice to the Philippines for Cope Thunder exercises (April/May 1981 and May 1985). The 199th TFS began exchanging its F-4Cs for F-15A/Bs in March 1987 and completed the conversion process in January 1988.

F-4Cs of the 199th TFS bore sole responsibility for the air defense of Hawaii from 1976 to 1987.

Idaho Air National Guard

Reconnaissance Weapons School, 189th Tactical Reconnaissance Training Flight, 190th Tactical Reconnaissance Squadron, 124th Tactical Reconnaissance Group

190th Fighter Squadron, 124th Fighter Group

Based at Gowen Field, Boise, the flying units of the Idaho ANG flew RF-4Cs beginning in the fall of 1975, when the 190th FIS converted from Convair F-102A/TF-102As and was redesignated 190th TRS. Sharing RF-4Cs with the 190th TRS, the Reconnaissance Weapons School was organized in March 1983 to teach advanced recce tactics to USAF and ANG crews, and the 189th TRTF was activated on 1 September 1984 to take over RF-4C training responsibility from the 190th TRS. While flying RF-4Cs, the tactical unit first deployed overseas in September/October 1979, when it went to Norway (Coronet Shetland). It won Photo Derby competitions in October 1980 and October 1982, and won three consecutive Photo Finish competitions in 1983-85. The 190th converted from RF-4Cs to F-4Gs during the summer of 1991 and

was redesignated the 190th Fighter Squadron on 16 March 1992. The Reconnaissance Weapons School was inactivated on 31 December 1991 and the training unit, which now trains both RF-4C and F-4G crews, was redesignated the 189th Training Flight on 16 March 1992.

Equipped with P-51Ds, the Idaho unit was federally recognized as the 190th Fighter Squadron (SE) in October 1946, served on active duty in the United States in 1951-52 and was reorganized as the 190th Fighter Interceptor Squadron in January 1953. It converted to F-86As in November 1953, to F-94Bs in December 1954, to F-89Bs in July 1956, to F-86Ls in April 1959 and to F-102As in April 1964. In October 1975, it became the 190th Tactical Reconnaissance Squadron and exchanged its Delta Daggers for RF-4Cs.

Above: Pictured at the moment of touchdown, this RF-4C is typical of those flown by the Idaho ANG's reconnaissance unit at Boise.

Right: In the summer of 1991, the Boise-based outfit acquired Wild Weasel F-4Gs for use in defense suppression taskings.

Illinois Air National Guard

170th Tactical Fighter Squadron, 183rd Tactical Fighter Group

When in November 1971 its Republic F-84Fs were grounded due to structural corrosion, the 170th TFS, 183rd TFG at the Capital airport in Springfield, was the last ANG unit equipped with the venerable Thunderstreak. Two months later it received F-4Cs and become the first Guard unit to fly Phantoms in the tactical fighter role. Between October 1973 and July 1975, the 170th TFS was also assigned a pair of RF-4Cs. F-4Ds replaced F-4Cs in early 1981, and in June 1982 the unit first deployed overseas with F-4Ds when it went to the UK for Coronet Bravo. Conversion from Phantoms to F-16A/Bs was

officially completed on 1 October 1989.

Organized in Springfield in September 1948, the 'Fly 'N Illini' had successively flown F-51Ds (including on active duty in Texas and California during the Korean War), F-86Es (from 1953) and F-84Fs (from 1955 and on active duty at their home base during the Berlin Crisis in 1961-62) prior to their conversion to Phantoms.

The 170th TFS was the first Guard unit to receive tactical fighter Phantoms, using F-4Cs and F-4Ds.

Indiana Air National Guard

113th Tactical Fighter Squadron, 181st Tactical Fighter Group

The 113th TFS at the Hulman regional airport in Terre Haute and the other flying squadron of the Indiana ANG, the 163rd TFS at Fort Wayne, share some unique historical features. Between 1962 and 1964 the two units, although designated tactical fighter squadrons, were equipped with RF-84F reconnaissance aircraft. In 1979, when they became the last Guard squadrons to relinquish F-100Ds for Phantoms, they received aircraft which had been modified as EF-4Cs for the Wild Weasel mission; however, neither the 113th nor the 163rd was given this specialized mission and both flew their Phantoms in the conventional strike role. Finally, having exchanged their F-4Cs for F-4Es in 1988, the two Indiana squadrons became the last ANG units to fly

F-4 fighters. They began their conversion to F-16C/Ds in the fall of 1991 and dropped 'Tactical' from their names in March 1992.

The first aviation unit in the Indiana Guard was organized as the 137th Squadron in 1921 and renumbered 113th Observation Squadron in 1923. During the war, it served on active duty in the US until it disbanded in November 1943. Postwar, it flew P-51Ds, F-51Hs, F-80Cs, F-86As, F-84Fs, RF-84Fs and F-100D/Fs prior to converting to Phantoms. With F-4C/EF-4Cs, the 113th TFS first deployed overseas when it went to Italy in May/June 1978 for Coronet Quail.

The 'HF' tailcode on this F-4E of the Indiana ANG signifies its home base at Hulman Field.

163rd Tactical Fighter Squadron, 122nd Tactical Fighter Wing

Extended federal recognition in October 1947, the 163rd Fighter Squadron was initially equipped with P-51Ds and remained at its home base while serving on active duty during the Korean War. It converted to F-80Cs in 1954, and went on to fly F-86As (from March 1956) and F-84Fs (from January 1958 and on active duty at Chambley AB, France, in 1961-62). Since receiving RF-84Fs after its return to state control in August 1962, the 163rd TFS has had a history paralleling that of the 113th TFS. Like the other Indiana flying squadron, it was equipped with F-84Fs (from May 1964) and F-100D/Fs (from June 1971), and it received Wild Weasel-modified EF-4Cs in 1979 but

did not fly this specialized defense suppression mission. In 1988, the 163rd TFS received F-4Es. Based at the Fort Wayne ANGS, Fort Wayne MAP, the unit began its conversion from F-4Es to F-16C/Ds in the fall of 1991 and was redesignated 163rd FS, 122nd FW, on 16 March 1992.

Indiana's other Phantom unit was also equipped with the F-4E.

Kansas Air National Guard

127th Tactical Fighter Squadron and 177th Tactical Fighter Training Squadron, 184th Tactical Fighter Group

Based at McConnell AFB, Kansas, two units of the 184th TFG have flown F-4Ds. The 127th TFS converted from F-105D/Fs during the winter of 1979 and, until the activation of the 177th TFTS on 1 February 1984, functioned both as an operational squadron and as the ANG F-4D Replacement Training Unit. As an operational squadron, the 127th TFS first took its F-4Ds overseas when it deployed to Southwest Asia in March 1984 for Sentry Tornado. The 127th TFS and the 177th TFTS retained their F-4Ds until converting to F-16A/Bs in 1990. Shared with the 161st TFTS, which was activated on 1 July 1987 as a Fighting Falcon RTU (Replacement Training Unit), the F-16A/Bs were replaced by F-16C/Ds in the spring of 1991.

Activated in the Kansas National Guard in August 1941, the 127th Observation Squadron was introduced into federal service two months later. In 1944-45, the 127th Liaison Squadron flew Stinson L-5s and Noorduyn C-64s as part of the 2nd Air Commando Group in India and Burma. The 127th FS received federal recognition in September 1946 and flew F-51Ds until converting to F-84Cs in 1950. In May 1952, 19 months after being activated once again,

it moved to Chaumont AB, France. After returning to state control, the 127th flew F-51Ds until June 1954, became a fighter interceptor squadron while flying F-80Cs and converted to F-86Ls in January 1958. As the 127th TFS, it flew F-100Cs from September 1961 and went on active duty in 1968-69 at Kunsan AB, Korea. In 1971, the squadron converted to F-105D/Fs and, as the 127th TFTS, became an RTU. Retaining that role and adding an operational mission, it converted to F-4Ds in 1979 and was redesignated 127th TFS on 8 October 1979.

Operating as an ANG training base, McConnell was home to a large F-4D fleet in the Phantom era.

Kentucky Air National Guard

165th Tactical Reconnaissance Squadron, 123rd Tactical Reconnaissance Wing

Receiving its first RF-4C at Standiford Field, Louisville, in February 1976, when it converted from McDonnell RF-101Cs, the 165th TRS, 123rd TRW flew recce Phantoms until 1989. The unit first deployed to Europe in February/March 1978 when it took its RF-4Cs to Norway for Coronet Snipe. On 8 January 1989, the unit was redesignated 165th TAS, 123rd TAW and was re-equipped with Lockheed C-130Bs. Redesignated 165th AS, 123rd AW, in March 1992, the Kentucky ANG unit is now equipped with new C-130Hs, which include the 2,000th Hercules built by Lockheed.

The 165th Fighter Squadron (SE) had originally been organized in February 1947 and flew North American F-51Ds until after being called to active duty. In November 1951, while still on active duty, the unit moved to England, where it flew F-84Es from RAF Manston. Returned to state control in July 1952, the 165th Fighter-Bomber Squadron was equipped first with F-51Hs and then again with F-51Ds. Becoming a fighter interceptor squadron in

July 1955, the 165th had to fly T-28A trainers for a few months before its facilities were ready for F-86As. The switch to tactical reconnaissance was made in January 1958, and the 165th TRS flew RB-57Bs, RF-84Fs, RF-101G/Hs (including active duty in 1968-69 when it operated from Richards-Gebaur AFB, Missouri, and from Itazuke AB, Japan) and RF-101Cs before converting to RF-4Cs in 1976.

Kentucky's 165th flew RF-4C Phantoms from 1976 until 1989.

Louisiana Air National Guard

122nd Tactical Fighter Squadron, 159th Tactical Fighter Group

Based at NAS New Orleans, the Louisiana ANG unit flew F-4Cs (including one conspicuously marked with its long-established but controversial 'Coonass Militia' nickname) between the spring of 1979 and the summer of 1985. The 122nd TFS took its F-4Cs to Iceland for Coronet Rodeo in August/September 1982, and it converted to McDonnell Douglas F-15A/Bs in 1985.

Organized in March 1941 as the 122nd Observation Squadron, the Louisiana Guard unit was called to active duty seven months later. It flew ASW sorties in the United States and North Africa before becoming an RTU for American and French pilots in Algeria. Redesignated the 885th Bombardment Squadron in May 1994 and

equipped with B-17s and B-24s as a special unit of the Fifteenth Air Force, the squadron flew partisan support missions in the Balkans. Postwar, the Louisiana unit first flew A-26s as the 122nd Bombardment Squadron. As the 122nd FIS, it briefly flew F-80Cs in 1957, prior to converting to F-86Ls later in that year and to F-102A/TF-102As in 1960. Becoming a tactical fighter unit in July 1970, the 122nd flew F-100D/Fs for nine years and then converted to F-4Cs in 1979.

F-4Cs served in the tactical role with the Louisiana Guard from New Orleans between 1979 and 1985.

Michigan Air National Guard

171st Fighter Interceptor Squadron, 191st Fighter Interceptor Group

The first ANG air defense unit to be assigned Phantoms, the 171st FIS converted from F-106A/Bs to F-4Cs at Selfridge ANGB in the spring of 1978. Maintaining an alert detachment at Seymour Johnson AFB, North Carolina, the squadron traded its F-4Cs for F-4Ds during the summer of 1986. It officially completed its conversion to Fighting Falcons, with its F-16A/Bs subsequently being upgraded to the ADF configuration, on 1 July 1990.

The 107th Fighter Squadron (SE) was extended federal recognition in April 1948, and flew F-51Ds and F-84Bs in the tactical

role before converting to F-51Hs and becoming the 171st FIS in October 1952. As an interceptor unit, the 171st then flew F-86Es and F-89Cs, but in February 1958 it was redesignated the 171st TRS and went on to fly RF-84Fs and RF-101Cs. Once again designated 171st FIS in January 1971, the squadron flew F-106A/Bs until 1978 when it converted to F-4Cs.

The air defense-dedicated F-4Cs of the Michigan ANG were among the most attractively marked Phantoms.

Minnesota Air National Guard

179th Tactical Reconnaissance Squadron, 148th Tactical Reconnaissance Group

179th Fighter Interceptor Squadron, 148th Fighter Interceptor Group

Currently flying F-16A/B ADFs from the Duluth IAP and, on alert, from Tyndall AFB, Florida, the northern Minnesota unit first received Phantoms during the winter of 1975 when the 179th FIS converted from McDonnell F-101B/Fs to RF-4Cs, and it was redesignated the 179th TRS on 10 January 1976. With its RF-4Cs, the 179th TRS first deployed to Germany in August 1979 (Coronet Bridle). In the fall of 1983, the unit converted to F-4Ds and from 15 November 1983 was again designated the 179th FIS. In 1986-87, it contributed F-4Ds, crews and maintenance personnel to Operation Creek Klaxon and Guardsmen assumed an air defense commitment at Ramstein AFB, Germany. During the winter of 1990, the 179th FIS completed its conversion to F-16A/B ADFs.

The 179th Fighter Squadron (SE) was extended federal recognition in September 1948 and flew F-51Ds until converting to F-94A/Bs in July 1954. Rocket-armed F-94Cs replaced gun-armed F-94A/Bs in April 1957, and were in turn supplanted by missile-carrying F-89Js in July 1959. Supersonic F-102A/TF-102As were received in November 1966 and were replaced by F-101B/Fs in April 1971. After serving as an interceptor squadron since its return from active duty in November 1952, the 179th became a tactical reconnaissance squadron

in January 1976 when it was re-equipped with RF-4Cs.

During 1976-83, the 179th TRS flew RF-4Cs from its base at Duluth on tactical reconnaissance duties.

Re-equipment with the F-4D Phantom coincided with a return to the air defense task in late 1983.

Mississippi Air National Guard

153rd Tactical Reconnaissance Squadron, 186th Tactical Reconnaissance Group

Based at Key Field in Meridian, the 153rd TRS flew RF-4Cs for 13 years starting in the fall of 1978. During that period, it made more varied overseas deployments than other ANG tactical units. It went to the UK in September/October 1980 (Coronet Cyro), to Southwest Asia in March 1984 (Sentry Tornado) and to Italy in July/August 1986 (Coronet Lake). Conversion from RF-4Cs to Boeing KC-135Rs was initiated in 1991, and

the unit was redesignated the 153rd Air Refueling Squadron, 186th Air Refueling Group, on 1 April 1992.

The 153rd TRS traces its origins to the 153rd Observation Squadron, which was organized in September 1939 and which served on active duty in Europe during World War II. As the 153rd Liaison Squadron, the unit distinguished itself during the Battle of the Bulge in the winter of 1944.

As the 153rd Fighter Squadron, it flew P-47Ns until reorganized as the 153rd TRS, and converted to RF-51Ds in December 1952. As the 153rd TRS, the squadron was then successively equipped with RF-80As (from June 1955), RF-84Fs (from October 1956, including 11 months on active duty at

Mississippi's 153rd TRS is still equipped with RF-4Cs, having converted from RF-101Cs in 1978.

home during the Berlin Crisis call-up in 1961-62), RF-101Cs (from November 1970) and RF-4Cs (since September 1978).

Missouri Air National Guard

110th Tactical Fighter Squadron, 131st Tactical Fighter Wing

Converting to McDonnell Douglas F-15A/Bs at the Lambert-St Louis ANGS in May 1991, the 110th TFS, 131st TFW had flown Phantoms since the beginning of 1979, when it traded North American F-100D/Fs for F-4Cs. It first deployed its F-4Cs to the UK in June/July 1982 for Coronet Cactus. Gun-armed F-4Es replaced F-4Cs in 1985.

With Charles Lindbergh among its early members, the 110th Observation Squadron was typical of the pre-World War II aviation units of the Guard. During the war, it served in the fighter reconnaissance role in the Southwest Pacific. Reorganized in 1946 as a fighter squadron with P-51Ds, the 110th became a bombardment squadron with B-26B/Cs in 1952, and returned to the fighter role in 1957. Since then, it has flown F-80Cs,

F-84Fs, F-100Cs (which it flew from Toul-Rosières AB, France, during the Berlin Crisis in 1961-62) and F-100D/Fs, before receiving F-4Cs in 1979.

The Phantom's home was also home to Missouri's 110th TFS, which had shark-mouthed F-4Es from 1985.

Nebraska Air National Guard

173rd Reconnaissance Squadron, 155th Reconnaissance Group

In keeping with current regulations, the Nebraska flying unit dropped 'Tactical' from its designation and, effective as of 16 March 1992, became the 173rd RS instead of the 173rd TRS. Based at Lincoln ANGS, the squadron and its parent group have been assigned RF-4Cs since converting from Republic RF-84Fs in February 1972. It first deployed to Turkey in May 1980 for Coronet Cannon. Plans for conversion to Boeing KC-135Rs and reorganization as an air refueling unit in 1994-95 are still to be confirmed.

The Nebraska unit was organized in July 1946 as the 173rd Fighter Squadron (SE) and was equipped with P-51Ds. In 1948, it became one of the first Guard units to fly jets when it received F-80Cs. However, these jets were turned over to the USAF during the Korean War, when the 173rd went on active duty and flew F-51Ds in the US. After return to state control, the unit briefly operated as a fighter-bomber

squadron with F-51Ds before converting again to F-80Cs and becoming the 173rd FIS. The Shooting Stars were replaced by F-86Ds in January 1957 and by F-86Ls in late 1959. Becoming the 173rd TRS in May 1964, the squadron flew RF-84Fs until February 1972 when it received RF-4Cs.

Nebraska's 173rd RS celebrated two decades of RF-4C operations during the early part of 1992.

Nevada Air National Guard

192nd Reconnaissance Squadron, 152nd Reconnaissance Group

In 1991, after returning from flying combat operations from Sheikh Isa AB, Bahrain, during Operation Desert Storm, the Nevada ANG flying unit began preparations for its conversion from RF-4Cs to F-4Gs. Although the unit did receive a Wild Weasel and painted it in its distinctive 'High Rollers' markings, plans for this conversion were canceled and the 192nd RS (a designation that became effective on 16 March 1992) continues to fly RF-4Cs from May ANGS at the Reno-Cannon IAP. Phantoms were first received during the summer of 1975 when the 192nd TRS converted from its unique McDonnell RF-101Bs. Since then, the squadron has made good use of its RF-4Cs

as it won Reconnaissance Air Meet competitions in November 1986 and November 1990. Less than a month after this second win, the 192nd TRS was called to active duty and flew 412 sorties during Operation Desert Shield/Desert Storm before being released from active duty on 20 April 1991.

Activated as the 192nd Fighter Squadron (SE) in April 1948, the Nevada unit was equipped with F-51Ds, served on active duty in the US in 1951-52, and returned to state control in December 1952. By then redesignated the 192nd Fighter-Bomber Squadron, the unit moved from Stead ANGB to the Reno Municipal Airport in January

1953. Two years later, the unit was redesignated the 192nd FIS and began jet training, but it did not complete its conversion from F-51Ds to F-86As until November 1955. The day-fighter F-86As were replaced by all-weather F-86Ls in

August 1958. Re-equipped with RB-57Bs, the squadron was redesignated the 192nd TRS in April 1961, converted to RF-101Hs in 1965, served on active duty in the US and Japan during the 1968-69 *Pueblo* Crisis call-up, and received RF-101Bs in 1971.

One of several ANG units which saw combat action during Desert Storm, the 192nd RS was due to convert to the F-4G in 1992 but continues to utilize the RF-4C, which it has flown from Reno since 1975.

New Jersey Air National Guard

141st Tactical Fighter Squadron, 108th Tactical Fighter Wing

After flying Phantoms from McGuire AFB since the spring of 1981, this New Jersey unit converted to KC-135Es in the fall of 1991 and was redesignated the 141st ARefS, 108th ARefW, on 19 October 1991. While equipped with F-4Ds, the 141st TFS first deployed to Norway in September 1982 (Coronet Rawhide) and, as a fighter unit, the 141st made its last deployment in May 1991 when it sent F-4Es to Ecuador for Blue Horizon.

Federally recognized in May 1949, the 141st Fighter Squadron (SE) flew F-47Ds for 3½ years, including 21 months on active duty in the United States during the Korean call-up. Back under state control, the 141st Fighter-Bomber Squadron was re-equipped with F-51Hs in December 1952 and with

F-86As in February 1954. Redesignated 141st FIS in July 1955, the squadron received F-86Es in February 1956 and F-84Fs in the spring of 1958. With Thunderstreaks, the unit was redesignated 141st TFS in November 1958, was called to active duty in October 1961 and was based at Chaumont AB, France, until October 1962. Back under state control, the 141st was successively equipped with F-86Hs (October 1962), F-105Bs (May 1964), F-4Ds (spring 1981) and F-4Es (July 1985).

Various color schemes are evident on this trio of F-4Es assigned to the 141st TFS at McGuire.

New York Air National Guard

136th Fighter Interceptor Squadron, 107th Fighter Interceptor Group

The 136th Fighter Squadron (SE) was granted federal recognition at Niagara Falls in December 1948 and, still equipped with its original F-51Ds, flew on active duty from its home base during the Korean War. As the 136th FIS, it was re-equipped with F-51Hs in late 1952 and with F-94Bs in January 1954. Redesignated 136th TFS in October 1957, the unit flew F-100Cs for 14 years, including while on active duty at its home base in 1961-62 and at Tuy Hoa AB, South Vietnam, in 1968-69. In June 1971, the 136th once again became a fighter interceptor unit. In that role, it has successively flown F-101B/Fs, F-4Cs (from spring 1982) and F-4Ds (from fall 1986). While equipped with Phantoms, the 136th FIS maintained an alert detachment at

Charleston AFB. In 1990, the 136th FIS began its conversion to Fighting Falcons with its initially assigned F-16A/Bs soon brought up to the ADF configuration.

F-4Cs and F-4Ds were flown by New York's 136th FIS on air defense tasks between 1982 and 1990.

North Dakota Air National Guard

178th Fighter Interceptor Squadron, 119th Fighter Interceptor Group

Based at the Hector Field ANGS in Fargo, the 'Happy Hooligans' (a nickname acquired as the result of a particularly boisterous celebration during summer encampment) flew F-4Ds between March 1977 and April 1990, prior to converting to F-16A ADFs. With its F-4Ds, the 178th FIS deployed twice overseas, flying 'Bear' patrols in Iceland in 1984 and becoming the first core unit to provide personnel and equipment for Operation Creek Klaxon at Ramstein AB,

Germany, in 1986-87.

Receiving federal recognition in January 1947, the 178th Fighter Squadron (SE) flew North American P-51Ds/F-51Ds until June 1954 (including active duty in Georgia and California during the Korean War), Lockheed F-94A/Bs and then F-94Cs until June 1958, Northrop F-89Ds and then F-89Js until July 1966, Convair F-102A/TF-102As until November 1969 and McDonnell F-101Bs until converting to Phantoms in March 1977.

*AIM-9 Sidewinder missiles form the armament of this **F-4D** of the **North Dakota** ANG's 178th FIS. It is seen at **Tyndall** AFB, during a **William Tell** air defense fighter meet in the early 1980s.*

Oregon Air National Guard

114th Tactical Fighter Training Squadron, 142nd Fighter Interceptor Group

Based at Kingsley Field in Klamath Falls, this squadron was organized on 1 February 1984 to serve as an RTU for F-4 crews assigned to fighter interceptor squadrons of the Air National Guard. This numerical designation had previously been used by a unit of the New York ANG, which had been organized in June 1947 as the 114th Bombardment Squadron (Light) to fly Douglas B-26B/C Invaders from Floyd Bennett Field. The New York ANG squadron was redesignated 114th FIS in June 1957 and was flying Lockheed F-94B Starfires when it was inactivated in September 1958. As a unit of the Oregon ANG, the 114th TFTS flew F-4Cs from its activation in 1984 until its conversion to F-16 ADFs during spring 1989.

*Although designated as a **TFTS**, the 114th was actually tasked with the training of **ANG** interceptor crews and flew **F-4Cs** on this duty from 1984 until 1989.*

123rd Fighter Interceptor Squadron, 142nd Fighter Interceptor Group

Based at the Portland ANGS, the 123rd FIS flew F-4Cs between the fall of 1982 and the fall of 1989. Its forebear, the 123rd Observation Squadron, was organized in April 1941. Ordered to active duty five months later, the Oregon unit first flew ASW missions and served as a training unit in the United States, before being redesignated the 35th Photographic Reconnaissance Squadron in August 1943. Equipped with Lockheed F-5s, the 35th PRS was sent to the CBI theater in September 1944. Federally recognized in August 1946, the 123rd Fighter Squadron (SE) was initially

equipped with P-51Ds and then flew F-86Fs while on active duty at Portland AFB during the Korean call-up. Returned to state control in December 1952, the 123rd FIS converted to F-86As shortly thereafter, received F-94Bs in October 1955, F-89Ds in June 1957, F-89Hs in November of the same year, F-89Js in September 1960, F-102A/TF-102As in January 1966 and F-101B/Fs in March 1971. Re-equipped with F-4Cs in 1982, the 123rd FIS phased out the Guard's last F-4Cs and T-33As in the fall of 1989 when it converted to F-15A/Bs.

Oregon's other Phantom-equipped ANG unit also utilized the F-4C version until 1989, this being the 123rd FIS which was tasked with air defense from Portland. An F-4C triple 'MiG killer' was among the fleet of aircraft assigned to the squadron before it received F-15s.

Texas Air National Guard

111th Fighter Interceptor Squadron, 147th Fighter Interceptor Group

With typical, but good humored, Texan bravado, the unit from Ellington ANGS, Houston, calls itself the 'National Air Force of Texas'! Tracing its origins to the 111th Observation Squadron, which was established in the Texas National Guard in June 1923 and which flew Douglas A-20s in Algeria and North American A-36s, P-51s and F-6s in Italy and France while on wartime active duty, the 111th was reorganized as a Guard fighter squadron in 1947. Back on active duty during the Korean War, the Texans flew combat missions with F-84Es between September 1951 and July 1952. Returned to state control in 1952, they flew F-51Hs, F-80Cs, F-86D/Ls, a mix of F/TF-102As and F-101B/Fs plus T-33As, and then F-101B/Fs prior to getting F-4Cs in 1982 and F-4Ds in 1987. The F-4Ds, with which the 111th FIS also kept an alert detachment at Holloman AFB, New Mexico, were short-

lived in Houston as the squadron began its conversion to F-16A/Bs in 1989. Its Fighting Falcons have now been upgraded to the ADF configuration.

F-4Cs and F-4Ds were employed by the 111th FIS from Ellington until this air defense-dedicated outfit acquired F-16s in 1989.

182nd Tactical Fighter Squadron, 149th Tactical Fighter Group

Based at Kelly AFB and equipped with F-4Cs between the spring of 1979 and the summer of 1986, the San Antonio unit had originally been activated as the 182nd Fighter Squadron (SE) in October 1947. Called to active duty in October 1950, the 182nd Fighter-Bomber Squadron converted from F-51Ds to F-84Es before flying combat operations in Korea between August 1951 and July 1952. Back under state control, the unit flew F-51Hs and F-80Cs as a fighter-bomber squadron, moved from Brooks AFB to Kelly AFB in August 1956, and became

the 182nd FIS in January 1957. In that role, the unit flew F-80Cs, F-86D/Ls (from December 1957) and F-102A/TF-102As (from summer 1960). It converted to F-84Fs and was redesignated 182nd TFS in September 1949, and it was re-equipped with F-100D/Fs in spring 1971 and with F-4Cs in spring 1979. The 182nd TFS first deployed outside the North American continent in August 1981 when it sent F-4Cs and crews to Iceland for Coronet Cruise. Since the summer of 1986, the 182nd TFS has been equipped with F-16A/Bs.

*In contrast, the other Texas **ANG** Phantom user was the 182nd **TFS** at Kelly AFB. This flew the F-4C from the spring of 1979 until summer in 1986, when it transitioned to the F-16 Fighting Falcon.*

Vermont Air National Guard

134th Tactical Fighter Squadron, 158th Tactical Fighter Group

The 'Green Mountain Boys' flew F-4Ds for just over four years from their Burlington ANGS. The Vermont ANG flying unit was organized in July 1946 as the 134th Fighter Squadron (SE) and was initially equipped with P-47Ds. Redesignated the 134th Fighter Interceptor Squadron in 1951, the unit successively flew F-51Ds, F-94A/Bs, F-89Ds and F-102A/TF-102As. In June 1974, it was redesignated 134th Defense Systems

Evaluation Squadron and converted from Delta Daggers to Martin EB-57s. Notwithstanding its long tradition as an ADC-gained unit, the squadron was redesignated 134th TFS in January 1982 when it converted to F-4Ds. Converting to Fighting Falcons from April 1986, the unit was once again designated 134th FIS on 1 July 1987. Redesignated as the 134th FS in March 1992, it now flies F-16A/B ADFs.

Residing at Burlington, Vermont, the 134th TFS operated F-4Ds for a period of four years, commencing in January 1982.

United States Navy

Originally developed for the US Navy, the Phantom II first went into squadron service on 30 December 1960, when F4H-1s were delivered to VF-121 at NAS Miramar, California. They first deployed aboard a carrier in February 1962, when the F4H-1s of VF-102 operated from the USS *Enterprise* (CVAN-65) during the shakedown cruise of the first nuclear carrier. Two and a half years later, at the time of the Gulf of Tonkin incident in August 1964, 13 of the 31 Navy-deployable fighter squadrons were equipped with F-4Bs, one had a mix of F-4Bs and F-4Gs, and one was converting from F-3Bs to F-4Bs. In addition, two RAG squadrons flew a mix of F-4As and F-4Bs.

During the war in Southeast Asia, 22 Navy squadrons and a Marine squadron made 84 war cruises to the Gulf of Tonkin (including 51 with F-4Bs, one with F-4Gs and 32 with F-4Js). They claimed 41 confirmed air combat kills, but 71 of their F-4s were lost in combat (five to enemy aircraft, 13 to SAMs and 53 to AAA and small arms fire) and 54 were lost in operational accidents during wartime deployments.

By the time US combat operations in Southeast Asia ended, Tomcats had begun supplementing Phantoms with deployable squadrons. The process continued until the end of 1983, when VF-21 and VF-154 became the last squadrons to trade F-4Ns for F-14As. Finally, the last two deployable squadrons, VF-151 and VF-161, transitioned from the F-4S to the F/A-18A in 1986.

With reserve units, F-4Bs were first assigned in the spring of 1969 to VF-22L1, a squadron belonging to the Naval Air Reserve Training Command and based at NAS Los Alamitos, California. However, VF-22L1 only had a brief existence as the Naval Air Reserve was reorganized in April 1970. Phantoms were then operated by four reserve squadrons, with the last F-4s being those of VF-202, which transitioned from the F-4S to the F-14A in 1987. In mid-1992, the only F-4s remaining in USN service are those assigned to the Naval Air Weapons Center for operations from NAS China Lake and NAS Point Mugu, California.

Distribution of variants

	F-4B	F-4G	F-4J	F-4N	F-4S
Atlantic Fleet fighter squadrons					
VF-11	65-73		73-80		
VF-14	63-74				
VF-31	63-68		68-81		
VF-32	65-70		70-74		
VF-33	65-68		68-81		
VF-41	62-67		67-74	74-76	
VF-74	61-72		72-82		82-83
VF-84	64-67		67-74	74-76	
VF-101	61-67		66-77		
VF-102	61-67		67-81		
VF-103	65-68		68-81		
VF-171				77-80	80-83
Pacific Fleet fighter squadrons					
VF-21	62-68		68-79	80-83	79-80
VF-51	71-74			74-78	
VF-92	64-68		68-75		
VF-96	62-68	63-64	68-75		
VF-111	71-74			74-78	
VF-114	61-70		70-75		
VF-121	60-68		67-80		80
VF-142	62-69		69-74		
VF-143	62-69		69-74		
VF-151	64-73		77-80	73-77	80-86
VF-154	66-68		68-79	80-83	79-80
VF-161	64-73		77-80	73-77	80-86
VF-191			76-78		
VF-194			76-78		
VF-213	66-70	64-66	70-75		
Reserve fighter squadrons					
VF-201				74-84	84-86
VF-202				74-84	84-87
VF-301	74-75			75-81	81-84
VF-302	74-75			75-80	80-85
Other squadrons					
VAQ-33	70 & 74-81 (F-4B & EF-4B)		74-81 (EF-4J)		
VX-4					
VX-5		68-73			
'Blue Angels'					

VF-11 'Red Rippers'

With their history tracing its origin to the commissioning of VF-5 in February 1927, the 'Red Rippers' were given numerous numerical designations over the years, prior to being designated VF-11 in 1948. When the first VF-11 was decommissioned in February 1959, VF-43 was renumbered to continue the 'Red Rippers' tradition.

VF-11 transitioned from F-8Es to F-4Bs in 1965. Embarked aboard the USS *Forrestal* (CVA-59), VF-11 had been on the line in the Gulf of Tonkin for five days when the carrier suffered serious damage and heavy casualties during a fire on 29 July 1967. With the exception of this aborted war cruise, VF-11 always deployed to the Atlantic and Mediterranean. Homeported at NAS Oceana, Virginia, the 'Red Rippers' converted to F-4Js during the second half of 1973 and transitioned to F-14As in October 1980.

Before converting to the Tomcat in 1980, VF-11 flew Phantoms for some 15 years, initially operating the F-4B version. In 1973, however, it re-equipped with F-4Js similar to the machines portrayed here.

VF-14 'Tophatters'

Laying claims to being the US Navy's oldest aircraft squadron, VF-14 traces its ancestry to an element of the Pacific Fleet Air Detachment organized in San Diego in 1919. Over the years, the squadron was given several designations (VF-1B, VT-5, VP-41, Combat Squadron Four, VB-3, VB-4, etc.) and used related names ('High Hat', 'High Hatters' and 'Top Hatters') until acquiring its present designation in 1949. The 'Tophatters' began flying jets in January 1954, converted from F3D-2s to F3H-2Ns in 1956, and became the third Atlantic Fleet deployable squadron to fly Phantoms when transitioning to F-4Bs at NAS Cecil Field, Florida, in August 1963.

Assigned to CVW-3 and homeported at NAS Oceana, Virginia, VF-14 first deployed aboard the USS *Franklin D. Roosevelt* (CVA-42) on 28 April 1964. Operating from that carrier during RefTra in the Caribbean, an F-4B of the 'Tophatters' gained some notoriety on 10 May 1966 when it was launched with wings spread but unlocked. Even though the wing outer panels folded upward, the aircraft flew 59 miles (95 km) to recover safely at Guantanamo Bay, Cuba. During their third Phantom cruise, the 'Tophatters' spent 95 days on the line in the Gulf of Tonkin. There were no victories and no combat losses, but an F-4B was lost in an operational accident. After five more deployments to the Mediterranean, VF-14 transitioned from F-4Bs to F-14As beginning in July 1974.

An F-4B of VF-14 is shown aboard the USS Roosevelt in the 1970s.

VF-21 'Freelancers'

Homeported at NAS Miramar, California, VF-21 transitioned from F-3Bs to F-4Bs during the fall of 1962 and first deployed with Phantoms aboard the USS *Midway* (CVA-41) in November 1963. During its second cruise aboard *Midway*, VF-21 spent 144 days on the line in the Gulf of Tonkin and was credited with the destruction of two MiG-17s for the loss of two F-4Bs (one to a SAM and one in an operational accident). During cruises aboard the USS *Coral Sea* (CVA-43) and USS *Ranger* (CVA-61) between July 1966 and June 1973, the 'Freelancers' claimed no enemy aircraft, but lost three F-4Bs in combat (two to AAA and one to an undetermined cause) and seven F-4Js in operational accidents.

During their 21 years on Phantoms, the 'Freelancers' successively flew the F-4B, F-4J, F-4S (VF-21 became the first fleet squadron to receive this model in December 1979, but was forced to 'trade down' to the F-4N prior to deploying aboard *Coral Sea*) and F-4N models. With F-4Ns, the squadron went around the world aboard *Coral Sea* when CV-43 was sent to the Norfolk Naval Shipyard for repair, modernization and subsequent reassignment to the Atlantic Fleet. On completion of this cruise, VF-21 returned to NAS Miramar to transition to the F-14A.

VF-21 of the Pacific Fleet was one of the longest-lived Phantom units of the US Navy and used examples from the final production batch of F-4Js for several years after they were delivered in the early 1970s.

VF-22L1

VF-22L1 was the first Naval Reserve Phantom squadron, which received '7L'-coded F-4Bs at its NAS Los Alamitos base in January 1969. These were used until October 1970.

The first Phantoms to be assigned to the US Navy Reserve were F-4Bs, which equipped VF-22L1 during the course of 1969. At the time, this outfit was based at Los Alamitos, California.

VF-31 'Tomcatters'

Commissioned as VF-1B in July 1935, the squadron which ultimately became VF-31 first flew Boeing F4B-4s from the first USS *Enterprise* (CV-6). After several unit redesignations, the squadron was numbered VF-31 in August 1948 and, later in that year, the 'Tomcatters' entered the jet era when they transitioned from F8F-1s to F9F-2s. VF-31 traded up from F-3Bs to F-4Bs in the fall of 1963, and first deployed with its

Phantoms aboard the USS *Saratoga* (CVA-60) in November 1964.

Relocated from NAS Cecil Field, Florida, to NAS Oceana, Virginia, VF-31 always deployed aboard *Saratoga* while operating F-4Bs and, from 1968, F-4Js. These deployments included a war cruise, during which VF-31 spent 173 days on the line between May 1972 and January 1973, claimed a MiG-21 and suffered no combat or operational losses. VF-31 received its first F-14A in January 1981, and it completed its transition from F-4Js shortly thereafter.

Displaying a 'Felix the Cat' motif on the center fuselage section, an F-4J of VF-31 sits at dispersal at this squadron's Oceana shore base.

VF-32 'Swordsmen'

At the time of the Gulf of Tonkin Incident, the 'Swordsmen' of VF-32 were still flying F-8Ds from NAS Cecil Field, Florida, as part of CVW-1. The squadron began transitioning to F-4Bs in the fall of 1965, and in December of that year moved to NAS Oceana, Virginia. With Phantoms, the 'Swordsmen' first deployed aboard the USS *Franklin D. Roosevelt* (CVA-42) in June 1966, when it

left Mayport, Florida, for the Gulf of Tonkin. During that war cruise, which ended when 'FDR' returned to Florida in February 1967, VF-32 scored no air-to-air victories and its only loss resulted from an operational accident.

From May 1968, when VF-32 went aboard the USS *John F. Kennedy* (CVA-67) as part of CVW-3, the 'Swordsmen' deployed aboard 'JFK'. They transitioned to F-4Js in 1970 and became the first Atlantic Fleet deployable F-14 squadron in 1974.

Hooked up to the catapult, an F-4B of VF-32 waits for a launch signal from the yellow-jacketed catapult control officer in a scene that was re-enacted thousands of times aboard Navy aircraft carriers.

VF-33 'Tarsiers'

After returning from their third cruise aboard the USS *Enterprise* (CVAN-65), in October 1964, the 'Tarsiers' transitioned from F-8Es to F-4Bs. While equipped with F-4Bs, VF-33

deployed to the Mediterranean but, after transitioning to F-4Js in 1968, the squadron joined VF-102 in introducing the F-4J in Southeast Asia. Embarked aboard the USS *America* (CVA-66), the 'Tarsiers' spent 112 days on the line between May and December 1968, shot down a MiG-21 and had three F-4Js shot down (one by AAA, one by a MiG and one by a SAM).

In 1980, VF-33 conducted tests with F-4Js painted in the experimental Keith Ferris camouflage scheme, and the following year the squadron transitioned to F-14As.

Black fins adorned the F-4Js that were assigned to VF-33 for a while in the mid-1970s.

VF-41 'Black Aces'

In October 1962, shortly after transitioning to F-4Bs to become one of the first Atlantic Fleet squadrons to fly Phantoms, VF-41 was sent from NAS Oceana, Virginia, to NAS Key West, Florida, to provide air defense during the Cuban Missile Crisis. Less than two years later, VF-41 became the first squadron to add the delivery of conventional attack weapons, a capability put to good use when the 'Black Aces' deployed to the Gulf of Tonkin aboard the USS *Independence* (CVA-62). Spending 100 days on the line

between June and November 1965, the 'Black Aces' lost two F-4Bs over North Vietnam to small-arms fire.

In mid-1967, VF-41 became the first deployable F-4J squadron. Retaining these aircraft, it made a Mediterranean cruise aboard the USS *Franklin D. Roosevelt* (CVA-42) in 1972-73, during which it operated 18 F-4Js, compared with the normal complement of 12, as it was the only fighter squadron aboard 'FDR'. After returning from this cruise, during which it supported US interests during the Yom Kippur War between Israel and its Arab

neighbors, VF-41 transitioned to F-4Ns. Finally, in April 1976, the 'Black Aces' began to transition to the Tomcat.

The origins of the squadron's name 'Black Aces' is clearly evident in this study of a VF-41 Phantom.

VF-51 'Screaming Eagles'

Homeported at NAS Miramar, California, the 'Screaming Eagles' made six war deployments to the Gulf of Tonkin with F-8Es, F-8Hs and F-8Js before transitioning to F-4Bs in 1971. With Phantoms, VF-51 made one final cruise to the Gulf of Tonkin in 1971-72, spending 148 days on the line aboard the USS *Coral Sea* (CVA-43), claiming four MiG-17s and losing two F-4Bs, one to North Vietnamese AAA and one in an operational accident.

The squadron then made a WestPac cruise with F-4Bs, and transitioned to F-4Ns, with which it deployed to WestPac aboard *Coral Sea* and then to the Mediterranean aboard the USS *Franklin D. Roosevelt* (CVA-42). It completed its transition to F-14As in October 1978.

With its wings folded, an F-4N of VF-51 is respotted during a lull in flight operations.

VF-74 'Be-devilers'

On 8 July 1961, VF-74 became the first deployable squadron to transition to Phantoms when it received F4H-1s at NAS Oceana, Virginia. It completed carquals (carrier qualifications) in October 1961, and took its Phantoms aboard the USS *Forrestal* (CVA-59) from August 1962 to March 1963 for the first full F-4B deployment. After three peacetime cruises to the Mediterranean, the F-4Bs of VF-74 were aboard *Forrestal* when it was forced out of the war due to a catastrophic fire, which occurred after only

five days on the line.

After transitioning to F-4Js in early 1972, VF-74 returned to the Gulf of Tonkin aboard the USS *America* (CVA-66) and spent 158 days on the line during Linebacker, Freedom Train and Linebacker II operations. The 'Be-devilers' scored no air combat victories and lost no aircraft in combat, but lost an F-4J and one of its crew in an operational accident during its third period on the line. Returning to Mediterranean cruises, VF-74 flew F-4Js and, finally, F-4Ss for a single cruise aboard *Forrestal* in 1982, before transitioning to F-14As at the beginning of 1983.

Sidewinder missiles form part of the armament carried by this VF-74 F-4J during a combat cruise to the Gulf of Tonkin aboard the USS America in 1972-73, when the unit was assigned to CVW-8.

VF-84 'Jolly Rogers'

After a final abbreviated cruise with Crusaders aboard the USS *Independence* (CVA-62), the colorful 'Jolly Rogers' received their F-4Bs at NAS Oceana, Virginia, at the end of 1964. Completing its transition quickly, VF-84 took its Phantoms to the Gulf of Tonkin in May 1965 when, as part of CVW-7, it deployed aboard *Independence*. Spending 100 days on the line between June and November 1965, VF-84 lost three F-4Bs to North Vietnamese AAA.

Returning to Mediterranean cruises in 1966, VF-84 made two deployments aboard the USS *Independence* (CVA-62), one with F-4Bs and one with F-4Js, and three with F-4Js aboard the USS *Franklin D. Roosevelt* (CVA-42), before transitioning from F-4Js to F-4Ns in 1974. After only one cruise with F-4Ns, the 'Jolly Rogers' began their transition to the F-14As in June 1976.

VF-84's final cruise as a Phantom-equipped unit was made with F-4Ns aboard the USS Roosevelt.

VF-92 'Silver Kings'

Sharing with sister squadron VF-96 the distinction of making eight war cruises (more than any other Navy F-4 squadron), VF-92 transitioned to F-4Bs in 1964. With this version of the Phantom, the 'Silver Kings' made one deployment aboard the USS *Ranger* (CVA-61) and three aboard the USS *Enterprise* (CVAN-65) before transitioning to F-4Js during the second semester of 1968. With their new Phantoms, the 'Silver Kings' then deployed four more times to the Gulf of Tonkin (once each aboard *Enterprise* and *America* and twice aboard *Constellation*). The wartime tally for VF-92 included 868 days on the line, a MiG-21 shot down, the loss of five F-4Bs and two F-4Js in combat and four F-4Bs and two F-4Js in operational accidents. In the postwar period, VF-92 and its F-4Js deployed once to WestPac before transitioning to the Tomcat in 1975.

VF-92 completed four combat tours with the F-4J model, utilizing it from USS America, Constellation *and* Enterprise *during 1968-73.*

VF-96 'Fighting Falcons'

On 1 June 1962, VF-142 was redesignated VF-96 at NAS Miramar, California, and the newly designated squadron soon supplemented the F-4Bs inherited from VF-142 with F-4Gs. With a mix of F-4Bs and F-4Gs, the 'Fighting Falcons' first deployed aboard the USS *Ranger* (CVA-61) for a peacetime cruise to WestPac. With F-4Bs, VF-96 flew combat operations in Vietnam from *Ranger* during a cruise between August 1964 and April 1965. On 9 April 1965, one of its crew got the first US Navy kill of the war when it shot down a PRC MiG-17, but the aircraft was subsequently shot down by another Chinese fighter. Still flying F-4Bs, the 'Fighting Falcons' made three combat cruises aboard the USS *Enterprise* (CVAN-65) between October 1965 and July 1968, claiming a MiG-21 on 9 May 1968 but losing three F-4Bs in combat and five F-4Bs in operational accidents.

After transitioning to F-4Js, VF-96 deployed again to the Gulf of Tonkin, once aboard *Enterprise* (January-July 1969, with neither victories nor losses), once aboard the USS *America* (CVA-66, April-December 1970, with neither victories nor losses) and twice aboard the USS *Constellation* (CVA-64, October 1971-June 1972, with six victories and one combat loss; and January-October 1973, with neither victories nor losses). In the postwar period, VF-96 deployed once more with F-4Js aboard *Constellation* before being disestablished on 1 November 1975.

VF-92's sister squadron in CVW-9 was VF-96, which enjoyed an almost identical combat career before it was disestablished in late 1975. A 'Fighting Falcons' F-4J is seen at Miramar between deployments.

VF-101 'Grim Reapers'

Commissioned on 1 May 1952, VF-101 assumed the old VF-10 'Grim Reapers' name. In 1958 it became a training unit, and in June 1960 its Det. A at NAS Oceana, Virginia, was selected to become the Atlantic Fleet F-4 RAG. Nevertheless, the squadron retained F4D-1 Skyrays and F3H-2N Demons until March 1962 and December 1962, respectively. Its initial batch of F4H-1Fs was supplemented during 1961 by F4H-1s.

In February 1963, Det. A was disestablished and F-4 training was transferred to NAS Key West, Florida, until 1 May 1966, when the 'Grim Reapers' once again established a detachment at NAS Oceana. On 23 December 1966, VF-101 became the first unit to receive F-4Js. The 'Grim Reapers' moved to NAS Oceana on 1 April 1971 and took on the additional job of training F-14A crews for the Atlantic Fleet in January 1976. VF-101 retained a detachment at NAS Key West until Atlantic Fleet F-4 training responsibility was transferred to VF-171 in August 1977.

VF-101 made one operational deployment when the F-4Js of its Det. 66 were assigned to CVW-8 for a Mediterranean cruise aboard the USS *America* (CVA-66) between July and December 1971.

Responsibility for the training of Atlantic Fleet air and ground crew was entrusted to VF-101 at Oceana.

VF-102 'Diamondbacks'

The second Atlantic Fleet deployable squadron to receive Phantoms, VF-102 first deployed with F-4Bs when it went aboard the USS *Enterprise* (CVAN-65) for the shakedown cruise of the first nuclear carrier (5 February-8 April 1962). After an around-the-world cruise aboard *Enterprise*, CVAN-65 was transferred to the Pacific Fleet in 1964 and the 'Diamondbacks' returned to NAS Oceana, Virginia, for more Mediterranean cruises.

After converting to F-4Js at the end of 1967, VF-102 embarked aboard USS *America* (CVA-66) and spent 112 days on the line in the Gulf of Tonkin between May and December 1968. Although they did not get an air combat victory, the 'Diamondbacks' were more fortunate than the 'Tarsiers', with which they made the first F-4J combat deployment, as they lost neither crew nor aircraft. The 'Diamondbacks' continued flying F-4Js from Oceana and during Mediterranean cruises until transitioning to F-14As in June 1981.

Pictured on one of Enterprise's *deck-edge elevators, this F-4B of VF-102 was embarked for the world cruise made by this carrier before reassignment to the Pacific Fleet.*

VF-103 'Sluggers'

The 'Sluggers' of VF-103 were still flying F-8Es aboard the USS *Forrestal* (CVA-59) at the time of the Gulf of Tonkin incident. After transitioning to the F-4B at NAS Oceana, Virginia, the squadron first deployed with Phantoms aboard the USS *Saratoga* (CVA-60) between March and October 1966. The 'Sluggers' traded their F-4Bs for F-4Js before making their third Mediterranean cruise aboard *Saratoga* in 1969. Two more peacetime cruises followed but, in April 1972, VF-103 and the other CVW-3 squadrons went aboard *Saratoga* on their way to the Gulf of Tonkin. Spending 173 days on the line during the hectic last phases of the war against North Vietnam, the 'Sluggers' were credited with a MiG-21 kill but lost three of their F-4Js (one each to a MiG, a SAM and AAA).

After that eventful cruise, the F-4Js of VF-103 again made several Mediterranean deployments aboard *Saratoga* and an abbreviated Atlantic cruise aboard *America* (CVA-66) in 1974. In 1981, the 'Sluggers' transitioned to the F-4S and were transferred from CVW-3 to CVW-17 for a final Phantom cruise aboard the USS *Forrestal* (CVA-59). The squadron began transitioning to the Tomcat in January 1983.

F-4Js from VF-103 formed part of a composite air wing on America *for a 1974 NATO exercise.*

VF-111 'Sundowners'

Veterans of seven war cruises on Crusaders, the 'Sundowners' transitioned from F-8Hs to F-4Bs at NAS Miramar, California, in early 1971, and in November of that year went back to the Gulf of Tonkin aboard the USS *Coral Sea* (CVA-43). Spending 148 days on the line, they claimed the destruction of a MiG-17 and lost an F-4B to a North Vietnamese SAM.

Postwar, VF-111 deployed twice to WestPac aboard *Coral Sea* (first with F-4Bs and then with F-4Ns) and once to the Mediterranean aboard the USS *Franklin D. Roosevelt* (CVA-42). The 'Sundowners' transitioned to the F-14A in June 1978.

A bicentennial motif at the base of the sunburst fin design helps date this VF-111 F-4N to the mid-1970s, shortly before it made its final deployment with the Phantom to the Mediterranean 6th Fleet.

VF-114 'Aardvarks'

Taking its recently acquired F-4Bs aboard the USS *Kitty Hawk* (CVA-63) in September 1962 for its first cruise, VF-114 became the first Pacific Fleet squadron to deploy with Phantoms. Remaining homeported at NAS Miramar, California, and assigned to CVW-11, the 'Aardvarks' deployed nine more times aboard *Kitty Hawk* before transitioning to F-14As in late 1975.

While equipped with Phantoms, with F-4Js replacing F-4Bs in 1970, VF-114 deployed six times to the Gulf of Tonkin for combat operations in Southeast Asia. During these cruises, the 'Aardvarks' claimed the destruction of two MiG-17s, two MiG-21s and an An-2, but lost no fewer than 20 Phantoms (nine F-4Bs and two F-4Js in combat and nine F-4Bs in accidents).

VF-114 claimed the distinction of being the first deployable Pacific Fleet Phantom squadron in 1962 and subsequently converted to the F-4J version in 1970, one of the latter machines being portrayed here.

VF-116 'Black Lions'

VF-116 never officially existed, since it was commissioned 'by mistake', and its commissioning order was immediately countermanded by the Pentagon. When VF-213 was reassigned from CVW-21 to CVW-11 it was planned to change the squadron designation to one in the 110-119 series, to continue the tradition of squadron numbers reflecting CVW assignment. Several aircraft were actually painted up in full VF-116 markings before it became clear that the system was unworkable, and that the same unit could change designation several times and redesignation was countermanded.

Even though it never officially existed, F-4Gs did display VF-116 inscriptions for a brief period at Miramar in the fall of 1964.

VF-121 'Pacemakers'

Commissioned on 1 July 1946 as a Ready Reserve unit equipped with F6F-5s at NAS Los Alamitos, California, VF-781 was called to active duty during the Korean War and flew F9F-2s from the USS *Bon Homme Richard* (CVA-31) during that conflict. The squadron was renumbered VF-121 in February 1953, and served as an active-duty deployable squadron until April 1958, when it assumed responsibility for training all-weather pilots and RIOs for the Pacific Fleet.

The 'Pacemakers', the West Coast RAG at NAS Miramar, California, received its first

F4H-1 on 30 December 1960, and trained Pacific Fleet F-4 crews until it was disestablished on 30 September 1980. Its initial Phantom complement of F4H-1Fs (F-4As after October 1962) and F4H-1s/F-4Bs was supplemented by TF-10Bs until 1965. On 27 April 1967, VF-121 became the first West Coast squadron to receive F-4Js, and the 'Pacemakers' retained this Phantom variant for 13 years.

Pacific Fleet crew training duties were the remit of VF-121, which flew F-4Js from 1967 to 1980.

VF-142 'Ghostriders'

Tracing its ancestry to VF-791, a Ready Reserve squadron established in November 1949 and called to active duty in July 1950, VF-142 transitioned from F8U-1s to F4H-1s in early 1962. Less than six months later, the first VF-142 was redesignated VF-96 in June 1962.

A new VF-142 was established at NAS Miramar, California, and transitioned from F-3Bs to F-4Bs in late 1963. With F-4Bs, the 'Ghostriders' made four deployments to the Gulf of Tonkin (aboard *Constellation* in May

1964-February 1965, aboard *Ranger* in December 1965-August 1966, and again aboard *Constellation* between April-December 1967 and May 1968 and January 1969).

The squadron transitioned to F-4Js during the first half of 1969 and again deployed to the Gulf of Tonkin, once aboard *Constellation* and twice aboard *Enterprise*. During its combat cruises, VF-142 claimed five victories and lost five aircraft in combat. After the war, VF-142 deployed once to the Mediterranean aboard the USS *America* (CVA-66) before transitioning to F-14As during the fall of 1974.

VF-142's first period of existence as a Phantom squadron came in 1962, but it soon evolved into VF-96.

The 'second' VF-142 Phantom era was destined to last much longer, this F-4J dating to about 1973.

VF-143 'Pukin' Dogs'

After transitioning from F-3Bs to F-4Bs at NAS Miramar, California, at the end of 1962, the 'Pukin' Dogs' of VF-143 first deployed with Phantoms aboard the USS *Constellation* (CVA-64) in February 1963. The squadron next went aboard the *Constellation* for its first war cruise to the Gulf of Tonkin and made six other war cruises aboard the USS *Ranger* (CVA-61),

Constellation (CVA-64) and *Enterprise* (CVAN-65), raking a record which included no fewer than 854 days on the line, an air combat victory over a MiG-21, five combat losses and three operational losses.

The 'Pukin' Dogs', which had transitioned to the F-4J in 1969, were then deployed in January 1974 to CVW-8 in the Atlantic Fleet for a cruise aboard the USS *America* (CVA-66). Afterward, they returned to the Pacific Fleet and NAS Miramar to transition to the Tomcat in the fall of 1974.

VF-143's final tour with Phantoms was as part of the Atlantic Fleet, even though it was still nominally a Pacific Fleet unit.

VF-151 'Vigilantes'

During the spring of 1964, the 'Vigilantes' of VF-151 transitioned from F-3Bs to F-4Bs at NAS Miramar, California. Later in the year, the squadron went aboard the USS *Coral Sea* (CVA-43) for the first of seven combat deployments to the Gulf of Tonkin. During the Vietnam War the 'Vigilantes' shot down a MiG-17 and lost 11 F-4Bs (six to enemy defenses).

Having transitioned to F-4Ns during the

spring of 1973, the 'Vigilantes' continued their association with CVW-5 and they were forward deployed to Japan in October 1973. For the next 12½ years, VF-151 remained homeported at NAS Atsugi, Japan, and deployed aboard the USS *Midway* (CVA-41) with F-4Ns, F-4Js (from May 1977) and F-4Ss (from December 1980). On 24 March 1986, one of its aircraft made the last Phantom's fleet trap aboard *Midway*. VF-151 transitioned to the Hornet during the summer of 1986.

VF-151 was one of the few US Navy fighter squadrons to be equipped with all four major versions. This F-4J served with the unit on the USS Midway in the late 1970s, just before VF-151 acquired the F-4S.

VF-154 'Black Knights'

The roots of VF-154 can be traced back to VBF-718, a Ready Reserve squadron established at NAS New York in July 1946. While in the Reserve, the squadron was successively redesignated VF-68A and VF-837. Called to active duty in April 1951, the squadron became a Regular Navy unit in February 1953, when it was renumbered VF-154. Equipped with F-8Ds, VF-154 made a combat cruise aboard the USS *Coral Sea* (CVA-43) at the onset of the Vietnam War.

After the shortest transition on record, the 'Black Knights' deployed with F-4Bs aboard *Coral Sea* to the Gulf of Tonkin (July 1966-February 1967) and lost four aircraft in combat over North Vietnam. Still equipped with F-4Bs, VF-154 deployed aboard the USS

Ranger (CVA-61) between November 1967 and May 1968. The squadron had no victories and no combat losses, but two F-4Bs were lost in operational accidents. Transitioning to F-4Js during the summer of 1968, VF-154 deployed four times aboard *Ranger* before combat operations in Southeast Asia ended. In the process, the 'Black Knights' again scored no victories and lost no aircraft in combat, but an F-4J was lost in an accident during the November 1969-May 1970 cruise.

In December 1979, VF-154 transitioned to the F-4S but within a year exchanged these aircraft for F-4Ns. Flying F-4Ns, the 'Black Knights' deployed twice again aboard *Coral Sea* before initiating their conversion to F-14As in December 1983. Flying Tomcats, VF-154 first deployed aboard the USS *Constellation* (CV-64) in February 1985.

Dull low-visibility markings were synonymous with VF-154's last tour of duty as a Phantom squadron and are epitomized by this rather drab F-4N. After two cruises on Coral Sea, VF-154 converted to F-14As.

VF-161 'Chargers'

Commissioned at NAS Cecil Field, Florida, on 1 September 1960 with F3H-2s, the 'Chargers' moved twice during the following year, being first relocated to NAS Key West, Florida, and then setting up shop at NAS Miramar, California. From that California station, the 'Chargers' flew F-3Bs until transitioning to F-4Bs in December 1964. Joining VF-151 aboard the USS *Constellation* (CVA-64) in November 1966, the 'Chargers' subsequently made the same deployments as the 'Vigilantes', moved to Japan at the same time, and made simultaneous transitions to the F-4N, F-4J and F-4S.

During their war cruises aboard *Constellation*, *Coral Sea* and *Midway*, the 'Chargers' lost five F-4Bs in combat and three in operational accidents, but they shot down six enemy aircraft (four MiG-17s and

two MiG-19s).

Homeported at NAS Atsugi, Japan, beginning in October 1973, VF-161 made numerous deployments aboard *Midway* during the following 12½ years, and on 25 March 1986 one of its F-4Ss (NF 210, BuNo. 153879) became the last US Navy Phantom to be launched from a carrier when it was catapulted off the waist of CV-41. The 'Chargers' then transitioned to the F/A-18A/B.

Like VF-151, VF-161 also operated no fewer than four Phantom models.

VF-171 'Aces'

When VF-101's mission was changed from F-4 to F-14 replacement training, VF-171 was established at NAS Oceana, Virginia, on 8 August 1977 as the Atlantic Fleet F-4 Fleet Replacement Squadron. Later adding a Key West detachment, the 'Aces' successively flew F-4Js and F-4Ss, as well as A-4Es, until being disestablished on 1 June 1984. At that time, responsibility for training the last US Navy F-4 crews was transferred to VMFAT-101.

After VF-101 gained responsibility for the training of Atlantic Fleet Tomcat crew members, VF-171 served as the Phantom FRS. It was mainly equipped with the F-4J and F-4S.

VF-191 'Satan's Kittens'

After eight war cruises to the Gulf of Tonkin, during which they flew Crusaders from the USS *Bon Homme Richard* (CVA-31), *Ticonderoga* (CVA-14) and *Oriskany* (CVA-34), the 'Satan's Kittens' transitioned from F-8Js to F-4Js in the spring of 1976. Equipped with the first F-4Js retrofitted with reduced smoke engines and solid-state radar, VF-191 made only one Phantom deployment, aboard the USS *Coral Sea* (CV-43), between 15 February 1977 and 5 October 1977, before being decommissioned on 1 March 1978.

VF-191's period as a Phantom unit was brief and it made just one sea cruise with the F-4J in 1977.

VF-194 'Red Lightnings'

The sister squadron to VF-191, VF-194 made the same war cruises with Crusaders and also transitioned to F-4Js at NAS Miramar, California, during the spring of 1976. With these Phantoms, the 'Red Lightnings' made a single WestPac deployment aboard the USS *Coral Sea* (CV-43) before being decommissioned on 1 March 1978.

Another short-lived Phantom outfit was VF-194, which flew F-4Js from 1976 until 1978 as the sister unit to VF-191. Like the latter, it was destined to deploy only once, on USS Coral Sea in 1977.

VF-201 'Renegades'

When Reserve Carrier Air Wing Twenty was established in April 1970, a shortage of fighters initially prevented the Navy from establishing its two fighter squadrons. That situation changed during the following year and the 'Renegades' of VF-201 were assigned F-8Hs at NAS Dallas, Texas. The squadron transitioned to F-4Ns in 1974 and phased out the last of these Phantoms in February 1984. VF-201 then flew F-4Ss until December 1986 when it transitioned to the F-14A.

One of two Atlantic Fleet Reserve Force squadrons, VF-201 converted to the F-4N in 1974 and continued to operate this version until 1984, when it re-equipped with the newer and more potent F-4S.

VF-202 'Superheats'

Like its sister squadron in CVWR-20, VF-202 was first equipped with F-8Hs. The squadron transitioned to the F-4N at NAS Dallas, Texas, in April 1976 and to the F-4S eight years later. The 'Superheats' made their last F-4 trap aboard the USS *America* (CV-66) on 21 October 1986 and flew their last F-4S, the last tactical Phantom in the USN inventory, to AMARC on 14 May 1987. VF-202 has since equipped with F-14As.

The brace of Phantoms visible in the foreground displays unit markings of VF-202, which flew McDonnell's classic warplane from NAS Dallas, Texas, between 1976 and 1987, using the F-4N and F-4S versions.

VF-213 'Black Lions'

In early 1964, when VF-213 transitioned from Demons to Phantoms, its initial complement of aircraft included two F-4Bs and 10 F-4Gs with the AN/ASW-13 datalink. The 'Black Lions' deployed with this mix of aircraft aboard the USS *Kitty Hawk* (CVA-63) and spent 122 days on the line in the Gulf of Tonkin between November 1965 and June 1966, losing an F-4B and an F-4G to North Vietnamese AAA. Re-equipped with F-4Bs, VF-213 made three more combat cruises and then transitioned to F-4Js (becoming, in November 1970, the first squadron to deploy with aircraft fitted with the Automatic Carrier Landing System, ACLS) for two final war cruises. While operating in the Gulf of Tonkin between November 1967 and November 1972, the 'Black Lions' claimed the destruction of an Antonov An-2, lost an F-4B and an F-4J in combat, and lost another F-4B in an operational accident.

After the end of combat operations in Southeast Asia, the 'Black Lions' made two WestPac deployments with F-4Js aboard *Kitty Hawk* and one short cruise to Europe aboard the USS *America* (CVA-66). Although assigned on this occasion to an Atlantic Fleet air wing (CVW-8) to take part in Exercise Northern Merger, VF-213 retained the tailcode 'NH' of its usual Pacific Fleet air wing (CVW-11). The 'Black Lions' transitioned to the Tomcat in late 1975.

Although normally operating in the WestPac area, VF-213 did complete a mini-cruise to European waters in late 1974 when it deployed with F-4Js aboard the USS America for NATO's Northern Merger exercise.

VF-301 'Devil's Disciples'

Established with F-8Ls at NAS Miramar, California, on 1 October 1970, the 'Devil's Disciples' transitioned to the F-4B in June 1974, to the F-4N during the summer of 1975 and to the F-4S in the spring of 1981. After 10 years with Phantoms, VF-301 began its transition to the F-14A in 1984.

West Coast reserve units also flew Phantoms for several years, VF-301 using the F-4B, F-4N and F-4S.

VF-302 'Stallions'

Established in 1970 at NAS Miramar, California, as the second fighter squadron in CVWR-30, VF-302 transitioned from the Crusader to the F-4B in 1974, to the F-4N in February 1975 and to the F-4S in November 1980. Prior to transitioning to the F-14A in March 1985, the 'Stallions' were the last to fly Phantoms from NAS Miramar, thus closing a chapter in Navy history which had begun in December 1960 with the assignment of the first F4H-1s to VF-121.

Also a reserve outfit, VF-302 used F-4B, F-4N and F-4S models between 1974 and 1985. This colorful F-4N dates back to 1975, shortly after the 'Stallions' took delivery of the updated version of the F-4B.

VAQ-33 'Firebirds'

After its Det. 67 made the last EA-1F deployment aboard the USS *John F. Kennedy* (CVA-67) in 1969, VAQ-33 was given a new mission as part of the Fleet Electronic Warfare Support Group. Its first jet, an F-4B, which was soon fitted by Westinghouse with electronic simulation gear, arrived at NAS Norfolk, Virginia, on 18 February 1970 but was lost less than three months later. Modified Phantoms again supplemented the squadron's mix of ERA-3Bs, EA-4Fs and NC-121Ks in 1974, and the 'Firebirds' operated EF-4B/Js (the EF designation being adopted in December 1976) until January 1981.

Tasked with the electronic warfare training role, VAQ-33 used barely a handful of Phantoms between 1970 and 1981 and never had more than a couple on hand. The F-4B seen here is typical of these aircraft.

VX-4 'Evaluators'

Air Development Squadron Four (VX-4) at NAS Point Mugu, California, flew all naval fighter versions of the Phantom to conduct evaluations and investigations of aircraft weapon systems and support system equipment under operational environment conditions, and to develop tactics and doctrines for the use of these weapons by Naval Air. Having received their first F4H-1s in 1961, the 'Evaluators' retired their last F-4Ss in 1986.

Operational test and evaluation of the Phantom was one of VX-4's main roles for almost three decades. It used all major versions, though few were as attractively finished as this pair.

VX-5 'Vampires'

Tasked with developing day and night tactics for the delivery of airborne conventional and special weapons, VX-5 operated F-4Bs during the early 1960s, primarily from NOTS China Lake, California, but also from Kirtland AFB, New Mexico, where its Det. A had Phantoms working with the Naval Weapons Evaluation Facility. The 'Vampires' later cleared other Phantom versions for the delivery of various airborne weapons.

Principally concerned with attack aircraft types, VX-5 did operate a few F-4Bs in the 1960s.

'Blue Angels'

Seven modified F-4Js were assigned to the 'Blue Angels', the Navy Flight Demonstration Squadron homeported at NAS Pensacola, Florida, in January 1969. The famous unit flew F-4Js until demonstrations were suspended in August 1973 after three pilots and six F-4Js had been lost in accidents. Later in the year, the energy crisis forced a switch to more fuel-efficient A-4Fs.

Like the Air Force's 'Thunderbirds', the Navy's 'Blue Angels' display team was equipped with the Phantom for a few years, using modified F-4Js from 1969 until it transitioned to the A-4F in late 1973.

Other USN F-4 operators

Phantoms were operated for a variety of tests by numerous Navy organizations including the Naval Air Test Center (NATC), which relinquished its last two F-4Ss on 6 October 1988, and the Naval Test Pilot School (NTPS) at NAS Patuxent River, Maryland; the Naval Weapons Evaluation Facility (NWEF) at Kirtland AFB, New Mexico; the Naval Air Test Facility (NATF) at NAS Lakehurst, New Jersey; the Naval Missile Center (NMC), the Pacific Missile Test Center (PMTC) and the Naval Weapons Station (NWS) at NAS Point Mugu, California; the Naval Ordnance Test Station (NOTS) and the Naval Air Weapons Center (NAWC) at NAS China Lake, California; the Naval Air Development Center (NADC) at Johnsville, Pennsylvania; and the National Parachute Test Range (NPTR) and the Aerospace Recovery Facility (ARF) at NAF El Centro, California. Only NAWC currently retains Phantoms, which are used as drones and drone directors in the development of missiles.

Numerous other agencies and units flew Phantoms in Navy colors, and these are represented here by an F-4S of the Naval Air Test Center (above); an F-4A from VC-7 (right); and a QF-4B from the Naval Air Weapons Center (below).

United States Marine Corps

The Marine Corps received its first F4H-1s in June 1962, when VMF(AW)-314 transitioned from Skyrays, and operated Phantoms until January 1992, when VMFA-112 became the last reserve squadron to transition to Hornets. Over the years, RF-4Bs had served with three composite squadrons and a reconnaissance squadron, and fighter versions (F-4B, F-4J, F-4N and F-4S) had equipped 15 active-duty fighter attack squadrons, two training squadrons and four reserve squadrons.

Beginning in April 1965, when the F-4Bs landed at Da Nang, Marine Phantoms took an active part in the Vietnam War from bases in Vietnam and Thailand and from the deck of the USS *America* (CVA-66). Marine crews claimed the destruction of three MiGs (two while flying on exchange duty with the USAF). Seventy-two fighters and three RF-4Bs were lost in combat, and four other Phantoms (one an RF-4B) were lost in operational accidents.

After the war had ended, Phantoms remained the only fighter aircraft in service with the Fleet Marine Force (FMF) until the advent of the F/A-18 in 1983. From their bases at MCAS Beaufort in South Carolina, MCAS El Toro in California and MCAS Kaneohe Bay in Hawaii, the 12 FMF squadrons went on regular six-month rotational deployments to Japan as part of the Unit Deployment program and made a few carrier deployments.

Distribution of variants

	F-4B	RF-4B	F-4J	F-4N	F-4S
VMCJ-1		66-75			
VMCJ-2		65-75			
VMCJ-3		65-75			
VMFA-112			83-84	76-83	84-92
VMFA-115	64-75		75-82		82-84
VMFA-122			75-84		84-85
VMFA-134				84-85	85-89
VMFA-212			68-81		81-88
VMFA-232			67-79		79-88
VMFA-235			68-81		81-89
VMFA-251	64-71			71-81	81-86
VMFA-312	66-73		73-83		83-87
VMFA-314	62-75			75-82	
VMFA-321	73-77			77-84	84-91
VMFA-323	64-79			79-82	
VMFA-333			68-79		79-87
VMFA-334			67-71		
VMFA-351				77-78	
VMFA-451			68-78		78-88
VMFA-513	63-70				
VMFA-531	62-75			75-83	
VMFA-542	63-70				
VMFAT-101			69-83	76-83	82-87
VMFAT-201	67-69				
VMFP-3		75-90			

VMCJ-1

Marine Composite Reconnaissance Squadron One added RF-4Bs to its mix of aircraft in 1966 while based at MCAS Iwakuni, Japan, and first took its Phantoms to Da Nang in October of that year. From then until the Marine withdrawal from Vietnam, VMCJ-1 sent RF-4B detachments from its home base at Iwakuni. In addition, a VMCJ-1 detachment was assigned to CVW-5 for deployment aboard the USS *Midway* (CVA-41) between July 1974 and August 1975. When *Midway* returned with the last of these detachments, VMCJ-1 transferred its RF-4Bs to the newly commissioned VMFP-3.

RF-4Bs were operated by VMCJ-1 at Iwakuni, Japan, and Da Nang, South Vietnam, from 1966 until 1975.

VMCJ-2 'Playboys'

VMCJ-2, the composite squadron assigned to the East Coast, began replacing its RF-8As with RF-4Bs in 1965. Based at MCAS Cherry Point, North Carolina, the squadron first underwent carquals aboard the USS *Independence* (CVA-62) in January 1966, and kept RF-4Bs as part of its mixed inventory for 10 years until turning its Phantoms over to VMFP-3.

Cherry Point-based composite unit VMCJ-2 used the specialized RF-4B between 1965 and 1975.

VMCJ-3

The first composite squadron to add RF-4Bs to its mixed inventory, VMCJ-3 received its first Phantoms at MCAS El Toro, California, in May 1965. It transferred its RF-4Bs to VMFP-3 in July 1975.

Reconnaissance-dedicated Phantoms were introduced to USMC service by VMCJ-3 at MCAS El Toro. This unit obtained its first example of the RF-4B version during the late spring of 1965.

VMFA-112 'Cowboys'

Formed on 1 March 1942, VMF-112 was involved in all phases of the Pacific war and obtained the Marines' third highest kill record. In 1946, the squadron was recommissioned as a reserve unit with FG-1D Corsairs. Remaining in the reserve, the squadron was redesignated from VMF(AW)-112 to VMFA-112 upon transitioning from F-8As to F-4Ns in 1976. Based at NAS Dallas, Texas, the 'Cowboys' switched to the F-4J in July 1983 and to the F-4S in December 1984. They retired the last tactical F-4S from the US Sea Service inventory during ceremony at NAS Dallas on 18 January 1992 and, soon afterward, completed the transition to the F/A-18A.

One of a handful of Marine reserve outfits that operated the Phantom, VMFA-112 was initially equipped with the F-4N model.

VMFA-115 'Silver Eagles'

Marine Fighter Attack Squadron 115 originated in July 1943, when VMF-115 was formed at Santa Barbara. With Corsairs, VMF-115 joined the Pacific campaign in February 1944 and ended the war in Peking. In 1949, the squadron achieved the distinction of becoming the first Marine squadron to be equipped with Panthers and, at the end of the following year, took these jets into combat. Designated VMF(AW)-115 after transitioning to the F4D-1, the squadron took its current designation after receiving F-4Bs in January 1964.

In January 1965, the 'Silver Eagles' took their F-4Bs to Vietnam, where they flew over 35,000 combat sorties in three detachments to Da Nang and Chu Lai, more than any other F-4 squadron, before being sent to Iwakuni. They were back in the fray between August 1970 and September 1972, first during two detachments at Da Nang and then from Nam Phong in Thailand. Until relocated at MCAS Beaufort, in June 1977, the squadron was at Iwakuni, where it transitioned to the F-4J in August 1975. At Beaufort, the 'Silver Eagles' initially kept flying F-4Js, and with this version of the Phantom made a Mediterranean deployment aboard the USS *Forrestal* (CV-59) in 1981. During the following year, VMFA-115 transitioned to the F-4S. The last of these aircraft were flown on 14 December 1984 and on 3 July 1985 VMFA-115 became the first Marine squadron on the East Coast to receive Hornets.

The 'AA' fincode is indicative of VMFA-115's period of duty with Carrier Air Wing 17 on the USS Forrestal in 1981. At that time, it was flying the F-4J, which gave way to the F-4S in 1982.

VMFA-122 'Crusaders'

During World War II, VMF-122 was one of the most successful fighter squadrons in the Pacific. It returned to MCAS Cherry Point in February 1945, and it was there that the squadron received its first Phantoms – FH-1s, not F-4s – in November 1947 to become the first operational Marine Corps squadron to fly jets. In September 1957, the squadron became the first Marine squadron to be equipped with Crusaders, transitioning to the F-4B at El Toro in July 1965. The squadron made two tours in Vietnam, at Da Nang in 1967-68 and at Chu Lai in 1969-70,

spending the interim at Iwakuni. Redeployed to MCAS Kaneohe Bay, Hawaii, in September 1970, VMFA-122 stood down to transition to the F-14A, inactivating when it was decided that Marine units would not receive Tomcats.

On 4 December 1975, the 'Crusaders' were reactivated at MCAS Beaufort, South Carolina, with F-4Js. In 1978-79, VMFA-122 deployed with its Phantoms for a one-year tour at MCAS Iwakuni, Japan. Back at MCAS Beaufort, VMFA-122 transitioned to the F-4S in 1984 and to the F/A-18A in early 1986.

Reactivation of VMFA-122 in late 1975 coincided with assignment of the F-4J version to the Beaufort-based outfit. In later years, this squadron converted to the F-4S and then to the F/A-18A Hornet.

VMFA-134 'Smokes'

This reserve unit transitioned from the A-4F to the F-4S at MCAS El Toro, California, changing name from 'Hawks' to 'Smokes'.

The 'Smokes' flew Phantoms until transitioning from the F-4S to the F/A-18A during the summer of 1989, to become the first Marine reserve squadron to fly Hornets.

One of the shortest-lived reserve Phantom units was VMFA-134 which flew the F-4S version from El Toro for a few years in the mid-1980s. It later became the first reserve unit to convert to the Hornet.

VMFA-212 'Lancers'

Tracing its origin to March 1942 when VMF-212 was commissioned at Ewa, Hawaii, VMFA-212 flew Phantoms for 20 years beginning in 1968. During World War II, its forebear had flown Wildcats and Corsairs in the Pacific. In the late 1940s the unit became an instrument training squadron (as VMT-2, VMIT-2 and VMIT-10), flying SNJ-6s and T-28Bs before switching back to the fighter mission. With F-8Es, VMF(AW)-212 made a combat cruise to the

Gulf of Tonkin in 1965 aboard the USS *Oriskany* (CVA-34).

VMF(AW)-212 transitioned from the Crusader to the F-4J during the spring of 1968 and was redesignated VMFA-212. In addition to their normal duties, the 'Lancers' trained F-4 crews between 1 January and 30 April 1972, deploying to Da Nang between April and June 1972 in response to the spring offensive. VMFA-212 transitioned to the F-4S in 1981 and retained these at MCAS Kaneohe Bay until 1988, when the 'Lancers' became the first Marines to receive F/A-18Cs.

The highly distinctive colors of this F-4S were carried for a brief period before VMFA-212 surrendered the Phantom for the Hornet as the first of three Kaneohe Bay units to obtain the F/A-18C version.

VMFA-232 'Red Devils'

Division 1, Fighting Plane Squadron 3M, the forebear of the 'Red Devils', was activated on 1 September 1925. After several changes of designations, combat operations during World War II with Dauntlesses, Avengers and Hellcats, the transition to jets in March 1953 and combat operations in Vietnam with Crusaders, VMF(AW)-232 was flying F-8Es when it was selected to transition to F-4Js. The squadron was redesignated VMFA-232 on 8 September 1967 and less than three weeks later received its first Phantoms at MCAS El Toro, California. VMFA-232 deployed to Chu Lai in March 1969 and

operated in Vietnam for five months. It was back in Vietnam in April 1972 and moved to Nam Phong, Thailand, in June of the same year. The 'Red Devils' and their F-4Js left Thailand in September 1973.

During the following years, VMFA-232 made several deployments to Japan, the Philippines and Korea, was based at MCAS Kaneohe Bay, Hawaii, between October 1977 and April 1978, and returned to Hawaii in March 1979, from where it flew F-4Ss for the next nine years. The last VMFA-232's F-4Ss left MCAS Kaneohe Bay on 11 October 1988 and, after participating for six weeks in exercises in CONUS, VMFA-232 transitioned to the F/A-18A.

Converting to the F-4J during the fall of 1967, VMFA-232 deployed to Vietnam during 1969 and was again in combat in 1972-73, when it flew many missions from Vietnam as well as Thailand.

VMFA-235 'Death Angels'

Commissioned in January 1943, Marine Scout Bombing Squadron 235 flew Dauntlesses during four tours in the Pacific. After World War II, the squadron became a reserve unit, but was recalled to active duty in 1951. Equipped with F-8Es, VMF(AW)-235 operated in Vietnam between February 1966 and May 1968. Later in that year, the squadron was transferred to MCAS Kaneohe Bay, Hawaii, where it transitioned to the F-4J and was redesignated VMFA-235 in October 1968.

With Phantoms, the 'Death Angels' made

the usual WestPac deployments until November 1981, when they were sent to MCAS Yuma, Arizona, to transition to the F-4S. Homeported at MCAS Kaneohe Bay, VMFA-235 continued making deployments until early 1989. The last Hawaiian-based F-4S Phantoms left MCAS Kaneohe Bay on 2 February 1989 and went to Nellis AFB, Nevada, where VMFA-235 – the last active-duty fighter squadron to fly Phantoms – took part in a Red Flag exercise before retiring their last F-4S Phantoms to AMARC and converting to F/A-18Cs.

VMFA-235 gained the distinction of being the last regular force USMC Phantom outfit, retiring the F-4S model in 1989. Before the F-4S, it had flown F-4Js like this aircraft between 1968 and 1981.

VMFA-251 'Thunderbolts'

VMO-251, the forebear of VMFA-251, was formed at North Island, California, in December 1951 and flew a tour of duty in the Solomons with photo-reconnaissance Wildcats. After converting to Corsairs, the squadron returned to the Pacific in 1944 and was redesignated VMF-251 in January 1945. After the war ended, the squadron was inactivated, but was soon reconstituted as a reserve fighter squadron in Detroit, Michigan. After being recalled to active duty, VMF-251 flew Furies and Crusaders from MCAS El Toro, California.

Transferred to MCAS Beaufort, South Carolina, the 'Thunderbolts' were redesignated from VMF(AW)-251 to VMFA-251 when transitioning to the F-4B in 1964. The F-4Bs were replaced with F-4Js in June 1971 and 10 years later VMFA-251 became the first Marine squadron to receive the F-4S. Transition to the Hornet took place at MCAS Beaufort in the spring of 1986.

VMFA-251 operated various Phantom models for more than 20 years.

VMFA-312 'Checkerboards'

Marine Fighting Squadron 312 was commissioned in June 1943 and flew Corsairs in combat operations from carriers and shore bases during World War II and the Korean War. Having transitioned to jets in June 1953, the squadron was redesignated VMF(AW)-312 in August 1963 and was flying F-8Es when it was sent to Da Nang AB in December 1965.

Back in CONUS within two months, the 'Checkerboards' transitioned to the F-4B at MCAS Cherry Point, North Carolina, in February 1966 (when it was redesignated VMFA-312) and to the F-4J in February 1973.

They conducted tests with F-4Js in Ferris disruptive camouflage during the spring of 1977, and in 1979 became the first fighter squadron in the Second Marine Aircraft Wing to deploy to WestPac under the Unit Deployment six-month rotation program. Beginning in 1983, VMFA-312 flew the F-4S from MCAS Beaufort, South Carolina, and on deployments. The last F-4S assigned to a squadron at MCAS Beaufort departed on 29 July 1987 for storage at AMARC. The 'Checkerboards' currently fly Hornets from MCAS Beaufort.

The Andrews-based reserve squadron VMFA-321 progressively utilized the F-4B, F-4N and F-4S models, but few were as attractively marked as the F-4N seen here heading skyward from its home base.

VMFA-312's period of residence at Cherry Point between 1971 and 1974 coincided with conversion from the F-4B to the F-4J. This Phantom is an example of the older sub-type which was first flown in 1966.

VMFA-314 'Black Knights'

The first Marines to be equipped with Phantoms, the 'Black Knights' trace their roots to October 1943 when VMF-314 was commissioned at Cherry Point. During the last year of the war, the squadron flew combat operations with Corsairs in Okinawa and Ryukyus. VMF-314 transitioned to Panthers in 1952 and, redesignated VMF(AW)-314 in 1957, was flying F4D-1s when it received its first F4H-1s in June 1962 at MCAS El Toro. On 1 August 1963,

the squadron became VMFA-314.

VMFA-314 made three deployments to Vietnam, at Da Nang (June 1965–April 1966 and August 1966–August 1967) and at Chu Lai (November 1967–August 1970). Having transitioned to F-4Ns in 1975, VMFA-314 continued flying Phantoms until 1982, when it began its transition to become the first Marine Hornet squadron. With F/A-18As, the squadron once again was operational at MCAS El Toro in January 1983.

VMFA-323 'Death Rattlers'

Marine Fighting Squadron 323 was formed on 1 August 1943 and flew Corsairs from carriers and shore bases during the last year of World War II and during the Korean War. Redesignated VMA-323 while in Korea, the squadron entered the jet era after its return to CONUS. The 'Death Rattlers' transitioned from Crusaders to Phantoms in 1963 at MCAS Cherry Point, North Carolina, and VMFA-323 took its F-4Bs to Vietnam in November 1965. After 18 months in combat from Da Nang and Chu Lai, VMFA-323 moved to Iwakuni, Japan, but later returned to Chu Lai. The squadron returned to MCAS El Toro, California, in March 1969.

Having transitioned to the F-4N in 1979, VMFA-323 deployed aboard the USS *Coral Sea* (CV-43) in 1979-80 and was in the Persian Gulf during the US Embassy hostage rescue attempt. On 14 September 1982, VMFA-323 retired its last F-4N and began its transition to the F/A-18A.

The death's head and rattlesnake motif of VMFA-323 adorned the side of many Phantoms over the years.

Caught performing a 'bolter' when engaged on carrier qualification, this VMFA-314 F-4N displays marks and insignia applied in the latter half of the 1970s when Phantoms of the USMC were very colorful.

VMFA-321 'Hell's Angels'

Commissioned on 1 February 1943, VMF-321 flew Corsairs and Hellcats from shore bases and carriers during the last two years of World War II. Decommissioned in February 1946, the unit was activated in the Organized Marine Corps Reserve Fighting Squadron at NAS Anacostia, District of Columbia, in July of that year. As Marine Attack Squadron 321, the 'Hell's Angels' transitioned to jets in 1961 and moved to Andrews AFB, Maryland.

Switching designation from attack to fighter in 1962, the squadron began the transition from F-8Ks to F-4Bs at the end of 1973 and was redesignated VMFA-321. F-4Ns replaced F-4Bs in 1977 and, in turn, were replaced by F-4Ss during the fall of 1984. The 'Hell's Angels' began their transition to the F/A-18A in early 1991 and bid their Phantom 'Pharewell' (F-4S) on 13 July 1991.

VMFA-323 was one of two Marine fighter-attack squadrons assigned to CVW-14 on the USS Coral Sea for a WestPac tour in 1979-80. At that time, it operated F-4Ns, which were retained until September 1982.

VMFA-333 'Shamrocks'

Activated in August 1943 as VMSB-333, the forebears of the 'Shamrocks' flew Dauntlesses and Corsairs in the Pacific, but did not take part in combat operations. Deactivated after the war, the squadron came to life again in August 1952 as VMA-333 and became VMF(AW)-333 in November 1959 when it transitioned to the F8U-2. After nine years on Crusaders, the 'Shamrocks', or 'Trip Treys', made the transition to the F-4J and the squadron was redesignated VMFA-333 at MCAS Beaufort, South Carolina.

Remaining stationed at that South

Carolina air station, VMFA-333 took its F-4Js aboard the USS *America* (CVA-66) and *Nimitz* (CVN-68) for four deployments. During its second deployment aboard *America*, the squadron spent 158 days on the line in the Gulf of Tonkin, claimed the only air combat victory (a MiG-21) by a Marine squadron during the Vietnam War, and lost one F-4J to a SAM and two to North Vietnamese AAA. After transitioning to the F-4J in December 1979, the 'Shamrocks' began participating in the Unit Deployment program and first went to MCAS Iwakuni, Japan, in July 1981. VMFA-333 stood up with F/A-18As in October 1987. Four and a half years later, on 31 March 1992, the long and distinguished history of VMFA-333 ended when the 'Trip Treys' were disestablished at MCAS Beaufort.

VMFA-333 secured a unique niche in USMC history when one of its F-4Js shot down a MiG-21, making it the only Marine Corps unit to score an air-to-air victory during the long and drawn-out Vietnam War.

VMFA-334 'Falcons'

In June 1967, while stationed at MCAS El Toro, California, VMFA-334 became the first Marine squadron to receive F-4Js. With these Phantoms, the 'Falcons' deployed to Da Nang in August 1968 and moved to Chu Lai in January 1969. Withdrawn to MCAS Iwakuni, Japan, in August 1969, VMFA-334 remained in Japan until March 1971. At that time the squadron returned to MCAS El Toro, California, where it was disestablished on 30 December 1971.

Noteworthy by virtue of being the first Marine squadron to receive the F-4J version, VMFA-334 existed for little more than four years, forming at El Toro in June 1967 as well as disestablishing there.

VMFA-351

This reserve squadron, which took over the numerical designation of VMF-351 and flew from escort carriers during the closing stages of World War II, had a brief existence. It flew F-4Ns from NAF Atlanta, Georgia, in 1977-78.

Another short-lived Marine reserve Phantom unit was VMFA-351. Formed at Atlanta, Georgia, in 1977, the squadron barely had time to receive a full complement of F-4Ns before it was disestablished during the course of 1978.

VMFA-451 'Warlords'

Activated in February 1944, VMF-451 went on to claim 30 Japanese aircraft while operating from the USS *Hornet* (CV-12). After World War II ended, the squadron was inactivated briefly before standing up as a reserve unit at NAS Willow Grove, Pennsylvania. Called to active duty during the Korean War, the squadron never returned to reserve status. Assigned Crusaders during the summer of 1961, the 'Warlords' made the first trans-Pacific flight with single-seat fighters when they deployed to Atsugi, Japan, in January 1962. Six years later, the squadron was redesignated VMFA-451 and became the first unit at MCAS Beaufort, South Carolina, to transition to the F-4J. The transition to the F-4S took place in June 1978, when the unit became the first in either the Navy or the Marine Corps to receive this version of the Phantom, and the 'Warlords' flew Phantoms until transitioning to Hornets in the spring of 1988.

Assigned to Carrier Air Wing 17 at the time of the bicentennial, the F-4Js of VMFA-451 were aboard USS Forrestal for a short cruise as part of the celebrations for the USA's 200th anniversary.

VMFA-513 'Flying Nightmares'

Formed in 1944, VMF-513 arrived in Saipan during the last month of World War II. After a checkered history, including service in Korea during which it scored 12 night kills, the 'Flying Nightmares' became the third Marine Corps to transition to the F-4B in January 1963. They deployed from El Toro to Atsugi in November 1964. Seven months later, the squadron relieved VMFA-531 in Da Nang. VMFA-513 left Vietnam in October 1965 and, for the next five years, flew F-4Bs from MCAS Cherry Point. In June 1970, the squadron was reduced to a cadre pending transition to the AV-8A.

Stationed at El Toro, VMFA-513 was the third USMC squadron to obtain the Phantom, accepting the F-4B in January 1963 and continuing to fly this model until reduced to cadre status in June 1970.

VMFA-531 'Gray Ghosts'

Activated on 16 November 1942 as the first Marine night-fighter squadron, VMF(N)-451 flew combat operations with specially-modified PV-1s during World War II and with F3D-2s during the 1950s. Redesignated VMF(AW)-531, the unit flew F4D-1s until becoming the first Marine squadron on the East Coast to transition to the Phantom, with training on F4H-1s starting during the summer of 1962. On 1 February 1963, the squadron deployed from MCAS Cherry Point, North Carolina, to NAS Key West, Florida, where it replaced VF-41 on NORAD air defense duty facing Cuba. Its designation was changed to VMFA-531 in August 1963.

In October 1963, VMFA-531 flew its F-4Bs to Atsugi, and on 10 April 1965 it left this Japanese base bound for Da Nang AB, where it became the first Marine F-4 unit in Vietnam. The 'Gray Ghosts' left the war zone on 15 June 1965 and returned to MCAS Cherry Point to train combat crews for duty in Vietnam. Less than three years later, they moved to MCAS El Toro, California.

While equipped with F-4Bs, VMFA-531 deployed to the Mediterranean aboard the USS *Forrestal* (CV-59) in 1972-73. After transitioning to the F-4N during the summer of 1975, VMFA-531 again went to sea when it deployed to WestPac, the Indian Ocean and the Persian Gulf aboard the USS *Coral Sea* (CV-43) in 1979-80. Transition training to the F/A-18A commenced in January 1983, and VMFA-531 received its first Hornets at MCAS El Toro on 29 May. The 'Gray Ghosts' of VMFA-531 were disestablished at MCAS El Toro on 31 March 1992.

*Pictured aboard USS **C**oral **S**ea when cruising in WestPac in 1979-80, an F-4N of VMFA-531 is made ready for launch at the start of a routine training mission. At the time, the squadron formed part of CVW-14.*

VMFA-542 'Bengals'

Heir of VMF(N)-542, a night-fighter squadron organized in August 1944 and which flew F6F-5Ns during the closing stages of the war in the Pacific, and F7F-3Ns in Korea, VMFA-542 transitioned to the F-4B at MCAS El Toro in the fall of 1963.

In April 1965, the 'Bengals' were forward deployed to Japan and three months later moved to Da Nang for combat operations in Vietnam. Alternating between their Japanese and Vietnamese bases, the 'Bengals' played a significant part in Marine operations during the Southeast Asia War. In 1969, they were returned to CONUS and were disestablished at El Toro, on 30 June 1970.

VMFA-542's seven-year career as a Phantom-equipped unit saw it face the rigors of combat in Vietnam between 1965 and 1969. Throughout this period, it only ever flew the initial F-4B version.

VMFAT-101 'Sharpshooters'

Marine Fighter Attack Training Squadron 101 was formed at MCAS El Toro, California, on 1 January 1969 and was assigned the primary mission of providing combat-ready pilots and RIOs for deployments with Fleet Marine Force F-4 squadrons. Eighteen months after taking on this mission, the 'Sharpshooters' were relocated to MCAS Yuma, Arizona.

When in June 1984 the Navy disestablished VF-171, its last F-4 RAG squadron, VMFAT-101 took over the responsibility for training the Navy F-4 crews. Initially equipped with F-4Js, VMFAT-101 later added F-4Ns, and was flying F-4Ss when it returned to MCAS El Toro on 1 October 1987 to transition to the Hornet.

Throughout the Phantom era, most USMC pilot and RIO training needs were satisfied by VMFAT-101 which was stationed at Yuma. In addition to F-4Ns like this, the F-4B, F-4J and F-4S versions were flown.

VMFAT-201

Based at MCAS Beaufort, South Carolina, this training squadron flew F-4Bs in 1967-69 before being disestablished.

East Coast training was entrusted to VMFAT-201 for a few years, with the F-4J version being used from Cherry Point in the early 1970s.

VMFP-3 'Eyes of the Corps'
VMFP-3 'Rhinos'

Marine Tactical Reconnaissance Squadron Three was established on 1 July 1975 from the photo-reconnaissance assets of VMCJ-1, VMCJ-2 and VMCJ-3. The 'Eye of the Corps'

were divided into a 13-aircraft main unit at MCAS El Toro, California, and three four-aircraft detachments operating in WestPac, Hawaii and CONUS. The squadron also sent detachments for operations aboard the USS *Midway* (CV-41) between 1975 and 1980.

Flying RF-4Bs throughout their existence, the 'Eyes of the Corps' were renamed the 'Rhinos' in 1987. VMFP-3 was deactivated on 30 September 1990, bringing to a close 25 years of RF-4B operations with the Marine Corps.

Consolidation of reconnaissance assets led to the creation of the specialist squadron VMFP-3 in July 1975. This duly inherited an RF-4B fleet from VMCJ-1, -2 and -3.

AUSTRALIA
Royal Australian Air Force

A reluctant and short-term Phantom operator, the Royal Australian Air Force (RAAF) leased 24 USAF F-4Es to maintain an effective front-line attack force when its acquisition of 24 General Dynamics F-111Cs went seriously awry. Due to have entered service from late 1967, the first F-111 was accepted a year later, but serious structural problems being experienced resulted in a long-term postponement of deliveries. Consequently, in May 1970 it was announced that arrivals in Australia could not be expected until 1974. The swing-wing bombers had been ordered to replace aging BAC Canberras of Nos 1 and 6 Squadrons, based at Amberley, Queensland, as part of No. 82 Wing. Although then still flying bombing missions over Vietnam, the radarless Canberra was a less than credible deterrent more than 20 years after its maiden flight, so on 22 June 1970 the Australian government signed an agreement to obtain Phantoms.

Codenamed Peace Reef, the program involved factory-fresh aircraft from USAF FY1969 contracts, which were to be leased at a cost of $34 million for the first two years, then, if required, $12 million per annum thereafter. The F-4E was assigned the out-of-sequence serial prefix A69 (previously used for the first 10 of a canceled order for 150 Curtiss A-25A Shrikes) to match the FY designator, but this was not painted on the aircraft, which retained their US serials. Flying via Hawaii and Guam, with their newly-trained Australian crews, the first five aircraft arrived at Amberley on 15 September 1970, led by 90304. Three more similarly-sized batches were accepted on 19 September, 26 September and 3 October, some being assigned to No. 2 OCU for crew training. The final machine, 97234, was damaged in a crash-landing at Amberley during its delivery flight on 10 October, and entered service after repair. The US trained 120 RAAF air- and groundcrews on the F-4 and stationed 38 USAF maintenance staff at Amberley to supervise acceptance of the aircraft and train remaining technicians. Command of No. 82 (Bomber) Wing during the Phantom era was in the hands of Group Captain V. J. Hill.

The aircraft supplied were 69-0304 to -0307, all F-4E-43-MCs; and 69-7201 to -7217, -7219, -7220 and -7234, all F-4E-44-MCs. Apart from kangaroo roundels (and no fin flashes) the only other markings were the last one or two digits of the serial applied to

the fin as an identification code, augmenting the black serial number. One was lost in service when 97203 crashed off Evans' Head on 16 June 1971 during night bombing practice, and under the terms of the lease agreement, Australia paid £2.7 million compensation to the USAF for the destroyed machine. It was with considerable reluctance that the RAAF gave up its Phantoms after the Australian government agreed in December 1971 that work on the F-111 could recommence.

In the fall of 1972, the US unsuccessfully offered to sell the 23 remaining F-4s for $54 million in order to augment the Mirage III force. This followed the abandonment of an earlier fallback plan under which the RAAF would have canceled the F-111 in favor of 48 Phantoms, including eight RF-4Es. This would have required the RAAF to buy eight Boeing KC-135 tankers and so increase the cost of the Phantom force to nearly twice that then estimated for the F-111. Redeliveries from Brisbane to Hill AFB, Utah, began with six aircraft on 25 October 1972 and was followed by a further batch of five on 8 November. On 1 June 1973, the first six F-111s arrived at Amberley, and on 21 June the last ex-RAAF Phantom arrived in the US. Interestingly, of the 23 survivors, 21 were converted to F-4G Wild Weasels, mostly for the 35th TFW.

Shortest-term Phantom operator was Australia, which acquired 24 as General Dynamics F-111C surrogates in 1970 and only returned them to the USAF with great reluctance two years later.

EGYPT
Al Quwwat al Jawwiya il Misriya

The historic Camp David peace agreement between Egypt and Israel resulted, during July 1979, in the abrupt cancelation of aid to Egypt by its oil-rich Arab neighbors in retaliation for what they viewed as a sellout. One victim was a batch of 50 Northrop F-5Es, which Saudi Arabia had ordered on behalf of the Egyptian Air Force (EAF). In its place, Washington offered a package of 35 ex-USAF F-4Es, 350 AIM-9 Sidewinder AAMs, 70 AIM-7 Sparrow radar-homing AAMs and 500 AGM-65A Maverick TV-guided ASMs for a total of £594 million. (At a later stage, Westinghouse AN/ALQ-119 jamming pods were obtained to enhance combat survivability.) Under the codename Peace Pharaoh, deliveries began rapidly, and the first 18 arrived in Egypt during September 1979, as the EAF's initial acquisition of US fighters. The Phantoms – early production machines – were taken from the 31st TFW at Homestead AFB, Florida, and included 67-9341, which had shot down a MiG-21 while serving with the 432nd TRW in Vietnam during 1972.

Assimilation of the F-4 into EAF service was hasty, as 16 former MiG-21 pilots were given a hurried conversion course at George AFB, California, and maintenance personnel had to make do with only OJT (on-the-job training). The aircraft were assigned to the 222nd TFB (Wing), which fielded the 76th and 88th Squadrons at Cairo West AB. As Exercise Proud Phantom, a test and evaluation group of 12 USAF Phantoms and their crews, plus 560 ground staff from the 347th TFW at Moody AFB, Georgia, flew to Cairo West in July 1980 and spent 90 days in Egypt demonstrating the aircraft's capabilities and providing some of the OJT. Immediately prior to that, the EAF was finding it difficult to raise nine serviceable Phantoms at any one time and squadrons could not achieve their weekly task of generating 50 sorties. The US detachment improved matters, although only slightly, and serviceability was 45-50 per

Orange fin stripes were applied to Egyptian Phantoms (and Mirage III/5s) to differentiate them from their Israeli counterparts. F-4Es wear both low-level and medium-altitude (gray) color schemes.

cent by spring 1982, following Egypt's assumption of all F-4 maintenance and support by late 1981. Still dissatisfied, Egypt considered selling the aircraft to Turkey for £300 million in order to fund 16 more of the GD F-16 Fighting Falcons it then had on order, but in May of the same year an initial two aircraft (with USAF insignia reapplied) were flown back to the US for extensive overhaul to improve their reliability. The effectiveness of the action may be judged from the fact that during its return to Egypt later in 1982, one of the F-4Es spent a month on the ground in England. By early 1983 the Turkish sale was back 'on' and US officials were admitting that the aircraft was 'totally beyond the capability of the EAF'. They added that the Phantom was the most complex fighter built by the US and a 'logistics nightmare'.

The aircraft were given a last chance when a US Technical Assistance Field Team arrived at Cairo West in mid-1983 and succeeded in boosting serviceability to 80 percent. Egypt then decided to keep them, helped in a negative way by Turkey, which had twice failed to meet deadlines for producing a deposit. Nevertheless, sales were discussed with Turkey early in 1985, by which time 33 aircraft remained, following a second loss on 8 May 1984 when two crew and 19 inhabitants of Ehzet beni Salama village were killed. The shadow of disposal had entirely lifted by early 1988 when Egypt considered buying a further seven ex-USAF Phantoms to increase its fleet to 40 and modifying the fleet with AN/APG-65 radars.

It is worth noting that two senior EAF F-4 pilots, Lieutenant Colonel Sakr Reda (Chief of Staff, 222nd TFB) and Lieutenant Colonel Ahmed Atef (222nd's Deputy Commander), reported scoring aerial victories against Israeli F-4Es in the October War (though Israel has, predictably, claimed that no Phantoms were lost in air-to-air action). Lieutenant Colonel Atef was flying his MiG-21F-13 day fighter when he engaged an Israeli F-4E. This marked the first time a former enemy of the F-4 claimed to have shot down an F-4 in combat and had then gone on to fly the same type of aircraft later.

Egyptian air force F-4Es have flown in both light gray and desert camouflage schemes and are issued with local serial numbers 7801-7835. At least three have crashed (the third in November 1989) and these have been replaced by 67-0328, -00332 and -00366. Those supplied were:

Egypt's own serial numbers are applied to F-4E noses in Persian characters, but the USAF tail number is retained, as on 702788/EAF 7835. EAF Phantoms have suffered from chronic unserviceability.

66-0337, 66-0340 (7814), 66-0341, 66-0343, 66-0349, 66-0353, 66-0358, 66-0360 (7802), 66-0362, 66-0364 (7801), 66-0366 (7813), 66-0375 (7804) 67-0211, 67-0212 (7825), 67-0213, 67-0220 (7831), 67-0231, 67-0236, 67-0238 (7811), 67-0239, 67-0242, 67-0264 (7809), 67-0278 (7835), 67-0289 (7817) 67-0305 (7820), 67-0307 (7816), 67-0309, 67-0313 (7815), 67-0317 (7806), 67-0322 (7812), 67-0328, 67-0332 (7824), 67-0341 (7832), 67-0355, 67-0366, 67-0371, 67-0373, 67-0388

GERMANY
Luftwaffe

An F-4F of JBG 35, with high-conspicuity Dayglo orange panels applied over the basic early gray and green camouflage scheme.

West Germany, as it then was, became a major Phantom operator partly in order to bridge the gap between obsolescence of the Lockheed F-104G Starfighter and the availability of Panavia Tornado interdictors. The initial two wings (Geschwader) to be equipped were the Lockheed RF-104G Starfighter reconnaissance units, which received RF-4E Phantoms from 1971 onwards. It was intended to upgrade to sensor systems more advanced than the visual-spectrum cameras carried by the RF-104, so after consideration of an upgraded, two-seat Starfighter and SEPECAT Jaguars, it was announced on 13 May 1968 that Germany would place a DM2,052-million contract for 88 RF-4Es – although the cost rose to DM2,134 million before the program was completed. Expecting increased serviceability and better operational effectiveness from the Phantom, the Luftwaffe cut wing strengths from 52 F-104s to 42 RF-4s – but the latter was more complex to maintain and needed a backseater (the Kampfbeobachter – KBO, literally 'combat observer'), so the 1,650 personnel on the staff of a Starfighter Geschwader had to be increased to 1,929 when F-4s arrived.

Early in 1970, well before delivery was due, six KBO instructors from Waffenschule 50 (WS 50, 50th Weapons Training Wing) attended a training course at St Louis. The first of 108 KBOs began training with WS 50 in April, and 108 pilots started five-week Phantom conversion courses with the USAF at George AFB, California, in October. At the same time, nine Luftwaffe instructor crews of two men each were at the 363rd TRW, Shaw AFB, South Carolina, learning reconnaissance techniques in eight-/nine-month courses between January 1970 and May 1971. Luftwaffe RF-4s had been assigned the USAF serials 69-7448 to -7535 and would be numbered 3501-3588 in service. The first three of these were handed over at St Louis on 22 October 1970 to begin training. Aircraft 3501 was the 3,861st Phantom built and 3588 emerged in 1971 as the 4,199th. There were minor differences between production blocks because, although the first eight were RF-4E-43-MCs, 3509-3515 were built as RF-4E-44-MCs, 3516-3534 as -45-MCs, 3535-3563 as -46-MCs and the rest as -47-MCs. All were built under McDonnell works order JO787.

Reconnaissance equipment

In all important aspects the aircraft were similar: KS-87B and KS-56D cameras in the nose; an AN/AAS-18A infrared linescan; attachment points for a Goodyear SLAR; Westinghouse QRC-335-4 ECM pods; and (fitted on arrival in Germany by technical support unit Schleuse RF-4E) Martin-Baker GH-7A ejection seats. In service only a few aircraft normally carried SLAR, its main role was probably gathering intelligence from flights along the East German border and the Baltic coast. Named 'Spirit of St Louis' after Charles Lindbergh's trans-Atlantic Ryan (New York-Paris), 3501 and three other RF-4Es left St Louis on 16 January 1971, arriving on German soil at Ramstein on 19th, and Bremgarten on 20th. Here, they were received by Inspekteur Gunther Rall on behalf of Aufklärungsgeschwader 51 (AKG 51 – Reconnaissance Wing 51). Others followed at the rate of about eight per month, crossing the Atlantic in USAF markings and being painted in Luftwaffe insignia on arrival. The assignment of aircraft was 42 each to AKG 51 and AKG 52, plus two for ground instruction at Technischeschule 1, Kaufbeuren, and two for trials with Erprobungsstelle 61 at Manching. Based at Leck, AKG 52 received its first RF-4E on 17 September 1971, although as AKG 51 was responsible for training, most aircraft initially operated from Bremgarten.

RF-4Es flew without armament, but it was decided in 1978 to give them the ability to mount ground attack missions if, in a wartime situation, that should prove to be more important than recce. The work began in November 1979 and was undertaken by MBB (at Ottobrunn and Manching), the German firm chosen in 1968 to be a 'foster parent' for Luftwaffe Phantoms. The RF-4Es were fitted with pylons beneath the wings for up to 5,000 lb (2270 kg) of weapons (such as six Hunting BL755 cluster bombs) or fuel (including two 370-US gal tanks), plus a weapon-aiming sight for the pilot and weapons selection switches. At the same time, the opportunity was taken to improve the aircraft's cameras and linescan, and add Tracor AN/ALE-40 chaff dispensers to decoy anti-aircraft missiles. The color scheme changed from standard NATO gray and green, with light gray undersides, to a wraparound two-tone green, plus gray. A government decision in 1988 resulted in the secondary attack tasking being abandoned.

It had been intended that RF-4Es should remain in service after the arrival of Tornado

*Inflight refueling from **USAF KC-135s** is not an operational requirement for Luftwaffe Phantoms, but is used for ferrying to and from training detachments at Goose Bay, Canada, for low-level flying.*

ECRs and they were thus expected to receive a further update involving modernized data recording equipment and undisclosed types of electronic warfare apparatus and passive sensors. However, the Conventional Forces in Europe arms limitation agreement, unification of the two Germanies and dissolution of the Warsaw Pact resulted in a reappraisal of requirements and the decision to disband both the RF-4E wings by 1994. Turkey was promised 45 RF-4Es from AKG 51, of which 15 were for breaking down as spares sources, but a political dispute between Ankara and Berlin resulted in the cancelation of the agreement in March 1992, and reinstatement in October 1992. Losses up to early 1992 totaled 15.

Phantom requirements

By 1970, it had become apparent that the MRCA (Panavia Tornado) could not be developed as an interceptor – as well as a strike/attack aircraft – in time to replace the Starfighter by the target date of 1975. Consequently, the Luftwaffe cut its MRCA requirement from 800 to 420 and began to look at alternatives including the Lockheed CL-1200 Lancer (an advanced Starfighter), Dassault Mirage F1, Northrop P-530 (later to become the F-18 Hornet) and both the single-seat F-4E(F) and standard two-place Phantom.

The purchase of 175 F-4F Phantoms was approved by the Bundestag (parliament) in August 1971 for DM3,900 million. In fact, the F-4F was specially-designed to German requirements, and is operated by no other air force. Special features include a reduced fuel capacity, no provision for AIM-7 Sparrow radar-guided missiles beneath the fuselage, no leading-edge slats in the stabilator and German-built versions of the General Electric J79-GE-17A engine. MTU was contracted to build 448 engines for the F-4F, while MBB, as with the RF-4E, received offset work from McDonnell Douglas. USAF serials 72-1111 to -1285 and German serials 3701-3875 were assigned, and the McDonnell line numbers ranged between 4330 and 4793 under company order number JO793. Production blocks were 3701-3714 F-4F-51-MC, then -52-MC up to 3727, 53-MC to 3740, -54-MC to 3754, -55-MC to 3772, -56-MC to 3796, -57-MC to 3820, -58-MC to 3864 and -59-MC to 3875.

The first F-4F flew on 18 March 1973 (but was not officially rolled out until 24 May!), while crew training began in the US in May 1973. About 12 aircraft were transferred to the 35th TFW at George AFB, California, where they flew in USAF serials and markings (e.g. 21116 'GA'). The first F-4F to arrive in Germany was 3704, which went to Kaufbeuren on 5 September 1973 for technical familiarization by Technischeschule 1.

On 1 January 1974, Jagdgeschwader (JG – Interceptor Wing) 71 'Richthofen' officially began training at George AFB, California, and its first aircraft arrived at Wittmundhafen on 7 March 1974 – although the unit did not officially transfer back to the Bundesrepublik until 1 April. At Neuburg, JG 74 'Mölders' flew its last Starfighter sortie on 30 June 1974 before converting, and when it was declared combat-ready in May 1976, re-equipment of the Luftwaffe's interceptor arm was at an end. In the attack role, Jagdbombergeschwader (JBG – Fighter-Bomber Wing) 36 at Rheine-Hopsten received its first F-4F in April 1975, and JBG 35 formed at Pferdsfeld from LKG 42 on 1 April 1975, and was also to receive Phantoms.

The final aircraft, 3875 'Spirit of Cooperation', was delivered to JBG 35 in April 1976, although eight early F-4Fs remained at George AFB, California. In order that they could be issued to combat units, Germany bought 10 standard F-4Es as replacements, with the additional advantage that they were more compatible with the based USAF F-4s. Serialed 75-00628 to -00637, these were delivered to the USAF in 1977 (its last Phantoms) and eight remain in service (50634 and 50637 collided and crashed on 21 November 1983). When the 35th Fighter Wing was disestablished in 1992, the German training aircraft passed to the Holloman-based 9th FS, 49th FW, which operates alongside F-117s at the New Mexico base. Seven of the F-4Fs flew to Germany by 1978, but 21118 was retained by USAF Systems Command for development work, designated NTF-4F, until it became 3708 with JG 71 in 1982.

German updates

Although they lacked a medium-range missile capability when delivered (having only early AIM-9 Sidewinders), the F-4Fs attached to both JG and JBG units were enhanced by the 'Peace Rhine' program of updates. Following trials of two prototypes, the first 'production' updated aircraft was redelivered by MBB to JG 74 in November 1980. This had received a digital weapons computer and the ability to operate with all the missiles and laser-guided bombs carried by USAF F-4Es, including AIM-9L Sidewinders and the Hughes AGM-65 Maverick. At the same time, ECM, all-weather systems and cockpit information displays were improved. By mid-1983, JBG 36, JG 71 and JBG 35 (in that order) had received the improved Phantom, so that the Jagdgeschwader could operate, if necessary, in the JaBo (Jagdbomber, fighter-bomber) role, and *vice versa*. As noted in reference to the RF-4E, this dual-tasking with a 40 percent air defense training commitment was abandoned on 1 July 1988.

Following cancelation of the Dornier Viper missile, AIM-9L Sidewinders assembled by Bodenseewerk have given the interceptor Phantoms an urgently-needed boost in capability, as previous armament consisted of only the internal M61A-1 Vulcan 20-mm cannon and four 'tail-chase' AIM-9Bs under the wings.

With unification of Germany on 3 October 1990, the Luftwaffe planned to redistribute assets to the eastern part of the country to replace withdrawn Soviet equipment. As an immediate step, six F-4Fs from Hopsten and Pferdsfeld were detached to Fassberg (still in 'old' West Germany) pending transfer of wings from both bases to Laage and Falkenberg. These changes include the disappearance of JBG 35 and JBG 36 and the creation of JG 72, JG 73 (alongside MiG-29s) and (later) JG 75, as explained below, the retasking from attack to interception being associated with an upgrade program that was started before unification.

Although the Peace Rhine program gave the Luftwaffe's F-4Fs additional capabilities which were highly valued by its crews, it was clear even before completion that this would be insufficient to keep the aircraft effective until the planned retirement date in 2005. After investigating the needs of a Phantom update, MBB was given a Bundeswehr (ministry of defence) contract in June 1986 to produce three prototypes of the Phantom KWS (Kampfwertsteigerung) – also known in English as ICE.

This is a two-part program, the first stage of which involved all the F-4Fs being modified from the first quarter of 1989 onwards. The most important change is the installation of a MIL STD 1553B digital databus for efficient communication between the aircraft's avionics and weapon systems. Other features include a Honeywell H-423 laser inertial gyroscope, a Litton AN/ALR-68(V)-2 radar-warning receiver and a Marconi CPU-143A digital air data computer, which act together to improve navigation, target-ranging and the prediction of weapon release points. With these new systems installed, 40 ground attack-tasked Phantoms will operate until retirement.

However, 107 intercept-tasked F-4Fs began a second phase of updating in the first quarter of 1991, greatly improving their interception capability. The original Westinghouse AN/APQ-120 radar is being replaced with the all-weather, lookdown Hughes AN/APG-65 built by TST (which is also making a new radar-control console), and there are also new Hughes information displays in the cockpit, a Litef digital fire-control computer, new IFF equipment and Frazer-Nash ejectors under the fuselage for four additional missiles (as well as the present AIM-9L Sidewinders under the wings): the advanced 'fire-and-forget' Hughes AIM-120 AMRAAM (Advanced Medium-Range Air-to-Air Missile). Three aircraft were upgraded to the new interceptor standard by MBB at Manching and used for live-firing trials of the AMRAAM against target drones at Point Mugu, in the USA, from September 1991. The remaining conversions will be undertaken by the Luftwaffe's Phantom overhaul unit, Luftwaffenwerft 62 (LwW 62) at Jever. MBB and LwW 62 are responsible for 600-hour minor overhauls and 1,200-hour

(or 54-month, whichever the sooner) major overhauls.

Future Phantom pilots continue to be trained on USAF and Luftwaffe F-4s at the 9th FS/49th FW which is otherwise known as 1 DtLwAusbildungsstaffel USA (No. 1 German Air Force Training Squadron). Following qualification on the Cessna T-37 and Northrop T-38 at US flying schools, pilots undergo a 28-week Phantom course which includes 36 hours in a simulator and 66 hours airborne. They then transfer to JG 72 at Hopsten, where the Zentrale Ausbildungsstaffel provides 'Europeanization' training of 10 simulator and 21 flying hours before pilots can join an operational geschwader. Kampfbeobachters receive navigation training on Boeing T-43s (737s) by the 455th FTS/323rd FT Wing at Mather AFB, California (to transfer to Randolph AFB, Texas). At Hopsten they undertake 14 simulator and 18 flying hours in nine weeks before being posted to an operational unit.

Combat training regularly takes place at Goose Bay, Canada, where there are no restrictions on low-level flying, as in Europe. Six aircraft from JBG 36 flew out to Goose on 21 July 1980 and returned in September after an assessment of the facilities, and now an average of 11 F-4Fs, nine RF-4Es, nine Alpha Jets and nine Tornados fly a combined total of some 3,200 sorties per year from the Canadian airfield. Beja, in Portugal, is used for similar training by RF-4Es.

Combat units in the western part of Germany are assigned to one of four divisions, which are in turn committed to either the 2nd or 4th Allied Tactical Air Forces of NATO's Allied Air Forces Central Europe. They are 1 Luftwaffendivision at Messstetten for 4th ATAF fighter-bombers, 2 Luftwaffendivision at Birkenfeld for 4th ATAF interceptors; 3 Luftwaffendivision at Kalkar for 2nd ATAF fighter-bombers and 4 Luftwaffendivision at Aurich for 2nd ATAF interceptors. Wings are divided into a Technical Group, an Air Base Group and a Flying Group of two squadrons (Staffeln). The last-mentioned are assigned NATO-style squadron numbers such as 351 and 352 within JBG 35, although the traditional manner of reference would be 1./JaBo 35 and 2./JaBo 35. Squadron badges are worn as shoulder patches and are not applied to the aircraft due to the pooled maintenance system. There are considerable variations in style and title of squadron insignia; for example, within JG 74 the components refer to themselves as '1/JG 74' and '742 FIS 'Zapata''.

Jagdbombergeschwader 35

The 35th Fighter-Bomber Wing began its Phantom era on 1 April 1975 when the former G91R operator, Leichtenkampfgeschwader 42, was redesignated at Pferdsfeld. Its last G91 departed on 11 April and the wing began the task of becoming the last German unit to convert to Phantoms. Personnel were converted at George AFB, California, and the unit began receiving its new aircraft in October 1975. Work up to operational status was accomplished most satisfactorily, and the wing won the Prince Heinrich's Prize for 1977 as the best unit in 1 Luftwaffendivision

– the attack group in southern Germany. The wing retained the badge of a stylized bird on a Greek cross, formerly used by LKG 42, and flew its 20,000th Phantom hour on 20 April 1978. Plans were canceled to redesignate the wing as JG 73 on 1 January 1991, and it has retained its attack tasking with the only German F-4Fs not earmarked to receive a radar update. In 1994, it is due to transfer to Falkenberg in former East Germany, where it will become JG 73 with one squadron of MiG-29s and one of F-4Fs.

JBG 35 is the last attack-tasked Phantom wing and its aircraft will not be updated with new radar.

Jagdbombergeschwader 36

Established on 13 March 1961, JBG 36 moved to Rheine-Hopsten on 31 August that year, first with Republic F-84F Thunderstreaks, and then with Lockheed F-104G Starfighters. Adopting the badge of a rampant, white horse it formed part of 3 Luftwaffendivision, which provides attack forces in northern Germany. F-4 deliveries began in April 1975, although it was not until mid-1976 that conversion was complete. A nonstandard feature of the wing was a third squadron, 3 Staffel, otherwise known as the

Zentrale Ausbildungsstaffel (Central Training Squadron), which is responsible for 'Europeanization' of pilots who are newly-qualified on the Phantom in the usually clear and uncluttered skies of the USA. With an allocation of 16 aircraft, the unit formed in mid-1981 and began its first course in April 1982. JBG 36 was redesignated JG 72 on 1 November 1990.

JBG 36 painted one F-4F in this eye-catching, if gaudy, color scheme to celebrate a squadron anniversary.

Aufklärungsgeschwader 51 'Immelmann'

The premier reconnaissance wing formed on 7 July 1959 with Republic RF-84F Thunderflashes and converted to Lockheed RF-104G Starfighters before taking up residence at Bremgarten in March 1969, its aircraft assigned to 1 Luftwaffendivision and

marked with the badge of an owl. Delivery of RF-4Es began on 20 January 1971 and the wing had flown 10,000 hours in them by September 1972, by which time it had only just disposed of its last F-104. On 19 April 1977, it celebrated 50,000 hours without a major accident. During 1993, AKG 51 will relinquish Phantoms and become a Tornado reconnaissance wing at Schleswig-Jagel when it takes over aircraft relinquished by the German navy.

RF-4Es were the first Phantoms in Luftwaffe service and will be replaced by reconnaissance-configured Panavia Tornados before the mid-1990s. Some RF-4Es are being transferred to Turkey for further NATO service.

Aufklärungsgeschwader 52

AG 52 formed on 12 December 1959 and flew RF-84Fs and RF-104Gs at Erding and Eggebeck before moving to Leck in October 1964. It was here that the first RF-4E arrived on 17 September 1971, with the Starfighter lingering on until May 1972. The first 10,000 RF-4 hours had been flown by March 1972. The unit badge is a panther, which is

sufficient to qualify it to attend NATO 'Tiger Meets'. In 1991, one of the wing's aircraft, 3513, became the first Luftwaffe jet combat aircraft to achieve 5,000 flying hours. Subordinate to 3 Luftwaffendivision, the wing will disband in 1993-94.

The current RF-4E camouflage of black and two-tone green was applied retrospectively.

Jagdgeschwader 71 'Richthofen'

Commissioned with North American F-86E Sabres on 6 June 1959, West Germany's first interceptor wing moved to Wittmundhafen in April 1963 to begin conversion to F-104G Starfighters. It is assigned to 4 Luftwaffendivision and the unit badge is a letter 'R' within a shield. Initially untitled, the wing adopted the name of one of Germany's most famous fighter pilots on 21 April 1961. The first pair of F-4Es arrived at Wittmundhafen on 7 March 1974,

and with conversion complete, the wing was declared combat-ready on 1 July 1975, passing its 50,000th Phantom flying hour in March 1980. In common with the fighter-bomber wings, JG 71 became dual-role in the early 1980s, but reverted to interception only on 1 July 1988.

Wearing the Norm 81 gray color scheme, an F-4F of JG 71 formates on an RF-4E. Like the other air defense wing, JG 71 had a secondary attack task until 1988.

Jagdgeschwader 72 'Westfalen'

An operator of Sabres and G91Rs between 1959 and 1964, JG 72 was re-established on 1 November 1990 when JBG 36 at Rheine-Hopsten was redesignated to reflect a change in operational tasking from attack to air defense. The wing retains the rampant, white horse badge of its predecessor, but is responsible to 4 Luftwaffendivision. It has also adopted a semi-official name to reflect

its location in the district of Westfalia, and 'Europeanization' training commitments are also maintained. In 1993-94, JG 72 will transfer to Laage, a former East German Su-22 'Fitter' base, reportedly changing its title once more to JG 75 and becoming part of 5 Luftwaffendivision.

Recently upgraded in the ICE program (note gray radome) is an F-4F of newly-formed JG 72. Note retention of the JBG 36 badge.

Jagdgeschwader 73

Plans to distribute air defense aircraft more evenly throughout unified Germany include establishment of JG 73 at Falkenberg in 1994. The wing will have one squadron of

MiG-29 'Fulcrums' and one of F-4F Phantoms provided by the disbandment of JBG 35, and it will be subordinate to 5 Luftwaffendivision.

Jagdgeschwader 74 'Mölders'

Commissioned at Neuburg on 5 May 1961 with F-86K Sabres, JG 74 then converted to Starfighters, the last mission with which was flown on 30 June 1974. Retraining on F-4Fs began immediately, and the wing was declared mission-ready in late May 1976. The wing's badge depicts an aircraft above a runway, and the name of fighter pilot Werner Mölders was awarded on 23

November 1973. From 1975 onwards, JG 74 undertook trials of several medium-altitude camouflage schemes, culminating in Graue Maus 2 (Grey Mouse 2) during 1980. This was adopted for general use under the less descriptive title of Norm 81.

High-viz tail markings compromise the medium-altitude camouflage of a Möldersgeschwader F-4F. Wing insignia is on the air intake.

Wehrtechnische Dienststelle fur Luftfahrtzeuge 61

The military technical headquarters for aircraft was originally known as Erprobungsstelle 61 and is based at Manching, although a move to Templin in

eastern Germany is planned by 1996. Subordinate to the government armaments agency, the Bundesamt fur Wehrtechnik und Beschaffung, it operates a mixed fleet of aircraft on development work. RF-4Es and F-4Fs are included, the latter currently being engaged in the KWS (ICE) avionics and armament upgrade program.

GREECE
Elliniki Polemiki Aeroporia

Taken out of the NATO command structure in January 1985, Greek-armed forces include four squadrons of Phantoms from new production and second-hand acquisition. An initial contract, codenamed Peace Icarus, was placed in 1971 for 36 F-4Es. These were delivered from March 1974 onwards, and two attrition replacements were delivered in June 1976. The second order was for 18 F-4Es costing $161 million and eight RF-4Es for $91 million. The delivery of the recce versions was effected between June 1978 and April 1979, while the remainder arrived between May and December 1978. Serials, which are worn in the USAF-style '01500' and '71743', are:

72-1500 to 72-1535	(36)	F-4E	JO797
74-1618 to 74-1619	(2)	F-4E	JO6FF
77-1743 to 77-1760	(18)	F-4E	JOM16
77-0357 to 77-0358	(2)	RF-4E	JOMDG
77-1761 to 77-1766	(6)	RF-4E	JOM17

Proposals for the US to supply 40 surplus F-4Es were revealed in 1987, and were later stated to involve 50 F-4Es and 19 F-4G Wild Weasels. As a first step, Greek signature (in July 1990) of an eight-year extension to the US bases agreement resulted in the promise of 28 F-4Es.

The following 28 F-4Es from the 113th TFS and 163rd TFS were delivered during late 1991. All had unit markings and tailcodes removed, and some had small Greek flags painted on their intakes.

67-0345, 67-0350, 67-0377, 67-0381, 68-0318, 68-0361, 68-0363, 68-0381, 68-0393, 68-0394, 68-0402, 68-0405, 68-0408, 68-0412, 68-0424, 68-0426, 68-0432, 68-0438, 68-0440, 68-0442, 68-0444, 68-0445, 68-0480, 68-0481, 68-0496, 68-0506, 68-0515, 68-0517

Greek Phantoms are used in the interception, fighter-bomber and reconnaissance roles by four squadrons, comprising two wings of the 28th TAF. Interceptors are armed with AIM-7E Sparrow and AIM-9 Sidewinder AAMs and have exchanged their two-tone green and brown camouflage for grayish-blue. The first aircraft to wear this new scheme was seen in November 1983.

110 Pterix Mahis

Based at Larissa, the 110th Combat Wing includes two Phantom squadrons.

Gray paint scheme denotes an interception-tasked F-4E of 337 Mira taxiing out for a training sortie.

337 Mira Dioseos 'Fantasma'

Equipped with F-5As in 1967 as part of 111 Wing at Nea Ankhialos, 337 Squadron moved to its present base to receive F-4Es from the initial batch. Its role is air defense.

348 Mira Taktikis Anagnoriseos 'Matla'

The 348th TRS took delivery of the RF-4Es but retained its RF-84F Thunderflashes in the training role until 1990.

Fitted with radar warning receivers on the air intakes and rear of the fin is an RF-4E reconnaissance Phantom of 348 Mira. Only eight of this variant were delivered to Greece, of which two have crashed.

338 Mira Dioseos Bombardismoy 'Ares'

This squadron was equipped in the fighter-bomber role following a brief period with LTV A-7H Corsairs in 1976-77.

The Phantom's naval origins are betrayed by the long nose-wheel leg of this F-4E operated by 338 Mira at Andravidha. More ex-USAF Phantoms have recently arrived.

339 Mira Dioseos 'Ajax'

This squadron converted to Phantoms in 1974, having previously flown Republic F-84Fs, and it is currently tasked with air defense.

Greek letters 'Pi Alpha' on the fuselage of an F-4E indicate Polemiki Aeroporia (Military Aviation). Interceptors received gray paint from 1983 onwards.

117 Pterix Mahis

Both current squadrons of 117 Wing are at Andravidha, where the first batch of Phantoms was delivered in 1974-75.

344 Mira Dioseos Bombardismoy

This was the partner squadron to 339 Squadron when first deliveries were made. It disbanded and was replaced by 338 Squadron with aircraft from the second batch.

IRAN
Imperial Iranian Air Force/ Islamic Republic of Iran Air Force

Large-scale arms purchases from the US characterized the final years of the Iranian monarchy, the Shah intending to make his nation the strongest in the region with the willing cooperation of Washington. Thus, the Imperial Iranian Air Force (IIAF) became the second largest overseas operator of Phantoms, with an eventual total of 32 F-4Ds, 177 F-4Es and 16 RF-4Es (plus eight F-4Es borrowed from the US and subsequently returned). The Islamic fundamentalist revolution, which swept the Shah from power and turned against his US backers, resulted in a 'stop production' instruction being issued on 28 February 1979. Orders were:

67-14869 to 67-14884	(16)	F-4D	JO764
68-6904 to 68-6919	(16)	F-4D	JO766
69-7711 to 69-7742	(32)	F-4E	JO786
71-1094 to 71-1166	(73)	F-4E	JO792
73-1519 to 73-1554	(36)	F-4E	JO6FC
75-0222 to 75-0257	(36)	F-4E	JO6FH
nil	(0)	F-4E	JOMDH (halted; 31 aircraft)
72-0266 to 72-0269	(4)	RF-4E	JO783
74-1725 to 74-1736	(12)	RF-4E	JO6FG
78-0751 to 78-0754	(0)	RF-4E	JOMDJ (halted; 4 aircraft)
78-0788	(0)	RF-4E	JOMDJ (halted; 1 aircraft)
78-0854 to 78-0864	(0)	RF-4E	JOMDK (halted; 11 aircraft)

(78-0751 to 0754, 78-0788 and 78-0854 were partly built, but then reduced to components after the cease-work order. Completion of all Iranian orders would have increased the number of McDonnell-built Phantom airframes to 5,115.)

Iran received its first F-4Ds in September 1968, initially for 306 Squadron. Only one other unit was equipped before the F-4E was received, in more considerable numbers. All were new-build machines.

The first to arrive in Iran were four F-4Ds ferried to Teheran/Mehrabad on 8 September 1968 as the first instalment towards 16 for 306 Fighter Squadron. In Iranian service, the aircraft were issued with local serial numbers beginning 3-601, 3-602, etc. The F-4Es followed between March 1971 and August 1979 and the RF-4s from February 1971, the initial reconnaissance aircraft for Iran having flown on 14 December 1970. The 225 Phantoms delivered gave the IIAF over a dozen squadrons; those in the interception role were armed with AIM-7E Sparrows and AIM-9J Sidewinders. The first combat use came in the ground attack role during 1975, when Iran provided assistance to the Sultan of Oman in combating rebels in the Dhofar region.

When Iraq attacked Iran in September 1980, the Islamic Republic of Iran Air Force (IRIAF) had some 190 Phantoms, of which only about 40 percent were operational due to a US spares embargo. Losses in the first nine months of the war were estimated at 60 F-4s, with many more out of action due to cannibalization. Israel secretly supplied spares, and other parts were obtained on the world market, while in 1985-86 the US broke its own embargo in the 'Irangate' scandal. Phantoms were reported making attacks on shipping in the Gulf shortly before the ceasefire of August 1988, but only 20-30 were then estimated to be airworthy.

There were also problems with Saudi Arabia. On 5 June 1984, two Iranian F-4Es were intercepted by two Saudi F-15C Eagles during border tensions, and one of the Phantoms was shot down – the only recorded time one McDonnell product scored an aerial victory over another. On 31 August 1984, an Iranian pilot defected with his Phantom to Saudi Arabia, where technicians minutely examined the aircraft and determined from serial numbers of components that some had come from Israel and NATO countries. There were reports in 1984 that Iranian Phantoms had been re-engined with Rolls-Royce Speys, but the magnitude of the task and the lack of any subsequent confirmation make this highly unlikely.

Before attrition took its heavy toll, the distribution of Phantoms was believed to be as follows: No. 1 Tactical Air Base, Mehrabad (two squadrons); No. 2 Tactical Air Base, Tabriz (two squadrons); No. 3 Tactical Air Base, Hamadan (two squadrons); No. 4 Tactical Air Base, Dezful (one squadron); No. 6 Tactical Air Base, Bushehr (two squadrons); No. 7 Tactical Air Base, Shiraz (two squadrons); No. 9 Tactical Air Base, Bandar Abbas (one squadron); No. 10 Tactical Air Base, Chabahar (one squadron).

Seen in pre-revolutionary markings, this F-4E may have been among those later kept airworthy by cannibalization and illicit supplies of spares. Iran was not too proud to accept parts from the USA, and even Israel.

ISRAEL

La Tsvah Haganah le Israel/Heyl Ha'Avir (Israel Defense Force/ Air Force)

By the time of the 1982 war over Lebanon, Phantoms had been relegated to attack, leaving F-15 Eagles and F-16 Fighting Falcons to undertake interception, although one F-4 scored the type's 116th air-to-air victory.

Israel first expressed an interest in the Phantom in 1965, during a visit to Washington by air force chief of staff Ezer Weizmann. Israeli interest was politely rebuffed, but losses during the Six Day War, imposition of an arms embargo by France and a flow of Soviet weapons to Arab countries served to increase pressure on the US government from its own powerful Jewish lobby. The sale of F-4s to Israel was approved in principle by Lyndon Johnson on 7 January 1968, and on 27 December 1968, the new US President, Richard Nixon, confirmed the sale of 44 F-4E and six RF-4E Phantoms to Israel under Operations Peace Echo and Peace Patch. This generated much controversy. Ten Israeli aircrew (including four navigators) began training at George AFB, California, with the 4452nd TFTS in March 1969, graduating on 25 July. The Israel Defense Force/Air Force (IDF/AF) received its first aircraft in September 1969. The four initial aircraft were delivered to Hatzor on 5 September 1969 for a formal acceptance ceremony presided over by Prime Minister Golda Meir and Minister of Defence Moshe Dayan. These went on to a newly-formed unit, sometimes described in the West as No. 201 Squadron. One rumour suggests that these may not have been the first Phantoms delivered to Israel, since an unknown number of unmarked US Navy F-4Bs were reportedly flown to Wheelus AFB, Libya, where they were picked up by civilian, Caucasian pilots and delivered eastwards during 1962. Israel's almost fanatical (and wholly understandable) obsession with security means that Israeli experts (and often non-Israeli Jewish writers) will never confirm such matters, and this means that all the squadron numbers given are speculative and based on information supplied solely by US and British sources. This information is often conflicting.

The original F-4Es were delivered by USAF (and later McDonnell) crews at a rate of four per month, initially (until November 1972) without leading-edge slats and TISEO. Sixty-eight new-build aircraft (some intended for the USAF) were delivered under Operation Peace Echo (along with six RF-4Es), and 12 more followed under Operation Peace Patch. Further deliveries included six more RF-4Es and 125 more F-4Es (sometimes quoted as 124 more), six of which were new-build aircraft and which also include the Nickel Grass aircraft (variously described as 36 or 40 ex-USAFE F-4Es). Aircraft from the second 24 aircraft batch of new-build F-4Es for Israel are compatible with the AGM-78 Standard ARM.

Into action

The aircraft were used operationally almost immediately, flying 'Prikha' (blossom) missions against Egyptian targets in the so-called (undeclared) War of Attrition. SAM sites were attacked in October and on 15 December, while other missions in 1969 included a sabre-rattling supersonic run by two F-4s over Cairo on 5 November and the downing of a MiG-21 on 11 November. On 7 January, F-4Es attacked a SAM training base at Dahashur and a commando HQ at Inchas. Warehouses at Hannak were attacked on 13 January, and ammunition dumps at Hexatat and an armored division HQ at Jabel Hoff were attacked on 18 January. On 23 January, it was the turn of an engineering corps at Helwan and Cairo's Watza camp. Finally, F-4Es hit a camp at Ma'adi and an armored corps HQ at Dahashur on 28 January.

Operations continued in February at much the same pace, although the F-4Es began to encounter some opposition, with Egyptian fighters being backed by a Soviet army air defense (AAA/SAM) division. An Egyptian MiG-21 was downed on 12 February, but F-4Es were intercepted and forced to break off their attacks on 26 February and on 18 April, when eight Soviet-flown MiG-21s were shaken off. On 2 April, an F-4E was shot down by an Egyptian MiG-21 and its crew were taken prisoner, and a further F-4E was lost after a mechanical failure earlier in the month. The crew were recovered since they ejected over Israeli territory.

The 'Prikha' campaign was canceled as a result of this engagement and publicity arising from the bombing of a civilian factory at Dahashur on 12 February (killing 70 civilians) and a school at Tshalchia on 8 April, killing 47 children. During the same period, Phantoms had flown 'boom flights' over five Syrian cities (following the dropping of a sonic bang over Haifa by an exuberant Syrian MiG-21 pilot) and had flown escort for A-4 Skyhawks which sank an Egyptian navy minelayer.

Sporadic attacks continued, but from March 1970 Egypt began to roll forward its SAM network towards the Suez Canal, and Phantom losses began to mount. Two were lost on 30 June and another fell on 5 July. Two more were lost on 18 July, one falling over enemy territory and killing the CO of No. 201 Squadron, and the other made it home but was lost in a forced landing at Refidim, although the crew survived. Another was lost in a similar crash landing at Refidim on 4 August. On the other side of the coin, eight Mirage IIIs and four F-4Es ambushed eight Russian-flown MiG-21s on 30 July, with two of the MiGs being downed by F-4s. A ceasefire ended the War of Attrition on 7 August 1971.

Proven in battle, the F-4E Phantom was Israel's most potent combat aircraft through the 1970s, both as interceptor and fighter-bomber. It announced its arrival to Egypt by a two-ship supersonic run over Cairo.

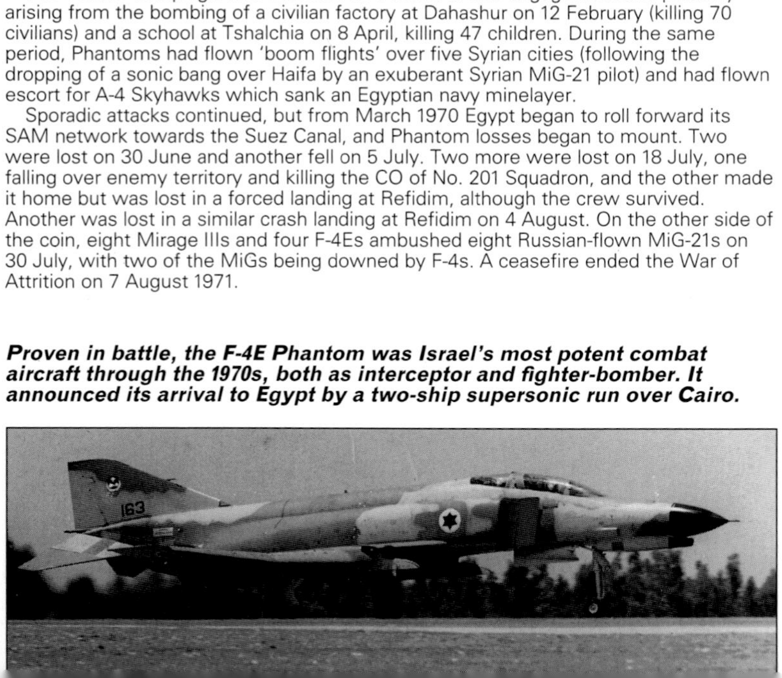

Operational flying did not altogether cease. In September 1971, Israeli F-4Es used the AGM-45 Shrike missile for the first time. The F-4's tally of kills also rose steadily, with two Syrian Su-7s falling to the first (No. 201) Squadron over the Golan on 9 September 1972, and four MiG-21s were downed in the same area on 8 January 1973. On 21 February, two F-4Es downed a Libyan Arab Airlines Boeing 727 which strayed over the Sinai and which refused to follow the F-4Es to Refidim. One hundred and five people were killed, but remarkably there were seven survivors. Another Syrian MiG-21 was downed on 13 September 1973.

By the outbreak of the Yom Kippur War, Israel had lost at least eight F-4Es (at least one and, probably two, of these to MiG-21s), but the Phantom crews had claimed 11 enemy aircraft. The 'score' during the Yom Kippur War is harder to discover, since both sides made wildly exaggerated claims and counter-claims. In the opening Egyptian attack on Ophir AB on 6 October 1973 by 28 MiG-17s and MiG-21s, a pair of QRA Phantoms were able to scramble and claimed seven enemy aircraft. Elsewhere, F-4s intercepted Mil Mi-8 'Hips' attempting to land commandos at key points in the Sinai. Five of these ungainly helicopters were claimed, of some 40 encountered.

The next day opened with hastily planned operations against Syrian SAM sites, but these cost six Phantoms, with two aircrew killed and nine captured. At least one more F-4E was able to land back at Ramat David, in flames! (It is unlikely to have been recoverable.) Attacks against Egyptian airfields were less costly. On 8 October, the Phantoms attacked Syrian airfields and Egyptian pontoon bridges across the Sinai and mounted CAPs in various areas. Four MiG-17s were downed when they tried to attack a C^3 post at Om Khasiba. On the debit side, a single F-4E on an undisclosed mission was lost, probably shot down by a Syrian MiG-21.

On 9 October, 16 Phantoms were launched in an attack against the Syrian army HQ in Damascus. Only eight were able to attack, due to the weather, but they scored some hits. One aircraft was lost (the pilot was killed and the navigator taken prisoner) and another crawled home with several 57-mm cannon hits! Another F-4 was lost, together with its crew, during attacks on power stations and Egyptian airfields. The following day, the Phantoms attacked various Egyptian and Syrian air bases, suffering no losses, but in similar operations on 11 October two F-4Es fell to Egyptian MiG-21s over Banbah airfield. No losses occurred on 12 October, but the next day an F-4 was badly damaged by AAA during an attack on El Mazza airfield near Damascus. It was nursed out over the sea and abandoned by its crew. The campaign against Syrian airfields ended on 14 October, while attacks on Egypt continued. During an attack on Mansurah, two MiG-21s were claimed (but only as probables), but the MiG's resistance was sufficient that two F-4Es ran out of fuel on their way home, forcing them to land at primitive strips at Baluza and Refidim.

On 15 October, 12 Phantoms attacked Tanta airfield and downed a MiG-21, but one F-4 and its navigator was lost (the pilot becoming a PoW) and another suffered severe damage but managed to limp home without an aileron. SAM positions at Port Said were attacked on 16 October, and more SAM positions were attacked during the following two days. Unfortunately, three Phantoms were shot down and a fourth was badly damaged. Four Syrian MiG-17s were intercepted and claimed destroyed near Kuneitra on 18 October – at least one using the new indigenous Rafael Shafrir AAM. On 20 October, two more Phantoms were shot down by Egyptian SAMs.

During 11,233 IDF/AF combat sorties (by all types), 37 Phantoms were lost (including those described above) and six more were so badly damaged that they had to be written off. This attrition rate was second only to that suffered by the A-4 Skyhawk, and was a result of the difficult anti-airfield and anti-SAM missions flown by the aircraft. The losses were largely made good by the transfer of 36 USAF F-4E Phantoms during Operation Nickel Grass (mainly from the 4th and 401st TFWs). These aircraft flew 200 combat missions, sometimes in USAF camouflage and with only national insignia and USAFE tailcodes overpainted. Reliable sources suggest that a number of USN F-4Bs were also transferred, although no photographs of such aircraft have ever emerged, nor have details of the aircraft involved. On the other hand, the four Phantom units, usually described as Nos 69, 107, 119 and 201 Squadrons, claimed a large number of enemy aircraft destroyed and did have a devastating effect on enemy airfields and SAM sites.

Israeli improvements

Since virtually every F-4 in the Israeli inventory had received damage of some sort during the Yom Kippur War, there was an urgent need for an extensive repair and refurbishment scheme. The opportunity to incorporate an avionics and equipment update at the same time was also taken, most notably adding a new radar warning receiver, and adding leading-edge slats and TISEO to surviving early aircraft. A series of other upgrade and improvement programs has since been instigated, and because the aircraft have amassed more flying hours than their US equivalents, such upgrades have been more numerous.

This has led to a number of different equipment standards among Israeli F-4s, most of which have a new Elbit Jason digital weapons delivery system, and some of which have strap-on external inflight refueling probes. The Jason, developed jointly by Elbit and Singer Kearfott, offers a navigation accuracy of 1.5 km per hour (0.9 miles per hour) and has an MTBF of 300 hours. A CRT display is provided for the navigator. Other upgrades have included the provision of a Litton LW-33 Digital Inertial Navigation Attack System, and some sources suggest that an ELTA radar has been fitted to some aircraft. Trial fitments have included twin 30-mm DEFA cannon and a variety of night-attack sensors. The latter program was initiated in 1973 and a number of optional locations for an electro-optical sensing/FLIR system were evaluated, including the

TISEO pod, the left forward missile bay and a palletized turret projecting from the gun bay. The three different locations could accommodate sensors of different lengths: 14½ in (37 cm), 16½ in (42 cm) and 20 in (51 cm), respectively. One of the first two options may have been adopted. Israeli F-4s can carry a number of different missiles, including Standard, Shrike, Maverick, Sidewinder and Sparrow, and indigenous AAMs like Shafrir and Python, and ASMs like the TV-guided Rafael Luz and Gabriel 3A/S anti-ship missile.

Between the end of the Yom Kippur War and the 1982 Lebanon War, the Israeli Phantoms saw constant use, flying many missions against PLO targets, and even being selected for use in Operation Opera – the raid on Iraq's Osirak nuclear reactor – before F-16s were substituted. One Egyptian MiG-21 was claimed on 6 December 1973, while two F-4Es were downed in April 1974 during the fight for Mount Hermon. One further F-4 unit was formed after the war, although the aircraft largely lost any air-to-air commitment after the introduction of the F-15 and F-16. During the Lebanon War, the F-4 operated almost exclusively in the air-to-ground role. The war opened on 9 June 1982 with a mass attack against the Syrian air defense network and included 24 Phantoms armed with Mavericks, Shrikes and Standard ARMs (the latter is apparently known as the 'Purple Fist' to Israeli crews) operating under cover of heavy jamming. Further F-4s attacked with iron bombs.

A single F-4E, using a Rafael Python, downed a Syrian MiG-21 over the Bekaa on 11 June, the last of 116 claimed air-to-air victories by Israeli F-4s. The unnamed pilot reportedly made 'ace' with this kill, having four previous kills to his credit. Since the Lebanon War, IDF/AF Phantoms have continued to mount operations against Syrian SAM sites and against PLO, Ammal and Hezbollah targets. Losses have continued to mount, with aircraft falling on 24 July 1982 and 16 October 1986, and perhaps on other occasions.

During the late 1970s it became clear that IDF/AF re-equipment plans were over-ambitious, and that replacement of the A-4 and Kfir by the IAI Lavi would leave insufficient money for procurement of the service's preferred F-4 replacement – the F/A-18 Hornet. Accordingly, the Kurnass 2000 update program was launched, aiming to bring the F-4 up to date with new engines and avionics.

Despite at least 55 admitted combat losses, in addition to normal peacetime attrition, Israel still operated some 120 F-4E/Kurnass 2000s, and two F-4E(S) and 14 RF-4Es were still in service by 1992. The Kurnass 2000 received its baptism of fire in February 1991. These equip four squadrons at Ramat David (usually described in the West as No. 69), Tel Nov (usually referred to as No. 119) and Hatzor (usually referred to as Nos 105 and 201).

IDF/AF Phantom deliveries

Operation Peace Echo I: 44 new-build F-4Es diverted from USAF orders, plus six RF-4Es, delivered from 7 September 1969.

69-0396 to 69-0399 (4)	69-0484 to 69-0487 (4)
69-0414 to 69-0417 (4)	69-0499 to 69-0502 (4)
69-0430 to 69-0433 (4)	69-0519 to 69-0525 (7)
69-0454 to 69-0457 (4)	69-0539 to 69-0547 (9)
69-0469 to 69-0472 (4)	69-7590 to 69-7595 (6) RF-4E

Operation Peace Echo II: six ex-USAF F-4Es delivered during 1970.

69-0294 to 69-0296 (3)
69-0299 to 69-0301 (3)

Operation Peace Echo III: 18 ex-USAF F-4Es delivered during 1970.

69-7224 to 69-7227 (4)
69-7237 to 69-7250 (14)

Operation Night Light: two USAF RF-4Cs loaned to Israel between August 1970 and March 1971.

Operation Peace Patch: 12 ex-USAF F-4Es delivered during early 1971. Last delivered 22 March 1971.

69-7547 (1) First with extended gun port
69-7549 (1)
69-7553 and 69-7554 (2)
69-7567 to 69-7570 (4)
69-7575 to 69-7578 (4)

69-7567, 69-7570 and 69-7576 later converted to F-4E(S) configuration.

Operation Peace Echo IV: 24 ex-USAF and 18 new-build (71-1779 to 71-1796) F-4Es delivered between April 1972 and October 1973, bringing cumulative total to 122 F-4Es and six RF-4Es.

71-0224 to 71-0236 (13)	71-1093 (1)
71-1071 (1) First slatted F-4E for Israel	71-1393 (1)
71-1080 (1)	71-1396 (1)
71-1082 (1)	71-1399 to 71-1402 (4)
71-1090 (1)	71-1779 to 71-1796 (18)

Operation Nickel Grass: transfer of USAF F-4Es to IDF/AF as attrition replacements during Yom Kippur War. Between 36 and 40 aircraft were transferred, and 34 are listed below. Dates given are dates of transfer to FMS, not to IDF/AF. Many were combat veterans from Vietnam.

66-0313 ex-33TFW 19 Oct 73	71-1394 ex-4TFW 16 Oct 73
66-0327 ex-33TFW 19 Oct 73	71-1395 ex-4TFW 14 Oct 73
66-0352 ex-33TFW 19 Oct 73	71-1398 ex-4TFW 14 Oct 73
67-0121 ex-33TFW 19 Oct 73	72-0121 ex-4TFW 16 Oct 73
67-0340 ex-33TFW 19 Oct 73	72-0123 ex-4TFW 15 Oct 73
67-0346 ex-33TFW 19 Oct 73	72-0127 ex-4TFW 14 Oct 73
67-0362 ex-33TFW 19 Oct 73	72-0129 ex-4TFW 14 Oct 73
67-0368 ex-33TFW 19 Oct 73	72-0130 ex-4TFW 16 Oct 73
67-0383 ex-33TFW 19 Oct 73	72-0131 ex-4TFW 14 Oct 73
68-0331 ex-33TFW 19 Oct 73	72-0132 ex-4TFW 14 Oct 73
68-0333 ex-33TFW 19 Oct 73	72-0133 ex-4TFW 16 Oct 73
68-0380 ex-33TFW 19 Oct 73	72-0137 ex-4TFW 15 Oct 73
69-7229 ex-33TFW 19 Oct 73	72-0138 ex-4TFW 14 Oct 73
69-7255 ex-33TFW 19 Oct 73	72-0157 ex-4TFW 14 Oct 73
71-0246 ex-4TFW 16 Oct 73	72-0158 ex-4TFW 15 Oct 73
71-1074 ex-57FWW 13 Oct 73	72-0163 ex-4TFW 15 Oct 73
71-1078 ex-57FWW 13 Oct 73	72-0164 ex-4TFW 16 Oct 73

Operation Peace Echo V: 24 ex-USAF and 24 new-build (74-1014 to 74-1037) F-4Es, plus two batches of six RF-4Es, delivered between 1974 and November 1976.

72-1480 to 72-1481 (2)	73-1169 to 73-1170 (2)
72-1487 to 72-1488 (2)	73-1178 to 73-1179 (2)
72-1491 to 72-1492 (2)	73-1190 to 73-1191 (2)
72-1495 to 72-1496 (2)	73-1201 to 73-1202 (2)
72-1497 to 72-1498 (2)	74-1014 to 74-1037 (24) First TISEO-equipped
72-1499 (1)	Israeli F-4Es. Standard ARM.
73-1157 to 73-1159 (3)	75-0418 to 75-0423 (6) RF-4E
73-1161 to 73-1162 (2)	75-656 to 75-661 (6) RF-4E

Known IDF/AF F-4E serials: 101, 106, 109, 110, 113, 114, 115, 119, 123, 129 (ex 69-7248, w/o 10/73), 141, 142, 144, 147, 151, 152, 153, 154, 156, 158, 160, 163, 164, 167, 170, 171, 172, 173, 175, 177, 181, 183, 184, 187, 189, 198, 201, 202, 206, 209, 210, 211, 214, 216, 218, 222, 226, 227, 228, 229, 230, 236, 237, 251, 253, 256, 260, 264, 270, 274, 280, 284, 288, 304, 307, 311, 315, 317, 327, 330, 334 (ex 66-0327), 584, 607, 608, 609, 610, 618, 620, 634, 640, 658, 668, 678, 680, 693. Total 86.

Known IDF/AF RF-4E serials: 191, 193, 195, 198, 216, 234, 489.

No. 69 Squadron 'Ha'patishim' ('The Hammers')

Israel's second F-4 unit, No. 69 Squadron, reformed with F-4Es in late 1969 at Ramat David under Avihu Ben-Nun. It was previously a B-17 unit between 1948 and 1956. The squadron's aircraft have black and yellow checkered rudders, and at least one RF-4E (489) was seen with the squadron's black and yellow rudder. Another has been seen with the red zigzag fuselage arrow marking often associated with another unit. Example aircraft: 209, 315, 327.

Rudder colors and badge of No. 69 Squadron, IDF/AF.

Land-based Phantoms have a manual wing-folding option for storage in confined spaces. It is here demonstrated by a slat-equipped F-4E from No. 69 Squadron, which also shows positioning of the underwing markings.

No. 105 Squadron 'Akrav' ('Scorpion')

Using updated Super Mystères during the Yom Kippur War, No. 105 Squadron re-equipped with F-4Es during the first half of 1974, passing its Super Mystères to Honduras. The aircraft have orange rudders and carry a scorpion badge and are believed to be based at Hatzor. The squadron may be the rightful owner of the red or red-outlined white fuselage arrow seen on some Israeli F-4s.

A fully-loaded F-4E from the Scorpion Squadron has little ground clearance for its underwing stores. Note the Israeli refueling probe for compatibility with the drogue system on KC-130s and Boeing 707s.

No. 107 Squadron 'Zanav Katom' ('Orange Tails')

No. 107 Squadron is believed to have formed during late 1970 or early 1971, and reportedly disbanded in 1981.

No. 113 Squadron

The most colorfully-marked Israeli Phantoms have been described as belonging to No. 113 Squadron, whose badge was supposed to be a lion's head. The aircraft also carried gaudy shark's mouths on the nose. Based at Tel Nov, the unit was said to have formed during 1971, retiring its Ouragans. It reportedly disbanded in 1979 or 1980 and has since re-equipped with the AH-64 Apache. The latest information suggests that the squadron may never have existed – the markings having been worn by another unit as a disinformation exercise.

No. 115 Squadron

The least known and most secretive Israeli Phantom unit is based at Tel Nov and flies the RF-4E and F-4E(S). Previously equipped with the Mosquito, and then the Vautour, the squadron received its first two RF-4s on loan from the USAF between August 1969 and March 1971 under the codename Peace Night Light. Their return reportedly coincided with the delivery of Israel's own RF-4s. Initially painted in the same tan, green and sand color scheme as the F-4Es, most, if not all, Israeli recce Phantoms are now believed to operate in an overall gray color scheme. No. 115 Squadron, like No. 113, may be a nonexistent disinformation exercise, and recent reports suggest that the RF-4s are spread among the fighter units.

No. 119 Squadron 'Atalev' ('Bat')

Another early F-4 unit was No. 119 Squadron, based at Ramat David, which passed its Mirage IIIs on to Nos 101 and 117 Squadrons. The squadron's aircraft carry a red arrowhead on the fin and a bat insignia. The aircraft were reportedly used for the test and development of new weapons and systems. No. 119 Squadron is now believed to be based at Tel Nov. The February 1992 IAF magazine reported the unit's conversion to the Kurnass 2000. Examples include non-TISEO, unslatted 114, 35 and 129, and slatted 119, 141 and 330.

No. 119's bat insignia now adorns Kurnass 2000 versions of Phantom.

Above: A slatted F-4E of No. 119 Squadron. The aircraft's serial may or may not be a coincidence.

No. 201 Squadron 'Ahat'

The first Israeli F-4 unit was No. 201 Squadron, which re-equipped with F-4s under the command of Shamuel Hetz. It initially acted as the Israeli F-4E OCU, although operations began immediately with an attack on a SAM site near Abu Sueir in October 1969. In November, the squadron's Phantoms dropped sonic bangs over Cairo. On 11 November 1969, Captain Ahud Hankin and his navigator, Major Saul Levy, scored the Israeli Phantom's first kill, downing a MiG-21 just south of Suez. Before the year's end, the squadron conducted another attack against eight SAM batteries on 15 December 1969. Hetz was killed on 18 July 1970 and his place was taken by Lieutenant Colonel Ran Peker, a former flying school commander. This officer's first operational sortie was only his ninth flight in the F-4E! The unit's aircraft can be identified by a red rudder with a blue/white/blue jagged flash

No. 201 Squadron's badge of a stylized blackbird upon a bull's-eye.

bisecting it. The squadron badge is a bull's-eye with a blackbird superimposed. The unit is believed to be based at Ramon, having moved south from Hatzor in early 1992 after becoming the first Kurnass 2000 squadron. Example aircraft include slatted 201, slatted Kurnass 2000 584 and slatted, TISEO-equipped Kurnass 2000 668, 678 and 680.

*Fitted with a **TISEO** sensor on the port wing is Kurnass 2000 of No. 201 Squadron. No. 201's earlier equipment included an F-4E serialed 201.*

Publisher's note: The above squadron designations cannot be confirmed. Some Israeli and Jewish aviation authors have refused to supply photographs or information because squadron numbers (some of which are said by some of them to be incorrect) have been included in this text. All non-European and non-industry suppliers of pictures used have individually requested that it is made clear that their assistance has been limited to the supply of uncaptioned photographs only.

JAPAN
Nihon Koku Jietai (Japan Air Self-Defense Force)

Japan acquired 154 Phantoms for air defense and reconnaissance, and is upgrading the aircraft for further service. First to arrive, at Komaki on 25 July 1971, were two F-4EJs from St Louis in airworthy condition, the prototype (F-4 No. 4,038) having made its initial flight on 14 January 1971. McDonnell also supplied Mitsubishi with 11 kits of parts (which are included in US production totals of 5,068) and two forward fuselages (which are not). The first Japanese-assembled aircraft (27-8303) flew on 12 May 1972 and the last (17-8440) was delivered to the Japan Air Self-Defense Force (JASDF) on 20 May 1981 – well after manufacture had ended in the US. In addition, 14 RF-4EJs were supplied for reconnaissance from US production, their delivery taking place between 26 November 1974 and 8 June 1975. ASDF aircraft have a four-digit serial with a two-digit prefix; the latter has '7' as its second element as the type number assigned to the Phantom and a variable first character to indicate the Western year of delivery. Numbers assigned are:

Serial range	Quantity	Year	Type
17-8301 to 17-8302	(2)	1971	F-4EJ (JO782)
27-8303 to 27-8306	(4)	1972	F-4EJ (JO782)
37-8307 to 37-8313	(7)	1973	F-4EJ (JO782)
37-8314 to 37-8323	(10)	1973	F-4EJ
47-8324 to 47-8352	(29)	1974	F-4EJ
57-8353 to 57-8376	(24)	1975	F-4EJ
67-8377 to 67-8391	(15)	1976	F-4EJ
77-8392 to 77-8403	(12)	1977	F-4EJ
87-8404 to 87-8415	(12)	1978	F-4EJ
97-8416 to 97-8427	(12)	1979	F-4EJ
07-8428 to 07-8436	(9)	1980	F-4EJ
17-8437 to 17-8440	(4)	1981	F-4EJ
47-6901 to 47-6905	(5)	1974	RF-4EJ
57-6906 to 57-6914	(9)	1975	RF-4EJ

F-4EJs were delivered with light gray upper surfaces and white undersides, but experimentation with blue and/or gray medium-altitude camouflage began in 1979. The RF-4Es arrived in light gray and white and changed to two-tone green and tan in 1977. Six squadrons of Air Defense Command received F-4EJs within the Northern, Central and Western Air Defense Forces, plus the Southwest Composite Air Wing; the RF-4EJ squadron reports directly to HQ Air Defense Command. F-4EJ strength is being reduced to three squadrons by April 1994, but they will have aircraft with enhanced capability. The upgraded aircraft, designated F-4EJ Kai (meaning 'plus'), has structural modifications to extend the airframe from 3,000 to 5,000 hours, Westinghouse AN/

APG-66J pulse-Doppler radar, indigenous J/APR-4 Kai radar-warning receivers, an INS, HUD and new central computer. The prototype (07-8431) flew on 17 July 1984 and the first eight conversions were authorized in the FY1987 budget, followed by 17, 20, 20 and 15 up to FY1992. The Kai aircraft have the latest AIM-7F Sparrow and AIM-9L Sidewinder AAMs, plus provision for the Mitsubishi ASM-1C anti-ship missile.

Mitsubishi's AAM-3 will eventually replace AIM-9; similarly, recce assets are being improved in a two-part program. The 13 surviving RF-4EJs are to gain a forward-looking radar, infrared surveillance system and INS, but in 1990 Mitsubishi began conversion of 17 F-4EJs to RF-4s capable of carrying one of three types of sensor pod: infrared, visual-spectrum camera or the French Thomson-CSF ASTAC Elint system.

301st Hikotai

301st Squadron formed on 16 October 1973 from a provisional squadron established in the previous year as the first principal JASDF Phantom unit. Assigned to operational conversion, it was a component of the 7th Kokudan (Air Wing) of the Central Air Defense Force until it moved to 5th Wing at Nyutabaru (Western ADF) in March 1985, receiving the F-4EJ Kai (the second wing to do so) during 1991. The squadron's aircraft wear a frog's head badge on their tail fins. The Shirokuno Gama frog inhabits Mount Tsukuba, close to the unit's Hyakuri base. The frog wears a scarf containing seven stars, indicating the 7th Kokudan.

A late production F-4EJ 07-8428 wears a color scheme designed to simulate a MiG-21 'Fishbed'.

302nd Hikotai

302nd Squadron formed on 1 October 1974 at Chitose as a squadron of the 2nd Kokudan (Air Wing) of the Northern ADF. It then moved to Naha, on the island of Okinawa, to replace the Starfighters of 207th Squadron, which disbanded in March 1986, and is currently the sole air defense squadron of the Southwest Composite Air Wing. The squadron's white-tailed eagle insignia represents the Ojiro Washi Eagle, which inhabits the high mountains near the unit's original base at Chitose. A very realistic black and white eagle was originally applied before the present stylized red, white and blue bird was adopted. This consists of blue swept-back wings representing the numeral '3', a triangular white tail in the shape of an '0' and yellow talons representing '2'. The 302nd Squadron will become the third squadron equipped with the Kai version.

Particularly attractive as a unit marking is the Ojiro Washi Eagle of 302 Squadron.

303rd Hikotai

Formed on 26 October 1976 at Komatsu within 6th Air Wing of the Central ADF, the unit adopted the old 205th Hikotai badge, which includes a stylized '6' on a blue disc. In November 1986, it began receiving F-15J Eagles and returned to operational status the following April.

Special high-visibility markings on an F-4EJ from Komatsu.

304th Hikotai

Formed on 1 August 1977 at Tsuiki as a squadron of 8th Air Wing, Western ADF, the squadron's badge depicts Tengu, the long-nosed, bearded goblin. Conversion to F-15Js began late in 1989 and the squadron became operational with the Eagle in April 1990.

Phantoms were flown for 12 years before F-15Js were received in 1989.

305th Hikotai

Formed on 1 December 1978 at Hyakuri, within 7th Kokudan, Central ADF, the squadron was due to convert to F-15Js in 1992. The badge is a representation of a plum flower on a red disc.

The type of mission to be flown from Hyakuri by this 305th Hikotai F-4EJ is obvious from the gunnery target carried beneath the port wing. All six F-4EJ squadrons were tasked with interception.

306th Hikotai

The squadron formed on 30 June 1981 as the last Phantom squadron and was attached to 6th Kokudan at Komatsu (Central ADF). The mountains near Komatsu are home to the golden eagle, or Inuwashi, which is the symbol of the local Ishikawa Prefecture. A golden eagle's head was thus adopted as the squadron badge, applied on a blue disc on the fin. The eagle's eye is the same shape as the insignia of the 205th Hikotai, the squadron's original parent unit. The squadron became the first with Kai versions of the F-4EJ when deliveries began in August 1989, and by March 1991 had increased its strength from 18 to 22 aircraft – as will be the case with other squadrons.

Several 306th Hikotai F-4EJs wore a dark gray camouflage pattern based on the unit's eagle badge.

501st Hikotai

Formed with RF-86F Sabres at Matsushima on 1 December 1961 and after moving to Iruma on 28 August 1962, received its first RF-4EJ on 3 December 1974. The squadron moved to Hyakuri on 1 October 1975, but maintained a Sabre detachment at its old base until 25 March 1977. It is currently the sole unit in the Teisatsu Kokutai (Reconnaissance Wing) and employs the badge of a woodpecker's head.

Phantoms have a standard low-level camouflage and wear a woodpecker badge.

Rinji F-4EJ Hikotai

The Provisional F-4EJ Squadron formed at Hyakuri on 1 August 1972, within the 7th Kokudan of the Central ADF. Initially having two aircraft, it expanded to become the nucleus of 301st Squadron.

The second of two US-assembled F-4EJs, 17-8302 was initially used by the Air Proving Wing at Gifu. In usual ASDF manner, early F-4EJs formed a provisional unit which later became 301st Hikotai.

KOREA
Hankook Kong Goon (Republic of Korea Air Force)

The Korean peninsula, where no peace agreement has replaced the 27 July 1953 ceasefire, remains one of the world's genuine potential flashpoints. More than a million men under arms face each other across a 2½-mile (4-km) DMZ (DeMilitarized Zone) and huge North Korean forces are poised on the northern side of the line, just 35 miles (56 km) from Seoul, the South's capital city. The Republic of Korea Air Force (RoKAF) ordered an initial 18 F-4D Phantoms in 1968, during a tense period when North Korea was sending guerrillas into the South; firefights raged along the DMZ; and the crew of the US spy ship *Pueblo* was held prisoner. The first six F-4Ds from this batch arrived at Seoul on 25 August 1969 to begin re-equipment of the 110th TFS of the 11th FW at Taegu. In 1972, the wing's 151st TFS gained a further 18 F-4Ds (from the USAF's locally-based 3rd TFW) in return for the RoKAF transferring 36 Northrop F-5s to South Vietnam under the Enhance Plus program. The second Phantom batch was officially on loan, but the transfer was eventually made permanent. A few USAF F-4Ds were used on short-term loan during the 1970s, but six were added to the RoKAF inventory in 1982, and a further 24 came from the US between December 1987 and April 1988 – this last batch equipped with Pave Spike laser designators. The 17th FW at Chongju received 19 new-build F-4Es in 1978 and 18 two years later, for the equipment of the 152nd and 153rd TFSs. The last of these, 68-0744, was also the 5,068th and final Phantom airframe built in the US. These 37 new-build F-4Es were delivered under Operation Peace Pheasant II. The US offered 24 surplus F-4Es in 1988 and 30 in 1989, but probably only the second batch was received. Some F-4s are equipped to carry the eight AN/AVQ-26 Pave Tack designators delivered in 1987. Finally, when the USAF's 460th TRG disbanded in 1988, 12 of its RF-4Cs and a quantity of AN/ALQ-131 jamming pods were transferred to Korea for the 131st TRS at Suwon. They have apparently been augmented by a few others.

F-4D deliveries ex-USAF:
In 1969: 64-0931, 64-0933, 64-0934, 64-0935, 64-0941, 64-0943, 64-0944, 64-0946, 64-0947, 64-0948, 64-0950, 64-0951, 64-0955, 64-0957, 64-0958, 64-0961, 64-0962, 64-0966
In 1970: 65-0709
In 1972: 64-0978, 65-0582, 65-0589, 65-0591, 65-0592, 65-0605, 65-0610, 65-0620, 65-0622, 65-0623, 65-0630, 65-0640, 65-0650, 65-0678, 65-0691, 65-0715, 65-0732, 65-0762

In 1973: 65-0663
In 1975: 65-0978
In 1982: 65-0679, 65-0755, 65-0797, plus three
In 1987/88: 66-7507, 66-7555, 66-7577, 66-7608, 66-7618, 66-7673, 66-7690, 66-7709, 66-7715, 66-7737, 66-7747, 66-7750, 66-7753, 66-7758, 66-7762, 66-8701, 66-8734, 66-8737, 66-8756, 66-8758, 66-8765, 66-8806, 66-8810, plus one
Date unknown: 66-0479

F-4E new manufacture:
76-0493 to 76-0511	(19)	JO6AK
78-0727 to 78-0744	(18)	JOMDH

F-4E ex-USAF: including: 68-0358, 68-0387, 68-0390, 68-0494

RF-4C ex-USAF: none identified

Operating units:
10th Tactical Fighter Wing, Suwon: 39th TRG/131st TRS,RF-4C
11th Tactical Fighter Wing, Taegu: 110th TFS, F-4D (detached to Kunsan); 151st TFS, F-4D
17th Tactical Fighter Wing, Chongju: 152nd TFS, F-4E; 153rd TFS, F-4E

A late delivery to South Korea, 66-7753 was an F-4D which saw two decades of service with the USAF. All RoKAF F-4Ds and some of its F-4Es have been handed down from its principal ally.

SPAIN
Ejercito del Aire

As a replacement for the Lockheed F-104G Starfighters and North American F-86F Sabres constituting Spain's front-line ADF, the Ejercito del Aire (EdA) obtained an initial batch of 36 Phantoms. Supplied via the Mutual Defense Aid Program, the aircraft were second-hand F-4Cs from USAFE's 81st TFW at Bentwaters, England, and received an overhaul by CASA at Getafe before being handed over to the EdA. In the local aircraft designation system the Phantom became C.12, as the 12th fighter (caza) type used since the civil war.

Ala 12 (12th Wing) at Torrejon was formed to operate the Phantom, and adopted the badge of a wildcat's face from Ala 6, which had been the Sabre and Starfighter unit. 121 Escuadron (Squadron) (callsign 'Poker') formed from Sabre-equipped 201 Escuadron in March 1971 with the first refurbished F-4Cs, followed on 31 May 1972 by 122 Escuadron (callsign 'Tennis') (ex-104 Escuadron, the appropriately-designated Starfighter unit). In the following month, Ala 12 formed 123 Squadron with three Boeing KC-97Ls to provide aerial refueling for Spain's first probe-equipped aircraft. The botijos (jugs) spent four years replenishing Phantom tanks (in all, 220,000 Imp-gal were transferred) and battling against unserviceability until replaced by KC-130H Hercules of the EdA's Transport Command.

Armed with AIM-9J (later AIM-9N) Sidewinders, AIM-7E Sparrows and SUU-16/A 20-mm gunpods, two Phantoms were kept on constant QRA to defend Spanish airspace. Serialed C.12-01 to -36, they were shared evenly between the two squadrons, so that C.12-35 was 121-18 of 121 Squadron and C.12-36 was 122-18 of 122 Squadron. In October 1978, attrition was more than covered by the addition of four F-4Cs (two ex-35th TFW and two from 58th TTW) and four RF-4Cs from 363rd TRW. None received codes, and the RF-4s – locally known as CR.12s – went to an individual flight (escuadrilla). Promises of replacement by at least 18 F-4Es and six RF-4Es failed to materialize, and, instead, the wing converted to McDonnell Douglas EF-18A/B Hornets, withdrawing its last F-4Cs from service in April 1979. A few aircraft managed to adopt the new style of unit codes before retirement, and existing machines were marked 12-01 upwards in serial number order, irrespective of squadron. Seven were lost in accidents.

That was not quite the end of the Spanish Phantom, for eight RF-4Cs had been obtained from the 123rd TRW, Kentucky ANG, the first six arriving at Torrejon on 11 January 1989 to form a new 123 Escuadron (callsign 'Titan') within Ala 12. These differed slightly from the original quartet of Spanish RF-4Es in that they were equipped with new radios, new RHAW gear, new VOR/ILS and KS-87 cameras, and were powered by smokeless J79-GE-15E engines. A single RF-4C from the first batch (CR.12-42) was retained, as were six F-4Cs (C.12-09, -10, -14, -19, -37 and -20), which served as target tugs and weapons test platforms until late 1990, when the last aircraft was finally relegated to use as a gate guard. The RF-4s are steadily being painted in the same pale gray color scheme as worn by Spain's Hornets, while updates have included AN/APQ-172 terrain-following radar, new ECM systems, laser INS, new electro-optical sensors and real-time datalinks, as well as inflight refueling probes similar to those applied to Israeli aircraft. Spain is reportedly keen to obtain ex-Luftwaffe RF-4Es to increase the unit's strength. They are intended to serve until the Hornet can be equipped with a reconnaissance pod in 1995.

F-4C ex-USAF:
In 1971: 64-0884, 64-0900, 64-0903, 64-0909, 64-0906 w/o, 64-0886 w/o, 64-0920, 64-0925, 64-0867, 64-0895, 64-0871, 64-0846, 64-0813 w/o, 64-0880, 64-0866, 64-0853, 64-0854, 64-0872, 64-0855, 64-0857 w/o, 64-0924, 64-0877, 64-0894 w/o, 64-0881 w/o, 64-0861, 64-0862, 64-0880, 64-0858, 64-0878, 64-0859, 64-0856, 64-0887, 64-0907, 64-0870 w/o, 64-0864 as C.12-01 to C.12-36, respectively
In 1978: 64-0820, 64-0882, 64-0892, 64-0896 as C.12-37 to C.12-40, respectively

RF-4C ex-USAF:
In 1978: 65-0936, 65-0937, 65-0942, 65-0943 as CR.12-41 to CR.12-44, respectively
In 1989: 64-1069, 64-1070, 64-1083, 65-0822, 65-0835, 65-0841, 65-0851, 65-0873 as CR.12-45 to CR.12-52, respectively

Above: RF-4Cs are the only Phantoms still operated by the Ejercito del Aire following the arrival of EF-18 Hornets, also from the McDonnell Douglas plant at St Louis.

Below: Black cat badge of 12 Wing prominently on its fin, an F-4C of 122 Squadron is pictured during a training flight. All Spanish Phantoms were secondhand, mostly from the USAF's 81st TFW.

Above: The start of a gunnery training sortie for a Phantom of 12 Wing is indicated by the towed target under the port wing.

TURKEY
Turk Hava Kuvvetleri

Turkey became a major Phantom user in the 1970s and employed F-4E aircraft as part of its commitment to NATO – a role taken very seriously by Ankara because of the proximity of the (then) Soviet Union. First deliveries were of 40 F-4Es ordered in FY1973 under Peace Diamond III, operators including 161 Filo (squadron) of 6 Ana Jet Us (Jet Air Base, JAB), now re-equipped with GD F-16C Fighting Falcons. Aircraft from this batch currently fly with 7 Air Base at Erhac, where they replaced F-5As in 171 and 172 Squadrons, later joined by 173 as the type OCU. Early crew training was undertaken by the Simsek Kit'a ('Simsek' flight) within 1 JAB at Eskisehir, this having disbanded by 1987. A FY1977 order for Phantoms comprised 32 more F-4Es and eight RF-4Es also under Peace Diamond III, now serving mainly with three squadrons of the 1st JAB at Eskisehir: as replacements for F-100D Super Sabres and Northrop RF-5As in 111 and 112 Squadrons and the recce aircraft with 113 Squadron. One Turk Hava Kuvvetleri (THK) Phantom, 77-0290, was the 5,000th of the type to be delivered, concurrent with the 20th anniversary, on 27 May 1958, of the F4H's first flight.

Several batches of former USAF F-4Es have been obtained subsequently starting with Peace Diamond IV in order to balance attrition and convert two squadrons (131 and 132) of 3 JAB at Konya. The latter wing, which previously flew F-100Ds, was a component of Air Training Command until the arrival of Phantoms allowed it to rejoin the front line in 1988. These supplementary batches have comprised 15 from June 1981 at a cost of £87 million to form 173 Squadron; 15 in mid-1984 for £70 million; 15 in 1986; 40 in June-October 1987; and, as 'payment' for Turkish support of UN forces in the 1991 Gulf War, 40 more beginning with an initial four on 25 March 1991. Phantom receipts thus have totaled 205. There is believed to be a long-standing requirement for 33 F-4Cs and four RF-4Cs stored in Spain, but their acquisition seems increasingly unlikely.

THK aircraft do not normally carry squadron badges, but their air base can be deduced from a coding system first noted in use with 1 JAB in mid-1981. This comprises the 'last three' of the USAF serial number prefixed by the air base (equivalent to a wing) number, for example '3-345' for a 3 JAB Phantom, 60345. All THK Phantom units are assigned primarily to attack, with interception as a secondary role and belong to the 1st or 2nd Tactical Air Force (THKK) according to their position west or east of the 35th meridian. Phantom deliveries to Turkey are as follows:

A 1992 delivery from the USAF to Turkey was 68-0473, formerly with the Missouri ANG at St Louis, and now with 7 Wing. The aircraft made a rare visit to the UK for a show at Boscombe Down.

As 'payment' for support in the Gulf War, Turkey is receiving 40 F-4Es from the USAF, drawn from the 110th TFS, the 141st TFS, the 457th TFS and the 35th Fighter Wing. Some are equipped with Pave Spike, and some of the aircraft from the 110th TFS were delivered still resplendent in their shark mouth markings. The 28 aircraft listed below were delivered between 25 March 1991 and December 1991, usually in flights of four.

66-0292, 66-0328, 66-0359, 67-0298, 67-0301, 67-0331, 67-0360, 67-0372, 67-0376, 67-0391, 67-0395, 67-0396, 67-0398, 68-0303, 68-0308, 68-0346, 68-0347, 68-0400, 68-0403, 68-0409, 68-0427, 68-0446, 68-0461, 68-0474, 68-0482, 68-0498, 68-0532, 69-7585.

Note: FY1973 aircraft are marked '01016' etc. Some FY1967 aircraft wear the same serials as FY1977 new-build F-4Es: e.g. (6)70280 and (7)70280.

New F-4E production:

73-1016 to 73-1055	(40)	F-4E	JO6FB
77-0277 to 77-0308	(32)	F-4E	JOMDC

New RF-4E production:

77-0309 to 77-0316	(8)	RF-4E	JOMDD

Ex-USAF F-4Es:

In 1982: 66-0293, 66-0312, 66-0373, 66-0374, 67-0215, 67-0227, 67-0242, 67-0251, 67-0259, 67-0262, 67-0304, 67-0336, 67-0338, 67-0307, plus one
In 1984: 66-0307, 66-0318, 67-0208, 67-0216, 67-0217, 67-0221, 67-0233, 67-0248, 67-0258, 67-0290, 67-0342, 67-0387, plus three
In 1986: 66-0272, 66-0305, 66-0323, 66-0346, 66-0377, 66-0397, 67-0222, 67-0273, 67-0318, 67-0321, 67-0331, 67-0334, 67-0377, 67-0389, 67-0390
In 1987: 66-0297, 66-0300, 66-0301, 66-0303, 66-0304, 66-0309, 66-0314, 66-0317, 66-0320, 66-0333, 66-0336, 66-0339, 66-0344, 66-0345, 66-0346, 66-0351, 66-0354, 66-0355, 66-0361, 66-0370, 66-0379, 67-0210, 67-0218, 67-0226, 67-0230, 67-0232, 67-0268, 67-0269, 67-0272, 67-0274, 67-0280, 67-0285, 67-0298, 67-0302, 67-0334, 67-0344, 67-0354, 68-0313, 68-0319, 68-0350

Below: All eight reconnaissance RF-4Es delivered to Turkey were new-build aircraft for 113 Squadron. These wear the standard NATO green and gray camouflage with light gray undersides.

Right: Operated by 1 Wing, as evidenced by the '1' prefix to the last three digits of its USAF serial number, 67-0230 was supplied to Turkey in 1987 and exhibits a rare camouflage pattern.

1ci Taktik Hava Kuvveti Komutabligi (1st Tactical Air Force)

1ci Ana Jet Us, Eskisehir
111 Filo F-4E
112 Filo F-4E
113 Filo RF-4E

2ci Taktik Hava Kuvveti Komutabligi (2nd Tactical Air Force)

3ci Ana Jet Us, Konya
131 Filo F-4E
132 Filo F-4E

7ci Ana Jet Us, Erhac
171 Filo F-4E
172 Filo F-4E
173 Filo F-4E

UNITED KINGDOM
Royal Navy (Fleet Air Arm)

The Royal Navy became the Phantom's first overseas customer as the result of not being able to agree with the Royal Air Force on a joint specification for the proposed bi-service Hawker Siddeley P.1154 V/STOL strike/attack aircraft. Discussions on a British Phantom with Rolls-Royce Spey turbofan engines were held in St Louis in January 1964, while in the following month the government admitted in its annual defence White Paper that the P.1154RN was unlikely to be a viable proposition. An official go-ahead for an RN Phantom was given by the government on 1 July 1964 and shortly afterward an order (JO740) was placed with McDonnell for two YF-4K-26 prototypes and two F-4K-27 production aircraft. The original RN plan was to obtain 143 Phantoms, but cuts in the aircraft carrier fleet resulted in reductions to 137, then 110, and then only 50, plus seven options. In the event, even this was optimistic and 14 of the 50 production F-4Ks went straight to the RAF when the decision was made not to modernize HMS *Eagle* for Phantom operations. Production was therefore:

XT595-XT596	(2)	YF-4K	JO740
XT597-XT598	(2)	F-4K	JO740
XT857-XT876	(20)	F-4K	JO748
XV565-XV592	(28)	F-4K	JO758
XV604-XV610	(0)	not taken up	
Total 52			

Royal Navy aircraft were designated Phantom FG.Mk 1 to indicate fighter and ground attack duties. They differed considerably in detail from the USN Navy F-4J from which they were derived, not only by powerplant but because of British avionics and equipment. In 1967, the unit cost was reckoned to be £1¼ million, of which 46 percent was accounted for by items produced in the UK.

XT595, the 1,449th Phantom built, first flew on 27 June 1966, followed by XT596 on 31 August. Both went to Edwards AFB, California, for engine trials, while XT597 (flown on 1 November 1966) began weapons trials, which included operations from USS *Coral Sea*. These early machines later served in the experimental role in the UK, flying with the Royal Aircraft Establishment at Bedford, the Aeroplane & Armament Experimental Establishment at Boscombe Down, Rolls-Royce at Hucknall and McDonnell's 'sister firm', Hawker Siddeley (later British Aerospace), at Brough. As the last airfield was too small for fast-jet operations, Phantoms flew from nearby Holme-on-Spalding-Moor until the flight-test facility was moved to RAF Scampton in December 1983.

Flown by US civilian crews, the first three RN Phantoms arrived at Royal Naval Air Station (RNAS) Yeovilton via the Azores on 29 April 1968. Serialed XT859-XT860, they wore extra-dark-sea-gray upper surfaces and white undersides, with large Type D national roundels. Initial trials and crew training were undertaken by 700P Squadron, following which 892 Squadron formed for carrier-based operations and 767 Squadron handled training. Ultimately, the requirement for crews was so small that the task was handed over to the RAF. Delivery of the last Phantom FG.Mk 1 (XV592; F-4 No. 3,394) was effected on 21 November 1969. On disbandment of 892 Squadron, all surviving Phantom FG.Mk 1s transferred to the RAF. The RN lost seven Phantoms in service and a further eight crashed with the RAF.

700P Squadron

On 30 April 1968, 700P Squadron formed at RNAS Yeovilton with the three Phantom FG.Mk 1s which had been delivered the previous day. Led by Commander A. M. G. Pearson, 700P was the Intensive Flight Trials Unit and marked its six aircraft with side numbers 722-727 and deck letters VL to indicate Yeovilton. The fin badge was McDonnell's 'Phantom' character wearing a Union Jack waistcoat. On completion of its task, the squadron's aircraft were distributed between 767 and 892 Squadrons, and formal disbandment took place on 31 March 1969.

First UK Phantom unit was the Royal Navy's 700P Squadron, tasked wih intensive flight trials from its base at Yeovilton.

767 Squadron

Twelve years after it had disbanded, 767 Squadron was re-established at Yeovilton on 14 January 1969 from a nucleus of 700P Squadron, and it expanded to become the Operational Conversion Unit (OCU) for all RN Phantom crews and the first RAF personnel to fly the aircraft. An adaptation of the unit's hawk badge appeared on the fin and aircraft were marked with codes ranging from 150/VL to 157/VL. Disbandment followed on 1 August 1972, but staff were immediately incorporated into the Phantom Post-Operational Conversion Unit (PPOCU) which was established at RAF Leuchars a month later.

Shore-based 767 Squadron was responsible for Phantom crew training in the Royal Navy until 1972, when the RAF took over.

892 Squadron

The only FAA squadron to conform to Their Lordships' plans to convert from DH Sea Vixens to Phantoms was 892, which disbanded at Yeovilton on 4 October 1968 and reformed at the same base on 31 March 1969 with aircraft and personnel from 700P Squadron. The sole RN aircraft carrier to operate Phantoms was HMS *Ark Royal*, and the squadron's aircraft accordingly carried deck letter 'R' on the fin, plus side numbers 010-018 (later 001-008) on the nose. Because it was destined to be the last operational fixed-wing unit to form in the RN (the Sea Harrier had yet to emerge for operation from smaller vessels), the squadron adopted the new fin marking of an omega – the last letter of the Greek alphabet. The main duty was to be air defense, with attack and close air support as secondary roles using BL755 cluster bombs, SNEB rocket pods and parachute-retarded bombs, but not the SUU-23/A podded gun.

An early and unusual mission for the squadron was participation in the London-New York race sponsored by the *Daily Mail* newspaper and on 11 May 1969, commanding officer, Lieutenant Commander Brian Davies and senior observer, Lieutenant Commander Peter Goddard, established a new FAI record of 4 hours, 46 minutes and 57 seconds in XT858, assisted by Handley Page Victor K.Mk 1A

To shorten their take-off run, British F-4Ks had a nose-wheel leg longer than that of other F-4s.

tankers. The first embarkation was aboard USS *Saratoga* in the Mediterranean on 12 October 1969 for trials during which four aircraft made 61 launches. The initial familiarization sorties were flown from HMS *Ark Royal* in Lyme Bay between 30 April and 15 May 1970, before a full embarkation on 12 June.

892 Squadron repositioned to RAF Leuchars on 17 July 1972 and remained there until its parent vessel was paid off. Following a farewell cruise calling at Naval Air Squadron (NAS) Roosevelt Roads, Cecil Field and Oceana, *Ark Royal* sailed into the Mediterranean and, from there catapulted its Buccaneers and final 10 Phantoms on 27 November 1978, the last one away was XT870. The Phantoms flew directly to the RAF maintenance unit at St Athan, and 892 Squadron officially disbanded on 15 December 1968. Previously, 892's aircraft had been maintained at Leuchars by the Navy-staffed Phantom Support Unit, which disbanded on 29 September.

Phantom Post-Operational Conversion Unit

Re-allocation of RN Phantom training to the RAF resulted in the PPOCU being formed at Leuchars on 1 September 1972 from 767 Squadron. Officially part of the RAF's No. 11 Group, and with a 'light blue' CO, it was known, unofficially, as the Phantom Training Flight, and provided FAA pilots and navigators with a naval-orientated version of the RAF Phantom course at Coningsby, comprising 70 flying hours, 25 hours in the simulator and 25 hours' intercept training over four months. Its four aircraft, which were on RAF charge, briefly wore deck letters LU before adopting single-letter identity codes on the fin together with the badge of an omega (like 892 Squadron) beneath a sword, point uppermost. The PPOCU's last aircraft was withdrawn on 15 March 1978, and it disbanded on 31 May.

Lacking naval 'side numbers', Phantom FG.Mk 1s of the PPOCU were operated by the RAF for training crews destined for the sole embarked squadron.

Royal Air Force

Cancelation of the RAF version of Hawker Siddeley's P.1154 on 2 February 1965 resulted in the launch of a two-type replacement program in the form of a militarized P.1127 (the Harrier) and Phantoms. The possibility of an RAF order for the aircraft had been communicated to St Louis when the F-4K was discussed in January 1984, and McDonnell prepared the F-4M to meet anticipated requirements. It therefore took only until 9 February 1965 for a Cooperative Logistics Agreement to be signed by the US and UK defense ministers, covering what the RAF would learn to call the Phantom FGR.Mk 2 (fighter, ground attack and reconnaissance). It was announced on 1 July 1965 that agreement had been reached on the first production batch of aircraft to be ordered for both the RAF and RN (discounting the four already ordered for the latter). These were two RAF YF-4M-29 prototypes, 20 F-4Ks and 38 F-4Ms, working towards a target of 200 for the RAF. That figure was soon reduced to 150, of which the final 32 were not taken up. Serial numbers and McDonnell contract numbers (JO) were as follows:

XT852-XT853	(2)	YF-4M	JO741
XT891-XT914	(24)	F-4M	JO744
XT915-XT928	(0)	transferred to following batch	
XV393-XV442	(50)	F-4M	JO757
XV460-XV501	(42)	F-4M	JO757
XV520-XV551	(0)	canceled	
Total 118			

Following its first flight on 17 February 1967, XT852 (the 1,950th Phantom) was delivered to Holloman AFB, New Mexico, for trials, while XT853 undertook similar duties at NAS Patuxent River. Both ultimately came to the UK to continue their development work with HSA/BAe and the A&AEE. The first Phantom in Britain was XT891, which arrived at Yeovilton on 18 July 1968 and two days later was transferred to No. 23 Maintenance Unit at Aldergrove, Northern Ireland. This unit accepted all the production F-4Ms in addition to 23 of the RN Phantoms. XV501 (F-4 No. 3,507) was received on 29 October 1969 to conclude the contract, although repairs to XV434, following a delivery flight accident, resulted in it being the last one accepted, on 16 June 1970. The colors for early service were a gloss dark-green and dark-sea-gray disruptive pattern on the upper surfaces, with light aircraft gray below and Type B roundels. As with RN aircraft, the radomes were black. These markings were also applied to the Phantom FG.Mk 1s which the RAF used to form No. 43 Squadron, but it also transpired that 767 Squadron received some in RAF camouflage.

Royal Air Force plans for the Phantom FGR.Mk 2 were that it should serve in the strike/attack role pending availability of the Anglo-French SEPECAT Jaguar, and then switch to air defense when the BAC Lightning ended its service career. Although early squadrons were based in the UK with No. 38 Group of Air Support Command, the main concentration was in Royal Air Force Germany, where No. II Squadron was, like No. 41 at home, assigned to tactical reconnaissance with a centerline pod. The strike/attack aircraft used bombs and rocket pods and could also be armed (Nos 14, 17 and 31 Squadrons) with US-controlled B57 nuclear weapons. In June 1972, XT891 of No. 6 Squadron became the first Phantom with matt camouflage and Type B (lacking white) roundels and fin flashes – the latter were 'swept-back'.

The change of tasking began in spring of 1974, when No. 54 Squadron re-equipped with Jaguars and passed its Phantoms to No. 111 Squadron for air defense. To reflect the change, the 'home' of the Phantom, moved from No. 38 Group to No. 11 Group in October 1974. Most interceptor squadrons were assigned to SACEUR, but No. 43 Squadron had been a SACLANT unit for TASMO (Tactical Air Support of Maritime Operations) since it became operational on 1 July 1970, and No. 29 was similarly assigned from 1 January 1980. The Germany-based squadrons likewise adopted Jaguars, but usually operated both aircraft types for some six months while personnel were retrained or replaced.

Beginning in 1975, the change to air defense was accompanied by the addition of Marconi ARI.18228 radar-warning receiver antennas in a fintip pod. By then, support

work was increasingly being undertaken by the Engineering Wing at St Athan, assisted by No. 60 MU at Leconfield, until its final Phantom (XV404) left on 19 November 1976. No. 23 MU closed in April 1978. Phantom XV474 was delivered to St Athan on 29 June 1978, emerging soon afterward in a new color scheme of medium-sea-gray, mixed-gray and (below) light-aircraft-gray. Initially, roundels were unaltered and radomes remained black, but they were soon changed to mixed-gray radomes and low-visibility-pink and light-blue nationality markings. Air defense armament comprised four AIM-7E2 Sparrow AAMs, two AIM-9G Sidewinder AAMs and an optional SUU-23/A 20-mm gunpod, the former pair giving way to BAe Sky Flash in 1979 and AIM-9L in the early 1980s.

Phantoms began operating in the southern hemisphere in 1982, when they bolstered the defenses of the Falkland Islands following their recapture from Argentina. At first flying from the short runway at Port Stanley Airport, they routinely used airfield arrester gear at the end of each sortie. In order to compensate NATO for the loss of aircraft diverted to the Falklands, the RAF took the unusual step of purchasing 15 ex-USN/USMC F-4Js for European use. They cost a fraction less than $1 million each, but by the time they had been refurbished at NARF North Island, the program price was $138 million. Retaining their J79 engines and the bulk of US avionics, these very non-standard machines arrived in Britain between 30 August 1984 and 4 January 1985, wearing the serials ZE350-ZE364. Nine of them sported a duck-egg-blue tint to their camouflage, as the result of a misunderstanding of the paint specification by the Mexican manufacturers. They adopted the designation F-4J(UK), instead of the more logical 'Phantom F.Mk 3', to avoid confusion with the Phantom F.Mk 3.

Phantom ranks were thinned during the late 1980s by conversion of squadrons to Tornado F.Mk 3s. The Mk 1s were first to be pensioned off, followed by the F-4J(UK) in January 1991, while 75 of the Mk 2s received new BAe-built outer wing panels from 1987 onwards to extend their fatigue lives. Dissolution of the Warsaw Pact and unification of Germany removed the need for the two air defense squadrons at Wildenrath and they disbanded in the second half of 1991. BAe completed the last Phantom overhaul in 1991. By the start of 1992, only Nos 56 and 74 Squadrons at Wattisham remained, before both disbanded in the fall, a short time after No. 1435 flight on the Falkland Islands converted to Tornados. Greece showed interest in buying 32 ex-RAF Phantoms in 1992, but had not placed an order at the time of writing. RAF losses totaled 32 Mk 2s and one F-4J in accidents.

No. II Squadron

The Phantom FGR.Mk 2 element of No. II Squadron formed at Brüggen on 7 December 1970 and moved to Laarbruch on 1 April 1971, when the squadron's Hunter FR.Mk 10 element disbanded. Tasked with tactical reconnaissance, the squadron's aircraft carried an EMI-built centerline pod with visual spectrum cameras and an infrared linescan, plus oblique cameras in the noses of the underwing drop-tanks. The insignia comprised a Wake Knot on a red disc, flanked by black bars containing red triangles. Replacement Jaguars began arriving in February 1976.

Phantoms of No. II Squadron carried a British-built reconnaissance pod on the centerline pylon in Germany.

No. 6 Squadron

This was the first operational Phantom squadron in the RAF, and it disbanded as a Canberra B.Mk 16 unit at Akrotiri on 13 January 1969. Three days later, No. 6 Squadron (Designate) was established at Coningsby, its crews at that time were on the first training course of No. 228 OCU. Official formation followed at Coningsby on

7 May 1969 and No. 6 was declared operational with FGR.Mk 2s in the attack role on the following 1 August. With Nos 41 and 54 Squadrons, it formed a ground attack wing in No. 38 Group, tasked with short-notice overseas deployment. The squadron's unofficial badge of a winged can-opener was applied. On 30 September 1974, No. 6 disbanded, to be reborn the next day with Jaguars.

The insignia of No. 6 Squadron includes the Royal Artillery 'gunner's stripe' on the fin and a flying can-opener badge on the nose. The unit was the first in the RAF to operate Phantoms.

No. 14 Squadron

Equipment of RAF Germany with Phantom FGR.Mk 2s began with the delivery of aircraft to Brüggen. The nucleus of a new squadron formed there on 1 June 1970 and became No. 14 Squadron when the old squadron of that name disbanded as a Canberra B(I).Mk 8 unit on 30 June. Retaining its interdiction tasking, No. 14 began receiving Jaguars on 7 April 1975, and it withdrew its final Phantom on 1 December the same year. The squadron's insignia was a winged disk, flanked by blue diamonds on a white field.

In 1970, No. 14 Squadron was the first Phantom unit in RAF Germany.

No. 17 Squadron

RAF Germany's second FGR.Mk 2 unit started to form at Wildenrath on 1 July 1970 and was commissioned on 1 September, although it did not take up residence at its permanent base of Brüggen until 16 September. Wearing the markings of a white arrowhead containing black zigzag lines, its aircraft were strike/attack dedicated. No. 17's first Jaguar arrived on 1 September and its last Phantom left in February 1976.

A Phantom FGR.Mk 2 of No. 17 Squadron bears the unusual 'sloping' fin flash.

No. 19 Squadron

The Phantom FGR.Mk 2's second tour of duty in Germany was as an air defense fighter, in which role Nos 19 and 92 Squadrons flew Lightnings at Gütersloh. No. 19 Squadron (Designate) formed at Wildenrath on 1 October 1976 (its first aircraft having arrived on 27 September) and became the 'proper' No. 19 when the Lightning unit disbanded on 1 January 1977. Its aircraft were marked with a dolphin on the fin, plus a white and blue checkerboard. Nos 19 and 92 Squadrons each provided one

aircraft for the QRA 'Battle Flight' tasked with defending the East/West German air defense zone, and they flew a symbolic mission at midnight on 2/3 October 1990, when united Germany became responsible for its own air defense. A year later, on 2 October 1991, No. 19 Squadron scrambled two aircraft on the last such mission. The squadron was 'de-declared' from NATO on 31 December 1991 and disbanded on 9 January 1992. Wildenrath's last Phantom, XT899, left the station on 16 January en route to the Czech Air Force museum.

Specially-marked XT899 of No. 19 Squadron was delivered to the Czech & Slovak Air Force museum at Kbely, thanks to personal intervention by the US ambassador in Prague – the former film star, Shirley Temple.

No. 23 Squadron

Equipped with Lightnings at Leuchars in the air defense role, No. 23 Squadron disbanded on 31 October 1975. On 6 October, however, No. 23 Squadron (Designate) had been established at Coningsby and it officially re-formed there from 17 November. Declared 'limited operational' on 20 February 1975, it transferred to Wattisham on 25 February, its Phantom FGR.Mk 2s marked

with the badge of an eagle. Fully operational on 14 May 1976, it was not until the night of 26/27 January 1978 that No. 23 Squadron mounted Wattisham's first Phantom QRA scramble to intercept a Soviet aircraft. The squadron moved to the Falkland Islands by sleight of hand on 1 April 1983, when it exchanged aircraft and number-plates with No. 29 Squadron. Operations transferred from Port Stanley Airport to the new RAF

Mount Pleasant on 20 April 1984, with strength reducing to four aircraft. The unit became No. 1435 Flight on 1 November 1988, when a new No. 23 formed at Leeming with Tornado F.Mk 3s.

No. 23 Squadron spent its last five F-4 years operating air defense Phantoms in the Falkland Islands before converting to Tornados.

No. 29 Squadron

No. 29 Squadron (Designate) was established on 1 October 1974 and was formed officially as a ready-made interceptor squadron at Coningsby on 1 January 1975. It was declared operational in May, although aircraft had received unit markings (an eagle preying on a buzzard) since the 25 October. The 'old' No. 29, equipped with Lightnings, had stood down to begin conversion on 19 July 1974, but was not disbanded until 31 December. It was a No. 29 Squadron Phantom that was the first aircraft in the UK to launch a BAe Sky Flash missile against a target (Gloster Meteor drone) over the Aberporth Range on 15 August 1979.

Following the Falklands war, nine Phantoms, known as the 'PhanDet', were based at Port Stanley, where the first (XV468) arrived on 17 October 1982. On 1 April 1983, No. 23 Squadron took over the South Atlantic detachment and No. 29 regrouped at Coningsby. After an eight-month period at Waddington due to runway repairs at its base, the unit returned to Coningsby on 1 November 1984 and took up residence in newly-built hardened accommodation – the first UK air defense squadron to do so. The squadron stood down from NATO on 1 December 1986, and it disbanded on 31 March 1987 becoming a Tornado F.Mk 3 unit a month later.

Type 'B' national identification is worn by a Phantom FGR.Mk 2 of No. 29 Squadron. The triple-X fin marking is based on the brewer's sign for 'extra strength' and is a long-term additional adornment for No. 29.

No. 31 Squadron

Disbanded as a Canberra PR.Mk 7 squadron at Laarbruch on 31 March 1971, No. 31 Squadron began reforming on 20 July 1971 and was formally established at Brüggen on 7 October in the strike/attack role. The squadron markings were a star, plus a

yellow and green checkerboard. Jaguars began arriving as replacements in January 1976, and the last five Phantoms left the unit on 1 July. The squadron had a reconnaissance commitment, but only a few aircraft received provision for the centerline pod late in the Phantom's era.

A quartet of No. 31 Squadron Phantom FGR.Mk 2s overflies West Germany during a sortie from Brüggen in the early 1970s. The unit was to be a third RAF reconnaissance Phantom squadron but was not fully equipped.

No. 41 Squadron

Some 18 months after disbanding as a Bloodhound SAM squadron, No. 41 Squadron reformed at Coningsby on 1 April 1972 as a reconnaissance unit with

secondary attack tasking, becoming operational on 12 July. Its badge was a double-armed cross. The squadron disbanded on 31 March 1977, instantly becoming a Jaguar unit at Coltishall.

The sole UK-based reconnaissance Phantom squadron was No. 41, which flew from Coningsby in the company of two similarly-equipped attack units.

No. 43 Squadron

Equipped with Phantom FG.Mk 1s that were surplus to naval requirements on their delivery, No. 43 Squadron was unusual in being tasked with air defense while other RAF Phantom units majored in strike/attack. After being dormant for two years, No. 43 reformed on 1 September 1969 to operate Phantoms at Leuchars. The aircraft were adorned with the badge of a fighting cock, plus a black and white checkerboard. The first QRA (Quick Reaction Alert) was mounted on 23 March 1970. Operational on 1 July 1970, the squadron was assigned to SACLANT for support of maritime operations. Single-letter codes were replaced by the group AA-AZ from July 1986, while a couple of Mk 2s were added from May 1988. No. 43 was 'de-declared' on 1 July 1989, and it flew its last Phantom

mission on 31 July, prior to beginning conversion to Tornado F.Mk 3s.

Operating naval F-4Ks, No. 43 was the RAF's only interceptor Phantom squadron in 1969-75.

No. 54 Squadron

On 1 September 1969, No. 54 Squadron disbanded as a Hunter FGA.Mk 9 squadron at West Raynham and formed with Phantom FGA.Mk 2s at Coningsby in the ground attack role. Squadron markings comprised a blue lion, plus a blue and yellow

checkerboard. The squadron disbanded on 23 April 1974 and passed its aircraft to No. 111 Squadron.

Attack-tasked Phantoms received fuel from Victors when training for overseas deployment.

No. 56 Squadron

Aircrew destined for No. 56 Squadron – otherwise known as the 'Firebirds' – began Phantom FGR.Mk 2 conversion on 22 March 1976, and the squadron moved to Wattisham on 8 July following the 28 June disbandment of the similarly-titled Lightning unit at the same base. Fully operational from

13 September 1976, the squadron's aircraft wore a Phoenix badge, plus a red and white checkerboard. The squadron was 'de-declared' on 30 June 1992, prior to disbanding the following day.

Red fins were a feature of No. 56 Squadron in later days, but this FGR.Mk 2 has gained some 'zaps'.

No. 64 Squadron

See No. 228 OCU.

No. 74 Squadron

Dormant for 13 years, this famous fighter squadron reformed on 1 July 1984 and spent its first two months training to fly the F-4J(UK) and ferrying aircraft to Wattisham, where it was commissioned on 19 October. The 'Tigers' were appropriately decorated with the badge of a tiger's face and fighter bars containing black and yellow triangles representing a tiger's pelt. Conversion to FGR.Mk 2s began with a first sortie on 15

January 1991 and was complete by the end of the month. Destined to be the RAF's last Phantom squadron, No. 74 stood down on 30 September 1992 and disbanded the following day.

The F-4J served only with No. 74 Squadron at Wattisham. Black fins were adopted later and perpetuated on the FGR.Mk 2.

No. 92 Squadron

The work-up of No. 92 (Phantom) Squadron for air defense in Germany began on 1 January 1977 and the unit officially formed on 1 April, coincident with the disbandment of No. 92 (Lightning) Squadron at Gütersloh. Markings comprised a cobra, plus an arrowhead containing red and yellow chevrons. No. 92 Squadron gained the RAF Phantom's only aerial 'victory' over a

manned aircraft on 25 May 1982, when Jaguar XX963 was destroyed by an accidentally-launched Sidewinder, thankfully without loss of life. In 1990, its CO, Wing Commander Dave Pollington, became the first RAF pilot to achieve 4,000 Phantom flying hours. No. 92 Squadron shared 'Battle Flight' duties with No. 19 Squadron until its final sortie was flown on 27 June 1991. The squadron stood down on 30 June 1991 and was disbanded on 5 July.

Representing the F-4M's appearance during the late 1980s, this aircraft has a fintip pod for the ARI 18228 RWR and is overall gray with toned-down Type B roundels. No. 92's arrowhead has been replaced by checks.

No. 111 Squadron

The training of a new 'Treble One' squadron began at Coningsby on 1 July 1974 and the unit officially came into being on 1 October when No. 111 (Lightning) Squadron disbanded at Wattisham. The squadron transferred to Leuchars on 3 November 1975 to assume air defense duties and converted to ex-Navy FG.Mk 1s between March 1978 and March 1980. It began using

two-letter codes BA-BZ in July 1986, its other markings included a black lightning flash and the badge of a cross potent quadrat. The squadron moved into hardened shelter accommodation in March 1986, followed by No. 43 Squadron in April. No. 111 Squadron 'de-declared' on 31 October 1989 and officially ceased being a Phantom unit on 31 January 1990, reforming with Tornado F.Mk 3s three months later.

Second and last RAF user of the naval F-4K, 'Treble One' Squadron led a busy life at Leuchars, helping to police the Iceland-UK Gap. The squadron's color scheme on gray aircraft was one of the RAF's best.

No. 1435 Flight

In March 1988, RAF Phantom squadrons in Europe began supplying crews in rotation to man the four-aircraft detachment at RAF Mount Pleasant in the Falkland Islands, although this retained the title of No. 23 Squadron until 30 October 1988. On the

following day it was renamed No. 1435 Flight, its aircraft wearing a large, red Maltese Cross on their fins and the individual names 'Faith', 'Hope', 'Charity' and 'Desperation'. Still supported by personnel on rotation, it undertook conversion to Tornado F.Mk 3s in July 1992.

No. 1435 Flight's aircraft were seldom seen in Europe. Their nose markings comprised the Falkland Islands' badge of a sheep and sailing ship upon a blue shield. ALE-40 chaff/flare dispensers were fitted.

No. 228 Operational Conversion Unit

Preparations for establishment of the RAF Phantom OCU began at Coningsby in December 1967, when No. 5 School of Technical Training formed to instruct ground crew. The OCU began to form in February 1968 and was officially established on 1 August, simultaneously absorbing No. 5 SoTT as its No. 3 Squadron. The first Phantom FGR.Mk 2 (XT891) was delivered on 23 August, and after instructors had been trained, the first course passed out on 2 May 1969. The 'shadow' identity of No. 64 (Reserve) Squadron was bestowed on 1 July 1970 and the aircraft received its badge of a scarab. Several types of course were provided; the one for *ab initio* crews lasted 19 weeks and involved 60-70 flying hours. Early in 1983, Nos 1 and 2 Squadrons (the flying component) were combined as No. 2 Squadron, and simulator operations became the new role of No. 1. Two-letter codes CA-CZ were applied from February 1987, and on 22 April the OCU transferred to Leuchars. One of its aircraft (XV470), then undergoing overhaul at the Phantom Aircraft Servicing Flight (PASF), left Coningsby on 16 October 1987, being the last Phantom to vacate the station. The OCU remained at

Leuchars until it was disbanded on 31 January 1991, although training had actually ended a couple of months before, and the last mission, a nine-ship formation, had been flown on 19 December 1990. The last Phantom of any unit to leave Leuchars was the OCU's XT906, which departed the relocated PASF on 21 March 1991.

Phantom Training Flight

Following disbandment of No. 228 OCU, the PTF formed at Wattisham on 1 February 1991, but only to 'retread' former Phantom crews returning to the aircraft after a tour elsewhere. The unit operated within No. 74 Squadron with an allocation of three of its aircraft, which wore the old PPOCU badge of an omega and a sword in addition to their No. 74 markings. The PTF disbanded on 31 December 1991.

Phantom Conversion Flight

Formed at Leuchars on 1 July 1969, the PCF trained Phantom FG.Mk 1 crews for No. 43 Squadron, the unit it became on 1 September that year.

The scarab badge of No. 64 (Reserve) Squadron was applied to the fins of No. 228 OCU aircraft. Although gray, this aircraft has yet to receive an RWR fin, dating the photograph as 1978-79.

Aircraft & Armament Evaluation Establishment

Several Phantoms have passed through Boscombe Down in the course of the aircraft's RAF and RN service. The sole resident is currently the only FG.Mk 1 flying: XT597, which has accurately-calibrated airspeed equipment for its duties as a chase aircraft.

The last Phantom flying in the UK is XT597, an FG.Mk 1 used for trials by the A&AEE.

Production Summary by Block Numbers

Block 1
YF4H-1 — USN — 142259 to 142260 — 2
F-4A-1-MC — USN — 143388 to 143392 — 5
Block 1 total/Cumulative total — 7/7

Block 2
F-4A-2-MC — USN — 145307 to 145317 — 11
Block 2 total/Cumulative total — 11/18

Block 3
F-4A-3-MC — USN — 146817 to 146821 — 5
Block 3 total/Cumulative total — 5/23

Block 4
F-4A-4-MC — USN — 148252 to 148261 — 10
Block 4 total/Cumulative total — 10/33

Block 5
F-4A-5-MC — USN — 148262 to 148275 — 14
Block 5 total/Cumulative total — 14/47

Block 6
F-4B-6-MC — USN — 148363 to 148386 — 24
Block 6 total/Cumulative total — 24/71

Block 7
F-4B-7-MC — USN — 148387 to 148410 — 24
Block 7 total/Cumulative total — 24/95

Block 8
F-4B-8-MC — USN — 148411 to 148434 — 24
Block 8 total/Cumulative total — 24/119

Block 9
F-4B-9-MC — USN — 149403 to 149426 — 24
Block 9 total/Cumulative total — 24/143

Block 10
F-4B-10-MC — USN — 149427 to 149450 — 24
Block 10 total/Cumulative total — 24/167

Block 11
F-4B-11-MC — USN — 149451 to 149474 — 24
Block 11 total/Cumulative total — 24/191

Block 12
F-4B-12-MC — USN — 150406 to 150435 — 30
Block 12 total/Cumulative total — 30/221

Block 13
F-4B-13-MC — USN — 150436 to 150479 — 44
Block 13 total/Cumulative total — 44/265

Block 14
F-4B-14-MC — USN — 150480 to 150493 & 150624 to 150651 — 42
YRF-4C-14-MC — USAF — 62-12200/62-12201 — 2
Block 14 total/Cumulative total — 44/309

Block 15
F-4B-15-MC — USN — 150652 to 150653, 150993 to 151021 & 151397 to 151398 — 33
F-4C-15-MC — USAF — 62-12199 & 63-7407 to 63-7420 — 15
Block 15 total/Cumulative total — 48/357

Block 16
F-4B-16-MC — USN — 151399 to 151426 — 28
F-4C-16-MC — USAF — 63-7421 to 63-7442 — 22
Block 16 total/Cumulative total — 50/407

Block 17
F-4B-17-MC — USN — 151427 to 151477 — 21
F-4C-17-MC — USAF — 63-7443 to 63-7468 — 26
RF-4C-17-MC — USAF — 63-7740 to 63-7742 — 3
Block 17 total/Cumulative total — 50/457

Block 18
F-4B-18-MC — USN — 151448 to 151472 — 25
F-4C-18-MC — USAF — 63-7469 to 63-7526 — 58
RF-4C-18-MC — USAF — 63-7743 to 63-7749 — 7
Block 18 total/Cumulative total — 90/547

Block 19
F-4B-19-MC — USN — 151473 to 151497 — 25
F-4C-19-MC — USAF — 63-7527 to 63-7597 — 71
RF-4C-19-MC — USAF — 63-7750 to 63-7763 — 14
Block 19 total/Cumulative total — 110/657

Block 20
F-4B-20-MC — USN — 151498 to 151519 & 152207 to 152215 — 31
RF-4B-20-MC — USMC — 151975 to 151977 — 3
F-4C-20-MC — USAF — 63-7598 to 63-7662 — 65
RF-4C-20-MC — USAF — 64-0997 to 64-1017 — 21
Block 20 total/Cumulative total — 120/777

Block 21
F-4B-21-MC — USN — 152216 to 152243 — 28
RF-4B-21-MC — USMC — 151978 to 151979 — 2
F-4C-21-MC — USAF — 63-7663 to 63-7713, 64-0654 to 64-0672 — 70
RF-4C-21-MC — USAF — 64-1018 to 64-1037 — 20
Block 21 total/Cumulative total — 120/897

Block 22
F-4B-22-MC — USN — 152244 to 152272 — 29
RF-4B-22-MC — USMC — 151980 to 151981 — 2
F-4C-22-MC — USAF — 64-0673 to 64-0737 — 65
RF-4C-22-MC — USAF — 64-1038 to 64-1061 — 24
Block 22 total/Cumulative total — 120/1,017

Block 23
F-4B-23-MC — USN — 152273 to 152304 — 32
RF-4B-23-MC — USMC — 151982 to 151983 — 2
F-4C-23-MC — USAF — 64-0738 to 64-0817 — 80
RF-4C-23-MC — USAF — 64-1062 to 64-1077 — 16
Block 23 total/Cumulative total — 130/1,147

Block 24
F-4B-24-MC — USN — 152305 to 152331 — 27
RF-4B-24-MC — USMC — 153089 to 153094 — 6
F-4C-24-MC — USAF — 64-0818 to 64-0881 — 64
RF-4C-24-MC — USAF — 64-1078 to 64-1085 & 65-0818 to 65-0838 — 29
F-4D-24-MC — USAF — 64-0929 to 64-0937 — 9
Block 24 total/Cumulative total — 135/1,282

Block 25
F-4B-25-MC — USN — 152965 to 152994 — 30
RF-4B-25-MC — USMC — 153095 to 153100 — 6
F-4C-25-MC — USAF — 64-0882 to 64-0928 — 47
RF-4C-25-MC — USAF — 65-0839 to 65-0864 — 26
F-4D-25-MC — USAF — 64-0938 to 64-0963 — 26
Block 25 total/Cumulative total — 135/1,417

Block 26
F-4B-26-MC — USN — 152995 to 153029 — 35
RF-4B-26-MC — USMC — 153101 to 153107 — 7
RF-4C-26-MC — USAF — 65-0865 to 65-0901 — 37
F-4D-26-MC — USAF — 64-0964 to 640980 & 65-0580 to 65-0611 — 49
F-4J-26-MC — USN — 153071 to 153075 — 5
YF-4K-26-MC — RN — XT595 to XT596 — 2
Block 26 total/Cumulative total — 135/1,552

Block 27
F-4B-27-MC — USN — 153030 to 153056 — 27
RF-4B-27-MC — USMC — 153108 to 153115 — 8
RF-4C-27-MC — USAF — 65-0902 to 65-0932 — 31
F-4D-27-MC — USAF — 65-0612 to 65-0665 — 54
F-4J-27-MC — USN — 153076 to 153088 — 13
F-4K-27-MC — RN — XT597 to XT598 — 2
Block 27 total/Cumulative total — 135/1,687

Block 28
F-4B-28-MC — USN — 153057 to 153070 & 153912 to 153915 — 18
RF-4C-28-MC — USAF — 65-0933 to 65-0945, 66-0383 to 66-0386 & 66-0388 — 18
F-4D-28-MC — USAF — 65-0666 to 65-0770 — 105
F-4J-28-MC — USN — 153768 to 153779 — 12
F-4J-38-MC — USN — 155875 to 155889 — 15
Block 28 total/Cumulative total — 168/1,855

Block 29
RF-4C-29-MC — USAF — 66-0387 & 66-0389 to 66-0406 — 19
F-4D-29-MC — USAF — 65-0771 to 65-0801, 66-0226 to 66-0283 & 66-7455 to 66-7504 — 139
F-4J-29-MC — USN — 153780 to 153799 — 20
YF-4M-29-MC — RAF — XT852 to XT853 — 2
Block 29 total/Cumulative total — 180/2,035

Block 30
RF-4C-30-MC — USAF — 66-0407 to 66-0428 — 22
F-4D-30-MC — USAF — 66-7505 to 66-7650 — 146
F-4J-30-MC — USN — 153800 to 153839 — 40
F-4K-30-MC — RN — XT857 to XT858 — 2
Block 30 total/Cumulative total — 210/2,245

Block 31
RF-4C-31-MC — USAF — 66-0429 to 66-0450 — 22
F-4D-31-MC — USAF — 66-7651 to 66-7774 & 66-8685 to 66-8698 — 138
F-4E-31-MC — USAF — 66-0284 to 66-0297 — 14
F-4J-31-MC — USN — 153840 to 153876 — 37
F-4K-31-MC — RN — XT859 to XT862 — 4
F-4M-31-MC — RAF — XT891 to XT895 — 5
Block 31 total/Cumulative total — 220/2,465

Block 32
RF-4C-32-MC — USAF — 66-0451 to 66-0472 — 22
F-4D-32-MC — USAF — 66-8699 to 66-8786 — 88
F-4E-32-MC — USAF — 66-0298 to 66-0338 — 41
F-4J-32-MC — USN — 153877 to 153911 & 154781 to 154785 — 40
F-4K-32-MC — RN — XT863 to XT870 — 8
F-4M-32-MC — RAF — XT896 to XT906 — 11
Block 32 total/Cumulative total — 210/2,675

Block 33
RF-4C-33-MC — USAF — 66-0473 to 66-0478 & 67-0428 to 67-0442 — 21
F-4D-33-MC — USAF — 66-8787 to 66-8825 — 39
F-4E-33-MC — USAF — 66-0339 to 66-0382 & 67-0208 to 67-0219 — 56
F-4J-33-MC — USN — 154786 to 154788 & 155504 to 155569 — 69
F-4K-33-MC — RN — XT871 to XT876 — 6
F-4M-33-MC — RAF — XT907 to XT914, XV393 to XV398 — 14
Block 33 total/Cumulative total — 205/2,880

Block 34
RF-4C-34-MC — USAF — 67-0443 to 67-0453 — 11
F-4E-34-MC — USAF — 67-0220 to 67-0282 — 63
F-4J-34-MC — USN — 155570 to 155580 & 155731 to 155784 — 65
F-4K-34-MC — RN — XV565 to XV571 — 7
F-4M-34-MC — RAF — XV399 to XV417 — 19
Block 34 total/Cumulative total — 165/3,045

Block 35
RF-4C-35-MC — USAF — 67-0454 to 67-0461 — 8
F-4D-35-MC — Iranian AF — 67-14869 to 67-14876 — 8
F-4E-35-MC — USAF — 67-0283 to 67-0341 — 59
F-4J-35-MC — USN — 155785 to 155843 — 59
F-4K-35-MC — RN — XV572 to XV578 — 7
F-4M-35-MC — RAF — XV418 to XV436 — 19
Block 35 total/Cumulative total — 160/3,205

Block 36
RF-4C-36-MC — USAF — 67-0462 to 67-0469 — 8
F-4D-36-MC — Iranian AF — 67-14877 to 67-14884 — 8
F-4E-36-MC — USAF — 67-0342 to 67-0398 — 57
F-4J-36-MC — USN — 155844 to 155866 — 23
F-4K-36-MC — RN — XV579 to XV585 — 7
F-4M-36-MC — RAF — XV437 to XV442, XV460 to XV475 — 22
Block 36 total/Cumulative total — 125/3,330

Block 37
RF-4C-37-MC — USAF — 68-0548 to 68-0561 — 14
F-4D-37-MC — Iranian AF — 68-6904 to 68-6911 — 8
F-4E-37-MC — USAF — 68-0303 to 68-0365 — 63
F-4J-37-MC — USN — 155867 to 155874 — 8
F-4K-37-MC — RN — XV586 to XV592 — 7
F-4M-37-MC — RAF — XV476 to XV495 — 20
Block 37 total/Cumulative total — 120/3,450

Block 38
RF-4C-38-MC — USAF — 68-0562 to 68-0576 — 15
F-4D-38-MC — Iranian AF — 68-6912 to 68-6919 — 8
F-4E-38-MC — USAF — 68-0366 to 68-0395 & 68-0400 to 68-0409 — 40
F-4E-38-MC — Israeli AF — 68-0396 to 68-0399 — 4
F-4M-38-MC — RAF — XV496 to XV501 — 6
Block 38 total/Cumulative total — 73/3,523

Block 39
RF-4C-39-MC — USAF — 68-0577 to 68-0593 — 17
F-4E-39-MC — USAF — 68-0410 to 68-0413, 68-0418 to 68-0433, & 68-0438 to 68-0451 — 34
F-4E-39-MC — Israeli AF — 68-0414 to 68-0417 & 68-0434 to 68-0437 — 8
F-4J-39-MC — USN — 155890 to 155902 — 13
Block 39 total/Cumulative total — 72/3,595

Block 40
RF-4C-40-MC — USAF — 68-0594 to 68-0611 — 18
F-4E-40-MC — USAF — 68-0452 to 68-0453, 68-0458 to 68-0468,

F-4E-40-MC	Israeli AF	68-0473 to 68-0483, & 68-0488 to 68-0494	31
		68-0454 to 68-0457, 68-0469 to 68-0472, & 68-0484 to 68-0487	12
F-4J-40-MC	USN	157242 to 157260	19

Block 40 total/Cumulative total 80/3,675

Block 41

RF-4B-41-MC	USMC	157342 to 157346	5
RF-4C-41-MC	USAF	69-0349 to 69-0357	9
F-4E-41-MC	USAF	68-0495 to 68-0498, 68-0503 to 68-0518, & 68-0526 to 68-0538	33
F-4E-41-MC	Israeli AF	68-0499 to 68-0502, 68-0519 to 68-0525, & 68-0539 to 68-0547	20
F-4J-41-MC	USN	157261 to 157273	13

Block 41 total/Cumulative total 80/3,755

Block 42

RF-4C-42-MC	USAF	69-0358 to 69-0366	9
F-4E-42-MC	USAF	69-0236 to 69-0303	68
F-4J-42-MC	USN	155903 & 157274 to 157285	13

Block 42 total/Cumulative total 90/3,845

Block 43

RF-4B-43-MC	USMC	157347 to 157351	5
RF-4C-43-MC	USAF	69-0367 to 69-0375	9
F-4E-43-MC	USAF	69-0304 to 69-0307 & 69-7201 to 69-7260	64
RF-4E-43-MC	Luftwaffe	3501 to 3508	8
F-4J-43-MC	USN	157286 to 157297	12

Block 43 total/Cumulative total 98/3,943

Block 44

RF-4C-44-MC	USAF	69-0376 to 69-0384	9
F-4E-44-MC	USAF	69-7261 to 69-7273, 69-7286 to 69-7303, & 69-7546 to 69-7578	64
RF-4E-44-MC	Luftwaffe	3509 to 3515	7
F-4J-44-MC	USN	157298 to 157309	12

Block 44 total/Cumulative total 92/4,035

Block 45

F-4E-45-MC	USAF	69-7579 to 69-7589	11
F-4EJ-45-MC	JASDF	17-8301 to 17-8302, 27-8303 to 27-8306, & 37-8307 to 37-8310	10
RF-4E-45-MC	Luftwaffe	3516 to 3534	19
RF-4E-45-MC	Israeli AF	69-7590 to 69-7595	6
F-4J-45-MC	USN	158346 to 158354	9

Block 45 total/Cumulative total 55/4,090

Block 46

F-4E-46-MC	Iranian AF	69-7711 to 69-7726	16
RF-4E-46-MC	Luftwaffe	3535 to 3563	29
F-4J-46-MC	USN	158355 TO 158365	11

Block 46 total/Cumulative total 56/4,146

Block 47

F-4E-47-MC	Iranian AF	69-7727 to 69-7742	16
F-4EJ-47-MC	JASDF	37-8311 to 37-8313	3
RF-4E-47-MC	Luftwaffe	3564 to 3588	25
F-4J-47-MC	USN	158366 to 158379	14

Block 47 total/Cumulative total 58/4,204

Block 48

RF-4C-48-MC	USAF	71-0248 to 71-0252	5
F-4E-48-MC	USAF	71-0224 to 71-0247	24
RF-4E-48-MC	Iranian AF	72-0266 to 72-0269	4

Block 48 total/Cumulative total 33/4,237

Block 49

RF-4C-49-MC	USAF	71-0253 to 71-0259	7
F-4E-49-MC	USAF	71-1070 to 71-1093	24

Block 49 total/Cumulative total 31/4,268

Block 50

F-4E-50-MC	USAF	71-1391 to 71-1402 & 72-0121 to 72-0138	30

Block 50 total/Cumulative total 30/4,298

Block 51

RF-4C-51-MC	USAF	72-0145 to 72-0150	6
F-4E-51-MC	USAF	72-0139 to 72-0144 & 72-0157 to 72-0159	9
F-4E-51-MC	Israeli AF	71-1779 to 71-1786	8
F-4E-51-MC	Iranian AF	71-1094 to 71-1101	8

Block 51 total/Cumulative total 31/4,329

Block 52

RF-4C-52-MC	USAF	72-0151 to 72-0153	3
F-4E-52-MC	USAF	72-0160 to 72-0165	6
F-4E-52-MC	Iranian AF	71-1102 to 71-1115	14
F-4E-52-MC	Israeli AF	71-1787 to 71-1793	7
F-4F-52-MC	Luftwaffe	3701 to 3709	9

Block 52 total/Cumulative total 39/4,368

Block 53

RF-4C-53-MC	USAF	72-0154 to 72-0156	3
RF-4E-53-MC	USAF	72-0166 to 72-0168 & 72-1407	4
F-4E-53-MC	Iranian AF	71-1116 to 71-1129	14
F-4E-53-MC	Israeli AF	71-1794 to 71-1796	3
F-4F-53-MC	Luftwaffe	3710 to 3724	15

Block 53 total/Cumulative total 39/4,407

Block 54

F-4E-54-MC	USAF	72-1476 to 72-1489	14
F-4E-54-MC	Iranian AF	71-1130 to 71-1142	13
F-4E-54-MC	Greek AF	72-1500 to 72-1507	8
F-4F-54-MC	Luftwaffe	3725 to 3748	24

Block 54 total/Cumulative total 59/4,466

Block 55

F-4E-55-MC	USAF	72-1490 to 72-1497	8
F-4E-55-MC	Iranian AF	71-1143 to 71-1152	10
F-4E-55-MC	Greek AF	72-1508 to 72-1523	16
F-4F-55-MC	Luftwaffe	3749 to 3772	24

Block 55 total/Cumulative total 58/4,524

Block 56

F-4E-56-MC	USAF	72-1498 to 72-1499	2
F-4E-56-MC	Turkish AF	73-1016 to 73-1027	12
F-4E-56-MC	Greek AF	72-1524 to 72-1535	12
F-4E-56-MC	Iranian AF	71-1153 to 71-1166	14
RF-4EJ-56-MC	JASDF	47-6901 to 47-6905	5
F-4F-56-MC	Luftwaffe	3773 to 3796	24

Block 56 total/Cumulative total 69/4,593

Block 57

F-4E-57-MC	USAF	73-1157 to 73-1164	8
F-4E-57-MC	Turkish AF	73-1028 to 73-1042	15
F-4E-57-MC	Iranian AF	73-1519 to 73-1534	16
RF-4EJ-57-MC	JASDF	57-6906 to 57-6914	9
F-4F-57-MC	Luftwaffe	3797 to 3820	24

Block 57 total/Cumulative total 72/4,665

Block 58

F-4E-58-MC	USAF	73-1165 to 73-1184	20
F-4E-58-MC	Turkish AF	73-1043 to 73-1055	13
F-4E-58-MC	Iranian AF	73-1535 to 73-1549	15
F-4F-58-MC	Luftwaffe	3821 to 3844	24

Block 58 total/Cumulative total 72/4,737

Block 59

F-4E-59-MC	USAF	73-1185 to 73-1204	20
F-4E-59-MC	Iranian AF	73-1550 to 73-1554	5
F-4F-59-MC	Luftwaffe	3845 to 3875	31

Block 59 total/Cumulative total 56/4,793

Block 60

F-4E-60-MC	USAF	74-0643 to 74-0666 & 74-1038 to 74-1049	36
F-4E-60-MC	Israeli AF	74-1014 to 74-1015	2
F-4E-60-MC	Greek AF	74-1618 to 74-1619	2

Block 60 total/Cumulative total 40/4,833

Block 61

F-4E-61-MC	USAF	74-1050 to 74-1061 & 74-1620 to 74-1637	30
F-4E-61-MC	Israeli AF	74-1016 to 74-1021	6
RF-4E-61-MC	Iranian AF	74-1725 to 74-1728	4

Block 61 total/Cumulative total 40/4,873

Block 62

F-4E-62-MC	USAF	74-1638 to 74-1653	16
F-4E-62-MC	Israeli AF	74-1022 to 74-1037	16
RF-4E-62-MC	Iranian AF	74-1729 to 74-1736	8

Block 62 total/Cumulative total 40/4,913

Block 63

F-4E-63-MC	USAF/Luftwaffe	75-0628 to 75-0637	10
F-4E-63-MC	Iranian AF	75-0222 to 75-0257	36
RF-4E-63-MC	Israeli AF	75-0418 to 75-0423	6

Block 63 total/Cumulative total 52/4,965

Block 64

F-4E-64-MC	RoKAF	76-0493 to 76-0511	19

Block 64 total/Cumulative total 19/4,984

Block 65

F-4E-65-MC	Turkish AF	77-0277 to 77-0300	24
F-4E-65-MC	Greek AF	77-1743 to 77-1750	8

Block 65 total/Cumulative total 32/5,016

Block 66

F-4E-66-MC	Turkish AF	77-0301 to 77-0308	8
F-4E-66-MC	Greek AF	77-1751 to 77-1760	10
RF-4E-66-MC	Turkish AF	77-0309 to 77-0316	8
RF-4E-66-MC	Greek AF	77-0357 to 77-0358 & 77-1761 to 77-1766	8

Block 66 total/Cumulative total 34/5,050

Block 67

F-4E-67-MC	RoKAF	78-0727 to 78-0744	18

Block 67 total/Cumulative total 18/5,068

F-4EJ (Mitsubishi built)

F-4EJ	JASDF	37-8314 to 37-8323	10
F-4EJ	JASDF	47-8324 to 47-8352	29
F-4EJ	JASDF	57-8353 to 57-8376	24
F-4EJ	JASDF	67-8377 to 67-8391	15
F-4EJ	JASDF	77-8392 to 77-8403	12
F-4EJ	JASDF	87-8404 to 87-8415	12
F-4EJ	JASDF	97-8416 to 97-8427	12
F-4EJ	JASDF	07-8428 to 07-8436	9
F-4EJ	JASDF	17-8437 to 17-8440	4

F-4EJ total (Mitsubishi) 127

For their disbandment, No. 74 Squadron painted up this F-4M Phantom FGR.Mk 2 in this vivid tiger-stripe color scheme. The aircraft had already been grounded.

F-4 Avionics

This listing of avionic equipment fitted to, or proposed for, different F-4 variants obviates the need to describe these items in the text.

A24 Central air-data computer; CPU-142/A is standard, or A24G.
AAA-4 IRST (IR search and track); only the second in service outside the USSR, it required radar for range information. ACF Industries.
AAD-5 IR reconnaissance (IR linescan), with high performance in dual fields and automatic control of V/H (velocity/height) ratio and conversion of video signals into permanent film record.
AAED Various kinds of advanced airborne expendable decoys, all designed to lure away hostile radars, see Maxi.
AAS-18 Advanced IR reconnaissance linescan, improved optics and up to 350 ft (107 m) of SO2498 film.
AAS-18A Modified for air-to-ground ejection of cassette.
ACE Elbit (Israel) produced ACE-3 and -4 mission computers, with cockpit display for digital radar, stores management and avionics integration.
AD-120 Standard British VHF/FM radio. GEC Avionics.
AD-980 Central suppression unit to avoid interference between com, TACAN, radar, IFF etc. GEC Avionics.
ADAS Auxiliary data annotation set for recording on recon film data, time, radar/baro altitude, latitude and heading, pitch/roll, drift angle and identity of unit.
Aero 1A Original Navy/Westinghouse designation of fire-control system of F-4A/B.
AIC-14 Baseline intercom system.
AIMS Updated APX-76 forming ATC radar beacon system plus IFF Mk XII.
AJB-3A Original weapon-delivery set incorporating loft/toss-bombing computer.
AJB-7 Upgraded delivery set for all-altitude nuclear release at various angles on timed basis from target or offset, with LADD timer and option of Bullpup guidance.
ALE-38 USAF high-capacity bulk chaff carrier, cutter and dispenser controlled by pilot or RWR/RHAWS; usual load six 50-lb (23-kg) rolls.
ALE-40 System developed for F-4, usually four dispensers for total of 120 cartridges, either RR-170 chaff or MJU-7/B flare; total weight about 133 lb (60 kg), drag similar to AIM-9 plus launcher.
ALE-41 Navy version of ALE-38.
ALE-43 Chaff cutter/dispenser pod with backseater control of dipole length to counter A to K-band; pod capacity is eight roving packs, total 320 lb (145 kg).
ALE-47 Tracor (as previous) upgrade to replace ALE-40.
ALQ-6 Mitsubishi jamming system for airborne radars, with control from cockpit or APR-2.
ALQ-71 External pod for jamming 1-8 GHz bands, powered by Garrett ram-air turbine. General Electric development, Hughes (production).
ALQ-72 Version of ALQ-71 for higher frequencies, mainly against airborne radars.
ALQ-87 External pod FM barrage jammer for countering from 1-8 GHz.
ALQ-100 Deception jamming pod operating against hostile radars from 2-8 GHz using noise or break-track technique. Sanders.
ALQ-101 Noise/deception jamming pod produced in five main configurations, the most common being 101(V)4 from 2-20 GHz and 101(V)8 with gondola adding trough compartment with two extra fore/aft antennas. Westinghouse.
ALQ-119 Developed 101 for noise and deception jamming over three bands covering terminal threat range; Westinghouse delivered over 1,600 in nine versions.
ALQ-119A Upgraded 119 by Seek Ice program using new Rotman lens technology and faster reprogramming.
ALQ-123 IR jamming pod emitting train of coded high-intensity IR pulses; weight 378 lb (171 kg). Loral.
ALQ-125 Originally called Pave Onyx. Terec (tactical electronic recon sensor), detects, identifies, locates and reports on surface threats (SAMs, AAA); two antennas provide coverage to left and right of track, and cockpit display reads out complete hostile electronic order of battle. Litton.
ALQ-126 DECM (deceptive ECM) instalation developed to replace Dash-100, giving wider coverage against AI, AAA and SAM systems.
ALQ-126B Increased frequency coverage, distributed microprocessor control for quick reaction to new threats, and integration with APR-43, ALR-67 or -68 and HARM missile. Sanders.
ALQ-127 Advanced development of 126A/B, shorter forward hemisphere antennas. Sanders.
ALQ-130 Tac communications jamming instalation using broadband radio and acoustic noise. Eaton.
ALQ-131 Advanced multimode jamming pod capable of housing a wide range of modules and with reprogrammable software for quick counter of all known SAM threats; variable length, typical weight 562 lb (255 kg). Westinghouse.
ALQ-140 IR countermeasure set using coded emission from hot ceramic block; installed in place of tail parachute doors. Sanders.
ALQ-162 Small (36 lb; 16 kg) radar jammer governed by existing on-board system or by own processor to give pulsed or CW emissions. Northrop.
ALQ-184 Large pod providing multi-beam (Rotman lens) architecture and many other advances based on the airframe of ALQ-119 series, giving protection against SAMs, AAA and hostile interceptors. Raytheon.
ALQ-187 Fully automatic internal ECM system quickly reprogrammable against pulse, PD or CW radars and integrated with RWRs and chaff/flare dispensers. Raytheon.
ALR-17 Basic ESM countermeasures warning receiver; as ELRAC identifies, classifies and locates surface threats on radar maps.
ALR-31 Early ESM surveillance system, withdrawn from 1985.
ALR-45 A standard USN RWR (radar warning receiver) using four spiral antennas to give all-round cover from 2-14 GHz, with fast digital threat processing.
ALR-46 USAF RWR giving fast digital processing from 2-18 GHz and cockpit display plus auto control of jamming assets. Itek.

The Wild Weasel F-4G employs a variety of sensors in its role of suppressing enemy air defenses, but most important is the AN/APR-38.

***An F-4N of VMFA-531, seen during a rare carrier deployment with CVW-14 aboard USS* Coral Sea.**

ALR-50 SAM missile alert and launch-warning receiver, normally covering 4-20 GHz, developed from APR-27, being replaced by Dash-68. Magnavox.
ALR-53 Long-range homing receiver for guiding towards surface threats.
ALR-67(V) Radar warning and countermeasures control system, incorporating ALR-45F. Itek.
ALR-68 Advanced digital threat-warning receiver developed for Luftwaffe by Litton with Itek computer able to give crew hands-off protection against surface, ship and air threats.
ALR-69 Over 3,500 of this RWR delivered, with frequency-selective system and low-band (Compass Sail) missile alert receiver; gives relative bearing of missile approach. Litton.
ALR-80 Latest drop-in retrofit RWR with library of 1,800+ modes and complete reprogramming possible on flight line in 90 seconds; many other new features. General Instrument.
ALR-606 Latest RWR available for F-4 retrofit, with single processor handling up to four separate antenna/receiver installations for 0.5-20 GHz cover via advanced display showing full details of threat type and location. General Instrument.
AN-1553B Standard digital databus system linking all avionic items.
AOR-45 Advanced CIS (control indicator set) to replace APR-38; related to APR-47.
APA-89 SIF (selective identification feature) for ATC.
APA-138 Fixed-optics gunsight.
APA-157 CW illuminator for AIM-7 family of Sparrow missiles.
APA-165 Radar set group incorporating APQ-109, APA-157 and ASG-22.
APD-10 Radar mapping set using SLAR (side-looking airborne radar).
APG-30 Original forward-looking AI radar for use with lead-computing gunsight.
APG-59 Pulse-Doppler radar with limited lookdown capability, original part of Aero 1A.
APG-65 Digital multimode radar (originally for F/A-18A); capabilities include Doppler velocity for MTI (moving target indication), ability to track target in ground clutter and to track multiple targets. Hughes.
APG-66J Lightweight and compact modular air-cooled radar, derived from F-16 set; 10 operating modes, weight 304 lb (138 kg). Westinghouse.
APN-22 Radar altimeter.
APN-141 Radar altimeter.
APN-159 Radar altimeter.
APN-194 High-resolution pulsed radar altimeter. Honeywell.
APN-202 Radar beacon receiver.
APQ-50 Radar of F3H-2 (F-3) Demon aircraft, installed in first F4H/F-4A aircraft to have radar. Thermionic valves; aperture (scanner diameter) 24 in (61 cm).
APQ-72 I/J-band interception radar with CW illuminator for Sparrow III missile. Thermionic valves; aperture (to aircraft 19) 24 in, (No. 20 onwards) 32 in. Westinghouse.
APQ-99 Small forward-looking radar with TA (terrain-avoidance) and TF (terrain-following) modes, plus ground-mapping facility; two-lobe monopulse J-band. Texas Instruments.
APQ-100 Modified Dash-72 integrated into fire-control system, with plan indication mode for ground mapping and range strobe for manual bombing. Westinghouse.
APQ-102 Reconnaissance SLAR with ability to track fixed and moving targets from any altitude; updated by UPD-4/6/8. Goodyear.
APQ-109 Dash-100 modified with partial solid-state electronics, air-to-ground slant range and movable cursor on display. Westinghouse.
APQ-120 Final F-4 radar in Westinghouse series, first all-solid-state (weight reduced to 639 lb; 290 kg), small elliptical (27.5 × 24.5 in) antennna, designed for proximity to gun, X-band, integrated guidance and illumination; 2,852 delivered.
APQ-162 Advanced compact forward-looking radar derived from Dash-99. Texas Instruments.
APQ-172 Further Dash-99 derivative, using LRUs (line-replaceable units) to create different solid-state set. Texas Instruments.
APR-2 Radar warning system developed from American APR-36/37, by 1988 being replaced by improved APR-4. Tokyo-Keiki.
APR-4 Kai Advanced radar warning receiver.
APR-6 Latest (1990) Japanese RHAW system, capable of processing multiple inputs simultaneously in dense EM (electromagnetic) environment.
APR-25 Upgraded RHAWS (radar homing and warning system); receiver giving direction of threats and assigning prioritization.
APR-26 SAM launch warning system, parallel with Dash-25.
APR-27 USN-sponsored SAM launch warning system.
APR-30 RHAWS using fin-cap antennas facing to front and rear.
APR-32 RHAWS derived from Dash-25 but using antennas in fin-cap trailing-edge fairing and in box beneath nose.
APR-36/37 Related USAF RHAWS installations.
APR-38 Large integrated CIS (control/indicator set) comprising seven internal modules that receive, locate and study all hostile emitters from about 0.01-25 GHz, with computer control to assign prioritization and feed cockpit display with scales to 200 nm (230 miles; 369 km); receiver IBM, CIS Loral, ESM Loral, computer. Texas Instruments.
APR-39 RWR from C- to J-band, four spiral plus one blade antennas. E-Systems.
APR-40 Auxiliary UHF receiver.
APR-43 Multimode tactical RWR (Compass Sail Clockwise) handling pulse and CW and linked with ALQ-126 and -162 for protection. Loral/AEL.
APR-47 New-generation CIS to replace Dash-38. McDonnell Douglas, plus Sperry (processor) and E-Systems (directional receiver).
APR-69 Auxiliary UHF receiver.
APS-107 Dash-107, -107A and -107B all related RHAWS installations, generally proved unreliable.
APX-68 IFF transponder.
APX-72 IFF transponder, autoradar ident, auto (digital) alt report and emergency signals.
APX-76 IFF interrogator; 76A standard air-to-air, 76B all solid-state.
APX-80 Drop-in retrofit IFF transponder.
APZ-79A Upgraded IFF transponder (all these IFFs Hazeltine).
ARA-25 ADF in UHF band.
ARC-52 Communications radio, VHF band.
ARC-105 Communications transceiver HF band, with large fin-skin shunt antennas.
ARC-159 Communications transceiver in UHF band. Collins.
ARC-182 Communications transceiver,

VHF (FM/AM) and UHF (FM/AM). Collins.
ARI.18228 RWR with antennas facing front and rear in fin-cap and rear-cockpit display showing quadrant of greatest threat; coverage 2-20 GHz. Marconi Defence Systems.
ARN-21 TACAN, tactical air navigation set giving bearing of friendly ground stations.
ARN-86 Later (1962) TACAN.
ARN-92 LORAN, long-range navigation receiver sensing waves emitted from distant ground stations, picked up by prominent 'towel rail' antenna along spine of fuselage.
ARN-101 Complete replacement of analog nav/attack system by digital, with addition of 'doghouse' antenna and blade antennas on fuselage spine. Lear Siegler.
ARN-118 Miniaturized and updated TACAN. Collins.
ARW-77 AGM-12C (Bullpup) control.
ASA-32 Analog autopilot and flight-control system, standard on early versions. General Electric.
ASG-22 LCOSS (lead-computing optical sight system), with lead-computing amplifier and gyro, with servoed output.
ASG-26 Lead-computing optical sight with HUD (head-up display) fed from ADC and other subsystems. General Electric.
ASN-39 Dead-reckoning navigation computer.
ASN-46A Analog navigation computer set.
ASN-48 Inertial navigation system; Litton LN-12A/B.
ASN-56 Inertial navigation system; like Dash-48, derived from CAINS (carrier aircraft INS).
ASN-63 Upgraded lightweight INS.
ASN-92 Further upgraded solid-state INS, installed in three arrangements.
ASQ-19 CNI (communications/nav/ident) package. Collins.
ASQ-88B Electronic central for integrated CNI package.
ASQ-90 CNI data display set.
ASQ-91 Weapons-release computer.
ASQ-153B Pave Spike laser target designator in 10 in (25 cm) diameter pod, for daytime target designation and ranging. Westinghouse.
ASQ-T-11 AIS (advanced instrumentation subsystem) pod replacing Sidewinders for training.
ASTAC French acronym for advanced tactical electronic recon system comprising multisensor ESM pod with secure datalink to ground station; can process 20 hostile emitters per second. Thomson-CSF.
ASW-21 Two-way secure datalink developed (1962) as part of NTDS.
ASW-25A One-way datalink derived from Dash-21.
ASW-25B Upgraded one-way digital datalink.
ASX-1 TISEO (target identification system electro-optical), auto daytime passive target acquisition and tracking sensor using closed-circuit TV with optics offering two magnifications, in pod on left wing leading edge. Northrop.

AVD-2 LRS (laser recon set) with laser mounted in either of three nose (forward or side) stations, giving picture quality surpassing optical photo.
AVQ-9 Laser target designator slaved to IR detecting set; provides slant range, can be used for terrain avoidance.
AVQ-10 Pave Knife pod with stabilized head housing boresighted TV camera and laser designator. Westinghouse/Dalmo Victor.
AVQ-26 Pave Tack package for day/night clear or adverse weather sensing, acquisition, tracking, ranging and attack of targets using free-fall or LG (laser-guided) bombs; comprises boresighted FLIR and laser, plus stabilization and display. Ford Aerospace.
AVS-IV Reconnaissance camera packaged in external pod.
AWG-10 Fire-control system to manage gun(s), Sparrow and Sidewinder missiles. Radar initially APG-59, later Dash-72, replaced in AWG-10 in 1966 by PD with look-down capability and BIT (built-in test). Westinghouse.
AWG-10A From 1973 reliability improved by solid-state transmitter with klystron and digital computer; servoed LCOSS added. Increased accuracy for missile launch and added air-to-ground weapon aiming.
AWG-10B Final upgrade to all-digital circuitry.
AWG-11 Incorporates Dash-10A upgrades but with some British changes, license-produced by Ferranti and with 180° folding radome.
AWG-12 Similar to Dash-11 but with further changes and interfaced with Ferranti INAS.
Cords Coherent-on-receive Doppler system, add-on to APQ-120 giving enhanced detection of small targets plus some air-to-ground MTI, but unreliable. Hughes.
CPU-143/A Digital air-data computer, linked with 1553B bus.
CP-XXX5 Upgraded ADC with Arinc 429 serial interface with 1553B bus; eight F-4 versions. All (like 143/A) GEC Avionics.
EL/L-8202 Compact 445-lb (202-kg) ECM jammer pod covering F- to J-bands, with ram-air/liquid cooling. Elta.
EL/M-2001B Compact (weight 105 lb; 48 kg) dual-mode PD radar in I/J-band, multiple modes feeding HUD or weapon control computer. Elta.
EL/M-2021 Large (3-kW) multimode radar for air-to-air and air-to-ground functions, I/J-band digital with lookup/lookdown. Elta.
EL/M-2032 Advanced all-digital multimode radar (1988). Elta.
El-Op Digital HUD. Elta.
ERAS Extended-range antenna system, in UPD-8.
Evade Airborne decoy system comprising dispensers for flares (10) or chaff cartridges (21). Wallop Systems.
EWACS Electronic wide-angle camera system giving 140° coverage with imagery on magnetic tape; 60 lb (27 kg), 1 cu ft (0.028 m³). Chicago Aerial Industries.

F.95 Reconnaissance optical camera, various focal lengths and any mounting attitude.
F.126 Reconnaissance optical camera for vertical medium altitudes, auto exposure control.
F.135 Reconnaissance optical stereo camera, one lens looking forward and the other aft, suitable for high-speed low-level day or night.
G-139 Reconnaissance pod, length 22 ft (6.7 m), housing various systems to weight of 4,000 lb (1814 kg), with full ECS (environmental control system). General Dynamics.
GVR-10 Vertical reference gyro.
H-423 Together with H-421 LINS (laser inertial navigation system), among the first in service using ring laser technology. Honeywell.
HIAC-1 Giant optical camera (HI-Alt Camera) in LOROP program, focal length 66 in (168 cm), resolution 240 lines/mm, capacity 1,000 ft of 5 in film. General Dynamics.
IFF 2720 Secondary surveillance transponder, pressurized for high altitude and with EW provisions. Cossor.
IFF 3500 Airborne interrogator, sensitive with narrow beam width. Cossor.
INAS Inertial navigation attack system comprising platform, computer, HUD and various secondary and interface units (with TACAN, radar alt, HSI, ADC and LCOSS) giving full air-to-ground capability. Ferranti.
KA-55A High-altitude panoramic optical camera, 12 in (30 cm) focal length, usually vertical.
KA-56A Low-altitude panoramic optical camera, 3 in (7.6 cm) focal length.
KA-91 High-altitude panoramic optical camera, 18 in (46 cm) focal length, vertical.
KC-1B Mapping camera, mounted on high-altitude station.
KS-1A Mapping camera, mounted on high-altitude station.
KS-56D Variant of KA-56A, vertical or forward oblique.
KS-72 Optical framing camera, forward oblique.
KS-74A Data-recording camera set or direct-scope recorder, camera, periscope and control unit.
KS-87/87A Most common family of optical cameras with focal length 3, 6, 12 or 18 in (7.6, 15, 30 or 46 cm) installed forward oblique, left or right, vertical or split vertical. Fairchild.
KS-127A LOROP (long-range oblique photography) reconnaissance camera, focal length usually 66 in (168 cm), fills camera stations 2 and 3.
KY-28 Speech security unit.
LA-285A Photoflash detector and camera control unit for night photography.
LA-311A Camera parameter control, for inflight alterations under crew control.
LA-313 Optical viewfinder for camera control, vertical optics giving HUD type presentation to pilot.

LA-429A Photoflash cartridge ejector dispensing 20 M185 cartridges.
Labs Low-altitude bombing system; see AJB-3A, AJB-7.
LN-39 Intertial navigation unit, basis of upgraded INS. Litton.
LORAN See ARN-92.
LOROP See KS-127A.
LS-58A Aircraft camera mount set with autostabilization.
LW-33 Digital inertial navigation attack system. Litton.
LWS-20 Laser warning system giving all-round cover, threat analysis and audio/visual warning. Part of SPS-20. Elisra.
M112 Flash cartridge, average 260 million cp.
M185 Flash cartridge, average 1 billion cp.
Masquerade External pod carrying 48 Radashield chaff cartridges and 42 Infrashield IR flare cartridges with microprocessor control from RWR, cockpit or IRWR. Wallop Systems.
Maxi Miniature F-4 cast in bronze, 37 in (94 cm) span and F-4 radar signature, released from 12-round pod. Brunswick.
MX-7933 Interference blanker between emitters.
NTDS Naval Tactical Data System, 1950s technology included ASW-21.
Pave Arrow Field (Vietnam) conversion to carry Sidewinder nose on external pod to detect IR from surface targets and give cockpit indication.
Pave Knife See AVQ-10.
Pave Onyx See ALQ-125.
Pave Tack See AVQ-26.
PTR 373 UHF receiver and transmitter amplifier. Plessey.
PTR 374 Emergency UHF transceiver. Plessey.
PTR 1721, 1751 Advanced UHF and UHF/VHF retrofit transceivers.
QRC-84-02 IR countermeasures pod with multithreat protection; ram-air turbine power. Northrop.
QRC-160 Designations (suffix A-2 to A-8) of early jammer pods later designated in ALQ-71, 72 and 87 series.
QRC-335 Designations with suffix A(V)3 to A(V)8 of early jammer pods later designated in ALQ-101 series.
QRC-353 Family of chaff cartridges, circular cross-section.
QRC-522, -529 Designations of early jammer pods later designated in ALQ-119 series.
Raphael Externally-mounted pod housing SLAR (side-looking airborne radar). Thomson-CSF.
RR-129 Chaff package (cartridge), partner to Mk 46 IR flare, both 40 mm (1.6 in) diameter.
RR-170 Chaff package (cartridge), partner to MJU series IR flares, square section 23 mm (0.9 in) each side.
RS-700 IRLS (infrared linescan) sensor in 8-14 micron band with roll stabilization. Texas Instruments.
RT-793 UHF transceiver.
SEAM Sidewinder expanded acquisition mode, affecting wiring and other items in carrier aircraft to make full use of upgraded missiles.
SPS-20 RWR self-protection over 0.7-18 GHz.
SPS-2000 Advanced digital integrated protection system over 0.7-18 GHz, handling AAA, SAM and fighter radars, displaying 16 threats simultaneously.
SSR 1500 IFF Mk 10A transponder. Cossor.
SSR 1503 IFF controller.
SST-181X Combat Skyspot radar guidance system for free-fall bombing.
T-11 Optical mapping camera, vertical mount on high-altitude station.
Tacan See ARN-21, 86, 118.
TD-709 Sequential timer.
Terec See ALQ-125.
TISEO See ASX-1.
UPD-4 SLAR reconnaissance system using APD-10 radar in WJ-bands plus displays, datalink and other items. Converts radar signals to optical film. Goodyear.
UPD-8 Upgraded UPD-4; produced like predecessor by Loral.
VTAS Visual target acquisition system, incorporating HMS (helmet-mounted sight).

The F-4S was the ultimate naval Phantom, with its slatted wings and upgraded avionics. This one served with VF-301, USN reserve.

Page numbers in **bold** refer to an illustration

228

Index

Picture acknowledgements

The publishers would like to thank the following organizations and individuals for supplying photographs for this book:

6: Robert L. Lawson. 7: Robert F. Dorr, Robert L. Lawson. 8: Robert F. Dorr (two). 9: Robert F. Dorr (two). 10: René J. Francillon, Robert L. Lawson. 11: Robert L. Lawson (five), Robert F. Dorr (two). 12: Robert L. Lawson, Robert F. Dorr. 15: Robert L. Lawson. 16: Robert F. Dorr. 17: Robert L. Lawson (two). 18: Robert L. Lawson (two). 19: Robert L. Lawson (two), Peter B. Mersky. 20: Robert L. Lawson. 21: Robert L. Lawson (three). 22-23: Robert L. Lawson (five). 24: Robert L. Lawson (two), Robert F. Dorr. 25: Robert F. Dorr (two), Robert L. Lawson. 26: Robert L. Lawson. 27: Robert L. Lawson, Robert F. Dorr (two). 28: M. J. Hooks, Robert L. Lawson. 29: Robert F. Dorr (two), Robert L. Lawson, Bruce Robertson. 30: Peter B. Mersky. 31: Robert F. Dorr, Peter B. Mersky. 32: Robert F. Dorr, Peter B. Mersky. 33: Dr Alfred Price. 36: Robert F. Dorr (two), Philip Chinnery. 37: Philip Chinnery. 38: Dr Alfred Price. 40: via Warren Thompson (two). 41: Robert F. Dorr, Robert L. Lawson. 45: Robert L. Lawson. 48: Robert L. Lawson. 50: Robert L. Lawson. 51: Mike Stroud (four), Robert F. Dorr. 52: Robert L. Lawson. 53: M. J. Hooks, Robert L. Lawson. 55: via Lon Nordeen. 59: Salvador Mafé Huertes. 60: Dr Alfred Price (two), Grant Race. 61: Dr Alfred Price (two). 62: M. J. Hooks, Dr Alfred Price (two). 63: Dr Alfred Price, M. J. Hooks. 66: Bruce Robertson (two), M. J. Hooks. 67: Robert L. Lawson (two). 68: Robert L. Lawson (three). 69: Chris Ryan, Robert L. Lawson. 70: Robert L. Lawson (three). 71: Robert L. Lawson, Michael Stroud. 73: Robert L. Lawson. 74: Michael Stroud, M. J. Hooks. 75: Chris Ryan. 76: Peter B. Mersky, Chris Ryan. 77: Robert L. Lawson (two). 78: via Warren Thompson, Chris Ryan, Robert L. Lawson. 79: AFFTC via Bob Archer. 80: Peter B. Mersky, P. Steinemann. 81: Jon Lake. 83: Robert L. Lawson. 84: Warren Thompson, Paul Bennett. 85: Robert L. Lawson, Warren Thompson. 88: James Benson (three). 89: Mark Hasara via Robert F. Dorr. 90: Robert F. Dorr, via Mule Holmburg. 91: Peter B. Mersky, Jeff Rankin-Lowe, Michelle Hamilton. 92: John Roberts, Jim Rotramel, via Pat Martin. 93: via John Roberts, John Roberts (two). 94: John Roberts, via Jim Rotramel, via Pat Martin. 95: via John Roberts, John Roberts, Jeff Rankin-Lowe. 96: via Jim Rotramel, US Air Force. 97: via Pat Martin, John Roberts (two), Hughes, via John Roberts. 99: via Jim Rotramel. 100: via Pat Martin, via Jim Rotramel (two). 101: Ministry of Defence. 102: Messerschmitt-Bölkow-Blohm (two), via M. J. Hooks, via Jim Rotramel. 103: McDonnell Douglas, Peter B. Mersky, Ministry of Defence. 104: . 105: Joe Cupido, Mike Stroud, via John Roberts, via Jim Rotramel (two). 106: Robert Hewson, via John Roberts, via Jim Rotramel. 107: via Pat Martin (two), Jim Rotramel (two), Jeff Rankin-Lowe. 108: Aerosphere Research, via Jim Rotramel (two). 109: via Jim Rotramel, via Pat Martin. 110: Frazer-Nash. 111: via Jim Rotramel, Rafael via BIAF Magazine. 112: Robert L. Lawson/Tailhook, Tailhook. 113: via Robert F. Dorr. 114: Robert L. Lawson/Tailhook, Tailhook. 115: John Lorentz/Tailhook, McDonnell Douglas via Robert F. Dorr. 116: Jim Rotramel, R. M. Hill/Tailhook. 117: Jim Rotramel, Carl E. Porter via René J. Francillon, Jeff Rankin-Lowe. 118: Jim Rotramel, Takeda. 119: McDonnell Douglas, Gary Frederick via Robert F. Dorr, Salvador Mafé Huertas. 120: David Donald, Mike Stroud, Claudio Toselli. 121: Georg Mader, Robert L. Lawson/Tailhook. 122: Robert L. Lawson /Tailhook. 123: Robert L. Lawson /Tailhook, René J. Francillon. 124: Robert F. Dorr (two). 125: Mike Stroud, Robert L. Lawson/Tailhook (two). 126: Robert L. Lawson/Tailhook, René J. Francillon. 127: Bruce Trombecky/Tailhook, Peter B. Mersky. 128: René J. Francillon. 129: Robert F. Dorr (two), Philip Chinnery, Peter B. Lewis via Robert F. Dorr. 130: René J. Francillon. 131: René J. Francillon. 132: Jim Rotramel (three), David Donald. 133: Joe Cupido (two), Jeff Rankin-Lowe (two). 134: via Robert F. Dorr. 135: via Robert F. Dorr (three), René J. Francillon. 137: Joe Cupido. 138: Jeff Rankin-Lowe (two), Carl Porter via René J. Francillon. 139: Robert F. Dorr, Peter R. Foster (two), M. J. Hooks, M. Ogawa via Bob Archer. 140: via Bob Archer, Malcolm J. Gault, Masahiko Takeda (two). 141: Masahiko Takeda, Jay Miller/Aerofax Inc. 142: via Robert F. Dorr. 143: via Robert F. Dorr, Peter Steinemann, Masahiko Takeda (two). 144: Masahiko Takeda, M. J. Hooks. 145: Mule Holmberg, via Mule Holmberg. 146: Mike Stroud, McDonnell Douglas. 147: Robert L. Lawson/Tailhook, René J. Francillon, M. J. Hooks. 148: McDonnell Douglas via John Roberts, Joe Cupido. 149: Robert L. Lawson, McDonnell Douglas via John Roberts. 150: Rick Burgess/Tailhook, Robert L. Lawson/Tailhook, Robert L. Lawson. 151: Jan Jacobs/Tailhook, via Robert F. Dorr, Robbie Shaw. 152: Bruce Trombecky/Tailhook, Bruce Robertson. 153: McDonnell Douglas via John Roberts, via Robert F. Dorr, Robbie Shaw, Mike Stroud, Dr Alfred Price. 156: Robbie Shaw, Denis J. Calvert, M. J. Hooks. 157: McDonnell Douglas via John Roberts. 158: Jon Lake. 159: Robert L. Lawson/Tailhook, Peter B. Mersky. 160: Bruce Trombecky/Tailhook, Peter B. Mersky, Robert L. Lawson/Tailhook. 161: Robert L. Lawson/Tailhook, Vance Vasquez/Tailhook (two), Richard Gennis, Jim Dunn (two). 162: René J. Francillon/Tailhook, Robert L. Lawson/Tailhook, René J. Francillon, Vance Vasquez/Tailhook. 163: Robbie Shaw. 164: Jay Miller/Aerofax Inc. 165: Paul Jackson, via BIAF Magazine. 166: McDonnell Douglas via Robert F. Dorr, Tailhook Photo Service. 167: Tailhook Photo Service, McDonnell Douglas. 168: Tailhook Photo Service. 169: McDonnell Douglas via Robert F. Dorr, Tailhook Photo Service. 170: McDonnell Douglas via Robert F. Dorr, Tailhook Photo Service. 172: McDonnell Douglas via John Roberts. 173: Dr Alfred Price. 174: McDonnell Douglas via Robert F. Dorr, John Roberts. 178-179: John Roberts. 180: Mick Roth/Tailhook, Georg Mader. 182: Robert L. Lawson, Denis J. Calvert, Greg Meggs. 183: Pat Martin, Robert F. Dorr (two), Photolink, Peter R. Foster, René J. Francillon. 184: Stefan Petersen, Peter B. Lewis via René J. Francillon, Robert L. Lawson, Lindsay T. Peacock. 185: Lindsay T. Peacock (three), Robert L. Lawson (two), Warren Thompson, Mick Taylor via Chris Ryan. 188: Robert F. Dorr (two), Mick Roth/Tailhook, Peter R. Foster. 189: Robert L. Lawson/Tailhook (four), René J. Francillon (three). 190: Robert L. Lawson/Tailhook, Robert L. Lawson (three), W. G. Turner, Peter B. Lewis via René J. Francillon (two). 191: Lindsay T. Peacock, Don Spering/AIR, Randy Jolly, René J. Francillon, Stephen J. Brennan. 192: Don Spering/AIR, Warren Thompson, Lindsay T. Peacock. 193: Don Spering/AIR (three), Jeff Rankin-Lowe, Mick Roth/Tailhook, René J. Francillon, Robbie Shaw. 194: Robert L. Lawson, Peter R. Foster, Don Spering/AIR, Randy Jolly, Jeff Rankin-Lowe, Don Spering/AIR. 195: Alex Hrapunov, Lindsay T. Peacock, Robert L. Lawson/Tailhook, Don Spering/AIR. 196: Robert L. Lawson/Tailhook, Jelle Sjoerdsma, Don Spering/AIR, Jeff Rankin-Lowe, Robert F. Dorr. 197: Denis Calvert, Pat Martin, James Benson, Philip Chinnery, Peter B. Mersky, René J. Francillon. 198: Peter B. Mersky, Chris Ryan, Robert L. Lawson/Tailhook (two), Chris Ryan. 199: Robert F. Dorr, Robert L. Lawson (two), Lindsay T. Peacock (two), Peter B. Mersky, Robert L. Lawson/Tailhook. 200: Robert L. Lawson (three), Lindsay T. Peacock, Robert L. Lawson, René J. Francillon (two). 201: Robert L. Lawson (five), René J. Francillon, Robert F. Dorr (two). 202: Don Spering/AIR, Robert L. Lawson/Tailhook, Robert L. Lawson (three), Lindsay T. Peacock, Jan C. Jacobs. 203: Lindsay T. Peacock, Robert L. Lawson (six), John Roberts. 204: Robert L. Lawson (four). 205: Robert L. Lawson (five), Peter R. Foster. 206: Lindsay T. Peacock, Robert L. Lawson (four). 207: Robert L. Lawson (five). 208: Robert L. Lawson (three), Peter R. Foster, Lindsay T. Peacock. 209: McDonnell Douglas via John Roberts, Lon Nordeen. 210: Graham Robson, Peter R. Foster. 211: Martin Baumann, John Waller, Peter R. Foster, Stefan Petersen. 212: Malcolm English, Pat Martin, Martin Baumann, Peter Steinemann. 213: Peter Steinemann, Mike Stroud, Peter R. Foster. 214: Robert F. Dorr. 215: Y. Borovik/BIAF Magazine, IAI via BIAF Magazine. 216: Y. Borovik/BIAF Magazine, via BIAF Magazine. 217: M. Yamasaki via Bob Archer, Lindsay T. Peacock (two), Robert F. Dorr, M. Ogawa via Bob Archer (two), Peter R. Foster, Robbie Shaw. 218: Peter Steinemann, D. Lamarque, Salvador Mafé Huertas (two). 219: Stuart Lewis, Marco Amatimaggio, Herman Sixma. 220: M. J. Hooks (two), Photolink, MAP via Grant Race. 221: Bruce Robertson, Dr Alfred Price (two), M. J. Hopper. 222: Peter R. Foster, Lindsay T. Peacock, Mick Taylor via Chris Ryan, T. Malcolm English. 223: Peter R. Foster, Lindsay T. Peacock (two), R. Gennis, F4 Aviation Photo Bank. 225: Jon Lake. 226: Robbie Shaw, Pete Clayton/Tailhook. 227: René J. Francillon.